THE HISTORY OF ENGLAND

VOLUME I

DAVID HUME ESQ.
HISTORY AND PIHLOSOPHY.

This portrait of the author is provided in all the earliest editions of his History.
The reversal of letters in the word "philosophy" remains uncorrected throughout.

THE HISTORY
OF ENGLAND

from the Invasion of Julius Caesar

to The Revolution in 1688

———

IN SIX VOLUMES

BY DAVID HUME, ESQ.

VOLUME I

Liberty Fund

The cuneiform inscription that serves as our logo and as the design motif for our endpapers is the earliest-known written appearance of the word "freedom" (*amagi*), or "liberty." It is taken from a clay document written about 2300 B.C. in the Sumerian city-state of Lagash.

Foreword copyright © 1983 by William B. Todd. All rights reserved. All inquiries should be addressed to Liberty Fund, Inc., 11301 North Meridian Street, Carmel, Indiana 46032. This book was manufactured in the United States of America.

This Liberty Fund edition is based on the edition of 1778, containing the author's last corrections and improvements. The only two recorded sets of that edition in the United States were consulted. One is a complete set at the Humanities Research Center of the University of Texas at Austin. The other is an incomplete set in the Boston Public Library. The publisher acknowledges with thanks the cooperation of both institutions as well as the advice of Professors William B. Todd and David Levy.

Design by Martin Lubin/Betty Binns Graphics. New York, New York.
Editorial services provided by Harkavy Publishing Service, New York, New York.

Library of Congress Cataloging in Publication Data

Hume, David, 1711–1776.
 The history of England.
 "Based on the edition of 1778, with the author's last corrections and improvements."
 Reprint. Originally published: London: T. Cadell, 1778. With new foreword.
 1. Great Britain—History—To 1485. 2. Great Britain—History—Tudors, 1485–1603. 3. Great Britain—History—Stuarts, 1603–1714. I. Title.
DA30 .H9 1983 942 82-25868
ISBN 0-86597-019-X (series)
ISBN 0-86597-020-3 (pbk. series)
ISBN 0-86597-021-1 (Volume I)
ISBN 0-86597-022-X (Volume I pbk.)

16 19 20 21 22   C 8 7 6 5 4
19 20 21 22 23   P 10 9 8 7 6

C O N T E N T S

OF THE FIRST VOLUME

I

*The Britons – Romans – Saxons – the Heptarchy –
The kingdom of Kent – of Northumberland –
of East-Anglia – of Mercia – of Essex –
of Sussex – of Wessex*

PAGE 3

I I

THE ANGLO-SAXONS

*Egbert – Ethelwolf –
Ethelbald and Ethelbert – Ethered –
Alfred the Great – Edward the Elder –
Athelstan – Edmund – Edred – Edwy –
Edgar – Edward the Martyr*

PAGE 55

III

APPENDIX I
THE ANGLO-SAXON
GOVERNMENT AND
MANNERS

IV
WILLIAM
THE CONQUEROR

V

WILLIAM RUFUS

VI

HENRY I

VII
STEPHEN

*Accession of Stephen – War with Scotland –
Insurrection in favour of Matilda – Stephen
taken prisoner – Matilda crowned – Stephen released –
Restored to the crown – Continuation of the civil wars –
Compromise between the King and prince Henry –
Death of the King*

VIII
HENRY II

*State of Europe – of France –
First acts of Henry's government –
Disputes between the civil and ecclesiastical powers –
Thomas a Becket, archbishop of Canterbury –
Quarrel between the King and Becket –
Constitutions of Clarendon – Banishment of Becket –
Compromise with him – His return
from banishment – His murder – Grief –
and submission of the King*

IX

*State of Ireland – Conquest of that island –
The King's accommodation with the court of Rome –
Revolt of young Henry and his brothers –*

X

RICHARD I

XI

JOHN

APPENDIX II
THE FEUDAL AND ANGLO-NORMAN GOVERNMENT AND MANNERS

FOREWORD

WHEN DAVID HUME began his *History of England* the under-taking came, not from any sudden resolve nor as an entirely new enterprise, but as one possibly contemplated thirteen years before, in 1739, probably attempted several times thereafter, and certainly considered, at least as a corollary discipline, in a philosophical discourse published in 1748. Even so, any concerted effort long sustained necessarily awaited appropriate conditions: all happily combining for Hume upon his election, January, 1752, as Keeper of the Advocates' Library in Edinburgh. With this appointment the author finally had "a genteel office," ready access to a collection of some thirty thousand volumes, and, no less desirable, leisure indefinitely extended to pursue his research. Heretofore, by mere exertion of his own commanding intellect, philosopher Hume had more than once set forth what he perceived to be the "constant and universal principles of human nature." Now, as a philosophical historian, he could ascertain from dreary chronicles all the aberrations of human behavior as there exhibited in "wars, intrigues, factions, and revolutions." These and other vagaries, previously recorded simply as odd phenomena, in Hume's more coherent view constituted a varied range of "materials" documenting the "science of man."

Once intent upon a history so formulated, the immediate question for this author was where to begin. In his own *Life* (an essay prefixed to the first, 1778, posthumous edition of the *History* and so reprinted here), Hume ingenuously speaks of being "frightened" away from the very start—that is, from the time of Caesar's invasion—and so at once passing over seventeen hundred years to "the accession of the House of Stuart [1603], an epoch when, I thought, the misrepresentations of faction began chiefly to take place." Indeed this was Hume's final decision, though he

FOREWORD

earlier admitted in a letter to Adam Smith, 24 September 1752, some inclination to commence with the preceding Tudor "epoch" [1485].

> I confess, I was once of the same Opinion with you, & thought that the best Period to begin an English History was about Henry the 7th. But you will please to observe, that the Change, which then happen'd in public Affairs, was very insensible, and did not display its Influence till many Years afterwards. Twas under James that the House of Commons began first to raise their Head, & then the Quarrel betwixt Privilege & Prerogative commenc'd. The Government, no longer opprest by the enormous Authority of the Crown, display'd its Genius; and the Factions, which then arose, having an Influence on our present Affairs, form the most curious, interesting, & instructive Part of our History. . . . I confess, that the Subject appears to me very fine; & I enter upon it with great Ardour & Pleasure. You need not doubt of my Perseverance.

For a historian tracing, in one period or another, the progress or decline of human welfare, the "influence" twice mentioned in the letter to Smith eventually required a "backward" narrative: from present effects to earlier precedents and then to causes earlier yet. Thus over the ensuing years Hume proceeded retrogressively, representing first the Stuart reigns (now volumes V–VI in this reprint), then the Tudors (III–IV), and finally all the "barbarous" times before Henry VII (I–II). Hence in surveying the development of this history, and the various reactions to its initial publication, we should remember that what Hume reports of his first two volumes (originally published 1754, 1757) is lastly conveyed here as V–VI (volumes not so designated until issue in 1762 of the "complete" edition).

About his early work, so ebulliently described to Smith, Hume has much else to say, all of it in great confidence as to the rectitude and efficacy of his own procedure. To one friend he observes: "You know that there is no post of honour in the English Parnassus more vacant than that of History. Style, judgement, impartiality, care—everything is wanting to our historians; and even Rapin, during this latter period, is extremely deficient." To another he confides that he has "more propos'd as my Model the concise manner of the antient Historians, than the prolix, tedious Style of

FOREWORD

some modern Compilers. I have inserted no original Papers, and enter'd into no Detail of minute, uninteresting Facts. The philosophical Spirit, which I have so much indulg'd in all my Writings, finds here ample Materials to work upon." To a third correspondent Hume is even more assured.

> The more I advance in my undertaking, the more am I convinced that the History of England has never yet been written, not only for style, which is notorious to all the world, but also for matter; such is the ignorance and partiality of all our historians. Rapin, whom I had an esteem for, is totally despicable. I may be liable to the reproach of ignorance, but I am certain of escaping that of partiality: The truth is, there is so much reason to blame and praise alternately King and Parliament, that I am afraid the mixture of both in my composition, being so equal, may pass sometimes for an affectation, and not the result of judgement and evidence.

In this last comment the allusion to troubles between King and Parliament—obviously in reference to Charles I rather than to his father, James I—provides a clue to the advance in Hume's narrative. On 26 May 1753 he reports that he is "now beginning the Long Parliament," i.e., chapter V (subsequently chapter LIV of this edition). Five months later, on 28 October, he had come to the execution of the King, representing the final chapter of his original volume. By then, as he realized, "the history of [these] two first Stuarts will be most agreeable to the Tories: That of the two last, to the Whigs. But we must endeavour to be above any Regard either to Whigs or Tories." The "two last," Charles II and James II, were of course to be considered in his next volume, one as yet hardly under way.

Early in 1754, and still affirming his conviction that "I am of no party, and have no bias," Hume sent off to press his first volume and on 1 September received his final proofs. During the course of printing, some of the sheets circulated among interested persons, with the Whigs and Tories among them alternately approving or disapproving, and "a few Christians" in some anguish reproaching this "Libertine in religion." The latter accusation, possibly quite unexpected, quickly prompted Hume to reassure his confidant that he was "tolerably reserved on this head."

FOREWORD

Whatever the author's claims, advanced perhaps all too complacently before issue, the charge of irreligion was hotly pursued upon publication of the volume, 20 November 1754. It may well be, as Hume discloses in his *Life,* that the primates of England and Ireland—surely much divergent in their own beliefs—both encouraged him to persevere; but the Bishop of Gloucester, in a violent outrage, privately denounced this historian as "an atheistical Jacobite, a monster as rare with us as a hippogriff." Even among the secular reviewers exception was at once taken, first in the opening chapter to the excessive "enthusiasm" Hume discerned in the Protestant Reformation, then in the next chapter to the intolerable "superstition" he discovered in the Roman Catholic Church. Always responsive to critical commentary, but only when it did not run counter to his own principles, or to the dictates of history itself, Hume in later editions prudentially withdrew both of these passages in their entirety, and thus excised some interior text apparently beyond the immediate cause of complaint. So that the present reader may determine whether, at the very beginning of his work, Hume has maintained in suitable language his own impartial attitude these suppressed sections are now reprinted.

The first, on the Protestants, appeared originally in Volume I of the first edition, pages 7–9 (1778 text, Volume VI, page 10) after the paragraph ending "reconcile both parties."

The first reformers, who made such furious and successful attacks on the Romish SUPERSTITION, and shook it to its lowest foundations, may safely be pronounced to have been universally inflamed with the highest ENTHUSIASM. These two species of religion, the superstitious and fanatical, stand in diametrical opposition to each other; and a large portion of the latter must necessarily fall to his share, who is so couragious as to control authority, and so assuming as to obtrude his own innovations upon the world. Hence that rage of dispute, which every where seized the new religionists; that disdain of ecclesiastical subjection; that contempt of ceremonies, and of all the exterior pomp and splendor of worship. And hence too, that inflexible intrepidity, with which they braved dangers, torments, and even death itself; while they preached the doctrine of peace, and carried the tumults of war, thro' every part of Christendom.

However obstinate and uncomplying this species of religion, it necessarily received some alteration, according to the different situ-

FOREWORD

ation of civil affairs, and the different species of government, which it met with in its progress.

In the electorates of Germany, in Denmark, and in Sweden, where the monarch was early converted, and, by putting himself at the head of the reformers, acquired authority amongst them; as the spirit of enthusiasm was somewhat tempered by a sense of order, episcopal jurisdiction, along with a few decent ceremonies, was preserved in the new establishment.

In Switzerland and Geneva, which were popular governments; in France, Scotland, and the low countries, where the people reformed themselves in opposition to the prince; the genius of fanaticism displayed itself in its full extent, and affected every circumstance of discipline and worship. A perfect equality was established among the ecclesiastics; and their inflamed imagination, unconfined by any forms of liturgy, had full liberty to pour out itself, in wild, unpremeditated addresses to the Divinity.

They were the preachers of Switzerland, France, and the low countries, who carried the reformation into England: But as the government was there monarchical, and the magistrate took the lead in this grand revolution; tho' the speculative doctrines were borrowed from the more fanatical churches, yet were the discipline and worship naturally mitigated with a more humane spirit of religion.

But after the persecutions of Mary had chased abroad all the most obstinate reformers, who escaped her fury; they had leisure to imbibe a stronger tincture of the enthusiastic genius; and when they returned, upon the accession of Elizabeth, they imported it, in its full force and virulence, into their native country.

That renowned Princess, whose good taste gave her a sense of order and decorum, and whose sound judgment taught her to abhor innovations, endeavored, by a steddy severity, to curb this obstinate enthusiasm, which, from the beginning, looked with an evil aspect, both on the church and monarchy. By an act of parliament in 1593, all persons above the age of sixteen, who were absent from church a month, or who, by word or writing, declared their sentiments against the established religion, were to be imprisoned, till they made an open declaration of their conformity. This if they refused during three months, they were to abjure the realm; and if they either refused such abjuration, or staid in England beyond the time limited, they were to suffer as felons, without benefit of clergy. To such extreme rigor was the severity pushed of Elizabeth's administration.

The Queen too had established the high commission court, which preserved an uniformity of worship thro' all the churches, and inflicted severe penalties on all innovators. The powers, with which this court was invested, were mostly discretionary; tho' by law it could exact a fine of twenty pound for every month that any one was absent from the established worship.

The second passage, on the Roman Catholics, occurred in the next chapter, pages 25–28 (1778 text, Volume VI, page 39) in the paragraph starting "The moderation" after the sentence ending "conformed himself to it."

Here it may not be improper, in a few words, to give some account of the Roman catholic superstition, its genius and spirit. History addresses itself to a more distant posterity than will ever be reached by any local or temporary theology; and the characters of sects may be studied, when their controversies shall be totally forgotten.

Before the reformation, all men of sense and virtue wished impatiently for some event, which might repress the exorbitant power of the clergy all over Europe, and put an end to the unbounded usurpations and pretensions of the Roman pontiff: But when the doctrine of Luther was promulgated, they were somewhat alarmed at the sharpness of the remedy; and it was easily foreseen, from the offensive zeal of the reformers, and defensive of the church, that all christendom must be thrown into combustion. In the preceeding state of ignorance and tranquillity, into which mankind were lulled, the attachment to superstition, tho' without reserve, was not extreme; and, like the antient pagan idolatry, the popular religion consisted more of exterior practices and observances, than of any principles, which either took possession of the heart, or influenced the conduct. It might have been hoped, that learning and knowledge, as of old in Greece, stealing in gradually, would have opened the eyes of men, and corrected such of the ecclesiastical abuses as were the grossest and most burthensome. It had been observed, that, upon the revival of letters, very generous and enlarged sentiments of religion prevailed thro'out all Italy; and that, during the reign of Leo, the court of Rome itself, in imitation of their illustrious prince, had not been wanting in a just sense of freedom. But when the enraged and fanatical reformers took arms against the papal hierarchy, and threatened to rend from the church at once all her riches and authority; no wonder she was animated with equal zeal and ardor, in defence of such antient and invaluable possessions. At the same time, that she employed the stake and gibbet against her avowed enemies, she extended her jealousy even towards learning and philosophy, whom, in her supine security, she had formerly overlooked, as harmless and inoffensive. Hence, the severe check, which knowlege received in Italy: Hence, its total extinction in Spain: And hence, the slow progress, which it made, in France, Germany, and England. From the admi-

FOREWORD

ration of antient literature, from the inquiry after new discoveries, the minds of the studious were every where turned to polemical science; and, in all schools and academies, the furious controversies of theology took place of the calm disquisitions of learning.

Mean while, the rage of dispute and the violence of opposition rivetted men more strongly in all their various delusions, and infected every intercourse of society with their malignant influence. The Roman pontiff, not armed with temporal force, sufficient for his defence, was obliged to point a-new all his spiritual artillery, and to propagate the doctrine of rebellion and even of assassination, in order to subdue or terrify his enemies. Priests, jealous and provoked, timorous and uncontroled, directed all the councils of that sect, and gave rise to such events as seem astonishing amid the mildness and humanity of modern manners. The massacre of Paris, that of Ireland, the murder of the two Henrys of France, the gunpowder conspiracy in England, are memorable, tho' temporary instances of the bigotry of that superstition. And the dreadful tribunal of the inquisition, that utmost instance of human depravity, is a durable monument to instruct us what a pitch iniquity and cruelty may rise to, when covered with the sacred mantle of religion.

Tho' the prospect of sharing the plunder of the church had engaged some princes to embrace the reformation, it may be affirmed, that the Romish system remained still the favorite religion of sovereigns. The blind submission, which is inculcated by all superstition, particularly by that of the catholics; the absolute resignation of all private judgment, reason, and inquiry; these are dispositions very advantageous to civil as well as ecclesiastical authority; and the liberty of the subject is more likely to suffer from such principles than the prerogatives of the chief magistrate. The splendor too and pomp of worship, which that religion carefully supports, are agreeable to the taste of magnificence, that prevails in courts, and form a species of devotion, which, while it flatters the pampered senses, gives little perplexity to the indolent understandings, of the great. That delicious country, where the Roman pontiff resides, was the source of all modern art and refinement, and diffused on its superstition an air of politeness, which distinguishes it from the gross rusticity of the other sects. And tho' policy made it assume, in some of its monastic orders, that austere mien, which is acceptable to the vulgar; all authority still resided in its prelates and spiritual princes, whose temper, more cultivated and humanized, inclined them to every decent pleasure and indulgence. Like all other species of superstition, it rouses the vain fears of unhappy mortals; but it knows also the secret of allaying these fears, and by exterior rites, ceremonies, and abasements, tho' sometimes at the expence of morals, it reconciles the penitent to his offended deity.

FOREWORD

> Employing all these various arts, along with a restless enter-
> prize, the catholic religion has acquired the favor of many mon-
> archs, who had received their education from its rival sect; and
> Sweden, as well as England, has felt the effect of its dangerous
> insinuations.

However one may regard these two influential religious movements, it must be conceded that Hume here betrays no unwonted
partiality and is quite even-handed in his censure. To all sectarian
objections then, both political and clerical, he may be allowed the
rejoinder that, while his book had been "extremely run down by
Faction . . . it has been met with such Indulgence by good Judges,
that I have no Reason to repent of my Undertaking." In later time
the critics could be more than indulgent, indeed lavish in their
praise, for upon completion of the work, essentially, in 1762, it had
been greatly improved in many respects: incidentally by more
precise and extensive footnoting, as well as by more careful ty-
pography; in its text by the gradual elimination of peculiarly Scottish spelling and idioms; in its authorities by reference to other
historical archives, especially those at the British Museum; and in
its scope by extending now, in other volumes, to less controversial
matters. All this achieved, the work received an extensive review by
Voltaire, himself an accomplished *philosophe* and historian, who
considered this English account to be "perhaps the best written in
any language." Moreover, he continued, the author thereof "is
neither parliamentarian, nor royalist, nor Anglican, nor Presby-
terian—he is simply judicial," one obviously of a "mind superior to
his materials; he speaks of weaknesses, blunders, cruelties as a
physician speaks of epidemic diseases." No less effusive was the
Earl of Chesterfield, who rightly predicted that this was "the only
History of England that will go down to Posterity."
    Still another way of assessing, now statistically, the continued
acceptance of the *History* may be discovered in the printers' own
accounts. Confronted by six massive quarto books, gradually appearing one or two at a time, even the most assiduous readers, as
Hume anticipated, would become less and less interested, especially when each succeeding volume took them backward to
epochs of lesser concern. Nonetheless, the complex printing
records, when reduced to tabular form, disclose a total quarto issue
hardly surpassed, in this period, for work of any kind.

FOREWORD

Printed		1754	1757	1759	1761	1762	1763	1764	Total
"Stuarts"	1 [5]	2,000		750		800	[225?]		3,775
	2 [6]		1,750	750		750	255		3,475
"Tudors"	1–2 [3–4]			2,250		750		250	3,225
"Ancient"	1–2 [1–2]				2,000	750			2,750

Before the long-produced, expensively priced but highly successful quarto issue had run its course, the *History* was already destined to appear in a more economical format designed for an even wider audience—and ultimately in a radical transformation of the text. The first hint of this new enterprise appears in a letter from Hume to his publisher concerning the full quarto edition then pending for 1762.

> I am very glad, that you are in so good a way, and that you think so soon of making a new Edition. I am running over both the antient History & the Tudors, and shall send you them up by the Waggon as soon as they are corrected. Please tell Mr Strahan [the printer] to keep carefully this Copy I send up, as well as that which I left of the Stuarts: For if you intend to print an Octavo Edition next Summer, it will be better to do it from these Copies which are corrected, than from the new Edition, where there will necessarily be some Errors of the Press.

Actually the octavo edition, a smaller format in eight volumes, did not appear until 1763 and then, effective 1 November, was sold either as a complete set leather bound for £2.8s., or under an ingenious installment plan of one volume a month unbound for 5s. Acting on what he believed to be sufficient warrant from the quarto sales, still continuing at £4.10s. a set, the publisher enthusiastically ordered five thousand copies of this cheaper issue, a printing far exceeding total production of all preceding editions. About this extraordinary venture Hume soon voiced nothing but contempt: Andrew Millar, the publisher, had been "rapacious"; the book was "ill-printed"; misleading statements about its lagging sales were quite "detestable"; and such an enormous issue effectively prevented him from introducing, in another, still further revisions.

FOREWORD

To promote these sales Millar eventually resorted to a deceptive technique which, it seems, went quite unnoticed by Hume at the time and has gone undetected ever since. Beginning with the quarto issue of 1762 all titles uniformly read *A New Edition, Corrected,* excepting only an octavo issue now appearing in 1767, which suggestively announced *A New Edition, With Corrections, and some Additions.* Close inspection of this "edition" discloses, however, that it is merely a reissue of the 1763 octavo with substitute titles.

Quite undeterred by his cheap 1763–1767 fiasco, Millar next imagined that he might profit still further from his more affluent clientele, and accordingly produced in 1770, under the imprint of Thomas Cadell, a magnificent "Royal Paper" quarto edition priced at £7.7s. Copies of this as well as the earlier £4.10s. quarto issue, then designated as "Small Paper," were still being advertised in 1778, a clear indication that the quality market had been saturated long before. Even so, the luxurious 1770 edition is not without merit, textually for the inclusion of numerous substantive revisions, many of them based on materials found 1763–65 during Hume's travels in France, and typographically for the transfer, to the end of the volumes, of all the longer footnotes. Almost from the outset certain of Hume's subtended commentaries had threatened to overwhelm the text; now as separate "Additional Notes" they could be steadily augmented, or occasionally increased in number, all without any restraint.

Eventually, when the supply of "that abominable Octavo Edition" had diminished, and the sale of the sumptuous quarto was "pretty well advanced," Hume on 20 July 1771 submitted to press yet another corrected copy, this now containing, as he advised printer Strahan, "many considerable Improvements, most of them in the Style; but some also in the matter." Stylistic refinements of old material variously introduced in times past admittedly would not be much appreciated; yet, Hume confesses, "I cannot help it, and they run mostly upon Trifles; at least they will be esteemd such by the Generality of Readers, who little attend to the extreme Accuracy of Style. It is one great advantage that results from the Art of printing, that an Author may correct his works, as long as he lives." The words are somewhat prophetic, for the edition then

FOREWORD

under way, and published in 1773, was the last in Hume's lifetime, though not the last to exhibit his continuing effort toward perfection.

Hume's final endeavor, appearing in 1778, was appropriately designated *A New Edition, with the Author's last Corrections and Improvements*. Amendments for this, first mentioned 13 November 1775, continued to be sent forward through 27 July 1776, when Hume asked Strahan to delete three passages relating to the Scottish clergy (1617), Philip IV of Spain (1624), and a message from Charles I to the House of Commons (1628). So at the first, on Protestants and Catholics, now also at the last on these other matters, careful excision of unnecessary parts generally improved the total performance.

Also directed in the revised copy and immediately evident upon a cursory review, are many other 1778 adjustments, among them these alterations in the "Additional Notes" to volumes VI–VII (volume V of this reprint):

    D.   Adds final clause, "who . . . *divine* right."

    K.   Adds paragraph in italics

    Q.   Substitutes for final sentence "the period . . . Malherbe" another reading "Machiavel . . . in Europe."

    Z.   Adds first introductory sentence and last sentence in italics.

    —.   Deletes 1773 note DD "In a Parliament . . . *parliament*, p. 61"; succeeding 1778 notes accordingly relettered.

  DD.   Adds second paragraph "with regard . . . *of the text*."

  GG.   Adds final sentence "His intended . . . in him."

  HH.   Adds last three sentences "In reality . . . enlarged views."

  NN.   Adds final paragraph "What a paradox . . . enterprize."

It is truly remarkable that, twenty-five years after he had begun writing on the early Stuart reigns, and on this eighth comprehensive revision of his work, Hume should find so much to amend.

FOREWORD

Apart from these substantive revisions, the 1778 edition also displays throughout Hume's fastidious concern over insignificant "trifles"—as seen, for example, in the single leaf in the set (volume II, signature I8, pages 127–28) cancelled and replaced, probably at Strahan's direction, to represent some authorial correction overlooked on first printing. (Reference here is to the paragraph introducing the variant, volume I, pages 476–477 of this reprint).

Paragraph	1773	1778
Such was	granted by his laws	ordained
The king	intitled	entitled
The escheats	revenue to the king	revenue
But besides	lands	land
" "	Where he sold	If he sold

Passing over the subtleties involved in this phraseology, we may agree that the minuscule specimen here scrutinized sufficiently establishes the general practice.

With this demonstration there can be little doubt that the present issue necessarily must reproduce the posthumous 1778 edition. The reprint here presented, from copies at the Humanities Research Center, University of Texas, and the Boston Public Library, now however extends to six volumes only: an arrangement which for the first time allows the final text to be recast according to Hume's original design of three "epochs." When for merely commercial reasons that grand concept was abandoned in the eight-volume 1763–1778 editions, all semblance of Hume's construction was lost. There Henry VII entirely and the initial chapter of Henry VIII were abruptly cut away from the Tudors and huddled in with the last of the Ancients. There too, among the Stuarts, both Charles I and Charles II were also dismembered, each being split between two volumes. Hume reluctantly acquiesced in this typographical butchery, insisting only that the divisions not occur *within* a chapter. Were he present now to witness his best text in its best form, an ideal state unobtainable in his

FOREWORD

own day, he would surely commend what the Liberty Fund has here accomplished. The only difficulty would be to restrain him from transforming this classic in historiography into yet another version!

WILLIAM B. TODD

26 April 1982

William B. Todd is The Mildred Caldwell and Baine Perkins Kerr Centennial Professor in English History and Culture at the University of Texas at Austin.

THE LIFE OF
DAVID HUME, ESQ.

WRITTEN BY HIMSELF

MY OWN LIFE

I**T IS DIFFICULT** for a man to speak long of himself without vanity; therefore, I shall be short. It may be thought an instance of vanity that I pretend at all to write my life; but this Narrative shall contain little more than the History of my Writings; as, indeed, almost all my life has been spent in literary pursuits and occupations. The first success of most of my writings was not such as to be an object of vanity.

I was born the 26th of April 1711, old style, at Edinburgh. I was of a good family, both by father and mother: my father's family is a branch of the Earl of Home's, or Hume's; and my ancestors had been proprietors of the estate, which my brother possesses, for several generations. My mother was daughter of Sir David Falconer, President of the College of Justice: the title of Lord Halkerton came by succession to her brother.

My family, however, was not rich, and being myself a younger brother, my patrimony, according to the mode of my country, was of course very slender. My father, who passed for a man of parts, died when I was an infant, leaving me, with an elder brother and a sister, under the care of our mother, a woman of singular merit, who though young and handsome, devoted herself entirely to the rearing and educating of her children. I passed through the ordinary course of education with success, and was seized very early with a passion for literature, which has been the ruling passion of my life, and the great source of my enjoyments. My studious disposition, my sobriety, and my industry, gave my family a notion that the law was a proper profession for me; but I found an unsurmountable aversion to every thing but the pursuits of philosophy and general learning; and while they fancied I was poring upon Voet and Vinnius, Cicero and Virgil were the authors which I was secretly devouring.

MY OWN LIFE

My very slender fortune, however, being unsuitable to this plan of life, and my health being a little broken by my ardent application, I was tempted, or rather forced, to make a very feeble trial for entering into a more active scene of life. In 1734, I went to Bristol, with some recommendations to eminent merchants, but in a few months found that scene totally unsuitable to me. I went over to France, with a view of prosecuting my studies in a country retreat; and I there laid that plan of life, which I have steadily and successfully pursued. I resolved to make a very rigid frugality supply my deficiency of fortune, to maintain unimpaired my independency, and to regard every object as contemptible, except the improvement of my talents in literature.

During my retreat in France, first at Reims, but chiefly at La Fleche, in Anjou, I composed my *Treatise of Human Nature*. After passing three years very agreeably in that country, I came over to London in 1737. In the end of 1738, I published my Treatise, and immediately went down to my mother and my brother, who lived at his country-house, and was employing himself very judiciously and successfully in the improvement of his fortune.

Never literary attempt was more unfortunate than my Treatise of Human Nature. It fell *dead-born from the press*, without reaching such distinction, as even to excite a murmur among the zealots. But being naturally of a cheerful and sanguine temper, I very soon recovered the blow, and prosecuted with great ardour my studies in the country. In 1742, I printed at Edinburgh the first part of my Essays: the work was favourably received, and soon made me entirely forget my former disappointment. I continued with my mother and brother in the country, and in that time recovered the knowledge of the Greek language, which I had too much neglected in my early youth.

In 1745, I received a letter from the Marquis of Annandale, inviting me to come and live with him in England; I found also, that the friends and family of that young nobleman were desirous of putting him under my care and direction, for the state of his mind and health required it.—I lived with him a twelvemonth. My appointments during that time made a considerable accession to my small fortune. I then received an invitation from General St. Clair to attend him as a secretary to his expedition, which was at

MY OWN LIFE

first meant against Canada, but ended in an incursion on the coast of France. Next year, to wit, 1747, I received an invitation from the General to attend him in the same station in his military embassy to the courts of Vienna and Turin. I then wore the uniform of an officer, and was introduced at these courts as aid-de-camp to the general, along with Sir Harry Erskine and Captain Grant, now General Grant. These two years were almost the only interruptions which my studies have received during the course of my life: I passed them agreeably, and in good company; and my appointments, with my frugality, had made me reach a fortune, which I called independent, though most of my friends were inclined to smile when I said so: in short, I was now master of near a thousand pounds.

I had always entertained a notion, that my want of success in publishing the Treatise of Human Nature, had proceeded more from the manner than the matter, and that I had been guilty of a very usual indiscretion, in going to the press too early. I, therefore, cast the first part of that work anew in the Enquiry concerning Human Understanding, which was published while I was at Turin. But this piece was at first little more successful than the Treatise of Human Nature. On my return from Italy, I had the mortification to find all England in a ferment, on account of Dr. Middleton's Free Enquiry, while my performance was entirely overlooked and neglected. A new edition, which had been published at London, of my Essays, moral and political, met not with a much better reception.

Such is the source of natural temper, that these disappointments made little or no impression on me. I went down in 1749, and lived two years with my brother at his country-house, for my mother was now dead. I there composed the second part of my Essay, which I called Political Discourses, and also my Enquiry concerning the Principles of Morals, which is another part of my treatise, that I cast anew. Meanwhile, my bookseller, A. Millar, informed me, that my former publications (all but the unfortunate Treatise) were beginning to be the subject of conversation; that the sale of them was gradually increasing, and that new editions were demanded. Answers by Reverends, and Right Reverends, came out two or three in a year; and I found, by Dr. Warburton's railing,

MY OWN LIFE

that the books were beginning to be esteemed in good company. However, I had fixed a resolution, which I inflexibly maintained, never to reply to any body; and not being very irascible in my temper, I have easily kept myself clear of all literary squabbles. These symptoms of a rising reputation gave me encouragement, as I was ever more disposed to see the favourable than unfavourable side of things; a turn of mind which it is more happy to possess, than to be born to an estate of ten thousand a-year.

In 1751, I removed from the country to the town, the true scene for a man of letters. In 1752, were published at Edinburgh, where I then lived, my Political Discourses, the only work of mine that was successful on the first publication. It was well received abroad and at home. In the same year was published at London, my Enquiry concerning the Principles of Morals; which, in my own opinion (who ought not to judge on that subject) is of all my writings, historical, philosophical, or literary, incomparably the best. It came unnoticed and unobserved into the world.

In 1752, the Faculty of Advocates chose me their Librarian, an office from which I received little or no emolument, but which gave me the command of a large library. I then formed the plan of writing the History of England; but being frightened with the notion of continuing a narrative through a period of 1700 years, I commenced with the accession of the House of Stuart, an epoch when, I thought, the misrepresentations of faction began chiefly to take place. I was, I own, sanguine in my expectation of the success of this work. I thought that I was the only historian, that had at once neglected present power, interest, and authority, and the cry of popular prejudices; and as the subject was suited to every capacity, I expected proportional applause. But miserable was my disappointment: I was assailed by one cry of reproach, disapprobation, and even detestation; English, Scotch, and Irish, Whig and Tory, churchman and sectary, freethinker and religionist, patriot and courtier, united in their rage against the man, who had presumed to shed a generous tear for the fate of Charles I, and the earl of Strafford; and after the first ebullitions of their fury were over, what was still more mortifying, the book seemed to sink into oblivion. Mr. Millar told me, that in a twelvemonth he sold only forty-five copies of it. I scarcely, indeed, heard of one man in the three

MY OWN LIFE

kingdoms, considerable for rank or letters, that could endure the book. I must only except the primate of England, Dr. Herring, and the primate of Ireland, Dr. Stone, which seem two odd exceptions. These dignified prelates separately sent me messages not to be discouraged.

I was, however, I confess, discouraged; and had not the war been at that time breaking out between France and England, I had certainly retired to some provincial town of the former kingdom, have changed my name, and never more have returned to my native country. But as this scheme was not now practicable, and the subsequent volume was considerably advanced, I resolved to pick up courage and to persevere.

In this interval, I published at London my Natural History of Religion, along with some other small pieces; its public entry was rather obscure except only that Dr. Hurd wrote a pamphlet against it, with all the illiberal petulance, arrogance, and scurrility, which distinguish the Warburtonian school. This pamphlet gave me some consolation for the otherwise indifferent reception of my performance.

In 1756, two years after the fall of the first volume, was published the second volume of my History, containing the period from the death of Charles I. till the Revolution. This performance happened to give less displeasure to the Whigs, and was better received. It not only rose itself, but helped to buoy up its unfortunate brother.

But though I had been taught by experience, that the Whig party were in possession of bestowing all places, both in the state and in literature, I was so little inclined to yield to their senseless clamour, that in above a hundred alterations, which farther study, reading, or reflection engaged me to make in the reigns of the two first Stuarts, I have made all of them invariably to the Tory side. It is ridiculous to consider the English constitution before that period as a regular plan of liberty.

In 1759, I published my History of the House of Tudor. The clamour against this performance was almost equal to that against the History of the two first Stuarts. The reign of Elizabeth was particularly obnoxious. But I was now callous against the impressions of public folly, and continued very peaceably and con-

MY OWN LIFE

tentedly in my retreat at Edinburgh, to finish, in two volumes, the
more early part of the English History, which I gave to the public
in 1761, with tolerable, and but tolerable success.

But, notwithstanding this variety of winds and seasons, to
which my writings had been exposed, they had still been making
such advances, that the copy-money given me by the booksellers,
much exceeded any thing formerly known in England; I was become not only independent, but opulent. I retired to my native
country of Scotland, determined never more to set my foot out
of it; and retaining the satisfaction of never having preferred a
request to one great man, or even making advances of friendship
to any of them. As I was now turned of fifty, I thought of passing
all the rest of my life in this philosophical manner, when I received,
in 1763, an invitation from the Earl of Hertford, with whom I was
not in the least acquainted, to attend him on his embassy to Paris,
with a near prospect of being appointed secretary to the embassy;
and, in the meanwhile, of performing the functions of that office.
This offer, however inviting, I at first declined, both because I was
reluctant to begin connexions with the great, and because I was
afraid that the civilities and gay company of Paris, would prove
disagreeable to a person of my age and humour: but on his lord-
ship's repeating the invitation, I accepted of it. I have every reason,
both of pleasure and interest, to think myself happy in my connexions with that nobleman, as well as afterwards with his brother,
General Conway.

Those who have not seen the strange effects of modes, will
never imagine the reception I met with at Paris, from men and
women of all ranks and stations. The more I recoiled from their
excessive civilities, the more I was loaded with them. There is,
however, a real satisfaction in living at Paris, from the great number of sensible, knowing and polite company with which that city
abounds above all places in the universe. I thought once of settling
there for life.

I was appointed secretary to the embassy; and, in summer
1765, Lord Hertford left me, being appointed Lord Lieutenant of
Ireland. I was *chargé d' affaires* till the arrival of the Duke of Richmond, towards the end of the year. In the beginning of 1766, I left
Paris, and next summer went to Edinburgh, with the same view as
formerly, of burying myself in a philosophical retreat. I returned

---

MY OWN LIFE

to that place, not richer, but with much more money, and a much larger income, by means of Lord Hertford's friendship, than I left it; and I was desirous of trying what superfluity could produce, as I had formerly made an experiment of a competency. But in 1767, I received from Mr. Conway an invitation to be Under-secretary and this invitation, both the character of the person, and my connexions with Lord Hertford, prevented me from declining. I returned to Edinburgh in 1769, very opulent (for I possessed a revenue of 1000 l. a-year), healthy, and though somewhat stricken in years, with the prospect of enjoying long my ease, and of seeing the increase of my reputation.

In spring 1775, I was struck with a disorder in my bowels, which at first gave me no alarm, but has since, as I apprehend it, become mortal and incurable. I now reckon upon a speedy dissolution. I have suffered very little pain from my disorder; and what is more strange, have, notwithstanding the great decline of my person, never suffered a moment's abatement of my spirits; insomuch, that were I to name a period of my life, which I should most choose to pass over again, I might be tempted to point to this later period. I possess the same ardour as ever in study, and the same gaiety in company. I consider besides, that a man of sixty-five, by dying, cuts off only a few years of infirmities; and though I see many symptoms of my literary reputation's breaking out at last with additional luster, I knew that I could have but few years to enjoy it. It is difficult to be more detached from life than I am at present.

To conclude historically with my own character. I am, or rather was (for that is the style I must now use in speaking of myself, which emboldens me the more to speak my sentiments); I was, I say, a man of mild disposition, of command of temper, of an open, social, and cheerful humour, capable of attachment, but little susceptible of enmity, and of great moderation in all my passions. Even my love of literary fame, my ruling passion, never soured my temper, notwithstanding my frequent disappointments. My company was not unacceptable to the young and careless, as well as to the studious and literary; and as I took a particular pleasure in the company of modest women, I had no reason to be displeased with the reception I met with from them. In a word, though most men, any wise eminent, have found reason to complain of calumny, I never was touched, or even attacked by her baleful tooth: and

MY OWN LIFE

though I wantonly exposed myself to the rage of both civil and
religious factions, they seemed to be disarmed in my behalf of their
wonted fury. My friends never had occasion to vindicate any one
circumstance of my character and conduct: Not but that the zealots, we may well suppose, would have been glad to invent and
propagate any story to my disadvantage, but they could never find
any which they thought would wear the face of probability. I cannot say there is no vanity in making this funeral oration of myself,
but I hope it is not a misplaced one; and this is a matter of fact
which is easily cleared and ascertained.

April 18, 1776.

LETTER FROM ADAM SMITH, LL.D. TO WILLIAM STRAHAN, ESQ.

Kirkaldy, Fifeshire, Nov. 9, 1776.

DEAR SIR,

It is with a real, though a very melancholy pleasure, that I sit down to give you some account of the behaviour of our late excellent friend, Mr. Hume, during his last illness.

Though, in his own judgment, his disease was mortal and incurable, yet he allowed himself to be prevailed upon, by the entreaty of his friends, to try what might be the effects of a long journey. A few days before he set out, he wrote that account of his own life, which, together with his other papers, he has left to your care. My account, therefore, shall begin where his ends.

He set out for London towards the end of April, and at Morpeth met with Mr. John Home and myself, who had both come down from London on purpose to see him, expecting to have found him at Edinburgh. Mr. Home returned with him, and attended him during the whole of his stay in England, with that care and attention which might be expected from a temper so perfectly friendly and affectionate. As I had written to my mother that she might expect me in Scotland, I was under the necessity of continuing my journey. His disease seemed to yield to exercise and change of air, and when he arrived in London, he was apparently in much better health than when he left Edinburgh. He was advised to go to Bath to drink the waters, which appeared for some time to have so good an effect upon him, that even he himself began to entertain, what he was not apt to do, a better opinion of

LETTER FROM ADAM SMITH

his own health. His symptoms, however, soon returned with their usual violence, and from that moment he gave up all thoughts of recovery, but submitted with the utmost cheerfulness, and the most perfect complacency and resignation. Upon his return to Edinburgh, though he found himself much weaker, yet his cheerfulness never abated, and he continued to divert himself, as usual, with correcting his own works for a new edition, with reading books of amusement, with the conversation of his friends; and, sometimes in the evening, with a party at his favourite game of whist. His cheerfulness was so great, and his conversation and amusements run so much in their usual strain, that, notwithstanding all bad symptoms, many people could not believe he was dying. "I shall tell your friend, Colonel Edmonstone," said Doctor Dundas to him one day, "that I left you much better, and in a fair way of recovery." "Doctor," said he, "as I believe you would not chuse to tell any thing but the truth, you had better tell him, that I am dying as fast as my enemies, if I have any, could wish, and as easily and cheerfully as my best friends could desire." Colonel Edmonstone soon afterwards came to see him, and take leave of him; and on his way home, he could not forbear writing him a letter bidding him once more all eternal adieu, and applying to him, as to a dying man, the beautiful French verses in which the Abbé Chaulieu, in expectation of his own death, laments his approaching separation from his friend, the Marquis de la Fare. Mr. Hume's magnanimity and firmness were such, that his more affectionate friends knew, that they hazarded nothing in talking or writing to him as to a dying man, and that so far from being hurt by this frankness, he was rather pleased and flattered by it. I happened to come into his room while he was reading this letter, which he had just received, and which he immediately showed me. I told him, that though I was sensible how very much he was weakened, and that appearances were in many respects very bad, yet his cheerfulness was still so great, the spirit of life seemed still to be so very strong in him, that I could not help entertaining some faint hopes. He answered, "Your hopes are groundless. An habitual diarrhoea of more than a year's standing, would be a very bad disease at any age: At my age it is a mortal one. When I lie down in the evening, I feel myself weaker than when I rose in the morning; and when I rise in the morning, weaker than when I lay down

LETTER FROM ADAM SMITH

in the evening. I am sensible, besides, that some of my vital parts are affected, so that I must soon die." "Well," said I, "if it must be so, you have at least the satisfaction of leaving all your friends, your brother's family in particular, in great prosperity." He said, that he felt that satisfaction so sensibly, that when he was reading, a few days before, Lucian's Dialogues of the Dead, among all the excuses which are alleged to Charon for not entering readily into his boat, he could not find one that fitted him; he had no house to finish, he had no daughter to provide for, he had no enemies upon whom he wished to revenge himself. "I could not well imagine," said he, "what excuse I could make to Charon in order to obtain a little delay. I have done everything of consequence which I ever meant to do, and I could at no time expect to leave my relations and friends in a better situation than that in which I am now likely to leave them: I, therefore, have all reason to die contented." He then diverted himself with inventing several jocular excuses which he supposed he might make to Charon, and with imagining the very surly answers which it might suit the character of Charon to return to them. "Upon further consideration," said he, "I thought I might say to him, Good Charon, I have been correcting my works for a new edition. Allow me a little time, that I may see how the Public receives the alterations." But Charon would answer, "When you have seen the effect of these, you will be for making other alterations. There will be no end of such excuses; so, honest friend, please step into the boat." But I might still urge, "Have a little patience, good Charon, I have been endeavouring to open the eyes of the Public. If I live a few years longer, I may have the satisfaction of seeing the downfal of some of the prevailing systems of superstition." But Charon would then lose all temper and decency. "You loitering rogue, that will not happen these many hundred years. Do you fancy I will grant you a lease for so long a term? Get into the boat this instant, you lazy, loitering rogue."

But, though Mr. Hume always talked of his approaching dissolution with great cheerfulness, he never affected to make any parade of his magnanimity. He never mentioned the subject but when the conversation naturally led to it, and never dwelt longer upon it than the course of the conversation happened to require: it was a subject indeed which occurred pretty frequently, in consequence of the inquiries which his friends, who came to see him,

LETTER FROM ADAM SMITH

naturally made concerning the state of his health. The conversation which I mentioned above, and which passed on Thursday the 8th of August, was the last, except one, that I ever had with him. He had now become so very weak, that the company of his most intimate friends fatigued him; for his cheerfulness was still so great, his complaisance and social disposition were still so entire, that when any friend was with him, he could not help talking more, and with greater exertion, than suited the weakness of his body. At his own desire, therefore, I agreed to leave Edinburgh, where I was staying partly upon his account, and returned to my mother's house here, at Kirkaldy, upon condition that he would send for me whenever he wished to see me; the physician who saw him most frequently, Doctor Black, undertaking, in the mean time, to write me occasionally an account of the state of his health.

On the 22d of August, the Doctor wrote me the following letter:

"Since my last, Mr. Hume has passed his time pretty easily, but is much weaker. He sits up, goes down stairs once a day, and amuses himself with reading, but seldom sees any body. He finds, that even the conversation of his most intimate friends fatigues and oppresses him; and it is happy that he does not need it, for he is quite free from anxiety, impatience, or low spirits, and passes his time very well with the assistance of amusing books."

I received the day after a letter from Mr. Hume himself, of which the following is an extract.

Edinburgh, 23d August, 1776.

"MY DEAREST FRIEND,

"I am obliged to make use of my nephew's hand in writing to you, as I do not rise to-day.

*　　*　　*　　*

"I go very fast to decline, and last night had a small fever, which I hoped might put a quicker period to this tedious illness; but unluckily it has, in a great measure, gone off. I cannot submit to your coming over here on my account, as it is possible for me to see you so small a part of the day, but Doctor Black can better inform you concerning the degree of strength which may from time to time remain with me. Adieu, &c."

LETTER FROM ADAM SMITH

Three days after I received the following letter from Doctor Black.

Edinburgh, Monday, 26th August, 1776.

"DEAR SIR,

"Yesterday about four o'clock afternoon, Mr. Hume expired. The near approach of his death became evident in the night between Thursday and Friday, when his disease became excessive, and soon weakened him so much, that he could no longer rise out of his bed. He continued to the last perfectly sensible, and free from much pain or feelings of distress. He never dropped the smallest expression of impatience; but when he had occasion to speak to the people about him, always did it with affection and tenderness. I thought it improper to write to bring you over, especially as I heard that he had dictated a letter to you, desiring you not to come. When he became very weak, it cost him an effort to speak, and he died in such a happy composure of mind, that nothing could exceed it."

Thus died our most excellent, and never to be forgotten friend; concerning whose philosophical opinions men will, no doubt, judge variously, every one approving, or condemning them, according as they happen to coincide or disagree with his own; but concerning whose character and conduct there can scarce be a difference of opinion. His temper, indeed, seemed to be more happily balanced, if I may be allowed such an expression, than that perhaps of any other man I have ever known. Even in the lowest state of his fortune, his great and necessary frugality never hindered him from exercising, upon proper occasions, acts both of charity and generosity. It was a frugality founded not upon avarice, but upon the love of independency. The extreme gentleness of his nature never weakened either the firmness of his mind, or the steadiness of his resolutions. His constant pleasantry was the genuine effusion of good-nature and good-humour, tempered with delicacy and modesty, and without even the slightest tincture of malignity, so frequently the disagreeable source of what is called wit in other men. It never was the meaning of his raillery to mortify; and therefore, far from offending, it seldom failed to please and delight, even those who were the objects of it. To his friends, who were frequently the objects of it, there was not perhaps any one of all his great and amiable qualities, which contributed more to endear his conversation. And that gaiety of temper, so agreeable in society, but which is so often accompanied with frivolous and superficial qualities, was in him certainly attended with the most severe application, the most extensive learning, the greatest depth of thought and a capacity in every respect the most comprehensive. Upon the whole, I have always considered him, both in his lifetime and since his death, as approaching as nearly to the idea of a perfectly wise and virtuous man, as perhaps the nature of human frailty will permit.

I ever am, dear Sir,

Most affectionately your's,

ADAM SMITH.

THE HISTORY
OF ENGLAND

VOLUME I

I

The Britons – Romans –
Saxons – the Heptarchy –
The Kingdom of Kent – of Northumberland –
of East-Anglia – of Mercia – of Essex–
of Sussex – of Wessex

🌿 🌿 🌿

THE BRITONS

THE CURIOSITY, entertained by all civilized nations, of enquiring into the exploits and adventures of their ancestors,
commonly excites a regret that the history of remote ages should
always be so much involved in obscurity, uncertainty, and contradiction. Ingenious men, possessed of leisure, are apt to push
their researches beyond the period, in which literary monuments
are framed or preserved; without reflecting, that the history of
past events is immediately lost or disfigured, when intrusted to
memory and oral tradition, and that the adventures of barbarous
nations, even if they were recorded, could afford little or no entertainment to men born in a more cultivated age. The convulsions of
a civilized state usually compose the most instructive and most
interesting part of its history; but the sudden, violent, and unprepared revolutions, incident to Barbarians, are so much guided
by caprice, and terminate so often in cruelty that they disgust us by

the uniformity of their appearance; and it is rather fortunate for letters that they are buried in silence and oblivion. The only certain means, by which nations can indulge their curiosity in researches concerning their remote origin, is to consider the language, manners, and customs of their ancestors, and to compare them with those of the neighbouring nations. The fables, which are commonly employed to supply the place of true history, ought entirely to be disregarded; or if any exception be admitted to this general rule, it can only be in favour of the ancient Grecian fictions, which are so celebrated and so agreeable, that they will ever be the objects of the attention of mankind. Neglecting, therefore, all traditions or rather tales concerning the more early history of Britain, we shall only consider the state of the inhabitants, as it appeared to the Romans on their invasion of this country: We shall briefly run over the events, which attended the conquest made by that empire, as belonging more to Roman than British story: We shall hasten through the obscure and uninteresting period of Saxon annals: And shall reserve a more full narration for those times, when the truth is both so well ascertained and so complete as to promise entertainment and instruction to the reader.

All ancient writers agree in representing the first inhabitants of Britain as a tribe of the Gauls or Celtae, who peopled that island from the neighbouring continent. Their language was the same, their manners, their government, their superstition; varied only by those small differences, which time or a communication with the bordering nations must necessarily introduce. The inhabitants of Gaul, especially in those parts which lie contiguous to Italy, had acquired, from a commerce with their southern neighbours, some refinement in the arts, which gradually diffused themselves northwards, and spread but a very faint light over this island. The Greek and Roman navigators or merchants (for there were scarcely any other travellers in those ages) brought back the most shocking accounts of the ferocity of the people, which they magnified, as usual, in order to excite the admiration of their countrymen. The south-east parts, however, of Britain, had already, before the age of Caesar, made the first and most requisite step toward a civil settlement; and the Britons, by tillage and agriculture, had there encreased to a great multitude.[a] The other inhabitants of the island

[a] Caesar, lib. 4.

still maintained themselves by pasture: They were clothed with skins of beasts: They dwelt in huts, which they reared in the forests and marshes, with which the country was covered: They shifted easily their habitation, when actuated either by the hopes of plunder or the fear of an enemy: The convenience of feeding their cattle was even a sufficient motive for removing their seats: And as they were ignorant of all the refinements of life, their wants and their possessions were equally scanty and limited.

The Britons were divided into many small nations or tribes; and being a military people, whose sole property was their arms and their cattle, it was impossible, after they had acquired a relish of liberty, for their princes or chieftains to establish any despotic authority over them. Their governments, though monarchical,[b] were free, as well as those of all the Celtic nations; and the common people seem even to have enjoyed more liberty among them,[c] than among the nations of Gaul,[d] from whom they were descended. Each state was divided into factions within itself.[e] It was agitated with jealousy or animosity against the neighbouring states: And while the arts of peace were yet unknown, wars were the chief occupation, and formed the chief object of ambition, among the people.

The religion of the Britons was one of the most considerable parts of their government; and the Druids, who were their priests, possessed great authority among them. Besides ministering at the altar, and directing all religious duties, they presided over the education of youth; they enjoyed an immunity from wars and taxes; they possessed both the civil and criminal jurisdiction; they decided all controversies among states as well as among private persons, and whoever refused to submit to their decree was exposed to the most severe penalties. The sentence of excommunication was pronounced against him: He was forbidden access to the sacrifices or public worship: He was debarred all intercourse with his fellow-citizens, even in the common affairs of life: His company was universally shunned, as profane and dangerous: He was refused the protection of law:[f] And death itself became an acceptable relief from the misery and infamy to which he was exposed. Thus, the bands of government, which were naturally

[b] Diod. Sic. lib. 4. Mela, lib. 3. cap. 6. Strabo, lib. 4. [c] Dion Cassius, lib. 75. [d] Caesar, lib. 6. [e] Tacit. Agr. [f] Caesar, lib. 6. Strabo, lib. 4.

loose among that rude and turbulent people, were happily corroborated by the terrors of their superstition.

No species of superstition was ever more terrible than that of the Druids. Besides the severe penalties, which it was in the power of the ecclesiastics to inflict in this world, they inculcated the eternal transmigration of souls; and thereby extended their authority as far as the fears of their timorous votaries. They practised their rites in dark groves or other secret recesses;[g] and in order to throw a greater mystery over their religion, they communicated their doctrines only to the initiated, and strictly forbad the committing of them to writing, lest they should at any time be exposed to the examination of the profane vulgar. Human sacrifices were practised among them: The spoils of war were often devoted to their divinities; and they punished with the severest tortures whoever dared to secrete any part of the consecrated offering: These treasures they kept in woods and forests, secured by no other guard than the terrors of their religion;[h] and this steddy conquest over human avidity may be regarded as more signal than their prompting men to the most extraordinary and most violent efforts. No idolatrous worship ever attained such an ascendant over mankind as that of the ancient Gauls and Britons; and the Romans, after their conquest, finding it impossible to reconcile those nations to the laws and institutions of their masters, while it maintained its authority, were at last obliged to abolish it by penal statutes; a violence, which had never in any other instance been practised by those tolerating conquerors.[i]

THE ROMANS

THE BRITONS had long remained in this rude but independent state, when Caesar, having over-run all Gaul by his victories, first cast his eye on their island. He was not allured either by its riches or its renown; but being ambitious of carrying the Roman arms into a new world, then mostly unknown, he took advantage of a short interval in his Gaulic wars, and made an

[g] Plin. lib. 12. cap. 1.   [h] Caesar, lib. 6.   [i] Sueton. in Vita Claudii.

CHAPTER I

invasion on Britain. The natives, informed of his intention, were sensible of the unequal contest, and endeavoured to appease him by submissions, which, however, retarded not the execution of his design. After some resistance, he landed, as is supposed, at Deal; and having obtained several advantages over the Britons and obliged them to promise hostages for their future obedience, he was constrained, by the necessity of his affairs, and the approach of winter, to withdraw his forces into Gaul. The Britons, relieved from the terror of his arms, neglected the performance of their stipulations; and that haughty conqueror resolved next summer to chastise them for this breach of treaty. He landed with a greater force; and though he found a more regular resistance from the Britons, who had united under Cassivelaunus, one of their petty princes; he discomfited them in every action. He advanced into the country; passed the Thames in the face of the enemy; took and burned the capital of Cassivelaunus; established his ally, Mandubratius, in the sovereignty of the Trinobantes; and having obliged the inhabitants to make him new submissions, he again returned with his army into Gaul, and left the authority of the Romans more nominal than real in this island.

Anno ante C. 55.

The civil wars, which ensued, and which prepared the way for the establishment of monarchy in Rome, saved the Britons from that yoke, which was ready to be imposed upon them. Augustus, the successor of Caesar, content with the victory obtained over the liberties of his own country, was little ambitious of acquiring fame by foreign wars; and being apprehensive lest the same unlimited extent of dominion, which had subverted the republic, might also overwhelm the empire, he recommended it to his successors never to enlarge the territories of the Romans. Tiberius, jealous of the fame, which might be acquired by his generals, made this advice of Augustus a pretence for his inactivity.[k] The mad sallies of Caligula, in which he menaced Britain with an invasion, served only to expose himself and the empire to ridicule: And the Britons had now, during almost a century, enjoyed their liberty unmolested; when the Romans, in the reign of Claudius, began to think seriously of reducing them under their dominion. Without seeking any more justifiable reasons of hostility than were employed by the

---

[k] Tacit. Agr.

A.D. 43. late Europeans in subjecting the Africans and Americans, they sent over an army under the command of Plautius, an able general, who gained some victories, and made a considerable progress in subduing the inhabitants. Claudius himself, finding matters sufficiently prepared for his reception, made a journey into Britain; and received the submission of several British states, the Cantii, Atrebates, Regni, and Trinobantes, who inhabited the southeast parts of the island, and whom their possessions and more cultivated manner of life rendered willing to purchase peace at the expence of their liberty. The other Britons, under the command of Caractacus, still maintained an obstinate resistance, and the Romans made little progress against them; till Ostorius Scapula was *A.D. 50.* sent over to command their armies. This general advanced the Roman conquests over the Britons; pierced into the country of the Silures, a warlike nation, who inhabited the banks of the Severne; defeated Caractacus in a great battle; took him prisoner, and sent him to Rome, where his magnanimous behaviour procured him better treatment than those conquerors usually bestowed on captive princes.[1]

Notwithstanding these misfortunes, the Britons were not subdued; and this island was regarded by the ambitious Romans as a field in which military honour might still be acquired. Under the *A.D. 59.* reign of Nero, Suetonius Paulinus was invested with the command, and prepared to signalize his name by victories over those barbarians. Finding that the island of Mona, now Anglesey, was the chief seat of the Druids, he resolved to attack it, and to subject a place, which was the center of their superstition, and which afforded protection to all their baffled forces. The Britons endeavoured to obstruct his landing on this sacred island, both by the force of their arms and the terrors of their religion. The women and priests were intermingled with the soldiers upon the shore; and running about with flaming torches in their hands, and tossing their dishevelled hair, they struck greater terror into the astonished Romans by their howlings, cries, and execrations, than the real danger from the armed forces was able to inspire. But Suetonius, exhorting his troops to despise the menaces of a superstition, which they despised, impelled them to the attack, drove the Britons off the field,

[1] Tacit. Ann. lib. 12.

burned the Druids in the same fires which those priests had prepared for their captive enemies, destroyed all the consecrated
groves and altars; and, having thus triumphed over the religion of
the Britons, he thought his future progress would be easy, in
reducing the people to subjection. But he was disappointed in his
expectations. The Britons, taking advantage of his absence, were
all in arms; and headed by Boadicea, queen of the Iceni, who had
been treated in the most ignominious manner by the Roman tri-
bunes, had already attacked with success several settlements of
their insulting conquerors. Suetonius hastened to the protection of
London, which was already a flourishing Roman colony; but he
found on his arrival, that it would be requisite for the general
safety to abandon that place to the merciless fury of the enemy.
London was reduced to ashes; such of the inhabitants as remained
in it, were cruelly massacred; the Romans and all strangers, to the
number of 70,000, were every where put to the sword without
distinction; and the Britons, by rendering the war thus bloody,
seemed determined to cut off all hopes of peace or composition
with the enemy. But this cruelty was revenged by Suetonius in a
great and decisive battle, where 80,000 of the Britons are said to
have perished; and Boadicea herself, rather than fall into the
hands of the enraged victor, put an end to her own life by poison.[m]
Nero soon after recalled Suetonius from a government, where, by
suffering and inflicting so many severities, he was judged improper for composing the angry and alarmed minds of the inhabitants. After some interval, Cerealis received the command from
Vespasian, and by his bravery propagated the terror of the Roman
arms. Julius Frontinus succeeded Cerealis both in authority and in
reputation: But the general, who finally established the dominion
of the Romans in this island, was Julius Agricola, who governed it
in the reigns of Vespasian, Titus, and Domitian, and distinguished
himself in that scene of action.

This great commander formed a regular plan for subduing
Britain, and rendering the acquisition useful to the conquerors.
He carried his victorious arms northwards, defeated the Britons in
every encounter, pierced into the inaccessible forests and mountains of Caledonia, reduced every state to subjection in the south-

[m] Tacit. Ann. lib. 14.

ern parts of the island, and chaced before him all the men of fiercer and more intractable spirits, who deemed war and death itself less intolerable than servitude under the victors. He even defeated them in a decisive action, which they sought under Galgacus, their leader; and having fixed a chain of garrisons, between the friths of Clyde and Forth, he thereby cut off the ruder and more barren parts of the island, and secured the Roman province from the incursions of the barbarous inhabitants.[n]

During these military enterprizes, he neglected not the arts of peace. He introduced laws and civility among the Britons, taught them to desire and raise all the conveniencies of life, reconciled them to the Roman language and manners, instructed them in letters and science, and employed every expedient to render those chains, which he had forged, both easy and agreeable to them.[o] The inhabitants, having experienced how unequal their own force was to resist that of the Romans, acquiesced in the dominion of their masters, and were gradually incorporated as a part of that mighty empire.

This was the last durable conquest made by the Romans; and Britain, once subdued, gave no farther inquietude to the victor. Caledonia alone, defended by barren mountains, and by the contempt which the Romans entertained for it, sometimes infested the more cultivated parts of the island by the incursions of its inhabitants. The better to secure the frontiers of the empire, Adrian, who visited this island, built a rampart between the river Tyne and the frith of Solway: Lollius Urbicus, under Antoninus Pius, erected one in the place where Agricola had formerly established his garrisons: Severus, who made an expedition into Britain, and carried his arms to the most northern extremity of it, added new fortifications to the wall of Adrian; and during the reign of all the Roman emperors, such a profound tranquillity prevailed in Britain, that little mention is made of the affairs of that island by any historian. The only incidents, which occur, are some seditions or rebellions of the Roman legions quartered there, and some usurpations of the imperial dignity by the Roman governors. The natives, disarmed, dispirited, and submissive, had left all desire and even idea of their former liberty and independence.

[n] Tacit. Agr.   [o] Tacit. Agr.

CHAPTER I

But the period was now come, when that enormous fabric of the Roman empire, which had diffused slavery and oppression, together with peace and civility, over so considerable a part of the globe, was approaching towards its final dissolution. Italy, and the center of the empire, removed, during so many ages, from all concern in the wars, had entirely lost the military spirit, and were peopled by an enervated race, equally disposed to submit to a foreign yoke, or to the tyranny of their own rulers. The emperors found themselves obliged to recruit their legions from the frontier provinces, where the genius of war, though languishing, was not totally extinct; and these mercenary forces, careless of laws and civil institutions, established a military government, no less dangerous to the sovereign than to the people. The farther progress of the same disorders introduced the bordering barbarians into the service of the Romans; and those fierce nations, having now added discipline to their native bravery, could no longer be restrained by the impotent policy of the emperors, who were accustomed to employ one in the destruction of the others. Sensible of their own force, and allured by the prospect of so rich a prize, the northern barbarians, in the reign of Arcadius and Honorius, assailed at once all the frontiers of the Roman empire; and having first satiated their avidity by plunder, began to think of fixing a settlement in the wasted provinces. The more distant barbarians, who occupied the deserted habitations of the former, advanced in their acquisitions, and pressed with their incumbent weight the Roman state, already unequal to the load which it sustained. Instead of arming the people in their own defence, the emperors recalled all the distant legions, in whom alone they could repose confidence; and collected the whole military force for the defence of the capital and center of the empire. The necessity of self-preservation had superseded the ambition of power; and the ancient point of honour, never to contract the limits of the empire, could no longer be attended to in this desperate extremity.

Britain by its situation was removed from the fury of these barbarous incursions; and being also a remote province, not much valued by the Romans, the legions, which defended it, were carried over to the protection of Italy and Gaul. But that province, though secured by the sea against the inroads of the greater tribes of barbarians, found enemies on its frontiers, who took advantage of its present defenceless situation. The Picts and Scots, who dwelt in the northern parts, beyond the wall of Antoninus, made incursions upon their peaceable and effeminate neighbours; and besides the temporary depredations which they committed, these combined nations threatened the whole province with subjection, or, what the inhabitants more dreaded, with plunder and devastation. The Picts seem to have been a tribe of the native British race, who, having been chaced into the northern parts by the conquests of Agricola, had there intermingled with the ancient inhabitants: The Scots were derived from the same Celtic origin, had first been established in Ireland, had migrated to the north-west coasts of this island, and had long been accustomed, as well from their old as their new feats, to infest the Roman province by pyracy and rapine.* These tribes, finding their more opulent neighbours exposed to invasion, soon broke over the Roman wall, no longer defended by the Roman arms; and though a contemptible enemy in themselves, met with no resistance from the unwarlike inhabitants. The Britons, accustomed to have recourse to the emperors for defence as well as government, made supplications to Rome; and one legion was sent over for their protection. This force was an over-match for the barbarians, repelled their invasion, routed them in every engagement, and having chaced them into their ancient limits, returned in triumph to the defence of the southern provinces of the empire.*° Their retreat brought on a new invasion of the enemy. The Britons made again an application to Rome, and again obtained the assistance of a legion, which proved effectual for their relief: But the Romans, reduced to extremities at home, and fatigued with those distant expeditions, informed the Britons that they must no longer look to them for succour, exhorted them to arm in their own defence, and urged, that, as they were now their own masters, it became them to protect by their valour that independence, which their ancient lords had conferred upon them.*9 That they might leave the island with the better grace, the Romans assisted them in erecting anew the wall of Severus, which was built entirely of stone, and which the Britons had not at that time artificers skilful enough to repair.* And having done this

---

*See Note [A] at the end of the Volume. *° Gildas, Bede, lib. 1. cap. 12. Paull. Diacon. *9 Bede, lib. 1. cap. 12. * Ibid.

CHAPTER I

last good office to the inhabitants, they bid a final adieu to Britain, about the year 448; after being masters of the more considerable part of it during the course of near four centuries.

THE BRITONS

THE ABJECT BRITONS regarded this present of liberty as fatal to them; and were in no condition to put in practice the prudent counsel given them by the Romans, to arm in their own defence. Unaccustomed both to the perils of war, and to the cares of civil government, they found themselves incapable of forming or executing any measures for resisting the incursions of the barbarians. Gratian also and Constantine, two Romans who had a little before assumed the purple in Britain, had carried over to the continent the flower of the British youth; and having perished in their unsuccessful attempts on the imperial throne, had despoiled the island of those, who, in this desperate extremity, were best able to defend it. The Picts and Scots, finding that the Romans had finally relinquished Britain, now regarded the whole as their prey, and attacked the northern wall with redoubled forces. The Britons, already subdued by their own fears, found the ramparts but a weak defence for them; and deserting their station, left the country entirely open to the inroads of the barbarous enemy. The invaders carried devastation and ruin along with them; and exerted to the utmost their native ferocity, which was not mitigated by the helpless condition and submissive behaviour of the inhabitants.[5] The unhappy Britons had a third time recourse to Rome, which had declared its resolution for ever to abandon them. Aetius, the patrician, sustained, at that time, by his valour and magnanimity, the towering ruins of the empire, and revived for a moment among the degenerate Romans the spirit, as well as discipline, of their ancestors. The British ambassadors carried to him the letter of their countrymen, which was inscribed, *The Groans of the Britons*. The tenor of the epistle was suitable to its superscription. *The barbarians*, say they, *on the one hand, chace us into the*

---

[5] Gildas, Bede, lib. 1. Ann Beverl. p. 45.

sea; the sea, on the other, throws us back upon the barbarians; and we have only the hard choice left us, of perishing by the sword or by the waves. But Aetius, pressed by the arms of Attila, the most terrible enemy that ever assailed the empire, had no leisure to attend to the complaints of allies, whom generosity alone could induce him to assist." The Britons, thus rejected, were reduced to despair, deserted their habitations, abandoned tillage, and flying for protection to the forests and mountains, suffered equally from hunger and from the enemy. The barbarians themselves began to feel the pressures of famine in a country which they had ravaged; and being harassed by the dispersed Britons, who had not dared to resist them in a body, they retreated with their spoils into their own country."

The Britons, taking advantage of this interval, returned to their usual occupations; and the favourable seasons which succeeded, seconding their industry, made them soon forget their past miseries, and restored to them great plenty of all the necessaries of life. No more can be imagined to have been possessed by a people so rude, who had not, without the assistance of the Romans, art of masonry sufficient to raise a stone rampart for their own defence: Yet the Monkish historians," who treat of those events, complain of the luxury of the Britons during this period, and ascribe to that vice, not to their cowardice or improvident counsels, all their subsequent calamities.

The Britons, entirely occupied in the enjoyment of the present interval of peace, made no provision for resisting the enemy, who, invited by their former timid behaviour, soon threatened them with a new invasion. We are not exactly informed what species of civil government the Romans on their departure had left among the Britons; but it appears probable, that the great men in the different districts assumed a kind of regal, though precarious authority; and lived in a great measure independant of each other." To this disunion of counsels were also added the disputes of theology; and the disciples of Pelagius, who was himself a native of Britain, having encreased to a great multitude, gave alarm to the clergy, who seem to have been more intent on suppressing them, than on opposing the public enemy." Labouring under these do-

---

' Gildas, Bede, lib. 1. cap. 13. Malmesbury, lib. 1. cap. 1. Ann. Beverl. p. 45.
" Chron. Sax. p. 11. Edit. 1692. " Ann. Beverl. p. 45. ˣ Gildas, Bede, lib.
1. cap. 14. ʸ Gildas, Usher Ant. Brit. p. 248, 347. ᶻ Gildas, Bede, lib. 1.
cap. 17. Constant. in vita Germ.

mestic evils, and menaced with a foreign invasion, the Britons attended only to the suggestions of their present fears; and following the counsels of Vortigern, prince of Dumnonium, who, though stained with every vice, possessed the chief authority among them,[a] they sent into Germany a deputation to invite over the Saxons for their protection and assistance.

THE SAXONS

O F ALL THE BARBAROUS NATIONS, known either in ancient or
modern times, the Germans seem to have been the most distinguished both by their manners and political institutions, and to have carried to the highest pitch the virtues of valour and love of liberty; the only virtues which can have place among an uncivilized people, where justice and humanity are commonly neglected. Kingly government, even when established among the Germans, (for it was not universal) possessed a very limited authority; and though the sovereign was usually chosen from among the royal family, he was directed in every measure by the common consent of the nation, over whom he presided. When any important affairs were transacted, all the warriors met in arms; the men of greatest authority employed persuasion to engage their consent; the people expressed their approbation by rattling their armour, or their dissent by murmurs; there was no necessity for a nice scrutiny of votes among a multitude, who were usually carried with a strong current to one side or the other; and the measure, thus suddenly chosen by general agreement, was executed with alacrity, and prosecuted with vigour. Even in war, the princes governed more by example than by authority: But in peace, the civil union was in a great measure dissolved, and the inferior leaders administered justice, after an independant manner, each in his particular district. These were elected by the votes of the people in their great councils; and though regard was paid to nobility in the choice, their personal qualities, chiefly their valour, procured them, from the suffrages of their fellow-citizens, that honorable but dangerous distinction. The warriors of each tribe attached

[a] Gildas, Gul. Malm. p. 8.

themselves to their leader, with the most devoted affection and most unshaken constancy. They attended him as his ornament in peace, as his defence in war, as his council in the administration of justice. Their constant emulation in military renown dissolved not that inviolable friendship which they professed to their chieftain and to each other. To die for the honour of their band was their chief ambition: To survive its disgrace, or the death of their leader, was infamous. They even carried into the field their women and children, who adopted all the martial sentiments of the men: and being thus impelled by every human motive, they were invincible; where they were not opposed, either by the similar manners and institutions of the neighbouring Germans, or by the superior discipline, arms, and numbers of the Romans.[b]

The leaders and their military companions were maintained by the labour of their slaves, or by that of the weaker and less warlike part of the community, whom they defended. The contributions, which they levied, went not beyond a bare subsistence; and the honours, acquired by a superior rank, were the only reward of their superior dangers and fatigues. All the refined arts of life were unknown among the Germans: Tillage itself was almost wholly neglected: They even seem to have been anxious to prevent any improvements of that nature; and the leaders, by annually distributing anew all the land among the inhabitants of each village, kept them from attaching themselves to particular possessions, or making such progress in agriculture as might divert their attention from military expeditions, the chief occupation of the community.[c]

The Saxons had been for some time regarded as one of the most warlike tribes of this fierce people, and had become the terror of the neighbouring nations.[d] They had diffused themselves from the northern parts of Germany and the Cimbrian Chersonesus, and had taken possession of all the sea-coast from the mouth of the Rhine to Jutland; whence they had long infested by their pyracies all the eastern and southern parts of Britain, and the northern of Gaul.[e] In order to oppose their inroads, the Romans had established an officer, whom they called *Count of the Saxon shore;* and as the naval arts can flourish among a civilized people alone, they

[b] Caesar, lib. 6. Tacit. de Mor. Germ. [c] Caesar, lib. 6. Tacit. ibid. [d] Amm. Marcell. lib. 28. Orosius. [e] Amm. Marcell. lib. 27. cap. 7. lib. 28. cap. 7.

CHAPTER I

seem to have been more successful in repelling the Saxons than any of the other barbarians, by whom they were invaded. The dissolution of the Roman power invited them to renew their inroads; and it was an acceptable circumstance, that the deputies of the Britons appeared among them, and prompted them to undertake an enterprize, to which they were of themselves sufficiently inclined.[f]

Hengist and Horsa, two brothers, possessed great credit among the Saxons, and were much celebrated both for their valour and nobility. They were reputed, as most of the Saxon princes, to be sprung from Woden, who was worshipped as a god among those nations, and they are said to be his great grandsons;[g] a circumstance which added much to their authority. We shall not attempt to trace any higher the origin of those princes and nations. It is evident what fruitless labour it must be to search, in those barbarous and illiterate ages, for the annals of a people, when their first leaders, known in any true history, were believed by them to be the fourth in descent from a fabulous deity, or from a man, exalted by ignorance into that character. The dark industry of antiquaries, led by imaginary analogies of names, or by uncertain traditions, would in vain attempt to pierce into that deep obscurity, which covers the remote history of those nations.

These two brothers, observing the other provinces of Germany to be occupied by a warlike and necessitous people, and the rich provinces of Gaul already conquered or over-run by other German tribes, found it easy to persuade their countrymen to embrace the sole enterprize, which promised a favourable opportunity of displaying their valour and gratifying their avidity. They embarked their troops in three vessels, and about the year 449 or 450,[h] carried over 1600 men, who landed in the isle of Thanet, and immediately marched to the defence of the Britons against the northern invaders. The Scots and Picts were unable to resist the valour of these auxiliaries; and the Britons, applauding their own wisdom in calling over the Saxons, hoped thenceforth to enjoy peace and security under the powerful protection of that warlike people.

[f] Will. Malm. p. 8.   [g] Bede, lib. 1. cap. 15. Saxon Chron. p. 13. Nennius, cap. 28.   [h] Saxon Chronicle, p. 12. Gul. Malm. p. 11. Huntington, lib. 2. p. 309. Ethelwerd. Brompton, p. 728.

But Hengist and Horsa, perceiving, from their easy victory over the Scots and Picts, with what facility they might subdue the Britons themselves, who had not been able to resist those feeble invaders, were determined to conquer and fight for their own grandeur, not for the defence of their degenerate allies. They sent intelligence to Saxony of the fertility and riches of Britain; and represented as certain the subjection of a people, so long disused to arms, who, being now cut off from the Roman empire, of which they had been a province during so many ages, had not yet acquired any union among themselves, and were destitute of all affection to their new liberties, and of all national attachments and regards.[i] The vices and pusillanimity of Vortigern, the British leader, were a new ground of hope; and the Saxons in Germany, following such agreeable prospects, soon reinforced Hengist and Horsa with 5000 men, who came over in seventeen vessels. The Britons now began to entertain apprehensions of their allies, whose numbers they found continually augmenting; but thought of no remedy, except a passive submission and connivance. This weak expedient soon failed them. The Saxons sought a quarrel by complaining, that their subsidies were ill paid, and their provisions withdrawn:[k] And immediately taking off the mask, they formed an alliance with the Picts and Scots, and proceeded to open hostility against the Britons.

The Britons, impelled by these violent extremities, and roused to indignation against their treacherous auxiliaries, were necessitated to take arms; and having deposed Vortigern, who had become odious from his vices, and from the bad event of his rash counsels, they put themselves under the command of his son, Vortimer. They fought many battles with their enemies; and though the victories in these actions be disputed between the British and Saxon annalists, the progress still made by the Saxons prove that the advantage was commonly on their side. In one battle, however, fought at Eglesford, now Ailsford, Horsa, the Saxon general, was slain; and left the sole command over his countrymen in the hands of Hengist. This active general, continually reinforced by fresh numbers from Germany, carried devastation

[i] Chron. Sax. p. 12. Ann. Beverl. p. 49.   [k] Bede, lib. 1. cap. 15. Nennius, cap. 35. Gildas, § 23.

into the most remote corners of Britain; and being chiefly anxious to spread the terror of his arms, he spared neither age, nor sex, nor condition, wherever he marched with his victorious forces. The private and public edifices of the Britons were reduced to ashes: The priests were slaughtered on the altars by those idolatrous ravagers: The bishops and nobility shared the fate of the vulgar: The people, flying to the mountains and deserts, were intercepted and butchered in heaps: Some were glad to accept of life and servitude under their victors: Others, deserting their native country, took shelter in the province of Armorica; where, being charitably received by a people of the same language and manners, they settled in great numbers, and gave the country the name of Brittany.[l]

The British writers assign one cause, which facilitated the entrance of the Saxons into this island; the love, with which Vortigern was at first seized for Rovena, the daughter of Hengist, and which that artful warrior made use of to blind the eyes of the imprudent monarch.[m] The same historians add, that Vortimer died; and that Vortigern, being restored to the throne, accepted of a banquet from Hengist, at Stonehenge; where 300 of his nobility were treacherously slaughtered, and himself detained captive.[n] But these stories seem to have been invented by the Welsh authors, in order to palliate the weak resistance made at first by their countrymen, and to account for the rapid progress and licentious devastations of the Saxons.[o]

After the death of Vortimer, Ambrosius, a Briton, though of Roman descent, was invested with the command over his countrymen, and endeavoured, not without success, to unite them in their resistance against the Saxons. Those contests encreased the animosity between the two nations, and roused the military spirit of the ancient inhabitants, which had before been sunk into a fatal lethargy. Hengist, however, notwithstanding their opposition, still maintained his ground in Britain; and in order to divide the forces and attention of the natives, he called over a new tribe of Saxons, under the command of his brother Octa, and of Ebissa, the son of Octa; and he settled them in Northumberland. He himself re-

---

[l] Bede, lib. 1. cap. 15. Usher, p. 226. Gildas, § 24.   [m] Nennius. Galfr. lib. 6. cap. 12.   [n] Nennius, cap. 47. Galfr.   [o] Stillingfleet's Orig. Britt. p. 324, 325.

mained in the southern parts of the island, and laid the foundation of the kingdom of Kent, comprehending the county of that name, Middlesex, Essex, and part of Surrey. He fixed his royal seat at Canterbury; where he governed about forty years, and he died in or near the year 488; leaving his new-acquired dominions to his posterity.

The success of Hengist excited the avidity of the other northern Germans; and at different times, and under different leaders, they flocked over in multitudes to the invasion of this island. These conquerors were chiefly composed of three tribes, the Saxons, Angles, and Jutes,[p] who all passed under the common appellation, sometimes of Saxons, sometimes of Angles; and speaking the same language, and being governed by the same institutions, they were naturally led, from these causes, as well as from their common interest, to unite themselves against the ancient inhabitants. The resistance however, though unequal, was still maintained by the Britons: but became every day more feeble: and their calamities admitted of few intervals, till they were driven into Cornwal and Wales, and received protection from the remote situation or inaccessible mountains of those countries.

The first Saxon state, after that of Kent, which was established in Britain, was the kingdom of South-Saxony. In the year 477,[q] Aella, a Saxon chief, brought over an army from Germany; and landing on the southern coast, proceeded to take possession of the neighbouring territory. The Britons, now armed, did not tamely abandon their possessions; nor were they expelled, till defeated in many battles by their warlike invaders. The most memorable action, mentioned by historians, is that of Mearcredes-Burn;[r] where, though the Saxons seem to have obtained the victory, they suffered so considerable a loss, as somewhat retarded the progress of their conquests. But Aella, reinforced by fresh numbers of his countrymen, again took the field against the Britons; and laid

[p] Bede, lib. 1. cap. 15. Ethelwerd, p. 833. edit. Camdeni. Chron. Sax. p. 12. Ann. Beverl. p. 78. The inhabitants of Kent and the Isle of Wight were Jutes. Essex, Middlesex, Surrey, Sussex, and all the southern counties to Cornwal, were peopled by Saxons: Mercia and other parts of the kingdom were inhabited by Angles.   [q] Chron. Sax. p. 14. Ann. Beverl. p. 81.
[r] Saxon. Chron. A. D. 485. Flor. Wigorn.

CHAPTER I

siege to Andred-Ceaster, which was defended by the garrison and inhabitants with desperate valour.[s] The Saxons, enraged by this resistance, and by the fatigues and dangers which they had sustained, redoubled their efforts against the place, and when masters of it, put all their enemies to the sword without distinction. This decisive advantage secured the conquests of Aella, who assumed the name of King, and extended his dominion over Sussex and a great part of Surrey. He was stopped in his progress to the east by the kingdom of Kent: In that to the west by another tribe of Saxons, who had taken possession of that territory.

These Saxons, from the situation of the country, in which they settled, were called the West-Saxons, and landed in the year 495, under the command of Cerdic, and of his son Kenric.[t] The Britons were, by past experience, so much on their guard, and so well prepared to receive the enemy, that they gave battle to Cerdic the very day of his landing; and though vanquished, still defended, for some time, their liberties against the invaders. None of the other tribes of Saxons met with such vigorous resistance, or exerted such valour and perseverance in pushing their conquests. Cerdic was even obliged to call for the assistance of his countrymen from the kingdoms of Kent and Sussex, as well as from Germany, and he was thence joined by a fresh army under the command of Porte, and of his sons Bleda and Megla.[u] Strengthened by these succours, he fought, in the year 508, a desperate battle with the Britons, commanded by Nazan-Leod, who was victorious in the beginning of the action, and routed the wing in which Cerdic himself commanded. But Kenric, who had prevailed in the other wing, brought timely assistance to his father, and restored the battle, which ended in a complete victory gained by the Saxons.[w] Nazan-Leod perished, with 5000 of his army: But left the Britons more weakened than discouraged by his death. The war still continued, though the success was commonly on the side of the Saxons, whose short swords and close manner of fighting gave them great advantage over the missile weapons of the Britons. Cerdic was not wanting to his good fortune; and in order to extend his conquests, he

[s] Hen. Huntin. lib. 2.   [t] Will. Malm. lib. 1. cap. 1. p. 12. Chron. Sax. p. 15.
[u] Chron. Sax. p. 17.   [w] H. Hunting. lib. 2. Ethelwerd, lib. 1. Chron. Sax. p. 17.

laid siege to Mount Badon or Banesdowne near Bath, whither the most obstinate of the discomfited Britons had retired. The southern Britons in this extremity applied for assistance to Arthur, Prince of the Silures, whose heroic valour now sustained the declining fate of this country.[x] This is that Arthur so much celebrated in the songs of Thaliessin, and the other British bards, and whose military atchievements have been blended with so many fables as even to give occasion for entertaining a doubt of his real existence. But poets, though they disfigure the most certain history by their fictions, and use strange liberties with truth where they are the sole historians, as among the Britons, have commonly some foundation for their wildest exaggerations. Certain it is, that the siege of Badon was raised by the Britons in the year 520; and the Saxons were there discomfited in a great battle.[y] This misfortune stopped the progress of Cerdic; but was not sufficient to wrest from him the conquests, which he had already made. He and his son, Kenric, who succeeded him, established the kingdom of the West-Saxons or of Wessex, over the counties of Hants, Dorset, Wilts, Berks, and the Isle of Wight, and left their new-acquired dominions to their posterity. Cerdic died in 534, Kenric in 560.

While the Saxons made this progress in the south, their countrymen were not less active in other quarters. In the year 527, a great tribe of adventurers, under several leaders, landed on the east-coast of Britain; and after fighting many battles, of which history has preserved no particular account, they established three new kingdoms in this island. Uffa assumed the title of king of the East-Angles in 575; Crida that of Mercia in 585;[z] and Erkenwin that of East-Saxony or Essex nearly about the same time; but the year is uncertain. This latter kingdom was dismembered from that of Kent, and comprehended Essex, Middlesex, and part of Hertfordshire. That of the East-Angles, the counties of Cambridge, Suffolk, and Norfolk: Mercia was extended over all the middle counties, from the banks of the Severn, to the frontiers of these two kingdoms.

The Saxons, soon after the landing of Hengist, had been planted in Northumberland; but as they met with an obstinate

[x] Hunting. lib. 2.   [y] Gildas, Saxon Chron. H. Hunting. lib. 2.   [z] Math. West. Huntingdon. lib. 2.

CHAPTER I

resistance, and made but small progress in subduing the inhabitants, their affairs were in so unsettled a condition, that none of their princes for a long time assumed the appellation of king. At last in 547,[a] Ida, a Saxon prince of great valour,[b] who claimed a descent, as did all the other princes of that nation, from Woden, brought over a reinforcement from Germany, and enabled the Northumbrians to carry on their conquests over the Britons. He entirely subdued the county now called Northumberland, the bishopric of Durham, as well as some of the south-east counties of Scotland; and he assumed the crown under the title of king of Bernicia. Nearly about the same time, Aella, another Saxon prince, having conquered Lancashire, and the greater part of Yorkshire, received the appellation of king of Deiri.[c] These two kingdoms were united in the person of Ethelfrid, grandson of Ida, who married Acca, the daughter of Aella; and expelling her brother, Edwin, established one of the most powerful of the Saxon kingdoms, by the title of Northumberland. How far his dominions extended into the country now called Scotland is uncertain; but it cannot be doubted, that all the lowlands, especially the east-coast of that country, were peopled in a great measure from Germany; though the expeditions, made by the several Saxon adventurers, have escaped the records of history. The language, spoken in those countries, which is purely Saxon, is a stronger proof of this event, than can be opposed by the imperfect, or rather fabulous annals, which are obtruded on us by the Scottish historians.

THE HEPTARCHY

THUS WAS ESTABLISHED, after a violent contest of near a hundred and fifty years, the Heptarchy, or seven Saxon kingdoms, in Britain; and the whole southern part of the island, except Wales and Cornwal, had totally changed its inhabitants, language, customs, and political institutions. The Britons, under the Roman dominion, had made such advances towards arts and civil manners, that they had built twenty-eight considerable cities

[a] Chron. Sax. p. 19.   [b] Will. Malms p. 19.   [c] Ann. Bever. p. 78.

within their province, besides a great number of villages and country-seats:[d] But the fierce conquerors, by whom they were now subdued, threw every thing back into ancient barbarity; and those few natives, who were not either massacred or expelled their habitations, were reduced to the most abject slavery. None of the other northern conquerors, the Franks, Goths, Vandals, or Burgundians, though they over-ran the southern provinces of the empire like a mighty torrent, made such devastations in the conquered territories, or were inflamed into so violent an animosity against the ancient inhabitants. As the Saxons came over at intervals in separate bodies, the Britons, however at first unwarlike, were tempted to make resistance; and hostilities, being thereby prolonged, proved more destructive to both parties, especially to the vanquished. The first invaders from Germany, instead of excluding other adventurers, who must share with them the spoils of the ancient inhabitants, were obliged to solicit fresh supplies from their own country; and a total extermination of the Britons became the sole expedient for providing a settlement and subsistence to the new planters. Hence there have been found in history few conquests more ruinous than that of the Saxons; and few revolutions more violent than that which they introduced.

So long as the contest was maintained with the natives, the several Saxon princes preserved a union of counsels and interests; but after the Britons were shut up in the barren countries of Cornwal and Wales, and gave no farther disturbance to the conquerors, the band of alliance was in a great measure dissolved among the princes of the Heptarchy. Though one prince seems still to have been allowed, or to have assumed, an ascendant over the whole, his authority, if it ought ever to be deemed regular or legal, was extremely limited; and each state acted as if it had been independant, and wholly separate from the rest. Wars, therefore, and revolutions and dissensions were unavoidable among a turbulent and military people; and these events, however intricate or confused, ought now to become the objects of our attention. But, added to the difficulty of carrying on at once the history of seven independant kingdoms, there is great discouragement to a writer, arising from the uncertainty, at least barrenness, of the accounts

---

[d] Gildas. Bede, lib. 1.

CHAPTER I

transmitted to us. The Monks, who were the only annalists during those ages, lived remote from public affairs, considered the civil transactions as entirely subordinate to the ecclesiastical, and besides partaking of the ignorance and barbarity, which were then universal, were strongly infected with credulity, with the love of wonder, and with a propensity to imposture; vices almost inseparable from their profession, and manner of life. The history of that period abounds in names, but is extremely barren of events; or the events are related so much without circumstances and causes, that the most profound or most eloquent writer must despair of rendering them either instructive or entertaining to the reader. Even the great learning and vigorous imagination of Milton sunk under the weight; and this author scruples not to declare, that the skirmishes of kites or crows as much merited a particular narrative, as the confused transactions and battles of the Saxon Heptarchy.[e] In order, however, to connect the events in some tolerable measure, we shall give a succinct account of the successions of kings, and of the more remarkable revolutions in each particular kingdom; beginning with that of Kent, which was the first established.

THE KINGDOM OF KENT

ESCUS SUCCEEDED HIS FATHER, Hengist, in the kingdom of Kent; but seems not to have possessed the military genius of that conqueror, who first made way for the entrance of the Saxon arms into Britain. All the Saxons, who sought either the fame of valour, or new establishments by arms, flocked to the standard of Aella, king of Sussex, who was carrying on successful war against the Britons, and laying the foundations of a new kingdom. Escus was content to possess in tranquillity the kingdom of Kent, which he left in 512 to his son Octa, in whose time the East-Saxons established their monarchy, and dismembered the provinces of Essex and Middlesex from that of Kent. His death, after a reign of twenty-two years, made room for his son Hermenric in 534, who performed nothing memorable during a reign of thirty-two

[e] Milton in Kennet, p. 50.

years; except associating with him his son, Ethelbert, in the government, that he might secure the succession in his family, and prevent such revolutions as are incident to a turbulent and barbarous monarchy.

Ethelbert revived the reputation of his family, which had languished for some generations. The inactivity of his predecessors, and the situation of his country, secured from all hostility with the Britons, seem to have much enfeebled the warlike genius of the Kentish Saxons; and Ethelbert, in his first attempt to aggrandize his country, and distinguish his own name, was unsuccessful.[f] He was twice discomfited in battle by Ceaulin, king of Wessex; and obliged to yield the superiority in the Heptarchy to that ambitious monarch, who preserved no moderation in his victory, and by reducing the kingdom of Sussex to subjection, excited jealousy in all the other princes. An association was formed against him; and Ethelbert, intrusted with the command of the allies, gave him battle, and obtained a decisive victory.[g] Ceaulin died soon after; and Ethelbert succeeded as well to his ascendant among the Saxon states, as to his other ambitious projects. He reduced all the princes, except the king of Northumberland, to a strict dependance upon him; and even established himself by force on the throne of Mercia, the most extensive of the Saxon kingdoms. Apprehensive, however, of a dangerous league against him, like that by which he himself had been enabled to overthrow Ceaulin, he had the prudence to resign the kingdom of Mercia to Webba, the rightful heir, the son of Crida, who had first founded that monarchy. But governed still by ambition more than by justice, he gave Webba possession of the crown on such conditions, as rendered him little better than a tributary prince under his artful benefactor.

But the most memorable event, which distinguished the reign of this great prince, was the introduction of the Christian religion among the English Saxons. The superstition of the Germans, particularly that of the Saxons, was of the grossest and most barbarous kind; and being founded on traditional tales, received from their ancestors, not reduced to any system, not supported by political institutions, like that of the Druids, it seems to have made little impression on its votaries, and to have easily resigned its place to

[f] Chron. Sax. p. 21.　　[g] H. Hunting. lib. 2.

CHAPTER I

the new doctrine, promulgated to them. Woden, whom they deemed the ancestor of all their princes, was regarded as the god of war, and, by a natural consequence, became their supreme deity, and the chief object of their religious worship. They believed, that, if they obtained the favour of this divinity by their valour, (for they made less account of the other virtues) they should be admitted after their death into his hall; and reposing on couches, should satiate themselves with ale from the skulls of their enemies, whom they had slain in battle. Incited by this idea of paradise, which gratified at once the passion of revenge and that of intemperance, the ruling inclinations of barbarians, they despised the dangers of war, and encreased their native ferocity against the vanquished by their religious prejudices. We know little of the other theological tenets of the Saxons: We only learn that they were polytheists; that they worshipped the sun and moon; that they adored the god of thunder, under the name of Thor; that they had images in their temples; that they practised sacrifices; believed firmly in spells and inchantments, and admitted in general a system of doctrines, which they held as sacred, but which, like all other superstitions, must carry the air of the wildest extravagance, if propounded to those who are not familiarized to it from their earliest infancy.

The constant hostilities, which the Saxons maintained against the Britons, would naturally indispose them for receiving the Christian faith, when preached to them by such inveterate enemies; and perhaps the Britons, as is objected to them by Gildas and Bede, were not overfond of communicating to their cruel invaders the doctrine of eternal life and salvation. But as a civilized people, however subdued by arms, still maintain a sensible superiority over barbarous and ignorant nations, all the other northern conquerors of Europe had been already induced to embrace the Christian faith, which they found established in the empire; and it was impossible but the Saxons informed of this event, must have regarded with some degree of veneration a doctrine, which had acquired the ascendant over all their brethren. However limited in their views, they could not but have perceived a degree of cultivation in the southern countries beyond what they themselves possessed; and it was natural for them to yield to that superior knowledge, as well as zeal, by which the inhabitants of the Christian kingdoms were even at that time distinguished.

But these causes might long have failed of producing any considerable effect, had not a favourable incident prepared the means of introducing Christianity into Kent. Ethelbert, in his father's lifetime, had married Bertha, the only daughter of Carlbert, king of Paris,[h] one of the descendants of Clovis, the conqueror of Gaul; but before he was admitted to this alliance, he was obliged to stipulate, that the princess should enjoy the free exercise of her religion; a concession not difficult to be obtained from the idolatrous Saxons.[i] Bertha brought over a French bishop to the court of Canterbury; and being zealous for the propagation of her religion, she had been very assiduous in her devotional exercises, had supported the credit of her faith by an irreproachable conduct, and had employed every art of insinuation and address to reconcile her husband to her religious principles. Her popularity in the court, and her influence over Ethelbert, had so well paved the way for the reception of the Christian doctrine, that Gregory, sirnamed the Great, then Roman pontiff, began to entertain hopes of effecting a project which he himself, before he mounted the papal throne, had once embraced, of converting the British Saxons.

It happened, that this prelate, at that time in a private station, had observed in the market-place of Rome some Saxon youth exposed to sale, whom the Roman merchants, in their trading voyages to Britain, had bought of their mercenary parents. Struck with the beauty of their fair complexions and blooming countenances, Gregory asked to what country they belonged; and being told they were *Angles,* he replied, that they ought more properly to be denominated *angels:* It were a pity that the Prince of Darkness should enjoy so fair a prey, and that so beautiful a frontispiece should cover a mind destitute of internal grace and righteousness. Enquiring farther concerning the name of their province, he was informed, that it was Deïri, a district of Northumberland: *Deïri!* replied he, *that is good! They are called to the mercy of God from his anger,* De ira. *But what is the name of the king of that province?* He was told it was *Aella* or *Alla: Alleluiah,* cried he: *We must endeavour, that the praises of God be sung in their country.* Moved by these allusions, which appeared to him so happy, he determined to undertake,

[h] Greg. of Tours, lib. 9. cap. 26. H. Hunting. lib. 2.   [i] Bede, lib. 1. cap. 25. Brompton, p. 729.

CHAPTER I

himself, a mission into Britain; and having obtained the Pope's approbation, he prepared for that perilous journey: But his popularity at home was so great, that the Romans, unwilling to expose him to such dangers, opposed his design; and he was obliged for the present to lay aside all farther thoughts of executing that pious purpose.[k]

The controversy between the Pagans and the Christians was not entirely cooled in that age; and no pontiff before Gregory had ever carried to greater excess an intemperate zeal against the former religion. He had waged war with all the precious monuments of the ancients, and even with their writings; which, as appears from the strain of his own wit, as well as from the style of his compositions, he had not taste or genius sufficient to comprehend. Ambitious to distinguish his pontificate by the conversion of the British Saxons, he pitched on Augustine, a Roman monk, and sent him with forty associates to preach the gospel in this island. These missionaries, terrified with the dangers which might attend their proposing a new doctrine to so fierce a people, of whose language they were ignorant, stopped some time in France, and sent back Augustine to lay the hazards and difficulties before the Pope, and crave his permission to desist from the undertaking. But Gregory exhorted them to persevere in their purpose, advised them to chuse some interpreters from among the Franks, who still spoke the same language with the Saxons,[l] and recommended them to the good offices of queen Brunehaut, who had at this time usurped the sovereign power in France. This princess, though stained with every vice of treachery and cruelty, either possessed or pretended great zeal for the cause; and Gregory acknowledged, that to her friendly assistance was, in a great measure, owing the success of that undertaking.[m]

Augustine, on his arrival in Kent in the year 597,[n] found the danger much less than he had apprehended. Ethelbert, already well-disposed towards the Christian faith, assigned him a habitation in the Isle of Thanet; and soon after admitted him to a conference. Apprehensive, however, lest spells or enchantments might be employed against him by priests, who brought an unknown worship from a distant country, he had the precaution to

[k] Bede, lib. 2. cap. 1. Spell. Conc. p. 91.   [l] Bede, lib. 1. cap. 23.   [m] Greg. Epist. lib. 9 epist. 56. Spell. Conc. p. 82.   [n] Higden, Polychron. lib. 5. Chron. Sax. p. 23.

receive them in the open air, where, he believed the force of their magic would be more easily dissipated.[o] Here Augustine, by means of his interpreters, delivered to him the tenets of the Christian faith, and promised him eternal joys above, and a kingdom in heaven without end, if he would be persuaded to receive that salutary doctrine. "Your words and promises," replied Ethelbert,[p] "are fair; but because they are new and uncertain, I cannot entirely yield to them, and relinquish the principles, which I and my ancestors have so long maintained. You are welcome, however, to remain here in peace; and as you have undertaken so long a journey, solely, as it appears, for what you believe to be for our advantage, I will supply you with all necessaries, and permit you to deliver your doctrine to my subjects."[q]

Augustine, encouraged by this favourable reception, and seeing now a prospect of success, proceeded with redoubled zeal to preach the gospel to the Kentish Saxons. He attracted their attention by the austerity of his manners, by the severe pennances to which he subjected himself, by the abstinence and self-denial which he practised: And having excited their wonder by a course of life, which appeared so contrary to nature, he procured more easily their belief of miracles, which, it was pretended, he wrought for their conversion.[r] Influenced by these motives, and by the declared favour of the court, numbers of the Kentish men were baptized; and the king himself was persuaded to submit to that rite of Christianity. His example had great influence with his subjects; but he employed no force to bring them over to the new doctrine. Augustine thought proper, in the commencement of his mission, to assume the appearance of the greatest lenity: He told Ethelbert, that the service of Christ must be entirely voluntary, and that no violence ought ever to be used in propagating so salutary a doctrine.[s]

The intelligence, received of these spiritual conquests, afforded great joy to the Romans; who now exulted as much in those peaceful trophies, as their ancestors had ever done in their most sanguinary triumphs, and most splendid victories. Gregory wrote

[o] Bede, lib. 1. cap. 25. H. Hunting. lib. 3. Brompton, p. 719. Parker Antiq. Brit. Eccl. p. 61.   [p] Bede, lib. 1. cap. 25. Chron. W. Thorn. p. 1759. [q] Bede, lib. 1. cap. 25. H. Hunting. lib. 3. Brompton, p. 729.   [r] Bede, lib. 1. cap. 26.   [s] Ibid. cap. 26. H. Hunting. lib. 3.

CHAPTER I

a letter to Ethelbert, in which, after informing him that the end of the world was approaching, he exhorted him to display his zeal in the conversion of his subjects, to exert rigour against the worship of idols, and to build up the good work of holiness by every expedient of exhortation, terror, blandishment, or correction:[t] A doctrine more suitable to that age, and to the usual papal maxims, than the tolerating principles, which Augustine had thought it prudent to inculcate. The pontiff also answered some questions, which the missionary had put concerning the government of the new church of Kent. Besides other queries, which it is not material here to relate, Augustine asked, *Whether cousin-germans might be allowed to marry?* Gregory answered, that that liberty had indeed been formerly granted by the Roman law; but that experience had shewn, that no issue could ever come from such marriages; and he therefore prohibited them. Augustine asked, *Whether a woman pregnant might be baptized?* Gregory answered, that he saw no objection. *How soon after the birth the child might receive baptism?* It was answered, Immediately, if necessary. *How soon a husband might have commerce with his wife after her delivery?* Not till she had given suck to her child: a practice to which Gregory exhorts all women. *How soon a man might enter the church, or receive the sacrament, after having had commerce with his wife?* It was replied, that, unless he had approached her without desire, merely for the sake of propagating his species, he was not without sin: But in all cases it was requisite for him, before he entered the church, or communicated, to purge himself by prayer and ablution; and he ought not, even after using these precautions, to participate immediately of the sacred duties.[u] There are some other questions and replies still more indecent and more ridiculous.[w] And on the whole it appears, that Gregory and his missionary, if sympathy of manners have any influence, were

[t] Bede, lib. 1. cap. 32. Brompton, p. 732. Spell. Conc. p. 86. [u] Bede, lib. 1 cap. 27. Spell. Conc. p. 97, 98, 99, &c. [w] Augustine asks, "Si mulier menstrua consuetudine tenetur, an ecclesiam intrare ei licet, aut sacrae communionis sacramenta percipere?" Gregory answers, "Santae communionis mysterium in eisdem diebus percipere non debet prohiberi. Si autem ex veneratione magna percipere non praesumitur, laudanda est." Augustine asks, "Si post illusionem, quae per somnum solet accidere, vel corpus Domini quilibet accipere valeat; vel, si sacerdos sit, sacra mysteria celebrare?" Gregory answers this learned question by many learned distinctions.

better calculated than men of more refined understandings, for making a progress with the ignorant and barbarous Saxons.

The more to facilitate the reception of Christianity, Gregory enjoined Augustine to remove the idols from the Heathen altars, but not to destroy the altars themselves; because the people, he said, would be allured to frequent the Christian worship, when they found it celebrated in a place, which they were accustomed to revere. And as the Pagans practised sacrifices, and feasted with the priests on their offerings, he also exhorted the missionary to persuade them, on Christian festivals, to kill their cattle in the neighbourhood of the church, and to indulge themselves in those cheerful entertainments, to which they had been habituated.[x] These political compliances shew, that, notwithstanding his ignorance and prejudices, he was not unacquainted with the arts of governing mankind. Augustine was consecrated archbishop of Canterbury, was endowed by Gregory with authority over all the British churches, and received the pall, a badge of ecclesiastical honour, from Rome.[y] Gregory also advised him not to be too much elated with his gift of working miracles;[z] and as Augustine, proud of the success of his mission, seemed to think himself entitled to extend his authority over the bishops of Gaul, the Pope informed him, that they lay entirely without the bounds of his jurisdiction.[a]

The marriage of Ethelbert with Bertha, and much more his embracing Christianity, begat a connexion of his subjects with the French, Italians, and other nations on the continent, and tended to reclaim them from that gross ignorance and barbarity, in which all the Saxon tribes had been hitherto involved.[b] Ethelbert also enacted,[c] with the consent of the states of his kingdom, a body of laws, the first written laws promulgated by any of the northern conquerors; and his reign was in every respect glorious to himself, and beneficial to his people. He governed the kingdom of Kent fifty years; and dying in 616, left the succession to his son, Eadbald. This prince, seduced by a passion for his mother-in-law, deserted for some time the Christian faith, which permitted not these incestuous marriages: His whole people immediately returned with him

---

[x] Bede, lib. 1. cap. 30. Spell. Conc. p. 89. Greg. Epist. lib. 9. epist. 71.
[y] Chron. Sax. p. 23, 24.   [z] H. Hunting. lib. 3. Spell. Conc. p. 83. Bede, lib.
1. Greg. Epist. lib. 9. epist. 6.   [a] Bede, lib. 1. cap. 27.   [b] Will. Malm. p. 10.
[c] Wilkins Leges Sax. p. 13.

to idolatry. Laurentius, the successor of Augustine, found the Christian worship wholly abandoned, and was prepared to return to France, in order to escape the mortification of preaching the gospel without fruit to the infidels. Mellitus and Justus, who had been consecrated bishops of London and Rochester, had already departed the kingdom;[d] when Laurentius, before he should entirely abandon his dignity, made one effort to reclaim the king. He appeared before that prince; and throwing off his vestments, showed his body all torn with bruises and stripes, which he had received. Eadbald, wondering that any man should have dared to treat in that manner a person of his rank, was told by Laurentius, that he had received this chastisement from St. Peter, the prince of the apostles, who had appeared to him in a vision, and severely reproving him for his intention to desert his charge, had inflicted on him these visible marks of his displeasure.[e] Whether Eadbald was struck with the miracle, or influenced by some other motive, he divorced himself from his mother-in-law, and returned to the profession of Christianity.[f] His whole people returned with him. Eadbald reached not the fame or authority of his father, and died in 640, after a reign of twenty-five years; leaving two sons, Erminfrid and Ercombert.

Ercombert, though the younger son, by Emma, a French princess, found means to mount the throne. He is celebrated by Bede for two exploits, for establishing the fast of Lent in his kingdom, and for utterly extirpating idolatry; which, notwithstanding the prevalence of Christianity, had hitherto been tolerated by the two preceding monarchs. He reigned twenty-four years; and left the crown to Egbert, his son, who reigned nine years. This prince is renowned for his encouragement of learning; but infamous for putting to death his two cousin-germans, sons of Erminfrid, his uncle. The ecclesiastical writers praise him for his bestowing on his sister, Domnona, some lands in the Isle of Thanet, where she founded a monastery.

The bloody precaution of Egbert could not fix the crown on the head of his son, Edric. Lothaire, brother of the deceased prince, took possession of the kingdom; and, in order to secure the power

---

[d] Bede, lib. 2. cap. 5.   [e] Ibid. cap. 6. Chron. Sax. p. 26. Higden, lib. 5.
[f] Brompton, p. 739.

in his family, he associated with him Richard, his son, in the administration of the government. Edric, the dispossessed prince, had recourse to Edilwach, king of Sussex, for assistance; and being supported by that prince, fought a battle with his uncle, who was defeated and slain. Richard fled into Germany, and afterwards died in Lucca, a city of Tuscany. William of Malmesbury ascribes Lothaire's bad fortune to two crimes, his concurrence in the murder of his cousins, and his contempt for reliques.[g]

Lothaire reigned eleven years; Edric, his successor, only two. Upon the death of the latter, which happened in 686, Widred, his brother, obtained possession of the crown. But as the succession had been of late so much disjointed by revolutions and usurpations, faction began to prevail among the nobility; which invited Cedwalla, king of Wessex, with his brother Mollo, to attack the kingdom. These invaders committed great devastations in Kent; but the death of Mollo, who was slain in a skirmish,[h] gave a short breathing-time to that kingdom. Widred restored the affairs of Kent; and after a reign of thirty-two years,[i] left the crown to his posterity. Eadbert, Ethelbert, and Alric, his descendants, successively mounted the throne. After the death of the last, which happened in 794, the royal family of Kent was extinguished; and every factious leader who could entertain hopes of ascending the throne, threw the state into confusion.[k] Egbert, who first succeeded, reigned but two years; Cuthred, brother to the King of Mercia, six years; Baldred, an illegitimate branch of the royal family, eighteen: And after a troublesome and precarious reign, he was, in the year 723, expelled by Egbert, king of Wessex, who dissolved the Saxon Heptarchy, and united the several kingdoms under his dominion.

THE KINGDOM OF
NORTHUMBERLAND

ADELFRID, KING OF BERNICIA, having married Acca, the daughter of Aella, king of Deïri, and expelled her infant brother, Edwin, had united all the counties north of Humber into

[g] Will. Malm. p. 11.   [h] Higden, lib. 5.   [i] Chron. Sax. p. 52.   [k] Will. Malmes. lib. 1. cap. 1. p. 11.

CHAPTER I

one monarchy, and acquired a great ascendant in the Heptarchy. He also spread the terror of the Saxon arms to the neighbouring people; and by his victories over the Scots and Picts, as well as Welsh, extended on all sides the bounds of his dominions. Having laid siege to Chester, the Britons marched out with all their forces to engage him; and they were attended by a body of 1250 monks from the monastery of Bangor, who stood at a small distance from the field of battle, in order to encourage the combatants by their presence and exhortations. Adelfrid enquiring the purpose of this unusual appearance, was told, that these priests had come to pray against him: *Then are they as such our enemies*, said he, *as those who intend to fight against us:*[l] And he immediately sent a detachment, who fell upon them, and did such execution, that only fifty escaped with their lives.[m] The Britons, astonished at this event, received a total defeat: Chester was obliged to surrender: and Adelfrid, pursuing his victory, made himself master of Bangor, and entirely demolished the monastery; a building so extensive, that there was a mile's distance from one gate of it to another; and it contained two thousand one hundred monks, who are said to have been there maintained by their own labour.[n]

Notwithstanding Adelfrid's success in war, he lived in inquietude on account of young Edwin, whom he had unjustly dispossessed of the crown of Deïri. This prince, now grown to man's estate, wandered from place to place, in continual danger from the attempts of Adelfrid; and received at last protection in the court of Redwald, king of the East-Angles; where his engaging and gallant deportment procured him general esteem and affection. Redwald, however, was strongly solicited by the king of Northumberland to kill or deliver up his guest: Rich presents were promised him, if he would comply; and war denounced against him in case of his refusal. After rejecting several messages of this kind, his generosity began to yield to the motives of interest: and he retained the last ambassador, till he should come to a resolution in a case of such importance. Edwin, informed of his friend's perplexity, was yet determined at all hazards to remain in East-Anglia; and thought, that if the protection of that court failed him, it were better to die than prolong a life so much exposed to the persecutions of his

[l] Brompton, p. 779.   [m] Trivet. apud Spell. Conc. p. 111.   [n] Bede, lib. 2. cap. 2. W. Malmes, lib. 1. cap. 3.

powerful rival. This confidence in Redwald's honour and friendship, with his other accomplishments, engaged the Queen on his
side; and she effectually represented to her husband the infamy of
delivering up to certain destruction their royal guest, who had fled
to them for protection against his cruel and jealous enemies.[o] Redwald, embracing more generous resolutions, thought it safest to
prevent Adelfrid, before that prince was aware of his intention,
and to attack him while he was yet unprepared for defence. He
marched suddenly with an army into the kingdom of Northumberland, and sought a battle with Adelfrid; in which that monarch was defeated and killed, after revenging himself by the death
of Regner, son of Redwald.[p] His own sons, Eanfrid, Oswald, and
Oswy, yet infants, were carried into Scotland; and Edwin obtained
possession of the crown of Northumberland.

Edwin was the greatest prince of the Heptarchy in that age, and
distinguished himself, both by his influence over the other kingdoms,[q] and by the strict execution of justice in his own dominions.
He reclaimed his subjects from the licentious life, to which they
had been accustomed; and it was a common saying, that during his
reign a woman or child might openly carry every where a purse of
gold, without any danger of violence or robbery. There is a remarkable instance, transmitted to us, of the affection borne him by
his servants. Cuichelme, king of Wessex, was his enemy; but finding himself unable to maintain open war against so gallant and
powerful a prince, he determined to use treachery against him,
and he employed one Eumer for that criminal purpose. The assassin, having obtained admittance, by pretending to deliver a message from Cuichelme, drew his dagger, and rushed upon the King.
Lilla, an officer of his army, seeing his master's danger, and having
no other means of defence, interposed with his own body between
the King and Eumer's dagger, which was pushed with such violence, that, after piercing Lilla, it even wounded Edwin: But before
the assassin could renew his blow, he was dispatched by the King's
attendants.

The East-Angles conspired against Redwald, their King; and
having put him to death, they offered their crown to Edwin, of
whose valour and capacity they had had experience, while he re-

---

[o] W. Malmes. lib. 1. cap. 3. H. Hunting. lib. 3. Bede.   [p] Bede, lib. 2. cap.
12. Brompton, p. 781.   [q] Chron. Sax. p. 27.

CHAPTER I

sided among them. But Edwin, from a sense of gratitude towards his benefactor, obliged them to submit to Earpwold, the son of Redwald; and that prince preserved his authority, though on a precarious footing, under the protection of the Northumbrian monarch.[r]

Edwin, after his accession to the crown, married Ethelburga, the daughter of Ethelbert, King of Kent. This princess, emulating the glory of her mother Bertha, who had been the instrument for converting her husband and his people to Christianity, carried Paullinus, a learned bishop, along with her;[s] and besides stipulating a toleration for the exercise of her own religion, which was readily granted her, she used every reason to persuade the King to embrace it. Edwin, like a prudent prince, hesitated on the proposal; but promised to examine the foundations of that doctrine; and declared, that, if he found them satisfactory, he was willing to be converted.[t] Accordingly he held several conferences with Paullinus; canvassed the arguments propounded with the wisest of his counsellors; retired frequently from company, in order to revolve alone that important question; and, after a serious and long enquiry, declared in favour of the Christian religion:[u] The people soon after imitated his example. Besides the authority and influence of the King, they were moved by another striking example. Coifi, the high priest, being converted after a public conference with Paullinus, led the way in destroying the images, which he had so long worshipped, and was forward in making this atonement for his past idolatry.[w]

This able prince perished with his son, Osfrid, in a great battle which he fought against Penda, king of Mercia, and Caedwalla, king of the Britons.[x] That event, which happened in the forty-eighth year of Edwin's age and seventeenth of his reign,[y] divided the monarchy of Northumberland, which that prince had united in his person. Eanfrid, the son of Adelfrid, returned with his brothers, Oswald and Oswy, from Scotland, and took possession of Bernicia, his paternal kingdom: Osric, Edwin's cousin-german, established himself in Deïri, the inheritance of his family; but to

---

[r] Gul. Malmes. lib. 1. cap. 3.   [s] H. Hunting. lib. 3.   [t] Bede, lib. 2. cap. 9.
[u] Bede, lib. 2. cap. 9. Malmes. lib. 1. cap. 3.   [w] Bede, lib. 2. cap. 13.
Brompton, Higden, lib. 5.   [x] Matth. West. p. 114. Chron. Sax. p. 29.
[y] W. Malmes. lib. 1. cap. 3.

which the sons of Edwin had a preferable title. Eanfrid, the elder surviving son, fled to Penda, by whom he was treacherously slain. The younger son, Vuscfraea, with Yffi, the grandson of Edwin, by Osfrid, sought protection in Kent, and not finding themselves in safety there, retired into France to King Dagobert, where they died.[z]

Osric, King of Deïri, and Eanfrid of Bernicia, returned to Paganism; and the whole people seem to have returned with them; since Paullinus, who was the first archbishop of York, and who had converted them, thought proper to retire with Ethelburga, the Queen Dowager, into Kent. Both these Northumbrian kings perished soon after, the first in battle against Caedwalla, the Briton; the second by the treachery of that prince. Oswald, the brother of Eanfrid, of the race of Bernicia, united again the kingdom of Northumberland in the year 634, and restored the Christian religion in his dominions. He gained a bloody and well-disputed battle against Caedwalla; the last vigorous effort which the Britons made against the Saxons. Oswald is much celebrated for his sanctity and charity by the Monkish historians; and they pretend, that his reliques wrought miracles, particularly the curing of a sick horse, which had approached the place of his interment.[a]

He died in battle against Penda, king of Mercia, and was succeeded by his brother, Oswy; who established himself in the government of the whole Northumbrian kingdom, by putting to death Oswin, the son of Osric, the last king of the race of Deïri. His son Egfrid succeeded him; who perishing in battle against the Picts, without leaving any children, because Adelthrid, his wife, refused to violate her vow of chastity, Alfred, his natural brother, acquired possession of the kingdom, which he governed for nineteen years; and he left it to Osred, his son, a boy of eight years of age. This prince, after a reign of eleven years, was murdered by Kenred his kinsman, who, after enjoying the crown only a year, perished by a like fate. Osric, and after him Celwulph the son of Kenred, next mounted the throne, which the latter relinquished in the year 738, in favour of Eadbert his cousin-german, who, imitating his predecessor, abdicated the crown, and retired into a monastery. Oswolf, son of Eadbert, was slain in a sedition, a year after his accession to

---

[z] Bede, lib. 2. cap. 20.　　[a] Bede, lib. 3. cap. 9.

CHAPTER I

the crown; and Mollo, who was not of the royal family, seized the crown. He perished by the treachery of Ailred, a prince of the blood; and Ailred, having succeeded in his design upon the throne, was soon after expelled by his subjects. Ethelred, his successor, the son of Mollo, underwent a like fate. Celwold, the next king, the brother of Ailred, was deposed and slain by the people, and his place was filled by Osred, his nephew, who, after a short reign of a year, made way for Ethelbert, another son of Mollo, whose death was equally tragical with that of almost all his predecessors. After Ethelbert's death an universal anarchy prevailed in Northumberland; and the people, having, by so many fatal revolutions, lost all attachment to their government and princes, were well prepared for subjection to a foreign yoke; which Egbert, king of Wessex, finally imposed upon them.

THE KINGDOM
OF EAST-ANGLIA

THE HISTORY of this kingdom contains nothing memorable, except the conversion of Earpwold, the fourth king, and great-grandson of Uffa, the founder of the monarchy. The authority of Edwin, king of Northumberland, on whom that prince entirely depended, engaged him to take this step: But soon after, his wife, who was an idolatress, brought him back to her religion; and he was found unable to resist those allurements, which have seduced the wisest of mankind. After his death, which was violent, like that of most of the Saxon princes, that did not early retire into monasteries, Sigebert, his successor, and half-brother, who had been educated in France, restored Christianity, and introduced learning among the East-Angles. Some pretend that he founded the university of Cambridge, or rather some schools in that place. It is almost impossible, and quite needless to be more particular in relating the transactions of the East-Angles. What instruction or entertainment can it give the reader to hear a long bead-roll of barbarous names, Egric, Annas, Ethelbert, Ethelwald, Aldulf, Elfwald, Beorne, Ethelred, Ethelbert, who successively murdered, expelled, or inherited from each other, and obscurely filled the throne of that kingdom. Ethelbert, the last of these princes was treacherously murdered by Offa, king of Mercia, in the year 792, and his state was thenceforth united with that of Offa, as we shall relate presently.

THE KINGDOM
OF MERCIA

MERCIA, the largest, if not the most powerful kingdom of the Heptarchy, comprehended all the middle counties of England; and as its frontiers extended to those of all the other six kingdoms, as well as to Wales, it received its name from that circumstance. Wibba, the son of Crida, founder of the monarchy, being placed on the throne by Ethelbert, king of Kent, governed his paternal dominions by a precarious authority; and after his death, Ceorl, his kinsman, was, by the influence of the Kentish monarch, preferred to his son, Penda, whose turbulent character appeared dangerous to that prince. Penda was thus fifty years of age before he mounted the throne; and his temerity and restless disposition were found nowise abated by time, experience, or reflection. He engaged in continual hostilities against all the neighbouring states; and, by his injustice and violence, rendered himself equally odious to his own subjects and to strangers. Sigebert, Egric, and Annas, three kings of East-Anglia, perished successively in battle against him; as did also Edwin and Oswald, the two greatest princes that had reigned over Northumberland. At last, Oswy, brother to Oswald, having defeated and slain him in a decisive battle, freed the world from this sanguinary tyrant. Peada, his son, mounted the throne of Mercia in 655, and lived under the protection of Oswy, whose daughter he had espoused. This princess was educated in the Christian faith, and she employed her influence with success, in converting her husband and his subjects to that religion. Thus the fair sex have had the merit of introducing the Christian doctrine into all the most considerable kingdoms of the Saxon Heptarchy. Peada died a violent death.[b] His son, Wolfhere,

[b] Hugo Candidus, p. 4. says that he was treacherously murdered by his queen, by whose persuasion he had embraced Christianity; but this account of the matter is found in that historian alone.

CHAPTER I

succeeded to the government; and after having reduced to dependance the kingdoms of Essex and East-Anglia, he left the
crown to his brother, Ethelred, who, though a lover of peace,
showed himself not unfit for military enterprizes. Besides making
a successful expedition into Kent, he repulsed Egfrid, king of
Northumberland, who had invaded his dominions; and he slew in
battle Elfwin, the brother of that prince. Desirous, however, of
composing all animosities with Egfrid, he payed him a sum of
money, as a compensation for the loss of his brother. After a
prosperous reign of thirty years, he resigned the crown to Kendred, son of Wolfhere, and retired into the monastery of Bardney.[c]
Kendred returned the present of the crown to Ceolred, the son of
Ethelred; and making a pilgrimage to Rome, passed his life there
in pennance and devotion. The place of Ceolred was supplied by
Ethelbald, great-grand-nephew to Penda by Alwy, his brother; and
this prince, being slain in a mutiny, was succeeded by Offa, who
was a degree more remote from Penda, by Eawa, another brother.

This prince, who mounted the throne in 755,[d] had some great
qualities, and was successful in his warlike enterprizes against Lothaire, king of Kent, and Kenwulph, king of Wessex. He defeated
the former in a bloody battle at Otford upon the Darent, and
reduced his kingdom to a state of dependance: he gained a victory
over the latter at Bensington in Oxfordshire; and conquering that
county, together with that of Glocester, annexed both to his dominions. But all these successes were stained by his treacherous
murder of Ethelbert, king of the East-Angles, and his violent seizing of that kingdom. This young prince, who is said to have possessed great merit, had paid his addresses to Elfrida, the daughter
of Offa, and was invited with all his retinue to Hereford, in order
to solemnize the nuptials. Amidst the joy and festivity of these
entertainments, he was seized by Offa, and secretly beheaded: and
though Elfrid, who abhorred her father's treachery, had time to
give warning to the East-Anglian nobility, who escaped into their
own country, Offa, having extinguished the royal family, succeeded in his design of subduing that kingdom.[e] The perfidious
prince, desirous of re-establishing his character in the world, and
perhaps of appeasing the remorses of his own conscience, payed
great court to the clergy, and practised all the monkish devotion,

[c] Bede, lib. 5.   [d] Chron. Sax. p. 59.   [e] Brompton, p. 750, 751, 752.

so much esteemed in that ignorant and superstitious age. He gave the tenth of his goods to the church;[f] bestowed rich donations on the cathedral of Hereford; and even made a pilgrimage to Rome, where his great power and riches could not fail of procuring him the papal absolution. The better to ingratiate himself with the sovereign pontiff, he engaged to pay him a yearly donation for the support of an English college at Rome,[g] and in order to raise the sum, he imposed a tax of a penny on each house possessed of thirty pence a year. This imposition, being afterwards levied on all England, was commonly denominated Peter's pence;[h] and though conferred at first as a gift, was afterwards claimed as a tribute by the Roman pontiff. Carrying his hypocrisy still farther, Offa, feigning to be directed by a vision from heaven, discovered at Verulam the reliques of St. Alban, the martyr, and endowed a magnificent monastery in that place.[i] Moved by all these acts of piety, Malmesbury, one of the best of the old English historians, declares himself at a loss to determine[k] whether the merits or crimes of this prince preponderated. Offa died, after a reign of thirty-nine years, in 794.[l]

This prince was become so considerable in the Heptarchy, that the emperor Charlemagne entered into an alliance and friendship with him; a circumstance, which did honour to Offa; as distant princes at that time had usually little communication with each other. That emperor being a great lover of learning and learned men, in an age very barren of that ornament, Offa, at his desire, sent him over Alcuin, a clergyman much celebrated for his knowledge, who received great honours from Charlemagne, and even became his preceptor in the sciences. The chief reason, why he had at first desired the company of Alcuin, was that he might oppose his learning to the heresy of Felix, bishop of Urgel in Catalonia; who maintained, that Jesus Christ, considered in his human nature, could, more properly, be denominated the adoptive than the natural son of God.[m] This heresy was condemned in the council of Francfort, held in 794, and consisting of 300 bishops. Such were the questions which were agitated in that age, and which employed

---

[f] Spell. Conc. p. 308. Brompton, p. 776.   [g] Spell. Conc. p. 230, 310, 312.
[h] Higden, lib. 5.   [i] Ingulph. p. 5. W. Malmes. lib. 1. cap. 4.   [k] Lib. 1. cap. 4.   [l] Chron. Sax. p. 65.   [m] Dupin, cent. 8. chap. 4.

the attention, not only of cloystered scholars, but of the wisest and greatest princes.[n]

Egfrith succeeded to his father, Offa, but survived him only five months;[o] when he made way for Kenulph, a descendant of the royal family. This prince waged war against Kent; and taking Egbert, the king, prisoner, he cut off his hands, and put out his eyes; leaving Cuthred, his own brother, in possession of the crown of that kingdom. Kenulph was killed in an insurrection of the East-Anglians, whose crown his predecessor, Offa, had usurped. He left his son, Kenelm, a minor; who was murdered the same year by his sister, Quendrade, who had entertained the ambitious views of assuming the government.[p] But she was supplanted by her uncle, Ceolulf; who, two years after, was dethroned by Beornulf. The reign of this usurper, who was not of the royal family, was short and unfortunate: He was defeated by the West-Saxons, and killed by his own subjects, the East-Angles.[q] Ludican, his successor, underwent the same fate;[r] and Wiglaff, who mounted this unstable throne, and found everything in the utmost confusion, could not withstand the fortune of Egbert, who united all the Saxon kingdoms into one great monarchy.

THE KINGDOM OF ESSEX

THIS KINGDOM made no great figure in the Heptarchy; and the history of it is very imperfect. Sleda succeeded to his father, Erkinwin, the founder of the monarchy; and made way for his son, Sebert, who, being nephew to Ethelbert, king of Kent, was persuaded by that prince to embrace the Christian faith.[s] His sons and conjunct successors, Sexted and Seward, relapsed into idolatry, and were soon after slain in a battle against the West-Saxons. To shew the rude manner of living in that age; Bede tells us,[t] that

[n] Offa, in order to protect his country from Wales, drew a rampart or ditch of a hundred miles in length from Basinwerke in Flintshire to the South-sea near Bristol. See *Speed's Description of Wales.* [o] Ingulph. p. 6. [p] Ingulph. p. 7. Brompton, p. 776. [q] Ingulph. p. 7. [r] Ann. Beverl. p. 87. [s] Chron. Sax. p. 24. [t] Lib. 2. cap. 5.

these two kings expressed great desire to eat the white bread, distributed by Mellitus, the bishop, at the communion.ᵘ But on his refusing them, unless they would submit to be baptized, they expelled him their dominions. The names of the other princes, who reigned successively in Essex, are Sigebert the little, Sigebert the good, who restored Christianity, Swithelm, Sigheri, Offa. This last prince, having made a vow of chastity, notwithstanding his marriage with Keneswitha, a Mercian princess, daughter to Penda, went in pilgrimage to Rome, and shut himself up during the rest of his life in a cloyster. Selred, his successor, reigned thirty-eight years; and was the last of the royal line: The failure of which threw the kingdom into great confusion, and reduced it to dependance under Mercia.ʷ Switherd first acquired the crown, by the concession of the Mercian princes; and his death made way for Sigeric, who ended his life in a pilgrimage to Rome. His successor, Sigered, unable to defend his kingdom, submitted to the victorious arms of Egbert.

THE KINGDOM
OF SUSSEX

THE HISTORY of this kingdom, the smallest in the Heptarchy, is still more imperfect than that of Essex. Aella, the founder of the monarchy, left the crown to his son, Cissa, who is chiefly remarkable for his long reign of seventy-six years. During his time, the South Saxons fell almost into a total dependance on the kingdom of Wessex; and we scarcely know the names of the princes, who were possessed of this titular sovereignty. Adelwalch, the last of them, was subdued in battle by Ceadwalla, king of Wessex, and was slain in the action; leaving two infant sons, who, falling into the hand of the conqueror, were murdered by him. The abbot of Redford opposed the order for this execution, but could only prevail on Ceadwalla to suspend it, till they should be baptized. Bercthun and Audhun, two noblemen of character, resisted some time the violence of the West-Saxons; but their op-

ᵘ H. Hunting. lib. 3. Brompton, p. 738, 743. Bede.   ʷ Malmes, lib. 1. cap. 6.

position served only to prolong the miseries of their country; and the subduing of this kingdom was the first step, which the West-Saxons made towards acquiring the sole monarchy of England.[x]

THE KINGDOM
OF WESSEX

THE KINGDOM OF WESSEX, which finally swallowed up all the other Saxon states, met with great resistance on its first establishment: and the Britons, who were now enured to arms, yielded not tamely their possessions to those invaders. Cerdic, the founder of the monarchy, and his son, Kenric, fought many successful, and some unsuccessful battles, against the natives; and the martial spirit, common to all the Saxons, was, by means of these hostilities, carried to the greatest height among this tribe. Ceaulin, who was the son and successor of Kenric, and who began his reign in 560, was still more ambitious and enterprizing than his predecessors; and by waging continual war against the Britons, he added a great part of the counties of Devon and Somerset to his other dominions. Carried along by the tide of success, he invaded the other Saxon states in his neighbourhood, and becoming terrible to all, he provoked a general confederacy against him. This alliance proved successful under the conduct of Ethelbert, king of Kent; and Ceaulin, who had lost the affections of his own subjects by his violent disposition, and had now fallen into contempt from his misfortunes, was expelled the throne,[y] and died in exile and misery. Cuichelme, and Cuthwin, his sons, governed jointly the kingdom, till the expulsion of the latter in 591, and the death of the former in 593, made way for Cealric, to whom succeeded Ceobald in 593, by whose death, which happened in 611, Kynegils inherited the crown. This prince embraced Christianity,[z] through the persuasion of Oswald, king of Northumberland, who had married his daughter, and who had attained a great ascendant in the Hep-

---

[x] Brompton, p. 800.   [y] Chron. Sax. p. 22.   [z] Higden, lib. 5. Chron. Sax. p. 15. Ann. Beverl. p. 94.

tarchy. Kenwalch next succeeded to the monarchy, and dying in 672, left the succession so much disputed, that Sexburga, his widow, a woman of spirit,[a] kept possession of the government till her death, which happened two years after. Escwin then peaceably acquired the crown; and, after a short reign of two years, made way for Kentwin, who governed nine years. Ceodwalla, his successor, mounted not the throne without opposition; but proved a great prince, according to the ideas of those times; that is, he was enterprizing, warlike, and successful. He entirely subdued the kingdom of Sussex, and annexed it to his own dominions. He made inroads into Kent; but met with resistance from Widred, the king, who proved successful against Mollo, brother to Ceodwalla, and slew him in a skirmish. Ceodwalla at last, tired with wars and bloodshed, was seized with a fit of devotion; bestowed several endowments on the church; and made a pilgrimage to Rome, where he received baptism, and died in 689. Ina, his successor, inherited the military virtues of Ceodwalla, and added to them the more valuable ones of justice, policy, and prudence. He made war upon the Britons in Somerset: and having finally subdued that province, he treated the vanquished with a humanity, hitherto unknown to the Saxon conquerors. He allowed the proprietors to retain possession of their lands, encouraged marriages and alliances between them and his ancient subjects, and gave them the privilege of being governed by the same laws. These laws he augmented and ascertained; and though he was disturbed by some insurrections at home, his long reign of thirty-seven years may be regarded as one of the most glorious and most prosperous of the Heptarchy. In the decline of his age he made a pilgrimage to Rome; and after his return, shut himself up in a cloyster, where he died.

Though the kings of Wessex had always been princes of the blood, descended from Cerdic, the founder of the monarchy, the order of succession had been far from exact; and a more remote prince had often found means to mount the throne, in preference to one descended from a nearer branch of the royal family. Ina, therefore, having no children of his own, and lying much under the influence of Ethelburga, his queen, left by will the succession to Adelard, her brother, who was his remote kinsman: But this

---

[a] Bede, lib. 4. cap. 12. Chron. Sax. p. 41.

CHAPTER I

destination did not take place without some difficulty. Oswald, a
prince more nearly allied to the crown, took arms against Adelard;
but he being suppressed, and dying soon after, the title of Adelard
was not any farther disputed; and in the year 741, he was succeeded by his cousin, Cudred. The reign of this prince was distinguished by a great victory, which he obtained, by means of
Edelhun, his general, over Ethelbald, king of Mercia. His death
made way for Sigebert, his kinsman, who governed so ill, that his
people rose in an insurrection, and dethroned him, crowning
Cenulph in his stead. The exiled prince found a refuge with duke
Cumbran, governor of Hampshire; who, that he might add new
obligations to Sigebert, gave him many salutary counsels for his
future conduct, accompanied with some reprehensions for the
past. But these were so much resented by the ungrateful prince,
that he conspired against the life of his protector, and treacherously murdered him. After this infamous action, he was forsaken
by all the world; and skulking about in the wilds and forests, was
at last discovered by a servant of Cumbran's, who instantly took
revenge upon him for the murder of his master.[b]

Cenulph, who had obtained the crown on the expulsion of
Sigebert, was fortunate in many expeditions against the Britons of
Cornwal; but afterwards lost some reputation by his ill success
against Offa, king of Mercia.[c] Kynehard also, brother to the deposed Sigebert, gave him disturbance; and though expelled the
kingdom, he hovered on the frontiers, and watched an opportunity for attacking his rival. The king had an intrigue with a
young woman, who lived at Merton in Surrey, whither having
secretly retired, he was on a sudden invironed, in the night-time,
by Kynehard and his followers, and after making a vigorous resistance, was murdered, with all his attendants. The nobility and
people of the neighbourhood, rising next day in arms, took revenge on Kynehard for the slaughter of their king, and put every
one to the sword, who had been engaged in that criminal enterprize. This event happened in 784.

Brithric next obtained possession of the government, though
remotely descended from the royal family; but he enjoyed not that
dignity without inquietude. Eoppa, nephew to king Ina, by his

[b] Higden, lib. 5. W. Malmes. lib. 1. cap. 2.   [c] W. Malmes. lib. 1. cap. 2.

brother Ingild, who died before that prince, had begot Eata, father to Alchmond, from whom sprung Egbert,[d] a young man of the most promising hopes, who gave great jealousy to Brithric, the reigning prince, both because he seemed by his birth better intitled to the crown, and because he had acquired, to an eminent degree, the affections of the people. Egbert, sensible of his danger from the suspicions of Brithric, secretly withdrew into France;[e] where he was well received by Charlemagne. By living in the court, and serving in the armies of that prince, the most able and most generous that had appeared in Europe during several ages, he acquired those accomplishments, which afterwards enabled him to make such a shining figure on the throne. And familiarizing himself to the manners of the French, who, as Malmesbury observes,[f] were eminent both for valour and civility, above all the western nations, he learned to polish the rudeness and barbarity of the Saxon character: His early misfortunes thus proved of singular advantage to him.

It was not long ere Egbert had opportunities of displaying his natural and acquired talents. Brithric, King of Wessex, had married Eadburga, natural daughter of Offa, king of Mercia, a profligate woman, equally infamous for cruelty and for incontinence. Having great influence over her husband, she often instigated him to destroy such of the nobility as were obnoxious to her; and where this expedient failed, she scrupled not being herself active in traiterous attempts against them. She had mixed a cup of poison for a young nobleman, who had acquired her husband's friendship, and had on that account become the object of her jealousy: But unfortunately, the king drank of the fatal cup along with his favourite, and soon after expired.[g] This tragical incident, joined to her other crimes, rendered Eadburga so odious, that she was obliged to fly into France; whence Egbert was at the same time recalled by the nobility, in order to ascend the throne of his ancestors.[h] He attained that dignity in the last year of the eighth century.

In the kingdoms of the Heptarchy, an exact rule of succession was either unknown or not strictly observed; and thence the reign-

[d] Chron. Sax. p. 16.   [e] H. Hunting. lib. 4.   [f] Lib. 2. cap. 11.   [g] Higden, lib. 5. M. West. p. 152. Asser. in vita Alfredi, p. 3. ex edit. Camdeni.   [h] Chron. Sax. A. D. 800. Brompton, p. 801.

CHAPTER I

ing prince was continually agitated with jealousy against all the princes of the blood, whom he still considered as rivals, and whose death alone could give him entire security in his possession of the throne. From this fatal cause, together with the admiration of the monastic life, and the opinion of merit, attending the preservation of chastity even in a married state, the royal families had been entirely extinguished in all the kingdoms except that of Wessex; and the emulations, suspicions, and conspiracies, which had formerly been confined to the princes of the blood alone, were now diffused among all the nobility in the several Saxon states. Egbert was the sole descendant of those first conquerors who subdued Britain, and who enhanced their authority by claiming a pedigree from Woden, the supreme divinity of their ancestors. But that prince, though invited by this favourable circumstance to make attempts on the neighbouring Saxons, gave them for some time no disturbance, and rather chose to turn his arms against the Britons in Cornwal, whom he defeated in several battles.[i] He was recalled from the conquest of that country by an invasion made upon his dominions by Bernulf, King of Mercia.

The Mercians, before the accession of Egbert, had very nearly attained the absolute sovereignty in the Heptarchy: They had reduced the East-Angles under subjection, and established tributary princes in the kingdoms of Kent and Essex. Northumberland was involved in anarchy; and no state of any consequence remained but that of Wessex, which, much inferior in extent to Mercia, was supported solely by the great qualities of its sovereign. Egbert led his army against the invaders; and encountering them at Ellandun in Wiltshire, obtained a complete victory, and by the great slaughter which he made of them in their flight, gave a mortal blow to the power of the Mercians. Whilst he himself, in prosecution of his victory, entered their country on the side of Oxfordshire, and threatened the heart of their dominions; he sent an army into Kent, commanded by Ethelwolph, his eldest son,[k] and expelling Baldred, the tributary king, soon made himself master of that country. The kingdom of Essex was conquered with equal facility; and the East-Angles, from their hatred to the Mercian government, which had been established over them by treachery and

---

[i] Chron. Sax. p. 69.   [k] Ethelwerd, lib. 3. cap. 2.

violence, and probably exercised with tyranny, immediately rose in arms, and craved the protection of Egbert.[l] Bernulf, the Mercian king, who marched against them, was defeated and slain; and two years after, Ludican, his successor, met with the same fate. These insurrections and calamities facilitated the enterprizes of Egbert, who advanced into the center of the Mercian territories, and made easy conquests over a dispirited and divided people. In order to engage them more easily to submission, he allowed Wiglef, their countryman, to retain the title of king, whilst he himself exercised the real powers of sovereignty.[m] The anarchy, which prevailed in Northumberland, tempted him to carry still farther his victorious arms; and the inhabitants, unable to resist his power, and desirous of possessing some established form of government, were forward, on his first appearance, to send deputies, who submitted to his authority, and swore allegiance to him as their sovereign. Egbert, however, still allowed to Northumberland, as he had done to Mercia and East-Anglia, the power of electing a king, who paid him tribute, and was dependant on him.

Thus were united all the kingdoms of the Heptarchy in one great state, near four hundred years after the first arrival of the Saxons in Britain; and the fortunate arms and prudent policy of Egbert at last effected what had been so often attempted in vain by so many princes.[n] Kent, Northumberland, and Mercia, which had successively aspired to general dominion, were now incorporated in his empire; and the other subordinate kingdoms seemed willingly to share the same fate. His territories were nearly of the same extent with what is now properly called England; and a favourable prospect was afforded to the Anglo-Saxons, of establishing a civilized monarchy, possessed of tranquillity within itself, and secure against foreign invasion. This great event happened in the year 827.[o]

The Saxons, though they had been so long settled in the island, seem not as yet to have been much improved beyond their German ancestors, either in arts, civility, knowledge, humanity, justice, or obedience to the laws. Even Christianity, though it opened the way to connexions between them and the more polished states of Eu-

---

[l] Ibid. lib. 3. cap. 3.   [m] Ingulph. p. 7, 8, 10.   [n] Chron. Sax. p. 71.
[o] Chron. Sax. p. 71.

rope, had not hitherto been very effectual, in banishing their ignorance, or softening their barbarous manners. As they received that doctrine through the corrupted channels of Rome, it carried along with it a great mixture of credulity and superstition, equally destructive to the understanding and to morals. The reverence towards saints and reliques seems to have almost supplanted the adoration of the Supreme Being: Monastic observances were esteemed more meritorious than the active virtues: The knowledge of natural causes was neglected from the universal belief of miraculous interpositions and judgments: Bounty to the church atoned for every violence against society: And the remorses for cruelty, murder, treachery, assassination, and the more robust vices, were appeased, not by amendment of life, but by pennances, servility to the monks, and an abject and illiberal devotion.[p] The reverence for the clergy had been carried to such a height, that, wherever a person appeared in a sacerdotal habit, though on the highway, the people flocked around him; and showing him all marks of profound respect, received every word he uttered as the most sacred oracle.[q] Even the military virtues, so inherent in all the Saxon tribes, began to be neglected; and the nobility, preferring the security and sloth of the cloyster to the tumults and glory of war, valued themselves chiefly on endowing monasteries, of which they assumed the government.[r] The several kings too, being extremely impoverished by continual benefactions to the church, to which the states of their kingdoms had weakly assented, could bestow no rewards on valour or military services, and retained not even sufficient influence to support their government.[s]

Another inconvenience, which attended this corrupt species of Christianity, was the superstitious attachment to Rome, and the gradual subjection of the kingdom to a foreign jurisdiction. The

[p] These abuses were common to all the European churches; but the priests in Italy, Spain and Gaul, made some atonement for them by other advantages, which they rendered society. For several ages, they were almost all Romans, or, in other words, the ancient natives; and they preserved the Roman language and laws, with some remains of the former civility. But the priests in the Heptarchy, after the first missionaries, were wholly Saxons, and almost as ignorant and barbarous as the laity. They contributed, therefore, little to the improvement of the society in knowledge or the arts.
[q] Bede, lib. 3. cap. 26.   [r] Ibid. lib. 5. cap. 23. Epistola Bedae ad Egbert.
[s] Bedae Epist. ad Egbert.

Britons, having never acknowledged any subordination to the Roman pontiff, had conducted all ecclesiastical government by their domestic synods and councils:[t] But the Saxons, receiving their religion from Roman monks, were taught at the same time a profound reverence for that see, and were naturally led to regard it as the capital of their religion. Pilgrimages to Rome were represented as the most meritorious acts of devotion. Not only noblemen and ladies of rank undertook this tedious journey;[u] but kings themselves, abdicating their crowns, sought for a secure passport to heaven at the feet of the Roman pontiff. New reliques, perpetually sent from that endless mint of superstition, and magnified by lying miracles, invented in convents, operated on the astonished minds of the multitude. And every prince has attained the eulogies of the monks, the only historians of those ages, not in proportion to his civil and military virtues, but to his devoted attachment towards their order, and his superstitious reverence for Rome.

The sovereign pontiff, encouraged by this blindness and submissive disposition of the people, advanced every day in his encroachments on the independance of the English churches. Wilfrid, bishop of Lindisferne, the sole prelate of the Northumbrian kingdom, encreased this subjection in the eighth century, by his making an appeal to Rome against the decisions of an English synod, which had abridged his diocese by the erection of some new bishoprics.[w] Agatho, the pope, readily embraced this precedent of an appeal to his court; and Wilfrid, though the haughtiest and most luxurious prelate of his age,[x] having obtained with the people the character of sanctity, was thus able to lay the foundation of this papal pretension.

The great topic, by which Wilfrid confounded the imaginations of men, was, that St. Peter, to whose custody the keys of heaven were entrusted, would certainly refuse admittance to every one who should be wanting in respect to his successor. This conceit, well suited to vulgar conceptions, made great impression on the people during several ages; and has not even at present lost all influence in the catholic countries.

---

[t] Append. to Bede, numb. 10. ex. edit. 1722. Spelm. Conc. p. 108, 109.
[u] Bede, lib. 5. cap. 7. [w] See Appendix to Bede, numb. 19. Higden, lib. 5.
[x] Eddius vita Vilfr. § 24, 60.

CHAPTER I

Had this abject superstition produced general peace and tranquillity, it had made some atonement for the ills attending it; but besides the usual avidity of men for power and riches, frivolous controversies in theology were engendered by it, which were so much the more fatal, as they admitted not, like the others, of any final determination from established possession. The disputes, excited in Britain, were of the most ridiculous kind, and entirely worthy of those ignorant and barbarous ages. There were some intricacies, observed by all the Christian churches, in adjusting the day of keeping Easter; which depended on a complicated consideration of the course of the sun and moon: And it happened that the missionaries, who had converted the Scots and Britons, had followed a different calendar from that which was observed at Rome, in the age when Augustine converted the Saxons. The priests also of all the Christian churches were accustomed to shave part of their head; but the form given to this tonsure, was different in the former from what was practised in the latter. The Scots and Britons pleaded the antiquity of *their* usages: The Romans, and their disciples, the Saxons, insisted on the universality of *theirs*. That Easter must necessarily be kept by a rule, which comprehended both the day of the year and age of the moon, was agreed by all; that the tonsure of a priest could not be omitted without the utmost impiety, was a point undisputed: But the Romans and Saxons called their antagonists schismatics; because they celebrated Easter on the very day of the full moon in March, if that day fell on a Sunday, instead of waiting till the Sunday following; and because they shaved the fore-part of their head from ear to ear, instead of making that tonsure on the crown of the head, and in a circular form. In order to render their antagonists odious, they affirmed, that, once in seven years, they concurred with the Jews in the time of celebrating that festival:[y] And that they might recommend their own form of tonsure, they maintained that it imitated symbolically the crown of thorns worn by Christ in his passion; whereas the other form was invented by Simon Magus, without any regard to that representation.[z] These controversies had, from the beginning, excited such animosity between the British and Romish priests, that, instead of concurring in their endeavours to

[y] Bede, lib. 2. cap. 19.   [z] Bede, lib. 5. cap. 21. Eddius, § 24.

convert the idolatrous Saxons, they refused all communion together, and each regarded his opponent as no better than a Pagan.[a] The dispute lasted more than a century; and was at last finished, not by men's discovering the folly of it, which would have been too great an effort for human reason to accomplish, but by the entire prevalence of the Romish ritual over the Scotch and British.[b] Wilfrid, bishop of Lindisferne, acquired great merit, both with the court of Rome and with all the southern Saxons, by expelling the quartodeciman schism, as it was called, from the Northumbrian kingdom, into which the neighbourhood of the Scots had formerly introduced it.[c]

Theodore, archbishop of Canterbury, called, in the year 680, a synod at Hatfield, consisting of all the bishops in Britain;[d] where was accepted and ratified the decree of the Lateran council, summoned by Martin, against the heresy of the Monothelites. The council and synod maintained, in opposition to these heretics, that, though the divine and human nature in Christ made but one person; yet had they different inclinations, wills, acts, and sentiments, and that the unity of the person implied not any unity in the consciousness.[e] This opinion it seems somewhat difficult to comprehend; and no one, unacquainted with the ecclesiastical history of those ages, could imagine the height of zeal and violence, with which it was then inculcated. The decree of the Lateran council calls the Monothelites impious, execrable, wicked, abominable, and even diabolical; and curses and anathematizes them to all eternity.[f]

The Saxons, from the first introduction of Christianity among them, had admitted the use of images; and perhaps, that religion, without some of those exterior ornaments, had not made so quick a progress with these idolaters: But they had not paid any species of worship or address to images; and this abuse never prevailed among Christians, till it received the sanction of the second council of Nice.

[a] Bede, lib. 2. cap. 2, 4, 20. Eddius, § 12.   [b] Bede, lib. 5. cap. 16, 22.
[c] Bede, lib. 3. cap. 25. Eddius, § 12.   [d] Spell. Conc. vol. 1. p. 168.   [e] Ibid.
p. 171.   [f] Spell. Conc. vol. 1. p. 172, 173, 174.

II

Egbert – Ethelwolf –
Ethelbald and Ethelbert – Ethered –
Alfred the Great – Edward the elder –
Athelstan – Edmund – Edred – Edwy –
Edgar – Edward the Martyr

EGBERT

THE KINGDOMS of the Heptarchy, though united by so recent a conquest, seemed to be firmly cemented into one state under Egbert; and the inhabitants of the several provinces had lost all desire of revolting from that monarch, or of restoring their former independent governments. Their language was every where nearly the same, their customs, laws, institutions civil and religious; and as the race of the ancient kings was totally extinct in all the subjected states, the people readily transferred their allegiance to a prince, who seemed to merit it, by the splendor of his victories, the vigour of his administration, and the superior nobility of his birth. A union also in government opened to them the agreeable prospect of future tranquillity; and it appeared more probable, that they would thenceforth become formidable to their neighbours, than be exposed to their inroads and devastations. But these flattering views were soon overcast by the appearance of the

827.

Danes, who, during some centuries, kept the Anglo-Saxons in perpetual inquietude, committed the most barbarous ravages upon them, and at last reduced them to grievous servitude.

The emperor Charlemagne, though naturally generous and humane, had been induced by bigotry to exercise great severities upon the Pagan Saxons in Germany, whom he subdued; and besides often ravaging their country with fire and sword, he had in cool blood decimated all the inhabitants for their revolts, and had obliged them, by the most rigorous edicts, to make a seeming compliance with the christian doctrine. That religion, which had easily made its way among the British-Saxons by insinuation and address, appeared shocking to their German brethren, when imposed on them by the violence of Charlemagne: and the more generous and warlike of these Pagans had fled northward into Jutland, in order to escape the fury of his persecutions. Meeting there with a people of similar manners, they were readily received among them; and they soon stimulated the natives to concur in enterprizes, which both promised revenge on the haughty conqueror, and afforded subsistence to those numerous inhabitants, with which the northern countries were now overburthened.[g] They invaded the provinces of France, which were exposed by the degeneracy and dissentions of Charlemagne's posterity; and being there known under the general name of Normans, which they received from their northern situation, they became the terror of all the maritime and even of the inland countries. They were also tempted to visit England in their frequent excursions; and being able, by sudden inroads, to make great progress over a people, who were not defended by any naval force, who had relaxed their military institutions, and who were sunk into a superstition, which had become odious to the Danes and ancient Saxons, they made no distinction in their hostilities between the French and English kingdoms. Their first appearance in this island was in the year 787,[h] when Brithric reigned in Wessex. A small body of them landed in that kingdom, with a view of learning the state of the country; and when the magistrate of the place questioned them concerning their enterprize, and summoned them to appear before the king, and account for their intentions, they killed him, and

[g] Ypod. Neustria, p. 414. [h] Chron. Sax. p. 64.

flying to their ships, escaped into their own country. The next
alarm was given to Northumberland in the year 794;[i] when a body
of these pirates pillaged a monastery; but their ships being much
damaged by a storm, and their leader slain in a skirmish, they were
at last defeated by the inhabitants, and the remainder of them put
to the sword. Five years after Egbert had established his monarchy   *832.*
over England, the Danes landed in the Isle of Shepey, and having
pillaged it, escaped with impunity.[k] They were not so fortunate in
their next year's enterprize, when they disembarked from thirty-
five ships, and were encountered by Egbert, at Charmouth in
Dorsetshire. The battle was bloody; but though the Danes lost
great numbers, they maintained the post, which they had taken,
and thence made good their retreat to their ships.[l] Having learned
by experience, that they must expect a vigorous resistance from
this warlike prince, they entered into an alliance with the Britons
of Cornwal; and landing two years after in that country, made an
inroad with their confederates into the county of Devon; but
were met at Hengesdown by Egbert, and totally defeated.[m] While
England remained in this state of anxiety, and defended itself
more by temporary expedients than by any regular plan of administration, Egbert, who alone was able to provide effectually against
this new evil, unfortunately died; and left the government to his   *838.*
son, Ethelwolf.

ETHELWOLF

THIS PRINCE had neither the abilities nor the vigour of his
father; and was better qualified for governing a convent than
a kingdom.[n] He began his reign with making a partition of his
dominions, and delivering over to his eldest son, Athelstan, the
new conquered provinces of Essex, Kent, and Sussex. But no
inconveniencies seem to have arisen from this partition; as the
continual terror of the Danish invasions prevented all domestic

---

[i] Chron. Sax. p. 66. Alur. Beverl. p. 108.   [k] Chron. Sax. p. 72.   [l] Ibid.
Ethelward, lib. 3. cap. 2.   [m] Chron. Sax. p. 71.   [n] Wm. Malmes. lib. 2.
cap. 2.

dissention. A fleet of these ravagers, consisting of thirty-three sail, appeared at Southampton; but were repulsed with loss by Wolfhere, governor of the neighbouring county.[o] The same year, Aethelhelm, governor of Dorsetshire, routed another band which had disembarked at Portsmouth; but he obtained the victory after a furious engagement, and he bought it with the loss of his life.[p] Next year, the Danes made several inroads into England; and fought battles, or rather skirmishes, in East-Anglia and Lindesey and Kent; where, though they were sometimes repulsed and defeated, they always obtained their end, of committing spoil upon the country, and carrying off their booty. They avoided coming to a general engagement, which was not suited to their plan of operations. Their vessels were small, and ran easily up the creeks and rivers; where they drew them ashore, and having formed an entrenchment round them, which they guarded with part of their number, the remainder scattered themselves every where, and carrying off the inhabitants and cattle and goods, they hastened to their ships, and quickly disappeared. If the military force of the county were assembled, (for there was no time for troops to march from a distance) the Danes either were able to repulse them and to continue their ravages with impunity, or they betook themselves to their vessels; and setting sail, suddenly invaded some distant quarter, which was not prepared for their reception. Every part of England was held in continual alarm; and the inhabitants of one county durst not give assistance to those of another, lest their own families and property should in the mean time be exposed by their absence to the fury of these barbarous ravagers.[q] All orders of men were involved in this calamity; and the priests and monks, who had been commonly spared in the domestic quarrels of the Heptarchy, were the chief objects on which the Danish idolaters exercised their rage and animosity. Every season of the year was dangerous; and the absence of the enemy was no reason why any man could esteem himself a moment in safety.

These incursions had now become almost annual; when the Danes, encouraged by their successes against France as well as England (for both kingdoms were alike exposed to this dreadful

851.

---

[o] Chron. Sax. p. 73. Ethelward, lib. 3. cap. 3. [p] Chron. Sax. p. 73. H. Hunting. lib. 5. [q] Alured Beverl. p. 108.

CHAPTER II

calamity), invaded the land in so numerous a body, as seemed to threaten it with universal subjection. But the English, more military than the Britons, whom, a few centuries before, they had treated with like violence, rouzed themselves with a vigour proportioned to the exigency. Ceorle, governor of Devonshire, sought a battle with one body of the Danes at Wiganburgh,[r] and put them to rout with great slaughter. King Athelstan attacked another at sea near Sandwich, sunk nine of their ships, and put the rest to flight.[s] A body of them however, ventured, for the first time, to take up winter-quarters in England; and receiving in the spring a strong reinforcement of their countrymen in 350 vessels, they advanced from the Isle of Thanet, where they had stationed themselves; burnt the cities of London and Canterbury; and having put to flight Brichtric, who now governed Mercia, under the title of King, they marched into the heart of Surrey, and laid every place waste around them. Ethelwolf, impelled by the urgency of the danger, marched against them, at the head of the West-Saxons; and carrying with him his second son, Ethelbald, gave them battle at Okely, and gained a bloody victory over them. This advantage procured but a short respite to the English. The Danes still maintained their settlement in the Isle of Thanet; and being attacked by Ealher and Huda, governors of Kent and Surrey, though defeated in the beginning of the action, they finally repulsed the assailants, and killed both the governors. They removed thence to the Isle of Shepey; where they took up their winter-quarters, that they might farther extend their devastation and ravages.

853.

This unsettled state of England hindered not Ethelwolf from making a pilgrimage to Rome; whither he carried his fourth, and favourite son, Alfred, then only six years of age.[t] He passed there a twelvemonth in exercises of devotion; and failed not in that most essential part of devotion, liberality to the church of Rome. Besides giving presents to the more distinguished ecclesiastics; he made a perpetual grant of three hundred mancuses[u] a year to that see; one third to support the lamps of St. Peter's, another those of St. Paul's, a third to the pope himself.[w] In his return home, he married

[r] H. Hunt. lib. 5. Ethelward, lib. 3. cap. 3. Simeon Dunelm. p. 120.
[s] Chron. Sax. p. 74. Asserius, p. 2.   [t] Asserius, p. 2. Chron. Sax. 76. Hunt. lib. 5.   [u] A mancus was about the weight of our present half crown: See Spelman's Glossary, in verbo Mancus.   [w] W. Malmes. lib. 2. cap. 2.

Judith, daughter of the emperor, Charles the Bald; but on his landing in England, he met with an opposition, which he little looked for.

His eldest son, Athelstan, being dead; Ethelbald, his second, who had assumed the government, formed, in concert with many of the nobles, the project of excluding his father from a throne, which his weakness and superstition seem to have rendered him so ill-qualified to fill. The people were divided between the two princes; and a bloody civil war, joined to all the other calamities under which the English laboured, appeared inevitable; when Ethelwolf had the facility to yield to the greater part of his son's pretensions. He made with him a partition of the kingdom; and taking to himself the eastern part, which was always at that time esteemed the least considerable, as well as the most exposed,[x] he delivered over to Ethelbald the sovereignty of the western. Immediately after, he summoned the states of the whole kingdom, and with the same facility conferred a perpetual and important donation on the church.

The ecclesiastics, in those days of ignorance, made rapid advances in the acquisition of power and grandeur; and inculcating the most absurd and most interested doctrines, though they sometimes met, from the contrary interests of the laity, with an opposition, which it required time and address to overcome, they found no obstacle in their reason or understanding. Not content with the donations of land made them by the Saxon princes and nobles, and with temporary oblations from the devotion of the people, they had cast a wishful eye on a vast revenue, which they claimed as belonging to them, by a sacred and indefeizable title. However little versed in the scriptures, they had been able to discover, that, under the Jewish law, a tenth of all the produce of land was conferred on the priest-hood; and forgetting, what they themselves taught, that the moral part only of that law was obligatory on Christians, they insisted, that this donation conveyed a perpetual property, inherent by divine right in those who officiated at the altar. During some centuries, the whole scope of sermons and homilies was directed to this purpose; and one would have imagined, from the general tenor of these discourses, that all

___

[x] Asserius, p. 3. W. Malm. lib. 2. cap. 2. Matth. West p. 1, 8.

the practical parts of Christianity were comprized in the exact and faithful payment of tythes to the clergy.[y] Encouraged by their success in inculcating these doctrines; they ventured farther than they were warranted even by the Levitical law, and pretended to draw the tenth of all industry, merchandize, wages of labourers, and pay of soldiers;[z] nay, some canonists went so far as to affirm, that the clergy were entitled to the tythe of the profits, made by courtezans in the exercise of their profession.[a] Though parishes had been instituted in England by Honorius, archbishop of Canterbury, near two centuries before,[b] the ecclesiastics had never yet been able to get possession of the tythes: they therefore seized the present favourable opportunity of making that acquisition; when a weak, superstitious prince filled the throne, and when the people, discouraged by their losses from the Danes, and terrified with the fear of future invasions, were susceptible of any impression, which bore the appearance of religion.[c] So meritorious was this concession deemed by the English, that, trusting entirely to supernatural assistance, they neglected the ordinary means of safety; and agreed, even in the present desperate extremity, that the revenues of the church should be exempted from all burthens, though imposed for national defence and security.[d]

ETHELBALD AND ETHELBERT

ETHELWOLF lived only two years after making this grant; and by his will he shared England between his two eldest sons, Ethelbald and Ethelbert, the west being assigned to the former; the east to the latter. Ethelbald was a profligate prince; and marrying Judith, his mother-in-law, gave great offence to the people; but moved by the remonstrances of Swithun, bishop of Winchester, he was at last prevailed on to divorce her. His reign

857.

---

[y] Padre Paolo, sopra beneficii ecclesiastici, p. 51, 52. edit. Colon. 1675.
[z] Spell. Conc. vol. 1. p. 268.   [a] Padre Paolo, p. 132.   [b] Parker, p. 77.
[c] Ingulf. p. 862. Selden's Hist. of tythes, c. 8.   [d] Asserius, p. 2. Chron. Sax. p. 76. W. Malmes. lib. 2. cap. 2. Ethelward, lib. 3. cap. 3. M. West. p. 158. Ingulf. p. 17. Ann. Beverl. p. 95.

860. was short; and Ethelbert, his brother, succeeding to the government, behaved himself, during a reign of five years, in a manner more worthy of his birth and station. The kingdom, however, was still infested by the Danes, who made an inroad and sacked Winchester; but were there defeated. A body also of these pirates, who were quartered in the Isle of Thanet, having deceived the English by a treaty, unexpectedly broke into Kent, and committed great outrages.

ETHERED

866. ETHELBERT was succeeded by his brother Ethered, who, though he defended himself with bravery, enjoyed, during his whole reign, no tranquillity from those Danish irruptions. His younger brother, Alfred, seconded him in all his enterprizes; and generously sacrificed to the public good all resentment, which he might entertain, on account of his being excluded by Ethered from a large patrimony, which had been left him by his father.

The first landing of the Danes in the reign of Ethered was among the East-Angles, who, more anxious for their present safety than for the common interest, entered into a separate treaty with the enemy; and furnished them with horses, which enabled them to make an irruption by land into the kingdom of Northumberland. They there seized the city of York; and defended it against Osbricht and Aella, two Northumbrian princes, who perished in the assault.[e] Encouraged by these successes, and by the superiority, which they had acquired in arms, they now ventured, under the command of Hinguar and Hubba, to leave the sea-coast, and penetrating into Mercia, they took up their winter-quarters at Nottingham, where they threatened the kingdom with a final subjection. The Mercians, in this extremity, applied to Ethered for succour; and that prince, with his brother, Alfred, conducting a *870.* great army to Nottingham, obliged the enemy to dislodge, and to retreat into Northumberland. Their restless disposition, and their avidity for plunder, allowed them not to remain long in those quarters: They broke into East-Anglia, defeated and took pris-

[e] Asser. p. 6. Chron. Sax. p. 79.

CHAPTER II

oner, Edmund, the king of that country, whom they afterwards murdered in cool blood; and committing the most barbarous ravages on the people, particularly on the monasteries, they gave the East-Angles cause to regret the temporary relief, which they had obtained, by assisting the common enemy.

The next station of the Danes was at Reading; whence they *871.* infested the neighbouring country by their incursions. The Mercians, desirous of shaking off their dependance on Ethered, refused to join him with their forces; and that prince, attended by Alfred, was obliged to march against the enemy, with the West Saxons alone, his hereditary subjects. The Danes, being defeated in an action, shut themselves up in their garrison; but quickly making thence an irruption, they routed the West-Saxons, and obliged them to raise the siege. An action soon after ensued at Aston, in Berkshire, where the English, in the beginning of the day, were in danger of a total defeat. Alfred, advancing with one division of the army, was surrounded by the enemy in disadvantageous ground; and Ethered, who was at that time hearing mass, refused to march to his assistance, till prayers should be finished.*f* But as he afterwards obtained the victory, this success, not the danger of Alfred, was ascribed by the monks to the piety of that monarch. This battle of Aston did not terminate the war: Another battle was a little after fought at Basing; where the Danes were more successful; and being reinforced by a new army from their own country, they became every day more terrible to the English. Amidst these confusions, Ethered died of a wound, which he had received in an action with the Danes; and left the inheritance of his cares and misfortunes, rather than of his grandeur, to his brother, Alfred, who was now twenty-two years of age.

ALFRED

THIS PRINCE gave very early marks of those great virtues *871.* and shining talents, by which, during the most difficult times, he saved his country from utter ruin and subversion. Ethel-

---

f Asser. p. 7. W. Malm. lib. 2. cap. 3. Simeon Dunelm. p. 125. Anglia Sacra, vol. i. p. 205.

wolf, his father, the year after his return with Alfred from Rome, had again sent the young prince thither with a numerous retinue; and a report being spread of the king's death, the pope, Leo III. gave Alfred the royal unction;[g] whether prognosticating his future greatness from the appearances of his pregnant genius, or willing to pretend even in that age, to the right of conferring kingdoms. Alfred, on his return home, became every day more the object of his father's affections; but being indulged in all youthful pleasures, he was much neglected in his education; and he had already reached his twelfth year, when he was yet totally ignorant of the lowest elements of literature. His genius was first rouzed by the recital of Saxon poems, in which the queen took delight; and this species of erudition, which is sometimes able to make a considerable progress even among barbarians, expanded those noble and elevated sentiments, which he had received from nature.[h] Encouraged by the queen, and stimulated by his own ardent inclination, he soon learned to read those compositions; and proceeded thence to acquire the knowledge of the Latin tongue, in which he met with authors, that better prompted his heroic spirit, and directed his generous views. Absorbed in these elegant pursuits, he regarded his accession to royalty rather as an object of regret than of triumph;[i] but being called to the throne, in preference to his brother's children, as well by the will of his father, a circumstance which had great authority with the Anglo-Saxons,[k] as by the vows of the whole nation and the urgency of public affairs, he shook off his literary indolence, and exerted himself in the defence of his people. He had scarcely buried his brother, when he was obliged to take the field, in order to oppose the Danes, who had seized Wilton, and were exercising their usual ravages on the countries around. He marched against them with the few troops, which he could assemble on a sudden; and giving them battle, gained at first an advantage, but by his pursuing the victory too far, the superiority of the enemy's numbers prevailed, and recovered them the day. Their loss, however, in the action was so considerable, that, fearing Alfred would receive daily reinforce-

[g] Asser. p. 2. W. Malm. lib. 2. cap. 2. Ingulf, p. 869. Simeon Dunelm. p. 120, 139.   [h] Asser. p. 5. M. West. p. 167.   [i] Asser. p. 7.   [k] Ibid. p. 22. Simeon Dunelm. p. 121.

ment from his subjects, they were content to stipulate for a safe retreat, and promised to depart the kingdom. For that purpose they were conducted to London, and allowed to take up winter-quarters there; but, careless of their engagements, they immediately set themselves to the committing of spoil on the neighbouring country. Burrhed, king of Mercia, in whose territories London was situated, made a new stipulation with them, and engaged them, by presents of money, to remove to Lindesey in Lincolnshire; a country which they had already reduced to ruin and desolation. Finding therefore no object in that place, either for their rapine or violence, they suddenly turned back upon Mercia, in a quarter where they expected to find it without defence; and fixing their station at Repton in Derbyshire, they laid the whole country desolate with fire and sword. Burrhed, despairing of success against an enemy, whom no force could resist, and no treaties bind, abandoned his kingdom, and flying to Rome, took shelter in a cloyster.[l] He was brother-in-law to Alfred, and the last who bore the title of King in Mercia.

The West-Saxons were now the only remaining power in England; and though supported by the vigour and abilities of Alfred, they were unable to sustain the efforts of those ravagers, who from all quarters invaded them. A new swarm of Danes came over this year under three princes, Guthrum, Oscitel, and Amund; and having first joined their countrymen at Repton, they soon found the necessity of separating, in order to provide for their subsistence. Part of them, under the command of Haldene, their chieftain,[m] marched into Northumberland, where they fixed their quarters; part of them took quarters at Cambridge, whence they dislodged in the ensuing summer, and seized Wereham, in the county of Dorset, the very center of Alfred's dominions. That prince so straitened them in these quarters, that they were content to come to a treaty with him, and stipulated to depart his country. Alfred, well acquainted with their usual perfidy, obliged them to swear upon the holy reliques to the observance of the treaty;[n] not that he expected they would pay any veneration to the reliques; but he hoped, that, if they now violated this oath, their impiety

875.

---

[l] Asser. p. 8. Chron. Sax. p. 82. Ethelward, lib. 4. cap. 4.   [m] Chron. Sax. p. 83.   [n] Asser. p. 8.

would infallibly draw down upon them the vengeance of heaven. But the Danes, little apprehensive of the danger, suddenly, without seeking any pretence, fell upon Alfred's army; and having put it to rout, marched westward, and took possession of Exeter. The prince collected new forces; and exerted such vigour, that he fought in one year eight battles with the enemy,[o] and reduced them to the utmost extremity. He hearkened however to new proposals of peace; and was satisfied to stipulate with them, that they would settle somewhere in England,[p] and would not permit the entrance of more ravagers into the kingdom. But while he was expecting the execution of this treaty, which it seemed the interest of the Danes themselves to fulfil, he heard that another body had landed, and having collected all the scattered troops of their countrymen, had surprized Chippenham, then a considerable town, and were exercising their usual ravages all around them.

This last incident quite broke the spirit of the Saxons, and reduced them to despair. Finding that, after all the miserable havoc, which they had undergone in their persons and in their property; after all the vigorous actions, which they had exerted in their own defence; a new band, equally greedy of spoil and slaughter, had disembarked among them; they believed themselves abandoned by heaven to destruction, and delivered over to those swarms of robbers, which the fertile north thus incessantly poured forth against them. Some left their country, and retired into Wales or fled beyond sea: Others submitted to the conquerors, in hopes of appeasing their fury by a servile obedience:[q] And every man's attention being now engrossed in concern for his own preservation, no one would hearken to the exhortations of the King, who summoned them to make, under his conduct, one effort more in defence of their prince, their country, and their liberties. Alfred himself was obliged to relinquish the ensigns of his dignity, to dismiss his servants, and to seek shelter, in the meanest disguises, from the pursuit and fury of his enemies. He concealed himself under a peasant's habit, and lived some time in the house of a neat-herd, who had been entrusted with the care of some of his cows.[r] There passed here an incident, which has been recorded by

---

[o] Asser. p. 8. The Saxon Chronicle, p. 82. says nine battles.   [p] Asser. p. 9. Alur. Beverl. p. 104.   [q] Chron. Sax. p. 84. Alured Beverl. p. 105.   [r] Asser. p. 9.

CHAPTER II

all the historians, and was long preserved by popular tradition; though it contains nothing memorable in itself, except so far as every circumstance is interesting, which attends so much virtue and dignity, reduced to such distress. The wife of the neat-herd was ignorant of the condition of her royal guest; and observing him one day busy by the fire-side in trimming his bow and arrows, she desired him to take care of some cakes, which were toasting, while she was employed elsewhere in other domestic affairs. But Alfred, whose thoughts were otherwise engaged, neglected this injunction; and the good woman, on her return, finding her cakes all burnt, rated the king very severely, and upbraided him, that he always seemed very well pleased to eat her warm cakes, though he was thus negligent in toasting them.[s]

By degrees, Alfred, as he found the search of the enemy become more remiss, collected some of his retainers, and retired into the center of a bog, formed by the stagnating waters of the Thone and Parret, in Somersetshire. He here found two acres of firm ground; and building a habitation on them, rendered himself secure by its fortifications, and still more by the unknown and inaccessible roads which led to it, and by the forests and morasses, with which it was every way environed. This place he called Aethelingay, or the Isle of Nobles;[t] and it now bears the name of Athelney. He thence made frequent and unexpected sallies upon the Danes, who often felt the vigour of his arm, but knew not from what quarter the blow came. He subsisted himself and his followers by the plunder which he acquired; he procured them consolation by revenge; and from small successes, he opened their minds to hope, that, notwithstanding his present low condition, more important victories might at length attend his valour.

Alfred lay here concealed, but not unactive, during a twelvemonth; when the news of a prosperous event reached his ears, and called him to the field. Hubba, the Dane, having spread devastation, fire, and slaughter, over Wales, had landed in Devonshire from twenty-three vessels, and laid siege to the castle of Kinwith, a place situated near the mouth of the small river Tau. Oddune, earl of Devonshire, with his followers, had taken shelter there; and being ill supplied with provisions, and even with water, he deter-

---

[s] Asser. p. 9. M. West. p. 170. [t] Chron. Sax. p. 85. W. Malm. lib. 2. cap. 4. Ethelward, lib. 4. cap. 4. Ingulf, p. 26.

mined, by some vigorous blow, to prevent the necessity of submitting to the barbarous enemy. He made a sudden sally on the Danes before sun-rising; and taking them unprepared, he put them to rout, pursued them with great slaughter, killed Hubba himself, and got possession of the famous *Reafen,* or enchanted standard, in which the Danes put great confidence.[u] It contained the figure of a raven, which had been inwoven by the three sisters of Hinguar and Hubba, with many magical incantations, and which, by its different movements, prognosticated, as the Danes believed, the good or bad success of any enterprize.[w]

When Alfred observed this symptom of successful resistance in his subjects, he left his retreat; but before he would assemble them in arms, or urge them to any attempt, which, if unfortunate, might, in their present despondency, prove fatal, he resolved to inspect, himself, the situation of the enemy, and to judge of the probability of success. For this purpose he entered their camp under the disguise of a harper, and passed unsuspected through every quarter. He so entertained them with his music and facetious humours, that he met with a welcome reception; and was even introduced to the tent of Guthrum, their prince, where he remained some days.[x] He remarked the supine security of the Danes, their contempt of the English, their negligence in foraging and plundering, and their dissolute wasting of what they gained by rapine and violence. Encouraged by these favourable appearances, he secretly sent emissaries to the most considerable of his subjects, and summoned them to a rendezvous, attended by their warlike followers, at Brixton, on the borders of Selwood forest.[y] The English, who had hoped to put an end to their calamities by servile submission, now found the insolence and rapine of the conqueror more intolerable than all past fatigues and dangers; and, at the appointed day, they joyfully resorted to their prince. On his appearance, they received him with shouts of applause;[z] and could not satiate their eyes with the sight of this beloved monarch, whom they had long regarded as dead, and who now with voice and looks expressing his confidence of success, called

---

[u] Asser. p. 10. Chron. Sax. p. 84. Abbas Rieval. p. 395. Alured Beverl. p. 105. [w] Asser. p. 10. [x] W. Malm. lib. 2. cap. 4. [y] Chron. Sax. p. 85.
[z] Asser. p. 10. Chron. Sax. p. 85. Simeon Dunelm. p. 128. Alured. Beverl. p. 105. Abbas Rieval. p. 354.

them to liberty and to vengeance. He instantly conducted them to Eddington, where the Danes were encamped: and taking advantage of his previous knowledge of the place, he directed his attack against the most unguarded quarter of the enemy. The Danes, surprised to see an army of English, whom they considered as totally subdued, and still more astonished to hear that Alfred was at their head, made but a faint resistance, notwithstanding their superiority of number; and were soon put to flight with great slaughter. The remainder of the routed army, with their prince, was besieged by Alfred in a fortified camp, to which they fled; but being reduced to extremity by want and hunger, they had recourse to the clemency of the victor, and offered to submit on any conditions. The king, no less generous than brave, gave them their lives; and even formed a scheme for converting them, from mortal enemies, into faithful subjects and confederates. He knew, that the kingdoms of East-Anglia and Northumberland were totally desolated by the frequent inroads of the Danes; and he now purposed to re-people them by settling there Guthrum and his followers. He hoped that the new planters would at last betake themselves to industry, when, by reason of his resistance, and the exhausted condition of the country, they could no longer subsist by plunder; and that they might serve him as a rampart against any future incursions of their countrymen. But before he ratified these mild conditions with the Danes, he required, that they should give him one pledge of their submission, and of their inclination to incorporate with the English, by declaring their conversion to Christianity.[a] Guthrum, and his army had no aversion to the proposal; and, without much instruction or argument or conference, they were all admitted to baptism. The king answered for Guthrum at the font, gave him the name of Athelstan, and received him as his adopted son.[b]

The success of this expedient seemed to correspond to Alfred's hopes: The greater part of the Danes settled peaceably in their new quarters: Some smaller bodies of the same nation, which were dispersed in Mercia, were distributed into the five cities of Darby, Leicester, Stamford, Lincoln, and Nottingham, and were thence called the Fif or Five-Burgers. The more turbulent and unquiet

880.

---

[a] Chron. Sax. p. 85.   [b] Asser. p. 10. Chron. Sax. p. 90.

made an expedition into France under the command of Hastings;[c] and except by a short incursion of Danes, who sailed up the Thames and landed at Fulham, but suddenly retreated to their ships, on finding the country in a posture of defence, Alfred was not for some years infested by the inroads of those barbarians.[d]

The king employed this interval of tranquillity in restoring order to the state, which had been shaken by so many violent convulsions; in establishing civil and military institutions; in composing the minds of men to industry and justice; and in providing against the return of like calamities. He was, more properly than his grandfather Egbert, the sole monarch of the English, (for so the Saxons were now universally called) because the kingdom of Mercia was at last incorporated in his state, and was governed by Ethelbert, his brother-in-law, who bore the title of Earl: and though the Danes, who peopled East-Anglia and Northumberland, were for some time ruled immediately by their own princes, they all acknowledged a subordination to Alfred, and submitted to his superior authority. As equality among subjects is the great source of concord, Alfred gave the same laws to the Danes and English, and put them entirely on a like footing in the administration both of civil and criminal justice. The fine for the murder of a Dane was the same with that for the murder of an Englishman; the great symbol of equality in those ages.

The king, after rebuilding the ruined cities, particularly London,[e] which had been destroyed by the Danes in the reign of Ethelwolf, established a regular militia for the defence of the kingdom. He ordained that all his people should be armed and registered; he assigned them a regular rotation of duty; he distributed part into the castles and fortresses, which he built at proper places;[f] he required another part to take the field on any alarm, and to assemble at stated places of rendezvous; and he left a sufficient number at home, who were employed in the cultivation of the land, and who afterwards took their turn in military service.[g] The whole kingdom was like one great garrison; and the Danes could no sooner appear in one place, than a sufficient number was assem-

[c] W. Malm. lib. 2. cap. 4. Ingulf, p. 26.   [d] Asser. p. 11.   [e] Asser. p. 15. Chron. Sax. p. 88. M. West. p. 171. Simeon Dunelm. p. 131. Brompton, p. 812. Alured Beverl. ex edit. Hearne, p. 106.   [f] Asser. p. 18. Ingulf, p. 27.   [g] Chron. Sax. p. 92, 93.

bled to oppose them, without leaving the other quarters defenceless or disarmed.[h]

But Alfred, sensible that the proper method of opposing an enemy, who made incursions by sea, was to meet them on their own element, took care to provide himself with a naval force,[i] which, though the most natural defence of an island, had hitherto been totally neglected by the English. He increased the shipping of his kingdom both in number and strength, and trained his subjects in the practice as well of sailing, as of naval action. He distributed his armed vessels in proper stations around the island, and was sure to meet the Danish ships either before or after they had landed their troops, and to pursue them in all their incursions. Though the Danes might suddenly, by surprize, disembark on the coast, which was generally become desolate by their frequent ravages, they were encountered by the English fleet in their retreat and escaped not, as formerly, by abandoning their booty, but paid, by their total destruction, the penalty of the disorders which they had committed.

In this manner, Alfred repelled several inroads of these pyratical Danes, and maintained his kingdom, during some years, in safety and tranquillity. A fleet of a hundred and twenty ships of war was stationed upon the coast; and being provided with warlike engines, as well as with expert seamen, both Frisians and English, (for Alfred supplied the defects of his own subjects by engaging able foreigners in his service) maintained a superiority over those smaller bands, with which England had so often been infested.[k] *893.* But at last Hastings the famous Danish chief, having ravaged all the provinces of France, both along the sea coast and the Loire and Seine, and being obliged to quit that country, more by the desolation which he himself had occasioned, than by the resistance of the inhabitants, appeared off the coast of Kent with a fleet of 330 sail. The greater part of the enemy disembarked in the Rother, and seized the fort of Apuldore. Hastings himself, commanding a fleet of eighty sail, entered the Thames, and fortifying Milton in Kent, began to spread his forces over the country, and to commit the most destructive ravages. But Alfred, on the first alarm of this descent, flew to the defence of his people, at the head of a select

[h] Spelman's life of Alfred, p. 147. edit. 1709.   [i] Asser. p. 9. M. West. p. 179.   [k] Asser. p. 11. Chron. Sax. p. 86, 87. M. West. p. 176.

band of soldiers, whom he always kept about his person;[l] and gathering to him the armed militia from all quarters, appeared in the field with a force superior to the enemy. All straggling parties, whom necessity or love of plunder had drawn to a distance from their chief encampment, were cut off by the English;[m] and these pyrates, instead of increasing their spoil, found themselves cooped up in their fortifications, and obliged to subsist by the plunder which they had brought from France. Tired of this situation, which must in the end prove ruinous to them, the Danes at Apuldore rose suddenly from their encampment, with an intention of marching towards the Thames, and passing over into Essex: But they escaped not the vigilance of Alfred, who encountered them at Farnham, put them to rout,[n] seized all their horses and baggage, and chaced the runaways on board their ships, which carried them up the Colne to Mersey in Essex, where they entrenched themselves. Hastings, at the same time, and probably by concert, made a like movement; and deserting Milton, took possession of Bamflete, near the Isle of Canvey in the same county;[o] where he hastily threw up fortifications for his defence against the power of Alfred.

Unfortunately for the English, Guthrum, prince of the East-Anglian Danes, was now dead; as was also Guthred, whom the king had appointed governor of the Northumbrians; and those restless tribes, being no longer restrained by the authority of their princes, and being encouraged by the appearance of so great a body of their countrymen, broke into rebellion, shook off the authority of Alfred, and yielding to their inveterate habits of war and depredation,[p] embarked on board two hundred and forty vessels, and appeared before Exeter in the west of England. Alfred lost not a moment in opposing this new enemy. Having left some forces at London to make head against Hastings and the other Danes, he marched suddenly to the west;[q] and falling on the rebels before they were aware, pursued them to their ships with great slaughter. These ravagers, sailing next to Sussex, began to plunder the country near Chichester; but the order which Alfred had every where established, sufficed here, without his presence, for the defence of

---

[l] Asser. p. 19. [m] Chron. Sax. p. 92. [n] Chron. Sax. p. 93. Flor. Wigorn. p. 595. [o] Chron. Sax. p. 93. [p] Chron. Sax. p. 92. [q] Chron. Sax. p. 93.

CHAPTER II

the place; and the rebels, meeting with a new repulse, in which many of them were killed, and some of their ships taken,[r] were obliged to put again to sea, and were discouraged from attempting any other enterprize.

Meanwhile, the Danish invaders in Essex, having united their force under the command of Hastings, advanced into the inland country, and made spoil of all around them; but soon had reason to repent of their temerity. The English army, left in London, assisted by a body of the citizens, attacked the enemy's entrenchments at Bamflete, overpowered the garrison, and having done great execution upon them, carried off the wife and two sons of Hastings.[s] Alfred generously spared these captives; and even restored them to Hastings,[t] on condition that he should depart the kingdom.

But though the king had thus honourably rid himself of this dangerous enemy, he had not entirely subdued or expelled the invaders. The pyratical Danes willingly followed in an excursion any prosperous leader, who gave them hopes of booty; but were not so easily induced to relinquish their enterprize, or submit to return, baffled and without plunder, into their native country. Great numbers of them, after the departure of Hastings, seized and fortified Shobury at the mouth of the Thames; and having left a garrison there, they marched along the river, till they came to Boddington in the county of Glocester, where, being reinforced by some Welsh, they threw up entrenchments, and prepared for their defence. The king here surrounded them with the whole force of his dominions;[u] and as he had now a certain prospect of victory, he resolved to trust nothing to chance, but rather to master his enemies by famine than assault. They were reduced to such extremities, that, having eaten their own horses, and having many of them perished with hunger,[w] they made a desperate sally upon the English; and though the greater number fell in the action, a considerable body made their escape.[x] These roved about for some time in England, still pursued by the vigilance of Alfred; they attacked Leicester with success, defended themselves in Hartford, and then fled to Quatford, where they were finally broken and

[r] Chron. Sax. p. 96. Flor. Wigorn. p. 596. [s] Chron. Sax. p. 94. M. West. p. 178. [t] M. West. p. 179. [u] Chron. Sax. p. 94. [w] Ibid. M. West. p. 179. Flor. Wigorn. p. 596. [x] Chron. Sax. p. 95.

subdued. The small remains of them either dispersed themselves among their countrymen in Northumberland and East-Anglia,^y or had recourse again to the sea, where they exercised pyracy, under the command of Sigefert, a Northumbrian. This free-booter, well acquainted with Alfred's naval preparations, had framed vessels of a new construction, higher, and longer, and swifter, than those of the English: But the king soon discovered his superior skill, by building vessels still higher, and longer, and swifter, than those of the Northumbrians; and falling upon them, while they were exercising their ravages in the west, he took twenty of their ships; and having tried all the prisoners at Winchester, he hanged them as pyrates, the common enemies of mankind.

The well-timed severity of this execution, together with the excellent posture of defence established every where, restored full tranquillity in England, and provided for the future security of the government. The East-Anglian and Northumbrian Danes, on the first appearance of Alfred upon their frontiers, made anew the most humble submissions to him; and he thought it prudent to take them under his immediate government, without establishing over them a viceroy of their own nation.^z The Welsh also acknowledged his authority; and this great prince had now, by prudence and justice and valour, established his sovereignty over all the southern parts of the island, from the English channel to the frontiers of Scotland; when he died, in the vigour of his age and the full strength of his faculties, after a glorious reign of twenty-nine years and a half;^a in which he deservedly attained the appellation of Alfred the Great, and the title of Founder of the English monarchy.

901.

The merit of this prince, both in private and public life, may with advantage be set in opposition to that of any monarch or citizen, which the annals of any age or any nation can present to us. He seems indeed to be the model of that perfect character, which, under the denomination of a sage or wise man, philosophers have been fond of delineating, rather as a fiction of their imagination, than in hopes of ever seeing it really existing. So happily were all his virtues tempered together; so justly were they blended; and so powerfully did each prevent the other from ex-

^y Ibid. p. 97.   ^z Flor. Wigorn. p. 598.   ^a Asser. p. 21. Chron. Sax. p. 99.

CHAPTER II

ceeding its proper boundaries! He knew how to reconcile the most enterprizing spirit with the coolest moderation; the most obstinate perseverance with the easiest flexibility; the most severe justice with the gentlest lenity; the greatest vigour in commanding with the most perfect affability of deportment;[b] the highest capacity and inclination for science, with the most shining talents for action. His civil and his military virtues are almost equally the objects of our admiration; excepting only, that the former, being more rare among princes, as well as more useful, seem chiefly to challenge our applause. Nature also, as if desirous that so bright a production of her skill should be set in the fairest light, had bestowed on him every bodily accomplishment, vigour of limbs, dignity of shape and air, with a pleasing, engaging, and open countenance.[c] Fortune alone, by throwing him into that barbarous age, deprived him of historians worthy to transmit his fame to posterity; and we wish to see him delineated in more lively colours, and with more particular strokes, that we may at least perceive some of those small specks and blemishes, from which, as a man, it is impossible he could be entirely exempted.

But we should give but an imperfect idea of Alfred's merit, were we to confine our narration to his military exploits, and were not more particular in our account of his institutions for the execution of justice, and of his zeal for the encouragement of arts and sciences.

After Alfred had subdued and had settled or expelled the Danes, he found the kingdom in the most wretched condition; desolated by the ravages of those barbarians, and thrown into disorders, which were calculated to perpetuate its misery. Though the great armies of the Danes were broken, the country was full of straggling troops of that nation, who, being accustomed to live by plunder, were become incapable of industry, and who, from the natural ferocity of their manners, indulged themselves in committing violence, even beyond what was requisite to supply their necessities. The English themselves, reduced to the most extreme indigence by these continued depredations, had shaken off all bands of government; and those who had been plundered to-day, betook themselves next day to a like disorderly life, and from

[b] Asser. p. 13.   [c] Asser. p. 5.

despair joined the robbers in pillaging and ruining their fellow-citizens. These were the evils, for which it was necessary that the vigilance and activity of Alfred should provide a remedy.

That he might render the execution of justice strict and regular, he divided all England into counties; these counties he subdivided into hundreds; and the hundreds into tithings. Every house-holder was answerable for the behaviour of his family and slaves, and even of his guests, if they lived above three days in his house. Ten neighbouring house-holders were formed into one corporation, who, under the name of a tithing, decennary, or fribourg, were answerable for each other's conduct, and over whom one person, called a tythingman, headbourg, or borsholder, was appointed to preside. Every man was punished as an outlaw, who did not register himself in some tything. And no man could change his habitation, without a warrant or certificate from the borsholder of the tything, to which he formerly belonged.

When any person in any tything or decennary was guilty of a crime, the borsholder was summoned to answer for him; and if he were not willing to be surety for his appearance and his clearing himself, the criminal was committed to prison, and there detained till his trial. If he fled, either before or after finding sureties, the borsholder and decennary became liable to enquiry, and were exposed to the penalties of law. Thirty-one days were allowed them for producing the criminal; and if that time elapsed without their being able to find him, the borsholder, with two other members of the decennary, was obliged to appear, and together with three chief members of the three neighbouring decennaries (making twelve in all) to swear that his decennary was free from all privity both of the crime committed, and of the escape of the criminal. If the borsholder could not find such a number to answer for their innocence, the decennary was compelled by fine to make satisfaction to the king, according to the degree of the offence.[d] By this institution every man was obliged from his own interest to keep a watchful eye over the conduct of his neighbours; and was in a manner surety for the behaviour of those who were placed under the division, to which he belonged: Whence these decennaries received the name of frank-pledges.

[d] Leges St. Edw. cap. 20. apud Wilkins, p. 202.

CHAPTER II

Such a regular distribution of the people, with such a strict confinement in their habitation, may not be necessary in times, when men are more enured to obedience and justice; and it might perhaps be regarded as destructive of liberty and commerce in a polished state; but it was well calculated to reduce that fierce and licentious people under the salutary restraint of law and government. But Alfred took care to temper these rigours by other institutions favourable to the freedom of the citizens; and nothing could be more popular and liberal than his plan for the administration of justice. The borsholder summoned together his whole decennary to assist him in deciding any lesser difference, which occurred among the members of this small community. In affairs of greater moment, in appeals from the decennary, or in controversies arising between members of different decennaries, the cause was brought before the hundred, which consisted of ten decennaries, or a hundred families of freemen, and which was regularly assembled once in four weeks, for the deciding of causes.[e] Their method of decision deserves to be noted, as being the origin of juries; an institution, admirable in itself, and the best calculated for the preservation of liberty and the administration of justice, that ever was devised by the wit of man. Twelve freeholders were chosen; who, having sworn, together with the hundreder or presiding magistrate of that division, to administer impartial justice,[f] proceeded to the examination of that cause, which was submitted to their jurisdiction. And beside these monthly meetings of the hundred, there was an annual meeting, appointed for a more general inspection of the police of the district; for the enquiry into crimes, the correction of abuses in magistrates, and the obliging of every person to shew the decennary in which he was registered. The people, in imitation of their ancestors, the ancient Germans, assembled there in arms, whence a hundred was sometimes called a wapen-take, and its court served both for the support of military discipline, and for the administration of civil justice.[g]

The next superior court to that of the hundred was the county-court, which met twice a year, after Michaelmas and Easter, and

[e] Leg. Edw. cap. 2.   [f] Faedus Alfred, and Gothurn, apud Wilkins, cap. 3. p. 47. Leg. Ethelstani, cap. 2. apud Wilkins, p. 58. LL. Ethelr. § 4. Wilkins, p. 117.   [g] Spellman in voce Wapentake.

consisted of the freeholders of the county, who possessed an equal vote in the decision of causes. The bishop presided in this court, together with the alderman; and the proper object of the court was the receiving of appeals from the hundreds and decennaries, and the deciding of such controversies as arose between men of different hundreds. Formerly, the alderman possessed both the civil and military authority; but Alfred, sensible that this conjunction of powers rendered the nobility dangerous and independant, appointed also a sheriff in each county; who enjoyed a co-ordinate authority with the former in the judicial function.[h] His office also impowered him to guard the rights of the crown in the county, and to levy the fines imposed; which in that age formed no contemptible part of the public revenue.

There lay an appeal, in default of justice, from all these courts to the king himself in council; and as the people, sensible of the equity and great talents of Alfred, placed their chief confidence in him, he was soon overwhelmed with appeals from all parts of England. He was indefatigable in the dispatch of these causes;[i] but finding that his time must be entirely engrossed by this branch of duty, he resolved to obviate the inconvenience, by correcting the ignorance or corruption of the inferior magistrates, from which it arose.[k] He took care to have his nobility instructed in letters and the laws:[l] He chose the earls and sheriffs from among the men most celebrated for probity and knowledge: He punished severely all malversation in office:[m] And he removed all the earls, whom he found unequal to the trust;[n] allowing only some of the more elderly to serve by a deputy, till their death should make room for more worthy successors.

The better to guide the magistrates in the administration of justice, Alfred framed a body of laws; which, though now lost, served long as the basis of English jurisprudence, and is generally deemed the origin of what is denominated the COMMON LAW. He appointed regular meetings of the states of England twice a year in London;[o] a city which he himself had repaired and beautified, and which he thus rendered the capital of the kingdom. The similarity of these institutions to the customs of the ancient Germans, to the practice of the other northern conquerors, and to the Saxon

[h] Ingulf. p. 870. [i] Asser. p. 20. [k] Ibid. p. 18, 21. Flor. Wigorn. p. 594. Abbas Rieval. p. 355. [l] Flor. Wigorn. p. 594. Brompton, p. 814. [m] Le Miroir de Justice, chap. 2. [n] Asser. p. 20. [o] Le Miroir de Justice.

laws during the Heptarchy, prevents us from regarding Alfred as the sole author of this plan of government; and leads us rather to think, that, like a wise man, he contented himself with reforming, extending, and executing the institutions, which he found previously established. But on the whole, such success attended his legislation, that every thing bore suddenly a new face in England: Robberies and iniquities of all kinds were repressed by the punishment or reformation of the criminals.[p] And so exact was the general police, that Alfred, it is said, hung up, by way of bravado, golden bracelets near the highways; and no man dared to touch them.[q] Yet amidst these rigours of justice, this great prince preserved the most sacred regard to the liberty of his people; and it is a memorable sentiment preserved in his will, that it was just the English should for ever remain as free as their own thoughts.[r]

As good morals and knowledge are almost inseparable, in every age, though not in every individual; the care of Alfred for the encouragement of learning among his subjects was another useful branch of his legislation, and tended to reclaim the English from their former dissolute and ferocious manners: But the King was guided in this pursuit, less by political views, than by his natural bent and propensity towards letters. When he came to the throne, he found the nation sunk into the grossest ignorance and barbarism, proceeding from the continued disorders in the government, and from the ravages of the Danes: The monasteries were destroyed, the monks butchered or dispersed, their libraries burnt; and thus the only feats of erudition in those ages were totally subverted. Alfred himself complains, that on his accession he knew not one person, south of the Thames, who could so much as interpret the Latin service; and very few in the northern parts, who had reached even that pitch of education. But this prince invited over the most celebrated scholars from all parts of Europe; he established schools every where for the instruction of his people; he founded, at least repaired the university of Oxford, and endowed it with many privileges, revenues and immunities; he enjoined by law all freeholders possessed of two hydes[s] of land or more to send their children to school for their instruction; he gave preferment

[p] Ingulf, p. 27.   [q] W. Malmes. lib. 2. cap. 4.   [r] Asser. p. 24.   [s] A hyde contained land sufficient to employ one plough. See H. Hunt. lib. 6. in A. D. 1008. Annal. Waverl. in A. D. 1083. Gervase of Tilbury says it commonly contained about 100 acres.

both in church and state to such only as had made some proficiency in knowledge: And by all these expedients he had the satisfaction, before his death, to see a great change in the face of affairs; and in a work of his, which is still extant, he congratulates himself on the progress which learning, under his patronage, had already made in England.

But the most effectual expedient, employed by Alfred, for the encouragement of learning, was his own example, and the constant assiduity, with which, notwithstanding the multiplicity and urgency of his affairs, he employed himself in the pursuits of knowledge. He usually divided his time into three equal portions: One was employed in sleep, and the refection of his body by diet and exercise; another in the dispatch of business; a third in study and devotion: And that he might more exactly measure the hours, he made use of burning tapers of equal length, which he fixed in lanthorns;[t] an expedient suited to that rude age, when the geometry of dialling and the mechanism of clocks and watches were totally unknown. And by such a regular distribution of his time, though he often laboured under great bodily infirmities,[u] this martial hero, who fought in person fifty-six battles by sea and land,[w] was able, during a life of no extraordinary length, to acquire more knowledge, and even to compose more books, than most studious men, though blest with the greatest leisure and application, have, in more fortunate ages, made the object of their uninterrupted industry.

Sensible, that the people, at all times, especially when their understandings are obstructed by ignorance and bad education, are not much susceptible of speculative instruction, Alfred endeavoured to convey his morality by apologues, parables, stories, apophthegms, couched in poetry; and besides propagating among his subjects, former compositions of that kind, which he found in the Saxon tongue,[x] he exercised his genius in inventing works of a like nature,[y] as well as in translating from the Greek the elegant fables of Aesop. He also gave Saxon translations of Orosius's and Bede's histories; and of Boethius concerning the consolation of philosophy.[z] And he deemed it nowise derogatory from his other great characters of sovereign, legislator, warrior, and politician,

---

[t] Asser. p. 20. W. Malm. lib. 2. cap. 4. Ingulf, p. 870.   [u] Asser. p. 4, 12, 13, 17.   [w] W. Malm. lib. 4. cap. 4.   [x] Asser. p. 13.   [y] Spelman, p. 124. Abas. Rieval. p. 355.   [z] W. Malm. lib. 2. cap. 4. Brompton, p. 814.

CHAPTER II

thus to lead the way to his people in the pursuits of literature.

Meanwhile, this prince was not negligent in encouraging the vulgar and mechanical arts, which have a more sensible, though not a closer connexion with the interests of society. He invited, from all quarters, industrious foreigners to re-people his country, which had been desolated by the ravages of the Danes.[a] He introduced and encouraged manufactures of all kinds; and no inventor or improver of any ingenious art did he suffer to go unrewarded.[b] He prompted men of activity to betake themselves to navigation, to push commerce into the most remote countries, and to acquire riches by propagating industry among their fellow-citizens. He set apart a seventh portion of his own revenue for maintaining a number of workmen, whom he constantly employed in rebuilding the ruined cities, castles, palaces, and monasteries.[c] Even the elegancies of life were brought to him from the Mediterranean and the Indies;[d] and his subjects, by seeing those productions of the peaceful arts, were taught to respect the virtues of justice and industry, from which alone they could arise. Both living and dead, Alfred was regarded, by foreigners, no less than by his own subjects, as the greatest prince after Charlemagne that had appeared in Europe during several ages, and as one of the wisest and best that had ever adorned the annals of any nation.

Alfred had, by his wife, Ethelswitha, daughter of a Mercian earl, three sons and three daughters. The eldest son, Edmund, died without issue, in his father's lifetime. The third, Ethelward, inherited his father's passion for letters, and lived a private life. The second, Edward, succeeded to his power; and passes by the appellation of Edward the Elder, being the first of that name who sat on the English throne.

EDWARD THE ELDER

THIS PRINCE, who equalled his father in military talents, though inferior to him in knowledge and erudition,[e] found immediately, on his accession, a specimen of that turbulent life, to

901.

[a] Asser. p. 13. Flor. Wigorn. p. 588. [b] Asser. p. 20. [c] Ibid. W. Malm lib. 2. cap. 4. [d] W. Malmes. lib. 2. cap. 4. [e] W. Malmes. lib. 2. cap. 5. Hoveden, p. 421.

which all princes, and even all individuals were exposed, in an age
when men, less restrained by law or justice, and less occupied by
industry, had no aliment for their inquietude, but wars, insurrections, convulsions, rapine, and depredation. Ethelwald, his
cousin-german, son of king Ethelbert, the elder brother of Alfred,
insisted on his preferable title;[f] and arming his partizans, took
possession of Winburne, where he seemed determined to defend
himself to the last extremity, and to await the issue of his pretensions.[g] But when the king approached the town with a great
army, Ethelwald, having the prospect of certain destruction, made
his escape, and fled first into Normandy, thence into Northumberland; where he hoped, that the people, who had been re-
cently subdued by Alfred, and who were impatient of peace,
would, on the intelligence of that great prince's death, seize the
first pretence or opportunity of rebellion. The event did not disappoint his expectations: The Northumbrians declared for him;[h] and
Ethelwald, having thus connected his interests with the Danish
tribes, went beyond sea, and collecting a body of these free-
booters, he excited the hopes of all those who had been accustomed to subsist by rapine and violence.[i] The East-Anglian Danes
joined his party: The Five-burgers, who were seated in the heart of
Mercia, began to put themselves in motion; and the English found
that they were again menaced with those convulsions, from which
the valour and policy of Alfred had so lately rescued them. The
rebels, headed by Ethelwald, made an incursion into the counties
of Glocester, Oxford, and Wilts; and having exercised their ravages in these places, they retired with their booty; before the king,
who had assembled an army, was able to approach them. Edward,
however, who was determined that his preparations should not be
fruitless, conducted his forces into East-Anglia, and retaliated the
injuries which the inhabitants had committed, by spreading the
like devastation among them. Satiated with revenge, and loaded
with booty, he gave orders to retire: But the authority of those
ancient kings, which was feeble in peace, was not much better
established in the field; and the Kentish men, greedy of more spoil,

[f] Chron. Sax. p. 99, 100.   [g] Ibid. p. 100. H. Hunting. lib. 5. p. 352.
[h] Chron. Sax. p. 100. H. Hunt. lib. 5. p. 352.   [i] Chron. Sax. p. 100. Chron.
Abb. St. Petri de Burgo, p. 24.

CHAPTER II

ventured, contrary to repeated orders, to stay behind him, and to take up their quarters in Bury. This disobedience proved in the issue fortunate to Edward. The Danes assaulted the Kentish men; but met with so vigorous a resistance, that, though they gained the field of battle, they bought that advantage by the loss of their bravest leaders, and among the rest, by that of Ethelwald, who perished in the action.[k] The king, freed from the fear of so dangerous a competitor, made peace on advantageous terms with the East-Angles.[l]

In order to restore England to such a state of tranquillity as it was then capable of attaining, naught was wanting but the subjection of the Northumbrians, who, assisted by the scattered Danes in Mercia, continually infested the bowels of the kingdom. Edward, in order to divert the force of these enemies, prepared a fleet to attack them by sea; hoping, that, when his ships appeared on their coast, they must at least remain at home, and provide for their defence. But the Northumbrians were less anxious to secure their own property than greedy to commit spoil on their enemy; and concluding, that the chief strength of the English was embarked on board the fleet, they thought the opportunity favourable, and entered Edward's territories with all their forces. The king, who was prepared against this event, attacked them on their return at Tetenhall in the county of Stafford, put them to rout, recovered all the booty, and pursued them with great slaughter into their own country.

All the rest of Edward's reign was a scene of continued and successful action against the Northumbrians, the East-Angles, the Five-burgers, and the foreign Danes, who invaded him from Normandy and Britanny. Nor was he less provident in putting his kingdom in a posture of defence, than vigorous in assaulting the enemy. He fortified the towns of Chester, Eddesbury, Warwic, Cherbury, Buckingham, Towcester, Maldon, Huntingdon, and Colchester. He fought two signal battles, at Temsford and Maldon.[m] He vanquished Thurketill, a great Danish chief, and obliged him to retire with his followers into France, in quest of spoil and adventures. He subdued the East Angles, and forced them to

[k] Chron. Sax. p. 101. Brompton, p. 832.   [l] Chron. Sax. p. 102. Brompton, p. 832. Math. West. p. 181.   [m] Chron. Sax. p. 108. Flor. Wigorn. p. 601.

swear allegiance to him: He expelled the two rival princes of Northumberland, Reginald and Sidroc, and acquired, for the present, the dominion of that province: Several tribes of the Britons were subjected by him; and even the Scots, who, during the reign of Egbert, had, under the conduct of Kenneth, their king, encreased their power, by the final subjection of the Picts, were nevertheless obliged to give him marks of submission.[n] In all these fortunate achievements he was assisted by the activity and prudence of his sister Ethelfleda, who was widow of Ethelbert, earl of Mercia, and who, after her husband's death, retained the government of that province. This princess, who had been reduced to extremity in child-bed, refused afterwards all commerce with her husband; not from any weak superstition, as was common in that age, but because she deemed all domestic occupations unworthy of her masculine and ambitious spirit.[o] She died before her brother; and Edward, during the remainder of his reign, took upon himself the immediate government of Mercia, which before had been entrusted to the authority of a governor.[p] The Saxon Chronicle fixes the death of this prince in 925:[q] His kingdom devolved to Athelstan, his natural son.

ATHELSTAN

925.

THE STAIN in this prince's birth was not, in those times, deemed so considerable as to exclude him from the throne; and Athelstan, being of an age, as well as of a capacity, fitted for government, obtained the preference to Edward's younger children, who, though legitimate, were of too tender years to rule a nation so much exposed both to foreign invasion and to domestic convulsions. Some discontents, however, prevailed on his accession; and Alfred, a nobleman of considerable power, was thence encouraged to enter into a conspiracy against him. This incident

---

[n] Chron. Sax. p. 110. Hoveden, p. 421.   [o] W. Malmes. lib. 2. cap. 5. Math. West. p. 182. Ingulf, p. 28. Higden, p. 261.   [p] Chron. Sax. p. 110. Brompton, p. 831.   [q] Page 110.

CHAPTER II

is related by historians with circumstances, which the reader, according to the degree of credit he is disposed to give them, may impute either to the invention of monks, who forged them, or to their artifice, who found means of making them real. Alfred, it is said, being seized upon strong suspicions, but without any certain proof, firmly denied the conspiracy imputed to him; and in order to justify himself, he offered to swear to his innocence before the pope, whose person, it was supposed, contained such superior sanctity, that no one could presume to give a false oath in his presence, and yet hope to escape the immediate vengeance of heaven. The king accepted of the condition, and Alfred was conducted to Rome; where, either conscious of his innocence, or neglecting the superstition, to which he appealed, he ventured to make the oath required of him, before John, who then filled the papal chair. But no sooner had he pronounced the fatal words, than he fell into convulsions, of which, three days after, he expired. The king, as if the guilt of the conspirator were now fully ascertained, confiscated his estate, and made a present of it to the monastery of Malmesbury;[r] secure that no doubts would ever thenceforth be entertained concerning the justice of his proceedings.

The dominion of Athelstan was no sooner established over his English subjects, than he endeavoured to give security to the government, by providing against the insurrections of the Danes, which had created so much disturbance to his predecessors. He marched into Northumberland; and finding, that the inhabitants bore with impatience the English yoke, he thought it prudent to confer on Sithric, a Danish nobleman, the title of King, and to attach him to his interest, by giving him his sister, Editha, in marriage. But this policy proved by accident the source of dangerous consequences. Sithric died in a twelvemonth after; and his two sons by a former marriage, Anlaf and Godfrid, founding pretensions on their father's elevation, assumed the sovereignty, without waiting for Athelstan's consent. They were soon expelled by the power of that monarch; and the former took shelter in Ireland, as the latter did in Scotland, where he received, during some time, protection from Constantine, who then enjoyed the crown of that

[r] W. Malmes. lib. 2. cap. 6. Spell. Conc. p. 407.

kingdom. The Scottish prince, however, continually solicited, and even menaced, by Athelstan, at last promised to deliver up his guest; but secretly detesting this treachery, he gave Godfrid warning to make his escape;[s] and that fugitive, after subsisting by pyracy for some years, freed the king, by his death, from any farther anxiety. Athelstan, resenting Constantine's behaviour, entered Scotland with an army; and ravaging the country with impunity,[t] he reduced the Scots to such distress, that their king was content to preserve his crown, by making submissions to the enemy. The English historians assert,[u] that Constantine did homage to Athelstan for his kingdom; and they add, that the latter prince, being urged by his courtiers to push the present favourable opportunity, and entirely subdue Scotland, replied, that it was more glorious to confer than conquer kingdoms.[w] But those annals, so uncertain and imperfect in themselves, lose all credit, when national prepossessions and animosities have place: And on that account, the Scotch historians, who, without having any more knowledge of the matter, strenuously deny the fact, seem more worthy of belief.

Constantine, whether he owed the retaining of his crown to the moderation of Athelstan, who was unwilling to employ all his advantages against him, or to the policy of that prince, who esteemed the humiliation of an enemy a greater acquisition than the subjection of a discontented and mutinous people, thought the behaviour of the English monarch more an object of resentment than of gratitude. He entered into a confederacy with Anlaf, who had collected a great body of Danish pyrates, whom he found hovering in the Irish seas; and with some Welsh princes, who were terrified at the growing power of Athelstan: and all these allies made by concert an irruption with a great army into England. Athelstan, collecting his forces, met the enemy near Brunsbury in Northumberland, and defeated them in a general engagement. This victory was chiefly ascribed to the valour of Turketul, the English chancellor: For in those turbulent ages, no one was so much oc-

[s] W. Malmes. lib. 2. cap. 6.   [t] Chron. Sax. p. 111. Hoveden, p. 422. H. Hunting. lib. 5. p. 354.   [u] Hoveden, p. 422.   [w] W. Malmes. lib. 2. cap. 6. Anglia Sacra, vol. I. p. 212.

CHAPTER II

cupied in civil employments, as wholly to lay aside the military character.[x]

There is a circumstance, not unworthy of notice, which historians relate with regard to the transactions of this war. Anlaf, on the approach of the English army, thought, that he could not venture too much to ensure a fortunate event; and employing the artifice formerly practised by Alfred against the Danes, he entered the enemy's camp in the habit of a minstrel. The stratagem was for the present attended with like success. He gave such satisfaction to the soldiers, who flocked about him, that they introduced him to the king's tent; and Anlaf, having played before that prince and his nobles during their repast, was dismissed with a handsome reward. His prudence kept him from refusing the present; but his pride determined him, on his departure, to bury it, while he fancied that he was unespied by all the world. But a soldier in Athelstan's camp, who had formerly served under Anlaf, had been struck with some suspicion on the first appearance of the minstrel; and was engaged by curiosity to observe all his motions. He regarded this last action as a full proof of Anlaf's disguise; and he immediately carried the intelligence to Athelstan, who blamed him for not sooner giving him information, that he might have seized his enemy. But the soldier told him that, as he had formerly sworn fealty to Anlaf, he could never have pardoned himself the treachery of betraying and ruining his ancient master; and that Athelstan himself, after such an instance of his criminal conduct, would have had equal reason to distrust his allegiance. Athelstan, having praised the generosity of the soldier's principles, reflected on the incident, which he foresaw might be attended with important consequences. He removed his station in the camp; and as a bishop arrived that evening with a reinforcement of troops, (for the ecclesiastics were then no less warlike than the civil magistrates) he occupied with his train that very place which had been left vacant by the king's removal. The precaution of Athelstan was found prudent: For no sooner had darkness fallen, than Anlaf broke into the camp, and hastening

---

[x] The office of chancellor among the Anglo-Saxons resembled more that of a secretary of state, than that of our present chancellor. See Spelman in *voce Cancellarius*.

directly to the place where he had left the king's tent, put the bishop to death, before he had time to prepare for his defence.[y]

There fell several Danish and Welsh princes in the action of Brunsbury;[z] and Constantine and Anlaf made their escape with difficulty, leaving the greater part of their army on the field of battle. After this success, Athelstan enjoyed his crown in tranquility; and he is regarded as one of the ablest and most active of those ancient princes. He passed a remarkable law, which was calculated for the encouragement of commerce, and which it required some liberality of mind, in that age, to have devised: That a merchant, who made three long sea-voyages on his own account, should be admitted to the rank of a thane or gentleman. This prince died at Glocester in the year 941,[a] after a reign of sixteen years; and was succeeded by Edmund, his legitimate brother.

EDMUND

941.

EDMUND, ON HIS ACCESSION, met with disturbance from the restless Northumbrians, who lay in wait for every opportunity of breaking into rebellion. But marching suddenly with his forces into their country, he so overawed the rebels, that they endeavoured to appease him by the most humble submissions.[b] In order to give him the surer pledge of their obedience, they offered to embrace Christianity; a religion which the English Danes had frequently professed, when reduced to difficulties, but which, for that very reason, they regarded as a badge of servitude, and shook off as soon as a favourable opportunity offered. Edmund, trusting little to their sincerity in this forced submission, used the precaution of removing the Five-burgers from the towns of Mercia, in which they had been allowed to settle; because it was always found, that they took advantage of every commotion, and introduced the rebellious or foreign Danes into the heart of the kingdom. He also conquered Cumberland from the Britons; and conferred that ter-

[y] W. Malmes. lib. 2. cap. 6. Higden, p. 263.   [z] Brompton, p. 859. Ingulf, p. 29.   [a] Chron. Sax. p. 114.   [b] W. Malmes. lib. 2. cap. 7. Brompton, p. 857.

ritory on Malcolm king of Scotland, on condition that he should do him homage for it, and protect the north from all future incursions of the Danes.

Edmund was young when he came to the crown, yet was his reign short, as his death was violent. One day, as he was solemnizing a festival in the county of Glocester, he remarked, that Leolf, a notorious robber, whom he had sentenced to banishment, had yet the boldness to enter the hall where he himself dined, and to sit at table with his attendants. Enraged at this insolence, he ordered him to leave the room; but on his refusing to obey, the king, whose temper, naturally choleric, was inflamed by this additional insult, leaped on him himself, and seized him by the hair: But the ruffian, pushed to extremity, drew his dagger, and gave Edmund a wound, of which he immediately expired. This event happened in the year 946, and in the sixth year of the king's reign. Edmund left male-issue, but so young, that they were incapable of governing the kingdom; and his brother, Edred, was promoted to the throne.

EDRED

THE REIGN of this prince, as those of his predecessors, was disturbed by the rebellions and incursions of the Northumbrian Danes, who, though frequently quelled, were never entirely subdued, nor had ever paid a sincere allegiance to the crown of England. The accession of a new king seemed to them a favourable opportunity for shaking off the yoke; but on Edred's appearance with an army, they made him their wonted submissions; and the king, having wasted the country with fire and sword, as a punishment of their rebellion, obliged them to renew their oaths of allegiance; and he straight retired with his forces. The obedience of the Danes lasted no longer than the present terror. Provoked at the devastations of Edred, and even reduced by necessity to subsist on plunder, they broke into a new rebellion, and were again subdued: But the king, now instructed by experience, took greater precautions against their future revolt. He fixed English garrisons in their most considerable towns; and placed over them an English

946.

HISTORY OF ENGLAND

governor, who might watch all their motions, and suppress any insurrection on its first appearance. He obliged also Malcolm, king of Scotland, to renew his homage for the lands which he held in England.

Edred, though not unwarlike, nor unfit for active life, lay under the influence of the lowest superstition, and had blindly delivered over his conscience to the guidance of Dunstan, commonly called St. Dunstan, abbot of Glastenbury, whom he advanced to the highest offices, and who covered, under the appearance of sanctity, the most violent and most insolent ambition. Taking advantage of the implicit confidence reposed in him by the king, this churchman imported into England a new order of monks, who much changed the state of ecclesiastical affairs, and excited, on their first establishment, the most violent commotions.

From the introduction of Christianity among the Saxons, there had been monasteries in England; and these establishments had extremely multiplied, by the donations of the princes and nobles; whose superstition, derived from their ignorance and precarious life, and encreased by remorses for the crimes into which they were so frequently betrayed, knew no other expedient for appeasing the Deity than a profuse liberality towards the ecclesiastics. But the monks had hitherto been a species of secular priests, who lived after the manner of the present canons or prebendaries, and were both intermingled, in some degree, with the world, and endeavoured to render themselves useful to it. They were employed in the education of youth:[c] They had the disposal of their own time and industry: They were not subjected to the rigid rules of an order: They had made no vows of implicit obedience to their superiors:[d] And they still retained the choice without quitting the convent, either of a married or a single life.[e] But a mistaken piety had produced in Italy a new species of monks, called Benedictines: who, carrying farther the plausible principles of mortification, secluded themselves entirely from the world, renounced all claim to liberty, and made a merit of the most inviolable chastity. These practices and principles, which superstition at first engendered, were greedily embraced and promoted by the policy of the court

[c] Osberne in Anglia Sacra, tom. 2. p. 92.   [d] Osberne, p. 91.   [e] See Wharton's notes to Anglia Sacra, tom. 2. p. 91. Gervase, p. 1645. Chron. Wint. MS. apud Spell. Conc. p. 434.

CHAPTER II

of Rome. The Roman pontiff, who was making every day great advances towards an absolute sovereignty over the ecclesiastics, perceived, that the celibacy of the clergy alone could break off entirely their connexion with the civil power, and depriving them of every other object of ambition, engage them to promote, with unceasing industry, the grandeur of their own order. He was sensible, that, so long as the monks were indulged in marriage, and were permitted to rear families, they never could be subjected to strict discipline, or reduced to that slavery under their superiors, which was requisite to procure to the mandates, issued from Rome, a ready and zealous obedience. Celibacy, therefore, began to be extolled, as the indispensible duty of priests; and the pope undertook to make all the clergy throughout the western world renounce at once the privilege of marriage: A fortunate policy, but at the same time an undertaking the most difficult of any, since he had the strongest propensities of human nature to encounter, and found, that the same connexions with the female sex, which generally encourage devotion, were here unfavourable to the success of his project. It is no wonder therefore, that this master-stroke of art should have met with violent contradiction, and that the interests of the hierarchy, and the inclinations of the priests, being now placed in this singular opposition, should, notwithstanding the continued efforts of Rome, have retarded the execution of that bold scheme, during the course of near three centuries.

As the bishops and parochial clergy lived apart with their families, and were more connected with the world, the hopes of success with them were fainter, and the pretence for making them renounce marriage was much less plausible. But the pope, having cast his eye on the monks as the basis of his authority, was determined to reduce them under strict rules of obedience, to procure them the credit of sanctity by an appearance of the most rigid mortification, and to break off all their other tyes which might interfere with his spiritual policy. Under pretence, therefore, of reforming abuses, which were, in some degree, unavoidable in the ancient establishments, he had already spread over the southern countries of Europe the severe laws of the monastic life, and began to form attempts towards a like innovation in England. The favourable opportunity offered itself (and it was greedily seized) arising from the weak superstition of Edred, and the violent impetuous character of Dunstan.

Dunstan was born of noble parents in the west of England; and being educated under his uncle, Aldhelm, then Archbishop of Canterbury, had betaken himself to the ecclesiastical life, and had acquired some character in the court of Edmund. He was, however, represented to that prince as a man of licentious manners;[f] and finding his fortune blasted by these suspicions, his ardent ambition prompted him to repair his indiscretions, by running into an opposite extreme. He secluded himself entirely from the world; he framed a cell so small that he could neither stand erect in it, nor stretch out his limbs during his repose; and he here employed himself perpetually either in devotion or in manual labour.[g] It is probable, that his brain became gradually crazed by these solitary occupations, and that his head was filled with chimeras, which, being believed by himself and his stupid votaries, procured him the general character of sanctity among the people. He fancied, that the devil, among the frequent visits, which he paid him, was one day more earnest than usual in his temptation; till Dunstan, provoked at his importunity, seized him by the nose with a pair of red hot pincers, as he put his head into the cell; and he held him there, till that malignant spirit made the whole neighbourhood resound with his bellowings. This notable exploit was seriously credited and extolled by the public; it is transmitted to posterity by one who, considering the age in which he lived, may pass for a writer of some elegance;[h] and it insured to Dunstan, a reputation, which no real piety, much less virtue, could, even in the most enlightened period, have ever procured him with the people.

Supported by the character obtained in his retreat, Dunstan appeared again in the world; and gained such an ascendant over Edred, who had succeeded to the crown, as made him, not only the director of that prince's conscience, but his counsellor in the most momentous affairs of government. He was placed at the head of the treasury;[i] and being thus possessed both of power at court, and of credit with the populace, he was enabled to attempt with success the most arduous enterprizes. Finding, that his advancement had

---

[f] Osberne, p. 95. Matth. West. p. 187.　[g] Osberne, p. 96.　[h] Osberne, p. 97.　[i] Osberne, p. 102. Wallingford, p. 541.

CHAPTER II

been owing to the opinion of his austerity, he professed himself a partizan of the rigid monastic rules; and after introducing that reformation into the convents of Glastenbury and Abingdon, he endeavoured to render it universal in the kingdom.

The minds of men were already well prepared for this innovation. The praises of an inviolable chastity had been carried to the highest extravagance by some of the first preachers of Christianity among the Saxons: The pleasures of love had been represented as incompatible with Christian perfection: And a total abstinence from all commerce with the sex was deemed such a meritorious pennance, as was sufficient to atone for the greatest enormities. The consequence seemed natural, that those at least who officiated at the altar should be clear of this pollution; and when the doctrine of transubstantiation, which was now creeping in,[k] was once fully established, the reverence to the real body of Christ in the eucharist bestowed on this argument an additional force and influence. The monks knew how to avail themselves of all these popular topics, and to set off their own character to the best advantage. They affected the greatest austerity of life and manners: They indulged themselves in the highest strains of devotion: They inveighed bitterly against the vices and pretended luxury of the age: They were particularly vehement against the dissolute lives of the secular clergy, their rivals: Every instance of libertinism in any individual of that order was represented as a general corruption: And where other topics of defamation were wanting, their marriage became a sure subject of invective, and their wives received the name of *concubine*, or other more opprobrious appellation. The secular clergy, on the other hand, who were numerous, and rich, and possessed of the ecclesiastical dignities, defended themselves with vigour, and endeavoured to retaliate upon their adversaries. The people were thrown into agitation; and few instances occur of more violent dissentions, excited by the most material differences in religion; or rather by the most frivolous: Since it is a just remark, that the more affinity there is between theological parties, the greater commonly is their animosity.

The progress of the monks, which was become considerable,

[k] Spell. Conc. vol. I. p. 452.

was somewhat retarded by the death of Edred, their partizan, who expired after a reign of nine years.[l] He left children; but as they were infants, his nephew, Edwy, son of Edmund, was placed on the throne.

EDWY

955.

E DWY, at the time of his accession, was not above sixteen or seventeen years of age, was possessed of the most amiable figure, and was even endowed, according to authentic accounts, with the most promising virtues.[m] He would have been the favourite of his people, had he not unhappily, at the commencement of his reign, been engaged in a controversy with the monks, whose rage neither the graces of the body nor virtues of the mind could mitigate, and who have pursued his memory with the same unrelenting vengeance, which they exercised against his person and dignity during his short and unfortunate reign. There was a beautiful princess of the royal blood, called Elgiva, who had made impression on the tender heart of Edwy; and as he was of an age, when the force of the passions first begins to be felt, he had ventured, contrary to the advice of his gravest counsellors, and the remonstrances of the more dignified ecclesiastics,[n] to espouse her; though she was within the degrees of affinity prohibited by the canon-law.[o] As the austerity, affected by the monks, made them particularly violent on this occasion, Edwy entertained a strong prepossession against them; and seemed on that account determined not to second their project, of expelling the seculars from all the convents, and of possessing themselves of those rich establishments. War was therefore declared between the king and the monks; and the former soon found reason to repent his provoking such dangerous enemies. On the day of his coronation, his nobility were assembled in a great hall, and were indulging themselves in that riot and disorder, which, from the example of their German ancestors, had become habitual to the English;[p] when Edwy, attracted by softer pleasures, retired into the Queen's apartment,

---

[l] Chron. Sax. p. 115.   [m] H. Hunting. lib. 5. p. 356.   [n] W. Malmes. lib. 2. cap. 7.   [o] Ibid.   [p] Wallingford, p. 542.

and in that privacy, gave reins to his fondness towards his wife, which was only moderately checked by the presence of her mother. Dunstan conjectured the reason of the king's retreat; and carrying along with him, Odo, archbishop of Canterbury, over whom he had gained an absolute ascendant, he burst into the apartment, upbraided Edwy with his lasciviousness, probably bestowed on the queen the most opprobrious epithet that can be applied to her sex, and tearing him from her arms, pushed him back, in a disgraceful manner, into the banquet of the nobles.[q] Edwy, though young and opposed by the prejudices of the people, found an opportunity of taking revenge for this public insult. He questioned Dunstan concerning the administration of the treasury during the reign of his predecessor;[r] and when that minister refused to give any account of money, expended, as he affirmed, by orders of the late king, he accused him of malversation in his office, and banished him the kingdom. But Dunstan's cabal was not unactive during his absence: They filled the public with high panegyrics on his sanctity: They exclaimed against the impiety of the king and queen: And having poisoned the minds of the people by these declamations, they proceeded to still more outrageous acts of violence against the royal authority. Archbishop Odo sent into the palace a party of soldiers, who seized the queen; and having burned her face with a red hot iron in order to destroy that fatal beauty, which had seduced Edwy, they carried her by force into Ireland, there to remain in perpetual exile.[s] Edwy, finding it in vain to resist, was obliged to consent to his divorce, which was pronounced by Odo;[t] and a catastrophe, still more dismal, awaited the unhappy Elgiva. That amiable princess, being cured of her wounds, and having even obliterated the scars, with which Odo had hoped to deface her beauty, returned into England, and was flying to the embraces of the king, whom she still regarded as her husband; when she fell into the hands of a party, whom the primate had sent to intercept her. Nothing but her death could now give security to Odo and the monks; and the most cruel death was requisite to satiate their vengeance. She was hamstringed; and expired a few days after at Glocester in the most acute torments.[u]

[q] W. Malmes. lib. 2. cap. 7. Osberne, p. 83, 105. M. West. p. 195, 196.
[r] Wallingford, p. 542. Alur. Beverl. p. 112. [s] Osberne, p. 84. Gervase, p. 1644. [t] Hoveden, p. 425. [u] Osberne, p. 84. Gervase, p. 1645, 1646.

The English, blinded with superstition, instead of being shocked with this inhumanity, exclaimed that the misfortunes of Edwy and his consort were a just judgment for their dissolute contempt of the ecclesiastical statutes. They even proceeded to rebellion against their sovereign: and having placed Edgar at their head, the younger brother of Edwy, a boy of thirteen years of age, they soon put him in possession of Mercia, Northumberland, East-Anglia; and chaced Edwy into the southern counties. That it might not be doubtful at whose instigation this revolt was undertaken; Dunstan returned into England, and took upon him the government of Edgar and his party. He was first installed in the see of Worcester, then in that of London,[w] and, on Odo's death, and the violent expulsion of Brithelm, his successor, in that of Canterbury;[x] of all which he long kept possession. Odo is transmitted to us by the monks under the character of a man of piety: Dunstan was even canonized; and is one of those numerous saints of the same stamp who disgrace the Romish calendar. Meanwhile the unhappy Edwy was excommunicated,[y] and pursued with unrelenting vengeance; but his death, which happened soon after, freed his enemies from all farther inquietude, and gave Edgar peaceable possession of the government.[*]

EDGAR

THIS PRINCE, who mounted the throne in such early youth, soon discovered an excellent capacity in the administration of affairs; and his reign is one of the most fortunate that we meet with in the ancient English history. He showed no aversion to war; he made the wisest preparations against invaders: And by this vigour and foresight, he was enabled, without any danger of suffering insults, to indulge his inclination towards peace, and to employ himself in supporting and improving the internal government of his kingdom. He maintained a body of disciplined troops; which he quartered in the north, in order to keep the mutinous North-

[w] Chron. Sax. p. 117. Flor. Wigorn. p. 605. Wallingford, p. 544.
[x] Hoveden, p. 425. Osberne, p. 109. [y] Brompton, p. 863. [*] See note [B] at the end of the volume.

CHAPTER II

umbrians in subjection, and to repel the inroads of the Scots. He built and supported a powerful navy;[z] and that he might retain the seamen in the practice of their duty, and always present a formidable armament to his enemies, he stationed three squadrons off the coast, and ordered them to make, from time to time, the circuit of his dominions.[*] The foreign Danes dared not to approach a country which appeared in such a posture of defence: The domestic Danes saw inevitable destruction to be the consequence of their tumults and insurrections: The neighbouring sovereigns, the king of Scotland, the princes of Wales, of the Isle of Man, of the Orkneys and even of Ireland,[a] were reduced to pay submission to so formidable a monarch. He carried his superiority to a great height, and might have excited an universal combination against him, had not his power been so well established, as to deprive his enemies of all hopes of shaking it. It is said, that, residing once at Chester, and having purposed to go by water to the abbey of St. John the Baptist, he obliged eight of his tributary princes to row him in a barge upon the Dee.[b] The English historians are fond of mentioning the name of Kenneth III, king of Scots among the number: The Scottish historians either deny the fact, or assert, that their king, if ever he acknowledged himself a vassal to Edgar, did him homage, not for his crown, but for the dominions which he held in England.

But the chief means, by which Edgar maintained his authority, and preserved public peace, was the paying of court to Dunstan and the monks, who had at first placed him on the throne, and who, by their pretensions to superior sanctity and purity of manners, had acquired an ascendant over the people. He favoured their scheme for dispossessing the secular canons of all the monasteries;[c] he bestowed preferment on none but their partizans; he allowed Dunstan to resign the see of Worcester into the hand of Oswald, one of his creatures,[d] and to place Ethelwold, another of them, in that of Winchester;[e] he consulted these prelates in the

---

[z] Higden, p. 265.   [*] See note [C] at the end of the volume.   [a] Spell. Conc. p. 432.   [b] W. Malmes. lib. 2. cap. 8. Hoveden, p. 406. H. Hunting. lib. 5. p. 356.   [c] Chron. Sax. p. 117, 118. W. Malmes. lib. 2. cap. 8. Hoveden, p. 425, 426. Osberne, p. 112.   [d] W. Malmes. lib. 2. cap. 8. Hoveden, p. 425.   [e] Gervase, p. 1616. Brompton, p. 864. Flor. Wigorn. p. 606. Chron. Abb. St. Petri de Burgo, p. 27, 28.

administration of all ecclesiastical, and even in that of many civil affairs; and though the vigour of his own genius prevented him from being implicitly guided by them, the king and the bishops found such advantages in their mutual agreement, that they always acted in concert, and united their influence in preserving the peace and tranquillity of the kingdom.

In order to compleat the great work of placing the new order of monks in all the convents, Edgar summoned a general council of the prelates and the heads of the religious orders. He here inveighed against the dissolute lives of the secular clergy; the smallness of their tonsure, which, it is probable, maintained no longer any resemblance to the crown of thorns; their negligence in attending the exercise of their function; their mixing with the laity in the pleasures of gaming, hunting, dancing, and singing; and their openly living with concubines, by which it is commonly supposed he meant their wives. He then turned himself to Dunstan the primate; and in the name of king Edred, whom he supposed to look down from heaven with indignation against all those enormities, he thus addressed him.

"It is you, Dunstan, by whose advice I founded monasteries, built churches, and expended my treasure in the support of religion and religious houses. You were my counsellor and assistant in all my schemes: You were the director of my conscience: To you I was obedient in all things. When did you call for supplies, which I refused you? Was my assistance ever wanting to the poor? Did I deny support and establishments to the clergy and the convents? Did I not hearken to your instructions, who told me, that these charities were, of all others, the most grateful to my Maker, and fixed a perpetual fund for the support of religion? And are all our pious endeavours now frustrated by the dissolute lives of the priests? Not that I throw any blame on you: You have reasoned, besought, inculcated, inveighed: But it now behoves you to use sharper and more vigorous remedies; and conjoining your spiritual authority with the civil power, to purge effectually the temple of God from thieves and intruders."[f]

It is easy to imagine, that this harangue had the desired effect: and that, when the king and prelates thus concurred with the popular

[f] Abbas Rieval. p. 360, 361. Spell. Conc. p. 476, 477, 478.

CHAPTER II

prejudices, it was not long before the monks prevailed, and established their new discipline in almost all the convents.

We may remark, that the declamations against the secular clergy are, both here and in all the historians, conveyed in general terms; and as that order of men are commonly restrained by the decency of their character, it is difficult to believe, that the complaints against their dissolute manners could be so universally just as is pretended. It is more probable, that the monks paid court to the populace by an affected austerity of life; and, representing the most innocent liberties, taken by the other clergy, as great and unpardonable enormities, thereby prepared the way for the encrease of their own power and influence. Edgar, however, like a true politician, concurred with the prevailing party; and he even indulged them in pretensions, which, though they might, when complied with, engage the monks to support royal authority during his own reign, proved afterwards dangerous to his successors, and gave disturbance to the whole civil power. He seconded the policy of the court of Rome, in granting to some monasteries an exemption from episcopal jurisdiction: He allowed the convents, even those of royal foundation, to usurp the election of their own abbot: and he admitted their forgeries of ancient charters, by which, from the pretended grant of former kings, they assumed many privileges and immunities.[g]

These merits of Edgar have procured him the highest panegyrics from the monks; and he is transmitted to us not only under the character of a consummate statesman and an active prince, praises to which he seems to have been justly entitled, but under that of a great saint and a man of virtue. But nothing could more betray both his hypocrisy in inveighing against the licentiousness of the secular clergy, and the interested spirit of his partizans, in bestowing such eulogies on his piety, than the usual tenor of his conduct, which was licentious to the highest degree, and violated every law, human and divine. Yet those very monks, who, as we are told by Ingulf, a very ancient historian, had no idea of any moral or religious merit, except chastity and obedience, not only connived at his enormities, but loaded him with the greatest praises.

[g] Chron. Sax. p. 118. W. Malmes. lib. 2. cap. 8. Seldeni Spicileg. ad Eadm. p. 149, 157.

History, however, has preserved some instance of his amours, from which, as from a specimen, we may form a conjecture of the rest.

Edgar broke into a convent, carried off Editha, a nun, by force, and even committed violence on her person.[h] For this act of sacrilege he was reprimanded by Dunstan; and that he might reconcile himself to the church, he was obliged, not to separate from his mistress, but to abstain from wearing his crown during seven years, and to deprive himself so long of that vain ornament.[i] A punishment very unequal to that which had been inflicted on the unfortunate Edwy, who, for a marriage, which, in the strictest sense, could only deserve the name of irregular, was expelled his kingdom, saw his queen treated with singular barbarity, was loaded with calumnies, and has been represented to us under the most odious colours. Such is the ascendant which may be attained, by hypocrisy and cabal, over mankind!

There was another mistress of Edgar's, with whom he first formed a connexion by a kind of accident. Passing one day by Andover, he lodged in the house of a nobleman, whose daughter, being endowed with all the graces of person and behaviour, enflamed him at first sight with the highest desire; and he resolved by any expedient to gratify it. As he had not leisure to employ courtship or address for attaining his purpose, he went directly to her mother, declared the violence of his passion, and desired that the young lady might be allowed to pass that very night with him. The mother was a woman of virtue, and determined not to dishonour her daughter and her family by compliance; but being well acquainted with the impetuosity of the king's temper, she thought it would be easier, as well as safer, to deceive, than refuse him. She feigned therefore a submission to his will; but secretly ordered a waiting-maid, of no disagreeable figure, to steal into the king's bed, after all the company should be retired to rest. In the morning, before day-break, the damsel, agreeably to the injunctions of her mistress, offered to retire; but Edgar, who had no reserve in his pleasures, and whose love to his bedfellow was rather enflamed by enjoyment, refused his consent, and employed force and entreaties to detain her. Elfleda (for that was the name of the maid)

---

[h] W. Malmes. lib. 2. cap. 8. Osberne, p. 3. Diceto, p. 457. Higden, p. 265, 267, 268. Spell. Conc. p. 481. [i] Osberne, p. 111.

CHAPTER II

trusting to her own charms, and to the love with which, she hoped, she had now inspired the king, made probably but a faint resistance; and the return of light discovered the deceit to Edgar. He had passed a night so much to his satisfaction, that he expressed no displeasure with the old lady on account of her fraud; his love was transferred to Elfleda; she became his favourite mistress; and maintained her ascendant over him, till his marriage with Elfrida.[k]

The circumstances of his marriage with this lady were more singular, and more criminal. Elfrida was daughter and heir of Olgar, earl of Devonshire; and though she had been educated in the country, and had never appeared at court, she had filled all England with the reputation of her beauty. Edgar himself, who was indifferent to no accounts of this nature, found his curiosity excited by the frequent panegyrics which he heard of Elfrida; and reflecting on her noble birth, he resolved, if he found her charms answerable to their fame, to obtain possession of her on honourable terms. He communicated his intention to earl Athelwold, his favourite; but used the precaution, before he made any advances to her parents, to order that nobleman, on some pretence, to pay them a visit, and to bring him a certain account of the beauty of their daughter. Athelwold, when introduced to the young lady, found general report to have fallen short of the truth; and being actuated by the most vehement love, he determined to sacrifice to this new passion his fidelity to his master, and to the trust reposed in him. He returned to Edgar, and told him, that the riches alone, and high quality of Elfrida, had been the ground of the admiration paid her, and that her charms, far from being any wise extraordinary, would have been overlooked in a woman of inferior station. When he had, by this deceit, diverted the king from his purpose, he took an opportunity after some interval, of turning again the conversation on Elfrida: He remarked, that, though the parentage and fortune of the lady had not produced on him, as on others, any illusion with regard to her beauty, he could not forbear reflecting, that she would on the whole be an advantageous match for him, and might, by her birth and riches, make him sufficient compensation for the homeliness of her person. If the king, therefore, gave his approbation, he was determined to make proposals in his own behalf to the earl of Devonshire, and doubted not to

[k] W. Malmes. lib. 2. cap. 8. Higden, p. 268.

obtain his, as well as the young lady's consent to the marriage. Edgar, pleased with an expedient for establishing his favourite's fortune, not only exhorted him to execute his purpose, but forwarded his success by his recommendations to the parents of Elfrida; and Athelwold was soon made happy in the possession of his mistress. Dreading, however, the detection of the artifice, he employed every pretence of detaining Elfrida in the country, and for keeping her at a distance from Edgar.

The violent passion of Athelwold had rendered him blind to the necessary consequences, which must attend his conduct, and the advantages, which the numerous enemies, that always pursue a royal favourite, would, by its means, be able to make against him. Edgar was soon informed of the truth; but before he would execute vengeance on Athelwold's treachery, he resolved to satisfy himself with his own eyes of the certainty and full extent of his guilt. He told him, that he intended to pay him a visit in his castle, and be introduced to the acquaintance of his new-married wife; and Athelwold, as he could not refuse the honour, only craved leave to go before him a few hours, that he might the better prepare every thing for his reception. He then discovered the whole matter to Elfrida; and begged her, if she had any regard, either to her own honour or his life, to conceal from Edgar, by every circumstance of dress and behaviour, that fatal beauty, which had seduced him from fidelity to his friend, and had betrayed him into so many falsehoods. Elfrida promised compliance, though nothing was farther from her intentions. She deemed herself little beholden to Athelwold for a passion, which had deprived her of a crown; and knowing the force of her own charms, she did not despair even yet of reaching that dignity, of which her husband's artifice had bereaved her. She appeared before the king with all the advantages, which the richest attire, and the most engaging airs could bestow upon her, and she excited at once in his bosom the highest love towards herself, and the most furious desire of revenge against her husband. He knew, however, to dissemble these passions; and seducing Athelwold into a wood, on pretence of hunting, he stabbed him with his own hand, and soon after publickly espoused Elfrida.[1]

[1] W. Malmes. lib. 2. cap. 8. Hoveden, p. 426. Brompton, p. 865, 866. Flor. Wigorn. p. 606. Higden, p. 268.

CHAPTER II

Before we conclude our account of this reign, we must mention two circumstances, which are remarked by historians. The reputation of Edgar allured a great number of foreigners to visit his court; and he gave them encouragement to settle in England.[m] We are told, that they imported all the vices of their respective countries, and contributed to corrupt the simple manners of the natives:[n] But as this simplicity of manners, so highly and often so injudiciously extolled, did not preserve them from barbarity and treachery, the greatest of all vices, and the most incident to a rude uncultivated people, we ought perhaps to deem their acquaintance with foreigners rather an advantage; as it tended to enlarge their views, and to cure them of those illiberal prejudices and rustic manners, to which islanders are often subject.

Another remarkable incident of this reign was the extirpation of wolves from England. This advantage was attained by the industrious policy of Edgar. He took great pains in hunting and pursuing those ravenous animals; and when he found, that all that escaped him had taken shelter in the mountains and forests of Wales, he changed the tribute of money imposed on the Welsh princes by Athelstan, his predecessor,[o] into an annual tribute of three hundred heads of wolves; which produced such diligence in hunting them, that the animal has been no more seen in this island.

Edgar died, after a reign of sixteen years, and in the thirty-third of his age. He was succeeded by Edward, whom he had by his first marriage with the daughter of earl Ordmer.

EDWARD THE MARTYR

THE SUCCESSION of this prince, who was only fifteen years of age at his father's death, did not take place without much difficulty and opposition. Elfrida, his step-mother, had a son, Ethelred, seven years old, whom she attempted to raise to the throne: She affirmed, that Edgar's marriage with the mother of Edward was exposed to insuperable objections; and as she had possessed great credit with her husband, she had found means to

957.

---

[m] Chron. Sax. p. 116. H. Hunting. lib. 5. p. 356. Brompton, p. 865.   [n] W. Malmes. lib. 2. cap. 8.   [o] W. Malmes. lib. 2. cap. 6. Brompton, p. 838.

acquire partizans, who seconded all her pretensions. But the title of Edward was supported by many advantages. He was appointed successor by the will of his father:[p] He was approaching to man's estate, and might soon be able to take into his own hands the reins of government: The principal nobility, dreading the imperious temper of Elfrida, were averse to her son's government, which must enlarge her authority, and probably put her in possession of the regency: Above all, Dunstan, whose character of sanctity had given him the highest credit with the people, had espoused the cause of Edward, over whom he had already acquired a great ascendant;[q] and he was determined to execute the will of Edgar in his favour. To cut off all opposite pretensions, Dunstan resolutely anointed and crowned the young prince at Kingston; and the whole kingdom, without farther dispute, submitted to him.[r]

It was of great importance to Dunstan and the monks, to place on the throne a king favourable to their cause: The secular clergy had still partizans in England, who wished to support them in the possession of the convents, and of the ecclesiastical authority. On the first intelligence of Edgar's death, Alfere, duke of Mercia, expelled the new orders of monks from all the monasteries which lay within his jurisdiction;[s] but Elfwin, duke of East-Anglia, and Brithnot, duke of the East-Saxons, protected them within their territories, and insisted upon the execution of the late laws enacted in their favour. In order to settle this controversy, there were summoned several synods, which, according to the practice of those times, consisted partly of ecclesiastical members, partly of the lay nobility. The monks were able to prevail in these assemblies; though, as it appears, contrary to the secret wishes, if not the declared inclination, of the leading men in the nation.[t] They had more invention in forging miracles to support their cause; or having been so fortunate as to obtain, by their pretended austerities, the character of piety, their miracles were more credited by the populace.

In one synod, Dunstan, finding the majority of votes against him, rose up, and informed the audience, that he had that instant,

[p] Hoveden, p. 427. Eadmer, p. 3.   [q] Eadmer, ex edit. Seldeni, p. 3.   [r] W. Malm. lib. 2. cap. 9. Hoveden, p. 427. Osberne, p. 113.   [s] Chron. Sax. p. 123. W. Malmes. lib. 2. cap. 9. Hoveden, p. 427. Brompton, p. 870. Flor. Wigorn, p. 607.   [t] W. Malmes. lib. 2. cap. 9.

CHAPTER II

received an immediate revelation in behalf of the monks: The assembly was so astonished at this intelligence, or probably so overawed by the populace, that they proceeded no farther in their deliberations. In another synod, a voice issued from the crucifix, and informed the members, that the establishment of the monks was founded on the will of heaven, and could not be opposed without impiety." But the miracle performed in the third synod was still more alarming: The floor of the hall in which the assembly met, sunk of a sudden, and a great number of the members were either bruised or killed by the fall. It was remarked, that Dunstan had that day prevented the king from attending the synod, and that the beam, on which his own chair stood, was the only one that did not sink under the weight of the assembly:" But these circumstances, instead of begetting any suspicion of contrivance, were regarded as the surest proof of the immediate interposition of providence, in behalf of those favourites of heaven.

Edward lived four years after his accession, and there passed nothing memorable during his reign. His death alone was memorable and tragical.* This young prince was endowed with the most amiable innocence of manners; and as his own intentions were always pure, he was incapable of entertaining any suspicion against others. Though his stepmother had opposed his succession, and had raised a party in favour of her own son, he always showed her marks of regard, and even expressed on all occasions, the most tender affection towards his brother. He was hunting one day in Dorsetshire; and being led by the chase near Corse-castle, where Elfrida resided, he took the opportunity of paying her a visit, unattended by any of his retinue, and he thereby presented her with the opportunity, which she had long wished for. After he had mounted his horse, he desired some liquor to be brought him: While he was holding the cup to his head, a servant of Elfrida approached him, and gave him a stab behind. The prince, finding himself wounded, put spurs to his horse; but becoming faint by loss of blood, he fell from the saddle, his foot stuck in the stirrup,

---

" W. Malmes. lib. 2. cap. 9. Osberne, p. 112. Gervase, p. 1647. Brompton, p. 870. Higden, p. 269. " Chron. Sax. p. 124. W. Malmes. lib. 2. cap. 9. Hoveden, p. 427. H. Hunting. lib. 5. p. 357. Gervase, p. 1647. Brompton, p. 870. Flor. Wigorn. p. 607. Higden, p. 269. Chron. Abb. St. Petri de Burgo, p. 29. * Chron. Sax. p. 124.

and he was dragged along by his unruly horse, till he expired. Being tracked by the blood, his body was found, and was privately interred at Wareham by his servants.

The youth and innocence of this prince, with his tragical death, begat such compassion among the people, that they believed miracles to be wrought at his tomb; and they gave him the appellation of martyr, though his murder had no connexion with any religious principle or opinion. Elfrida built monasteries, and performed many pennances, in order to atone for her guilt; but could never, by all her hypocrisy or remorses, recover the good opinion of the public, though so easily deluded in those ignorant ages.

III

Ethelred – Settlement of the Normans –
Edmund Ironside – Canute – Harold Harefoot –
Hardicanute – Edward the Confessor – Harold

ETHELRED

T HE FREEDOM, which England had so long enjoyed from the 978.
depredations of the Danes, seems to have proceeded, partly
from the establishments, which that pyratical nation had obtained
in the north of France, and which employed all their superfluous
hands to people and maintain them; partly from the vigour and
warlike spirit of a long race of English princes, who preserved the
kingdom in a posture of defence by sea and land, and either prevented or repelled every attempt of the invaders. But a new gener-
ation of men being now sprung up in the northern regions, who
could no longer disburthen themselves on Normandy; the English
had reason to dread, that the Danes would again visit an island, to
which they were invited, both by the memory of their past successes, and by the expectation of assistance from their countrymen, who, though long established in the kingdom, were not
yet thoroughly incorporated with the natives, nor had entirely

forgotten their inveterate habits of war and depredation. And as the reigning prince was a minor, and even when he attained to man's estate, never discovered either courage or capacity sufficient to govern his own subjects, much less to repel a formidable enemy, the people might justly apprehend the worst calamities from so dangerous a crisis.

The Danes, before they durst attempt any important enterprize against England, made an inconsiderable descent by way of trial;

981. and having landed from seven vessels near Southampton, they ravaged the country, enriched themselves by spoil, and departed with impunity. Six years after, they made a like attempt in the west, and met with like success. The invaders, having now found affairs in a very different situation from that in which they formerly appeared, encouraged their countrymen to assemble a greater

991. force, and to hope for more considerable advantages. They landed in Essex under the command of two leaders; and having defeated and slain at Maldon, Brithnot, duke of that county, who ventured, with a small body, to attack them, they spread their devastations over all the neighbouring provinces. In this extremity, Ethelred, to whom historians give the epithet of the *Unready,* instead of rousing his people to defend with courage their honour and their property, hearkened to the advice of Siricius, archbishop of Canterbury, which was seconded by many of the degenerate nobility; and paying the enemy the sum of ten thousand pounds, he bribed them to depart the kingdom. This shameful expedient was attended with the success which might be expected. The Danes next year appeared off the eastern coast, in hopes of subduing a people, who defended themselves by their money, which invited assailants, instead of their arms, which repelled them. But the English, sensible of their folly, had, in the interval, assembled in a great council, and had determined to collect at London a fleet able to give battle to the enemy;[y] though that judicious measure failed of success, from the treachery of Alfric, duke of Mercia, whose name is infamous in the annals of that age, by the calamities which his repeated perfidy brought upon his country. This nobleman had, in 983, succeeded to his father, Alfere, in that extensive command; but being deprived of it two years after, and banished the king-

[y] Chron. Sax. p. 126.

CHAPTER III

dom, he was obliged to employ all his intrigue, and all his power, which was too great for a subject, to be restored to his country, and reinstated in his authority. Having had experience of the credit and malevolence of his enemies, he thenceforth trusted for security, not to his services or to the affections of his fellow citizens, but to the influence which he had obtained over his vassals, and to the public calamities, which, he thought, must, in every revolution, render his assistance necessary. Having fixed this resolution, he determined to prevent all such successes as might establish the royal authority, or render his own situation dependant or precarious. As the English had formed the plan of surrounding and destroying the Danish fleet in harbour, he privately informed the enemy of their danger; and when they put to sea, in consequence of this intelligence, he deserted to them, with the squadron under his command, the night before the engagement, and thereby disappointed all the efforts of his countrymen.[z] Ethelred, enraged at his perfidy, seized his son, Alfgar, and ordered his eyes to be put out.[a] But such was the power of Alfric, that he again forced himself into authority; and though he had given this specimen of his character, and received this grievous provocation, it was found necessary to entrust him anew with the government of Mercia. This conduct of the court, which, in all its circumstances, is so barbarous, weak, and imprudent, both merited and prognosticated the most grievous calamities.

The northern invaders, now well acquainted with the defenceless condition of England, made a powerful descent under the command of Sweyn, king of Denmark, and Olave, king of Norway; and sailing up the Humber, spread on all sides their destructive ravages. Lindesey was laid waste; Banbury was destroyed; and all the Northumbrians, though mostly of Danish descent, were constrained either to join the invaders, or to suffer under their depredations. A powerful army was assembled to oppose the Danes, and a general action ensued; but the English were deserted in the battle, from the cowardice or treachery of their three leaders, all of them men of Danish race, Frena, Frithegist, and Godwin, who gave the example of a shameful flight to the troops under their command. *993.*

[z] Chron. Sax. p. 127. W. Malm. p. 62. Higden, p. 270.　[a] Chron. Sax. p. 128. W. Malm. p. 62.

Encouraged by this success, and still more by the contempt which it inspired for their enemy, the pirates ventured to attack the center of the kingdom; and entering the Thames in ninety-four vessels, laid siege to London, and threatened it with total destruction. But the citizens, alarmed at the danger, and firmly united among themselves, made a bolder defence than the cowardice of the nobility and gentry gave the invaders reason to apprehend; and the besiegers, after suffering the greatest hardships, were finally frustrated in their attempt. In order to revenge themselves, they laid waste Essex, Sussex, and Hampshire; and having there procured horses, they were thereby enabled to spread, through the more inland counties, the fury of their depredations. In this extremity, Ethelred and his nobles had recourse to the former expedient; and sending ambassadors to the two northern kings, they promised them subsistence and tribute, on condition they would, for the present, put an end to their ravages, and soon after depart the kingdom. Sweyn and Olave agreed to the terms, and peaceably took up their quarters at Southampton, where the sum of sixteen thousand pounds was paid to them. Olave even made a journey to Andover, where Ethelred resided; and he received the rite of confirmation from the English bishops, as well as many rich presents from the king. He here promised, that he would never more infest the English territories; and he faithfully fulfilled the engagement. This prince receives the appellation of St. Olave from the church of Rome; and notwithstanding the general presumption, which lies, either against the understanding or morals of every one, who in those ignorant ages was dignified with that title, he seems to have been a man of merit and of virtue. Sweyn, though less scrupulous than Olave, was constrained, upon the departure of the Norwegian prince, to evacuate also the kingdom with all his followers.

997.   This composition brought only a short interval to the miseries of the English. The Danish pirates appeared soon after in the Severne; and having committed spoil in Wales, as well as in Cornwall and Devonshire, they sailed round to the south-coast, and entering the Tamar, completed the devastation of these two counties. They then returned to the Bristol-channel; and penetrating into the country by the Avon, spread themselves over all that neighbourhood, and carried fire and sword even into Dorsetshire.

CHAPTER III

They next changed the seat of war; and after ravaging the Isle of   *998.*
Wight, they entered the Thames and Medway, and laid siege to
Rochester, where they defeated the Kentish-men in a pitched battle. After this victory the whole province of Kent was made a scene
of slaughter, fire, and devastation. The extremity of these miseries
forced the English into counsels for common defence both by sea
and land; but the weakness of the king, the divisions among the
nobility, the treachery of some, the cowardice of others, the want
of concert in all, frustrated every endeavour: Their fleets and
armies either came too late to attack the enemy, or were repulsed
with dishonour; and the people were thus equally ruined by resistance or by submission. The English, therefore, destitute both of
prudence and unanimity in council, of courage and conduct in the
field, had recourse to the same weak expedient, which by experience they had already found so ineffectual: They offered the
Danes to buy peace by paying them a large sum of money. These
ravagers rose continually in their demands; and now required the
payment of 24,000 pounds, to which the English were so mean and
imprudent as to submit.[b] The departure of the Danes procured
them another short interval of repose, which they enjoyed as if it
were to be perpetual, without making any effectual preparations
for a more vigorous resistance upon the next return of the enemy.

Besides receiving this sum, the Danes were engaged by another
motive to depart a kingdom, which appeared so little in a situation
to resist their efforts: They were invited over by their countrymen
in Normandy, who at this time were hard pressed by the arms of
Robert, king of France, and who found it difficult to defend the
settlement, which, with so much advantage to themselves and
glory to their nation, they had made in that country. It is probable,
also, that Ethelred, observing the close connexions thus maintained among all the Danes, however divided in government or
situation, was desirous of forming an alliance with that formidable
people: For this purpose, being now a widower, he made his addresses to Emma, sister to Richard II. duke of Normandy, and he
soon succeeded in his negociation. The princess came over this
year to England, and was married to Ethelred.[c]   *1001.*

[b] Hoveden, p. 429. Chron. Mailr. p. 153.   [c] H. Hunt. p. 359. Higden,
p. 271.

*Settlement
of the
Normans.*

In the end of the ninth and beginning of the tenth century; when the north, not yet exhausted by that multitude of people or rather nations, which she had successively emitted, sent forth a new race, not of conquerors, as before, but of pirates and ravagers, who infested the countries possessed by her once warlike sons; lived Rollo, a petty prince or chieftain in Denmark, whose valour and abilities soon engaged the attention of his countrymen. He was exposed in his youth to the jealousy of the king of Denmark, who attacked his small, but independant principality; and who, being foiled in every assault, had recourse at last to perfidy for effecting his purpose, which he had often attempted in vain by force of arms:[d] He lulled Rollo into security by an insidious peace; and falling suddenly upon him, murdered his brother and his bravest officers, and forced him to fly for safety into Scandinavia. Here many of his ancient subjects, induced partly by affection to their prince, partly by the oppressions of the Danish monarch, ranged themselves under his standard, and offered to follow him in every enterprize. Rollo, instead of attempting to recover his paternal dominions, where he must expect a vigorous resistance from the Danes, determined to pursue an easier, but more important undertaking, and to make his fortune, in imitation of his countrymen, by pillaging the richer and more southern coasts of Europe. He collected a body of troops, which, like that of all those ravagers, was composed of Norwegians, Swedes, Frisians, Danes, and adventurers of all nations, who, being accustomed to a roving, unsettled life, took delight in nothing but war and plunder. His reputation brought him associates from all quarters; and a vision, which he pretended to have appeared to him in his sleep, and which, according to his interpretation of it, prognosticated the greatest successes, proved also a powerful incentive with those ignorant and superstitious people.[e]

The first attempt, made by Rollo, was on England, near the end of Alfred's reign; when that great monarch, having settled Guthrun and his followers in East-Anglia, and others of those freebooters in Northumberland, and having restored peace to his harassed country, had established the most excellent military as well

[d] Dudo, ex edit. Duchesne, p. 70, 71. Gul. Gemeticenis, lib. 2. cap. 2, 3.
[e] Dudo, p. 71. Gul. Gem. in epist. ad Gul. Conq.

CHAPTER III

as civil institutions among the English. The prudent Dane, finding that no advantages could be gained over such a people, governed by such a prince, soon turned his enterprizes against France, which he found more exposed to his inroads;[f] and during the reigns of Eudes, an usurper, and of Charles the Simple, a weak prince, he committed the most destructive ravages both on the inland and maritime provinces of that kingdom. The French, having no means of defence against a leader, who united all the valour of his countrymen with the policy of more civilized nations, were obliged to submit to the expedient practised by Alfred, and to offer the invaders a settlement in some of those provinces, which they had depopulated by their arms.[g]

The reason why the Danes for many years pursued measures so different from those which had been embraced by the Goths, Vandals, Franks, Burgundians, Lombards, and other northern conquerors, was the great difference, in the method of attack, which was practised by these several nations, and to which the nature of their respective situations necessarily confined them. The latter tribes, living in an inland country, made incursions by land upon the Roman empire; and when they entered far into the frontiers, they were obliged to carry along with them their wives and families, whom they had no hopes of soon re-visiting, and who could not otherwise participate of their plunder. This circumstance quickly made them think of forcing a settlement in the provinces, which they had over-run; and these barbarians, spreading themselves over the country, found an interest in protecting the property and industry of the people, whom they had subdued. But the Danes and Norwegians, invited by their maritime situation, and obliged to maintain themselves in their uncultivated country by fishing, had acquired some experience of navigation; and in their military excursions pursued the method practised against the Roman empire by the more early Saxons: They made descents in small bodies from their ships or rather boats, and ravaging the coasts, returned with the booty to their families, whom they could not conveniently carry along with them in those hazardous enterprizes. But when they encreased their armaments, made incursions into the inland countries, and found it safe to remain longer

[f] Gul. Gemet. lib. 2. cap. 6. [g] Dudo, p. 82.

in the midst of the enfeebled enemy, they had been accustomed to crowd their vessels with their wives and children, and having no longer any temptation to return to their own country, they willingly embraced an opportunity of settling in the warm climates and cultivated fields of the south.

Affairs were in this situation with Rollo and his followers, when Charles proposed to relinquish to them part of the province formerly called Neustria, and to purchase peace on these hard conditions. After all the terms were fully settled, there appeared only one circumstance shocking to the haughty Dane: He was required to do homage to Charles for this province, and to put himself in that humiliating posture, imposed on vassals by the rites of the feudal law. He long refused to submit to this indignity; but being unwilling to lose such important advantages for a mere ceremony, he made a sacrifice of his pride to his interest, and acknowledged himself in form the vassal of the French monarch.[h] Charles gave him his daughter, Gisla, in marriage; and that he might bind him faster to his interests, made him a donation of a considerable territory, besides that which he was obliged to surrender to him by his stipulations. When some of the French nobles informed him, that, in return for so generous a present, it was expected, that he should throw himself at the king's feet, and make suitable acknowledgments for his bounty; Rollo replied, that he would rather decline the present; and it was with some difficulty they could persuade him to make that compliment by one of his captains. The Dane, commissioned for this purpose, full of indignation at the order, and despising so unwarlike a prince, caught Charles by the foot, and pretending to carry it to his mouth, that he might kiss it, overthrew him before all his courtiers. The French, sensible of their present weakness, found it prudent to overlook this insult.[i]

Rollo, who was now in the decline of life, and was tired of wars and depredations, applied himself, with mature counsels, to the settlement of his new-acquired territory, which was thenceforth called Normandy; and he parcelled it out among his captains and followers. He followed in this partition the customs of the feudal law, which was then universally established in the southern coun-

[h] Ypod. Neust. p. 417.   [i] Gul. Gemet. lib. 2. cap. 17.

CHAPTER III

tries of Europe, and which suited the peculiar circumstances of that age. He treated the French subjects who submitted to him, with mildness and justice; he reclaimed his ancient followers from their ferocious violence; he established law and order throughout his state; and after a life spent in tumults and ravages, he died peaceably in a good old age, and left his dominions to his posterity.[k]

William I. who succeeded him, governed the dutchy twenty-five years; and during that time, the Normans were thoroughly intermingled with the French, had acquired their language, had imitated their manners, and had made such progress towards cultivation, that, on the death of William, his son, Richard, though a minor,[l] inherited his dominions: A sure proof, that the Normans were already somewhat advanced in civility, and that their government could now rest secure on its laws and civil institutions, and was not wholly sustained by the abilities of the Sovereign. Richard, after a long reign of fifty-four years, was succeeded by his son of the same name in the year 996;[m] which was eighty-five years after the first establishment of the Normans in France. This was the duke, who gave his sister, Emma, in marriage to Ethelred, king of England, and who thereby formed connections with a country, which his posterity was so soon after destined to subdue.

The Danes had been established during a longer period in England than in France; and though the similarity of their original language to that of the Saxons invited them to a more early coalition with the natives, they had hitherto found so little example of civilized manners among the English, that they retained all their ancient ferocity, and valued themselves only on their national character of military bravery. The recent, as well as more ancient atchievements of their countrymen, tended to support this idea; and the English princes, particularly Athelstan and Edgar, sensible of that superiority, had been accustomed to keep in pay bodies of Danish troops, who were quartered about the country, and committed many violences upon the inhabitants. These mercenaries had attained to such a height of luxury, according to the old English writers,[n] that they combed their hair once a day, bathed

[k] Gul. Gemet. lib. 2. cap. 19, 20, 21.   [l] Order. Vitalis, p. 459. Gul. Gemet. lib. 4. cap. 1.   [m] Order. Vitalis, p. 459.   [n] Wallingford, p. 547.

themselves once a week, changed their cloaths frequently; and by all these arts of effeminacy, as well as by their military character, had rendered themselves so agreeable to the fair sex, that they debauched the wives and daughters of the English, and dishonoured many families. But what most provoked the inhabitants, was, that, instead of defending them against invaders, they were ever ready to betray them to the foreign Danes, and to associate themselves with all straggling parties of that nation. The animosity, between the inhabitants of English and Danish race, had, from these repeated injuries, risen to a great height; when Ethelred, from a policy incident to weak princes, embraced the cruel resolution of massacring the latter throughout all his dominions.[*] Secret orders were dispatched to commence the execution every where on the same day; and the festival of St. Brice, which fell on a Sunday, the day on which the Danes usually bathed themselves, was chosen for that purpose. It is needless to repeat the accounts transmitted concerning the barbarity of this massacre: The rage of the populace, excited by so many injuries, sanctified by authority, and stimulated by example, distinguished not between innocence and guilt, spared neither sex nor age, and was not satiated without the tortures, as well as death, of the unhappy victims. Even Gunilda, sister to the king of Denmark, who had married Earl Paling, and had embraced Christianity, was, by the advice of Edric, earl of Wilts, seized and condemned to death by Ethelred, after seeing her husband and children butchered before her face. This unhappy princess foretold, in the agonies of despair, that her murder would soon be avenged by the total ruin of the English nation.

1003. Never was prophecy better fulfilled; and never did barbarous policy prove more fatal to the authors. Sweyn and his Danes, who wanted but a pretence for invading the English, appeared off the Western coast, and threatened to take full revenge for the slaughter of their countrymen. Exeter fell first into their hands, from the negligence or treachery of earl Hugh, a Norman, who had been made governor by the interest of Queen Emma. They began to spread their devastations over the country; when the English, sensible what outrages they must now expect from their barbarous and offended enemy, assembled more early and in

1002.

Nov. 13.

---

[*] See note [D] at the end of the volume.

CHAPTER III

greater numbers than usual, and made an appearance of vigorous resistance. But all these preparations were frustrated by the treachery of duke Alfric, who was intrusted with the command, and who, feigning sickness, refused to lead the army against the Danes, till it was dispirited, and at last dissipated, by his fatal misconduct. Alfric soon after died; and Edric, a greater traitor than he, who had married the king's daughter, and had acquired a total ascendant over him, succeeded Alfric in the government of Mercia, and in the command of the English armies. A great famine, proceeding partly from the bad seasons, partly from the decay of agriculture, added to all the other miseries of the inhabitants. The country, wasted by the Danes, harassed by the fruitless expeditions of its own forces, was reduced to the utmost desolation; and at last submitted to the infamy of purchasing a precarious peace   *1007.* from the enemy, by the payment of 30,000 pounds.

The English endeavoured to employ this interval in making preparations against the return of the Danes, which they had reason soon to expect. A law was made, ordering the proprietors of eight hydes of land to provide each a horseman and a complete suit of armour; and those of 310 hydes to equip a ship for the defence of the coast. When this navy was assembled, which must have consisted of near eight hundred vessels,[o] all hopes of its success were disappointed by the factions, animosities, and dissentions of the nobility. Edric had impelled his brother Brightric to prefer an accusation of treason against Wolfnoth, governor of Sussex, the father of the famous earl Godwin; and that nobleman, well acquainted with the malevolence as well as power of his enemy, found no means of safety but in deserting with twenty ships to the Danes. Brightric pursued him with a fleet of eighty sail; but his ships being shattered in a tempest, and stranded on the coast, he was suddenly attacked by Wolfnoth, and all his vessels burnt and destroyed. The imbecility of the king was little capable of repairing this misfortune: The treachery of Edric frustrated every plan for future defence: And the English navy, disconcerted, discouraged, and divided, was at last scattered into its several harbours.

It is almost impossible, or would be tedious, to relate particularly all the miseries to which the English were thenceforth ex-

[o] There were 243,600 hydes in England. Consequently the ships equipped must be 785. The cavalry was 30,450 men.

posed. We hear of nothing but the sacking and burning of towns; the devastation of the open country; the appearance of the enemy in every quarter of the kingdom; their cruel diligence in discovering any corner, which had not been ransacked by their former violence. The broken and disjointed narration of the antient historians is here well adapted to the nature of the war, which was conducted by such sudden inroads, as would have been dangerous even to an united and well governed kingdom, but proved fatal, where nothing but a general consternation, and mutual diffidence and dissention prevailed. The governors of one province refused to march to the assistance of another, and were at last terrified from assembling their forces for the defence of their own province. General councils were summoned; but either no resolution was taken, or none was carried into execution. And the only expedient, in which the English agreed, was the base and imprudent one, of buying a new peace from the Danes by the payment of 48,000 pounds.

1011.   This measure did not bring them even that short interval of repose, which they had expected from it. The Danes, disregarding all engagements, continued their devastations and hostilities; levied a new contribution of 8000 pounds upon the county of Kent alone; murdered the archbishop of Canterbury, who had refused to countenance this exaction; and the English nobility found no other resource than that of submitting every where to the Danish monarch, swearing allegiance to him, and delivering him *1013.*   hostages for their fidelity. Ethelred, equally afraid of the violence of the enemy and the treachery of his own subjects, fled into Normandy, whither he had sent before him Queen Emma, and her two sons, Alfred and Edward. Richard received his unhappy guests with a generosity that does honour to his memory.

1014.   The King had not been above six weeks in Normandy, when he heard of the death of Sweyn, who expired at Gainsborough, before he had time to establish himself in his new-acquired dominions. The English prelates and nobility, taking advantage of this event, sent over a deputation to Normandy; inviting Ethelred to return to them, expressing a desire of being again governed by their native prince, and intimating their hopes, that, being now tutored by experience, he would avoid all those errors, which had been attended with such misfortunes to himself and to his people.

CHAPTER III

But the misconduct of Ethelred was incurable; and on his re-suming the government, he discovered the same incapacity, in-dolence, cowardice, and credulity, which had so often exposed him to the insults of his enemies. His son-in-law, Edric, notwithstand-ing his repeated treasons, retained such influence at court, as to instil into the king jealousies of Sigefert and Morcar, two of the chief nobles of Mercia: Edric allured them into his house, where he murdered them; while Ethelred participated in the infamy of the action, by confiscating their estates, and thrusting into a convent the widow of Sigefert. She was a woman of singular beauty and merit; and in a visit which was paid her, during her confinement, by prince Edmond, the king's eldest son, she inspired him with so violent an affection, that he released her from the convent, and soon after married her, without the consent of his father.

Meanwhile the English found in Canute, the son and successor of Sweyn, an enemy no less terrible than the prince, from whom death had so lately delivered them. He ravaged the eastern coast with merciless fury, and put ashore all the English hostages at Sandwich, after having cut off their hands and noses. He was obliged, by the necessity of his affairs, to make a voyage to Den-mark; but returning soon after, he continued his depredations along the southern coast: He even broke into the counties of Dor-set, Wilts, and Somerset; where an army was assembled against him, under the command of prince Edmond and duke Edric. The latter still continued his perfidious machinations; and after en-deavouring in vain to get the prince into his power, he found *1015.* means to disperse the army; and he then openly deserted to Canute with forty vessels.

Notwithstanding this misfortune, Edmond was not discon-certed; but assembling all the force of England, was in a condition to give battle to the enemy. The king had had such frequent ex-perience of perfidy among his subjects, that he had lost all con-fidence in them: He remained at London, pretending sickness, but really from apprehensions, that they intended to buy their peace, by delivering him into the hands of his enemies. The army called aloud for their sovereign to march at their head against the Danes; and on his refusal to take the field, they were so discouraged, that those vast preparations became ineffectual for the defence of the kingdom. Edmond, deprived of all regular supplies to maintain his soldiers, was obliged to commit equal ravages with those which were practised by the Danes, and after making some fruitless expeditions into the north, which had submitted entirely to Canute's power, he retired to London, determined there to maintain to the last extremity the small remains of English liberty. He here found *1016.* every thing in confusion by the death of the king, who expired after an unhappy and inglorious reign of thirty-five years. He left two sons by his first marriage, Edmond, who succeeded him, and Edwy, whom Canute afterwards murdered. His two sons by the second marriage, Alfred and Edward, were, immediately upon Ethelred's death, conveyed into Normandy by Queen Emma.

EDMOND IRONSIDE

THIS PRINCE, who received the name of Ironside from his hardy valour, possessed courage and abilities, sufficient to have prevented his country from sinking into those calamities, but not to raise it from that abyss of misery, into which it had already fallen. Among the other misfortunes of the English, treachery and disaffection had creeped in among the nobility and prelates; and Edmond found no better expedient for stopping the farther progress of these fatal evils, than to lead his army instantly into the field, and to employ them against the common enemy. After meeting with some success at Gillingham, he prepared himself to decide in one general engagement the fate of his crown, and at Scoerston, in the county of Glocester, he offered battle to the enemy, who were commanded by Canute and Edric. Fortune in the beginning of the day declared for him; but Edric, having cut off the head of one Osmer, whose countenance resembled that of Edmond, fixed it on a spear, carried it through the ranks in triumph, and called aloud to the English, that it was time to fly; for behold! the head of their sovereign. And though Edmond, observing the consternation of the troops, took off his helmet and showed himself to them, the utmost he could gain by his activity and valour was to leave the victory undecided. Edric now took a surer method to ruin him, by pretending to desert to him; and as Edmond was well acquainted with his power, and probably knew no other of the chief nobility in whom he could repose more confidence, he was obliged, notwithstanding the repeated perfidy of the man, to give him a considerable command in the army. A battle soon after ensued at Assington in Essex; where Edric, flying in the beginning of the day, occasioned the total defeat of the English, followed by a great slaughter of the nobility. The indefatigable Edmond, how-ever, had still resources. Assembling a new army at Glocester, he was again in a condition to dispute the field; when the Danish and English nobility, equally harassed with those convulsions, obliged their kings to come to a compromise, and to divide the kingdom between them by treaty. Canute reserved to himself the northern division, consisting of Mercia, East-Anglia, and Northumberland, which he had entirely subdued: The southern parts were left to Edmond. This prince survived the treaty about a month: He was murdered at Oxford by two of his chamberlains, accomplices of Edric, who thereby made way for the succession of Canute the Dane to the crown of England.

CANUTE

THE ENGLISH, who had been unable to defend their country, *1017.* and maintain their independency, under so active and brave a prince as Edmond, could, after his death, expect nothing but total subjection from Canute, who, active and brave himself, and at the head of a great force, was ready to take advantage of the minority of Edwin and Edward, the two sons of Edmond. Yet this conqueror, who was commonly so little scrupulous, showed him-self anxious to cover his injustice under plausible pretences: Be-fore he seized the dominions of the English princes, he summoned a general assembly of the states, in order to fix the succession of the kingdom. He here suborned some nobles to depose, that, in the treaty of Glocester, it had been verbally agreed, either to name Canute, in case of Edmond's death, successor to his dominions, or tutor to his children (for historians vary in this particular): And that evidence, supported by the great power of Canute, deter-mined the states immediately to put the Danish monarch in pos-session of the government. Canute, jealous of the two princes, but sensible that he should render himself extremely odious, if he ordered them to be dispatched in England, sent them abroad to his ally, the king of Sweden, whom he desired, as soon as they arrived at his court, to free him, by their death, from all farther anxiety. The Swedish monarch was too generous to comply with the request; but being afraid of drawing on himself a quarrel with Canute, by protecting the young princes, he sent them to Solomon, king of Hungary, to be educated in his court. The elder, Edwin, was afterwards married to the sister of the king of Hungary; but the English prince dying without issue, Solomon gave his sister-in-law, Agatha, daughter of the emperor Henry II. in marriage to Edward, the younger brother; and she bore him Edgar Atheling, Margaret, afterwards queen of Scotland, and Christina, who retired into a convent.

Canute, though he had reached the great point of his ambition, in obtaining possession of the English crown, was obliged at first to make great sacrifices to it; and to gratify the chief of the nobility, by bestowing on them the most extensive governments and jurisdictions. He created Thurkill earl or duke of East-Anglia, (for these titles were then nearly of the same import) Yric of Northumberland, and Edric of Mercia; reserving only to himself the administration of Wessex. But seizing afterwards a favourable opportunity, he expelled Thurkill and Yric from their governments, and banished them the kingdom: He put to death many of the English nobility, on whose fidelity he could not rely, and whom he hated on account of their disloyalty to their native prince. And even the traitor, Edric, having had the assurance to reproach him with his services, was condemned to be executed, and his body to be thrown into the Thames; a suitable reward for his multiplied acts of perfidy and rebellion.

Canute also found himself obliged, in the beginning of his reign, to load the people with heavy taxes, in order to reward his Danish followers: He exacted from them at one time the sum of 72,000 pounds; besides 11,000 pounds, which he levied on London alone. He was probably willing, from political motives, to mulct severely that city, on account of the affection which it had borne to Edmond, and the resistance which it had made to the Danish power in two obstinate sieges.[p] But these rigors were im-

---

[p] W. Malm. p. 72. In one of these sieges, Canute diverted the course of the Thames, and by that means brought his ships above London bridge.

CHAPTER III

puted to necessity; and Canute, like a wise prince, was determined, that the English, now deprived of all their dangerous leaders, should be reconciled to the Danish yoke, by the justice and impartiality of his administration. He sent back to Denmark as many of his followers as he could safely spare: He restored the Saxon customs in a general assembly of the states: He made no distinction between Danes and English in the distribution of justice: And he took care, by a strict execution of law, to protect the lives and properties of all his people. The Danes were gradually incorporated with his new subjects; and both were glad to obtain a little respite from those multiplied calamities, from which the one, no less than the other, had, in their fierce contest for power, experienced such fatal consequences.

The removal of Edmond's children into so distant a country as Hungary, was, next to their death, regarded by Canute as the greatest security to his government: He had no farther anxiety, except with regard to Alfred and Edward, who were protected and supported by their uncle, Richard, duke of Normandy. Richard even fitted out a great armament, in order to restore the English princes to the throne of their ancestors; and though the navy was dispersed by a storm, Canute saw the danger to which he was exposed, from the enmity of so warlike a people as the Normans. In order to acquire the friendship of the duke, he paid his addresses to queen Emma, sister of that prince; and promised, that he would leave the children, whom he should have by that marriage, in possession of the crown of England. Richard complied with his demand, and sent over Emma to England, where she was soon after married to Canute.[q] The English, though they disapproved of her espousing the mortal enemy of her former husband and his family, were pleased to find at court a sovereign, to whom they were accustomed, and who had already formed connections with them: And thus Canute, besides securing, by this marriage, the alliance of Normandy, gradually acquired, by the same means, the confidence of his own subjects.[r] The Norman prince did not long survive the marriage of Emma; and he left the inheritance of the dutchy to his eldest son of the same name; who, dying a year

[q] Chron. Sax. p. 151. W. Malmes. p. 73.   [r] W. Malmes. p. 73. Higden, p. 275.

after him without children, was succeeded by his brother Robert, a man of valour and abilities.

Canute, having settled his power in England, beyond all danger of a revolution, made a voyage to Denmark, in order to resist the attacks of the king of Sweden; and he carried along with him a great body of the English, under the command of earl Godwin. This nobleman had here an opportunity of performing a service, by which he both reconciled the king's mind to the English nation, and gaining to himself the friendship of his sovereign, laid the foundation of that immense fortune which he acquired to his family. He was stationed next the Swedish camp; and observing a favourable opportunity, which he was obliged suddenly to seize, he attacked the enemy in the night, drove them from their trenches, threw them into disorder, pursued his advantage, and obtained a decisive victory over them. Next morning, Canute, seeing the English camp entirely abandoned, imagined that those disaffected troops had deserted to the enemy: He was agreeably surprised to find, that they were at that time engaged in pursuit of the discomfited Swedes. He was so pleased with this success, and with the manner of obtaining it, that he bestowed his daughter in marriage upon Godwin, and treated him ever after with entire confidence and regard.

1028.   In another voyage, which he made afterwards to Denmark, Canute attacked Norway, and expelling the just, but unwarlike Olaus, kept possession of his kingdom, till the death of that prince. He had now by his conquests and valour attained the utmost height of grandeur: Having leisure from wars and intrigues, he felt the unsatisfactory nature of all human enjoyments; and equally weary of the glories and turmoils of this life, he began to cast his view towards that future existence, which it is so natural for the human mind, whether satiated by prosperity or disgusted with adversity, to make the object of its attention. Unfortunately, the spirit which prevailed in that age gave a wrong direction to his devotion: Instead of making compensation to those whom he had injured by his former acts of violence, he employed himself entirely in those exercises of piety, which the monks represented as the most meritorious. He built churches, he endowed monasteries, he enriched the ecclesiastics, and he bestowed revenues for the support of chantries at Assington and other places; where he ap-

CHAPTER III

pointed prayers to be said for the souls of those who had there fallen in battle against him. He even undertook a pilgrimage to Rome, where he resided a considerable time: Besides obtaining from the pope some privileges for the English school erected there, he engaged all the princes, through whose dominions he was obliged to pass, to desist from those heavy impositions and tolls, which they were accustomed to exact from the English pilgrims. By this spirit of devotion, no less than by his equitable and politic administration, he gained, in a good measure, the affections of his subjects.

Canute, the greatest and most powerful monarch of his time, sovereign of Denmark and Norway, as well as of England, could not fail of meeting with adulation from his courtiers; a tribute which is liberally paid even to the meanest and weakest princes. Some of his flatterers breaking out, one day, in admiration of his grandeur, exclaimed that every thing was possible for him: Upon which the monarch, it is said, ordered his chair to be set on the sea-shore, while the tide was rising; and as the waters approached, he commanded them to retire, and to obey the voice of him who was lord of the ocean. He feigned to sit some time in expectation of their submission; but when the sea still advanced towards him, and began to wash him with its billows, he turned to his courtiers, and remarked to them, that every creature in the universe was feeble and impotent, and that power resided with one Being alone, in whose hands were all the elements of nature; who could say to the ocean, *Thus far shalt thou go, and no farther;* and who could level with his nod the most towering piles of human pride and ambition.

The only memorable action, which Canute performed after *1031.* his return from Rome, was an expedition against Malcolm, king of Scotland. During the reign of Ethelred, a tax of a shilling a hyde had been imposed on all the lands of England. It was commonly called *Danegelt;* because the revenue had been employed, either in buying peace with the Danes, or in making preparations against the inroads of that hostile nation. That monarch had required, that the same tax should be paid by Cumberland, which was held by the Scots; but Malcolm, a warlike prince, told him, that, as he was always able to repulse the Danes by his own power, he would neither submit to buy peace of his enemies, nor pay others for resisting them. Ethelred, offended at this reply, which contained a secret reproach on his own conduct, undertook an expedition against Cumberland; but though he committed ravages upon the country, he could never bring Malcolm to a temper more humble or submissive. Canute, after his accession, summoned the Scottish king to acknowledge himself a vassal for Cumberland to the crown of England; but Malcolm refused compliance, on pretence that he owed homage to those princes only, who inherited that kingdom by right of blood. Canute was not of a temper to bear this insult; and the king of Scotland soon found, that the sceptre was in very different hands from those of the feeble and irresolute Ethelred. Upon Canute's appearing on the frontiers with a formidable army, Malcolm agreed, that his grandson and heir, Duncan, whom he put in possession of Cumberland, should make the submissions required, and that the heirs of Scotland should always acknowledge themselves vassals to England for that province.[5]

Canute passed four years in peace after this enterprize, and he died at Shaftsbury;[t] leaving three sons, Sweyn, Harold, and Hardicanute. Sweyn, whom he had by his first marriage with Alfwen, daughter of the earl of Hampshire, was crowned in Norway: Hardicanute, whom Emma had born him, was in possession of Denmark: Harold, who was of the same marriage with Sweyn, was at that time in England.

HAROLD HAREFOOT

1035. THOUGH CANUTE, in his treaty with Richard, duke of Normandy, had stipulated, that his children by Emma should succeed to the crown of England, he had either considered himself as released from that engagement by the death of Richard, or esteemed it dangerous to leave an unsettled and newly conquered kingdom in the hands of so young a prince as Hardicanute: He therefore appointed, by his will, Harold successor to the crown. This prince was besides present, to maintain his claim; he was favoured by all the Danes; and he got immediately possession of his father's treasures, which might be equally useful, whether he

[5] W. Malm. p. 74. [t] Chron. Sax. p. 154. W. Malm. p. 76.

CHAPTER III

found it necessary to proceed by force or intrigue, in insuring his succession. On the other hand, Hardicanute had the suffrages of the English, who, on account of his being born among them of queen Emma, regarded him as their countryman; he was favoured by the articles of treaty with the duke of Normandy; and above all, his party was espoused by earl Godwin, the most powerful nobleman in the kingdom, especially in the province of Wessex, the chief seat of the ancient English. Affairs were likely to terminate in a civil war; when, by the interposition of the nobility of both parties, a compromise was made; and it was agreed, that Harold should enjoy, together with London, all the provinces north of the Thames, while the possession of the south should remain to Hardicanute: And till that prince should appear and take possession of his dominions, Emma fixed her residence at Winchester, and established her authority over her son's share of the partition.

Meanwhile, Robert, duke of Normandy, died in a pilgrimage to the Holy Land, and being succeeded by a son, yet a minor, the two English princes, Alfred and Edward, who found no longer any countenance or protection in that country, gladly embraced the opportunity of paying a visit, with a numerous retinue, to their mother Emma, who seemed to be placed in a state of so much power and splendor at Winchester. But the face of affairs soon wore a melancholy aspect. Earl Godwin had been gained by the arts of Harold, who promised to espouse the daughter of that nobleman; and while the treaty was yet a secret, these two tyrants laid a plan for the destruction of the English princes. Alfred was invited to London by Harold with many professions of friendship; but when he had reached Guilford, he was set upon by Godwin's vassals, about six hundred of his train were murdered in the most cruel manner, he himself was taken prisoner, his eyes were put out, and he was conducted to the monastery of Ely, where he died soon after.[u] Edward and Emma, apprized of the fate which was awaiting them, fled beyond sea, the former into Normandy, the latter into Flanders. While Harold, triumphing in his bloody pol-

---

[u] H. Hunt. p. 365. Ypod. Neustr. p. 434. Hoveden. p. 438. Chron. Mailr. p. 156. Higden, p. 277. Chron. St. Petri di Burgo, p. 39. Sim. Dun. p. 179. Abbas Rieval. p. 366, 374. Brompton, p. 935. Gul. Gem. lib. 7. cap. 11. Matth. West. p. 209. Flor. Wigorn. p. 622. Alur. Beverl. p. 118.

icy, took possession, without resistance, of all the dominions as-signed to his brother.

This is the only memorable action, performed, during a reign of four years, by this prince, who gave so bad a specimen of his character, and whose bodily accomplishments alone are known to us, by his appellation of *Harefoot,* which he acquired from his agility in running and walking. He died on the 14th of April, 1039; little regretted or esteemed by his subjects; and left the succession open to his brother, Hardicanute.

HARDICANUTE

1039.

HARDICANUTE, or Canute the Hardy, that is, the robust (for he too is chiefly known by his bodily accomplishments), though, by remaining so long in Denmark, he had been deprived of his share in the partition of the kingdom, had not abandoned his pretensions; and he had determined, before Harold's death, to recover by arms, what he had lost, either by his own negligence, or by the necessity of his affairs. On pretence of paying a visit to the queen dowager in Flanders, he had assembled a fleet of sixty sail, and was preparing to make a descent on England, when intel-ligence of his brother's death induced him to sail immediately to London, where he was received in triumph, and acknowledged king without opposition.

The first act of Hardicanute's government afforded his subjects a bad prognostic of his future conduct. He was so enraged at Harold, for depriving him of his share of the kingdom, and for the cruel treatment of his brother Alfred, that, in an impotent desire of revenge against the dead, he ordered his body to be dug up, and to be thrown into the Thames: And when it was found by some fishermen, and buried in London, he ordered it again to be dug up, and to be thrown again into the river: But it was fished up a second time, and then interred with great secrecy. Godwin, equally servile and insolent, submitted to be his instrument in this un-natural and brutal action.

CHAPTER III

That nobleman knew, that he was universally believed to have been an accomplice in the barbarity exercised on Alfred, and that he was on that account obnoxious to Hardicanute; and perhaps he hoped, by displaying this rage against Harold's memory, to justify himself from having had any participation in his counsels. But prince Edward, being invited over by the king, immediately on his appearance, preferred an accusation against Godwin for the murder of Alfred, and demanded justice for that crime. Godwin, in order to appease the king, made him a magnificent present of a galley with a gilt stern, rowed by fourscore men, who wore each of them a gold bracelet on his arm, weighing sixteen ounces, and were armed and cloathed in the most sumptuous manner. Hardicanute, pleased with the splendor of this spectacle, quickly forgot his brother's murder; and on Godwin's swearing that he was innocent of the crime, he allowed him to be acquitted.

Though Hardicanute, before his accession, had been called over by the vows of the English, he soon lost the affections of the nation by his misconduct; but nothing appeared more grievous to them, than his renewing the imposition of Danegelt, and obliging the nation to pay a great sum of money to the fleet, which brought him from Denmark. The discontents ran high in many places: In Worcester the populace rose, and put to death two of the collectors. The king, enraged at this opposition, swore vengeance against the city, and ordered three noblemen, Godwin, duke of Wessex, Siward, duke of Northumberland, and Leofric, duke of Mercia, to execute his menaces with the utmost rigour. They were obliged to set fire to the city, and deliver it up to be plundered by their soldiers; but they saved the lives of the inhabitants; whom they confined in a small island of the Severn, called Beverey, till, by their intercession, they were able to appease the king, and obtain the pardon of the supplicants.

This violent government was of short duration. Hardicanute died in two years after his accession, at the nuptials of a Danish lord, which he had honoured with his presence. His usual habits of intemperance were so well known, that, notwithstanding his robust constitution, his sudden death gave as little surprize, as it did sorrow, to his subjects.

EDWARD
THE CONFESSOR

1041. THE ENGLISH, on the death of Hardicanute, saw a favourable opportunity for recovering their liberty, and for shaking
off the Danish yoke, under which they had so long laboured.
Sweyn, king of Norway, the eldest son of Canute, was absent; and
as the two last kings had died without issue, none of that race
presented himself, nor any whom the Danes could support as
successor to the throne. Prince Edward was fortunately at court on
his brother's demise; and though the descendants of Edmond
Ironside were the true heirs of the Saxon family, yet their absence
in so remote a country as Hungary, appeared a sufficient reason
for their exclusion, to a people like the English, so little accustomed to observe a regular order in the succession of their monarchs. All delays might be dangerous; and the present occasion
must hastily be embraced; while the Danes, without concert, without a leader, astonished at the present incident, and anxious only
for their personal safety, durst not oppose the united voice of the
nation.

But this concurrence of circumstances in favour of Edward,
might have failed of its effect, had his succession been opposed by
Godwin, whose power, alliances, and abilities gave him a great
influence at all times, especially amidst those sudden opportunities, which always attend a revolution of government, and
which, either seized or neglected, commonly prove decisive. There
were opposite reasons, which divided men's hopes and fears with
regard to Godwin's conduct. On the one hand, the credit of that
nobleman lay chiefly in Wessex, which was almost entirely inhabited by English: It was therefore presumed, that he would second
the wishes of that people, in restoring the Saxon line, and in
humbling the Danes, from whom he, as well as they, had reason to
dread, as they had already felt, the most grievous oppressions. On
the other hand, there subsisted a declared animosity between Edward and Godwin, on account of Alfred's murder; of which the
latter had publicly been accused by the prince, and which he might
believe so deep an offence, as could never, on account of any
subsequent merits, be sincerely pardoned. But their common

CHAPTER III

friends here interposed; and representing the necessity of their good correspondence, obliged them to lay aside all jealousy and rancour, and concur in restoring liberty to their native country. Godwin only stipulated, that Edward, as a pledge of his sincere reconciliation, should promise to marry his daughter Editha; and having fortified himself by this alliance, he summoned a general council at Gillingham, and prepared every measure for securing the succession to Edward. The English were unanimous and zealous in their resolutions; the Danes were divided and dispirited: Any small opposition, which appeared in this assembly, was browbeaten and suppressed; and Edward was crowned king, with every demonstration of duty and affection.

The triumph of the English, upon this signal and decisive advantage, was at first attended with some insult and violence against the Danes; but the king, by the mildness of his character, soon reconciled the latter to his administration, and the distinction between the two nations gradually disappeared. The Danes were interspersed with the English in most of the provinces; they spoke nearly the same language; they differed little in their manners and laws; domestic dissentions in Denmark prevented, for some years, any powerful invasion from thence, which might awaken past animosities; and as the Norman conquest, which ensued soon after, reduced both nations to equal subjection, there is no farther mention in history of any difference between them. The joy, however, of their present deliverance made such impression on the minds of the English, that they instituted an annual festival for celebrating that great event; and it was observed in some counties, even to the time of Spellman.[w]

The popularity, which Edward enjoyed on his accession, was not destroyed by the first act of his administration, his resuming all the grants of his immediate predecessors; an attempt, which is commonly attended with the most dangerous consequences. The poverty of the crown convinced the nation, that this act of violence was become absolutely necessary; and as the loss fell chiefly on the Danes, who had obtained large grants from the late kings, their countrymen, on account of their services in subduing the kingdom, the English were rather pleased to see them reduced to their

---

[w] Spellm. Glossary in verbo *Hocday*.

primitive poverty. The king's severity also towards his mother, the queen-dowager, though exposed to some more censure, met not with very general disapprobation. He had hitherto lived on indifferent terms with that princess: He accused her of neglecting him and his brother during their adverse fortune;[x] He remarked, that, as the superior qualities of Canute, and his better treatment of her, had made her entirely indifferent to the memory of Ethelred, she also gave the preference to her children of the second bed, and always regarded Hardicanute as her favourite. The same reasons had probably made her unpopular in England; and though her benefactions to the monks obtained her the favour of that order, the nation was not, in general, displeased to see her stripped by Edward of immense treasures which she had amassed. He confined her, during the remainder of her life, in a monastery at Winchester; but carried his rigour against her no farther. The stories of his accusing her of a participation in her son Alfred's murder, and of a criminal correspondence with the bishop of Winchester, and also of her justifying herself by treading barefoot, without receiving any hurt, over nine burning plough-shares, were the inventions of the monkish historians, and were propagated and believed from the silly wonder of posterity.[y]

The English flattered themselves, that, by the accession of Edward, they were delivered for ever from the dominion of foreigners; but they soon found, that this evil was not yet entirely removed. The king had been educated in Normandy; and had contracted many intimacies with the natives of that country, as well as an affection for their manners.[z] The court of England was soon filled with Normans, who, being distinguished both by the favour of Edward, and by a degree of cultivation superior to that which was attained by the English in those ages, soon rendered their language, customs, and laws fashionable in the kingdom. The study of the French tongue became general among the people. The courtiers affected to imitate that nation in their dress, equipage, and entertainments: Even the lawyers employed a foreign language in their deeds and papers:[a] But above all, the church felt the influence and dominion of those strangers: Ulf and William, two Normans, who had formerly been the king's chaplains, were

---

[x] Anglia Sacra, vol. I. p. 237.   [y] Higden, p. 277.   [z] Ingulf, p. 62.   [a] Ibid.

133

CHAPTER III

created bishops of Dorchester and London. Robert, a Norman also, was promoted to the see of Canterbury,[b] and always enjoyed the highest favour of his master, of which his abilities rendered him not unworthy. And though the king's prudence, or his want of authority, made him confer almost all the civil and military employments on the natives, the ecclesiastical preferments fell often to the share of the Normans; and as the latter possessed Edward's confidence, they had secretly a great influence on public affairs, and excited the jealousy of the English, particularly of earl Godwin.[c]

This powerful nobleman, besides being duke or earl of Wessex, had the counties of Kent and Sussex annexed to his government. His eldest son, Sweyn, possessed the same authority in the counties of Oxford, Berks, Glocester, and Hereford: And Harold, his second son, was duke of East-Anglia, and at the same time governor of Essex. The great authority of this family was supported by immense possessions and powerful alliances; and the abilities, as well as ambition, of Godwin himself, contributed to render it still more dangerous. A prince of greater capacity and vigour than Edward, would have found it difficult to support the dignity of the crown under such circumstances; and as the haughty temper of Godwin made him often forget the respect due to his prince, Edward's animosity against him was grounded on personal as well as political considerations, on recent as well as more ancient injuries. The king, in pursuance of his engagements, had indeed married Editha, the daughter of Godwin;[d] but this alliance became a fresh source of enmity between them. Edward's hatred of the father was transferred to that princess; and Editha, though possessed of many amiable accomplishments, could never acquire the confidence and affection of her husband. It is even pretended, that, during the whole course of her life, he abstained from all commerce of love with her; and such was the absurd admiration paid to an inviolable chastity during those ages, that his conduct in this *1048.* particular is highly celebrated by the monkish historians, and greatly contributed to his acquiring the title of saint and confessor.[e]

[b] Chron. Sax. p. 161.   [c] W. Malm. p. 80.   [d] Chron. Sax. p. 157.   [e] W. Malm. p. 80. Higden, p. 277. Abbas Rieval. p. 366, 377. Matth. West. p. 221. Chron. Thom. Wykes, p. 21. Anglia Sacra, vol. I. p. 241.

The most popular pretence on which Godwin could ground his disaffection to the king and his administration, was to complain of the influence of the Normans in the government; and a declared opposition had thence arisen between him and these favourites. It was not long before this animosity broke into action. Eustace, count of Bologne, having paid a visit to the king, passed by Dover in his return: One of his train, being refused entrance to a lodging, which had been assigned him, attempted to make his way by force, and in the contest he wounded the master of the house. The inhabitants revenged this insult by the death of the stranger; the count and his train took arms, and murdered the wounded towns-man; a tumult ensued; near twenty persons were killed on each side; and Eustace, being overpowered by numbers, was obliged to save his life by flight from the fury of the populace. He hurried immediately to court and complained of the usage he had met with: The king entered zealously into the quarrel, and was highly displeased that a stranger of such distinction, whom he had invited over to his court, should, without any just cause, as he believed, have felt so sensibly the insolence and animosity of his people. He gave orders to Godwin, in whose government Dover lay, to repair immediately to the place, and to punish the inhabitants for the crime: But Godwin, who desired rather to encourage, than re-press, the popular discontents against foreigners, refused obe-dience, and endeavoured to throw the whole blame of the riot on the count of Bologne, and his retinue.[f] Edward, touched in so sensible a point, saw the necessity of exerting the royal authority, and he threatened Godwin, if he persisted in his disobedience to make him feel the utmost effects of his resentment.

The earl, perceiving a rupture to be unavoidable, and pleased to embark in a cause, where, it was likely, he should be supported by his countrymen, made preparations for his own defence, or rather for an attack on Edward. Under pretence of repressing some disorders on the Welsh frontier, he secretly assembled a great army, and was approaching the king, who resided, without any military force, and without suspicion, at Glocester.[g] Edward applied for protection to Siward, duke of Northumberland, and

---

[f] Chron. Sax. p. 163. W. Malm. p. 81. Higden, p. 279.   [g] Chron. Sax. p. 163. W. Malm. p. 81.

CHAPTER III

Leofric, duke of Mercia, two powerful noblemen, whose jealousy of Godwin's greatness, as well as their duty to the crown, engaged them to defend the king in this extremity. They hastened to him with such of their followers as they could assemble on a sudden; and finding the danger much greater than they had at first apprehended, they issued orders for mustering all the forces within their respective governments, and for marching them without delay to the defence of the king's person and authority. Edward, meanwhile, endeavoured to gain time by negociation; while Godwin, who thought the king entirely in his power, and who was willing to save appearances, fell into the snare; and not sensible, that he ought to have no farther reserve after he had proceeded so far, he lost the favourable opportunity of rendering himself master of the government.

The English, though they had no high idea of Edward's vigour and capacity, bore him great affection on account of his humanity, justice, and piety, as well as the long race of their native kings, from whom he was descended; and they hastened from all quarters to defend him from the present danger. His army was now so considerable, that he ventured to take the field; and marching to London, he summoned a great council to judge of the rebellion of Godwin and his sons. These noblemen pretended at first that they were willing to stand their trial; but having in vain endeavoured to make their adherents persist in rebellion, they offered to come to London, provided they might receive hostages for their safety: This proposal being rejected, they were obliged to disband the remains of their forces, and have recourse to flight. Baldwin, earl of Flanders, gave protection to Godwin and his three sons, Gurth, Sweyn, and Tosti; the latter of whom had married the daughter of that prince: Harold and Leofwin, two others of his sons, took shelter in Ireland. The estates of the father and sons were confiscated: Their governments were given to others: Queen Editha was confined in a monastery at Warewel: And the greatness of this family, once so formidable, seemed now to be totally supplanted and overthrown.

But Godwin had fixed his authority on too firm a basis, and he was too strongly supported by alliances both foreign and domestic, not to occasion farther disturbances, and make new efforts for his re-establishment. The earl of Flanders permitted him to purchase *1052.*

and hire ships within his harbours; and Godwin, having manned them with his followers, and with free-booters of all nations, put to sea, and attempted to make a descent at Sandwich. The king, informed of his preparations, had equipped a considerable fleet, much superior to that of the enemy; and the earl hastily, before their appearance, made his retreat into the Flemish harbours.[h] The English court, allured by the present security, and destitute of all vigorous counsels, allowed the seamen to disband, and the fleet to go to decay;[i] while Godwin, expecting this event, kept his men in readiness for action. He put to sea immediately, and sailed to the Isle of Wight, where he was joined by Harold with a squadron, which that nobleman had collected in Ireland. He was now master of the sea; and entering every harbour in the southern coast, he seized all the ships,[k] and summoned his followers in those counties, which had so long been subject to his government, to assist him in procuring justice to himself, his family, and his country, against the tyranny of foreigners. Reinforced by great numbers from all quarters, he entered the Thames; and appearing before London, threw every thing into confusion. The king alone seemed resolute to defend himself to the last extremity; but the interposition of the English nobility, many of whom favoured Godwin's pretensions, made Edward hearken to terms of accommodation; and the feigned humility of the earl, who disclaimed all intentions of offering violence to his sovereign, and desired only to justify himself by a fair and open trial, paved the way for his more easy admission. It was stipulated, that he should give hostages for his good behaviour, and that the primate and all the foreigners should be banished: By this treaty, the present danger of a civil war was obviated, but the authority of the crown was considerably impaired or rather entirely annihilated. Edward, sensible that he had not power sufficient to secure Godwin's hostages in England, sent them over to his kinsman, the young duke of Normandy.

Godwin's death, which happened soon after, while he was sitting at table with the king, prevented him from farther establishing the authority which he had acquired, and from reducing Edward to still greater subjection.[*] He was succeeded in the government of Wessex, Sussex, Kent, and Essex, and in the office of steward of

[h] Sim. Dun. p. 186.   [i] Chron. Sax. p. 166.   [k] Ibid.   [*] See note [E] at the end of the volume.

CHAPTER III

the household, a place of great power, by his son, Harold, who was actuated by an ambition equal to that of his father, and was superior to him in address, in insinuation, and in virtue. By a modest and gentle demeanor, he acquired the good-will of Edward; at least, softened that hatred which the prince had so long borne his family;[l] and gaining every day new partizans by his bounty and affability, he proceeded, in a more silent, and therefore a more dangerous manner, to the encrease of his authority. The king, who had not sufficient vigour directly to oppose his progress, knew of no other expedient than that hazardous one, of raising him a rival in the family of Leofric, duke of Mercia, whose son, Algar, was invested with the government of East-Anglia, which, before the banishment of Harold, had belonged to the latter nobleman. But this policy, of balancing opposite parties, required a more steady hand to manage it than that of Edward, and naturally produced faction, and even civil broils, among nobles of such mighty and independant authority. Algar was soon after expelled his government by the intrigues and power of Harold; but being protected by Griffith, prince of Wales, who had married his daughter, as well as by the power of his father, Leofric, he obliged Harold to submit to an accommodation, and was reinstated in the government of East-Anglia. This peace was not of long duration: Harold, taking advantage of Leofric's death, which happened soon after, expelled Algar anew, and banished him the kingdom: And though that nobleman made a fresh irruption into East-Anglia with an army of Norwegians, and over-ran the country, his death soon freed Harold from the pretensions of so dangerous a rival. Edward, the eldest son of Algar, was indeed advanced to the government of Mercia; but the balance, which the king desired to establish between those potent families, was wholly lost, and the influence of Harold greatly preponderated.

The death of Siward, duke of Northumberland, made the way still more open to the ambition of that nobleman. Siward, besides his other merits, had acquired honour to England, by his successful conduct in the only foreign enterprize undertaken during the reign of Edward. Duncan, king of Scotland, was a prince of a gentle disposition, but possessed not the genius requisite for

1055.

---

[l] Brompton, p. 948.

governing a country so turbulent, and so much infested by the intrigues and animosities of the great. Macbeth, a powerful nobleman, and nearly allied to the crown, not content with curbing the king's authority, carried still farther his pestilent ambition: He put his sovereign to death; chaced Malcolm Kenmore, his son and heir, into England; and usurped the crown. Siward, whose daughter was married to Duncan, embraced, by Edward's orders, the protection of this distressed family: He marched an army into Scotland; and having defeated and killed Macbeth in battle, he restored Malcolm to the throne of his ancestors.[m] This service, added to his former connections with the royal family of Scotland, brought a great accession to the authority of Siward in the north; but as he had lost his eldest son, Osbern, in the action with Macbeth, it proved in the issue fatal to his family. His second son, Walthoef, appeared, on his father's death, too young to be entrusted with the government of Northumberland; and Harold's influence obtained that dukedom for his own brother Tosti.

There are two circumstances related of Siward, which discover his high sense of honour, and his martial disposition. When intelligence was brought him of his son Osberne's death, he was inconsolable; till he heard, that the wound was received in the breast, and that he had behaved with great gallantry in the action. When he found his own death approaching, he ordered his servants to clothe him in a complete suit of armour; and sitting erect on the couch, with a spear in his hand, declared, that, in that posture, the only one worthy of a warrior, he would patiently await the fatal moment.

The king, now worn out with cares and infirmities, felt himself far advanced in the decline of life; and having no issue himself, began to think of appointing a successor to the kingdom. He sent a deputation to Hungary, to invite over his nephew, Edward, son of his elder brother, and the only remaining heir of the Saxon line. That prince, whose succession to the crown would have been easy and undisputed, came to England with his children, Edgar, surnamed Atheling, Margaret and Christina; but his death, which happened a few days after his arrival, threw the king into new

[m] W. Malm. p. 79. Hoveden, p. 443. Chron. Mailr, p. 158. Buchanan, p. 115. edit. 1715.

CHAPTER III

difficulties. He saw, that the great power and ambition of Harold had tempted him to think of obtaining possession of the throne on the first vacancy, and that Edgar, on account of his youth and inexperience, was very unfit to oppose the pretensions of so popular and enterprising a rival. The animosity, which he had long borne to earl Godwin, made him averse to the succession of his son; and he could not, without extreme reluctance, think of an encrease of grandeur to a family, which had risen on the ruins of royal authority, and which, by the murder of Alfred, his brother, had contributed so much to the weakening of the Saxon line. In this uncertainty, he secretly cast his eye towards his kinsman, William duke of Normandy, as the only person whose power, and reputation, and capacity, could support any detestation, which he might make in his favour, to the exclusion of Harold, and his family.[n]

This famous prince was natural son of Robert, duke of Normandy, by Harlotta, daughter of a tanner in Falaise,[o] and was very early established in that grandeur, from which his birth seemed to have set him at so great a distance. While he was but nine years of age, his father had resolved to undertake a pilgrimage to Jerusalem; a fashionable act of devotion, which had taken place of the pilgrimages to Rome, and which, as it was attended with more difficulty and danger, and carried those religious adventurers to the first sources of Christianity, appeared to them more meritorious. Before his departure, he assembled the states of the dutchy; and informing them of his design, he engaged them to swear allegiance to his natural son, William, whom, as he had no legitimate issue, he intended, in case he should die in the pilgrimage, to leave successor to his dominions.[p] As he was a prudent prince, he could not but foresee the great inconveniences which must attend this journey, and this settlement of his succession; arising from the perpetual turbulency of the great, the claims of other branches of the ducal family, and the power of the French monarch: But all these considerations were surmounted by the prevailing zeal for pilgrimages;[q] and probably, the more important they were, the more would Robert exult in sacrificing them to what he imagined to be his religious duty.

[n] Ingulf, p. 68. [o] Brompton, p. 910. [p] W. Malm. p. 95. [q] Ypod. Neust. p. 452.

This prince, as he had apprehended, died in his pilgrimage; and the minority of his son was attended with all those disorders, which were almost unavoidable in that situation. The licentious nobles, freed from the awe of sovereign authority, broke out into personal animosities against each other, and made the whole country a scene of war and devastation.[r] Roger, count of Toni, and Alain, count of Britanny, advanced claims to the dominion of the state; and Henry I. king of France, thought the opportunity favourable for reducing the power of a vassal, who had originally acquired his settlement in so violent and invidious a manner, and who had long appeared formidable to his sovereign.[s] The regency established by Robert encountered great difficulties in supporting the government under this complication of dangers; and the young prince, when he came to maturity, found himself reduced to a very low condition. But the great qualities, which he soon displayed in the field and in the cabinet, gave encouragement to his friends, and struck a terror into his enemies. He opposed himself on all sides against his rebellious subjects, and against foreign invaders; and by his valour and conduct prevailed in every action. He obliged the French king to grant him peace on reasonable terms; he expelled all pretenders to the sovereignty; and he reduced his turbulent barons to pay submission to his authority, and to suspend their mutual animosities. The natural severity of his temper appeared in a rigorous administration of justice; and having found the happy effects of this plan of government, without which the laws in those ages became totally impotent, he regarded it as a fixed maxim, that an inflexible conduct was the first duty of a sovereign.

The tranquillity, which he had established in his dominions, had given William leisure to pay a visit to the king of England during the time of Godwin's banishment; and he was received in a manner suitable to the great reputation which he had acquired, to the relation by which he was connected with Edward, and to the obligations which that prince owed to his family.[t] On the return of Godwin, and the expulsion of the Norman favourites, Robert, archbishop of Canterbury, had, before his departure, persuaded

[r] W. Malm. p. 95. Gul. Gemet. lib. 7. cap. 1.   [s] W. Malm. p. 97.
[t] Hoveden, p. 442. Ingulf, p. 65. Chron. Mailr. p. 157. Higden, p. 279.

CHAPTER III

Edward to think of adopting William as his successor; a counsel, which was favoured by the king's aversion to Godwin, his prepossessions for the Normans, and his esteem of the duke. That prelate, therefore, received a commission to inform William of the king's intentions in his favour; and he was the first person that opened the mind of the prince to entertain those ambitious hopes.[u] But Edward, irresolute and feeble in his purpose, finding that the English would more easily acquiesce in that restoration of the Saxon line, had, in the mean time, invited his brother's descendants from Hungary, with a view of having them recognized heirs to the crown. The death of his nephew, and the inexperience and unpromising qualities of young Edgar, made him resume his former intentions in favour of the duke of Normandy; though his aversion to hazardous enterprizes engaged him to postpone the execution, and even to keep his purpose secret from all his ministers.

Harold, mean while, proceeded, after a more open manner, in encreasing his popularity, in establishing his power, and in preparing the way for his advancement on the first vacancy; an event which, from the age and infirmities of the king, appeared not very distant. But there was still an obstacle, which it was requisite for him previously to overcome. Earl Godwin, when restored to his power and fortune, had given hostages for his good behaviour; and among the rest one son and one grandson, whom Edward, for greater security, as has been related, had consigned to the custody of the duke of Normandy. Harold, though not aware of the duke's being his competitor, was uneasy, that such near relations should be detained prisoners in a foreign country; and he was afraid, lest William should, in favour of Edgar, retain these pledges as a check on the ambition of any other pretender. He represented, therefore, to the king, his unfeigned submission to royal authority, his steady duty to his prince, and the little necessity there was, after such a uniform trial of his obedience, to detain any longer those hostages, who had been required on the first composing of civil discords. By these topics, enforced by his great power, he extorted the king's consent to release them; and in order to effect his purpose, he immediately proceeded, with a numerous retinue, on his

[u] Ingulf, p. 68. Gul. Gemet. lib. 7. cap. 31. Order. Vitalis, p. 492.

journey to Normandy. A tempest drove him on the territory of
Guy count of Ponthieu, who, being informed of his quality, immediately detained him prisoner, and demanded an exorbitant sum
for his ransom. Harold found means to convey intelligence of his
situation to the duke of Normandy; and represented, that, while
he was proceeding to *his* court, in execution of a commission from
the king of England, he had met with this harsh treatment from
the mercenary disposition of the count of Ponthieu.

William was immediately sensible of the importance of the incident. He foresaw, that, if he could once gain Harold, either by
favours or menaces, his way to the throne of England would be
open, and Edward would meet with no farther obstacle in executing the favourable intentions, which he had entertained in his
behalf. He sent, therefore, a messenger to Guy, in order to demand the liberty of his prisoner; and that nobleman, not daring to
refuse so great a prince, put Harold into the hands of the Norman,
who conducted him to Roüen. William received him with every
demonstration of respect and friendship; and after showing himself disposed to comply with his desire, in delivering up the hostages, he took an opportunity of disclosing to him the great secret,
of his pretensions to the crown of England, and of the will which
Edward intended to make in his favour. He desired the assistance
of Harold in perfecting that design; he made professions of the
utmost gratitude in return for so great an obligation; he promised
that the present grandeur of Harold's family, which supported
itself with difficulty under the jealousy and hatred of Edward,
should receive new encrease from a successor, who would be so
greatly beholden to him for his advancement. Harold was surprized at this declaration of the duke; but being sensible that he
should never recover his own liberty, much less that of his brother
and nephew, if he refused the demand, he feigned a compliance
with William, renounced all hopes of the crown for himself, and
professed his sincere intention of supporting the will of Edward,
and seconding the pretensions of the duke of Normandy. William,
to bind him faster to his interests, besides offering him one of his
daughters in marriage, required him to take an oath, that he would
fulfil his promises; and in order to render the oath more obligatory, he employed an artifice, well suited to the ignorance and
superstition of the age. He secretly conveyed under the altar, on

CHAPTER III

which Harold agreed to swear, the reliques of some of the most revered martyrs; and when Harold had taken the oath, he showed him the reliques, and admonished him to observe religiously an engagement, which had been ratified by so tremendous a sanction.[w] The English nobleman was astonished; but dissembling his concern, he renewed the same professions, and was dismissed with all the marks of mutual confidence by the duke of Normandy.

When Harold found himself at liberty, his ambition suggested casuistry sufficient to justify to him the violation of an oath, which had been extorted from him by fear, and which, if fulfilled, might be attended with the subjection of his native country to a foreign power. He continued still to practise every art of popularity; to encrease the number of his partizans; to reconcile the minds of the English to the idea of his succession; to revive their hatred of the Normans; and by an ostentation of his power an influence, to deter the timorous Edward from executing his intended destination in favour of William. Fortune, about this time, threw two incidents in his way, by which he was enabled to acquire general favour, and to encrease the character, which he had already attained, of virtue and abilities.

The Welsh, though a less formidable enemy than the Danes, had long been accustomed to infest the western borders; and after committing spoil on the low countries, they usually made a hasty retreat into their mountains, where they were sheltered from the pursuit of their enemies, and were ready to seize the first favourable opportunity of renewing their depredations. Griffith, the reigning prince, had greatly distinguished himself in those incursions; and his name had become so terrible to the English, that Harold found he could do nothing more acceptable to the public, and more honourable for himself, than the suppressing of so dangerous an enemy. He formed the plan of an expedition against Wales; and having prepared some light-armed foot to pursue the natives into their fastnesses, some cavalry to scour the open country, and a squadron of ships to attack the sea-coast, he employed at once all these forces against the Welsh, prosecuted his advantages with vigour, made no intermission in his assaults, and at last

---

[w] Wace, p. 459, 460. MS. penes Carte, p. 354. W. Malm. p. 93. H. Hunt. p. 366. Hoveden, p. 449. Brompton, p. 947.

reduced the enemy to such distress, that, in order to prevent their total destruction, they made a sacrifice of their prince, whose head they cut off, and sent to Harold; and they were content to receive as their sovereigns two Welsh noblemen appointed by Edward to rule over them. The other incident was no less honourable to Harold.

Tosti, brother of this nobleman, who had been created duke of Northumberland, being of a violent, tyrannical temper, had acted with such cruelty and injustice, that the inhabitants rose in rebellion, and chased him from his government. Morcar and Edwin, two brothers, who possessed great power in those parts, and who were grandsons of the great duke, Leofric, concurred in the insurrection; and the former, being elected duke, advanced with an army, to oppose Harold, who was commissioned by the king to reduce and chastise the Northumbrians. Before the armies came to action, Morcar, well acquainted with the generous disposition of the English commander, endeavoured to justify his own conduct. He represented to Harold, that Tosti had behaved in a manner unworthy of the station to which he was advanced, and no one, not even a brother, could support such tyranny, without participating, in some degree, of the infamy attending it; that the Northumbrians, accustomed to a legal administration, and regarding it as their birthright, were willing to submit to the king, but required a governor who would pay regard to their rights and privileges; that they had been taught by their ancestors, that death was preferable to servitude, and had taken the field determined to perish, rather than suffer a renewal of those indignities, to which they had so long been exposed; and they trusted, that Harold, on reflection, would not defend in another that violent conduct, from which he himself, in his own government, had always kept at so great a distance. This vigorous remonstrance was accompanied with such a detail of facts, so well supported, that Harold found it prudent to abandon his brother's cause; and returning to Edward, he persuaded him to pardon the Northumbrians, and to confirm Morcar in the government. He even married the sister of that nobleman;[x] and by his interest procured Edwin, the younger brother, to be elected into the government of Mercia. Tosti in rage departed the

[x] Order. Vitalis, p. 492.

CHAPTER III

kingdom, and took shelter in Flanders with earl Baldwin, his father-in-law.

By this marriage, Harold broke all measures with the duke of Normandy; and William clearly perceived, that he could no longer rely on the oaths and promises, which he had extorted from him. But the English nobleman was now in such a situation, that he deemed it no longer necessary to dissemble. He had, in his conduct towards the Northumbrians, given such a specimen of his moderation as had gained him the affections of his countrymen. He saw, that almost all England was engaged in his interests; while he himself possessed the government of Wessex, Morcar that of Northumberland, and Edwin that of Mercia. He now openly aspired to the succession; and insisted, that, since it was necessary, by the confession of all, to set aside the royal family, on account of the imbecility of Edgar, the sole surviving heir, there was no one so capable of filling the throne, as a nobleman, of great power, of mature age, of long experience, of approved courage and abilities, who, being a native of the kingdom, would effectually secure it against the dominion and tyranny of foreigners. Edward, broken with age and infirmities, saw the difficulties too great for him to encounter; and though his inveterate prepossessions kept him from seconding the pretensions of Harold, he took but feeble and irresolute steps for securing the succession to the duke of Normandy.* While he continued in this uncertainty, he was surprised by sickness, which brought him to his grave, on the fifth of January 1066, in the sixty-fifth year of his age, and twenty-fifth of his reign.

This prince, to whom the monks give the title of saint and confessor, was the last of the Saxon line, that ruled in England. Though his reign was peaceable and fortunate, he owed his prosperity less to his own abilities than to the conjunctures of the times. The Danes, employed in other enterprizes, attempted not those incursions, which had been so troublesome to all his predecessors, and fatal to some of them. The facility of his disposition made him acquiesce under the government of Godwin, and his son Harold; and the abilities, as well as the power of these noblemen, enabled them while they were entrusted with authority, to preserve domestic peace and tranquillity. The most commendable circumstance of

* See note [F] at the end of the volume.

Edward's government was his attention to the administration of justice, and his compiling for that purpose a body of laws, which he collected from the laws of Ethelbert, Ina, and Alfred. This compilation, though now lost (for the laws that pass under Edward's name were composed afterwards[y]) was long the object of affection to the English nation.

Edward the Confessor was the first that touched for the king's evil: The opinion of his sanctity procured belief to this cure among the people: His successors regarded it as a part of their state and grandeur to uphold the same opinion. It has been continued down to our time; and the practice was first dropped by the present royal family, who observed, that it could no longer give amazement even to the populace, and was attended with ridicule in the eyes of all men of understanding.

HAROLD

1066.
January.

HAROLD had so well prepared matters before the death of Edward, that he immediately stepped into the vacant throne; and his accession was attended with as little opposition and disturbance, as if he had succeeded by the most undoubted hereditary title. The citizens of London were his zealous partizans: The bishops and clergy had adopted his cause: And all the powerful nobility, connected with him by alliance or friendship, willingly seconded his pretensions. The title of Edgar Atheling, was scarcely mentioned: Much less, the claim of the duke of Normandy: And Harold, assembling his partizans, received the crown from their hands, without waiting for the free deliberation of the states, or regularly submitting the question to their determination.[z] If any were averse to this measure, they were obliged to conceal their sentiments; and the new prince, taking a general silence for consent, and founding his title on the supposed suffrages of the peo-

---

[y] Spelm. in verbo *Belliva.*   [z] G. Pict. p. 196. Ypod. Neust. p. 436. Order. Vitalis, p. 492. M. West. p. 221. W. Malm. p. 93. Ingulf, p. 68. Brompton, p. 957. Knyghton, p. 2339. H. Hunt. p. 210. Many of the historians say, that Harold was regularly elected by the states: Some, that Edward left him his successor by will.

CHAPTER III

ple, which appeared unanimous, was, on the day immediately succeeding Edward's death, crowned and anointed King, by Aldred, archbishop of York. The whole nation seemed joyfully to acquiesce in his elevation.

The first symptoms of danger, which the king discovered, came from abroad, and from his own brother, Tosti, who had submitted to a voluntary banishment in Flanders. Enraged at the successful ambition of Harold, to which he himself had fallen a victim, he filled the court of Baldwin with complaints of the injustice, which he had suffered: He engaged the interest of that family against his brother: He endeavoured to form intrigues with some of the discontented nobles in England: He sent his emissaries to Norway, in order to rouze to arms the free-booters of that kingdom and to excite their hopes of reaping advantage from the unsettled state of affairs on the usurpation of the new king: And that he might render the combination more formidable, he made a journey to Normandy; in expectation that the duke, who had married Matilda, another daughter of Baldwin, would, in revenge of his own wrongs, as well as those of Tosti, second, by his counsels and forces, the projected invasion of England.[a]

The duke of Normandy, when he first received intelligence of Harold's intrigues and accession, had been moved to the highest pitch of indignation; but that he might give the better colour to his pretensions, he sent an embassy to England, upbraiding that prince with his breach of faith, and summoning him to resign immediately possession of the kingdom. Harold replied to the Norman ambassadors, that the oath, with which he was reproached, had been extorted by the well-grounded fear of violence, and could never, for that reason, be regarded as obligatory: That he had had no commission, either from the late king or the states of England, who alone could dispose of the crown, to make any tender of the succession to the duke of Normandy; and if he, a private person, had assumed so much authority, and had even voluntarily sworn to support the duke's pretensions, the oath was unlawful, and it was his duty to seize the first opportunity of breaking it: That he had obtained the crown by the unanimous suffrages of the people; and should prove himself totally unworthy

[a] Order. Vitalis, p. 492.

of their favour, did he not strenuously maintain those national liberties, with whose protection they had entrusted him: And that the duke, if he made any attempt by force of arms, should experience the power of an united nation, conducted by a prince, who, sensible of the obligations imposed on him by his royal dignity, was determined, that the same moment should put a period to his life and to his government.[b]

This answer was no other than William expected; and he had previously fixed his resolution of making an attempt upon England. Consulting only his courage, his resentment, and his ambition, he overlooked all the difficulties, inseparable from an attack on a great kingdom by such inferior force, and he saw only the circumstances, which would facilitate his enterprize. He considered, that England, ever since the accession of Canute, had enjoyed profound tranquillity, during a period of near fifty years; and it would require time for its soldiers, enervated by long peace, to learn discipline, and its generals experience. He knew, that it was entirely unprovided with fortified towns, by which it could prolong the war; but must venture its whole fortune in one decisive action against a veteran enemy, who, being once master of the field, would be in a condition to over-run the kingdom. He saw that Harold, though he had given proofs of vigour and bravery, had newly mounted a throne, which he had acquired by faction, from which he had excluded a very ancient royal family, and which was likely to totter under him by its own instability, much more if shaken by any violent external impulse. And he hoped, that the very circumstance of his crossing the sea, quitting his own country, and leaving himself no hopes of retreat; as it would astonish the enemy by the boldness of the enterprize, would inspirit his soldiers by despair, and rouze them to sustain the reputation of the Norman arms.

The Normans, as they had long been distinguished by valour among all the European nations, had at this time attained to the highest pitch of military glory. Besides acquiring by arms such a noble territory in France, besides defending it against continual attempts of the French monarch and all its neighbours, besides

[b] W. Malm. p. 99. Higden, p. 285. Matth. West. p. 222. De Gest. Angel. incerto auctore, p. 331.

CHAPTER III

exerting many acts of vigour under their present sovereign; they had, about this very time, revived their ancient fame, by the most hazardous exploits, and the most wonderful successes, in the other extremity of Europe. A few Norman adventurers in Italy had acquired such an ascendant, not only over the Italians and Greeks, but the Germans and Saracens, that they expelled those foreigners, procured to themselves ample establishments, and laid the foundation of the opulent kingdom of Naples and Sicily.[c] These enterprizes of men, who were all of them vassals in Normandy, many of them banished for faction and rebellion, excited the ambition of the haughty William; who disdained, after such examples of fortune and valour, to be deterred from making an attack on a neighbouring country, where he could be supported by the whole force of his principality.

The situation also of Europe inspired William with hopes, that, besides his brave Normans, he might employ against England the flower of the military force, which was dispersed in all the neighbouring states. France, Germany, and the Low Countries, by the progress of the feudal institutions, were divided and subdivided into many principalities and baronies; and the possessors, enjoying the civil jurisdiction within themselves, as well as the right of arms, acted, in many respects, as independant sovereigns, and maintained their properties and privileges, less by the authority of laws, than by their own force and valour. A military spirit had universally diffused itself throughout Europe; and the several leaders, whose minds were elevated by their princely situation, greedily embraced the most hazardous enterprizes; and being accustomed to nothing from their infancy but recitals of the success attending wars and battles, they were prompted by a natural ambition to imitate those adventures, which they heard so much celebrated, and which were so much exaggerated by the credulity of the age. United, however loosely, by their duty to one superior lord, and by their connexions with the great body of the community, to which they belonged, they desired to spread their fame each beyond his own district; and in all assemblies, whether instituted for civil deliberations, for military expeditions, or merely for show and entertainment, to outshine each other by the reputation

[c] Gul. Gemet. lib. 7. cap. 30.

of strength and prowess. Hence their genius for chivalry; hence their impatience of peace and tranquillity; and hence their readiness to embark in any dangerous enterprize, how little soever interested in its failure or success.

William, by his power, his courage, and his abilities, had long maintained a pre-eminence among those haughty chieftains; and every one who desired to signalize himself by his address in military exercises, or his valour in action, had been ambitious of acquiring a reputation in the court and in the armies of Normandy. Entertained with that hospitality and courtesy, which distinguished the age, they had formed attachments with the prince, and greedily attended to the prospects of the signal glory and elevation, which he promised them in return for their concurrence in an expedition against England. The more grandeur there appeared in the attempt, the more it suited their romantic spirit: The fame of the intended invasion was already diffused every where: Multitudes crowded to tender to the duke their service, with that of their vassals and retainers:[d] And William found less difficulty in compleating his levies, than in chusing the most veteran forces, and in rejecting the offers of those, who were impatient to acquire fame under so renowned a leader.

Besides these advantages, which William owed to his personal valour and good conduct; he was indebted to fortune for procuring him some assistance, and also for removing many obstacles, which it was natural for him to expect in an undertaking, in which all his neighbours were so deeply interested. Conan, count of Britany, was his mortal enemy: In order to throw a damp upon the duke's enterprize, he chose this conjuncture for reviving his claim to Normandy itself; and he required, that, in case of William's success against England, the possession of that dutchy should devolve to him.[e] But Conan died suddenly after making this demand; and Hoel, his successor, instead of adopting the malignity, or more properly speaking, the prudence of his predecessor, zealously seconded the duke's views, and sent his eldest son, Alain Fergant, to serve under him with a body of five thousand Bretons. The counts of Anjou and of Flanders encouraged their subjects to engage in the expedition; and even the court of France, though it

[d] Gul. Pictavensis, p. 198.   [e] Gul. Gemet. lib. 7. cap. 33.

CHAPTER III

might justly fear the aggrandizement of so dangerous a vassal, pursued not its interests on this occasion with sufficient vigour and resolution. Philip I. the reigning monarch, was a minor; and William, having communicated his project to the council, having desired assistance, and offered to do homage, in case of his success, for the crown of England, was indeed openly ordered to lay aside all thoughts of the enterprize; but the earl of Flanders, his father-in-law, being at the head of the regency, favoured under-hand his levies, and secretly encouraged the adventurous nobility to inlist under the standard of the duke of Normandy.

The emperor, Henry IV. besides openly giving all his vassals permission to embark in this expedition, which so much engaged the attention of Europe, promised his protection to the dutchy of Normandy during the absence of the prince, and thereby enabled him to employ his whole force in the invasion of England.*f* But the most important ally, whom William gained by his negociations, was the pope, who had a mighty influence over the ancient barons, no less devout in their religious principles than valorous in their military enterprizes. The Roman pontiff, after an insensible progress during several ages of darkness and ignorance, began now to lift his head openly above all the princes of Europe; to assume the office of a mediator, or even an arbiter, in the quarrels of the greatest monarchs; to interpose in all secular affairs; and to obtrude his dictates as sovereign laws on his obsequious disciples. It was a sufficient motive to Alexander II. the reigning pope, for embracing William's quarrel, that he alone had made an appeal to his tribunal, and rendered him umpire of the dispute between him and Harold; but there were other advantages, which, that pontiff foresaw, must result from the conquest of England by the Norman arms. That kingdom, though at first converted by Romish missionaries, though it had afterwards advanced some farther steps towards subjection to Rome, maintained still a considerable independance in its ecclesiastical administration; and forming a world within itself, entirely separated from the rest of Europe, it had hitherto proved inaccessible to those exorbitant claims, which supported the grandeur of the papacy. Alexander, therefore, hoped, that the French and Norman barons, if successful in their enter-

f Gul. Pict. p. 198.

prize, might import into that country a more devoted reverence to the holy see, and bring the English churches to a nearer conformity with those of the continent. He declared immediately in favour of William's claim; pronounced Harold a perjured usurper; denounced excommunication against him and his adherents; and the more to encourage the duke of Normandy in his enterprize, he sent him a consecrated banner, and a ring with one of St. Peter's hairs in it.[g] Thus were all the ambition and violence of that invasion covered over safely with the broad mantle of religion.

The greatest difficulty, which William had to encounter in his preparations, arose from his own subjects in Normandy. The states of the dutchy were assembled at Lislebonne; and supplies being demanded for the intended enterprize, which promised so much glory and advantage to their country, there appeared a reluctance in many members, both to grant sums so much beyond the common measure of taxes in that age, and to set a precedent of performing their military service at a distance from their own country. The duke, finding it dangerous to solicit them in a body, conferred separately with the richest individuals in the province; and beginning with those on whose affections he most relied, he gradually engaged all of them to advance the sums demanded. The count of Longueville seconded him in this negociation; as did the count of Mortaigne, Odo bishop of Baieux, and especially William Fitz-Osborne, count of Breteüil, and constable of the dutchy. Every person, when he himself was once engaged, endeavoured to bring over others; and at last the states themselves, after stipulating that this concession should be no precedent, voted, that they would assist their prince to the utmost in his intended enterprize.[h]

William had now assembled a fleet of 3000 vessels, great and small,[i] and had selected an army of 60,000 men from among those numerous supplies, which from every quarter solicited to be received into his service. The camp bore a splendid, yet a martial appearance, from the discipline of the men, the beauty and vigour of the horses, the lustre of the arms, and the accoutrements of both; but above all, from the high names of nobility who engaged under the banners of the duke of Normandy. The most celebrated

[g] Baker, p. 22. edit. 1684. [h] Camden. introd. ad Britann. p. 212. 2d edit. Gibs. Verstegan, p. 173. [i] Gul. Gemet. lib. 7. cap. 34.

CHAPTER III

were Eustace, count of Boulogne, Aimeri de Thouars, Hugh d'Estaples, William d'Evreux, Geoffrey de Rotrou, Roger de Beaumont, William de Warenne, Roger de Montgomery, Hugh de Grantmesnil, Charles Martel, and Geoffrey Giffard.[k] To these bold chieftains William held up the spoils of England as the prize of their valour; and pointing to the opposite shore, called to them, that *there* was the field, on which they must erect trophies to their name, and fix their establishments.

While he was making these mighty preparations, the duke, that he might encrease the number of Harold's enemies, excited the inveterate rancour of Tosti, and encouraged him, in concert with Harold Halfager, king of Norway, to infest the coasts of England. Tosti, having collected about sixty vessels in the ports of Flanders, put to sea; and after committing some depredations on the south and east coasts, he sailed to Northumberland, and was there joined by Halfager, who came over with a great armament of three hundred sail. The combined fleets entered the Humber, and disembarked the troops, who began to extend their depredations on all sides; when Morcar earl of Northumberland, and Edwin earl of Mercia, the king's brother-in-law, having hastily collected some forces, ventured to give them battle. The action ended in the defeat and flight of these two noblemen.

Harold, informed of this defeat, hastened with an army to the protection of his people; and expressed the utmost ardour to show himself worthy of the crown, which had been conferred upon him. This prince, though he was not sensible of the full extent of his danger, from the great combination against him, had employed every art of popularity to acquire the affections of the public; and he gave so many proofs of an equitable and prudent administration, that the English found no reason to repent the choice which they had made of a sovereign. They flocked from all quarters to join his standard; and as soon as he reached the enemy at Standford, he found himself in a condition to give them battle. *September 25.* The action was bloody; but the victory was decisive on the side of Harold, and ended in the total rout of the Norvegians, together with the death of Tosti and Halfager. Even the Norvegian fleet fell into the hands of Harold; who had the generosity to give prince

[k] Ordericus Vitalis, p. 501.

Olave, the son of Halfager, his liberty, and allow him to depart with twenty vessels. But he had scarcely time to rejoice for this victory, when he received intelligence, that the duke of Normandy was landed with a great army in the south of England.

The Norman fleet and army had been assembled, early in the summer, at the mouth of the small river Dive, and all the troops had been instantly embarked; but the winds proved long contrary, and detained them in that harbour. The authority, however, of the duke, the good discipline maintained among the seamen and soldiers, and the great care in supplying them with provisions, had prevented any disorder; when at last the wind became favourable, and enabled them to sail along the coast, till they reached St. Valori. There were, however, several vessels lost in this short passage; and as the wind again proved contrary, the army began to imagine, that heaven had declared against them, and that, notwithstanding the pope's benediction, they were destined to certain destruction. These bold warriors, who despised real dangers, were very subject to the dread of imaginary ones; and many of them began to mutiny, some of them even to desert their colours; when the duke, in order to support their drooping hopes, ordered a procession to be made with the reliques of St. Valori,[l] and prayers to be said for more favourable weather. The wind instantly changed; and as this incident happened on the eve of the feast of St. Michael, the tutelar saint of Normandy, the soldiers, fancying they saw the hand of heaven in all these concurring circumstances, set out with the greatest alacrity: They met with no opposition on their passage: A great fleet, which Harold had assembled, and which had cruized all summer off the Isle of Wight, had been dismissed, on his receiving false intelligence, that William, discouraged by contrary winds and other accidents, had laid aside his preparations. The Norman armament, proceeding in great order, arrived, without any material loss, at Pevensey in Sussex; and the army quietly disembarked. The duke himself, as he leaped on shore, happened to stumble and fall; but had the presence of mind, it is said, to turn the omen to his advantage, by calling aloud, that he had taken possession of the country. And a soldier, run-

---

[l] Higden, p. 285. Order. Vitalis, p. 500. Matth. Paris, edit. Parisis anno 1644. p. 2.

CHAPTER III

ning to a neighbouring cottage, plucked some thatch, which, as if giving him seizine of the kingdom, he presented to his general. The joy and alacrity of William and his whole army was so great, that they were nowise discouraged, even when they heard of Harold's great victory over the Norvegians: They seemed rather to wait with impatience the arrival of the enemy.

The victory of Harold, though great and honourable, had proved in the main prejudicial to his interest and may be regarded as the immediate cause of his ruin. He lost many of his bravest officers and soldiers in the action; and he disgusted the rest, by refusing to distribute the Norvegian spoils among them: A conduct which was little agreeable to his usual generosity of temper; but which his desire of sparing the people, in the war that impended over him from the duke of Normandy, had probably occasioned. He hastened by quick marches to reach this new invader; but though he was reinforced at London and other places with fresh troops, he found himself also weakened by the desertion of his old soldiers, who from fatigue and discontent secretly withdrew from their colours. His brother Gurth, a man of bravery and conduct, began to entertain apprehensions of the event; and remonstrated with the king, that it would be better policy to prolong the war; at least, to spare his own person in the action. He urged to him, that the desperate situation of the duke of Normandy made it requisite for that prince to bring matters to a speedy decision, and put his whole fortune on the issue of a battle; but that the king of England, in his own country, beloved by his subjects, provided with every supply, had more certain and less dangerous means of ensuring to himself the victory: That the Norman troops, elated on the one hand with the highest hopes, and seeing, on the other, no resource in case of a discomfiture, would fight to the last extremity; and being the flower of all the warriors of the continent, must be regarded as formidable to the English: That if their first fire, which is always the most dangerous, were allowed to languish for want of action; if they were harassed with small skirmishes, straitened in provisions, and fatigued with the bad weather and deep roads during the winter-season, which was approaching, they must fall an easy and a bloodless prey to their enemy: That if a general action were delayed, the English, sensible of the imminent danger, to which their properties, as well as liberties, were exposed from those rapacious invaders, would hasten from all quarters to his assistance, and would render his army invincible: That, at least, if he thought it necessary to hazard a battle, he ought not to expose his own person; but reserve, in case of disastrous accidents, some resource to the liberty and independance of the kingdom: And that having once been so unfortunate, as to be constrained to swear, and that upon the holy reliques, to support the pretensions of the duke of Normandy, it were better that the command of the army should be entrusted to another, who, not being bound by those sacred ties, might give the soldiers more assured hopes of a prosperous issue to the combat.

Harold was deaf to all these remonstrances: Elated with his past prosperity, as well as stimulated by his native courage, he resolved to give battle in person; and for that purpose, he drew near to the Normans, who had removed their camp and fleet to Hastings, where they fixed their quarters. He was so confident of success, that he sent a message to the duke, promising him a sum of money, if he would depart the kingdom without effusion of blood: But his offer was rejected with disdain; and William, not to be behind with his enemy in vaunting, sent him a message by some monks, requiring him either to resign the kingdom, or to hold it of him in fealty, or to submit their cause to the arbitration of the pope, or to fight him in single combat. Harold replied, that the God of battles would soon be the arbiter of all their differences.[m]

14th October. The English and Normans now prepared themselves for this important decision; but the aspect of things, on the night before the battle, was very different in the two camps. The English spent the time in riot, and jollity, and disorder; the Normans in silence and in prayer, and in the other functions of their religion.[n] On the morning, the duke called together the most considerable of his commanders, and made them a speech suitable to the occasion. He represented to them, that the event, which they and he had long wished for, was approaching; the whole fortune of the war now depended on their swords, and would be decided in a single action: That never army had greater motives for exerting a vigorous courage, whether they considered the prize which would attend their victory, or the inevitable destruction which must ensue upon their

---

[m] Higden, p. 286.   [n] W. Malm. p. 101. De Gest. Angl. p. 332.

CHAPTER III

discomfiture: That if their martial and veteran bands could once break those raw soldiers, who had rashly dared to approach them, they conquered a kingdom at one blow, and were justly entitled to all its possessions as the reward of their prosperous valour: That, on the contrary, if they remitted in the least their wonted prowess, an enraged enemy hung upon their rear, the sea met them in their retreat, and an ignominious death was the certain punishment of their imprudent cowardice: That by collecting so numerous and brave a host, he had ensured every human means of conquest; and the commander of the enemy, by his criminal conduct, had given him just cause to hope for the favour of the Almighty, in whose hands alone lay the event of wars and battles: And that a perjured usurper, anathematized by the sovereign pontiff, and conscious of his own breach of faith, would be struck with terror on their appearance, and would prognosticate to himself that fate which his multiplied crimes had so justly merited.[o] The duke next divided his army into three lines: The first, led by Montgomery, consisted of archers and light armed infantry. The second, commanded by Martel, was composed of his bravest battalions, heavy armed, and ranged in close order: His cavalry, at whose head he placed himself, formed the third line; and were so disposed, that they stretched beyond the infantry, and flanked each wing of the army.[p] He ordered the signal of battle to be given; and the whole army, moving at once, and singing the hymn or song of Roland, the famous peer of Charlemagne,[q] advanced, in order and with alacrity, towards the enemy.

Harold had seized the advantage of a rising ground, and having likewise drawn some trenches to secure his flanks, he resolved to stand upon the defensive, and to avoid all action with the cavalry, in which he was inferior. The Kentish men were placed in the van; a post which they had always claimed as their due: The Londoners guarded the standard: And the king himself, accompanied by his two valiant brothers, Gurth and Leofwin, dismounting, placed himself at the head of his infantry, and expressed his resolution to conquer or to perish in the action. The first attack of the Normans

---

[o] H. Hunt. p. 363. Brompton, p. 959. Gul. Pict. p. 201. [p] Gul. Pict. 201. Order. Vital. p. 501. [q] W. Malm. p. 101. Higden, p. 286. Matth. West. p. 223. Du Gange's Glossary in verbo *Cantilena Rolandi.*

was desperate, but was received with equal valour by the English; and after a furious combat, which remained long undecided, the former, overcome by the difficulty of the ground, and hard pressed by the enemy, began first to relax their vigour, then to retreat; and confusion was spreading among the ranks; when William, who found himself on the brink of destruction, hastened with a select band, to the relief of his dismayed forces. His presence restored the action; the English were obliged to retire with loss; and the duke ordering his second line to advance, renewed the attack with fresh forces and with redoubled courage. Finding, that the enemy, aided by the advantage of ground, and animated by the example of their prince, still made a vigorous resistance, he tried a stratagem, which was very delicate in its management, but which seemed adviseable in his desperate situation, where, if he gained not a decisive victory, he was totally undone: He commanded his troops to make a hasty retreat, and to allure the enemy from their ground by the appearance of flight. The artifice succeeded against those unexperienced soldiers, who, heated by the action and sanguine in their hopes, precipitately followed the Normans into the plain. William gave orders, that at once the infantry should face about upon their pursuers, and the cavalry make an assault upon their wings, and both of them pursue the advantage, which the surprize and terror of the enemy must give them in that critical and decisive moment. The English were repulsed with great slaughter, and driven back to the hill; where, being rallied by the bravery of Harold, they were able, notwithstanding their loss, to maintain the post and continue the combat. The duke tried the same stratagem a second time with the same success; but even after this double advantage, he still found a great body of the English, who, maintaining themselves in firm array, seemed determined to dispute the victory to the last extremity. He ordered his heavy-armed infantry to make an assault upon them; while his archers, placed behind, should gall the enemy, who were exposed by the situation of the ground, and who were intent in defending themselves against the swords and spears of the assailants. By this disposition he at last prevailed: Harold was slain by an arrow, while he was combating with great bravery at the head of his men: His two brothers shared the same fate: And the English, discouraged by the fall of those princes, gave ground on all sides, and were pur-

CHAPTER III

sued with great slaughter by the victorious Normans. A few troops however of the vanquished had still the courage to turn upon their pursuers; and attacking them in deep and miry ground, obtained some revenge for the slaughter and dishonour of the day. But the appearance of the duke obliged them to seek their safety by flight; and darkness saved them from any farther pursuit by the enemy.

Thus was gained by William, duke of Normandy, the great and decisive victory of Hastings, after a battle which was fought from morning till sunset, and which seemed worthy, by the heroic valour displayed by both armies and by both commanders, to decide the fate of a mighty kingdom. William had three horses killed under him; and there fell near fifteen thousand men on the side of the Normans: The loss was still more considerable on that of the vanquished; besides the death of the king and his two brothers. The dead body of Harold was brought to William, and was generously restored without ransom to his mother. The Norman army left not the field of battle without giving thanks to heaven, in the most solemn manner, for their victory: And the prince, having refreshed his troops, prepared to push to the utmost his advantage against the divided, dismayed, and discomfited English.

APPENDIX I
THE ANGLO-SAXON
GOVERNMENT AND
MANNERS

First Saxon government –
Succession of the Kings – The Wittenagemot –
The aristocracy – The several orders of men –
Courts of Justice – Criminal law – Rules of proof –
Military force – Public revenue –
Value of Money – Manners

THE GOVERNMENT of the Germans, and that of all the northern nations, who established themselves on the ruins of Rome, was always extremely free; and those fierce people, accustomed to independance and enured to arms, were more guided by persuasion than authority, in the submission which they paid to their princes. The military despotism, which had taken place in the Roman empire, and which, previously to the irruption of those conquerors, had sunk the genius of men, and destroyed every noble principle of science and virtue, was unable to resist the vigorous efforts of a free people; and Europe, as from a new epoch, rekindled her ancient spirit, and shook off the base servitude to arbitrary will and authority, under which she had so long laboured. The free constitutions then established, however impaired by the encroachments of succeeding princes, still preserve an air of independance and legal administration, which distinguish

APPENDIX I

the European nations; and if that part of the globe maintain sentiments of liberty, honour, equity, and valour superior to the rest of mankind, it owes these advantages chiefly to the seeds implanted by those generous barbarians.

The Saxons, who subdued Britain, as they enjoyed great liberty in their own country, obstinately retained that invaluable possession in their new settlement; and they imported into this island the same principles of independance, which they had inherited from their ancestors. The chieftains (for such they were, more properly than kings or princes) who commanded them in those military expeditions, still possessed a very limited authority; and as the Saxons exterminated, rather than subdued the ancient inhabitants, they were indeed transplanted into a new territory, but preserved unaltered all their civil and military institutions. The language was pure Saxon; even the names of places, which often remain while the tongue entirely changes, were almost all affixed by the conquerors; the manners and customs were wholly German; and the same picture of a fierce and bold liberty, which is drawn by the masterly pencil of Tacitus, will suit those founders of the English government. The king, so far from being invested with arbitrary power, was only considered as the first among the citizens; his authority depended more on his personal qualities than on his station; he was even so far on a level with the people, that a stated price was fixed for his head, and a legal fine was levied upon his murderer, which, though proportionate to his station, and superior to that paid for the life of a subject, was a sensible mark of his subordination to the community. *First Saxon government.*

It is easy to imagine, that an independant people, so little restrained by law, and cultivated by science, would not be very strict in maintaining a regular succession of their princes. Though they paid great regard to the royal family, and ascribed to it an undisputed superiority, they either had no rule, or none that was steadily observed, in filling the vacant throne; and present convenience, in that emergency, was more attended to than general principles. We are not however to suppose, that the crown was considered as altogether elective; and that a regular plan was traced by the constitution for supplying, by the suffrages of the people, every vacancy made by the demise of the first magistrate. If any king left a son of an age and capacity fit for government, the *Succession of the kings.*

young prince naturally stepped into the throne: If he was a minor, his uncle, or the next prince of the blood, was promoted to the government, and left the sceptre to his posterity: Any sovereign, by taking previous measures with the leading men, had it greatly in his power to appoint his successor: All these changes, and indeed the ordinary administration of government, required the express concurrence; or at least the tacit acquiescence of the people; but possession, however obtained, was extremely apt to secure their obedience, and the idea of any right, which was once excluded, was but feeble and imperfect. This is so much the case in all barbarous monarchies, and occurs so often in the history of the Anglo-Saxons, that we cannot consistently entertain any other notion of their government. The idea of an hereditary succession in authority is so natural to men, and is so much fortified by the usual rule in transmitting private possessions, that it must retain a great influence on every society, which does not exclude it by the refinements of a republican constitution. But as there is a material difference between government and private possessions, and every man is not as much qualified for exercising the one, as for enjoying the other, a people, who are not sensible of the general advantages attending a fixed rule, are apt to make great leaps in the succession, and frequently to pass over the person, who, had he possessed the requisite years and abilities, would have been thought entitled to the sovereignty. Thus, these monarchies are not, strictly speaking, either elective or hereditary; and though the destination of a prince may often be followed in appointing his successor, they can as little be regarded as wholly testamentary. The states by their suffrage may sometimes establish a sovereign; but they more frequently recognize the person, whom they find established: A few great men take the lead; the people, overawed and influenced, acquiesce in the government; and the reigning prince, provided he be of the royal family, passes undisputedly for the legal sovereign.

The Witte-nagemot.   It is confessed, that our knowledge of the Anglo-Saxon history and antiquities is too imperfect to afford us means of determining with certainty all the prerogatives of the crown and privileges of the people, or of giving an exact delineation of that government. It is probable also, that the constitution might be somewhat different in the different kingdoms of the Heptarchy, and that it changed considerably during the course of six centuries, which

APPENDIX I

elapsed from the first invasion of the Saxons till the Norman conquest.[r] But most of these differences and changes, with their causes and effects, are unknown to us: It only appears, that, at all times, and in all the kingdoms, there was a national council, called a Wittenagemot or assembly of the wise men, (for that is the import of the term) whose consent was requisite for enacting laws, and for ratifying the chief acts of public administration. The preambles to all the laws of Ethelbert, Ina, Alfred, Edward the Elder, Athelstan, Edmond, Edgar, Ethelred, and Edward the Confessor; even those to the laws of Canute, though a kind of conqueror, put this matter beyond controversy, and carry proofs every where of a limited and legal government. But who were the constituent members of this Wittenagemot has not been determined with certainty by antiquaries. It is agreed, that the bishops and abbots[s] were an essential part; and it is also evident, from the tenor of those ancient laws, that the Wittenagemot enacted statutes which regulated the ecclesiastical as well as civil government, and that those dangerous principles, by which the church is totally severed from the state, were hitherto unknown to the Anglo-Saxons.[t] It also appears, that the aldermen or governors of counties, who, after the Danish times, were often called earls,[*] were admitted into this council, and gave their consent to the public statutes. But besides the prelates and aldermen, there is also mention of the wites or wise-men, as a component part of the Wittenagemot; but who *these* were, is not so clearly ascertained by the laws or the history of that period. The matter would probably be of difficult discussion, even were it examined impartially; but as our modern parties have chosen to divide on this point, the question has been disputed with the

[r] We know of one change, not inconsiderable in the Saxon constitution. The Saxon Annals, p. 49. inform us, that it was in early times the prerogative of the king to name the dukes, earls, aldermen and sheriffs of the counties. Asser, a contemporary writer, informs us, that Alfred deposed all the ignorant aldermen, and appointed men of more capacity in their place: Yet the laws of Edward the Confessor, § 35. say expressly, that the heretoghs or dukes, and the sheriffs were chosen by the freeholders in the folkmote, a county court, which was assembled once a-year, and where all the freeholders swore allegiance to the king. [s] Sometimes abbesses were admitted; at least, they often sign the king's charters or grants. Spellm. Gloss. in verbo *parliamentum*. [t] Wilkins passim. [*] See note [G] at the end of the volume.

greater obstinacy, and the arguments on both sides have become, on that account, the more captious and deceitful. Our monarchical faction maintain, that these *wites* or *sapientes* were the judges, or men learned in the law: The popular faction assert them to be representatives of the boroughs, or what we now call the commons.

The expressions, employed by all ancient historians in mentioning the Wittenagemot, seem to contradict the latter supposition. The members are almost always called the *principes, satrapae, optimates, magnates, proceres;* terms which seem to suppose an aristocracy, and to exclude the commons. The boroughs also, from the low state of commerce, were so small and so poor, and the inhabitants lived in such dependance on the great men,[u] that it seems nowise probable they would be admitted as a part of the national councils. The commons are well known to have had no share in the governments established by the Franks, Burgundians, and other northern nations; and we may conclude, that the Saxons, who remained longer barbarous and uncivilized than those tribes, would never think of conferring such an extraordinary privilege on trade and industry. The military profession alone was honourable among all those conquerors: The warriors subsisted by their possessions in land: They became considerable by their influence over their vassals, retainers, tenants, and slaves: And it requires strong proof to convince us that they would admit any of a rank so much inferior as the burgesses, to share with them in the legislative authority. Tacitus indeed affirms, that, among the ancient Germans, the consent of all the members of the community was required in every important deliberation; but he speaks not of representatives; and this ancient practice, mentioned by the Roman historian, could only have place in small tribes, where every citizen might without inconvenience be assembled upon any extraordinary emergency. After principalities became extensive; after the difference of property had formed distinctions more important than those which arose from personal strength and valour; we may conclude, that the national assemblies must have been more limited in their number, and composed only of the more considerable citizens.

[u] Brady's treatise of English boroughs, p. 3, 4, 5, & c.

APPENDIX I

But though we must exclude the burgesses or commons from the Saxon Wittenagemot, there is some necessity for supposing, that this assembly consisted of other members than the prelates, abbots, aldermen, and the judges or privy council. For as all these, excepting some of the ecclesiastics,[w] were anciently appointed by the king, had there been no other legislative authority, the royal power had been in a great measure absolute, contrary to the tenor of all the historians, and to the practice of all the northern nations. We may, therefore, conclude, that the more considerable proprietors of land were, without any election, constituent members of the national assembly: There is reason to think, that forty hydes, or between four and five thousand acres, was the estate requisite for entitling the possessor to this honourable privilege. We find a passage in an ancient author,[x] by which it appears, that a person of very noble birth, even one allied to the crown, was not esteemed a *princeps* (the term usually employed by ancient historians when the Wittenagemot is mentioned) till he had acquired a fortune of that amount. Nor need we imagine, that the public council would become disorderly or confused by admitting so great a multitude. The landed property of England was probably in few hands during the Saxon times; at least, during the later part of that period: And as men had hardly any ambition to attend those public councils, there was no danger of the assembly's becoming too numerous for the dispatch of the little business, which was brought before them.

It is certain, that, whatever we may determine concerning the constituent members of the Wittenagemot, in whom, with the king, the legislature resided, the Anglo-Saxon government, in the period preceding the Norman conquest, was become extremely aristocratical: The royal authority was very limited; the people, even if admitted to that assembly, were of little or no weight and consideration. We have hints given us in historians of the great

The Aristocracy.

[w] There is some reason to think, that the bishops were sometimes chosen by the Wittenagemot, and confirmed by the king. Eddius, cap. 2. The abbots in the monasteries of royal foundation were anciently named by the king; though Edgar gave the monks the election, and only reserved to himself the ratification. This destination was afterwards frequently violated; and the abbots as well as bishops were afterwards all appointed by the king; as we learn from Ingulf, a writer contemporary to the conquest.
[x] Hist. Eliensis, lib. 2. cap. 40.

power and riches of particular noblemen: And it could not but happen, after the abolition of the Heptarchy, when the king lived at a distance from the provinces, that those great proprietors, who resided on their estates, would much augment their authority over their vassals and retainers, and over all the inhabitants of the neighbourhood. Hence the immeasurable power assumed by Harold, Godwin, Leofric, Siward, Morcar, Edwin, Edric and Alfric, who controlled the authority of the kings, and rendered themselves quite necessary in the government. The two latter, though detested by the people, on account of their joining a foreign enemy, still preserved their power and influence; and we may therefore conclude, that their authority was founded, not on popularity, but on family rights and possessions. There is one Athelstan, mentioned in the reign of the king of that name, who is called alderman of all England, and is said to be half-king; though the monarch himself was a prince of valour and abilities.[y] And we find, that in the later Saxon times, and in these alone, the great offices went from father to son, and became, in a manner, hereditary in the families.[z]

The circumstances, attending the invasions of the Danes, would also serve much to encrease the power of the principal nobility. Those free-booters made unexpected inroads on all quarters; and there was a necessity, that each county should resist them by its own force, and under the conduct of its own nobility and its own magistrates. For the same reason, that a general war, managed by the united efforts of the whole state, commonly augments the power of the crown; those private wars and inroads turned to the advantage of the aldermen and nobles.

Among that military and turbulent people, so averse to commerce and the arts, and so little enured to industry, justice was commonly very ill administered, and great oppression and violence seem to have prevailed. These disorders would be encreased

[y] Hist. Rames. § 3. p. 387.   [z] Roger Hoveden, giving the reason why William the Conqueror made Cospatric earl of Northumberland, says, *Nam ex materno sanguine attinebat ad eum honor illius comitatus. Erat enim ex matre Algitha, filia Uthredi comitis.* See also Sim. Dun. p. 205. We see in those instances, the same tendency towards rendering offices hereditary, which took place, during a more early period, on the continent; and which had already produced there its full effect.

APPENDIX I

by the exorbitant power of the aristocracy, and would, in their turn, contribute to encrease it. Men, not daring to rely on the guardianship of the laws, were obliged to devote themselves to the service of some chieftain, whose orders they followed even to the disturbance of the government or the injury of their fellow-citizens, and who afforded them in return protection from any insult or injustice by strangers. Hence we find, by the extracts which Dr. Brady has given us from Domesday, that almost all the inhabitants even of towns, had placed themselves under the clientship of some particular nobleman, whose patronage they purchased by annual payments, and whom they were obliged to consider as their sovereign, more than the king himself, or even the legislature.[a] A client, though a freeman, was supposed so much to belong to his patron, that his murderer was obliged by law to pay a fine to the latter, as a compensation for his loss; in like manner as he paid a fine to the master for the murder of his slave.[b] Men, who were of a more considerable rank, but not powerful enough, each to support himself by his own independant authority, entered into formal confederacies with each other, and composed a kind of separate community, which rendered itself formidable to all aggressors. Dr. Hickes has preserved a curious Saxon bond of this kind, which he calls a *Sodalitium,* and which contains many particulars characteristical of the manners and customs of the times.[c] All the associates are there said to be gentlemen of Cambridgeshire; and they swear before the holy reliques to observe their confederacy, and to be faithful to each other: They promise to bury any of the associates who dies, in whatever place he had appointed; to contribute to his funeral charges; and to attend at his interment; and whoever is wanting in this last duty, binds himself to pay a measure of honey. When any of the associates is in danger, and calls for the assistance of his fellows, they promise, besides flying to his succour, to give information to the sheriff; and if he be negligent in protecting the person exposed to danger, they engage to levy a fine of one pound upon him: If the president of the society himself be wanting in this particular, he binds himself to

[a] Brady's treatise of boroughs, 3, 4, 5, & c. The case was the same with the freemen in the country. See pref. to his hist. p. 8, 9, 10, & c.   [b] LL. Edw. Conf. § 8. apud Ingulf.   [c] Dissert. Epist. p. 21.

pay one pound; unless he has the reasonable excuse of sickness, or of duty to his superior. When any of the associates is murdered, they are to exact eight pounds from the murderer; and if he refuse to pay it, they are to prosecute him for the sum at their joint expence. If any of the associates, who happens to be poor, kill a man, the society are to contribute by a certain proportion to pay his fine. A mark a piece, if the fine be 700 shillings; less if the person killed be a clown or ceorle; the half of that sum, again, if he be a Welshman. But where any of the associates kills a man, wilfully and without provocation, he must himself pay the fine. If any of the associates kill any of his fellows, in a like criminal manner, besides paying the usual fine to the relations of the deceased, he must pay eight pounds to the society, or renounce the benefit of it: In which case they bind themselves, under the penalty of one pound, never to eat or drink with him, except in the presence of the king, bishop, or alderman. There are other regulations to protect themselves and their servants from all injuries, to revenge such as are committed, and to prevent their giving abusive language to each other; and the fine, which they engage to pay for this last offence, is a measure of honey.

It is not to be doubted, but a confederacy of this kind must have been a great source of friendship and attachment; when men lived in perpetual danger from enemies, robbers, and oppressors, and received protection chiefly from their personal valour, and from the assistance of their friends or patrons. As animosities were then more violent, connexions were also more intimate, whether voluntary or derived from blood: The most remote degree of propinquity was regarded: An indelible memory of benefits was preserved: Severe vengeance was taken for injuries, both from a point of honour, and as the best means of future security: And the civil union being weak, many private engagements were contracted, in order to supply its place, and to procure men that safety, which the laws and their own innocence were not alone able to insure to them.

On the whole, notwithstanding the seeming liberty or rather licentiousness of the Anglo-Saxons, the great body even of the free citizens, in those ages, really enjoyed much less true liberty, than where the execution of the laws is the most severe, and where subjects are reduced to the strictest subordination and dependance

APPENDIX I

on the civil magistrate. The reason is derived from the excess itself of that liberty. Men must guard themselves at any price against insults and injuries; and where they receive not protection from the laws and magistrate, they will seek it by submission to superiors, and by herding in some private confederacy, which acts under the direction of a powerful leader. And thus all anarchy is the immediate cause of tyranny, if not over the state, at least over many of the individuals.

Security was provided by the Saxon laws to all members of the Wittenagemot, both in going and returning, *except they were notorious thieves and robbers.*

The German Saxons, as the other nations of that continent, were divided into three ranks of men, the noble, the free, and the slaves.[d] This distinction they brought over with them into Britain. *The several orders of men.*

The nobles were called thanes; and were of two kinds, the king's thanes and lesser thanes. The latter seem to have been dependant on the former; and to have received lands, for which they paid rent, services, or attendance in peace and war.[e] We know of no title, which raised any one to the rank of thane, except noble birth and the possession of land. The former was always much regarded by all the German nations even in their most barbarous state; and as the Saxon nobility, having little credit, could scarcely burthen their estates with much debt, and as the commons had little trade or industry by which they could accumulate riches, these two ranks of men, even though they were not separated by positive laws, might remain long distinct, and the noble families continue many ages in opulence and splendor. There were no middle rank of men, that could gradually mix with their superiors, and insensibly procure to themselves honour and distinction. If by any extraordinary accident, a mean person acquired riches, a circumstance so singular made him be known and remarked; he became the object of envy, as well as of indignation, to all the nobles; he would have great difficulty to defend what he had acquired; and he would find it impossible to protect himself from oppression, except by courting the patronage of some great chieftain, and paying a large price for his safety.

There are two statutes among the Saxon laws, which seem

[d] Nithard. hist. lib. 4.   [e] Spelm. Feus and Tenures, p. 40.

HISTORY OF ENGLAND

calculated to confound those different ranks of men; that of Athelstan, by which a merchant, who had made three long sea-voyages
on his own account, was intitled to the quality of thane;[f] and that
of the same prince, by which a ceorle or husbandman, who had
been able to purchase five hydes of land, and had a chapel, a
kitchen, a hall, and a bell, was raised to the same distinction.[g] But
the opportunities were so few, by which a merchant or ceorle could
thus exalt himself above his rank, that the law could never overcome the reigning prejudices; the distinction between noble and
base blood would still be indelible; and the well-born thanes would
entertain the highest contempt for those legal and factitious ones.
Though we are not informed of any of these circumstances by
ancient historians, they are so much founded on the nature of
things, that we may admit them as a necessary and infallible consequence of the situation of the kingdom during those ages.

The cities appear by Domesday-book to have been at the conquest little better than villages.[h] York itself, though it was always
the second, at least the third[i] city in England, and was the capital
of a great province, which never was thoroughly united with the
rest, contained then but 1418 families.[k] Malmesbury tells us[l] that
the great distinction between the Anglo-Saxon nobility and the
French or Norman, was that the latter built magnificent and stately
castles; whereas the former consumed their immense fortunes in
riot and hospitality, and in mean houses. We may thence infer, that
the arts in general were much less advanced in England than in
France; a greater number of idle servants and retainers lived about
the great families; and as these, even in France, were powerful
enough to disturb the execution of the laws, we may judge of the
authority, acquired by the aristocracy in England. When earl Godwin besieged the Confessor in London, he summoned from all

[f] Wilkins, p. 71.   [g] Selden, Titles of honour, p. 515. Wilkins, p. 70.
[h] Winchester, being the capital of the West Saxon monarchy, was anciently
a considerable city. Gul. Pict. p. 210.   [i] Norwich contained 738 houses,
Exeter, 315, Ipswich, 538, Northampton, 60, Hertford, 146, Canterbury,
262, Bath, 64, Southampton, 84, Warwick, 225. See Brady of Boroughs,
p. 3, 4, 5, 6, & c. These are the most considerable he mentions. The account
of them is extracted from Domesday-book.   [k] Brady's treatise of boroughs, p. 10. There were six wards, besides the archbishop's palace; and
five of these wards contained the number of families here mentioned,
which at the rate of five persons to a family makes about 7000 souls. The
sixth ward was laid waste.   [l] P. 102. See also de Gest. Angl. p. 333.

parts his huscarles, or houseceorles and retainers, and thereby constrained his sovereign to accept of the conditions, which he was pleased to impose upon him.

The lower rank of freemen were denominated ceorles among the Anglo-Saxons; and where they were industrious, they were chiefly employed in husbandry: Whence a ceorle, and a husbandman, became in a manner synonimous terms. They cultivated the farms of the nobility or thanes for which they paid rent: and they seem to have been removeable at pleasure. For there is little mention of leases among the Anglo-Saxons: The pride of the nobility, together with the general ignorance of writing, must have rendered those contracts very rare, and must have kept the husbandmen in a dependant condition. The rents of farms were then chiefly paid in kind.[m]

But the most numerous rank by far in the community seems to have been the slaves or villains, who were the property of their lords, and were consequently incapable, themselves, of possessing any property. Dr. Brady assures us, from a survey of Domesday-book,[n] that, in all the counties of England, the far greater part of the land was occupied by them, and that the husbandmen, and still more the socmen, who were tenants that could not be removed at pleasure, were very few in comparison. This was not the case with the German nations, as far as we can collect from the account given us by Tacitus. The perpetual wars in the Heptarchy, and the depredations of the Danes, seem to have been the cause of this great alteration with the Anglo-Saxons. Prisoners taken in battle, or carried off in the frequent inroads, were then reduced to slavery; and became, by right of war,[o] entirely at the disposal of their lords. Great property in the nobles, especially if joined to an irregular administration of justice, naturally favours the power of the aristocracy; but still more so, if the practice of slavery be admitted, and has become very common. The nobility not only possess the influence which always attends riches, but also the power which the laws give them over their slaves and villains. It then becomes difficult, and almost impossible, for a private man to remain altogether free and independant.

---

[m] LL. Inae, § 70. These laws fixed the rents for a hyde; but it is difficult to convert it into modern measures.   [n] General preface to his hist. p. 7, 8, 9, & c.   [o] LL. Edg. § 14. apud Spellm. Conc. vol. i. p. 471.

HISTORY OF ENGLAND

There were two kinds of slaves among the Anglo-Saxons; household slaves, after the manner of the ancients, and praedial or rustic, after the manner of the Germans.[p] These latter resembled the serfs, which are at present to be met with in Poland, Denmark, and some parts of Germany. The power of a master over his slaves was not unlimited among the Anglo-Saxons, as it was among their ancestors. If a man beat out his slave's eye or teeth, the slave recovered his liberty:[q] If he killed him, he paid a fine to the king; provided the slave died within a day after the wound or blow: Otherwise it passed unpunished.[r] The selling of themselves or children to slavery was always the practice among the German nations,[s] and was continued by the Anglo-Saxons.[t]

The great lords and abbots among the Anglo-Saxons possessed a criminal jurisdiction within their territories and could punish without appeal any thieves or robbers whom they caught there.[u] This institution must have had a very contrary effect to that which was intended, and must have procured robbers a sure protection on the lands of such noblemen as did not sincerely mean to discourage crimes and violence.

Courts of justice. But though the general strain of the Anglo-Saxon government seems to have become aristocratical, there were still considerable remains of the ancient democracy, which were not indeed sufficient to protect the lowest of the people, without the patronage of some great lord, but might give security, and even some degree of dignity, to the gentry or inferior nobility. The administration of justice, in particular, by the courts of the Decennary, the Hundred, and the County, was well calculated to defend general liberty, and to restrain the power of the nobles. In the county courts or shire-motes, all the freeholders were assembled twice a-year, and received appeals from the inferior courts. They there decided all causes, ecclesiastical as well as civil; and the bishop, together with the alderman or earl, presided over them.[w] The affair was determined in a summary manner, without much pleading, formality, or delay, by a majority of voices; and the bishop and alderman had

---

[p] Spellm. Gloss. in verb. *Servus.*   [q] LL. Aelf. § 20.   [r] Ibid. § 17.   [s] Tacit. de morib. Germ.   [t] LL. Inae, § 11. LL. Aelf. § 12.   [u] Higden, lib. 1. cap. 50. LL. Edw. Conf. § 26. Spellm. Conc. vol. i. p. 415. Gloss. in verb. *Haligemot et Infangenthefe.*   [w] LL. Edg. § 5. Wilkins, p. 78. LL. Canut. § 17. Wilkins, p. 136.

APPENDIX I

no further authority than to keep order among the freeholders, and interpose with their opinion.[x] Where justice was denied during three sessions by the Hundred, and then by the County court, there lay an appeal to the king's court;[y] but this was not practised on slight occasions. The aldermen received a third of the fines levied in those courts;[z] and as most of the punishments were then pecuniary, this perquisite formed a considerable part of the profits belonging to his office. The two thirds also, which went to the king, made no contemptible part of the public revenue. Any freeholder was fined who absented himself thrice from these courts.[a]

As the extreme ignorance of the age made deeds and writings very rare, the County or Hundred court was the place where the most remarkable civil transactions were finished, in order to preserve the memory of them, and prevent all future disputes. Here testaments were promulgated, slaves manumitted, bargains of sale concluded; and sometimes, for greater security, the most considerable of these deeds were inserted in the blank leaves of the parish Bible, which thus became a kind of register, too sacred to be falsified. It was not unusual to add to the deed an imprecation on all such as should be guilty of that crime.[b]

Among a people, who lived in so simple a manner as the Anglo-Saxons, the judicial power is always of greater importance than the legislative. There were few or no taxes imposed by the states: There were few statutes enacted; and the nation was less governed by laws, than by customs, which admitted a great latitude of interpretation. Though it should, therefore, be allowed, that the Wittenagemot was altogether composed of the principal nobility, the county-courts, where all the free-holders were admitted, and which regulated all the daily occurrences of life, formed a wide basis for the government, and were no contemptible checks on the aristocracy. But there is another power still more important than either the judicial or legislative; to wit, the power of injuring or serving by immediate force and violence, for which it is difficult to obtain redress in courts of justice. In all extensive governments, where the execution of the laws is feeble, this power naturally falls into the hands of the principal nobility; and the degree of it which

[x] Hickes Dissert. Epist. p. 2, 3, 4, 5, 6, 7, 8.   [y] LL. Edg. § 2. Wilkins, p. 77. LL. Canut. § 18. apud Wilkins, p. 136.   [z] LL. Edw. Conf. § 31.   [a] LL. Ethelst. § 20.   [b] Hickes Dissert. Epist.

prevails, cannot be determined so much by the public statutes, as by small incidents in history, by particular customs, and sometimes by the reason and nature of things. The Highlands of Scotland have long been entitled by law to every privilege of British subjects; but it was not till very lately that the common people could in fact enjoy these privileges.

The powers of all the members of the Anglo-Saxon government are disputed among historians and antiquaries: The extreme obscurity of the subject, even though faction had never entered into the question, would naturally have begotten those controversies. But the great influence of the lords over their slaves and tenants, the clientship of the burghers, the total want of a middling rank of men, the extent of the monarchy, the loose execution of the laws, the continued disorders and convulsions of the state; all these circumstances evince, that the Anglo-Saxon government became at last extremely aristocratical; and the events, during the period immediately preceding the conquest, confirm this inference or conjecture.

Criminal law. Both the punishments inflicted by the Anglo-Saxon courts of judicature, and the methods of proof employed in all causes, appear somewhat singular, and are very different from those which prevail at present among all civilized nations.

We must conceive, that the ancient Germans were little removed from the original state of nature: The social confederacy among them was more martial than civil: They had chiefly in view the means of attack or defence against public enemies, not those of protection against their fellow-citizens: Their possessions were so slender and so equal, that they were not exposed to great danger; and the natural bravery of the people made every man trust to himself and to his particular friends for his defence or vengeance. This defect in the political union drew much closer the knot of particular confederacies: An insult upon any man was regarded by all his relations and associates as a common injury: They were bound by honour, as well as by a sense of common interest, to revenge his death, or any violence which he had suffered: They retaliated on the aggressor by like acts of violence; and if he were protected, as was natural and usual, by his own clan, the quarrel was spread still wider, and bred endless disorders in the nation.

APPENDIX I

The Frisians, a tribe of the Germans, had never advanced beyond this wild and imperfect state of society; and the right of private revenge still remained among them unlimited and uncontrouled.[c] But the other German nations, in the age of Tacitus, had made one step farther towards completing the political or civil union. Though it still continued to be an indispensable point of honour for every clan to revenge the death or injury of a member, the magistrate had acquired a right of interposing in the quarrel, and of accommodating the difference. He obliged the person maimed or injured, and the relations of one killed, to accept of a present from the aggressor and his relations,[d] as a compensation for the injury,[e] and to drop all farther prosecution of revenge. That the accommodation of one quarrel might not be the source of more, this present was fixed and certain, according to the rank of the person killed or injured, and was commonly paid in cattle, the chief property of those rude and uncultivated nations. A present of this kind gratified the revenge of the injured family by the loss which the aggressor suffered: It satisfied their pride by the submission which it expressed: It diminished their regret for the loss or injury of a kinsman by their acquisition of new property, and thus general peace was for a moment restored to the society.[f]

But when the German nations had been settled some time in the provinces of the Roman empire, they made still another step towards a more cultivated life, and their criminal justice gradually improved and refined itself. The magistrate, whose office it was to guard public peace and to suppress private animosities, conceived himself to be injured by every injury done to any of his people; and besides the compensation to the person who suffered, or to his family, he thought himself entitled to exact a fine, called the Fridwit, as an atonement for the breach of peace, and as reward for the pains which he had taken in accommodating the quarrel. When this idea, which is so natural, was once suggested, it was willingly received both by sovereign and people. The numerous fines which were levied, augmented the revenue of the king: And the people were sensible, that he would be more vigilant in interposing with

---

[c] LL. Fris. tit. 2. apud Lindenbrog. p. 491.   [d] LL. Aethelb. § 23. LL. Aelf. § 27.   [e] Called by the Saxons *maegbota*.   [f] Tacit de morib. Germ. The author says, that the price of the composition was fixed; which must have been by the laws and the interposition of the magistrates.

his good offices, when he reaped such immediate advantage from them; and that injuries would be less frequent, when, besides compensation to the person injured, they were exposed to this additional penalty.[g]

This short abstract contains the history of the criminal jurisprudence of the northern nations for several centuries. The state of England in this particular, during the period of the Anglo-Saxons, may be judged of by the collection of ancient laws, published by Lambard and Wilkins. The chief purport of these laws is not to prevent or entirely suppress private quarrels, which the legislator knew to be impossible, but only to regulate and moderate them. The laws of Alfred enjoin, that, if any one know, that his enemy or aggressor, after doing him an injury, resolves to keep within his own house *and his own lands,*[h] he shall not fight him, till he require compensation for the injury. If he be strong enough to besiege him in his house, he may do it for seven days without attacking him; and if the aggressor be willing, during that time, to surrender himself and his arms, his adversary must detain him thirty days, but is afterwards obliged to restore him safe to his kindred, *and be content with the compensation.* If the criminal fly to the temple, that sanctuary must not be violated. Where the assailant has not force sufficient to besiege the criminal in his house, he must apply to the alderman for assistance; and if the alderman refuse aid, the assailant must have recourse to the king: And he is not allowed to assault the house, till after this supreme magistrate has refused assistance. If any one meet with his enemy, and be ignorant that he was resolved to keep within his own lands, he must, before he attack him, require him to surrender himself prisoner, and deliver up his arms; in which case he may detain him thirty days: But if he refuse to deliver up his arms, it is then lawful to fight him. A slave may fight in his master's quarrel: A father may fight in his son's with any one, except with his master.[i]

It was enacted by king Ina, that no man should take revenge for

---

[g] Besides paying money to the relations of the deceased and to the king, the murderer was also obliged to pay the master of a slave or vassal a sum as a compensation for his loss. This was called the *Manbote.* See Spell. Gloss. in verb. *Fredum, Manbot.*   [h] The addition of these last words in Italics appears necessary from what follows in the same law.   [i] LL. Aelfr. § 28. Wilkins, p. 43.

an injury till he had first demanded compensation, and had been refused it.[k]

King Edmond, in the preamble to his laws, mentions the general misery, occasioned by the multiplicity of private feuds and battles; and he establishes several expedients for remedying this grievance. He ordains, that, if any one commit murder, he may, with the assistance of his kindred, pay within a twelvemonth the fine of his crime, and if they abandon him, he shall alone sustain the deadly feud or quarrel with the kindred of the murdered person. His own kindred are free from the feud, but on condition that they neither converse with the criminal, nor supply him with meat *or other necessaries:* If any of them, after renouncing him, receive him into their house, *or give him assistance,* they are finable to the king, and are involved in the feud. If the kindred of the murdered person take revenge on any but the criminal himself, *after he is abandoned by his kindred,* all their property is forfeited, and they are declared to be enemies to the king and all his friends.[l] It is also ordained, that the fine for murder shall never be remitted by the king,[m] and that no criminal shall be killed who flies to the church, or any of the king's towns;[n] and the king himself declares, that his house shall give no protection to murderers, till they have satisfied the church by their pennance, and the kindred of the deceased, by making compensation.[o] The method appointed for transacting this composition is found in the same law.[p]

These attempts of Edmond, to contract and diminish the feuds, were contrary to the ancient spirit of the northern barbarians, and were a step towards a more regular administration of justice. By the Salic law, any man might, by a public declaration, exempt himself from his family quarrels: But then he was considered by the law as no longer belonging to the family; and he was deprived of all right of succession, as the punishment of his cowardice.[q]

The price of the king's head, or his weregild, as it was then called, was by law 30,000 thrimsas, near 1300 pounds of present money. The price of the prince's head was 15,000 thrimsas; that of a bishop's or alderman's 8000; a sheriff's 4000; a thane's or clergyman's 2000; a ceorle's 266. These prices were fixed by the laws

---

[k] LL. Inae, § 9.   [l] LL. Edm. § 1. Wilkins, p. 73.   [m] LL. Edm. § 3.   [n] LL. Edm. § 2.   [o] LL. Edm. § 4.   [p] LL. Edm. § 7.   [q] Tit. 63.

of the Angles. By the Mercian law, the price of a ceorle's head was 200 shillings; that of a thane's six times as much; that of a king's six times more.[r] By the laws of Kent, the price of the archbishop's head was higher than that of the king's.[s] Such respect was then paid to the ecclesiastics! It must be understood, that, where a person was unable or unwilling to pay the fine, he was put out of the protection of law and the kindred of the deceased had liberty to punish him as they thought proper.

Some antiquaries[t] have thought, that these compensations were only given for man-slaughter, not for wilful murder: But no such distinction appears in the laws; and it is contradicted by the practice of all the other barbarous nations,[u] by that of the ancient Germans,[w] and by that curious monument above mentioned of Saxon antiquity, preserved by Hickes. There is indeed a law of Alfred's which makes wilful murder capital;[x] but this seems only to have been an attempt of that great legislator towards establishing a better police in the kingdom, and it probably remained without execution. By the laws of the same prince, a conspiracy against the life of the king might be redeemed by a fine.[y]

The price of all kinds of wounds was likewise fixed by the Saxon laws: A wound of an inch long under the hair was paid with one shilling: One of a like size in the face, two shillings: Thirty shillings for the loss of an ear; and so forth.[z] There seems not to have been any difference made, according to the dignity of the person. By the laws of Ethelbert, any one who committed adultery with his neighbour's wife was obliged to pay him a fine, and buy him another wife.[a]

These institutions are not peculiar to the ancient Germans. They seem to be the necessary progress of criminal jurisprudence among every free people, where the will of the sovereign is not implicitly obeyed. We find them among the ancient Greeks during the time of the Trojan war. Compositions for murder are mentioned in Nestor's speech to Achilles in the ninth Iliad, and are

---

[r] Wilkins, p. 71, 72. [s] LL. Elthredi, apud Wilkins, p. 110. [t] Tyrrel introduct. vol. i. p. 126. Carte, vol. i. p. 366. [u] Lindenbrogius, passim. [w] Tac. de mor. Germ. [x] LL. Aelf. § 12. Wilkins, p. 29. It is probable, that by wilful murder Alfred means a treacherous murder, committed by one who has no declared feud with another. [y] LL. Aelf. § 4. Wilkins, p. 35. [z] LL. Aelf. § 40. See also LL. Ethelb. § 34, & c. [a] LL. Ethelb. § 32.

APPENDIX I

called απoιvαι. The Irish, who never had any connections with the German nations, adopted the same practice till very lately; and the price of a man's head was called among them his *eric;* as we learn from Sir John Davis. The same custom seems also to have prevailed among the Jews.[b]

Theft and robbery were frequent among the Anglo-Saxons. In order to impose some check upon these crimes, it was ordained, that no man should sell or buy any thing above twenty pence value, except in open market;[c] and every bargain of sale must be executed before witnesses.[d] Gangs of robbers much disturbed the peace of the country; and the law determined, that a tribe of banditti, consisting of between seven and thirty-five persons, was to be called a *turma,* or troop: Any greater company was denominated an army.[e] The punishments for this crime were various, but none of them capital.[f] If any man could track his stolen cattle into another's ground, the latter was obliged to show the tracks out of it, or pay their value.[g]

Rebellion, to whatever excess it was carried, was not capital, but might be redeemed by a sum of money.[h] The legislators, knowing it impossible to prevent all disorders, only imposed a higher fine on breaches of the peace committed in the king's court, or before an alderman or bishop. An alehouse too seems to have been considered as a privileged place; and any quarrels that arose there were more severely punished than elsewhere.[i]

If the manner of punishing crimes among the Anglo-Saxons appear singular, the proofs were not less so; and were also the natural result of the situation of those people. Whatever we may imagine concerning the usual truth and sincerity of men, who live in a rude and barbarous state, there is much more falsehood, and even perjury among them, than among civilized nations: Virtue, which is nothing but a more enlarged and more cultivated reason, never flourishes to any degree, nor is founded on steady principles of honour, except where a good education becomes general; and

Rules of proof.

[b] Exod. cap. xxi. 29, 30.   [c] LL. Aethelst. § 12.   [d] LL. Aethelst. § 10, 12. LL. Edg. apud Wilkins, p. 80. LL. Ethelredi, § 4 apud Wilkins, p. 103. Hloth. & Eadm. § 16. LL. Canut. § 22.   [e] LL. Inae, § 12.   [f] LL. Inae, § 37.   [g] LL. Aethelst. § 2. Wilkins, p. 63.   [h] LL. Ethelredi, apud Wilkins, p. 110. LL. Aelf. § 4. Wilkins, p. 35.   [i] LL. Hloth. & Eadm. § 12, 13. LL. Ethelr. apud Wilkins, p. 117.

where men are taught the pernicious consequences of vice, treachery, and immorality. Even superstition, though more prevalent among ignorant nations, is but a poor supply for the defects in knowledge and education: Our European ancestors, who employed every moment the expedient of swearing on extraordinary crosses and reliques, were less honourable in all engagements than their posterity, who from experience have omitted those ineffectual securities. This general proneness to perjury was much encreased by the usual want of discernment in judges, who could not discuss an intricate evidence, and were obliged to number, not weigh, the testimony of the witnesses.[k] Hence the ridiculous practice of obliging men to bring compurgators, who, as they did not pretend to know any thing of the fact, expressed upon oath, that they believed the person spoke true; and these compurgators were in some cases multiplied to the number of three hundred.[l] The practice also of single combat was employed by most nations on the continent as a remedy against false evidence;[m] and though it was frequently dropped, from the opposition of the clergy, it was continually revived, from experience of the falsehood attending the testimony of witnesses.[n] It became at last a species of jurisprudence: The cases were determined by law, in which the party might challenge his adversary, or the witnesses, or the judge himself:[o] And though these customs were absurd, they were rather an improvement on the methods of trial, which had formerly been practised among those barbarous nations, and which still prevailed among the Anglo-Saxons.

When any controversy about a fact became too intricate for those ignorant judges to unravel, they had recourse to what they called the judgment of God, that is, to fortune: Their methods of consulting this oracle were various. One of them was the decision by the cross: It was practised in this manner. When a person was accused of any crime, he first cleared himself by oath, and he was

---

[k] Sometimes the laws fixed easy general rules for weighing the credibility of witnesses. A man whose life was estimated at 120 shillings counterbalanced six ceorles, each of whose lives was only valued at twenty shillings, and his oath was esteemed equivalent to that of all the six. See Wilkins, p. 72. [l] Praef. Nicol. ad Wilkins, p. 11. [m] LL. Burgund. cap. 45. LL. Lomb. lib. 2. tit. 55. cap. 34. [n] LL. Longob. lib. 2. tit. 55. cap. 23. apud Lindenb. p. 661. [o] See Desfontaines and Beaumanoir.

APPENDIX I

attended by eleven compurgators. He next took two pieces of wood, one of which was marked with the sign of the cross; and wrapping both up in wool, he placed them on the altar, or on some celebrated relique. After solemn prayers for the success of the experiment, a priest, or in his stead some unexperienced youth, took up one of the pieces of wood, and if he happened upon that which was marked with the figure of the cross, the person was pronounced innocent; if otherwise, guilty.[p] This practice, as it arose from superstition, was abolished by it in France. The emperor, Lewis the Debonnaire, prohibited that method of trial, not because it was uncertain, but lest that sacred figure, says he, of the cross should be prostituted in common disputes and controversies.[q]

The ordeal was another established method of trial among the Anglo-Saxons. It was practised either by boiling water or red-hot iron. The former was appropriated to the common people; the latter to the nobility. The water or iron was consecrated by many prayers, masses, fastings, and exorcisms;[r] after which, the person accused either took up a stone sunk in the water[s] to a certain depth, or carried the iron to a certain distance; and his hand being wrapped up, and the covering sealed for three days, if there appeared, on examining it, no marks of burning, he was pronounced innocent; if otherwise, guilty.[t] The trial by cold water was different: The person was thrown into consecrated water; if he swam, he was guilty; if he sunk, innocent.[u] It is difficult for us to conceive, how any innocent person could ever escape by the one trial, or any criminal be convicted by the other. But there was another usage admirably calculated for allowing every criminal to escape, who had confidence enough to try it. A consecrated cake, called a corsned, was produced; which if the person could swallow and digest, he was pronounced innocent.[w]

The feudal law, if it had place at all among the Anglo-Saxons, which is doubtful, was not certainly extended over all the landed property, and was not attended with those consequences of hom-

Military force.

---

[p] LL. Frison. tit. 14. apud Lindenbrogium, p. 496.   [q] Du Cange in verb. Crux.   [r] Spellm. in verb. Ordeal. Parker, p. 155. Lindenbrog, p. 1299.   [s] LL. Inae, § 77.   [t] Sometimes the person accused walked barefoot over red hot iron.   [u] Spellman in verb. Ordealium.   [w] Spellm. in verb. Corsned. Parker, p. 156. Text. Roffens. p. 33.

age, reliefs,[x] wardship, marriage, and other burthens, which were inseparable from it in the kingdoms of the continent. As the Saxons expelled or almost entirely destroyed the ancient Britons, they planted themselves in this island on the same footing with their ancestors in Germany, and found no occasion for the feudal institutions,[y] which were calculated to maintain a kind of standing army, always in readiness to suppress any insurrection among the conquered people. The trouble and expence of defending the state in England lay equally upon all the land; and it was usual for every five hides to equip a man for the service. The *trinoda necessitas*, as it was called, or the burthen of military expeditions, of repairing highways, and of building and supporting bridges, was inseparable from landed property, even though it belonged to the church or monasteries, unless exempted by a particular charter.[z] The ceorles or husbandmen were provided with arms, and were obliged to take their turn in military duty.[a] There were computed to be 243,600 hides in England;[b] consequently the ordinary military force of the kingdom consisted of 48,720 men; though, no doubt, on extraordinary occasions, a greater number might be assembled. The king and nobility had some military tenants, who were called Sithcun-men.[c] And there were some lands annexed to the office of aldermen, and to other offices; but these probably were not of great extent, and were possessed only during pleasure, as in the commencement of the feudal law in other countries of Europe.

Public revenue. The revenue of the king seems to have consisted chiefly in his demesnes, which were large; and in the tolls and imposts which he probably levied at discretion on the boroughs and sea-ports, that lay within his demesnes. He could not alienate any part of the crown lands, even to religious uses, without the consent of the states.[d] Danegelt was a land-tax of a shilling a hide, imposed by the

---

[x] On the death of an alderman, a greater or lesser thane, there was a payment made to the king of his best arms; and this was called his heriot: But this was not of the nature of a relief. See Spellm. of tenures, p. 2. The value of this heriot was fixed by Canute's laws, § 69.   [y] Bracton de Acqu. rer. domin. lib. 2. cap. 16. See more fully Spellman of feuds and tenures, and Craigius de jure feud. lib. 1. dieg. 7.   [z] Spellm. Conc. vol. i. p. 256.   [a] Inae, § 51.   [b] Spellm. of feuds and tenures, p. 17.   [c] Spellm. Conc. vol. i. p. 195.   [d] Spellm. Conc. vol. i. p. 340.

183

APPENDIX I

states,[e] either for payment of the sums exacted by the Danes, or for putting the kingdom in a posture of defence against those invaders.[f]

The Saxon pound, as likewise that which was coined for some centuries after the conquest, was near three times the weight of our present money: There were forty-eight shillings in the pound, and five pence in a shilling,[g] consequently a Saxon shilling was near a fifth heavier than ours, and a Saxon penny near three times as heavy.[h] As to the value of money in those times, compared to commodities, there are some, though not very certain, means of computation. A sheep by the laws of Athelstan was estimated at a shilling; that is, fifteen-pence of our money. The fleece was two-fifths of the value of the whole sheep;[i] much above its present estimation; and the reason probably was, that the Saxons, like the ancients, were little acquainted with any clothing but what was made of wool. Silk and cotton were quite unknown: Linen was not much used. An ox was computed at six times the value of a sheep; a cow at four.[k] If we suppose, that the cattle in that age, from the defects in husbandry, were not so large as they are at present in England, we may compute, that money was then near ten times of greater value. A horse was valued at about thirty-six shillings of our money, or thirty Saxon shillings;[l] a mare a third less. A man at three pounds.[m] The board-wages of a child the first year was eight shillings, together with a cow's pasture in summer, and an ox's in winter.[n] William of Malmesbury mentions it as a remarkably high price that William Rufus gave fifteen marks for a horse, or about thirty pounds of our present money.[o] Between the years 900 and 1000, Ednoth bought a hide of land for about 118 shillings of present money.[p] This was little more than a shilling an acre, which indeed appears to have been the usual price, as we may learn from other accounts.[q] A palfrey was sold for twelve shillings about the year 966.[r] The value of an ox in king Ethelred's time was between seven and eight shillings; a cow about six shillings.[s] Gervas of Tilbury says, that in Henry I.'s time, bread which would suffice a

Value of money.

[e] Chron. Sax. p. 128.   [f] LL. Edw. Con. § 12.   [g] LL. Aelf. § 40.
[h] Fleetwood's Chron. Pretiosum, p. 27, 28, & c.   [i] LL. Inae, § 69.
[k] Wilkins, p. 66.   [l] Ibid. p. 126.   [m] Ibid.   [n] LL. Inae, § 38.   [o] P. 121.
[p] Hist. Rames. p. 415.   [q] Hist. Eliens. p. 473.   [r] Hist. Eliens. p. 471.
[s] Wilkins, p. 126.

hundred men for a day was rated at three shillings, or a shilling of that age; for it is thought that soon after the conquest a pound sterling was divided into twenty shillings: A sheep was rated at a shilling, and so of other things in proportion. In Athelstan's time a ram was valued at a shilling, or four-pence Saxon.[t] The tenants of Shireburn were obliged, at their choice, to pay either sixpence or four hens.[u] About 1232, the abbot of St. Albans, going on a journey, hired seven handsome stout horses; and agreed, if any of them died on the road, to pay the owner 30 shillings a piece of our present money.[w] It is to be remarked, that in all ancient times, the raising of corn, especially wheat, being a species of manufactory, that commodity always bore a higher price, compared to cattle, than it does in our times.[x] The Saxon Chronicle tells us,[y] that in the reign of Edward the Confessor there was the most terrible famine ever known; in so much that a quarter of wheat rose to sixty pennies, or fifteen shillings of our present money. Consequently it was as dear as if it now cost seven pounds ten shillings. This much exceeds the great famine in the end of queen Elizabeth; when a quarter of wheat was sold for four pounds. Money in this last period was nearly of the same value as in our time. These severe famines are a certain proof of bad husbandry.

On the whole, there are three things to be considered, wherever a sum of money is mentioned in ancient times. First the change of denomination, by which a pound has been reduced to the third part of its ancient weight in silver. Secondly, the change in value by the greater plenty of money, which has reduced the same weight of silver to ten times less value, compared to commodities; and consequently a pound sterling to the thirtieth part of the ancient value. Thirdly, the fewer people and less industry, which were then to be found in every European kingdom. This circumstance made even the thirtieth part of the sum more difficult to levy, and caused any sum to have more than thirty times greater weight and influence both abroad and at home, than in our times; in the same manner that a sum, a hundred thousand pounds for instance, is at present more difficult to levy in a small state, such as Bavaria, and can produce greater effects on such a small com-

[t] Wilkins, p. 56. [u] Monast. Anglic. vol. ii. p. 528. [w] Mat. Paris.
[x] Fleetwood, p. 83, 94, 96, 98. [y] P. 157.

APPENDIX I

munity, than on England. This last difference is not easy to be calculated: But allowing, that England has now six times more industry, and three times more people than it had at the conquest and for some reigns after that period, we are, upon that supposition, to conceive taking all circumstances together, every sum of money mentioned by historians, as if it were multiplied more than a hundred fold above a sum of the same denomination at present.

In the Saxon times, land was divided equally among all the male-children of the deceased, according to the custom of Gavelkind. The practice of entails is to be found in those times.[z] Land was chiefly of two kinds, bookland, or land held by book or charter, which was regarded as full property, and defended to the heirs of the possessor, and folkland, or the land held by the ceorles and common people, who were removeable at pleasure, and were indeed only tenants during the will of their lords.

The first attempt, which we find in England to separate the ecclesiastical from the civil jurisdiction, was that law of Edgar, by which all disputes among the clergy were ordered to be carried before the bishop.[a] The pennances were then very severe; but as a man could buy them off with money, or might substitute others to perform them, they lay easy upon the rich.[b]

With regard to the manners of the Anglo-Saxons we can say *Manners.* little, but that they were in general a rude, uncultivated people, ignorant of letters, unskilled in the mechanical arts, untamed to submission under law and government, addicted to intemperance, riot, and disorder. Their best quality was their military courage, which yet was not supported by discipline or conduct. Their want of fidelity to the prince, or to any trust reposed in them, appears strongly in the history of their later period; and their want of humanity in all their history. Even the Norman historians, notwithstanding the low state of the arts in their own country, speak of them as barbarians, when they mention the invasion made upon them by the duke of Normandy.[c] The conquest put the people in a situation of receiving slowly, from abroad, the rudiments of science and cultivation, and of correcting their rough and licentious manners.

[z] LL. Aelf. § 37. apud Wilkins, p. 43.   [a] Wilkins, p. 83.   [b] Ibid. p. 96, 97. Spell. Conc. p. 473.   [c] Gul. Pict. p. 202.

IV

WILLIAM
THE CONQUEROR

Consequences of the battle of Hastings – Submission of the English – Settlement of the government – King's return to Normandy – Discontents of the English – Their insurrections – Rigours of the Norman government – New insurrections – New rigours of the government – Introduction of the feudal law – Innovation in ecclesiastical government – Insurrection of the Norman barons – Dispute about investitures – Revolt of prince Robert – Doomsday book – The New forest – War with France – Death – and character of William the Conqueror

🌼 🌼 🌼

1066. Conse- quences of the battle of Hastings **N**OTHING COULD exceed the consternation which seized the English, when they received intelligence of the unfortunate battle of Hastings, the death of their king, the slaughter of their principal nobility and of their bravest warriors, and the rout and dispersion of the remainder. But though the loss, which they had sustained in that fatal action, was considerable, it might have been repaired by a great nation; where the people were generally armed, and where there resided so many powerful noblemen in every province, who could have assembled their retainers, and

CHAPTER IV

have obliged the duke of Normandy to divide his army, and probably to waste it in a variety of actions and rencounters. It was thus
that the kingdom had formerly resisted, for many years, its invaders, and had been gradually subdued, by the continued efforts
of the Romans, Saxons, and Danes; and equal difficulties might
have been apprehended by William in this bold and hazardous
enterprize. But there were several vices in the Anglo-Saxon constitution, which rendered it difficult for the English to defend their
liberties in so critical an emergency. The people had in a great
measure lost all national pride and spirit, by their recent and long
subjection to the Danes; and as Canute had, in the course of his
administration, much abated the rigors of conquest, and had governed them equitably by their own laws, they regarded with the
less terror the ignominy of a foreign yoke, and deemed the inconveniences of submission less formidable than those of bloodshed,
war, and resistance. Their attachment also to the ancient royal
family had been much weakened by their habits of submission to
the Danish princes, and by their late election of Harold, or their
acquiescence in his usurpation. And as they had long been accustomed to regard Edgar Atheling, the only heir of the Saxon line,
as unfit to govern them even in times of order and tranquillity;
they could entertain small hopes of his being able to repair such
great losses as they had sustained, or to withstand the victorious
arms of the duke of Normandy.

That they might not, however, be altogether wanting to themselves in this extreme necessity, the English took some steps towards adjusting their disjointed government, and uniting themselves against the common enemy. The two potent earls, Edwin
and Morcar, who had fled to London with the remains of the
broken army, took the lead on this occasion: In concert with
Stigand, archbishop of Canterbury, a man possessed of great
authority, and of ample revenues, they proclaimed Edgar, and
endeavoured to put the people in a posture of defence, and encourage them to resist the Normans.[d] But the terror of the late
defeat, and the near neighbourhood of the invaders, encreased the
confusion, inseparable from great revolutions; and every resolu-

[d] Gul. Pictav. p. 205. Order. Vitalis, p. 502. Hoveden, p. 449. Knyghton,
p. 2343.

tion proposed was hasty, fluctuating, tumultuary; disconcerted by fear or faction; ill planned, and worse executed.

William, that his enemies might have no leisure to recover from their consternation or unite their counsels, immediately put himself in motion after his victory, and resolved to prosecute an enterprize, which nothing but celerity and vigour could render finally successful. His first attempt was against Romney, whose inhabitants he severely punished, on account of their cruel treatment of some Norman seamen and soldiers, who had been carried thither by stress of weather, or by a mistake in their course:[e] And foreseeing that his conquest of England might still be attended with many difficulties and with much opposition, he deemed it necessary, before he should advance farther into the country, to make himself master of Dover, which would both secure him a retreat in case of adverse fortune, and afford him a safe landing-place for such supplies as might be requisite for pushing his advantages. The terror diffused by his victory at Hastings was so great, that the garrison of Dover, though numerous and well provided, immediately capitulated; and as the Normans, rushing in to take possession of the town, hastily set fire to some of the houses, William, desirous to conciliate the minds of the English by an appearance of lenity and justice, made compensation to the inhabitants for their losses.[f]

The Norman army, being much distressed with a dysentery, was obliged to remain here eight days; but the duke, on their recovery, advanced with quick marches towards London, and by his approach encreased the confusions, which were already so prevalent in the English counsels. The ecclesiastics in particular, whose influence was great over the people, began to declare in his favour, and as most of the bishops and dignified clergymen were even then Frenchmen or Normans, the pope's bull, by which his enterprize was avowed and hallowed, was now openly insisted on as a reason for general submission. The superior learning of those prelates, which, during the Confessor's reign, had raised them above the ignorant Saxons, made their opinions be received with implicit faith; and a young prince, like Edgar, whose capacity was deemed so mean, was but ill qualified to resist the impression, which they made on the minds of the people. A repulse, which a

[e] Gul. Pictav. p. 204.   [f] Ibid.

CHAPTER IV

body of Londoners received from five hundred Norman horse, renewed in the city the terror of the great defeat at Hastings; the easy submission of all the inhabitants of Kent was an additional discouragement to them; the burning of Southwark before their eyes made them dread a like fate to their own city; and no man any longer entertained thoughts but of immediate safety and of self-preservation. Even the earls, Edwin and Morcar, in despair of making effectual resistance, retired with their troops to their own provinces; and the people thenceforth disposed themselves unanimously to yield to the victor. As soon as he passed the Thames at Wallingford, and reached Berkhamstead, Stigand, the primate, made submissions to him: Before he came within sight of the city, all the chief nobility, and Edgar Atheling himself, the new elected king, came into his camp, and declared their intention of yielding to his authority.[g] They requested him to mount their throne, which they now considered as vacant; and declared to him, that, as they had always been ruled by regal power, they desired to follow, in this particular, the example of their ancestors, and knew of no one more worthy than himself to hold the reins of government.[h]

Submission of the English.

Though this was the great object, to which the duke's enterprize tended, he feigned to deliberate on the offer; and being desirous, at first, of preserving the appearance of a legal administration, he wished to obtain a more explicit and formal consent of the English nation:[i] But Aimar of Aquitain, a man equally respected for valour in the field, and for prudence in council, remonstrating with him on the danger of delay in so critical a conjuncture, he laid aside all farther scruples, and accepted of the crown which was tendered him. Orders were immediately issued to prepare every thing for the ceremony of his coronation; but as he was yet afraid to place entire confidence in the Londoners, who were numerous and warlike, he meanwhile commanded fortresses to be erected in order to curb the inhabitants, and to secure his person and government.[k]

Stigand was not much in the duke's favour, both because he had intruded into the see on the expulsion of Robert, the Norman, and because he possessed such influence and authority over the English[l] as might be dangerous to a new established monarch.

[g] Hoveden, p. 450. Flor. Wigorn. p. 634.   [h] Gul. Pict. p. 205. Ord. Vital. p. 503.   [i] Gul. Pictav. p. 205.   [k] Ibid.   [l] Eadmer, p. 6.

William, therefore, pretending that the primate had obtained his pall in an irregular manner from pope Benedict IX. who was himself an usurper, refused to be consecrated by him, and conferred this honour on Aldred, archbishop of York. Westminster abbey was the place appointed for that magnificent ceremony; the most considerable of the nobility, both English and Norman, attended the duke on this occasion; Aldred in a short speech asked the former, whether they agreed to accept of William as their king; the bishop of Coutance put the same question to the latter; and both being answered with acclamations,[m] Aldred administered to the duke the usual coronation oath, by which he bound himself to protect the church, to administer justice, and to repress violence: He then anointed him and put the crown upon his head.[n] There appeared nothing but joy in the countenance of the spectators: But in that very moment, there burst forth the strongest symptoms of the jealousy and animosity which prevailed between the nations, and which continually encreased during the reign of this prince. The Norman soldiers, who were placed without in order to guard the church, hearing the shouts within, fancied that the English were offering violence to their duke; and they immediately assaulted the populace, and set fire to the neighbouring houses. The alarm was conveyed to the nobility who surrounded the prince; both English and Normans, full of apprehensions, rushed out to secure themselves from the present danger; and it was with difficulty that William himself was able to appease the tumult.[o]

1067. Settlement of the government. The king, thus possessed of the throne by a pretended destination of king Edward, and by an irregular election of the people, but still more by force of arms, retired from London to Berking in Essex; and there received the submissions of all the nobility, who had not attended his coronation. Edric, sirnamed the Forester, grand-nephew to that Edric so noted for his repeated acts of perfidy during the reigns of Ethelred and Edmond; earl Coxo, a man famous for bravery; even Edwin and Morcar, earls of Mercia and Northumberland; with the other principal noblemen of England, came and swore fealty to him; were received into

26th Dec.

[m] Order. Vital. p. 503. [n] Malmesbury, p. 271, says, that he also promised to govern the Normans and English by equal laws; and this addition to the usual oath seems not improbable, considering the circumstances of the times. [o] Gul. Pict. p. 206. Order Vitalis, p. 503.

CHAPTER IV

favour; and were confirmed in the possession of their estates and dignities.*p* Every thing bore the appearance of peace and tranquillity; and William had no other occupation than to give contentment to the foreigners who had assisted him to mount the throne, and to his new subjects, who had so readily submitted to him.

He had got possession of the treasure of Harold, which was considerable; and being also supplied with rich presents from the opulent men in all parts of England, who were solicitous to gain the favour of their new sovereign, he distributed great sums among his troops, and by this liberality gave them hopes of obtaining at length those more durable establishments, which they had expected from his enterprize.*q* The ecclesiastics, both at home and abroad, had much forwarded his success; and he failed not, in return, to express his gratitude and devotion in the manner which was most acceptable to them: He sent Harold's standard to the pope, accompanied with many valuable presents: All the considerable monasteries and churches in France, where prayers had been put up for his success, now tasted of his bounty:*r* The English monks found him well disposed to favour their order: And he built a new convent near Hastings, which he called *Battle-Abbey,* and which, on pretence of supporting monks to pray for his own soul, and for that of Harold, served as a lasting memorial of his victory.*s*

He introduced into England that strict execution of justice, for which his administration had been much celebrated in Normandy; and even during this violent revolution, every disorder or oppression met with rigorous punishment.*t* His army in particular was governed with severe discipline; and notwithstanding the insolence of victory, care was taken to give as little offence as possible to the jealousy of the vanquished. The king appeared solicitous to unite in an amicable manner the Normans and the English, by intermarriages and alliances; and all his new subjects who approached his person were received with affability and regard. No signs of suspicion appeared, not even towards Edgar Atheling, the heir of the ancient royal family, whom William confirmed in the

---

p Gul. Pictav. p. 208. Order. Vital. p. 506.   *q* Gul. Pict. 206.   *r* Ibid.
s Gul. Gemet. p. 288. Chron. Sax. p. 189. M. West. p. 226. M. Paris, p. 9. Diceto, p. 482. This convent was freed by him from all episcopal jurisdiction. Monast. Ang. tom. 1. p. 311, 312.   *t* Gul. Pict. p. 208. Order. Vital. p. 506.

honours of earl of Oxford, conferred on him by Harold, and whom he affected to treat with the highest kindness, as nephew to the Confessor, his great friend and benefactor. Though he confiscated the estates of Harold, and of those who had fought in the battle of Hastings on the side of that prince, whom he represented as an usurper, he seemed willing to admit of every plausible excuse for past opposition to his pretensions, and he received many into favour, who had carried arms against him. He confirmed the liberties and immunities of London and the other cities of England; and appeared desirous of replacing every thing on ancient establishments. In his whole administration, he bore the semblance of the lawful prince, not of the conqueror; and the English began to flatter themselves, that they had changed, not the form of their government, but the succession only of their sovereigns, a matter which gave them small concern. The better to reconcile his new subjects to his authority, William made a progress through some parts of England; and besides a splendid court and majestic presence, which overawed the people, already struck with his military fame, the appearance of his clemency and justice gained the approbation of the wise, attentive to the first steps of their new sovereign.

But amidst this confidence and friendship, which he expressed for the English, the king took care to place all real power in the hands of his Normans, and still to keep possession of the sword, to which, he was sensible, he had owed his advancement to sovereign authority. He disarmed the city of London and other places, which appeared most warlike and populous; and building citadels in that capital, as well as in Winchester, Hereford, and the cities best situated for commanding the kingdom, he quartered Norman soldiers in all of them, and left no where any power able to resist or oppose him. He bestowed the forfeited estates on the most eminent of his captains, and established funds for the payment of his soldiers. And thus, while his civil administration carried the face of a legal magistrate, his military institutions were those of a master and tyrant; at least of one, who reserved to himself, whenever he pleased, the power of assuming that character.

King's return to Normandy. By this mixture, however, of vigour and lenity, he had so soothed the minds of the English, that he thought he might safely revisit his native country, and enjoy the triumph and congratulation of his ancient subjects. He left the administration in the

CHAPTER IV

hands of his uterine brother, Odo, bishop of Baieux, and of William Fitz Osberne. That their authority might be exposed to less danger, he carried over with him all the most considerable nobility of England, who, while they served to grace his court by their presence and magnificent retinues, were in reality hostages for the fidelity of the nation. Among these, were Edgar Atheling, Stigand the primate, the earls Edwin and Morcar, Waltheof, the son of the brave earl Siward, with others, eminent for the greatness of their fortunes and families, or for their ecclesiastical and civil dignities. He was visited at the abbey of Fescamp, where he resided during some time, by Rodulph, uncle to the king of France, and by many powerful princes and nobles, who, having contributed to his enterprize, were desirous of participating in the joy and advantages of its success. His English courtiers, willing to ingratiate themselves with their new sovereign, outvyed each other in equipages and entertainments; and made a display of riches, which struck the foreigners with astonishment. William of Poictiers, a Norman historian,[u] who was present, speaks with admiration of the beauty of their persons, the size and workmanship of their silver plate, the costliness of their embroideries, an art in which the English then excelled; and he expresses himself in such terms, as tend much to exalt our idea of the opulence and cultivation of the people.[w] But though every thing bore the face of joy and festivity, and William himself treated his new courtiers with great appearance of kindness, it was impossible altogether to prevent the insolence of the Normans; and the English nobles derived little satisfaction from those entertainments, where they considered themselves as led in triumph by their ostentatious conqueror.

In England affairs took still a worse turn during the absence of the sovereign. Discontents and complaints multiplied every where; secret conspiracies were entered into against the government; hostilities were already begun in many places; and every thing seemed to menace a revolution as rapid as that which had placed William on the throne. The historian above mentioned, who is a panegyrist of his master, throws the blame entirely on the fickle and mutinous

March.

Discontents of the English.

[u] P. 211, 212. [w] As the historian chiefly insists on the silver plate, his panegyrics on the English magnificence shows only how incompetent a judge he was of the matter. Silver was then of ten times the value, and was more than twenty times more rare than at present; and consequently, of all species of luxury, plate must have been the rarest.

disposition of the English, and highly celebrates the justice and lenity of Odo's and Fitz Osberne's administration.[x] But other historians, with more probability, impute the cause chiefly to the Normans, who, despising a people that had so easily submitted to the yoke, envying their riches, and grudging the restraints imposed upon their own rapine, were desirous of provoking them to a rebellion, by which they expected to acquire new confiscations and forfeitures, and to gratify those unbounded hopes, which they had formed in entering on this enterprize.[y]

It is evident, that the chief reason of this alteration in the sentiments of the English, must be ascribed to the departure of William, who was alone able to curb the violence of his captains, and to overawe the mutinies of the people. Nothing indeed appears more strange, than that this prince, in less than three months after the conquest of a great, warlike, and turbulent nation, should absent himself, in order to revisit his own country, which remained in profound tranquillity, and was not menaced by any of its neighbours; and should so long leave his jealous subjects at the mercy of an insolent and licentious army. Were we not assured of the solidity of his genius, and the good sense displayed in all other circumstances of his conduct, we might ascribe this measure to a vain ostentation, which rendered him impatient to display his pomp and magnificence among his ancient subjects. It is therefore more natural to believe, that, in so extraordinary a step, he was guided by a concealed policy; and that, though he had thought proper at first to allure the people to submission by the semblance of a legal administration, he found, that he could neither satisfy his rapacious captains, nor secure his unstable government, without farther exerting the rights of conquest, and seizing the possessions of the English. In order to have a pretext for this violence, he endeavoured, without discovering his intentions, to provoke and allure them into insurrections, which, he thought, could never prove dangerous, while he detained all the principal nobility in Normandy, while a great and victorious army was quartered in England, and while he himself was so near to suppress any tumult or rebellion. But as no ancient writer has ascribed this tyrannical purpose to William, it scarcely seems allowable, from conjecture alone, to throw such an imputation upon him.

[x] P. 212.   [y] Order. Vital. p. 507.

CHAPTER IV

But whether we are to account for that measure from the king's *Their* vanity or from his policy, it was the immediate cause of all the *insurrec-* calamities which the English endured during this and the sub- *tions.* sequent reigns, and gave rise to those mutual jealousies and animosities between them and the Normans, which were never appeased, till a long tract of time had gradually united the two nations, and made them one people. The inhabitants of Kent, who had first submitted to the Conqueror, were the first that attempted to throw off the yoke; and in confederacy with Eustace, count of Bologne, who had also been disgusted by the Normans, they made an attempt, though without success, on the garrison of Dover.[z] Edric, the Forester, whose possessions lay on the banks of the Severne, being provoked at the depredations of some Norman captains in his neighbourhood, formed an alliance with Blethyn and Rowallan, two Welsh princes; and endeavoured, with their assistance, to repel force by force.[a] But though these open hostilities were not very considerable, the disaffection was general among the English, who had become sensible, though too late, of their defenceless condition, and began already to experience those insults and injuries, which a nation must always expect, that allows itself to be reduced to that abject situation. A secret conspiracy was entered into to perpetrate in one day a general massacre of the Normans, like that which had formerly been executed upon the Danes; and the quarrel was become so general and national, that the vassals of earl Coxo, having desired him to head them in an insurrection, and finding him resolute in maintaining his fidelity to William, put him to death as a traitor to his country.

The king, informed of these dangerous discontents, hastened *Decemb.* over to England; and by his presence, and the vigorous measures *6.* which he pursued, disconcerted all the schemes of the conspirators. Such of them as had been more violent in their mutiny betrayed their guilt, by flying or concealing themselves; and the confiscation of their estates, while it increased the number of malcontents, both enabled William to gratify farther the rapacity of his Norman captains, and gave them the prospect of new forfeitures and attainders. The king began to regard all his English subjects as inveterate and irreclaimable enemies; and thenceforth either embraced, or was more fully confirmed in the resolution, of

[z] Gul. Gemet. p. 289. Order. Vital. p. 508. Anglia Sacra, vol. i. p. 245.
[a] Hoveden, p. 450. M. West. p. 226. Sim. Dunelm. p. 197.

seizing their possessions, and of reducing them to the most abject slavery. Though the natural violence and severity of his temper made him incapable of feeling any remorse in the execution of this tyrannical purpose, he had art enough to conceal his intention, and to preserve still some appearance of justice in his oppressions. He ordered all the English, who had been arbitrarily expelled by the Normans, during his absence, to be restored to their estates:[b] But at the same time, he imposed a general tax on the people, that of Danegelt, which had been abolished by the Confessor, and which had always been extremely odious to the nation.[c]

1068.   As the vigilance of William overawed the malcontents, their insurrections were more the result of an impatient humour in the people, than of any regular conspiracy, which could give them a rational hope of success against the established power of the Normans. The inhabitants of Exeter, instigated by Githa, mother to king Harold, refused to admit a Norman garrison, and betaking themselves to arms, were strengthened by the accession of the neighbouring inhabitants of Devonshire and Cornwal.[d] The king hastened with his forces to chastize this revolt; and on his approach, the wiser and more considerable citizens, sensible of the unequal contest, persuaded the people to submit, and to deliver hostages for their obedience. A sudden mutiny of the populace broke this agreement; and William, appearing before the walls, ordered the eyes of one of the hostages to be put out, as an earnest of that severity, which the rebels must expect, if they persevered in their revolt.[e] The inhabitants were anew seized with terror, and surrendering at discretion, threw themselves at the king's feet, and supplicated his clemency and forgiveness. William was not destitute of generosity, when his temper was not hardened either by policy or passion: He was prevailed on to pardon the rebels, and he set guards on all the gates, in order to prevent the rapacity and insolence of his soldiery.[f] Githa escaped with her treasures to Flanders. The malcontents of Cornwal imitated the example of Exeter, and met with like treatment: And the king, having built a citadel in that city, which he put under the command of Baldwin,

---

[b] Chron. Sax. p. 173. This fact is a full proof, that the Normans had committed great injustice, and were the real cause of the insurrections of the English.   [c] Hoveden, p. 450. Sim. Dunelm. p. 197. Alur. Beverl. p. 127.   [d] Order. Vital. p. 510.   [e] Ibid.   [f] Ibid.

CHAPTER IV

son of earl Gilbert, returned to Winchester, and dispersed his army into their quarters. He was here joined by his wife, Matilda, who had not before visited England, and whom he now ordered to be crowned by archbishop Aldred. Soon after, she brought him an accession to his family, by the birth of a fourth son, whom he named Henry. His three elder sons, Robert, Richard, and William, still resided in Normandy.

But though the king appeared thus fortunate both in public and domestic life, the discontents of his English subjects augmented daily; and the injuries, committed and suffered on both sides, rendered the quarrel between them and the Normans absolutely incurable. The insolence of victorious masters, dispersed throughout the kingdom, seemed intolerable to the natives; and where-ever they found the Normans, separate or assembled in small bodies, they secretly set upon them, and gratified their vengeance by the slaughter of their enemies. But an insurrection in the north drew thither the general attention, and seemed to threaten more important consequences. Edwin and Morcar appeared at the head of this rebellion; and these potent noblemen, before they took arms, stipulated for foreign succours, from their nephew Blethin, prince of North-Wales, from Malcolm, king of Scotland, and from Sweyn, king of Denmark. Besides the general discontent, which had seized the English; the two earls were incited to this revolt by private injuries. William, in order to insure them to his interests, had, on his accession, promised his daughter in marriage to Edwin; but either he had never seriously intended to perform this engagement, or having changed his plan of administration in England from clemency to rigour, he thought it was to little purpose, if he gained one family, while he enraged the whole nation. When Edwin, therefore, renewed his applications, he gave him an absolute denial;[g] and this disappointment, added to so many other reasons of disgust, induced that nobleman and his brother to concur with their incensed countrymen, and to make one general effort for the recovery of their ancient liberties. William knew the importance of celerity in quelling an insurrection, supported by such powerful leaders, and so agreeable to the wishes of the people; and having his troops always in readiness, he ad-

---

[g] Order. Vital. p. 511.

vanced by great journies to the north. On his march he gave orders to fortify the castle of Warwic, of which he left Henry de Beaumont governor, and that of Nottingham, which he committed to the custody of William Peverell, another Norman captain.[h] He reached York before the rebels were in any condition for resistance, or were joined by any of the foreign succours, which they expected, except a small reinforcement from Wales;[i] and the two earls found no means of safety, but having recourse to the clemency of the victor. Archil, a potent nobleman in those parts, imitated their example, and delivered his son as a hostage for his fidelity;[k] nor were the people, thus deserted by their leaders, able to make any farther resistance. But the treatment, which William gave the chiefs, was very different from that which fell to the share of their followers. He observed religiously the terms, which he had granted to the former; and allowed them, for the present, to keep possession of their estates; but he extended the rigors of his confiscations over the latter, and gave away their lands to his foreign adventurers. These, planted throughout the whole country, and in possession of the military power, left Edwin and Morcar, whom he pretended to spare, destitute of all support, and ready to fall, whenever he should think proper to command their ruin. A peace, which he made with Malcolm, who did him homage for Cumberland, seemed, at the same time, to deprive them of all prospect of foreign assistance.[l]

Rigors of the Norman government. The English were now sensible that their final destruction was intended; and that, instead of a sovereign, whom they had hoped to gain by their submission, they had tamely surrendered themselves, without resistance, to a tyrant and a conqueror. Though the early confiscation of Harold's followers might seem iniquitous; being inflicted on men who had never sworn fealty to the duke of Normandy, who were ignorant of his pretensions, and who only fought in defence of the government, which they themselves had established in their own country: Yet were these rigors, however contrary to the ancient Saxon laws, excused on account of the urgent necessities of the prince; and those who were not involved in the present ruin, hoped, that they should thenceforth enjoy without molestation their possessions and their dignities. But the

[h] Order. Vital. p. 511.   [i] Ibid.   [k] Ibid.   [l] Ibid.

199

CHAPTER IV

successive destruction of so many other families convinced them, that the king intended to rely entirely on the support and affections of foreigners; and they foresaw new forfeitures, attainders, and acts of violence, as the necessary result of this destructive plan of administration. They observed, that no Englishman possessed his confidence, or was entrusted with any command or authority; and that the strangers, whom a rigorous discipline could have but ill restrained, were encouraged in their insolence and tyranny against them. The easy submission of the kingdom on its first invasion had exposed the natives to contempt; the subsequent proofs of their animosity and resentment had made them the object of hatred; and they were now deprived of every expedient, by which they could hope to make themselves either regarded or beloved by their sovereign. Impressed with the sense of this dismal situation, many Englishmen fled into foreign countries, with an intention of passing their lives abroad free from oppression, or of returning on a favourable opportunity to assist their friends in the recovery of their native liberties.[m] Edgar Atheling himself, dreading the insidious caresses of William, was persuaded by Cospatric, a powerful Northumbrian, to escape with him into Scotland; and he carried thither his two sisters Margaret and Christina. They were well received by Malcolm, who soon after espoused Margaret, the elder sister; and partly with a view of strengthening his kingdom by the accession of so many strangers, partly in hopes of employing them against the growing power of William, he gave great countenance to all the English exiles. Many of them settled there; and laid the foundation of families which afterwards made a figure in that country.

While the English suffered under these oppressions, even the foreigners were not much at their ease; but finding themselves surrounded on all hands by enraged enemies, who took every advantage against them, and menaced them with still more bloody effects of the public resentment, they began to wish again for the tranquillity and security of their native country. Hugh de Grentmesnil, and Humphry de Teliol, though entrusted with great commands, desired to be dismissed the service; and some others imitated their example: A desertion which was highly resented by the

[m] Order. Vital. p. 508. M. West. p. 225. M. Paris, p. 4. Sim. Dun. p. 197.

king, and which he punished by the confiscation of all their possessions in England.[n] But William's bounty to his followers could not fail of alluring many new adventurers into his service; and the rage of the vanquished English served only to excite the attention of the king and those warlike chiefs, and keep them in readiness to suppress every commencement of domestic rebellion or foreign invasion.

1069.
New
insurrec-
tions.

It was not long before they found occupation for their prowess and military conduct. Godwin, Edmond, and Magnus, three sons of Harold, had, immediately after the defeat at Hastings, sought a retreat in Ireland; where, having met with a kind reception from Dermot and other princes of that country, they projected an invasion on England, and they hoped that all the exiles from Denmark, Scotland, and Wales, assisted by forces from these several countries, would at once commence hostilities, and rouze the indignation of the English against their haughty conquerors. They landed in Devonshire; but found Brian, son of the count of Britanny, at the head of some foreign troops, ready to oppose them; and being defeated in several actions, they were obliged to retreat to their ships, and to return with great loss to Ireland.[o] The efforts of the Normans were now directed to the north, where affairs had fallen into the utmost confusion. The more impatient of the Northumbrians had attacked Robert de Comyn, who was appointed governor of Durham; and gaining the advantage over him from his negligence, they put him to death in that city, with seven hundred of his followers.[p] This success animated the inhabitants of York, who, rising in arms, slew Robert Fitz-Richard, their governor;[q] and besieged in the castle William Mallet, on whom the command now devolved. A little after, the Danish troops landed from 300 vessels: Osberne, brother to king Sweyn, was entrusted with the command of these forces, and he was accompanied by Harold and Canute, two sons of that monarch. Edgar Atheling appeared from Scotland, and brought along with him Cospatric, Waltheof, Siward, Bearne, Merleswain, Adelin, and other leaders, who, partly from the hopes which they gave of Scottish succours, partly from their authority in those parts,

[n] Order. Vitalis, p. 512.   [o] Gul. Gemet. p. 290. Order. Vital. p. 513. Anglia Sacra, vol. i. p. 246.   [p] Order. Vital. p. 512. Chron. de Mailr. p. 116. Hoveden, p. 450. M. Paris, p. 5. Sim. Dun. p. 198.   [q] Order. Vital. p. 512.

CHAPTER IV

easily persuaded the warlike and discontented Northumbrians to join the insurrection. Mallet, that he might better provide for the defence of the citadel of York, set fire to some houses, which lay contiguous; but this expedient proved the immediate cause of his destruction. The flames, spreading into the neighbouring streets, reduced the whole city to ashes: The enraged inhabitants, aided by the Danes, took advantage of the confusion to attack the castle, which they carried by assault; and the garrison, to the number of 3000 men, was put to the sword without mercy.[r]

This success proved a signal to many other parts of England, and gave the people an opportunity of showing their malevolence to the Normans. Hereward, a nobleman in East-Anglia, celebrated for valour, assembled his followers, and taking shelter in the Isle of Ely, made inroads on all the neighbouring country.[s] The English in the counties of Somerset and Dorset rose in arms, and assaulted Montacute, the Norman governor; while the inhabitants of Cornwal and Devon invested Exeter, which, from the memory of William's clemency, still remained faithful to him. Edric, the forester, calling in the assistance of the Welsh, laid siege to Shrewsbury, and made head against earl Brient and Fitz-Osberne, who commanded in those quarters.[t] The English every where, repenting their former easy submission, seemed determined to make by concert one great effort for the recovery of their liberties, and for the expulsion of their oppressors.

William, undismayed amidst this scene of confusion, assembled his forces, and animating them with the prospect of new confiscations and forfeitures, he marched against the rebels in the north, whom he regarded as the most formidable, and whose defeat he knew would strike a terror into all the other malcontents. Joining policy to force, he tried, before his approach, to weaken the enemy, by detaching the Danes from them; and he engaged Osberne, by large presents, and by offering him the liberty of plundering the sea-coast, to retire, without committing farther hostilities, into Denmark.[u] Cospatric also, in despair of success, made his peace with the king, and paying a sum of money as an atonement for his insurrection, was received into favour, and even invested with the

---

[r] Order. Vital. p. 513. Hoveden, p. 451.　[s] Ingulf. p. 71. Chron. Abb. St. Petri de Burgo, p. 47.　[t] Order. Vital. p. 514.　[u] Hoveden, p. 451. Chron. Abb. St. Petri di Burgo, p. 47. Sim. Dun. p. 199.

earldom of Northumberland. Waltheof, who long defended York with great courage, was allured with this appearance of clemency; and as William knew how to esteem valour even in an enemy, that nobleman had no reason to repent of this confidence.[w] Even Edric, compelled by necessity, submitted to the Conqueror, and received forgiveness, which was soon after followed by some degree of trust and favour. Malcolm, coming too late to support his confederates, was constrained to retire; and all the English rebels in other parts, except Hereward, who still kept in his fastnesses, dispersed themselves, and left the Normans undisputed masters of the kingdom. Edgar Atheling, with his followers, sought again a retreat in Scotland from the pursuit of his enemies.

1070.
New rigors of the government.

But the seeming clemency of William towards the English leaders proceeded only from artifice, or from his esteem of individuals: His heart was hardened against all compassion towards the people; and he scrupled no measure, however violent or severe, which seemed requisite to support his plan of tyrannical administration. Sensible of the restless disposition of the Northumbrians, he determined to incapacitate them ever after from giving him disturbance, and he issued orders for laying entirely waste that fertile country, which, for the extent of sixty miles, lies between the Humber and the Tees.[x] The houses were reduced to ashes by the merciless Normans, the cattle seized and driven away; the instruments of husbandry destroyed; and the inhabitants compelled either to seek for a subsistence in the southern parts of Scotland, or if they lingered in England, from a reluctance to abandon their ancient habitations, they perished miserably in the woods from cold and hunger. The lives of a hundred thousand persons are computed to have been sacrificed to this stroke of barbarous policy,[y] which, by seeking a remedy for a temporary evil, thus inflicted a lasting wound on the power and populousness of the nation.

But William, finding himself entirely master of a people, who had given him such sensible proofs of their impotent rage and animosity now resolved to proceed to extremities against all the

[w] Malmes. p. 104. H. Hunt. p. 369.   [x] Chron. Sax. p. 174. Ingulf, p. 79. Malmes. p. 103. Hoveden, p. 451. Chron. Abb. St. Petri de Burgo, p. 47. M. Paris, p. 5. Sim. Dun. p. 199. Brompton, p. 966. Knyghton, p. 2344. Anglia Sacra, vol. i. p. 702.   [y] Order. Vital. p. 515.

CHAPTER IV

natives of England; and to reduce them to a condition, in which they should no longer be formidable to his government. The insurrections and conspiracies in so many parts of the kingdom had involved the bulk of the landed proprietors, more or less, in the guilt of treason; and the king took advantage of executing against them, with the utmost rigour, the laws of forfeiture and attainder. Their lives were indeed commonly spared; but their estates were confiscated, and either annexed to the royal demesnes, or conferred with the most profuse bounty on the Normans and other foreigners.[z] While the king's declared intention was to depress or rather entirely extirpate the English gentry,[a] it is easy to believe that scarcely the form of justice would be observed in those violent proceedings;[*] and that any suspicions served as the most undoubted proofs of guilt against a people thus devoted to destruction. It was crime sufficient in an Englishman to be opulent or noble or powerful; and the policy of the king, concurring with the rapacity of foreign adventurers, produced almost a total revolution in the landed property of the kingdom. Ancient and honourable families were reduced to beggary; the nobles themselves were every where treated with ignominy and contempt; they had the mortification of seeing their castles and manors possessed by Normans of the meanest birth and lowest stations;[b] and they found themselves carefully excluded from every road, which led either to riches or preferment.[†]

As power naturally follows property, this revolution alone gave great security to the foreigners; but William, by the new institutions which he established, took also care to retain for ever the military authority in those hands, which had enabled him to subdue the kingdom. He introduced into England the feudal law, which he found established in France and Normandy, and which, during that age, was the foundation both of the stability and of the disorders, in most of the monarchial governments of Europe. He divided all the lands of England, with very few exceptions, beside the royal demesnes, into baronies; and he conferred these, with the reservation of stated services and payments, on the most considerable of his adventurers. These great barons, who held imme-

Introduction of the feudal law.

[z] Malmes. p. 104.   [a] H. Hunt. p. 370.   [*] See note [H] at the end of the volume.   [b] Order. Vitalis, p. 521. M. West, p. 229.   [†] See note [I] at the end of the volume.

diately of the crown, shared out a great part of their lands to other foreigners, who were denominated knights or vassals, and who paid their lord the same duty and submission in peace and war, which he himself owed to his sovereign. The whole kingdom contained about 700 chief tenants, and 60,215 knights-fees;[c] and as none of the native English were admitted into the first rank, the few, who retained their landed property, were glad to be received into the second, and under the protection of some powerful Norman, to load themselves and their posterity with this grievous burthen, for estates which they had received free from their ancestors.[d] The small mixture of English, which entered into this civil or military fabric, (for it partook of both species) was so restrained by subordination under the foreigners, that the Norman dominion seemed now to be fixed on the most durable basis, and to defy all the efforts of its enemies.

The better to unite the parts of the government, and to bind them into one system, which might serve both for defence against foreigners, and for the support of domestic tranquillity, William reduced the ecclesiastical revenues under the same feudal law; and though he had courted the church on his invasion and accession, he now subjected it to services, which the clergy regarded as a grievous slavery, and as totally unbefitting their profession. The bishops and abbots were obliged, when required, to furnish to the king during war a number of knights or military tenants, proportioned to the extent of property possessed by each see or abbey; and they were liable, in case of failure, to the same penalties which were exacted from the laity.[e] The pope and the ecclesiastics exclaimed against this tyranny, as they called it; but the king's authority was so well established over the army, who held every thing from his bounty, that superstition itself, even in that age, when it was most prevalent, was constrained to bend under his superior influence.

But as the great body of the clergy were still natives, the king had much reason to dread the effects of their resentment: He therefore used the precaution of expelling the English from all the

[c] Order. Vital. p. 523. Secretum Abbatis, apud Selden, Titles of Honour, p. 573. Spellm. Gloss. in verbo *Feodum*. Sir Robert Cotton.   [d] M. West. p. 225. M. Paris, p. 4. Bracton, lib. 1. cap. 11. num. 1. Fleta, lib. 1. cap. 8. n. 2.
[e] M. Paris, p. 5. Anglia Sacra, vol. i. p. 248.

CHAPTER IV

considerable dignities, and of advancing foreigners in their place. The partiality of the Confessor towards the Normans had been so great, that, aided by their superior learning, it had promoted them to many of the sees in England; and even before the period of the conquest, scarcely more than six or seven of the prelates were natives of the country. But among these was Stigand, archbishop of Canterbury; a man, who, by his address and vigour, by the greatness of his family and alliances, by the extent of his possessions, as well as by the dignity of his office, and his authority among the English, gave jealousy to the king.[f] Though William had, on his accession, affronted this prelate, by employing the archbishop of York to officiate at his consecration, he was careful, on other occasions, to load him with honours and caresses, and to avoid giving him farther offence till the opportunity should offer of effecting his final destruction.[g] The suppression of the late rebellions, and the total subjection of the English, made him hope, that an attempt against Stigand, however violent, would be covered by his great successes, and be overlooked amidst the other important revolutions, which affected so deeply the property and liberty of the kingdom. Yet, notwithstanding these great advantages, he did not think it safe to violate the reverence usually paid to the primate, but under cover of a new superstition, which he was the great instrument of introducing into England.

The doctrine, which exalted the papacy above all human power, had gradually diffused itself from the city and court of Rome; and was, during that age, much more prevalent in the southern than in the northern kingdoms of Europe. Pope Alexander, who had assisted William in his conquests, naturally expected, that the French and Normans would import into England, the same reverence for his sacred character, with which they were impressed in their own country; and would break the spiritual, as well as civil independency of the Saxons, who had hitherto conducted their ecclesiastical government, with an acknowledgment indeed of primacy in the see of Rome, but without much idea of its title to dominion or authority. As soon, therefore, as the Norman prince seemed fully established on the throne, the Pope dispatched Ermenfroy, bishop of Sion, as his legate into England; and

Innovation in ecclesiastical government.

[f] Parker, p. 161.   [g] Ibid. p. 164.

this prelate was the first that had ever appeared with that character in any part of the British islands. The king, though he was probably led by principle to pay this submission to Rome, determined, as is usual, to employ the incident as a means of serving his political purposes, and of degrading those English prelates, who were become obnoxious to him. The legate submitted to become the instrument of his tyranny; and thought, that the more violent the exertion of power, the more certainly did it confirm the authority of that court, from which he derived his commission. He summoned, therefore, a council of the prelates and abbots at Winchester; and being assisted by two cardinals, Peter and John, he cited before him Stigand, archbishop of Canterbury, to answer for his conduct. The primate was accused of three crimes; the holding of the see of Winchester together with that of Canterbury; the officiating in the pall of Robert, his predecessor; and the having received his own pall from Benedict IX. who was afterwards deposed for symony, and for intrusion into the papacy.[h] These crimes of Stigand were mere pretences; since the first had been a practice not unusual in England, and was never any where subjected to a higher penalty than a resignation of one of the sees; the second was a pure ceremonial; and as Benedict was the only pope who then officiated, and his acts were never repealed, all the prelates of the church, especially those who lay at a distance, were excusable for making their applications to him. Stigand's ruin, however, was resolved on, and was prosecuted with great severity. The legate degraded him from his dignity: The king confiscated his estate, and cast him into prison, where he continued, in poverty and want, during the remainder of his life. Like rigour was exercised against the other English prelates: Agelric, bishop of Selesey, and Agelmare, of Elmham, were deposed by the legate, and imprisoned by the king. Many considerable abbots shared the same fate: Egelwin, bishop of Durham, fled the kingdom: Wulstan, of Worcester, a man of an inoffensive character, was the only English prelate that escaped this general proscription,[i] and remained in

[h] Hoveden, p. 453. Diceto, p. 482. Knyghton, p. 2345. Anglia Sacra, vol. i. p. 5, 6. Ypod. Neust. p. 438.   [i] Brompton relates, that Wulstan was also deprived by the synod; but refusing to deliver his pastoral staff and ring to any but the person from whom he first received it, he went immediately to king Edward's tomb, and struck the staff so deeply into the stone, that none

possession of his dignity. Aldred, archbishop of York, who had set the crown on William's head, had died a little before of grief and vexation, and had left his malediction to that prince, on account of the breach of his coronation oath, and of the extreme tyranny with which, he saw, he was determined to treat his English subjects.[k]

It was a fixed maxim in this reign, as well as in some of the subsequent, that no native of the island should ever be advanced to any dignity, ecclesiastical, civil, or military.[l] The king therefore, upon Stigand's deposition, promoted Lanfranc, a Milanese monk, celebrated for his learning and piety, to the vacant see. This prelate was rigid in defending the prerogatives of his station; and after a long process before the pope, he obliged Thomas, a Norman monk, who had been appointed to the see of York, to acknowledge the primacy of the archbishop of Canterbury. Where ambition can be so happy as to cover its enterprizes, even to the person himself, under the appearance of principle, it is the most incurable and inflexible of all human passions. Hence Lanfranc's zeal in promoting the interests of the papacy, by which he himself augmented his own authority, was indefatigable; and met with proportionable success. The devoted attachment to Rome continually encreased in England; and being favoured by the sentiments of the conquerors, as well as by the monastic establishments formerly introduced by Edred and by Edgar, it soon reached the same height, at which it had, during some time, stood in France and Italy.[m] It afterwards went much farther; being favoured by that very remote situation, which had at first obstructed its progress; and being less checked by knowledge and a liberal education, which were still somewhat more common in the southern countries.

The prevalence of this superstitious spirit became dangerous to some of William's successors, and incommodious to most of them: But the arbitrary sway of this king over the English, and his extensive authority over the foreigners, kept him from feeling any im-

but himself was able to pull it out: Upon which he was allowed to keep his bishopric. This instance may serve, instead of many, as a specimen of the monkish miracles. See also the Annals of Burton, p. 284.   [k] Malmes. de gest. Pont. p. 154.   [l] Ingulf, p. 70, 71.   [m] M. West. p. 228. Lanfranc wrote in defence of the real presence against Berengarius; and in these ages of stupidity and ignorance, he was greatly applauded for that performance.

mediate inconveniencies from it. He retained the church in great subjection, as well as his lay subjects; and would allow none, of whatever character, to dispute his sovereign will and pleasure. He prohibited his subjects from acknowledging any one for pope whom he himself had not previously received: He required, that all the ecclesiastical canons, voted in any synod, should first be laid before him, and be ratified by his authority: Even bulls or letters from Rome could not legally be produced, till they received the same sanction: And none of his ministers or barons, whatever offences they were guilty of, could be subjected to spiritual censures, till he himself had given his consent to their excommunication.[n] These regulations were worthy of a sovereign, and kept united the civil and ecclesiastical powers, which the principles, introduced by this prince himself, had an immediate tendency to separate.

But the English had the cruel mortification to find, that their king's authority, however acquired or however extended, was all employed in their oppression; and that the scheme of their subjection, attended with every circumstance of insult and indignity,[o] was deliberately formed by the prince, and wantonly prosecuted by his followers.[p] William had even entertained the difficult project of totally abolishing the English language; and, for that purpose, he ordered, that, in all schools throughout the kingdom, the youth should be instructed in the French tongue, a practice which was continued from custom till after the reign of Edward III. and was never indeed totally discontinued in England. The pleadings in the supreme courts of judicature were in French:[q] The deeds were often drawn in the same language: The laws were composed in that idiom:[r] No other tongue was used at court: It became the language of all fashionable company; and the English themselves, ashamed of their own country, affected to excel in that foreign dialect. From this attention of William, and from the extensive foreign dominions, long annexed to the crown of England, proceeded that mixture of French, which is at present to be found in the English tongue, and which composes the greatest and best part

[n] Eadmer, p. 6.   [o] Order. Vital. p. 523. H. Hunt. p. 370.   [p] Ingulf, p. 71.
[q] 36 Ed. III. cap. 15. Selden Spicileg. ad Eadmer, p. 189. Fortescue de laud. leg. Angl. cap. 48.   [r] Chron. Rothom. A. D. 1066.

of our language. But amidst those endeavours to depress the English nation, the king, moved by the remonstrances of some of his prelates, and by the earnest desires of the people, restored a few of the laws of king Edward;[s] which, though seemingly of no great importance towards the protection of general liberty, gave them extreme satisfaction, as a memorial of their ancient government, and an unusual mark of complaisance in their imperious conquerors.*

The situation of the two great earls, Morcar and Edwin, *1071.* became now very disagreeable. Though they had retained their allegiance, during this general insurrection of their countrymen, they had not gained the king's confidence, and they found themselves exposed to the malignity of the courtiers, who envied them on account of their opulence and greatness, and at the same time involved them in that general contempt which they entertained for the English. Sensible that they had entirely lost their dignity, and could not even hope to remain long in safety; they determined, though too late, to share the same fate with their countrymen. While Edwin retired to his estate in the north, with a view of commencing an insurrection, Morcar took shelter in the Isle of Ely with the brave Hereward, who, secured by the inaccessible situation of the place, still defended himself against the Normans. But this attempt served only to accelerate the ruin of the few English, who had hitherto been able to preserve their rank or fortune during the past convulsions. William employed all his endeavours to subdue the Isle of Ely; and having surrounded it with flat-bottomed boats, and made a causeway through the morasses to the extent of two miles, he obliged the rebels to surrender at discretion. Hereward alone forced his way, sword in hand, through the enemy; and still continued his hostilities by sea against the Normans, till at last William, charmed with his bravery, received him into favour, and restored him to his estate. Earl Morcar, and Egelwin, bishop of Durham, who had joined the malcontents, were thrown into prison, and the latter soon after died in confinement. Edwin, attempting to make his escape into Scotland, was betrayed by some of his followers; and was killed by a party of Normans, to

[s] Ingulf, p. 88. Brompton, p. 982. Knyghton, p. 2355. Hoveden, p. 600.
* See note [J] at the end of the volume.

the great affliction of the English, and even to that of William, who paid a tribute of generous tears to the memory of this gallant and beautiful youth. The king of Scotland, in hopes of profiting by these convulsions, had fallen upon the northern counties; but on the approach of William he retired; and when the king entered his country, he was glad to make peace, and to pay the usual homage to the English crown. To complete the king's prosperity, Edgar Atheling himself, despairing of success, and weary of a fugitive life, submitted to his enemy; and receiving a decent pension for his subsistence, was permitted to live in England unmolested. But these acts of generosity towards the leaders were disgraced, as usual, by William's rigour against the inferior malcontents. He ordered the hands to be lopt off, and the eyes to be put out, of many of the prisoners, whom he had taken in the Isle of Ely; and he dispersed them in that miserable condition throughout the country, as monuments of his severity.

1073. The province of Maine in France had, by the will of Hebert, the last count, fallen under the dominion of William some years before his conquest of England; but the inhabitants, dissatisfied with the Norman government, and instigated by Fulk count of Anjou, who had some pretensions to the succession, now rose in rebellion, and expelled the magistrates, whom the king had placed over them. The full settlement of England afforded him leisure to punish this insult on his authority; but being unwilling to remove his Norman forces from this island, he carried over a considerable army, composed almost entirely of English, and joining them to some troops levied in Normandy, he entered the revolted province. The English appeared ambitious of distinguishing themselves on this occasion, and of retrieving that character of valour, which had long been national among them; but which their late easy subjection under the Normans had somewhat degraded and obscured. Perhaps too they hoped that, by their zeal and activity, they might recover the confidence of their sovereign, as their ancestors had formerly, by like means, gained the affections of Canute; and might conquer his inveterate prejudices in favour of his own countrymen. The king's military conduct, seconded by these brave troops, soon overcame all opposition in Maine: The inhabitants were obliged to submit, and the count of Anjou relinquished his pretensions.

CHAPTER IV

But during these transactions, the government of England was greatly disturbed; and that too by those very foreigners, who owed every thing to the king's bounty, and who were the sole object of his friendship and regard. The Norman barons, who had engaged with their duke in the conquest of England, were men of the most independant spirit; and though they obeyed their leader in the field, they would have regarded with disdain the richest acquisitions, had they been required, in return, to submit, in their civil government, to the arbitrary will of one man. But the imperious character of William, encouraged by his absolute dominion over the English, and often impelled by the necessity of his affairs, had prompted him to stretch his authority over the Normans themselves beyond what the free genius of that victorious people could easily bear. The discontents were become general among those haughty nobles; and even Roger, earl of Hereford, son and heir of Fitz-Osberne, the king's chief favourite, was strongly infected with them. This nobleman, intending to marry his sister to Ralph de Guader, earl of Norfolk, had thought it his duty to inform the king of his purpose, and to desire the royal consent; but meeting with a refusal, he proceeded nevertheless to complete the nuptials, and assembled all his friends, and those of Guader, to attend the solemnity. The two earls, disgusted by the denial of their request, and dreading William's resentment for their disobedience, here prepared measures for a revolt; and during the gaiety of the festival, while the company was heated with wine, they opened the design to their guests. They inveighed against the arbitrary conduct of the king; his tyranny over the English, whom they affected on this occasion to commiserate; his imperious behaviour to his barons of the noblest birth; and his apparent intention of reducing the victors and the vanquished to a like ignominious servitude. Amidst their complaints, the indignity of submitting to a bastard[f] was not forgotten; the certain prospect of success in a revolt, by the assistance of the Danes and the discontented English, was insisted on; and the whole company, inflamed with the same sentiments, and warmed by the jollity of the entertainment, entered, by a solemn engagement, into the design of shaking off the royal authority.

1074. Insurrection of the Norman barons.

[f] William was so little ashamed of his birth, that he assumed the appellation of Bastard in some of his letters and charters. Spellm. Gloss. in verb. *Bastardus.* Camden in *Richmondshire.*

Even earl Waltheof, who was present, inconsiderately expressed his approbation of the conspiracy, and promised his concurrence towards its success.

This nobleman, the last of the English, who, for some generations, possessed any power or authority, had, after his capitulation at York, been received into favour by the Conqueror; had even married Judith, niece to that prince; and had been promoted to the earldoms of Huntingdon and Northampton.[u] Cospatric, earl of Northumberland, having, on some new disgust from William, retired into Scotland, where he received the earldom of Dunbar from the bounty of Malcolm; Waltheof was appointed his successor in that important command, and seemed still to possess the confidence and friendship of his sovereign.[w] But as he was a man of generous principles, and loved his country, it is probable, that the tyranny exercised over the English lay heavy upon his mind, and destroyed all the satisfaction, which he could reap from his own grandeur and advancement. When a prospect, therefore, was opened of retrieving their liberty, he hastily embraced it; while the fumes of the liquor, and the ardour of the company, prevented him from reflecting on the consequences of that rash attempt. But after his cool judgment returned, he foresaw, that the conspiracy of those discontented barons was not likely to prove successful against the established power of William; or if it did, that the slavery of the English, instead of being alleviated by that event, would become more grievous, under a multitude of foreign leaders, factious and ambitious, whose union and whose discord would be equally oppressive to the people. Tormented with these reflections, he opened his mind to his wife, Judith, of whose fidelity he entertained no suspicion, but who, having secretly fixed her affections on another, took this opportunity of ruining her easy and credulous husband. She conveyed intelligence of the conspiracy to the king, and aggravated every circumstance, which, she believed, would tend to incense him against Waltheof, and render him absolutely implacable.[x] Meanwhile, the earl, still dubious with regard to the part which he should act, discovered the secret in confession to Lanfranc, on whose probity and judgment he had a great reliance: He was persuaded by the prelate, that he owed no fidelity to those

[u] Order. Vital. p. 522. Hoveden, p. 454.   [w] Sim. Dun. p. 205.   [x] Order. Vital. p. 536.

CHAPTER IV

rebellious barons, who had by surprise gained his consent to a crime; that his first duty was to his sovereign and benefactor, his next to himself and his family; and that, if he seized not the opportunity of making atonement for his guilt, by revealing it, the temerity of the conspirators was so great, that they would give some other person the means of acquiring the merit of the discovery. Waltheof, convinced by these arguments, went over to Normandy; but, though he was well received by the king, and thanked for his fidelity, the account, previously transmitted by Judith, had sunk deep into William's mind, and had destroyed all the merit of her husband's repentance.

The conspirators, hearing of Waltheof's departure, immediately concluded their design to be betrayed; and they flew to arms, before their schemes were ripe for execution, and before the arrival of the Danes, in whose aid they placed their chief confidence. The earl of Hereford was checked by Walter de Lacy, a great baron in those parts, who, supported by the bishop of Worcester and the abbot of Evesham, raised some forces, and prevented the earl from passing the Severne, or advancing into the heart of the kingdom. The earl of Norfolk was defeated at Fagadun, near Cambridge, by Odo, the regent, assisted by Richard de Bienfaite, and William de Warrenne, the two justiciaries. The prisoners taken in this action had their right foot cut off, as a punishment of their treason: The earl himself escaped to Norwich, thence to Denmark; where the Danish fleet, which had made an unsuccessful attempt upon the coast of England,[y] soon after arrived, and brought him intelligence, that all his confederates were suppressed and were either killed, banished, or taken prisoners.[z] Ralph retired in despair to Britanny, where he possessed a large estate, and extensive jurisdictions.

The king, who hastened over to England, in order to suppress the insurrection, found, that nothing remained but the punishment of the criminals, which he executed with great severity. Many of the rebels were hanged; some had their eyes put out; others their hands cut off. But William, agreeably to his usual

[y] Chron. Sax. p. 183. M. Paris, p. 7.   [z] Many of the fugitive Normans are supposed to have fled into Scotland; where they were protected, as well as the fugitive English, by Malcolm. Whence come the many French and Norman families, which are found at present in that country.

maxims, showed more lenity to their leader, the earl of Hereford, who was only condemned to a forfeiture of his estate, and to imprisonment during pleasure. The king seemed even disposed to remit this last part of the punishment; had not Roger, by a fresh insolence, provoked him to render his confinement perpetual. But Waltheof, being an Englishman, was not treated with so much humanity; though his guilt, always much inferior to that of the other conspirators, was atoned for by an early repentance and return to his duty. William, instigated by his niece, as well as by his rapacious courtiers, who longed for so rich a forfeiture, ordered him to be tried, condemned, and executed. The English, who considered this nobleman as the last resource of their nation, grievously lamented his fate, and fancied that miracles were wrought by his reliques, as a testimony of his innocence and sanctity. The infamous Judith, falling soon after under the king's displeasure, was abandoned by all the world, and passed the rest of her life in contempt, remorse, and misery.

1075.

29th April.

Nothing remained to complete William's satisfaction but the punishment of Ralph de Guader; and he hastened over to Normandy, in order to gratify his vengeance on that criminal. But though the contest seemed very unequal between a private nobleman and the king of England, Ralph was so well supported both by the earl of Britanny and the King of France, that William, after besieging him for some time in Dol, was obliged to abandon the enterprize, and make with those powerful princes a peace, in which Ralph himself was included. England, during his absence, remained in tranquillity; and nothing remarkable occurred, except two ecclesiastical synods, which were summoned, one at London, another at Winchester. In the former, the precedency among the episcopal sees was settled, and the seat of some of them was removed from small villages to the most considerable town within the diocese. In the second was transacted a business of more importance.

1076.
Dispute about investitures.

The industry and perseverance are surprising, with which the popes had been treasuring up powers and pretensions during so many ages of ignorance; while each pontiff employed every fraud for advancing purposes of imaginary piety, and cherished all claims which might turn to the advantage of his successors, though he himself could not expect ever to reap any benefit from them. All

CHAPTER IV

this immense store of spiritual and civil authority was now devolved on Gregory VII. of the name of Hildebrand, the most enterprising pontiff that had ever filled that chair, and the least restrained by fear, decency, or moderation. Not content with shaking off the yoke of the emperors, who had hitherto exercised the power of appointing the pope on every vacancy, at least of ratifying his election; he undertook the arduous task of entirely disjoining the ecclesiastical from the civil power, and of excluding profane laymen from the right which they had assumed, of filling the vacancies of bishoprics, abbies, and other spiritual dignities.[a] The sovereigns, who had long exercised this power, and who had acquired it, not by encroachments on the church, but on the people, to whom it originally belonged,[b] made great opposition to this claim of the court of Rome; and Henry IV. the reigning emperor, defended this prerogative of his crown with a vigour and resolution suitable to its importance. The few offices, either civil or military, which the feudal institutions left the sovereign the power of bestowing, made the prerogative of conferring the pastoral ring and staff the most valuable jewel of the royal diadem; especially as the general ignorance of the age bestowed a consequence on the ecclesiastical offices, even beyond the great extent of power and property which belonged to them. Superstition, the child of ignorance, invested the clergy with an authority almost sacred; and as they ingrossed the little learning of the age, their interposition became requisite in all civil business, and a real usefulness in common life was thus superadded to the spiritual sanctity of their character.

When the usurpations, therefore, of the church had come to such maturity as to embolden her to attempt extorting the right of investitures from the temporal power, Europe, especially Italy and Germany, was thrown into the most violent convulsions, and the pope and the emperor waged implacable war on each other. Gregory dared to fulminate the sentence of excommunication against Henry and his adherents, to pronounce him rightfully deposed, to free his subjects from their oaths of allegiance; and, instead of shocking mankind by this gross encroachment on the civil authority, he found the stupid people ready to second his most exorbitant

[a] L'Abbe Conc. tom. 10. p. 371, 372. com. 2.   [b] Padre Paolo sopra benef. eccles. p. 30.

pretensions. Every minister, servant, or vassal of the emperor, who received any disgust, covered his rebellion under the pretence of principle; and even the mother of this monarch, forgetting all the ties of nature, was seduced to countenance the insolence of his enemies. Princes themselves, not attentive to the pernicious consequences of those papal claims, employed them for their present purposes: And the controversy, spreading into every city of Italy, engendered the parties of Guelf and Ghibbelin; the most durable and most inveterate factions that ever arose from the mixture of ambition and religious zeal. Besides numberless assassinations, tumults, and convulsions, to which they gave rise, it is computed that the quarrel occasioned no less than sixty battles in the reign of Henry IV. and eighteen in that of his successor, Henry V. when the claims of the sovereign pontiff finally prevailed.[c]

But the bold spirit of Gregory, not dismayed with the vigorous opposition, which he met with from the emperor, extended his usurpations all over Europe; and well knowing the nature of mankind, whose blind astonishment ever inclines them to yield to the most impudent pretensions, he seemed determined to set no bounds to the spiritual, or rather temporal monarchy, which he had undertaken to erect. He pronounced the sentence of excommunication against Nicephorus, emperor of the East; Robert Guiscard, the adventurous Norman, who had acquired the dominion of Naples, was attacked by the same dangerous weapon: He degraded Boleslas, king of Poland, from the rank of king; and even deprived Poland of the title of a kingdom: He attempted to treat Philip king of France with the same rigour, which he had employed against the emperor:[d] He pretended to the entire property and dominion of Spain; and he parcelled it out amongst adventurers, who undertook to conquer it from the Saracens, and to hold it in vassalage under the see of Rome:[e] Even the Christian bishops, on whose aid he relied for subduing the temporal princes, saw that he was determined to reduce them to servitude, and by assuming the whole legislative and judicial power of the church, to center all authority in the sovereign pontiff.[f]

William the Conqueror, the most potent, the most haughty,

[c] Padre Paolo sopra benef. eccles. p. 113. [d] Epist. Greg. VII. epist. 32, 35. lib. 2. epist. 5. [e] Epist. Greg. VII. lib. 1. epist. 7. [f] Greg. Epist. lib. 2. epist. 55.

CHAPTER IV

and the most vigorous prince in Europe, was not, amidst all his splendid successes, secure from the attacks of this enterprizing pontiff. Gregory wrote him a letter, requiring him to fulfil his promise in doing homage for the kingdom of England to the see of Rome, and to send him over that tribute, which all his predecessors had been accustomed to pay to the vicar of Christ. By the tribute, he meant Peter's pence; which, though at first a charitable donation of the Saxon princes, was interpreted, according to the usual practice of the Romish court, to be a badge of subjection acknowledged by the kingdom. William replied, that the money should be remitted as usual; but that neither had he promised to do homage to Rome, nor was it in the least his purpose to impose that servitude on his state.[g] And the better to show Gregory his independance, he ventured, notwithstanding the frequent complaints of the pope, to refuse to the English bishops the liberty of attending a general council, which that pontiff had summoned against his enemies.

But though the king displayed this vigour in supporting the royal dignity, he was infected with the general superstition of the age, and he did not perceive the ambitious scope of those institutions, which, under colour of strictness in religion, were introduced or promoted by the court of Rome. Gregory, while he was throwing all Europe into combustion by his violence and impostures, affected an anxious care for the purity of manners; and even the chaste pleasures of the marriage-bed were inconsistent, in his opinion, with the sanctity of the sacerdotal character. He had issued a decree prohibiting the marriage of priests, excommunicating all clergymen who retained their wives, declaring such unlawful commerce to be fornication, and rendering it criminal in the laity to attend divine worship, when such profane priests officiated at the altar.[h] This point was a great object in the politics of the Roman pontiffs; and it cost them infinitely more pains to establish it than the propagation of any speculative absurdity, which they had ever attempted to introduce. Many synods were summoned in different parts of Europe, before it was finally settled; and it was there constantly remarked, that the younger clergymen complied chearfully with the pope's decrees in this particu-

[g] Spicileg. Seldeni ad Eadmer, p. 4.　[h] Hoveden, p. 455, 457. Flor. Wigorn. p. 638. Spell. Concil. fol. 13. A. D. 1076.

lar, and that the chief reluctance appeared in those who were more advanced in years: An event so little consonant to men's natural expectations, that it could not fail to be glossed on, even in that blind and superstitious age. William allowed the pope's legate to assemble, in his absence, a synod at Winchester, in order to establish the celibacy of the clergy; but the church of England could not yet be carried the whole length expected. The synod was content with decreeing, that the bishops should not thenceforth ordain any priests or deacons without exacting from them a promise of celibacy; but they enacted, that none, except those who belonged to collegiate or cathedral churches, should be obliged to separate from their wives.

Revolt of prince Robert.   The king passed some years in Normandy; but his long residence there was not entirely owing to his declared preference of that dutchy: His presence was also necessary for composing those disturbances, which had arisen in that favourite territory, and which had even originally proceeded from his own family. Robert, his eldest son, sirnamed Gambaron or Courthose, from his short legs, was a prince, who inherited all the bravery of his family and nation; but without that policy and dissimulation, by which his father was so much distinguished, and which, no less than his military valour, had contributed to his great successes. Greedy of fame, impatient of contradiction, without reserve in his friendships, declared in his enmities, this prince could endure no controul even from his imperious father, and openly aspired to that independance, to which his temper, as well as some circumstances in his situation, strongly invited him.[i] When William first received the submissions of the province of Maine, he had promised the inhabitants, that Robert should be their prince; and before he undertook the expedition against England, he had, on the application of the French court, declared him his successor in Normandy, and had obliged the barons of that dutchy to do him homage as their future sovereign. By this artifice, he had endeavoured to appease the jealousy of his neighbours, as affording them a prospect of separating England from his dominions on the continent; but when Robert demanded of him the execution of those engagements, he gave him an absolute refusal, and told him, according to

[i] Order. Vital. p. 545. Hoveden, p. 457. Flor. Wigorn. p. 639.

CHAPTER IV

the homely saying, that he never intended to throw off his cloaths, till he went to bed.[k] Robert openly declared his discontent; and was suspected of secretly instigating the king of France and the earl of Britanny to the opposition, which they made to William, and which had formerly frustrated his attempts upon the town of Dol. And as the quarrel still augmented, Robert proceeded to entertain a strong jealousy of his two surviving brothers, William and Henry, (for Richard was killed in hunting, by a stag) who, by greater submission and complaisance, had acquired the affections of their father. In this disposition, on both sides, the greatest trifle sufficed to produce a rupture between them.

The three princes, residing with their father in the castle of l'Aigle in Normandy, were one day engaged in sport together; and after some mirth and jollity, the two younger took a fancy of throwing over some water on Robert as he passed through the court on leaving their apartment;[l] a frolic, which he would naturally have regarded as innocent, had it not been for the suggestions of Alberic de Grentmesnil, son of that Hugh de Grentmesnil, whom William had formerly deprived of his fortunes, when that baron deserted him during his greatest difficulties in England. The young man, mindful of the injury, persuaded the prince, that this action was meant as a public affront, which it behoved him in honour to resent; and the choleric Robert, drawing his sword, ran up stairs, with an intention of taking revenge on his brothers.[m] The whole castle was filled with tumult, which the king himself, who hastened from his apartment, found some difficulty to appease. But he could by no means appease the resentment of his eldest son, who, complaining of his partiality, and fancying that no proper atonement had been made him for the insult, left the court that very evening, and hastened to Roüen, with an intention of seizing the citadel of that place.[n] But being disappointed in this view by the precaution and vigilance of Roger de Ivery, the governor, he fled to Hugh de Neufchatel, a powerful Norman baron, who gave him protection in his castles; and he openly levied war against his father.[o] The popular character of the prince, and a similarity of manners, engaged all the young nobility of Normandy and Maine, as well as of Anjou and Britanny, to take part with him;

[k] Chron. de Mailr. p. 160.   [l] Order. Vital. p. 545.   [m] Ibid.   [n] Ibid.
[o] Order Vital. p. 545. Hoveden, p. 457. Sim. Dun. p. 210. Diceto, p. 487.

and it was suspected that Matilda, his mother, whose favourite he was, supported him in his rebellion by secret remittances of money, and by the encouragement which she gave his partizans. All the hereditary provinces of William, as well as his family, were during several years thrown into convulsions by this war; and he was at last obliged to have recourse to England, where that species of military government, which he had established, gave him greater authority than the ancient feudal institutions permitted him to exercise in Normandy. He called over an army of English under his ancient captains, who soon expelled Robert and his adherents from their retreats, and restored the authority of the sovereign in all his dominions. The young prince was obliged to take shelter in the castle of Gerberoy in the Beauvoisis, which the king of France, who secretly fomented all these dissensions, had provided for him. In this fortress he was closely besieged by his father, against whom, having a strong garrison, he made an obstinate defence. There passed under the walls of this place many rencounters, which resembled more the single combats of chivalry, than the military actions of armies; but one of them was remarkable for its circumstances and its event. Robert happened to engage the king, who was concealed by his helmet; and both of them being valiant, a fierce combat ensued, till at last the young prince wounded his father in the arm, and unhorsed him. On his calling out for assistance, his voice discovered him to his son, who, struck with remorse for his past guilt, and astonished with the apprehensions of one much greater, which he had so nearly incurred, instantly threw himself at his father's feet, craved pardon for his offences, and offered to purchase forgiveness by any atonement.[p] The resentment, harboured by William, was so implacable, that he did not immediately correspond to this dutiful submission of his son with like tenderness; but giving him his malediction, departed for his own camp, on Robert's horse, which that prince had assisted him to mount. He soon after raised the siege, and marched with his army to Normandy; where the interposition of the queen and other common friends brought about a reconcilement, which was probably not a little forwarded by the generosity of the son's behaviour in this action, and by the returning sense of his past mis-

1079.

[p] Malmes. p. 106. H. Hunt. p. 369. Hoveden, p. 457. Flor. Wig. p. 639. Sim. Dun. p. 210. Diceto, p. 287. Knyghton, p. 2351. Alur. Beverl. p. 135.

CHAPTER IV

conduct. The king seemed so fully appeased, that he even took
Robert with him into England; where he intrusted him with the
command of an army, in order to repel an inroad of Malcolm king
of Scotland, and to retaliate by a like inroad into that country. The
Welsh, unable to resist William's power, were, about the same
time, necessitated to pay a compensation for their incursions; and
every thing was reduced to full tranquillity on this island.

This state of affairs gave William leisure to begin and finish
an undertaking, which proves his extensive genius, and does honour to his memory: It was a general survey of all the lands in the
kingdom, their extent in each district, their proprietors, tenures,
value; the quantity of meadow, pasture, wood, and arable land,
which they contained; and in some counties the number of tenants, cottagers, and slaves of all denominations, who lived upon
them. He appointed commissioners for this purpose, who entered
every particular in their register by the verdict of juries; and after
a labour of six years (for the work was so long in finishing) brought
him an exact account of all the landed property of his kingdom.[q]
This monument, called Domesday-book, the most valuable piece
of antiquity possessed by any nation, is still preserved in the Exchequer; and though only some extracts of it have hitherto been
published, it serves to illustrate to us in many particulars the ancient state of England. The great Alfred had finished a like survey
of the kingdom in his time which was long kept at Winchester, and
which probably served as a model to William in this undertaking.[r]

The king was naturally a great economist; and though no
prince had ever been more bountiful to his officers and servants,
it was merely because he had rendered himself universal proprietor of England, and had a whole kingdom to bestow. He reserved
an ample revenue for the crown; and in the general distribution of
land among his followers, he kept possession of no less than 1422
manors in different parts of England,[s] which paid him rent either
in money, or in corn, cattle, and the usual produce of the soil. An

*1081.
Domesday-
book.*

[q] Chron. Sax. p. 190. Ingulf, p. 79. Chron. T. Tykes, p. 23. H. Hunt. p. 370.
Hoveden, p. 460. M. West. p. 229. Flor. Wigorn. p. 641. Chron. Abb. St.
Petri de Burgo, p. 51. M. Paris, p. 8. The more northern counties were not
comprehended in this survey; I suppose because of their wild, uncultivated
state.   [r] Ingulf, p. 8.   [s] West's enquiry into the manner of creating peers,
p. 24.

ancient historian computes, that his annual fixed income, besides escheats, fines, reliefs, and other casual profits to a great value, amounted to near 400,000 pounds a-year;[t] a sum, which, if all circumstances be attended to, will appear wholly incredible. A pound in that age, as we have already observed, contained three times the weight of silver that it does at present; and the same weight of silver, by the most probable computation, would purchase near ten times more of the necessaries of life, though not in the same proportion of the finer manufactures. This revenue, therefore, of William would be equal to at least nine or ten millions at present; and as that prince had neither fleet nor army to support, the former being only an occasional expence, and the latter being maintained, without any charge to him, by his military vassals, we must thence conclude, that no emperor or prince, in any age or nation, can be compared to the Conqueror for opulence and riches. This leads us to suspect a great mistake in the computation of the historian; though, if we consider that avarice is always imputed to William as one of his vices, and that, having by the sword rendered himself master of all the lands in the kingdom, he would certainly in the partition retain a great proportion for his own share; we can scarcely be guilty of any error in asserting, that perhaps no king of England was ever more opulent, was more able to support by his revenue the splendor and magnificence of a court, or could bestow more on his pleasures or in liberalities to his servants and favourites.[u]

The new forest. There was one pleasure, to which William, as well as all the Normans and ancient Saxons, was extremely addicted; and that was hunting: But this pleasure he indulged more at the expence of his unhappy subjects, whose interests he always disregarded, than to the loss or diminution of his own revenue. Not content with those large forests, which former kings possessed in all parts of England; he resolved to make a new forest near Winchester, the usual place of his residence: And for that purpose, he laid waste the country in Hampshire for an extent of thirty miles, expelled the inhabitants from their houses, seized their property, even demolished churches and convents, and made the sufferers no com-

[t] Order. Vital. p. 523. He says 1060 pounds and some odd shillings and pence a-day   [u] Fortescue, de Dom. reg. & politic. cap. 111.

CHAPTER IV

pensation for the injury.[w] At the same time, he enacted new laws, by which he prohibited all his subjects from hunting in any of his forests, and rendered the penalties more severe than ever had been inflicted for such offences. The killing of a deer or boar, or even a hare, was punished with the loss of the delinquent's eyes; and that at a time, when the killing of a man could be atoned for by paying a moderate fine or composition.

The transactions, recorded during the remainder of this reign, may be considered more as domestic occurrences, which concern the prince, than as national events, which regard England. Odo, bishop of Baieux, the king's uterine brother, whom he had created earl of Kent, and entrusted with a great share of power during his whole reign, had amassed immense riches; and agreeably to the usual progress of human wishes, he began to regard his present acquisitions but as a step to farther grandeur. He had formed the chimerical project of buying the papacy; and though Gregory, the reigning pope, was not of advanced years, the prelate had confided so much in the predictions of an astrologer, that he reckoned upon the pontiff's death, and upon attaining, by his own intrigues and money, that envied state of greatness. Resolving, therefore, to remit all his riches to Italy, he had persuaded many considerable barons, and among the rest, Hugh earl of Chester, to take the same course; in hopes, that when he should mount the papal throne, he would bestow on them more considerable establishments in that country. The king, from whom all these projects had been carefully concealed, at last got intelligence of the design, and ordered Odo to be arrested. His officers, from respect to the immunities, which the ecclesiastics now assumed, scrupled to execute the command, till the king himself was obliged in person to seize him; and when Odo insisted that he was a prelate, and exempt from all temporal jurisdiction, William replied, that he arrested him, not as bishop of Baieux, but as earl of Kent. He was sent prisoner to Normandy; and notwithstanding the remonstrances and menaces of Gregory, was detained in custody during the remainder of this reign.

Another domestic event gave the king much more concern: It was the death of Matilda, his consort, whom he tenderly

1082.

1083.

[w] Malmes. p. 3. H. Hunt. p. 731. Anglia Sacra, vol. i. p. 258.

loved, and for whom he had ever preserved the most sincere friendship. Three years afterwards he passed into Normandy, and carried with him Edgar Atheling, to whom he willingly granted permission to make a pilgrimage to the Holy Land. He was detained on the continent by a misunderstanding, which broke out between him and the king of France, and which was occasioned by inroads made into Normandy by some French barons on the frontiers. It was little in the power of princes at that time to restrain their licentious nobility; but William suspected, that these barons durst not have provoked his indignation, had they not been assured of the countenance and protection of Philip. His displeasure was encreased by the account he received of some railleries which that monarch had thrown out against him. William, who was become corpulent, had been detained in bed some time by sickness; upon which Philip expressed his surprise that his brother of England should be so long in being delivered of his big belly. The king sent him word, that, as soon as he was up, he would present so many lights at Notre-dame, as would perhaps give little pleasure to the king of France; alluding to the usual practice at that time of women after child-birth. Immediately on his recovery, he led an army into L'Isle de France, and laid every thing waste with fire and sword. He took the town of Mante, which he reduced to ashes. But the progress of these hostilities was stopped by an accident, which soon after put an end to William's life. His horse starting aside of a sudden, he bruised his belly on the pommel of the saddle; and being in a bad habit of body, as well as somewhat advanced in years, he began to apprehend the consequences, and ordered himself to be carried in a litter to the monastery of St. Gervas. Finding his illness encrease, and being sensible of the approach of death, he discovered at last the vanity of all human grandeur, and was struck with remorse for those horrible cruelties and acts of violence, which, in the attainment and defence of it, he had committed during the course of his reign over England. He endeavoured to make atonement by presents to churches and monasteries; and he issued orders, that earl Morcar, Siward Bearne, and other English prisoners, should be set at liberty. He was even prevailed on, though not without reluctance, to consent, with his dying breath, to release his brother, Odo, against whom he was extremely incensed. He left Normandy and Maine to his eldest son, Robert: He wrote to Lanfranc, desiring him to crown William

1087.
War with
France.

CHAPTER IV

king of England: He bequeathed to Henry nothing but the possessions of his mother, Matilda; but foretold, that he would one
day surpass both his brothers in power and opulence. He expired
in the sixty-third year of his age, in the twenty-first year of his
reign over England, and in the fifty-fourth of that over Normandy.

Few princes have been more fortunate than this great monarch, or were better entitled to grandeur and prosperity, from the
abilities and the vigour of mind which he displayed in all his conduct. His spirit was bold and enterprising, yet guided by prudence:
His ambition, which was exorbitant, and lay little under the
restraints of justice, still less under those of humanity, ever submitted to the dictates of sound policy. Born in an age when the
minds of men were intractable and unacquainted with submission,
he was yet able to direct them to his purposes; and partly from the
ascendant of his vehement character, partly from art and dissimulation, to establish an unlimited authority. Though not insensible
to generosity, he was hardened against compassion; and he
seemed equally ostentatious and equally ambitious of show and
parade in his clemency and in his severity. The maxims of his
administration were austere; but might have been useful, had they
been solely employed to preserve order in an established government:[x] They were ill calculated for softening the rigours, which,
under the most gentle management, are inseparable from conquest. His attempt against England was the last great enterprize of
the kind, which, during the course of seven hundred years, has
fully succeeded in Europe; and the force of his genius broke
through those limits, which first the feudal institutions, then the
refined policy of princes, have fixed to the several states of Christendom. Though he rendered himself infinitely odious to his
English subjects, he transmitted his power to his posterity, and the
throne is still filled by his descendants: A proof, that the foundations which he laid were firm and solid, and that, amidst all his
violence, while he seemed only to gratify the present passion, he
had still an eye towards futurity.

Some writers have been desirous of refusing to this prince the
title of Conqueror, in the sense which that term commonly bears;
and on pretence, that the word is sometimes in old books applied
to such as make an acquisition of territory by any means, they are

*9th Sept.
Death
and char-
acter of
William
the Con-
queror.*

---

[x] M. West. p. 230. Anglia Sacra, vol. i. p. 258.

willing to reject William's title, by right of war, to the crown of
England. It is needless to enter into a controversy, which, by the
terms of it, must necessarily degenerate into a dispute of words. It
suffices to say, that the duke of Normandy's first invasion of the
island was hostile; that his subsequent administration was entirely
supported by arms, that in the very frame of his laws he made a
distinction between the Normans and English, to the advantage of
the former;[y] that he acted in every thing as absolute master over
the natives, whose interests and affections he totally disregarded;
and that if there was an interval when he assumed the appearance
of a legal sovereign, the period was very short, and was nothing but
a temporary sacrifice, which he, as has been the case with most
conquerors, was obliged to make, of his inclination to his present
policy. Scarce any of those revolutions, which, both in history and
in common language, have always been denominated conquests,
appear equally violent, or were attended with so sudden an alteration both of power and property. The Roman state, which spread
its dominion over Europe, left the rights of individuals, in a great
measure, untouched; and those civilized conquerors, while they
made their own country the seat of empire, found, that they could
draw most advantage from the subjected provinces, by securing to
the natives the free enjoyment of their own laws and of their
private possessions. The barbarians, who subdued the Roman empire, though they settled in the conquered countries, yet being
accustomed to a rude uncultivated life, found a part only of the
land sufficient to supply all their wants; and they were not tempted
to seize extensive possessions, which they knew neither how to
cultivate nor enjoy. But the Normans and other foreigners, who
followed the standard of William, while they made the vanquished
kingdom the seat of government, were yet so far advanced in arts
as to be acquainted with the advantages of a large property; and
having totally subdued the natives, they pushed the rights of conquest (very extensive in the eyes of avarice and ambition, however
narrow in those of reason) to the utmost extremity against them.
Except the former conquest of England by the Saxons themselves,
who were induced, by peculiar circumstances, to proceed even to
the extermination of the natives, it would be difficult to find in all

[y] Hoveden, p. 600.

CHAPTER IV

history a revolution more destructive, or attended with a more complete subjection of the antient inhabitants. Contumely seems even to have been wantonly added to oppression;[z] and the natives were universally reduced to such a state of meanness and poverty, that the English name became a term of reproach; and several generations elapsed before one family of Saxon pedigree was raised to any considerable honours, or could so much as attain the rank of baron of the realm.[a] These facts are so apparent from the whole tenor of the English history, that none would have been tempted to deny or elude them, were they not heated by the controversies of faction; while one party was *absurdly* afraid of those *absurd* consequences, which they saw the other party inclined to draw from this event. But it is evident, that the present rights and privileges of the people, who are a mixture of English and Normans, can never be affected by a transaction, which passed seven hundred years ago; and as all ancient authors,[*] who lived nearest the time, and best knew the state of the country, unanimously speak of the Norman dominion as a conquest by war and arms, no reasonable man, from the fear of imaginary consequences, will ever be tempted to reject their concurring and undoubted testimony.

King William had issue, besides his three sons, who survived him, five daughters, to wit, (1.) Cicily, a nun in the monastery of Feschamp, afterwards abbess in the holy Trinity at Caen, where she died in 1127. (2.) Constantia, married to Alan Fergant, earl of Britanny. She died without issue. (3.) Alice, contracted to Harold. (4.) Adela, married to Stephen, earl of Blois, by whom she had four sons, William, Theobald, Henry, and Stephen; of whom the elder was neglected, on account of the imbecillity of his understanding. (5.) Agatha, who died a virgin, but was betrothed to the king of Gallicia. She died on her journey thither, before she joined her bridegroom.

---

[z] H. Hunt. p. 370. Brompton, p. 980. [a] So late as the reign of king Stephen, the earl of Albemarle, before the battle of the Standard, addressed the officers of his army in these terms, *Proceres Angliae clarissimi, & genere Normanni, &c.* Brompton, p. 1026. See farther Abbas Rieval, p. 339, &c. All the barons and military men of England still called themselves Normans.
[*] See note [K] at the end of the volume.

V

WILLIAM RUFUS

*Accession of William Rufus –
Conspiracy against the King – Invasion
of Normandy – The Crusades – Acquisition of
Normandy – Quarrel with Anselm, the primate –
Death – and character of William Rufus*

🌸 🌸 🌸

*1087.
Accession
of Wil-
liam
Rufus.*

WILLIAM, sirnamed *Rufus* or the *Red,* from the colour of his hair, had no sooner procured his father's recommendatory letter to Lanfranc, the primate, than he hastened to take measures for securing to himself the government of England. Sensible, that a deed so unformal, and so little prepared, which violated Robert's right of primogeniture, might meet with great opposition, he trusted entirely for success to his own celerity; and having left St. Gervais, while William was breathing his last, he arrived in England, before intelligence of his father's death had reached that kingdom.[b] Pretending orders from the king, he secured the fortresses of Dover, Pevensey, and Hastings, whose situation rendered them of the greatest importance; and he got possession of the royal treasure at Winchester, amounting to the sum of sixty

---

[b] W. Malmes. p. 120. M. Paris, p. 10.

thousand pounds, by which he hoped to encourage and encrease his partizans.[c] The primate, whose rank and reputation in the kingdom gave him great authority, had been entrusted with the care of his education, and had conferred on him the honour of knighthood;[d] and being connected with him by these ties, and probably deeming his pretensions just, declared that he would pay a willing obedience to the last will of the Conqueror, his friend and benefactor. Having assembled some bishops and some of the principal nobility, he instantly proceeded to the ceremony of crowning the new king;[e] and by this dispatch endeavoured to prevent all faction and resistance. At the same time, Robert, who had been already acknowledged successor to Normandy, took peaceable possession of that dutchy.

But though this partition appeared to have been made without any violence or opposition, there remained in England many causes of discontent, which seemed to menace that kingdom with a sudden revolution. *Conspiracy against the king.* The barons, who generally possessed large estates both in England and in Normandy, were uneasy at the separation of those territories; and foresaw, that, as it would be impossible for them to preserve long their allegiance to two masters, they must necessarily resign either their ancient patrimony or their new acquisitions.[f] Robert's title to the dutchy they esteemed incontestible; his claim to the kingdom plausible; and they all desired that this prince, who alone had any pretensions to unite these states, should be put in possession of both. A comparison also of the personal qualities of the two brothers led them to give the preference to the elder. The duke was brave, open, sincere, generous: Even his predominant faults, his extreme indolence and facility, were not disagreeable to those haughty barons, who affected independance, and submitted with reluctance to a vigorous administration in their sovereign. The king, though equally brave, was violent, haughty, tyrannical; and seemed disposed to govern more by the fear than by the love of his subjects. Odo, bishop of Baieux, and Robert earl of Mortaigne, maternal brothers of the conqueror, envying the great credit of Lanfranc, which was encreased by his late services, enforced all these motives with their partizans, and

[c] Chron. Sax. p. 192. Brompton, p. 983.   [d] W. Malmes. p. 120. M. Paris, p. 10. Thom. Rudborne, p. 263.   [e] Hoveden, p. 461.   [f] Order. Vitalis, p. 666.

engaged them in a formal conspiracy to dethrone the king. They communicated their design to Eustace, count of Bologne, Roger earl of Shrewsbury and Arundel, Robert Belesme, his eldest son, William bishop of Durham, Robert de Moubray, Roger Bigod, Hugh de Grentmesnil; and they easily procured the assent of these potent noblemen. The conspirators, retiring to their castles, hastened to put themselves in a military posture; and expecting to be soon supported by a powerful army from Normandy, they had already begun hostilities in many places.

The king, sensible of his perilous situation, endeavoured to engage the affections of the native English. As that people were now so thoroughly subdued that they no longer aspired to the recovery of their ancient liberties, and were content with the prospect of some mitigation in the tyranny of the Norman princes, they zealously embraced William's cause, upon receiving general promises of good treatment, and of enjoying the licence of hunting in the royal forests. The king was soon in a situation to take the field; and as he knew the danger of delay, he suddenly marched into Kent; where his uncles had already seized the fortresses of Pevensey and Rochester. These places he successively reduced by famine; and though he was prevailed on by the earl of Chester, William de Warrenne, and Robert Fitz Hammon, who had embraced his cause, to spare the lives of the rebels, he confiscated all their estates, and banished them the kingdom.[g] This success gave authority to his negotiations with Roger earl of Shrewsbury, whom he detached from the confederates: And as his powerful fleet, joined to the indolent conduct of Robert, prevented the arrival of the Norman succours, all the other rebels found no resource but in flight or submission. Some of them received a pardon; but the greater part were attainted and the king bestowed their estates on the Norman barons, who had remained faithful to him.

1089.   William, freed from the danger of these insurrections, took little care of fulfilling his promises to the English, who still found themselves exposed to the same oppressions, which they had undergone during the reign of the Conqueror, and which were rather augmented by the violent, impetuous temper of the present

[g] Chron. Sax. p. 195. Order. Vital. p. 668.

CHAPTER V

monarch. The death of Lanfranc, who retained great influence over him, gave soon after a full career to his tyranny; and all orders of men found reason to complain of an arbitrary and illegal administration. Even the privileges of the church, held sacred in those days, were a feeble rampart against his usurpations. He seized the temporalities of all the vacant bishoprics and abbies; he delayed the appointing of successors to those dignities, that he might the longer enjoy the profits of their revenue; he bestowed some of the church-lands in property on his captains and favourites; and he openly set to sale such sees and abbies as he thought proper to dispose of. Though the murmurs of the ecclesiastics, which were quickly propagated to the nation, rose high against this grievance, the terror of William's authority, confirmed by the suppression of the late insurrections, retained every one in subjection and preserved general tranquillity in England.

The king even thought himself enabled to disturb his brother in the possession of Normandy. The loose and negligent administration of that prince had emboldened the Norman barons to affect a great independancy; and their mutual quarrels and devastations had rendered that whole territory a scene of violence and outrage. Two of them, Walter and Odo, were bribed by William to deliver the fortresses of St. Valori and Albemarle into his hands: Others soon after imitated the example of revolt; while Philip, king of France, who ought to have protected his vassal in the possession of his fief, was, after making some efforts in his favour, engaged by large presents to remain neuter. The duke had also reason to apprehend danger from the intrigues of his brother Henry. This young prince, who had inherited nothing of his father's great possessions but some of his money, had furnished Robert, while he was making his preparations against England, with the sum of three thousand marks; and in return for so slender a supply, had been put in possession of the Cotentin, which comprehended near a third of the dutchy of Normandy. Robert afterwards upon some suspicion threw him into prison; but finding himself exposed to invasion from the king of England, and dreading the conjunction of the two brothers against him, he now gave Henry his liberty, and even made use of his assistance in suppressing the insurrections of his rebellious subjects. Conan, a rich burgess of Roüen, had entered into a conspiracy to deliver that city to William; but Henry,

*1090.
Invasion
of Normandy.*

on the detection of his guilt, carried the traitor up to a high tower, and with his own hands flung him from the battlements.

The king appeared in Normandy at the head of an army; and affairs seemed to have come to extremity between the brothers; when the nobility on both sides, strongly connected by interest and alliances, interposed and mediated an accommodation. The chief advantage of this treaty accrued to William, who obtained possession of the territory of Eu, the towns of Aumale, Fescamp, and other places: But in return he promised, that he would assist his brother in subduing Maine, which had rebelled; and that the Norman barons, attainted in Robert's cause, should be restored to their estates in England. The two brothers also stipulated, that, on the demise of either without issue, the survivor should inherit all his dominions; and twelve of the most powerful barons on each side swore, that they would employ their power to insure the effectual execution of the whole treaty:[h] A strong proof of the great independance and authority of the nobles in those ages!

Prince Henry, disgusted, that so little care had been taken of his interests in this accommodation, retired to St. Michael's Mount, a strong fortress on the coast of Normandy, and infested the neighbourhood with his incursions. Robert and William with their joint forces besieged him in this place, and had nearly reduced him by the scarcity of water; when the elder, hearing of his distress, granted him permission to supply himself, and also sent him some pipes of wine for his own table. Being reproved by William for this ill-timed generosity, he replied, *What, shall I suffer my brother to die of thirst? Where shall we find another, when he is gone?* The king also, during this siege, performed an act of generosity, which was less suitable to his character. Riding out one day alone, to take a survey of the fortress, he was attacked by two soldiers, and dismounted. One of them drew his sword in order to dispatch him; when the king exclaimed, *Hold knave! I am the king of England.* The soldier suspended his blow; and raising the king from the ground, with expressions of respect, received a handsome reward, and was taken into his service. Prince Henry was soon after obliged to

---

[h] Chron. Sax. p. 197. W. Malm. p. 121. Hoveden, p. 462. M. Paris, p. 11. Annal. Waverl. p. 137. W. Heming. p. 463. Sim. Dunelm. p. 216. Brompton, p. 986.

CHAPTER V

capitulate; and being despoiled of all his patrimony, wandered about for some time with very few attendants, and often in great poverty.

The continued intestine discord among the barons was alone in that age destructive: The public wars were commonly short and feeble, produced little bloodshed, and were attended with no memorable event. To this Norman war, which was so soon concluded, there succeeded hostilities with Scotland, which were not of longer duration. Robert here commanded his brother's army, and obliged Malcolm to accept of peace and do homage to the crown of England. This peace was not more durable. Malcolm, two years after, levying an army, invaded England, and after ravaging Northumberland, he laid siege to Alnwic, where a party of earl Moubray's troops falling upon him by surprize, a sharp action ensued, in which Malcolm was slain. This incident interrupted for some years the regular succession to the Scottish crown. Though Malcolm left legitimate sons, his brother, Donald, on account of the youth of these princes, was advanced to the throne; but kept not long possession of it. Duncan, natural son of Malcolm, formed a conspiracy against him; and being assisted by William with a small force, made himself master of the kingdom. New broils ensued with Normandy. The frank, open, remiss temper of Robert was ill-fitted to withstand the interested, rapacious character of William, who, supported by greater power, was still encroaching on his brother's possessions, and instigating his turbulent barons to rebellion against him. The king, having gone over to Normandy to support his partizans, ordered an army of twenty thousand men to be levied in England, and to be conducted to the sea-coast, as if they were instantly to be embarked. Here Ralph Flambard, the king's minister, and the chief instrument of his extortions, exacted ten shillings a piece from them, in lieu of their service, and then dismissed them into their several counties. This money was so skilfully employed by William, that it rendered him better service than he could have expected from the army. He engaged the French king by new presents to depart from the protection of Robert; and he daily bribed the Norman barons to desert his service: But was prevented from pushing his advantages by an incursion of the Welsh, which obliged him to return to England. He found no difficulty in repelling the enemy; but was not able to

1091.

1093.

1094.

1095.

make any considerable impression on a country, guarded by its mountainous situation. A conspiracy of his own barons, which was detected at this time, appeared a more serious concern, and engrossed all his attention. Robert Moubray, earl of Northumberland, was at the head of this combination; and he engaged in it the count d'Eu, Richard de Tunbridge, Roger de Lacey, and many others. The purpose of the conspirators was to dethrone the king, and to advance in his stead, Stephen, count of Aumalc, nephew to the Conqueror. William's dispatch prevented the design from taking effect, and disconcerted the conspirators. Moubray made some resistance; but being taken prisoner, was attainted, and thrown into confinement, where he died about thirty

1096.

years after. The count d'Eu denied his concurrence in the plot; and to justify himself, fought, in the presence of the court at Windsor, a duel with Geoffrey Bainard, who accused him. But being worsted in the combat, he was condemned to be castrated, and to have his eyes put out. William de Alderi, another conspirator, was supposed to be treated with more rigour, when he was sentenced to be hanged.

The Crusades.

But the noise of these petty wars and commotions was quite sunk in the tumult of the Crusades, which now engrossed the attention of Europe, and have ever since engaged the curiosity of mankind, as the most signal and most durable monument of human folly, that has yet appeared in any age or nation. After Mahomet had, by means of his pretended revelations, united the dispersed Arabians under one head, they issued forth from their desarts in great multitudes; and being animated with zeal for their new religion, and supported by the vigour of their new government, they made deep impression on the eastern empire, which was far in the decline, with regard both to military discipline and to civil policy. Jerusalem, by its situation, became one of their most early conquests; and the Christians had the mortification to see the holy sepulchre, and the other places, consecrated by the presence of their religious founder, fallen into the possession of infidels. But the Arabians or Saracens were so employed in military enterprizes, by which they spread their empire, in a few years, from the banks of the Ganges, to the Streights of Gibraltar, that they had no leisure for theological controversy: And though the Alcoran, the original monument of their faith, seems to contain some violent

CHAPTER V

precepts, they were much less infected with the spirit of bigotry and persecution than the indolent and speculative Greeks, who were continually refining on the several articles of their religious system. They gave little disturbance to those zealous pilgrims, who daily flocked to Jerusalem; and they allowed every man, after paying a moderate tribute, to visit the holy sepulchre, to perform his religious duties, and to return in peace. But the Turcomans or Turks, a tribe of Tartars, who had embraced Mahometanism, having wrested Syria from the Saracens, and having in the year 1065 made themselves masters of Jerusalem, rendered the pilgrimage much more difficult and dangerous to the Christians. The barbarity of their manners, and the confusions attending their unsettled government, exposed the pilgrims to many insults, robberies, and extortions; and these zealots, returning from their meritorious fatigues and sufferings, filled all Christendom with indignation against the infidels, who profaned the holy city by their presence, and derided the sacred mysteries in the very place of their completion. Gregory VII. among the other vast ideas which he entertained, had formed the design of uniting all the western Christians against the Mahometans; but the egregious and violent invasions of that pontiff on the civil power of princes, had created him so many enemies, and had rendered his schemes so suspicious, that he was not able to make great progress in this undertaking. The work was reserved for a meaner instrument, whose low condition in life exposed him to no jealousy, and whose folly was well calculated to coincide with the prevailing principles of the times.

Peter, commonly called the Hermit, a native of Amiens in Picardy, had made the pilgrimage to Jerusalem. Being deeply affected with the dangers, to which that act of piety now exposed the pilgrims, as well as with the instances of oppression, under which the eastern Christians laboured, he entertained the bold, and in all appearance, impracticable project of leading into Asia, from the farthest extremities of the West, armies sufficient to subdue those potent and warlike nations, which now held the holy city in subjection.[i] He proposed his views to Martin II. who filled the papal chair, and who, though sensible of the advantages, which the head of the Christian religion must reap from a religious war, and

[i] Gul. Tyrius, lib. i. cap. 11. M. Paris, p. 17.

though he esteemed the blind zeal of Peter a proper means for effecting the purpose,[k] resolved not to interpose his authority, till he saw a greater probability of success. He summoned a council at Placentia, which consisted of four thousand ecclesiastics and thirty thousand seculars; and which was so numerous, that no hall could contain the multitude, and it was necessary to hold the assembly in a plain. The harangues of the pope, and of Peter himself, representing the dismal situation of their brethren in the east, and the indignity, suffered by the Christian name, in allowing the holy city to remain in the hands of infidels, here found the minds of men so well prepared, that the whole multitude, suddenly and violently, declared for the war, and solemnly devoted themselves to perform this service, so meritorious, as they believed it, to God and religion.

But though Italy seemed thus to have zealously embraced the enterprize, Martin knew, that, in order to insure success, it was necessary to inlist the greater and more warlike nations in the same engagement; and having previously exhorted Peter to visit the chief cities and sovereigns of Christendom, he summoned another council at Clermont in Auvergne.[l] The fame of this great and pious design, being now universally diffused, procured the attendance of the greatest prelates, nobles, and princes; and when the pope and the hermit renewed their pathetic exhortations, the whole assembly, as if impelled by an immediate inspiration, not moved by their preceding impressions, exclaimed with one voice, *It is the will of God, It is the will of God:* Words deemed so memorable, and so much the result of a divine influence, that they were employed as the signal of rendezvous and battle in all the future exploits of those adventurers.[m] Men of all ranks flew to arms with the utmost ardour; and an exterior symbol too, a circumstance of chief moment, was here chosen by the devoted combatants. The sign of the cross, which had been hitherto so much revered among Christians, and which, the more it was an object of reproach among the pagan world, was the more passionately cherished by them, became the badge of union, and was affixed to their right shoulder, by all who enlisted themselves in this sacred warfare.[n]

[k] Gul. Tyrius, lib. i. cap. 13.   [l] Concil. tom. x. Concil. Clarom. Matth. Paris, p. 16. M. West. p. 233.   [m] Historia Bell. Sacri, tom. i. Musaei Ital.   [n] Hist. Bell. Sacri, tom. 1. Mus. Ital. Order. Vital. p. 721.

CHAPTER V

Europe was at this time sunk into profound ignorance and
superstition: The ecclesiastics had acquired the greatest ascendant
over the human mind: The people, who, being little restrained by
honour, and less by law, abandoned themselves to the worst crimes
and disorders, knew of no other expiation than the observances
imposed on them by their spiritual pastors: and it was easy to
represent the holy war as an equivalent for all penances,[o] and an
atonement for every violation of justice and humanity. But amidst
the abject superstition, which now prevailed, the military spirit also
had universally diffused itself; and though not supported by art or
discipline, was become the general passion of the nations, governed by the feudal law. All the great lords possessed the right of
peace and war: They were engaged in perpetual hostilities with
each other: The open country was become a scene of outrage and
disorder: The cities, still mean and poor, were neither guarded by
walls, nor protected by privileges, and were exposed to every insult: Individuals were obliged to depend for safety on their own
force, or their private alliances: And valour was the only excel-
lence, which was held in esteem, or gave one man the pre-
eminence above another. When all the particular superstitions,
therefore, were here united in one great object, the ardour for
military enterprizes took the same direction; and Europe, impelled
by its two ruling passions, was loosened, as it were, from its foundations, and seemed to precipitate itself in one united body upon
the east.

All orders of men, deeming the crusades the only road to
heaven, enlisted themselves under these sacred banners, and were
impatient to open the way with their sword to the holy city. Nobles,
artizans, peasants, even priests[p] inrolled their names; and to decline this meritorious service was branded with the reproach of
impiety, or what perhaps was esteemed still more disgraceful, of
cowardice and pusillanimity.[q] The infirm and aged contributed to
the expedition by presents and money; and many of them, not
satisfied with the merit of this atonement, attended it in person,
and were determined, if possible, to breathe their last, in sight of
that city where their Saviour had died for them. Women themselves, concealing their sex under the disguise of armour, attended

[o] Order. Vital. p. 720.   [p] Order. Vital. p. 720.   [q] W. Malm. p. 133.

the camp; and commonly forgot still more the duty of their sex, by prostituting themselves, without reserve, to the army.[r] The greatest criminals were forward in a service, which they regarded as a propitiation for all crimes; and the most enormous disorders were, during the course of those expeditions, committed by men, enured to wickedness, encouraged by example, and impelled by necessity. The multitude of the adventurers soon became so great, that their more sagacious leaders, Hugh count of Vermandois, brother to the French king, Raymond count of Toulouse, Godfrey of Boüillon, prince of Brabant, and Stephen count of Blois,[s] became apprehensive lest the greatness itself of the armament should disappoint its purpose; and they permitted an undisciplined multitude, computed at 300,000 men, to go before them, under the command of Peter the Hermit, and Walter the Moneyless.[t] These men took the road towards Constantinople through Hungary and Bulgaria; and trusting, that Heaven, by supernatural assistance, would supply all their necessities, they made no provision for subsistence on their march. They soon found themselves obliged to obtain by plunder what they had vainly expected from miracles; and the enraged inhabitants of the countries through which they passed, gathering together in arms, attacked the disorderly multitude, and put them to slaughter without resistance. The more disciplined armies followed after; and passing the streights at Constantinople, they were mustered in the plains of Asia, and amounted in the whole to the number of 700,000 combatants.[u]

Amidst this universal frenzy, which spread itself by contagion throughout Europe, especially in France and Germany, men were not entirely forgetful of their present interest; and both those who went on this expedition, and those who stayed behind, entertained schemes of gratifying, by its means, their avarice or their ambition. The nobles who enlisted themselves were moved, from the romantic spirit of the age, to hope for opulent establishments in the east, the chief seat of arts and commerce during those ages; and in pursuit of these chimerical projects, they sold at the lowest price their ancient castles and inheritances, which had now lost all value in their eyes. The greater princes, who remained at home, besides

[r] Vertot Hist. de Chev. de Malte, vol. i. p. 46.   [s] Sim. Dunelm. p. 222.
[t] Matth. Paris, p. 17.   [u] Matth. Paris, p. 20, 21.

CHAPTER V

establishing peace in their dominions by giving occupation abroad to the inquietude and martial disposition of their subjects, took the opportunity of annexing to their crown many considerable fiefs, either by purchase or by the extinction of heirs. The pope frequently turned the zeal of the crusaders from the infidels against his own enemies, whom he represented as equally criminal with the enemies of Christ. The convents and other religious societies bought the possessions of the adventurers; and as the contributions of the faithful were commonly entrusted to their management, they often diverted to this purpose what was intended to be employed against the infidels.[w] But no one was a more immediate gainer by this epidemic fury than the king of England, who kept aloof from all connections with those fanatical and romantic warriors.

Robert, duke of Normandy, impelled by the bravery and mistaken generosity of his spirit, had early enlisted himself in the crusade; but being always unprovided with money, he found, that it would be impracticable for him to appear in a manner suitable to his rank and station, at the head of his numerous vassals and subjects, who, transported with the general rage, were determined to follow him into Asia. He resolved, therefore, to mortgage or rather to sell his dominions, which he had not talents to govern; and he offered them to his brother William, for the very unequal sum of ten thousand marks.[x] The bargain was soon concluded: The king raised the money by violent extortions on his subjects of all ranks, even on the convents, who were obliged to melt their plate in order to furnish the quota demanded of them:[y] He was put in possession of Normandy and Maine; and Robert, providing himself with a magnificent train, set out for the Holy Land, in pursuit of glory, and in full confidence of securing his eternal salvation.

Acquisition of Normandy.

The smallness of this sum, with the difficulties which William found in raising it, suffices alone to refute the account which is heedlessly adopted by historians, of the enormous revenue of the conqueror. Is it credible, that Robert would consign to the rapa-

[w] Padre Paolo Hist. delle benef. ecclesiast. p. 128. [x] W. Malm. p. 123. Chron. T. Wykes, p. 24. Annal. Waverl. p. 139. W. Heming. p. 467. Flor. Wig. p. 648. Sim. Dunelm. p. 222. Knyghton, p. 2364. [y] Eadmer, p. 35. W. Malm. p. 123. W. Heming. p. 467.

cious hands of his brother such considerable dominions, for a sum, which, according to that account, made not a week's income of his father's English revenue alone? Or that the king of England could not on demand, without oppressing his subjects, have been able to pay him the money? The conqueror, it is agreed, was frugal as well as rapacious; yet his treasure, at his death, exceeded not 60,000 pounds, which hardly amounted to his income for two months: Another certain refutation of that exaggerated account.

The fury of the crusades, during this age, less infected England than the neighbouring kingdoms; probably because the Norman conquerors, finding their settlement in that kingdom still somewhat precarious, durst not abandon their homes, in quest of distant adventures. The selfish interested spirit also of the king, which kept him from kindling in the general flame, checked its progress among his subjects; and as he is accused of open profaneness,[z] and was endued with a sharp wit,[a] it is likely that he made the romantic chivalry of the crusaders the object of his perpetual raillery. As an instance of his irreligion, we are told, that he once accepted of sixty marks from a Jew, whose son had been converted to Christianity, and who engaged him by that present to assist him in bringing back the youth to Judaism. William employed both menaces and persuasion for that purpose; but finding the convert obstinate in his new faith, he sent for the father, and told him, that as he had not succeeded, it was not just that he should keep the present; but as he had done his utmost, it was but equitable that he should be paid for his pains; and he would therefore retain only thirty marks of the money.[b] At another time, it is said, he sent for some learned Christian theologians and some rabbies, and bade them fairly dispute the question of their religion in his presence: He was perfectly indifferent between them; had his ears open to reason and conviction; and would embrace that doctrine, which upon comparison should be found supported by the most solid arguments.[c] If this story be true, it is probable that he meant only to amuse himself by turning both into ridicule: But we must be cautious of admitting every thing related by the monkish historians to the disadvantage of this prince: He had the misfortune to be

---

[z] G. Newbr. p. 358. W. Gemet. p. 292.   [a] W. Malm. p. 121.
[b] Eadmer, p. 47.   [c] W. Malm. p. 123.

CHAPTER V

engaged in quarrels with the ecclesiastics, particularly with Anselm, commonly called St. Anselm, archbishop of Canterbury; and
it is no wonder his memory should be blackened by the historians
of that order.

After the death of Lanfranc, the king, for several years, re- *Quarrel*
tained in his own hands the revenues of Canterbury, as he did *with An-*
those of many other vacant bishoprics: but falling into a dangerous *selm, the*
sickness, he was seized with remorse, and the clergy represented to *primate.*
him, that he was in danger of eternal perdition, if before his death
he did not make atonement for those multiplied impieties and
sacrileges, of which he had been guilty.[d] He resolved therefore to
supply instantly the vacancy of Canterbury; and for that purpose
he sent for Anselm, a Piedmontese by birth, abbot of Bec in Normandy, who was much celebrated for his learning and piety. The
abbot earnestly refused the dignity, fell on his knees, wept, and
entreated the king to change his purpose;[e] and when he found the
prince obstinate in forcing the pastoral staff upon him, he kept his
fist so fast clenched, that it required the utmost violence of the
bystanders to open it, and force him to receive that ensign of
spiritual dignity.[f] William soon after recovered; and his passions
regaining their wonted vigour, he returned to his former violence
and rapine. He detained in prison several persons whom he had
ordered to be freed during the time of his penitence; he still
preyed upon the ecclesiastical benefices; the sale of spiritual dignities continued as open as ever; and he kept possession of a considerable part of the revenues belonging to the see of Canterbury.[g]
But he found in Anselm that persevering opposition, which he had
reason to expect from the ostentatious humility, which that prelate
had displayed in refusing his promotion.

The opposition, made by Anselm, was the more dangerous
on account of the character of piety, which he soon acquired in
England, by his great zeal against all abuses, particularly those in
dress and ornament. There was a mode, which, in that age, prevailed throughout Europe, both among men and women, to give
an enormous length to their shoes, to draw the toe to a sharp point,
and to affix to it the figure of a bird's bill, or some such ornament,

[d] Eadmer, p. 16. Chron. Sax. p. 198.   [e] Eadmer, p. 17. Diceto, p. 494.
[f] Eadmer, p. 18.   [g] Eadmer, p. 19, 43. Chron. Sax. p. 199.

which was turned upwards, and which was often sustained by gold or silver chains tied to the knee.[h] The ecclesiastics took exception at this ornament, which, they said, was an attempt to bely the Scripture, where it is affirmed, that no man can add a cubit to his stature; and they declaimed against it with great vehemence, nay assembled some synods, who absolutely condemned it. But, such are the strange contradictions in human nature! Though the clergy, at that time, could overturn thrones, and had authority sufficient to send above a million of men on *their* errand to the desarts of Asia, they could never prevail against these long-pointed shoes: On the contrary, that caprice, contrary to all other modes, maintained its ground during several centuries; and if the clergy had not at last desisted from their persecution of it, it might still have been the prevailing fashion in Europe.

But Anselm was more fortunate in decrying the particular mode, which was the object of his aversion, and which probably had not taken such fast hold of the affections of the people. He preached zealously against the long hair and curled locks, which were then fashionable among the courtiers; he refused the ashes on Ash-Wednesday to those who were so accoutered; and his authority and eloquence had such influence, that the young men universally abandoned that ornament, and appeared in the cropt hair, which was recommended to them by the sermons of the primate. The noted historian of Anselm, who was also his companion and secretary, celebrates highly this effort of his zeal and piety.[i]

When William's profaneness therefore returned to him with his health, he was soon engaged in controversies with this austere prelate. There was at that time a schism in the church, between Urban and Clement, who both pretended to the papacy;[k] and Anselm, who, as abbot of Bec, had already acknowledged the former, was determined, without the king's consent, to introduce his authority into England.[l] William, who, imitating his father's example, had prohibited his subjects from recognizing any pope, whom he had not previously received, was enraged at this attempt;

[h] Order. Vital. p. 682. W. Malmes. p. 123. Knyghton, p. 2369.   [i] Eadmer, p. 23.   [k] Hoveden, p. 463.   [l] Eadmer, p. 25. M. Paris, p. 13. Diceto, p. 494. Spelm. Conc. vol. ii. p. 16.

CHAPTER V

and summoned a synod at Rockingham, with an intention of deposing Anselm: But the prelate's suffragans declared, that, without the papal authority, they knew of no expedient for inflicting that punishment on their primate.[m] The king was at last engaged by other motives to give the preference to Urban's title; Anselm received the pall from that pontiff; and matters seemed to be accommodated between the king and the primate,[n] when the quarrel broke out afresh from a new cause. William had undertaken an expedition against Wales, and required the archbishop to furnish his quota of soldiers for that service; but Anselm, who regarded the demand as an oppression on the church, and yet durst not refuse compliance, sent them so miserably accoutered, that the king was extremely displeased, and threatened him with a prosecution.[o] Anselm, on the other hand, demanded positively that all the revenues of his see should be restored to him; appealed to Rome against the king's injustice;[p] and affairs came to such extremities, that the primate, finding it dangerous to remain in the kingdom, desired and obtained the king's permission to retire beyond sea. All his temporalities were seized;[q] but he was received with great respect by Urban, who considered him as a martyr in the cause of religion, and even menaced the king, on account of his proceedings against the primate and the church, with the sentence of excommunication. Anselm assisted at the council of Bari, where, besides fixing the controversy between the Greek and Latin churches, concerning the procession of the Holy Ghost,[r] the right of election to church preferments was declared to belong to the clergy alone, and spiritual censures were denounced against all ecclesiastics, who did homage to laymen for their sees or benefices, and against all laymen who exacted it.[s] The rite of homage, by the feudal customs, was, that the vassal should throw himself on his knees, should put his joined hands between those of his superior, and should in that posture swear fealty to him.[t] But the council declared it execrable, that pure hands, which could create God, and could offer him up as a sacrifice for the salvation of mankind,

---

[m] Eadmer, p. 30.   [n] Diceto, p. 495.   [o] Eadmer, p. 37, 43.   [p] Ibid. p. 40.
[q] M. Paris, p. 13. Parker, p. 178.   [r] Eadmer, p. 49. M. Paris, p. 13. Sim. Dun. p. 224.   [s] M. Paris, p. 14.   [t] Spellman, Du Cange, in verb. *Hominium.*

should be put, after this humiliating manner, between profane hands, which, besides being inured to rapine and bloodshed, were employed day and night in impure purposes and obscene contacts.[u] Such were the reasonings prevalent in that age; reasonings, which, though they cannot be passed over in silence, without omitting the most curious and, perhaps, not the least instructive part of history, can scarcely be delivered with the requisite decency and gravity.

1097. The cession of Normandy and Maine by duke Robert encreased the king's territories; but brought him no great encrease of power, because of the unsettled state of those countries, the mutinous disposition of the barons, and the vicinity of the French king, who supported them in all their insurrections. Even Helie, lord of la Fleche, a small town in Anjou, was able to give him inquietude; and this great monarch was obliged to make several expeditions abroad, without being able to prevail over so petty a baron, who had acquired the confidence and affections of the inhabitants of Maine. He was, however, so fortunate, as at last to take him prisoner in a rencounter; but having released him, at the intercession of the French king and the count of Anjou, he found the province of Maine still exposed to his intrigues and incursions. Helie, being introduced by the citizens into the town of Mans,

1099. besieged the garrison in the citadel: William, who was hunting in the new forest, when he received intelligence of this hostile attempt, was so provoked, that he immediately turned his horse, and galloped to the sea-shore at Dartmouth; declaring, that he would not stop a moment till he had taken vengeance for the offence. He found the weather so cloudy and tempestuous, that the mariners thought it dangerous to put to sea: But the king hurried on board, and ordered them to set sail instantly; telling them that they never yet heard of a king that was drowned.[w] By this vigour and celerity, he delivered the citadel of Mans from its present danger; and pursuing Helie into his own territories, he laid siege to Majol, a small castle in those parts: But a wound,

1100. which he received before this place, obliged him to raise the siege; and he returned to England.

[u] W. Heming. p. 467. Flor. Wigorn. p. 649. Sim. Dunelm. p. 224. Brompton, p. 994.   [w] W. Malm. p. 124. H. Hunt. p. 378. M. Paris, p. 36. Ypod. Neust. p. 442.

CHAPTER V

The weakness of the greatest monarchs, during this age, in their military expeditions against their nearest neighbours, appears the more surprising, when we consider the prodigious numbers, which even petty princes, seconding the enthusiastic rage of the people, were able to assemble, and to conduct in dangerous enterprizes to the remote provinces of Asia. William, earl of Poitiers and duke of Guienne, enflamed with the glory, and not discouraged by the misfortunes, which had attended the former adventurers in the crusades, had put himself at the head of an immense multitude, computed by some historians to amount to 60,000 horse, and a much greater number of foot,[x] and he purposed to lead them into the Holy Land against the infidels. He wanted money to forward the preparations requisite for this expedition, and he offered to mortgage all his dominions to William, without entertaining any scruple on account of that rapacious and iniquitous hand, to which he resolved to consign them.[y] The king accepted the offer; and had prepared a fleet, and an army, in order to escort the money, and take possession of the rich provinces of Guienne and Poictou; when an accident put an end to his life, and to all his ambitious projects. He was engaged in hunting, the sole amusement, and indeed the chief occupation of princes in those rude times, when society was little cultivated, and the arts afforded few objects worthy of attention. Walter Tyrrel, a French gentleman, remarkable for his address in archery, attended him in this recreation, of which the new forest was the scene; and as William had dismounted after a chace, Tyrrel, impatient to show his dexterity, let fly an arrow at a stag, which suddenly started before him. The arrow, glancing from a tree, struck the king in the breast, and instantly slew him;[z] while Tyrrel, without informing any one of the accident, put spurs to his horse, hastened to the sea-shore, embarked for France, and joined the crusade in an expedition to Jerusalem; a pennance which he imposed on himself for this involuntary crime. The body of William was found in the forest by the country-people, and was buried without any pomp or ceremony at Winchester. His courtiers were negligent in performing the last duties to a master who was so little beloved; and every one

3d August.

Death

---

[x] W. Malm. p. 149. The whole is said by Order. Vital. p. 789, to amount to 300,000 men. [y] W. Malmes. p. 127. [z] W. Malm. p. 125. H. Hunt. p. 378. M. Paris, p. 37. Petr. Bles. p. 110.

was too much occupied in the interesting object of fixing his successor, to attend the funerals of a dead sovereign.

and char-
acter of
William
Rufus.

The memory of this monarch is transmitted to us with little
advantage by the churchmen, whom he had offended; and though
we may suspect in general, that their account of his vices is somewhat exaggerated, his conduct affords little reason for con-
tradicting the character which they have assigned him, or for at-
tributing to him any very estimable qualities. He seems to have
been a violent and tyrannical prince; a perfidious, encroaching,
and dangerous neighbour; an unkind and ungenerous relation.
He was equally prodigal and rapacious in the management of his
treasury; and if he possessed abilities, he lay so much under the
government of impetuous passions, that he made little use of them
in his administration; and he indulged, without reserve, that domineering policy, which suited his temper, and which, if supported,
as it was in him, with courage and vigour, proves often more
successful in disorderly times, than the deepest foresight and most
refined artifice.

The monuments which remained of this prince in England are
the Tower, Westminster-hall, and London-bridge, which he built.
The most laudable foreign enterprize which he undertook, was the
sending of Edgar Atheling, three years before his death, into Scotland with a small army, to restore prince Edgar the true heir of that
kingdom, son of Malcolm, and of Margaret, sister of Edgar Atheling; and the enterprize proved successful. It was remarked in that
age, that Richard, an elder brother of William's, perished by an
accident in the new forest; Richard, his nephew, natural son of
duke Robert, lost his life in the same place, after the same manner:
And all men, upon the king's fate, exclaimed, that, as the Conqueror had been guilty of extreme violence, in expelling all the
inhabitants of that large district, to make room for his game, the
just vengeance of heaven was signalized, in the same place, by the
slaughter of his posterity. William was killed in the thirteenth year
of his reign, and about the fortieth of his age. As he was never
married, he left no legitimate issue.

In the eleventh year of this reign, Magnus king of Norway
made a descent on the isle of Anglesea; but was repulsed by Hugh,
earl of Shrewsbury. This is the last attempt made by the northern
nations upon England. That restless people seem about this time

CHAPTER V

to have learned the practice of tillage, which thenceforth kept them at home, and freed the other nations of Europe from the devastations spread over them by those pyratical invaders. This proved one great cause of the subsequent settlement and improvement of the southern nations.

VI

HENRY I

The Crusades – Accession of Henry –
Marriage of the king – Invasion by duke
Robert – Accommodation with Robert –
Attack of Normandy – Conquest of Normandy –
Continuation of the quarrel with Anselm,
the primate – Compromise with him –
Wars abroad – Death of prince William –
King's second marriage – Death –
and character of Henry

1100.
The cru-
sades.

AFTER THE ADVENTURERS in the holy war were assembled on the banks of the Bosphorus, opposite to Constantinople, they proceeded on their enterprize; but immediately experienced those difficulties, which their zeal had hitherto concealed from them, and for which, even if they had foreseen them, it would have been almost impossible to provide a remedy. The Greek emperor, Alexis Comnenus, who had applied to the western Christians for succour against the Turks, entertained hopes, and those but feeble ones, of obtaining such a moderate supply, as, acting under his command, might enable him to repulse the enemy: But he was extremely astonished to see his dominions overwhelmed, on a sudden, by such an inundation of licentious barbarians, who, though they pretended friendship, despised his subjects as un-warlike, and detested them as heretical. By all the arts of policy, in which he excelled, he endeavoured to divert the torrent; but while

CHAPTER VI

he employed professions, caresses, civilities, and seeming services towards the leaders of the crusade, he secretly regarded those imperious allies as more dangerous than the open enemies, by whom his empire had been formerly invaded. Having effected that difficult point of disembarking them safely in Asia, he entered into a private correspondence with Soliman, emperor of the Turks; and practised every insidious art, which his genius, his power, or his situation enabled him to employ, for disappointing the enterprize, and discouraging the Latins from making thenceforward any such prodigious migrations. His dangerous policy was seconded by the disorders, inseparable from so vast a multitude, who were not united under one head, and were conducted by leaders of the most independant, intractable spirit, unacquainted with military discipline, and determined enemies to civil authority and submission. The scarcity of provisions, the excesses of fatigue, the influence of unknown climates, joined to the want of concert in their operations, and to the sword of a warlike enemy, destroyed the adventurers by thousands, and would have abated the ardour of men, impelled to war by less powerful motives. Their zeal, however, their bravery, and their irresistible force still carried them forward, and continually advanced them to the great end of their enterprize. After an obstinate siege, they took Nice, the seat of the Turkish empire; they defeated Soliman in two great battles; they made themselves masters of Antioch; and entirely broke the force of the Turks, who had so long retained those countries in subjection. The soldan of Egypt, whose alliance they had hitherto courted, recovered, on the fall of the Turkish power, his former authority in Jerusalem; and he informed them by his ambassadors, that, if they came disarmed to that city, they might now perform their religious vows, and that all Christian pilgrims, who should thenceforth visit the holy sepulchre, might expect the same good treatment, which they had ever received from his predecessors. The offer was rejected; the soldan was required to yield up the city to the Christians; and on his refusal, the champions of the cross advanced to the siege of Jerusalem, which they regarded as the consummation of their labours. By the detachments which they had made, and the disasters which they had undergone, they were diminished to the number of twenty thousand foot and fifteen hundred horse; but these were still formidable, from their valour, their experience, and the obedience, which, from past calamities, they had learned to pay to their leaders. After a siege of five weeks, they took Jerusalem by assault; and, impelled by a mixture of military and religious rage, they put the numerous garrison and inhabitants to the sword without distinction. Neither arms defended the valiant, nor submission the timorous: No age or sex was spared: Infants on the breast were pierced by the same blow with their mothers, who implored for mercy: Even a multitude, to the number of ten thousand persons, who had surrendered themselves prisoners, and were promised quarter, were butchered in cool blood by those ferocious conquerors.[a] The streets of Jerusalem were covered with dead bodies;[b] and the triumphant warriors, after every enemy was subdued and slaughtered, immediately turned themselves, with the sentiments of humiliation and contrition, towards the holy sepulchre. They threw aside their arms, still streaming with blood: They advanced with reclined bodies, and naked feet and heads to that sacred monument: They sung anthems to their Saviour, who had there purchased their salvation by his death and agony: And their devotion, enlivened by the presence of the place where he had suffered, so overcame their fury, that they dissolved in tears, and bore the appearance of every soft and tender sentiment. So inconsistent is human nature with itself! And so easily does the most effeminate superstition ally, both with the most heroic courage, and with the fiercest barbarity!

This great event happened on the fifth of July in the last year of the eleventh century. The Christian princes and nobles, after chusing Godfrey of Boüillion king of Jerusalem, began to settle themselves in their new conquests; while some of them returned to Europe, in order to enjoy at home that glory, which their valour had acquired them in this popular and meritorious enterprize. Among these, was Robert, duke of Normandy, who, as he had relinquished the greatest dominions of any prince that attended the crusade, had all along distinguished himself by the most intrepid courage, as well as by that affable disposition and unbounded generosity, which gain the hearts of soldiers, and qualify a prince to shine in a military life. In passing through Italy, he became acquainted with Sibylla, daughter of the count of Con-

[a] Vertot, vol. i. p. 57.   [b] M. Paris, p. 34. Order. Vital. p. 756. Diceto, p. 498.

CHAPTER VI

versana, a young lady of great beauty and merit, whom he espoused: Indulging himself in this new passion, as well as fond of enjoying ease and pleasure, after the fatigues of so many rough campaigns, he lingered a twelvemonth in that delicious climate; and though his friends in the north looked every moment for his arrival none of them knew when they could with certainty expect it. By this delay, he lost the kingdom of England, which the great fame he had acquired during the crusades, as well as his undoubted title, both by birth, and by the preceding agreement with his deceased brother, would, had he been present, have infallibly secured to him.

Prince Henry was hunting with Rufus in the new forest, when intelligence of that monarch's death was brought him; and being sensible of the advantage attending the conjuncture, he hurried to Winchester, in order to secure the royal treasure, which he knew to be a necessary implement for facilitating his designs on the crown. He had scarcely reached the place when William de Breteuil, keeper of the treasure, arrived, and opposed himself to Henry's pretensions. This nobleman, who had been engaged in the same party of hunting, had no sooner heard of his master's death, than he hastened to take care of his charge; and he told the prince, that this treasure, as well as the crown, belonged to his elder brother, who was now his sovereign; and that he himself, for his part, was determined, in spite of all other pretensions, to maintain his allegiance to him. But Henry, drawing his sword, threatened him with instant death, if he dared to disobey him; and as others of the late king's retinue, who came every moment to Winchester, joined the prince's party, Breteuil was obliged to withdraw his opposition, and to acquiesce in this violence.[c]

Henry, without losing a moment, hastened with the money to London; and having assembled some noblemen and prelates, whom his address, or abilities, or presents, gained to his side, he was suddenly elected, or rather saluted king; and immediately proceeded to the exercise of royal authority. In less than three days after his brother's death, the ceremony of his coronation was performed by Maurice, bishop of London, who was persuaded to officiate on that occasion;[d] and thus, by his courage and celerity, he

Accession of Henry.

---

[c] Order. Vital. p. 782.   [d] Chron. Sax. p. 208. Order. Vital. p. 783.

intruded himself into the vacant throne. No one had sufficient spirit or sense of duty to appear in defence of the absent prince: All men were seduced or intimidated: Present possession supplied the apparent defects in Henry's title, which was indeed founded on plain usurpation: And the barons, as well as the people, acquiesced in a claim, which, though it could neither be justified nor comprehended, could now, they found, be opposed through the perils alone of civil war and rebellion.

But as Henry foresaw, that a crown, usurped against all rules of justice, would sit unsteady on his head, he resolved, by fair professions at least, to gain the affections of all his subjects. Besides taking the usual coronation-oath to maintain the laws and execute justice, he passed a charter, which was calculated to remedy many of the grievous oppressions, which had been complained of during the reigns of his father and brother.[f] He there promised, that, at the death of any bishop or abbot, he never would seize the revenues of the see or abbey during the vacancy, but would leave the whole to be reaped by the successor; and that he would never let to farm any ecclesiastical benefice, nor dispose of it for money. After this concession to the church, whose favour was of so great importance, he proceeded to enumerate the civil grievances, which he purposed to redress. He promised, that, upon the death of any earl, baron, or military tenant, his heir should be admitted to the possession of his estate, on paying a just and lawful relief; without being exposed to such violent exactions as had been usual during the late reigns: He remitted the wardship of minors, and allowed guardians to be appointed, who should be answerable for the trust: He promised not to dispose of any heiress in marriage, but by the advice of all the barons; and if any baron intended to give his daughter, sister, niece, or kinswoman, in marriage, it should only be necessary for him to consult the king, who promised to take no money for his consent, nor ever to refuse permission, unless the person, to whom it was purposed to marry her, should happen to be his enemy: He granted his barons and military tenants the power of bequeathing by will their money or personal estates; and if they neglected to make a will, he promised, that their heirs should succeed to them: He renounced the right of

[f] Chron. Sax. p. 208. Sim. Dunelm. p. 225.

CHAPTER VI

imposing moneyage, and of levying taxes at pleasure on the farms, which the barons retained in their own hands:[f] He made some general professions of moderating fines; he offered a pardon for all offences; and he remitted all debts due to the crown: He required, that the vassals of the barons should enjoy the same privileges, which he granted to his own barons; and he promised a general confirmation and observance of the laws of king Edward. This is the substance of the chief articles contained in that famous charter.[g]

To give greater authenticity to these concessions, Henry lodged a copy of his charter in some abbey of each county; as if desirous that it should be exposed to the view of all his subjects, and remain a perpetual rule for the limitation and direction of his government: Yet it is certain, that, after the present purpose was served, he never once thought, during his reign, of observing one single article of it; and the whole fell so much into neglect and oblivion, that, in the following century, when the barons, who had heard an obscure tradition of it, desired to make it the model of the great charter, which they exacted from king John, they could with difficulty find a copy of it in the kingdom. But as to the grievances here meant to be redressed, they were still continued in their full extent; and the royal authority, in all those particulars, lay under no manner of restriction. Reliefs of heirs, so capital an article, were never effectually fixed till the time of Magna Charta;[h] and it is evident, that the general promise here given, of accepting a just and lawful relief, ought to have been reduced to more precision, in order to give security to the subject. The oppression of wardship and marriage was perpetuated even till the reign of Charles II.: And it appears from Glanville,[i] the famous justiciary of Henry II. that, in his time, where any man died intestate, an accident which must have been very frequent, when the art of writing was so little

[f] See Appendix II.   [g] Matth. Paris, p. 38. Hoveden, p. 468. Brompton, p. 1021. Hagulstad, p. 310.   [h] Glanv. lib. 2. cap. 36. What is called a relief in the Conqueror's laws, preserved by Ingulf, seems to have been the heriot; since reliefs, as well as the other burdens of the feudal law, were unknown in the age of the Confessor, whose laws these originally were.
[i] Lib. 7. cap. 16. This practice was contrary to the laws of king Edward, ratified by the Conqueror, as we learn from Ingulf, p. 91. But laws had at that time very little influence: Power and violence governed every thing.

known, the king, or the lord of the fief, pretended to seize all the moveables, and to exclude every heir, even the children of the deceased: A sure mark of a tyrannical and arbitrary government.

The Normans indeed, who domineered in England, were, during this age, so licentious a people, that they may be pronounced incapable of any true or regular liberty; which requires such improvement in knowledge and morals, as can only be the result of reflection and experience, and must grow to perfection during several ages of settled and established government. A people, so insensible to the rights of their sovereign, as to disjoint, without necessity, the hereditary succession, and permit a younger brother to intrude himself into the place of the elder, whom they esteemed, and who was guilty of no crime but being absent, could not expect, that that prince would pay any greater regard to their privileges, or allow his engagements to fetter his power, and debar him from any considerable interest or convenience. They had indeed arms in their hands, which prevented the establishment of a total despotism, and left their posterity sufficient power, whenever they should attain a sufficient degree of reason, to assume true liberty: But their turbulent disposition frequently prompted them to make such use of their arms, that they were more fitted to obstruct the execution of justice, than to stop the career of violence and oppression. The prince, finding that greater opposition was often made to him when he enforced the laws, than when he violated them, was apt to render his own will and pleasure the sole rule of government; and on every emergence to consider more the power of the persons whom he might offend, than the rights of those whom he might injure. The very form of this charter of Henry proves, that the Norman barons (for they, rather than the people of England, are chiefly concerned in it) were totally ignorant of the nature of limited monarchy, and were ill qualified to conduct, in conjunction with their sovereign, the machine of government. It is an act of his sole power, is the result of his free grace, contains some articles which bind others as well as himself, and is therefore unfit to be the deed of any one who possesses not the whole legislative power, and who may not at pleasure revoke all his concessions.

Henry, farther to encrease his popularity, degraded and committed to prison Ralph Flambard, bishop of Durham, who had been the chief instrument of oppression under his brother:[k] But this act was followed by another, which was a direct violation of his own charter, and was a bad prognostic of his sincere intentions to observe it: He kept the see of Durham vacant for five years, and during that time retained possession of all its revenues. Sensible of the great authority, which Anselm had acquired by his character of piety, and by the persecutions which he had undergone from William, he sent repeated messages to him at Lyons, where he resided, and invited him to return and take possession of his dignities.[l] On the arrival of the prelate, he proposed to him the renewal of that homage which he had done his brother and which had never been refused by any English bishop: But Anselm had acquired other sentiments by his journey to Rome, and gave the king an absolute refusal. He objected the decrees of the council of Bari, at which he himself had assisted; and he declared, that, so far from doing homage for his spiritual dignity, he would not so much as communicate with any ecclesiastic, who paid that submission or who accepted of investitures from laymen. Henry, who expected, in his present delicate situation, to reap great advantages from the authority and popularity of Anselm, durst not insist on his demand:[m] He only desired that the controversy might be suspended; and that messengers might be sent to Rome, in order to accommodate matters with the pope, and obtain his confirmation of the laws and customs of England.

There immediately occurred an important affair, in which the king was obliged to have recourse to the authority of Anselm. *Marriage of the king.* Matilda, daughter of Malcolm III. king of Scotland, and niece to Edgar Atheling, had, on her father's death, and the subsequent revolutions in the Scottish government, been brought to England, and educated under her aunt, Christina, in the nunnery of Rumsey. This princess Henry purposed to marry; but as she had worn the veil, though never taken the vows, doubts might arise concerning the lawfulness of the act; and it behoved him to be very careful not to shock, in any particular, the religious prejudices of his subjects. The affair was examined by Anselm in a council of the

---

[k] Chron. Sax. p. 208. W. Malm. p. 156. Matth. Paris, p. 39. Alur. Beverl. p. 144. [l] Chron. Sax. p. 208. Order. Vital. p. 783. Matth. Paris, p. 39. T. Rudborne, p. 273. [m] W. Malm. p. 225.

prelates and nobles, which was summoned at Lambeth: Matilda there proved, that she had put on the veil, not with a view of entering into a religious life, but merely in consequence of a custom, familiar to the English ladies, who protected their chastity from the brutal violence of the Normans, by taking shelter under that habit,[n] which amidst the horrible licentiousness of the times, was yet generally revered. The council, sensible that even a princess had otherwise no security for her honour, admitted this reason as valid: They pronounced, that Matilda was still free to marry;[o] and her espousals with Henry were celebrated by Anselm with great pomp and solemnity.[p] No act of the king's reign rendered him equally popular with his English subjects, and tended more to establish him on the throne. Though Matilda, during the life of her uncle and brothers, was not heir of the Saxon line, she was become very dear to the English on account of her connexions with it: And that people, who, before the conquest, had fallen into a kind of indifference towards their ancient royal family, had felt so severely the tyranny of the Normans, that they reflected with extreme regret on their former liberty, and hoped for a more equal and mild administration, when the blood of their native princes should be mingled with that of their new sovereigns.[q]

Invasion by duke Robert.

But the policy and prudence of Henry, which, if time had been allowed for these virtues to produce their full effect, would have secured him possession of the crown, ran great hazard of being frustrated by the sudden appearance of Robert, who returned to Normandy about a month after the death of his brother William.

1101.

He took possession, without opposition, of that dutchy; and immediately made preparations for recovering England, of which, during his absence, he had, by Henry's intrigues, been so unjustly defrauded. The great fame, which he had acquired in the East, forwarded his pretensions; and the Norman barons, sensible of the consequences, expressed the same discontent at the separation of the dutchy and kingdom, which had appeared on the accession of William. Robert de Belesme, earl of Shrewsbury and Arundel, William de la Warrenne, earl of Surrey, Arnulf de Montgomery, Walter Giffard, Robert de Pontefract, Robert de Mallet, Yvo de Grentmesnil, and many others of the principal nobility,[r] invited

[n] Eadmer, p. 57.   [o] Ibid.   [p] Hoveden, p. 468.   [q] M. Paris, p. 40.
[r] Order. Vital. p. 785.

CHAPTER VI

Robert to make an attempt upon England, and promised, on his landing, to join him with all their forces. Even the seamen were affected with the general popularity of his name, and they carried over to him the greater part of a fleet, which had been equipped to oppose his passage. Henry, in this extremity, began to be apprehensive for his life, as well as for his crown; and had recourse to the superstition of the people, in order to oppose their sentiment of justice. He paid diligent court to Anselm, whose sanctity and wisdom he pretended to revere. He consulted him in all difficult emergencies; seemed to be governed by him in every measure; promised a strict regard to ecclesiastical privileges; professed a great attachment to Rome, and a resolution of persevering in an implicit obedience to the decrees of councils, and to the will of the sovereign pontiff. By these caresses and declarations, he entirely gained the confidence of the primate, whose influence over the people, and authority with the barons, were of the utmost service to him, in his present situation. Anselm scrupled not to assure the nobles of the king's sincerity in those professions which he made, of avoiding the tyrannical and oppressive government of his father and brother: He even rode through the ranks of the army, recommended to the soldiers the defence of their prince, represented the duty of keeping their oaths of allegiance, and prognosticated to them the greatest happiness from the government of so wise and just a sovereign. By this expedient, joined to the influence of the earls of Warwic and Mellent, of Roger Bigod, Richard de Redvers, and Robert Fitz-Hamon, powerful barons, who still adhered to the present government, the army was retained in the king's interest, and marched, with seeming union and firmness, to oppose Robert, who had landed with his forces at Portsmouth.

The two armies lay in sight of each other for some days without coming to action; and both princes, being apprehensive of the event, which would probably be decisive, hearkened the more willingly to the counsels of Anselm and the other great men, who mediated an accommodation between them. After employing some negociation, it was agreed, that Robert should resign his pretensions to England, and receive in lieu of them an annual pension of 300 marks; that, if either of the princes died without issue, the other should succeed to his dominions; that the adherents of each should be pardoned, and restored to all their pos-

*Accommo-
dation
with
Robert.*

sessions either in Normandy or England; and that neither Robert nor Henry should thenceforth encourage, receive, or protect the enemies of the other.[5]

1102.   This treaty, though calculated so much for Henry's advantage, he was the first to violate. He restored indeed the estates of all Robert's adherents; but was secretly determined, that noblemen so powerful and so ill affected, who had both inclination and ability to disturb his government, should not long remain unmolested in their present opulence and grandeur. He began with the earl of Shrewsbury, who was watched for some time by spies, and then indicted on a charge, consisting of forty-five articles. This turbulent nobleman, knowing his own guilt, as well as the prejudices of his judges, and the power of his prosecutor, had recourse to arms for defence: But being soon suppressed by the activity and address of Henry, he was banished the kingdom, and his great estate was confiscated. His ruin involved that of his two brothers, Arnulf de Montgomery, and Roger earl of Lancaster. Soon after followed the prosecution and condemnation of Robert de Pontefract and Robert de Mallet, who had distinguished themselves among Robert's adherents. William de Warenne was the

1103.   next victim: Even William earl of Cornwal, son of the earl of Mortaigne, the king's uncle, having given matter of suspicion ٫gainst him, lost all the vast acquisitions of his family in England. Though the usual violence and tyranny of the Norman barons afforded a plausible pretence for those prosecutions, and it is probable that none of the sentences, pronounced against these noblemen, was wholly iniquituous; men easily saw or conjectured, that the chief part of their guilt was not the injustice or illegality of their conduct. Robert, enraged at the fate of his friends, imprudently ventured to come into England; and he remonstrated with his brother, in severe terms, against this breach of treaty: But met with so bad a reception, that he began to apprehend danger to his own liberty, and was glad to purchase an escape, by resigning his pension.

The indiscretion of Robert soon exposed him to more fatal injuries. This prince, whose bravery and candor procured him respect, while at a distance, had no sooner attained the possession

[5] Chron. Sax. p. 209. W. Malmes. p. 156.

CHAPTER VI

of power, and enjoyment of peace, than all the vigour of his mind
relaxed; and he fell into contempt among those who approached
his person, or were subjected to his authority. Alternately abandoned to dissolute pleasures and to womanish superstition, he was
so remiss, both in the care of his treasure and the exercise of his
government, that his servants pillaged his money with impunity,
stole from him his very clothes, and proceeded thence to practise
every species of extortion on his defenceless subjects. The barons,
whom a severe administration alone could have restrained, gave *Attack*
reins to their unbounded rapine upon their vassals, and inveterate *of Nor-*
animosities against each other; and all Normandy, during the *mandy.*
reign of this benign prince, was become a scene of violence and
depredation. The Normans at last, observing the regular government, which Henry, notwithstanding his usurped title, had been
able to establish in England, applied to him, that he might use his
authority for the suppression of these disorders; and they thereby
afforded him a pretence for interposing in the affairs of Normandy. Instead of employing his mediation, to render his
brother's government respectable, or to redress the grievances of
the Normans; he was only attentive to support his own partizans,
and to encrease their number by every art of bribery, intrigue, and
insinuation. Having found, in a visit, which he made to that
dutchy, that the nobility were more disposed to pay submission to
him than to their legal sovereign; he collected, by arbitrary extortions on England, a great army and treasure, and returned next
year to Normandy, in a situation to obtain, either by violence or
corruption, the dominion of that province. He took Bayeux by *1105.*
storm after an obstinate siege: He made himself master of Caen by
the voluntary submission of the inhabitants: But being repulsed at
Falaise, and obliged, by the winter season, to raise the siege, he
returned into England; after giving assurances to his adherents,
that he would persevere in supporting and protecting them.

Next year he opened the campaign with the siege of Tenche- *1106.*
bray; and it became evident, from his preparation and progress, *Conquest*
that he intended to usurp the entire possession of Normandy. *of Nor-*
Robert was at last rouzed from his lethargy; and being supported *mandy.*
by the earl of Mortaigne and Robert de Belesme, the king's inveterate enemies, he raised a considerable army, and approached his
brother's camp, with a view of finishing, in one decisive battle, the

quarrel between them. He was now entered on that scene of action, in which alone he was qualified to excel; and he so animated his troops by his example, that they threw the English into disorder, and had nearly obtained the victory;[t] when the flight of Bellesme spread a panic among the Normans, and occasioned their total defeat. Henry, besides doing great execution on the enemy, made near ten thousand prisoners; among whom was duke Robert himself, and all the most considerable barons, who adhered to his interest.[u] This victory was followed by the final reduction of Normandy: Roüen immediately submitted to the conqueror: Falaise, after some negotiation, opened its gates; and by this acquisition, besides rendering himself master of an important fortress, he got into his hands prince William, the only son of Robert: He assembled the states of Normandy; and having received the homage of all the vassals of the dutchy, having settled the government, revoked his brother's donations, and dismantled the castles, lately built, he returned into England, and carried along with him the duke as prisoner. That unfortunate prince was detained in custody during the remainder of his life, which was no less than twenty-eight years, and he died in the castle of Cardiff in Glamorganshire; happy if, without losing his liberty, he could have relinquished that power, which he was not qualified either to hold or exercise. Prince William was committed to the care of Helie de St. Saen, who had married Robert's natural daughter, and who, being a man of probity and honour, beyond what was usual in those ages, executed the trust with great affection and fidelity. Edgar Atheling, who had followed Robert in the expedition to Jerusalem, and who had lived with him ever since in Normandy, was another illustrious prisoner, taken in the battle of Tenchebray.[w] Henry gave him his liberty, and settled a small pension on him, with which he retired; and he lived to a good old age in England, totally neglected and forgotten. This prince was distinguished by personal bravery: But nothing can be a stronger proof of his mean talents in every other respect, than that, notwithstanding he possessed the affections of the English, and enjoyed the only legal title to the throne, he was allowed,

[t] H. Hunt. p. 379. M. Paris, p. 43. Brompton, p. 1002. [u] Eadmer, p. 90. Chron. Sax. p. 214. Order. Vital. p. 821. [w] Chron. Sax. p. 214. Ann. Waverl. p. 144.

CHAPTER VI

during the reigns of so many violent and jealous usurpers, to live unmolested, and go to his grave in peace.

A little after Henry had completed the conquest of Normandy, and settled the government of that province, he finished a controversy, which had been long depending between him and the pope, with regard to the investitures in ecclesiastical benefices; and though he was here obliged to relinquish some of the ancient rights of the crown, he extricated himself from the difficulty on easier terms than most princes, who, in that age, were so unhappy as to be engaged in disputes with the apostolic see. The king's situation, in the beginning of his reign, obliged him to pay great court to Anselm: The advantages, which he had reaped from the zealous friendship of that prelate, had made him sensible how prone the minds of his people were to superstition, and what an ascendant the ecclesiastics had been able to assume over them. He had seen, on the accession of his brother Rufus, that, though the rights of primogeniture were then violated, and the inclinations of almost all the barons thwarted, yet the authority of Lanfranc, the primate, had prevailed over all other considerations: His own case, which was still more unfavourable, afforded an instance, in which the clergy had more evidently shown their influence and authority. These recent examples, while they made him cautious not to offend that powerful body, convinced him, at the same time, that it was extremely his interest to retain the former prerogative of the crown in filling offices of such vast importance, and to check the ecclesiastics in that independance to which they visibly aspired. The choice, which his brother, in a fit of penitence, had made of Anselm, was so far unfortunate to the king's pretensions, that this prelate was celebrated for his piety and zeal and austerity of manners; and though his monkish devotion and narrow principles prognosticated no great knowledge of the world or depth of policy, he was, on that very account, a more dangerous instrument in the hands of politicians, and retained a greater ascendant over the bigotted populace. The prudence and temper of the king appear in nothing more conspicuous than in the management of this delicate affair; where he was always sensible that it had become necessary for him to risque his whole crown, in order to preserve the most invaluable jewel of it.[x]

1107.
Continuation of the quarrel with Anselm the primate.

[x] Eadmer, p. 56.

Anselm had no sooner returned from banishment, than his refusal to do homage to the king raised a dispute, which Henry evaded at that critical juncture, by promising to send a messenger, in order to compound the matter with Pascal II. who then filled the papal throne. The messenger, as was probably foreseen, returned with an absolute refusal of the king's demands;[y] and that fortified by many reasons, which were well qualified to operate on the understandings of men in those ages. Pascal quoted the scriptures to prove that Christ was the door; and he thence inferred, that all ecclesiastics must enter into the church through Christ alone, not through the civil magistrate, or any profane laymen.[z] "It is monstrous," added the pontiff, "that a son should pretend to beget his father, or a man to create his God: Priests are called Gods in scripture, as being the vicars of God: And will you, by your abominable pretensions to grant them their investiture, assume the right of creating them."[a]

But how convincing soever these arguments, they could not persuade Henry to resign so important a prerogative; and perhaps, as he was possessed of great reflection and learning, he thought, that the absurdity of a man's creating his God, even allowing priests to be gods, was not urged with the best grace by the Roman pontiff. But as he desired still to avoid, at least to delay, the coming to any dangerous extremity with the church, he persuaded Anselm, that he should be able, by farther negociation, to attain some composition with Pascal; and for that purpose, he dispatched three bishops to Rome, while Anselm sent two messengers of his own, to be more fully assured of the pope's intentions.[b] Pascal wrote back letters equally positive and arrogant both to the king and primate; urging to the former, that, by assuming the right of investitures, he committed a kind of spiritual adultery with the church, who was the spouse of Christ, and who must not admit of such a commerce with any other person;[c] and insisting with the latter, that the pretension of kings to confer benefices was the

---

[y] W. Malm. p. 225.   [z] Eadmer, p. 60. This topic is farther enforced in p. 73, 74. See also W. Malm. p. 163.   [a] Eadmer, p. 61. I much suspect, that this text of scripture is a forgery of his holiness: For I have not been able to find it. Yet it passed current in those ages, and was often quoted by the clergy as the foundation of their power. See Epist. St. Thom. p. 169.
[b] Eadmer, p. 62. W. Malm. p. 225.   [c] Eadmer, p. 63.

CHAPTER VI

source of all simony; a topic which had but too much foundation in those ages.[d]

Henry had now no other expedient than to suppress the letter addressed to himself, and to persuade the three bishops to prevaricate, and assert, upon their episcopal faith, that Pascal had assured them in private of his good intentions towards Henry, and of his resolution not to resent any future exertion of his prerogative in granting investitures; though he himself scrupled to give this assurance under his hand, lest other princes should copy the example and assume a like privilege.[e] Anselm's two messengers, who were monks, affirmed to him, that it was impossible this story could have any foundation: But their word was not deemed equal to that of three bishops; and the king, as if he had finally gained his cause, proceeded to fill the sees of Hereford and Salisbury, and to invest the new bishops in the usual manner.[f] But Anselm, who, as he had good reason, gave no credit to the asseveration of the king's messengers, refused not only to consecrate them, but even to communicate with them; and the bishops themselves, finding how odious they were become, returned to Henry the ensigns of their dignity. The quarrel every-day encreased between the king and the primate: The former, notwithstanding the prudence and moderation of his temper, threw out menaces against such as should pretend to oppose him in exerting the ancient prerogatives of his crown: And Anselm, sensible of his own dangerous situation, desired leave to make a journey to Rome, in order to lay the case before the sovereign pontiff. Henry, well pleased to rid himself without violence of so inflexible an antagonist, readily granted him permission. The prelate was attended to the shore by infinite multitudes, not only monks and clergymen, but people of all ranks, who scrupled not in this manner to declare for their primate against their sovereign, and who regarded his departure as the final abolition of religion and true piety in the kingdom.[g] The king, however, seized all the revenues of his see; and sent William de Warelwast to negociate with Pascal, and to find some means of accommodation in this delicate affair.

The English minister told Pascal, that his master would rather

---

[d] Eadmer, p. 64, 66. [e] Eadmer, p. 65. W. Malm. p. 225. [f] Eadmer, p. 66. W. Malm. p. 225. Hoveden, p. 469. Sim. Dunelm. p. 228. [g] Eadmer, p. 71.

lose his crown than part with the right of granting investitures. "And I," replied Pascal, "would rather lose my head than allow him to retain it."[h] Henry secretly prohibited Anselm from returning, unless he resolved to conform himself to the laws and usages of the kingdom; and the primate took up his residence at Lyons, in expectation, that the king would at last be obliged to yield the point, which was the present object of controversy between them. Soon after, he was permitted to return to his monastery at Bec in Normandy; and Henry, besides restoring to him the revenues of his see, treated him with the greatest respect, and held several conferences with him, in order to soften his opposition, and bend him to submission.[i] The people of England, who thought all differences now accommodated, were inclined to blame their primate for absenting himself so long from his charge; and he daily received letters from his partizans, representing the necessity of his speedy return. The total extinction, they told him, of religion and Christianity was likely to ensue from the want of his fatherly care: The most shocking customs prevail in England: And the dread of his severity being now removed, sodomy and the practice of wearing long hair gain ground among all ranks of men, and these enormities openly appear every where, without sense of shame or fear of punishment.[k]

The policy of the court of Rome has commonly been much admired; and men, judging by success, have bestowed the highest eulogies on that prudence by which a power, from such slender beginnings, could advance, without force of arms, to establish an universal and almost absolute monarchy in Europe. But the wisdom of so long a succession of men, who filled the papal throne, and who were of such different ages, tempers, and interests, is not intelligible, and could never have place in nature. The instrument, indeed, with which they wrought, the ignorance and superstition of the people, is so gross an engine, of such universal prevalence, and so little liable to accident or disorder, that it may be successful even in the most unskilful hands; and scarce any indiscretion can frustrate its operations. While the court of Rome was openly abandoned to the most flagrant disorders, even while it was torn with

[h] Eadmer, p. 73. W. Malm. p. 226. M. Paris, p. 40.   [i] Hoveden, p. 471.
[k] Eadmer, p. 81.

CHAPTER VI

schisms and factions, the power of the church daily made a sensible progress in Europe; and the temerity of Gregory and caution of Pascal were equally fortunate in promoting it. The clergy, feeling the necessity, which they lay under, of being protected against the violence of princes, or vigour of the laws, were well pleased to adhere to a foreign head, who being removed from the fear of the civil authority, could freely employ the power of the whole church in defending her ancient or usurped properties and privileges, when invaded in any particular country: The monks, desirous of an independance on their diocesans, professed a still more devoted attachment to the triple crown; and the stupid people possessed no science or reason, which they could oppose to the most exorbitant pretensions. Nonsense passed for demonstration: The most criminal means were sanctified by the piety of the end: Treaties were not supposed to be binding, where the interests of God were concerned: The ancient laws and customs of states had no authority against a divine right: Impudent forgeries were received as authentic monuments of antiquity: And the champions of holy church, if successful, were celebrated as heroes; if unfortunate, were worshipped as martyrs; and all events thus turned out equally to the advantage of clerical usurpations. Pascal himself, the reigning pope, was, in the course of this very controversy concerning investitures, involved in circumstances, and necessitated to follow a conduct, which would have drawn disgrace and ruin on any temporal prince, that had been so unfortunate as to fall into a like situation. His person was seized by the emperor Henry V. and he was obliged, by a formal treaty, to resign to that monarch, the right of granting investitures, for which they had so long contended.[1] In order to add greater solemnity to this agreement, the emperor and pope communicated together on the same hoste; one half of which was given to the prince, the other taken by the pontiff: The most tremendous imprecations were publicly denounced on either of them who should violate the treaty: Yet no sooner did Pascal recover his liberty, than he revoked all his concessions, and pronounced the sentence of excommunication against the emperor, who, in the end, was obliged to submit to the terms required of

[1] W. Malm. p. 167.

him, and to yield up all his pretensions, which he never could resume.[m]

The king of England had very nearly fallen into the same dangerous situation: Pascal had already excommunicated the earl of Mallont, and the other ministers of Henry, who were instrumental in supporting his pretensions:[n] He daily menaced the king himself with a like sentence; and he suspended the blow only to give him leisure to prevent it by a timely submission. The malcontents waited impatiently for the opportunity of disturbing his government by conspiracies and insurrections:[o] The king's best friends were anxious at the prospect of an incident, which would set their religious and civil duties at variance: And the countess of Blois, his sister, a princess of piety, who had great influence over him, was affrighted with the danger of her brother's eternal damnation.[p] Henry, on the other hand, seemed determined to run all hazards, rather than resign a prerogative of such importance, which had been enjoyed by all his predecessors; and it seemed probable, from his great prudence and abilities, that he might be able to sustain his rights, and finally prevail in the contest. While Pascal and Henry thus stood mutually in awe of each other, it was the more easy to bring about an accommodation between them, and to find a medium, in which they might agree.

Compromise with Anselm. Before bishops took possession of their dignities, they had formerly been accustomed to pass through two ceremonies: They received from the hands of the sovereign a ring and crosier, as symbols of their office; and this was called their *investiture:* They also made those submissions to the prince, which were required of vassals by the rites of the feudal law, and which received the name of *homage.* And as the king might refuse, both to grant the *investiture* and to receive the *homage,* though the chapter had, by some canons of the middle age, been endowed with the right of election, the sovereign had in reality the sole power of appointing prelates. Urban II. had equally deprived laymen of the rights of granting investiture and of receiving homage:[q] The emperors never were able, by all their wars and negociations, to make any

[m] Padre Paolo sopra benef. eccles. p. 112. W. Malmes. p. 170. Chron. Abb. St. Petri de Burgo, p. 63. Sim. Dunelm. p. 233.   [n] Eadmer, p. 79.   [o] Ibid. p. 80.   [p] Ibid. p. 79.   [q] Eadmer, p. 91. W. Malm. p. 163. Sim. Dunelm. p. 230.

distinction be admitted between them: The interposition of profane laymen, in any particular, was still represented as impious and abominable: And the church openly aspired to a total independance on the state. But Henry had put England, as well as Normandy, in such a situation as gave greater weight to his negotiations; and Pascal was for the present satisfied with his resigning the right of granting investitures, by which the spiritual dignity was supposed to be conferred; and he allowed the bishops to do homage for their temporal properties and privileges.ʳ The pontiff was well pleased to have made this acquisition, which, he hoped, would in time involve the whole: And the king, anxious to procure an escape from a very dangerous situation, was content to retain some, though a more precarious authority, in the election of prelates.

After the principal controversy was accommodated, it was not difficult to adjust the other differences. The pope allowed Anselm to communicate with the prelates, who had already received investitures from the crown; and he only required of them some submissions for their past misconduct.ˢ He also granted Anselm a plenary power of remedying every other disorder, which, he said, might arise from the barbarousness of the country.ᵗ Such was the idea which the popes then entertained of the English: and nothing can be a stronger proof of the miserable ignorance in which that people were then plunged, than that a man, who sat on the papal throne, and who subsisted by absurdities and nonsense, should think himself intitled to treat them as barbarians.

During the course of these controversies, a synod was held at Westminster, where the king, intent only on the main dispute, allowed some canons of less importance to be enacted, which tended to promote the usurpations of the clergy. The celibacy of priests was enjoined; a point which it was still found very difficult to carry into execution: And even laymen were not allowed to marry within the seventh degree of affinity.ᵘ By this contrivance, the pope augmented the profits, which he reaped from granting dispensations; and likewise those from divorces. For as the art of

ʳ Eadmer, p. 91. W. Malm. p. 164, 227. Hoveden, p. 471. M. Paris, p. 43. T. Rudb. p. 274. Brompton, p. 1000. Wilkins, p. 303. Chron. Dunst. p. 21. ˢ Eadmer, p. 87. ᵗ Ibid. p. 91. ᵘ Eadmer, p. 67, 68. Spelm. Conc. vol. ii. p. 22.

writing was then rare, and parish registers were not regularly kept, it was not easy to ascertain the degrees of affinity even among people of rank; and any man, who had money sufficient to pay for it, might obtain a divorce, on pretence that his wife was more nearly related to him than was permitted by the canons. The synod also passed a vote, prohibiting the laity from wearing long hair.[w] The aversion of the clergy to this mode was not confined to England. When the king went to Normandy, before he had conquered that province, the bishop of Seeze, in a formal harangue, earnestly exhorted him to redress the manifold disorders under which the government laboured, and to oblige the people to poll their hair in a decent form. Henry, though he would not resign his prerogatives to the church, willingly parted with his hair: He cut it in the form which they required of him, and obliged all the courtiers to imitate his example.[x]

Wars abroad.

The acquisition of Normandy was a great point of Henry's ambition; being the ancient patrimony of his family, and the only territory, which, while in his possession, gave him any weight or consideration on the continent: But the injustice of his usurpation was the source of great inquietude, involved him in frequent wars, and obliged him to impose on his English subjects those many heavy and arbitrary taxes, of which all the historians of that age unanimously complain.[y] His nephew, William, was but six years of age, when he committed him to the care of Helie de St. Saen; and it is probable, that his reason for intrusting that important charge to a man of so unblemished a character, was to prevent all malignant suspicions, in case any accident should befal the life of the young prince. He soon repented of his choice; but when he desired to recover possession of William's person, Helie withdrew his pupil, and carried him to the court of Fulk, count of Anjou, who gave him protection.[z] In proportion as the prince grew up to man's estate, he discovered virtues becoming his birth; and wandering through different courts of Europe, he excited the friendly compassion of many princes, and raised a general indignation against his uncle, who had so unjustly bereaved him of his inheritance. Lewis the Gross, son of Philip, was at this time king of France, a

1110.

[w] Eadmer, p. 68.　[x] Order. Vital. p. 816.　[y] Eadmer, p. 83. Chron. Sax. p. 211, 212, 213, 219, 220, 228. H. Hunt. p. 380. Hoveden, p. 470. Ann. Waverl. p. 143.　[z] Order. Vital. p. 837.

CHAPTER VI

brave and generous prince, who, having been obliged, during the life-time of his father, to fly into England, in order to escape the persecutions of his step-mother Bertrude, had been protected by Henry, and had thence conceived a personal friendship for him. But these ties were soon dissolved after the accession of Lewis, who found his interest to be in so many particulars opposite to those of the English monarch, and who became sensible of the danger attending the annexation of Normandy to England. He joined, therefore, the counts of Anjou and Flanders in giving disquiet to Henry's government; and this monarch, in order to defend his foreign dominions, found himself obliged to go over to Normandy, where he resided two years. The war which ensued among those princes was attended with no memorable event, and produced only slight skirmishes on the frontiers, agreeably to the weak condition of the sovereigns in that age, whenever their subjects were not rouzed by some great and urgent occasion. Henry, by contracting his eldest son, William, to the daughter of Fulk, detached that prince from the alliance, and obliged the others to come to an accommodation with him. This peace was not of long duration. His nephew, William, retired to the court of Baldwin, earl of Flanders, who espoused his cause; and the king of France, having soon after, for other reasons, joined the party, a new war was kindled in Normandy, which produced no event more memorable than had attended the former. At last the death of Baldwin, who was slain in an action near Eu, gave some respite to Henry, and enabled him to carry on war with more advantage against his enemies.

1118.

Lewis, finding himself unable to wrest Normandy from the king by force of arms, had recourse to the dangerous expedient, of applying to the spiritual power, and of affording the ecclesiastics a pretence to interpose in the temporal concerns of princes. He carried young William to a general council, which was assembled at Rheims by pope Calixtus II. presented the Norman prince to them, complained of the manifest usurpation and injustice of Henry, craved the assistance of the church for reinstating the true heir in his dominions, and represented the enormity of detaining in captivity so brave a prince as Robert, one of the most eminent champions of the cross, and who, by that very quality, was placed under the immediate protection of the holy see. Henry knew how to defend the rights of his crown with vigour, and yet with dexterity. He had sent over the English bishops to this synod; but at the same time had warned them, that, if any farther claims were started by the pope or the ecclesiastics, he was determined to adhere to the laws and customs of England, and maintain the prerogatives transmitted to him by his predecessors. "Go," said he to them, "salute the pope in my name; hear his apostolical precepts; but take care to bring none of his new inventions into my kingdom." Finding, however, that it would be easier for him to elude than oppose the efforts of Calixtus, he gave his ambassadors orders to gain the pope and his favourites by liberal presents and promises. The complaints of the Norman prince were thenceforth heard with great coldness by the council; and Calixtus confessed, after a conference, which he had the same summer with Henry, and when that prince probably renewed his presents, that, of all men, whom he had ever yet been acquainted with, he was, beyond comparison, the most eloquent and persuasive.

The warlike measures of Lewis proved as ineffectual as his intrigues. He had laid a scheme for surprising Noyon; but Henry, having received intelligence of the design, marched to the relief of the place, and suddenly attacked the French at Brenneville, as they were advancing towards it. A sharp conflict ensued; where prince William behaved with great bravery, and the king himself was in the most imminent danger. He was wounded in the head by Crispin, a gallant Norman officer, who had followed the fortunes of William;[a] but being rather animated than terrified by the blow, he immediately beat his antagonist to the ground, and so encouraged his troops by the example, that they put the French to total rout, and had very nearly taken their king prisoner. The dignity of the persons, engaged in this skirmish, rendered it the most memorable action of the war: For in other respects, it was not of great importance. There were nine hundred horsemen, who fought on both sides; yet were there only two persons slain. The rest were defended by that heavy armour, worn by the cavalry in those times.[b] An accommodation soon after ensued between the kings of France and England; and the interests of young William were entirely neglected in it.

[a] H. Hunt. p. 381. M. Paris, p. 47. Diceto, p. 503.   [b] Order. Vital. p. 854.

CHAPTER VI

But this public prosperity of Henry was much overbalanced by a domestic calamity, which befel him. His only son, William, had now reached his eighteenth year; and the king, from the facility with which he himself had usurped the crown, dreading that a like revolution might subvert his family, had taken care to have him recognized successor by the states of the kingdom, and had carried him over to Normandy, that he might receive the homage of the barons of that dutchy. The king, on his return, set sail from Barfleur, and was soon carried by a fair wind out of sight of land. The prince was detained by some accident; and his sailors, as well as their captain, Thomas Fitz-Stephens, having spent the interval in drinking, were so flustered, that, being in a hurry to follow the king, they heedlessly carried the ship on a rock, where she immediately foundered. William was put into the long-boat, and had got clear of the ship; when hearing the cries of his natural sister, the countess of Perche, he ordered the seamen to row back in hopes of saving her: But the numbers, who then crowded in, soon sunk the boat; and the prince with all his retinue perished. Above a hundred and forty young noblemen, of the principal families of England and Normandy, were lost on this occasion. A butcher of Roüen was the only person on board who escaped:[c] He clung to the mast, and was taken up next morning by fishermen. Fitz-Stephens also took hold of the mast; but being informed by the butcher, that prince William had perished, he said, that he would not survive the disaster; and he threw himself headlong into the sea.[d] Henry entertained hopes for three days, that his son had put into some distant port of England: But when certain intelligence of the calamity was brought him, he fainted away; and it was remarked, that he never after was seen to smile, nor ever recovered his wonted chearfulness.[e]

The death of William may be regarded, in one respect, as a misfortune to the English; because it was the immediate source of those civil wars, which, after the demise of the king, caused such confusion in the kingdom: But it is remarkable, that the young prince had entertained a violent aversion to the natives; and had been heard to threaten, that, when he should be king, he would

*1120.
Death of
prince
William.*

[c] Sim. Dunelm. p. 242. Alured Beverl. p. 148.   [d] Order. Vital. p. 868.
[e] Hoveden, p. 476. Order. Vital. p. 869.

make them draw the plough, and would turn them into beasts of burthen. These prepossessions he inherited from his father, who, though he was wont, when it might serve his purpose, to value himself on his birth, as a native of England,[f] showed, in the course of his government, an extreme prejudice against that people. All hopes of preferment, to ecclesiastical as well as civil dignities, were denied them during this whole reign; and any foreigner, however ignorant or worthless, was sure to have the preference in every competition.[g] As the English had given no disturbance to the government during the course of fifty years, this inveterate antipathy, in a prince of so much temper as well as penetration, forms a presumption, that the English of that age were still a rude and barbarous people even compared to the Normans, and impresses us with no very favourable idea of the Anglo-Saxon manners.

Prince William left no children; and the king had not now any legitimate issue; except one daughter, Matilda, whom, in 1110, he had betrothed, though only eight years of age,[h] to the emperor Henry V. and whom he had then sent over to be educated in Germany.[*] But as her absence from the kingdom, and her marriage into a foreign family, might endanger the succession, Henry, who was now a widower, was induced to marry in hopes of having *King's* male heirs; and he made his addresses to Adelais, daughter of *second* Godfrey, duke of Lovaine, and niece of pope Calixtus, a young *marriage.* princess of an amiable person.[i] But Adelais brought him no chil-
1121. dren; and the prince, who was most likely to dispute the succession, and even the immediate possession of the crown, recovered hopes of subverting his rival, who had successively seized all his patrimonial dominions. William, the son of duke Robert, was still protected in the French court; and as Henry's connections with the count of Anjou were broken off by the death of his son, Fulk joined the party of the unfortunate prince, gave him his daughter in marriage, and aided him in raising disturbances in Normandy. But Henry found the means of drawing off the count of Anjou, by forming anew with him a nearer connexion than the former, and one more material to the interests of that count's family. The *1127.* emperor, his son-in-law, dying without issue, he bestowed his

[f] Gul. Neub. lib. 1. cap. 3.   [g] Eadmer, p. 110.   [h] Chron. Sax. p. 215. W. Malm. p. 166. Order. Vital. p. 83.   [*] See note [L] at the end of the volume.   [i] Chron. Sax. p. 223. W. Malm. p. 165.

CHAPTER VI

daughter on Geoffrey, the eldest son of Fulk, and endeavoured to ensure her succession, by having her recognized heir to all his dominions, and obliging the barons both of Normandy and England to swear fealty to her. He hoped, that the choice of this husband would be more agreeable to all his subjects than that of the emperor; as securing them from the danger of falling under the dominion of a great and distant potentate, who might bring them into subjection, and reduce their country to the rank of a province: But the barons were displeased, that a step so material to national interests had been taken without consulting them;[k] and Henry had too sensibly experienced the turbulence of their disposition, not to dread the effects of their resentment. It seemed probable, that his nephew's party might gain force from the encrease of the malcontents: An accession of power, which that prince acquired a little after, tended to render his pretensions still more dangerous. Charles, earl of Flanders, being assassinated during the celebration of divine service, king Lewis immediately put the young prince in possession of that county, to which he had pretensions, in the right of his grandmother Matilda, wife to the Conqueror. But William survived a very little time this piece of good fortune, which seemed to open the way to still farther prosperity. He was killed in a skirmish with the landgrave of Alsace, his competitor for Flanders; and his death put an end, for the present, to the jealousy and inquietude of Henry.

The chief merit of this monarch's government consists in the profound tranquillity, which he established and maintained throughout all his dominions during the greater part of his reign. The mutinous barons were retained in subjection; and his neighbours, in every attempt which they made upon him, found him so well prepared, that they were discouraged from continuing or renewing their enterprizes. In order to repress the incursions of the Welsh, he brought over some Flemings in the year 1111, and settled them in Pembrokeshire, where they long maintained a different language, and customs, and manners, from their neighbours. Though his government seems to have been arbitrary in England, it was judicious and prudent; and was as little oppressive

1128.

---

[k] W. Malm. p. 175. The annals of Waverly, p. 150, say, that the king asked and obtained the consent of all the barons.

as the necessity of his affairs would permit. He wanted not attention to the redress of grievances; and historians mention in particular the levying of purveyance, which he endeavoured to moderate and restrain. The tenants in the king's demesne lands were at that time obliged to supply *gratis* the court with provisions, and to furnish carriages on the same hard terms, when the king made a progress, as he did frequently, into any of the counties. These exactions were so grievous, and levied in so licentious a manner, that the farmers, when they heard of the approach of the court, often deserted their houses, as if an enemy had invaded the country;[l] and sheltered their persons and families in the woods, from the insults of the king's retinue. Henry prohibited those enormities, and punished the persons guilty of them by cutting off their hands, legs, or other members.[m] But the prerogative was perpetual; the remedy applied by Henry was temporary; and the violence itself of this remedy, so far from giving security to the people, was only a proof of the ferocity of the government, and threatened a quick return of like abuses.

One great and difficult object of the king's prudence was the guarding against the encroachments of the court of Rome, and protecting the liberties of the church of England. The pope, in the year 1101, had sent Guy, archbishop of Vienne, as legate into Britain; and though he was the first that for many years had appeared there in that character, and his commission gave general surprize,[n] the king, who was then in the commencement of his reign, and was involved in many difficulties, was obliged to submit to this encroachment on his authority. But in the year 1116, Anselm, abbot of St. Sabas, who was coming over with a like legantine commission, was prohibited from entering the kingdom;[o] and pope Calixtus, who in his turn was then labouring under many difficulties, by reason of the pretensions of Gregory, an antipope, was obliged to promise, that he never would for the future, except when solicited by the king himself, send any legate into England.[p] Notwithstanding this engagement, the pope, as soon as he had suppressed his antagonist, granted the cardinal de Crema a legantine commission over the kingdom; and the king, who by reason

---

[l] Eadmer, p. 94. Chron. Sax. p. 212.   [m] Eadmer, p. 94.   [n] Ibid. p. 58.
[o] Hoveden, p. 474.   [p] Eadmer, p. 125, 137, 138.

CHAPTER VI

of his nephew's intrigues and invasions, found himself at that time in a dangerous situation, was obliged to submit to the exercise of this commission.[q] A synod was called by the legate at London; where, among other canons, a vote passed, enacting severe penalties on the marriages of the clergy.[r] The cardinal, in a public harangue, declared it to be an unpardonable enormity, that a priest should dare to consecrate and touch the body of Christ immediately after he had risen from the side of a strumpet: For that was the decent appellation which he gave to the wives of the clergy. But it happened, that the very next night, the officers of justice, breaking into a disorderly house, found the cardinal in bed with a courtezan;[s] an incident which threw such ridicule upon him, that he immediately stole out of the kingdom: The synod broke up; and the canons against the marriage of clergymen were worse executed than ever.[t]

Henry, in order to prevent this alternate revolution of concessions and encroachments, sent William, then archbishop of Canterbury, to remonstrate with the court of Rome against those abuses, and to assert the liberties of the English church. It was a usual maxim with every pope, when he found that he could not prevail in any pretension, to grant princes or states a power which they had always exercised, to resume at a proper juncture the claim which seemed to be resigned, and to pretend, that the civil magistrate had possessed the authority only from a special indulgence of the Roman pontiff. After this manner, the pope, finding that the French nations would not admit his claim of granting investitures, had passed a bull, giving the king that authority; and he now practised a like invention to elude the complaints of the king of England. He made the archbishop of Canterbury his legate, renewed his commission from time to time, and still pretended, that the rights, which that prelate had ever exercised as metropolitan, were entirely derived from the indulgence of the apostolic see. The English princes, and Henry in particular, who were glad to avoid

[q] Chron. Sax. p. 229. [r] Spelm. Conc. vol. ii. p. 34. [s] Hoveden, p. 478. M. Paris, p. 48. Matth. West. ad ann. 1125. H. Huntingdon, p. 382. It is remarkable, that this last writer, who was a clergyman as well as the others, makes an apology for using such freedom with the fathers of the church; but says, that the fact was notorious, and ought not to be concealed. [t] Chron. Sax. p. 234.

any immediate contest of so dangerous a nature, commonly acquiesced by their silence in these pretensions of the court of Rome.*

1131. As every thing in England remained in tranquillity, Henry took the opportunity of paying a visit to Normandy, to which he was invited, as well by his affection for that country, as by his tenderness for his daughter, the empress Matilda, who was always *1132.* his favourite. Some time after, that princess was delivered of a son, who received the name of Henry; and the king, farther to ensure her succession, made all the nobility of England and Normandy renew the oath of fealty, which they had already sworn to her.ᵘ The joy of this event, and the satisfaction which he reaped from his daughter's company, who bore successively two other sons, made his residence in Normandy very agreeable to him;ʷ and he seemed determined to pass the remainder of his days in that *1135.* country; when an incursion of the Welsh obliged him to think of returning into England. He was preparing for the journey, but was *1st of* seized with a sudden illness at St. Dennis le Forment, from eating *Dec.* too plentifully of lampreys, a food which always agreed better with *Death* his palate than his constitution.ˣ He died in the sixty-seventh year of his age, and the thirty-fifth year of his reign; leaving by will his daughter, Matilda, heir of all his dominions, without making any mention of her husband Geoffrey, who had given him several causes of displeasure.ʸ

and character of Henry. This prince was one of the most accomplished that has filled the English throne, and possessed all the great qualities both of body and mind, natural and acquired, which could fit him for the high station, to which he attained. His person was manly, his countenance engaging, his eyes clear, serene, and penetrating. The affability of his address encouraged those who might be overawed by the sense of his dignity or of his wisdom; and though he often indulged his facetious humour, he knew how to temper it with discretion, and ever kept at a distance from all indecent familiarities with his courtiers. His superior eloquence and judgment would have given him an ascendant even had he been born in a private station; and his personal bravery would have procured him respect, though it had been less supported by art and policy. By his

---

* See note [M] at the end of the volume. ᵘ W. Malm. p. 177. ʷ H. Hunt. p. 315. ˣ H. Hunt. p. 385. M. Paris, p. 50. ʸ W. Malm. p. 178.

CHAPTER VI

great progress in literature, he acquired the name of *Beau-clerc* or the scholar: But his application to those sedentary pursuits, abated nothing of the activity and vigilance of his government; and though the learning of that age was better fitted to corrupt than improve the understanding, his natural good sense preserved itself untainted both from the pedantry and superstition, which were then so prevalent among men of letters. His temper was susceptible of the sentiments as well of friendship as of resentment;[z] and his ambition, though high, might be deemed moderate and reasonable, had not his conduct towards his brother and nephew showed that he was too much disposed to sacrifice to it all the maxims of justice and equity. But the total incapacity of Robert for government afforded his younger brother a reason or pretence for seizing the scepter both of England and Normandy; and when violence and usurpation are once begun, necessity obliges a prince to continue in the same criminal course, and engages him in measures, which his better judgment and sounder principles would otherwise have induced him to reject with warmth and indignation.

King Henry was much addicted to women; and historians mention no less than seven illegitimate sons and six daughters born to him.[a] Hunting was also one of his favourite amusements; and he exercised great rigour against those who encroached on the royal forests, which were augmented during his reign,[b] though their number and extent were already too great. To kill a stag was as criminal as to murder a man: He made all the dogs be mutilated, which were kept on the borders of his forest: And he sometimes deprived his subjects of the liberty of hunting on their own lands, or even cutting their own woods. In other respects, he executed justice, and that with rigour; the best maxim which a prince in that age could follow. Stealing was first made capital in this reign:[c] False coining, which was then a very common crime, and by which the money had been extremely debased, was severely punished by Henry.[d] Near fifty criminals of this kind were at one time hanged or mutilated; and though these punishments seem to have been

[z] Order. Vital. p. 805.   [a] Gul. Gemet. lib. 8. cap. 29.   [b] W. Malm. p. 179.
[c] Sim. Dunelm. p. 231. Brompton, p. 1000. Flor. Wigorn. p. 653. Hoveden, p. 471.   [d] Sim. Dunelm. p. 231. Brompton, p. 1000. Hoveden, p. 471. Annal. Waverl. p. 149.

exercised in a manner somewhat arbitrary, they were grateful to the people, more attentive to present advantages, than jealous of general laws. There is a code, which passes under the name of Henry I. but the best antiquaries have agreed to think it spurious. It is however a very ancient compilation, and may be useful to instruct us in the manners and customs of the times. We learn from it, that a great distinction was then made between the English and Normans, much to the advantage of the latter.[e] The deadly feuds and the liberty of private revenge, which had been avowed by the Saxon laws, were still continued, and were not yet wholly illegal.[f]

Among the laws, granted on the king's accession, it is remarkable that the re-union of the civil and ecclesiastical courts, as in the Saxon times, was enacted.[g] But this law, like the articles of his charter, remained without effect, probably from the opposition of archbishop Anselm.

Henry, on his accession, granted a charter to London, which seems to have been the first step towards rendering that city a corporation. By this charter, the city was empowered to keep the farm of Middlesex at three hundred pounds a year, to elect its own sheriff and justiciary and to hold pleas of the crown; and it was exempted from Scot, Danegelt, trials by combat, and lodging the king's retinue. These, with a confirmation of the privileges of their court of Hustings, wardmotes, and common halls, and their liberty of hunting in Middlesex and Surrey, are the chief articles of this charter.[h]

It is said,[i] that this prince, from indulgence to his tenants, changed the rents of his demesnes, which were formerly paid in kind, into money, which was more easily remitted to the Exchequer. But the great scarcity of coin would render that commutation difficult to be executed, while at the same time provisions could not be sent to a distant quarter of the kingdom. This affords a probable reason, why the ancient kings of England so frequently changed their place of abode: They carried their court from one palace to another, that they might consume upon the spot the revenue of their several demesnes.

---

[e] LL. Hen. 1. § 18, 75.　[f] LL. Hen. § 82.　[g] Spellm. p. 305. Blackstone, vol. iii. p. 63. Coke, 2. Inst. 70.　[h] Lambardi Archaionomia ex edit. Twisden Wilkins, p. 235.　[i] Dial. de Scaccario, lib. 1. cap. 7.

VII

STEPHEN

*Accession of Stephen – War with Scotland –
Insurrection in favour of Matilda –
Stephen taken prisoner – Matilda crowned –
Stephen released – Restored to the crown –
Continuation of the civil wars –
Compromise between the king and prince
Henry – Death of the king*

I N THE PROGRESS and settlement of the feudal law, the male
succession to fiefs had taken place some time before the female
was admitted; and estates, being considered as military benefices,
not as property, were transmitted to such only as could serve in the
armies, and perform in person the conditions upon which they
were originally granted. But when the continuance of rights, during some generations, in the same family, had, in a great measure,
obliterated the primitive idea, the females were gradually admitted
to the possession of feudal property; and the same revolution of
principles, which procured them the inheritance of private estates,
naturally introduced their succession to government and authority. The failure, therefore, of male-heirs to the kingdom of
England and dutchy of Normandy, seemed to leave the succession
open, without a rival, to the empress Matilda; and as Henry had
made all his vassals in both states swear fealty to her, he presumed,

1135.

279

that they would not easily be induced to depart at once from her hereditary right, and from their own reiterated oaths and engagements. But the irregular manner, in which he himself had acquired the crown, might have instructed him, that neither his Norman nor English subjects were as yet capable of adhering to a strict rule of government; and as every precedent of this kind seems to give authority to new usurpations, he had reason to dread, even from his own family, some invasion of his daughter's title, which he had taken such pains to establish.

Adela, daughter of William the conqueror, had been married to Stephen, count of Blois, and had brought him several sons; among whom, Stephen and Henry, the two youngest, had been invited over to England by the late king, and had received great honours, riches, and preferment from the zealous friendship, which that prince bore to every one, that had been so fortunate as to acquire his favour and good opinion. Henry, who had betaken himself to the ecclesiastical profession, was created abbot of Glastenbury and bishop of Winchester; and though these dignities were considerable, Stephen had, from his uncle's liberality, attained establishments still more solid and durable.[k] The king had married him to Matilda, who was daughter and heir of Eustace count of Boulogne, and who brought him, besides that feudal sovereignty in France, an immense property in England, which, in the distribution of lands, had been conferred by the conqueror on the family of Boulogne. Stephen also by this marriage acquired a new connexion with the royal family of England; as Mary, his wife's mother, was sister to David, the reigning king of Scotland, and to Matilda, the first wife of Henry, and mother of the empress. The king, still imagining, that he strengthened the interests of his family by the aggrandizement of Stephen, took pleasure in enriching him by the grant of new possessions; and he conferred on him the great estate forfeited by Robert Mallet in England and that forfeited by the earl of Montaigne in Normandy. Stephen, in return, professed great attachment to his uncle; and appeared so zealous for the succession of Matilda, that, when the barons swore fealty to that princess, he contended with Robert, earl of Glocester, the king's natural son, who should first be admitted to give her this

[k] Gul. Neubr. p. 360. Brompton, p. 1023.

CHAPTER VII

testimony of devoted zeal and fidelity.[l] Meanwhile, he continued to
cultivate, by every art of popularity, the friendship of the English
nation; and many virtues, with which he seemed to be endowed,
favoured the success of his intentions. By his bravery, activity and
vigour, he acquired the esteem of the barons: By his generosity,
and by an affable and familiar address, unusual in that age among
men of his high quality, he obtained the affections of the people,
particularly of the Londoners.[m] And though he dared not to take
any steps towards his farther grandeur, lest he should expose
himself to the jealousy of so penetrating a prince as Henry; he still
hoped, that, by accumulating riches and power, and by acquiring
popularity, he might in time be able to open his way to the throne.

No sooner had Henry breathed his last, than Stephen, insensible to all the ties of gratitude and fidelity, and blind to danger,
gave full reins to his criminal ambition, and trusted, that, even
without any previous intrigue, the celerity of his enterprize and
the boldness of his attempt might overcome the weak attachment,
which the English and Normans in that age bore to the laws, and
to the rights of their sovereign. He hastened over to England; and
though the citizens of Dover, and those of Canterbury, apprized of
his purpose, shut their gates against him, he stopped not till he
arrived at London, where some of the lower rank, instigated by his
emissaries, as well as moved by his general popularity, immediately
saluted him king. His next point was to acquire the good will of the
clergy; and by performing the ceremony of his coronation, to put
himself in possession of the throne, from which, he was confident,
it would not be easy afterwards to expel him. His brother, the
bishop of Winchester, was useful to him in these capital articles:
Having gained Roger, bishop of Salisbury, who, though he owed
a great fortune and advancement to the favour of the late king,
preserved no sense of gratitude to that prince's family, he applied,
in conjunction with that prelate, to William, archbishop of Canterbury, and required him, in virtue of his office, to give the royal
unction to Stephen. The primate, who, as all the others, had sworn
fealty to Matilda, refused to perform this ceremony; but his opposition was overcome by an expedient equally dishonourable with
the other steps by which this revolution was effected. Hugh Bigod,

[l] W. Malm. p. 192.　[m] Ibid. p. 179. Gest. Steph. p. 928.

steward of the household, made oath before the primate, that the late king, on his death-bed, had shown a dissatisfaction with his daughter Matilda, and had expressed his intention of leaving the count of Boulogne heir to all his dominions.[n] William, either believing or feigning to believe Bigod's testimony, anointed Stephen, and put the crown upon his head; and from this religious ceremony, that prince, without any shadow either of hereditary title or consent of the nobility or people, was allowed to proceed to the exercise of sovereign authority. Very few barons attended his coronation.[o] But none opposed his usurpation, however unjust or flagrant. The sentiment of religion, which, if corrupted into superstition, has often little efficacy in fortifying the duties of civil society, was not affected by the multiplied oaths, taken in favour of Matilda, and only rendered the people obedient to a prince, who was countenanced by the clergy, and who had received from the primate the rite of royal unction and consecration.[p]

22d Decem.

Stephen, that he might farther secure his tottering throne, passed a charter, in which he made liberal promises to all orders of men; to the clergy, that he would speedily fill all vacant benefices, and would never levy the rents of any of them during the vacancy; to the nobility, that he would reduce the royal forests to their ancient boundaries, and correct all encroachments; and to the people, that he would remit the tax of Danegelt and restore the laws of king Edward.[q] The late king had a great treasure at Winchester, amounting to a hundred thousand pounds: And Stephen, by seizing this money, immediately turned against Henry's family the precaution, which that prince had employed for their grandeur and security: An event, which naturally attends the policy of amassing treasures. By means of this money, the usurper insured the compliance, though not the attachment, of the principal clergy and nobility; but not trusting to this frail security, he invited over from the continent, particularly from Britanny and Flanders, great numbers of those bravoes or disorderly soldiers, with whom every

[n] Matth. Paris, p. 51. Diceto, p. 505. Chron. Dunst. p. 23. [o] Brompton, p. 1023. [p] Such stress was formerly laid on the rite of coronation, that the monkish writers never give any prince the title of king, till he is crowned; though he had for some time been in possession of the crown, and exercised all the powers of sovereignty. [q] W. Malmes. p. 179. Hoveden, p. 482.

CHAPTER VII

country in Europe, by reason of the general ill police and turbulent government, extremely abounded.' These mercenary troops guarded his throne, by the terrors of the sword; and Stephen, that he might also overawe all malcontents by new and additional terrors of religion, procured a bull from Rome, which ratified his title, and which the pope, seeing this prince in possession of the throne, and pleased with an appeal to his authority in secular controversies, very readily granted him.'

Matilda and her husband Geoffrey, were as unfortunate in *1136.* Normandy as they had been in England. The Norman nobility, moved by an hereditary animosity against the Angevins, first applied to Theobald, count of Blois, Stephen's elder brother, for protection and assistance; but hearing afterwards, that Stephen had got possession of the English crown, and having many of them the same reasons as formerly for desiring a continuance of their union with that kingdom, they transferred their allegiance to Stephen, and put him in possession of their government. Lewis the younger, the reigning king of France, accepted the homage of Eustace, Stephen's eldest son, for the dutchy; and the more to corroborate his connexions with that family, he betrothed his sister, Constantia, to the young prince. The count of Blois resigned all his pretensions, and received in lieu of them, an annual pension of two thousand marks; and Geoffrey himself was obliged to conclude a truce for two years with Stephen, on condition of the king's paying him, during that time, a pension of five thousand.' Stephen, who had taken a journey to Normandy, finished all these transactions in person, and soon after returned to England.

Robert, earl of Glocester, natural son of the late king, was a man of honour and abilities; and as he was much attached to the interests of his sister, Matilda, and zealous for the lineal succession, it was chiefly from his intrigues and resistance, that the king had reason to dread a new revolution of government. This nobleman, who was in Normandy when he received intelligence of Stephen's accession, found himself much embarrassed concerning the measures, which he should pursue in that difficult emergency. To swear allegiance to the usurper appeared to him dishonourable, and a breach of his oath to Matilda: To refuse giving this pledge

---

' W. Malm. p. 179. ' Hagulstad. p. 259, 313. ' M. Paris, p. 52.

of his fidelity was to banish himself from England, and be totally incapacitated from serving the royal family, or contributing to their restoration.[u] He offered Stephen to do him homage and to take the oath of fealty; but with an express condition, that the king should maintain all his stipulations, and should never invade any of Robert's rights or dignities: And Stephen, though sensible, that this reserve, so unusual in itself, and so unbefitting the duty of a subject, was meant only to afford Robert a pretence for a revolt on the first favourable opportunity, was obliged, by the numerous friends and retainers of that nobleman, to receive him on those terms.[w] The clergy, who could scarcely, at this time, be deemed subjects to the crown, imitated that dangerous example: They annexed to their oaths of allegiance this condition, that they were only bound so long as the king defended the ecclesiastical liberties, and supported the discipline of the church.[x] The barons, in return for their submission, exacted terms still more destructive of public peace, as well as of royal authority: Many of them required the right of fortifying their castles, and of putting themselves in a posture of defence; and the king found himself totally unable to refuse his consent to this exorbitant demand.[y] All England was immediately filled with those fortresses which the noblemen garrisoned either with their vassals, or with licentious soldiers, who flocked to them from all quarters. Unbounded rapine was exercised upon the people for the maintenance of these troops; and private animosities, which had with difficulty been restrained by law, now breaking out without controul, rendered England a scene of uninterrupted violence and devastation. Wars between the nobles were carried on with the utmost fury in every quarter; the barons even assumed the right of coining money, and of exercising, without appeal, every act of jurisdiction;[z] and the inferior gentry, as well as the people, finding no defence from the laws, during this total dissolution of sovereign authority, were obliged, for their immediate safety, to pay court to some neighbouring chieftain, and to purchase his protection both by submitting to his exactions, and by assisting him in his rapine upon others. The erection of one castle proved the immediate cause of building

[u] Malmes. p. 179. [w] Ibid. M. Paris, p. 51. [x] W. Malm. p. 179. [y] Ibid. p. 180. [z] Trivet, p. 19. Gul. Neub. p. 372. Chron. Heming. p. 487. Brompton, p. 1035.

CHAPTER VII

many others; and even those who obtained not the king's permission, thought that they were entitled, by the great principle of self-preservation, to put themselves on an equal footing with their neighbours, who commonly were also their enemies and rivals. The aristocratical power, which is usually so oppressive in the feudal governments, had now risen to its utmost height, during the reign of a prince, who, though endowed with vigour and abilities, had usurped the throne without the pretence of a title, and who was necessitated to tolerate in others the same violence, to which he himself had been beholden for his sovereignty.

But Stephen was not of a disposition to submit long to these usurpations, without making some effort for the recovery of royal authority. Finding that the legal prerogatives of the crown were resisted and abridged, he was also tempted to make his power the sole measure of his conduct; and to violate all those concessions, which he himself had made on his accession,[a] as well as the ancient privileges of his subjects. The mercenary soldiers, who chiefly supported his authority, having exhausted the royal treasure, subsisted by depredations; and every place was filled with the best grounded complaints against the government. The earl of Glocester, having now settled with his friends the plan of an insurrection, retired beyond sea, sent the king a defiance, solemnly renounced his allegiance, and upbraided him with the breach of those conditions, which had been annexed to the oath of fealty, sworn by that nobleman.[b] David, king of Scotland, appeared at the head of an army in defence of his niece's title, and penetrating into Yorkshire, committed the most barbarous devastations on that country. The fury of his massacres and ravages enraged the northern nobility, who might otherwise have been inclined to join him; and William earl of Albemarle, Robert de Ferrers, William Piercy, Robert de Brus, Roger Moubray, Ilbert Lacy, Walter l'Espec, powerful barons in those parts, assembled an army, with which they encamped at North-Allerton, and awaited the arrival of the enemy. A great battle was here fought, called the battle of the *Standard,* from a high crucifix, erected by the English on a waggon, and carried along with the army as a military ensign. The king of Scots was defeated, and he himself, as well as his son Henry, narrowly

1137.

1138.
War with Scotland.

22d August.

---

[a] W. Malm. p. 180. M. Paris, p. 51.   [b] W. Malm. p. 180.

escaped falling into the hands of the English. This success over-awed the malcontents in England, and might have given some stability to Stephen's throne, had he not been so elated with pros-perity as to engage in a controversy with the clergy, who were at that time an overmatch for any monarch.

Though the great power of the church, in ancient times, weak-ened the authority of the crown, and interrupted the course of the laws, it may be doubted, whether, in ages of such violence and outrage, it was not rather advantageous that some limits were set to the power of the sword, both in the hands of the prince and nobles, and that men were taught to pay regard to some principles and privileges. The chief misfortune was, that the prelates, on some occasions, acted entirely as barons, employed military power against their sovereign or their neighbours, and thereby often encreased those disorders, which it was their duty to repress. The bishop of Salisbury, in imitation of the nobility, had built two strong castles, one at Sherborne, another at the Devizes, and had laid the foundations of a third at Malmesbury: His nephew, Alex-ander, bishop of Lincoln, had erected a fortress at Newark: And Stephen, who was now sensible from experience of the mischiefs attending these multiplied citadels, resolved to begin with de-stroying those of the clergy, who by their function seemed less intitled than the barons to such military securities.[c] Making pre-tence of a fray, which had arisen in court between the retinue of the bishop of Salisbury and that of the earl of Britanny, he seized both that prelate and the bishop of Lincoln, threw them into prison, and obliged them by menaces to deliver up those places of strength which they had lately erected.[d]

Henry, bishop of Winchester, the king's brother, being armed with a legantine commission, now conceived himself to be an ec-clesiastical sovereign no less powerful than the civil; and forgetting the ties of blood which connected him with the king, he resolved to vindicate the clerical privileges, which, he pretended, were here openly violated. He assembled a synod at Westminster, and there complained of the impiety of Stephen's measures, who had em-ployed violence against the dignitaries of the church, and had not awaited the sentence of a spiritual court, by which alone, he af-

1139.

30th Aug.

[c] Gul. Neubr. p. 362. [d] Chron. Sax. p. 238. W. Malmes. p. 181.

CHAPTER VII

firmed, they could lawfully be tried and condemned, if their conduct had any wise merited censure or punishment.[e] The synod ventured to send a summons to the king, charging him to appear before them, and to justify his measures;[f] and Stephen, instead of resenting this indignity, sent Aubrey de Vere to plead his cause before that assembly. De Vere accused the two prelates of treason and sedition; but the synod refused to try the cause, or examine their conduct, till those castles, of which they had been dispossessed, were previously restored to them.[g] The bishop of Salisbury declared, that he would appeal to the pope; and had not Stephen and his partizans employed menaces, and even shown a disposition of executing violence by the hands of the soldiery, affairs had instantly come to extremity between the crown and the mitre.[h]

While this quarrel, joined to so many other grievances, encreased the discontents among the people, the Empress, invited by the opportunity, and secretly encouraged by the legate himself, landed in England, with Robert earl of Glocester, and a retinue of a hundred and forty knights. She fixed her residence at Arundel castle, whose gates were opened to her by Adelais, the queendowager, now married to William de Albini, earl of Sussex; and she excited by messengers her partizans to take arms in every county of England. Adelais, who had expected that her daughter-in-law would have invaded the kingdom with a much greater force, became apprehensive of danger; and Matilda, to ease her of her fears, removed first to Bristol, which belonged to her brother Robert, thence to Glocester, where she remained under the protection of Milo, a gallant nobleman in those parts, who had embraced her cause. Soon after, Geoffrey Talbot, William Mohun, Ralph Lovel, William Fitz-John, William Fitz-Alan, Paganell, and many other barons, declared for her; and her party, which was generally favoured in the kingdom, seemed every day to gain ground upon that of her antagonist.

22d
Sept.
Insurrection in
favour of
Matilda.

Were we to relate all the military events transmitted to us by contemporary and authentic historians, it would be easy to swell our accounts of this reign into a large volume: But those incidents, so little memorable in themselves, and so confused both in time and place, could afford neither instruction nor entertainment to

[e] W. Malm. p. 182. [f] W. Malm. p. 182. M. Paris, p. 53. [g] W. Malm. p. 183. [h] Ibid.

the reader. It suffices to say, that the war was spread into every quarter; and that those turbulent barons, who had already shaken off, in a great measure, the restraint of government, having now obtained the pretence of a public cause, carried on their devastations with redoubled fury, exercised implacable vengeance on each other, and set no bounds to their oppressions over the people. The castles of the nobility were become receptacles of licensed robbers, who, sallying forth day and night, committed spoil on the open country, on the villages, and even on the cities; put the captives to torture, in order to make them reveal their treasures; sold their persons to slavery; and set fire to their houses, after they had pillaged them of everything valuable. The fierceness of their disposition, leading them to commit wanton destruction, frustrated their rapacity of its purpose; and the property and persons even of the ecclesiastics, generally so much revered, were at last, from necessity, exposed to the same outrage, which had laid waste the rest of the kingdom. The land was left untilled; the instruments of husbandry were destroyed or abandoned; and a grievous famine, the natural result of those disorders, affected equally both parties, and reduced the spoilers, as well as the defenceless people, to the most extreme want and indigence.

After several fruitless negociations and treaties of peace, which never interrupted these destructive hostilities, there happened at *1140.* last an event, which seemed to promise some end of the public calamities. Ralph, earl of Chester, and his half brother, William de Roumara, partizans of Matilda, had surprised the castle of Lincoln; but the citizens, who were better affected to Stephen, having invited him to their aid, that prince laid close siege to the castle, in hopes of soon rendering himself master of the place, either by assault or by famine. The earl of Glocester hastened with an army *1141.* to the relief of his friends; and Stephen, informed of his approach, *2d Feb.* took the field with a resolution of giving him battle. After a violent shock, the two wings of the royalists were put to flight; and Stephen himself, surrounded by the enemy, was at last, after exerting great efforts of valour, borne down by numbers, and taken *Stephen taken prisoner.* prisoner. He was conducted to Glocester; and though at first treated with humanity, was soon after, on some suspicion, thrown into prison, and loaded with irons.

<hr>

[i] Chron. Sax. p. 238. W. Malmes. p. 185. Gest. Steph. p. 961.

CHAPTER VII

Stephen's party was entirely broken by the captivity of their leader, and the barons came in daily from all quarters, and did homage to Matilda. The princess, however, amidst all her prosperity, knew, that she was not secure of success, unless she could gain the confidence of the clergy; and as the conduct of the legate had been of late very ambiguous, and showed his intentions to have rather aimed at humbling his brother, than totally ruining him, she employed every endeavour to fix him in her interests. She held a conference with him in an open plain near Winchester; where she promised upon oath, that, if he would acknowledge her for sovereign, would recognize her title as the sole descendant of the late king, and would again submit to the allegiance, which he, as well as the rest of the kingdom, had sworn to her, he should in return be entire master of the administration and in particular should, at his pleasure, dispose of all vacant bishoprics and abbies. Earl Robert, her brother, Brian Fitz-Count, Milo of Glocester, and other great men, became guarantees for her observing these engagements;[k] and the prelate was at last induced to promise her allegiance, but that still burdened with the express condition, that she should on her part fulfil her promises. He then conducted her to Winchester, led her in procession to the cathedral, and with great solemnity, in the presence of many bishops and abbots, denounced curses against all those who cursed her, poured out blessings on those who blessed her, granted absolution to such as were obedient to her, and excommunicated such as were rebellious.[l] Theobald, archbishop of Canterbury, soon after came also to court, and swore allegiance to the empress.[m]

Matilda, that she might farther ensure the attachment of the clergy, was willing to receive the crown from their hands; and instead of assembling the states of the kingdom, the measure which the constitution, had it been either fixed or regarded, seemed necessarily to require, she was content, that the legate should summon an ecclesiastical synod, and that her title to the throne should there be acknowledged. The legate, addressing himself to the assembly, told them, that, in the absence of the empress, Stephen, his brother, had been permitted to reign, and, previously to his ascending the throne, had seduced them by many fair promises, of honouring and exalting the church, of maintain-

Matilda crowned.

---

[k] W. Malm. p. 187. [l] Chron. Sax. p. 242. Contin. Flor. Wig. p. 676. [m] W. Malmes. p. 187.

ing the laws, and of reforming all abuses: That it grieved him to observe how much that prince had in every particular been wanting to his engagements; public peace was interrupted, crimes were daily committed with impunity, bishops were thrown into prison and forced to surrender their possessions, abbies were put to sale, churches were pillaged, and the most enormous disorders prevailed in the administration: That he himself, in order to procure a redress of these grievances, had formerly summoned the king before a council of bishops; but instead of inducing him to amend his conduct, had rather offended him by that expedient: That, how much soever misguided, that prince was still his brother, and the object of his affections; but his interests, however, must be regarded as subordinate to those of their heavenly father, who had now rejected him, and thrown him into the hands of his enemies: That it principally belonged to the clergy to elect and ordain kings; he had summoned them together for that purpose; and having invoked the divine assistance, he now pronounced Matilda, the only descendant of Henry, their late sovereign, queen of England. The whole assembly, by their acclamations or silence, gave, or seemed to give, their assent to this declaration.[n]

The only laymen summoned to this council, which decided the fate of the crown, were the Londoners; and even these were required, not to give their opinion, but to submit to the decrees of the synod. The deputies of London, however, were not so passive: They insisted, that their king should be delivered from prison; but were told by the legate, that it became not the Londoners, who were regarded as noblemen in England, to take part with those barons, who had basely forsaken their lord in battle, and who had treated holy church with contumely.[o] It is with reason that the citizens of London assumed so much authority, if it be true, what is related by Fitz-Stephen, a contemporary author, that that city could at this time bring into the field no less than 80,000 combatants.[p]

[n] W. Malmes. p. 188. This author, a judicious man, was present, and says, that he was very attentive to what passed. This speech, therefore, may be regarded as entirely genuine. [o] W. Malmes. p. 188. [p] P. 4. Were this account to be depended on, London must at that time have contained near 400,000 inhabitants, which is above double the number it contained at the death of queen Elizabeth. But these loose calculations, or rather guesses,

CHAPTER VII

London, notwithstanding its great power, and its attachment to Stephen, was at length obliged to submit to Matilda; and her authority, by the prudent conduct of earl Robert, seemed to be established over the whole kingdom: But affairs remained not long in this situation. That princess, besides the disadvantages of her sex, which weakened her influence over a turbulent and martial people, was of a passionate, imperious spirit, and knew not how to temper with affability the harshness of a refusal. Stephen's queen, seconded by many of the nobility, petitioned for the liberty of her husband; and offered, that, on this condition, he should renounce the crown, and retire into a convent. The legate desired, that prince Eustace, his nephew, might inherit Boulogne and the other patrimonial estates of his father:[q] The Londoners applied for the establishment of king Edward's laws, instead of those of king Henry, which, they said, were grievous and oppressive.[r] All these petitions were rejected in the most haughty and peremptory manner.

The legate, who had probably never been sincere in his compliance with Matilda's government, availed himself of the ill-humour excited by this imperious conduct, and secretly instigated the Londoners to a revolt. A conspiracy was entered into to seize the person of the empress; and she saved herself from the danger by a precipitate retreat. She fled to Oxford: Soon after she went to Winchester; whither the legate, desirous to save appearances, and watching the opportunity to ruin her cause, had retired. But having assembled all his retainers, he openly joined his force to that of the Londoners, and to Stephen's mercenary troops, who had not yet evacuated the kingdom; and he besieged Matilda in Winchester. The princess, being hard pressed by famine, made her escape; but in the flight, earl Robert, her brother, fell into the hands of the enemy. This nobleman, though a subject, was as much the life and soul of his own party, as Stephen was of the

---

deserve very little credit. Peter of Blois, a contemporary writer, and a man of sense, says there were then only forty thousand inhabitants in London, which is much more likely. See Epist. 151. What Fitz-Stephen says of the prodigious riches, splendor and commerce of London, proves only the great poverty of the other towns of the kingdom, and indeed of all the northern parts of Europe. [q] Brompton, p. 1031. [r] Contin. Flor. Wig. p. 677. Gervase, p. 1355.

Stephen
released.

1142.

1143.

1146.
Continu-
ation of
the civil
wars.

other; and the empress, sensible of his merit and importance, consented to exchange the prisoners on equal terms. The civil war was again kindled with greater fury than ever.

Earl Robert, finding the successes on both sides nearly balanced, went over to Normandy, which, during Stephen's captivity, had submitted to the earl of Anjou; and he persuaded Geoffrey to allow his eldest son, Henry, a young prince of great hopes, to take a journey into England, and appear at the head of his partizans. This expedient, however, produced nothing decisive. Stephen took Oxford after a long siege: He was defeated by earl Robert at Wilton: And the empress, though of a masculine spirit, yet being harassed with a variety of good and bad fortune, and alarmed with continual dangers to her person and family, at last retired into Normandy, whither she had sent her son some time before. The death of her brother, which happened nearly about the same time, would have proved fatal to her interests, had not some incidents occurred, which checked the course of Stephen's prosperity. This prince, finding that the castles built by the noblemen of his own party encouraged the spirit of independance, and were little less dangerous than those which remained in the hands of the enemy, endeavoured to extort from them a surrender of those fortresses; and he alienated the affections of many of them by this equitable demand. The artillery also of the church, which his brother had brought over to his side, had, after some interval, joined the other party. Eugenius III. had mounted the papal throne; the bishop of Winchester was deprived of the legantine commission, which was conferred on Theobald, archbishop of Canterbury, the enemy and rival of the former legate. That pontiff also, having summoned a general council at Rheims in Champagne, instead of allowing the church of England, as had been usual, to elect its own deputies, nominated five English bishops to represent that church, and required their attendance in the council. Stephen, who, notwithstanding his present difficulties, was jealous of the rights of his crown, refused them permission to attend;[s] and the pope, sensible of his advantage in contending with a prince who reigned by a disputed title, took revenge by laying all Stephen's party under an interdict.[t] The discontents of the royal-

[s] Epist. St. Thom. p. 225. [t] Chron. W. Thorn. p. 1807.

ists at being thrown into this situation, were augmented by a com-   *1147.*
parison with Matilda's party, who enjoyed all the benefits of the
sacred ordinances; and Stephen was at last obliged, by making
proper submissions to the see of Rome, to remove the reproach
from his party.[u]

The weakness of both sides, rather than any decrease of   *1148.*
mutual animosity, having produced a tacit cessation of arms in
England, many of the nobility, Roger de Moubray, William de
Warenne, and others, finding no opportunity to exert their military ardor at home, inlisted themselves in a new crusade, which
with surprising success, after former disappointments and misfortunes, was now preached by St. Barnard.[w] But an event soon after
happened, which threatened a revival of hostilities in England.
Prince Henry, who had reached his sixteenth year, was desirous of
receiving the honour of knighthood; a ceremony which every gentleman in that age passed through before he was admitted to the
use of arms, and which was even deemed requisite for the greatest
princes. He intended to receive his admission from his great-uncle,
David king of Scotland; and for that purpose he passed through
England with a great retinue, and was attended by the most considerable of his partizans. He remained some time with the king of
Scotland; made incursions into England; and by his dexterity and
vigour in all manly exercises, by his valour in war, and his prudent
conduct in every occurrence, he rouzed the hopes of his party, and
gave symptoms of those great qualities, which he afterwards displayed when he mounted the throne of England. Soon after his   *1150.*
return to Normandy, he was, by Matilda's consent, invested in that
dutchy; and upon the death of his father, Geoffrey, which happened in the subsequent year, he took possession both of Anjou
and Maine, and concluded a marriage, which brought him a great
accession of power, and rendered him extremely formidable to his
rival. Eleanor, the daughter and heir of William, duke of Guienne,
and earl of Poictou, had been married sixteen years to Lewis VII.
king of France, and had attended him in a crusade, which that
monarch conducted against the infidels: But having there lost the
affections of her husband, and even fallen under some suspicion
of gallantry with a handsome Saracen, Lewis, more delicate than

[u] Epist. St. Thom. p. 226.   [w] Hagulst. p. 275, 276.

1152. politic, procured a divorce from her, and restored her those rich provinces, which by her marriage she had annexed to the crown of France. Young Henry, neither discouraged by the inequality of years, nor by the reports of Eleanor's gallantries, made successful courtship to that princess, and, espousing her six weeks after her divorce, got possession of all her dominions as her dowry. The lustre which he received from this acquisition, and the prospect of his rising fortune, had such an effect in England, that, when Stephen, desirous to ensure the crown to his son Eustace, required the archbishop of Canterbury to anoint that prince as his successor, the primate refused compliance, and made his escape beyond sea, to avoid the violence and resentment of Stephen.

1153. Henry, informed of these dispositions in the people, made an invasion on England: Having gained some advantage over Stephen at Malmesbury, and having taken that place, he proceeded thence to throw succours into Wallingford, which the king had advanced with a superior army to besiege. A decisive action was every day expected; when the great men of both sides, terrified at the prospect of farther bloodshed and confusion, interposed with their good offices, and set on foot a negociation between the rival princes. The death of Eustace, during the course of the treaty, facilitated its conclusion: An accommodation was settled, *Compro-* by which it was agreed, that Stephen should possess the crown *mise be-* during his lifetime, that justice should be administered in his *tween the* name, even in the provinces which had submitted to Henry, and *king and* that this latter prince should, on Stephen's demise, succeed to the *prince* kingdom, and William, Stephen's son, to Boulogne and his patri-*Henry.* monial estate. After all the barons had sworn to the observance of *Death of* this treaty, and done homage to Henry, as to the heir of the crown, *the king.* that prince evacuated the kingdom; and the death of Stephen, *1154.* which happened next year, after a short illness, prevented all those *October* quarrels and jealousies, which were likely to have ensued in so *25.* delicate a situation.

England suffered great miseries during the reign of this prince: But his personal character, allowing for the temerity and injustice of his usurpation, appears not liable to any great exception; and he seems to have been well qualified, had he succeeded by a just title, to have promoted the happiness and prosperity of his subjects.[x] He

---

[x] W. Malmes. p. 180.

CHAPTER VII

was possessed of industry, activity, and courage, to a great degree; though not endowed with a sound judgment, he was not deficient in abilities; he had the talent of gaining men's affections; and notwithstanding his precarious situation, he never indulged himself in the exercise of any cruelty or revenge.[y] His advancement to the throne procured him neither tranquillity nor happiness; and though the situation of England prevented the neighbouring states from taking any durable advantage of her confusions, her intestine disorders were to the last degree ruinous and destructive. The court of Rome was also permitted, during those civil wars, to make farther advances in her usurpations; and appeals to the pope, which had always been strictly prohibited by the English laws, became now common in every ecclesiastical controversy.[z]

[y] M. Paris, p. 51. Hagul. p. 312. [z] H. Hunt. p. 395.

VIII

HENRY II

State of Europe – of France –
First acts of Henry's government –
Disputes between the civil and ecclesiastical
powers – Thomas a Becket, archbishop of
Canterbury – Quarrel between the king
and Becket – Constitutions of Clarendon –
Banishment of Becket – Compromise
with him – His return from banishment –
His murder – Grief –
and submission of the king

🌀 🌀 🌀

1154.
State of
Europe.

THE EXTENSIVE CONFEDERACIES, by which the European potentates are now at once united and set in opposition to each other, and which, though they are apt to diffuse the least spark of dissention throughout the whole, are at least attended with this advantage, that they prevent any violent revolutions or conquests in particular states, were totally unknown in ancient ages; and the theory of foreign politics, in each kingdom, formed a speculation much less complicated and involved than at present. Commerce had not yet bound together the most distant nations in so close a chain: Wars, finished in one campaign and often in one battle, were little affected by the movements of remote states: The imperfect communication among the kingdoms, and their ignorance of each other's situation, made it impracticable for a great number of them to combine in one project or effort: And above all, the tur-

CHAPTER VIII

bulent spirit and independant situation of the barons or great vassals in each state gave so much occupation to the sovereign, that he was obliged to confine his attention chiefly to his own state and his own system of government, and was more indifferent about what passed among his neighbours. Religion alone, not politics, carried abroad the views of princes; while it either fixed their thoughts on the Holy Land, whose conquest and defence was deemed a point of common honour and interest, or engaged them in intrigues with the Roman pontiff, to whom they had yielded the direction of ecclesiastical affairs, and who was every day assuming more authority than they were willing to allow him.

Before the conquest of England by the duke of Normandy, this island was as much separated from the rest of the world in politics as in situation: and except from the inroads of the Danish pirates, the English, happily confined at home, had neither enemies nor allies on the continent. The foreign dominions of William connected them with the king and great vassals of France; and while the opposite pretensions of the pope and emperor in Italy produced a continual intercourse between Germany and that country, the two great monarchs of France and England formed, in another part of Europe, a separate system, and carried on their wars and negotiations, without meeting either with opposition or support from the others.

On the decline of the Carlovingian race, the nobles, in every province of France, taking advantage of the weakness of the sovereign, and obliged to provide, each for his own defence, against the ravages of the Norman freebooters, had assumed, both in civil and military affairs, an authority almost independant, and had reduced, within very narrow limits, the prerogative of their princes. The accession of Hugh Capet, by annexing a great fief to the crown, had brought some addition to the royal dignity; but this fief, though considerable for a subject, appeared a narrow basis of power for a prince who was placed at the head of so great a community. The royal demesnes consisted only of Paris, Orleans, Estampes, Compiegne, and a few places, scattered over the northern provinces: In the rest of the kingdom, the prince's authority was rather nominal than real: The vassals were accustomed, nay entitled to make war, without his permission, on each other: They were even entitled, if they conceived themselves injured, to turn

State of France.

their arms against their sovereign: They exercised all civil jurisdiction, without appeal, over their tenants and inferior vassals: Their common jealousy of the crown easily united them against any attempt on their exorbitant privileges; and as some of them had attained the power and authority of great princes, even the smallest baron was sure of immediate and effectual protection. Besides six ecclesiastical peerages, which, with the other immunities of the church, cramped extremely the general execution of justice; there were six lay peerages, Burgundy, Normandy, Guienne, Flanders, Toulouse, and Champagne, which formed very extensive and puissant sovereignties. And though the combination of all those princes and barons could, on urgent occasions, muster a mighty power: Yet was it very difficult to set that great machine in movement; it was almost impossible to preserve harmony in its parts; a sense of common interest alone could, for a time, unite them under their sovereign against a common enemy; but if the king attempted to turn the force of the community against any mutinous vassal, the same sense of common interest made the others oppose themselves to the success of his pretensions. Lewis the Gross, the last sovereign, marched, at one time, to his frontiers against the Germans at the head of an army of two hundred thousand men; but a petty lord of Corbeil, of Puiset, of Couci, was able, at another period, to set that prince at defiance, and to maintain open war against him.

The authority of the English monarch was much more extensive within his kingdom, and the disproportion much greater between him and the most powerful of his vassals. His demesnes and revenue were large, compared to the greatness of his state: He was accustomed to levy arbitrary exactions on his subjects: His courts of judicature extended their jurisdiction into every part of the kingdom: He could crush by his power, or by a judicial sentence, well or ill founded, any obnoxious baron: And though the feudal institutions which prevailed in his kingdom, had the same tendency, as in other states, to exalt the aristocracy, and depress the monarchy, it required, in England, according to its present constitution, a great combination of the vassals to oppose their sovereign lord, and there had not hitherto arisen any baron so powerful, as of himself to levy war against the prince, and afford protection to the inferior barons.

CHAPTER VIII

While such were the different situations of France and England, and the latter enjoyed so many advantages above the former; the accession of Henry II. a prince of great abilities, possessed of so many rich provinces on the continent, might appear an event dangerous, if not fatal, to the French monarchy, and sufficient to break entirely the balance between the states. He was master, in the right of his father, of Anjou, and Touraine; in that of his mother, of Normandy and Maine; in that of his wife, of Guienne, Poictou, Xaintonge, Auvergne, Perigord, Angoumois, the Limousin. He soon after annexed Britanny to his other states, and was already possessed of the superiority over that province, which, on the first cession of Normandy to Rollo the Dane, had been granted by Charles the Simple in vassalage to that formidable ravager. These provinces composed above a third of the whole French monarchy, and were much superior, in extent and opulence, to those territories, which were subjected to the immediate jurisdiction and government of the king. The vassal was here more powerful than his liege lord: The situation, which had enabled Hugh Capet to depose the Carlovingian princes, seemed to be renewed, and that with much greater advantages on the side of the vassal: And when England was added to so many provinces, the French king had reason to apprehend, from this conjuncture, some great disaster to himself and to his family. But in reality, it was this circumstance, which appeared so formidable, that saved the Capetian race, and, by its consequences, exalted them to that pitch of grandeur, which they at present enjoy.

The limited authority of the prince in the feudal constitutions prevented the king of England from employing with advantage the force of so many states, which were subjected to his government; and these different members, disjoined in situation, and disagreeing in laws, language, and manners, were never thoroughly cemented into one monarchy. He soon became, both from his distant place of residence and from the incompatibility of interests, a kind of foreigner to his French dominions; and his subjects on the continent considered their allegiance as more naturally due to their superior lord, who lived in their neighbourhood, and who was acknowledged to be the supreme head of their nation. He was always at hand to invade them; their immediate lord was often at too great a distance to protect them; and any disorder in any part of his dispersed dominions gave advantages against him. The other powerful vassals of the French crown were rather pleased to see the expulsion of the English, and were not affected with that jealousy, which would have arisen from the oppression of a co-vassal, who was of the same rank with themselves. By this means, the king of France found it more easy to conquer those numerous provinces from England, than to subdue a duke of Normandy or Guienne, a count of Anjou, Maine, or Poictou. And after reducing such extensive territories, which immediately incorporated with the body of the monarchy, he found greater facility in uniting to the crown the other great fiefs, which still remained separate and independant.

But as these important consequences could not be foreseen by human wisdom, the king of France remarked with terror the rising grandeur of the house of Anjou or Plantagenet; and in order to retard its progress, he had ever maintained a strict union with Stephen, and had endeavoured to support the tottering fortunes of that bold usurper. But after this prince's death, it was too late to think of opposing the succession of Henry, or preventing the performance of those stipulations, which, with the unanimous consent of the nation he had made with his predecessor. The English, harassed with civil wars, and disgusted with the bloodshed and depredations, which, during the course of so many years, had attended them, were little disposed to violate their oaths, by excluding the lawful heir from the succession of their monarchy.[a] Many of the most considerable fortresses were in the hands of his partizans; the whole nation had had occasion to see the noble qualities with which he was endowed,[b] and to compare them with the mean talents of William, the son of Stephen; and as they were acquainted with his great power, and were rather pleased to see the accession of so many foreign dominions to the crown of England, they never entertained the least thoughts of resisting them. Henry himself, sensible of the advantages attending his present situation, was in no hurry to arrive in England; and being engaged in the siege of a castle on the frontiers of Normandy, when he received intelligence of Stephen's death, he made it a point of honour not to depart from his enterprize, till he had brought it to an issue. He

---

[a] Matth. Paris, p. 65.   [b] Gul. Neubr. p. 381.

then set out on his journey, and was received in England with the acclamations of all orders of men, who swore with pleasure the oath of fealty and allegiance to him.

8th December.

The first act of Henry's government corresponded to the high idea entertained of his abilities, and prognosticated the reestablishment of justice and tranquillity, of which the kingdom had so long been bereaved. He immediately dismissed all those mercenary soldiers, who had committed great disorders in the nation; and he sent them abroad, together with William of Ypres, their leader, the friend and confident of Stephen.[c] He revoked all the grants made by his predecessor,[d] even those which necessity had extorted from the empress Matilda; and that princess, who had resigned her rights in favour of Henry, made no opposition to a measure so necessary for supporting the dignity of the crown. He repaired the coin, which had been extremely debased during the reign of his predecessor; and he took proper measures against the return of a like abuse.[e] He was rigorous in the execution of justice, and in the suppression of robbery and violence; and that he might restore authority to the laws, he caused all the new erected castles to be demolished, which had proved so many sanctuaries to freebooters and rebels.[f] The earl of Albemarle, Hugh Mortimer, and Roger, the son of Milo of Glocester, were inclined to make some resistance to this salutary measure; but the approach of the king with his forces soon obliged them to submit.

*1155.
First
acts of
Henry's
government.*

Every thing being restored to full tranquillity in England, Henry went abroad in order to oppose the attempts of his brother Geoffrey, who, during his absence, had made an incursion into Anjou and Maine, had advanced some pretensions to those provinces, and had got possession of a considerable part of them.[*] On the king's appearance, the people returned to their allegiance; and Geoffrey, resigning his claim for an annual pension of a thousand pounds, departed and took possession of the county of Nantz, which the inhabitants, who had expelled count Hoei, their prince, had put into his hands. Henry returned to England the following year: The incursions of the Welsh then provoked him to make an

1157.

[c] Fitz-Steph. p. 13. M. Paris, p. 65. Neubr. p. 381. Chron. T. Wykes, p. 30.
[d] Neubr. p. 382. [e] Hoveden, p. 491. [f] Hoveden, p. 491. Fitz-Steph.
p. 13. M. Paris, p. 65. Neubr. p. 381. Brompton, p. 1043. [*] See note [N]
at the end of the volume.

invasion upon them; where the natural fastnesses of the country occasioned him great difficulties, and even brought him into danger. His vanguard, being engaged in a narrow pass, was put to rout: Henry de Essex, the hereditary standard-bearer, seized with a panic, threw down the standard, took to flight, and exclaimed that the king was slain: And had not the prince immediately appeared in person, and led on his troops with great gallantry, the consequences might have proved fatal to the whole army.[g] For this misbehaviour, Essex was afterwards accused of felony by Robert de Montfort; was vanquished in single combat; his estate was confiscated; and he himself was thrust into a convent.[h] The submissions of the Welsh procured them an accommodation with England.

1158. The martial disposition of the princes in that age engaged them to head their own armies in every enterprize, even the most frivolous; and their feeble authority made it commonly impracticable for them to delegate, on occasion, the command to their generals. Geoffrey, the king's brother, died soon after he had acquired possession of Nantz: Though he had no other title to that county, than the voluntary submission or election of the inhabitants two years before, Henry laid claim to the territory as devolved to him by hereditary right, and he went over to support his pretensions by force of arms. Conan, duke or earl of Britanny (for these titles are given indifferently by historians to those princes) pretended that Nantz had been lately separated by rebellion from his principality, to which of right it belonged; and immediately on Geoffrey's death, he took possession of the disputed territory. Lest Lewis, the French king, should interpose in the controversy, Henry paid him a visit; and so allured him by caresses and civilities, that an alliance was contracted between them; and they agreed, that young Henry, heir to the English monarchy, should be affianced to Margaret of France, though the former was only five years of age, the latter was still in her cradle. Henry, now secure of meeting with no interruption on this side, advanced with his army into Britanny; and Conan, in despair of being able to make resistance, delivered up the county of Nantz to him. The able conduct of the king procured him farther and more important advan-

[g] Neubr. p. 383. Chron. W. Heming. p. 492.   [h] M. Paris, p. 70. Neubr. p. 383.

tages from this incident. Conan, harassed with the turbulent disposition of his subjects, was desirous of procuring to himself the support of so great a monarch; and he betrothed his daughter and only child, yet an infant, to Geoffrey, the king's third son, who was of the same tender years. The duke of Britanny died about seven years after; and Henry, being *mesne* lord and also natural guardian to his son and daughter-in-law, put himself in possession of that principality, and annexed it for the present to his other great dominions.

The king had a prospect of making still farther acquisi- *1159.* tions; and the activity of his temper suffered no opportunity of that kind to escape him. Philippa, duchess of Guienne, mother of Queen Eleanor, was the only issue of William IV. count of Toulouse; and would have inherited his dominions, had not that prince, desirous of preserving the succession in the male-line, conveyed the principality to his brother, Raymond de St. Gilles, by a contract of sale which was in that age regarded as fictitious and illusory. By this means the title to the county of Toulouse came to be disputed between the male and female heirs; and the one or the other, as opportunities favoured them, had obtained possession. Raymond, grandson of Raymond de St. Gilles, was the reigning sovereign; and on Henry's reviving his wife's claim, this prince had recourse for protection to the king of France, who was so much concerned in policy to prevent the farther aggrandizement of the English monarch. Lewis himself, when married to Eleanor, had asserted the justice of her claim, and had demanded possession of Toulouse;[i] but his sentiments changing with his interest, he now determined to defend, by his power and authority, the title of Raymond. Henry found, that it would be requisite to support his pretensions against potent antagonists; and that nothing but a formidable army could maintain a claim, which he had in vain asserted by arguments and manifestos.

An army, composed of feudal vassals, was commonly very intractable and undisciplined, both because of the independant spirit of the persons who served in it, and because the commands were not given either by the choice of the sovereign or from the military capacity and experience of the officers. Each baron con-

[i] Neubr. p. 387. Chron. W. Heming. p. 494.

ducted his own vassals: His rank was greater or less, proportioned to the extent of his property: Even the supreme command under the prince was often attached to birth: And as the military vassals were obliged to serve only forty days at their own charge; though, if the expedition were distant, they were put to great expence; the prince reaped little benefit from their attendance. Henry, sensible of these inconveniencies, levied upon his vassals in Normandy and other provinces, which were remote from Toulouse, a sum of money in lieu of their service; and this commutation, by reason of the great distance, was still more advantageous to his English vassals. He imposed, therefore, a scutage of 180,000 pounds on the knight's fees, a commutation, to which, though it was unusual, and the first perhaps to be met with in history,* the military tenants willingly submitted; and with this money, he levied an army which was more under his command, and whose service was more durable and constant. Assisted by Berenger, count of Barcelona, and Trincaval, count of Nismes, whom he had gained to his party, he invaded the county of Toulouse; and after taking Verdun, Castlenau, and other places, he besieged the capital of the province, and was likely to prevail in the enterprize; when Lewis, advancing before the arrival of his main body, threw himself into the place with a small reinforcement. Henry was urged by some of his ministers to prosecute the siege, to take Lewis prisoner, and to impose his own terms in the pacification; but he either thought it so much his interest to maintain the feudal principles, by which his foreign dominions were secured, or bore so much respect to his superior lord, that, he declared, he would not attack a place defended by him in person; and he immediately raised the siege.ᵏ He marched into Normandy to protect that province against an incursion which the count of Dreux, instigated by king Lewis, his brother, had made upon it. War was now openly carried on between the two monarchs, but produced no memorable event: It soon ended in a cessation of arms, and that followed by a peace, which was not, however, attended with any confidence or good correspondence between those rival princes. The fortress of Gisors, being part of the dowry stipulated to Margaret of France, had been consigned by

1160.

* Madox, p. 435. Gervase, p. 1381. See note [O] at the end of the volume.
ᵏ Fitz-Steph. p. 22. Diceto, p. 531.

CHAPTER VIII

agreement to the knights templars, on condition that it should be *1161.*
delivered into Henry's hands, after the celebration of the nuptials.
The king, that he might have a pretence for immediately de-
manding the place, ordered the marriage to be solemnized between the prince and princess, though both infants;[l] and he engaged the grand-master of the templars, by large presents, as was
generally suspected, to put him in possession of Gisors.[m] Lewis
resenting this fraudulent conduct, banished the templars, and
would have made war upon the king of England, had it not been
for the mediation and authority of pope Alexander III. who had
been chaced from Rome by the anti-pope, Victor IV. and resided
at that time in France. That we may form an idea of the authority
possessed by the Roman pontiff during those ages, it may be
proper to observe, that the two kings had, the year before, met the
pope at the castle of Torci on the Loir; and they gave him such
marks of respect, that both dismounted to receive him, and holding each of them one of the reins of his bridle, walked on foot by
his side, and conducted him in that submissive manner into the
castle.[n] *A spectacle,* cries Baronius in an ecstacy, *to God, angels, and
men; and such as had never before been exhibited to the world!*

Henry, soon after he had accommodated his differences with *1162.*
Lewis by the pope's mediation, returned to England; where he
commenced an enterprize, which, though required by sound policy, and even conducted in the main with prudence, bred him great
disquietude, involved him in danger, and was not concluded without some loss and dishonour.

The usurpations of the clergy, which had at first been gradual, *Disputes*
were now become so rapid, and had mounted to such a height, that *between*
the contest between the regale and pontificale was really arrived at *the civil*
a crisis in England; and it became necessary to determine whether *and ec-*
the king or the priests, particularly the archbishop of Canterbury, *clesias-*
should be sovereign of the kingdom.[o] The aspiring spirit of Henry, *tical*
which gave inquietude to all his neighbours, was not likely long to *powers.*
pay a tame submission to the encroachments of subjects; and as

[l] Hoveden, p. 492. Neubr. p. 400. Diceto, p. 532. Brompton, p. 1450.
[m] Since the first publication of this history, Lord Lyttelton has published
a copy of the treaty between Henry and Lewis, by which it appears, if there
was no secret article, that Henry was not guilty of any fraud in this
transaction.   [n] Trivet, p. 48.   [o] Fitz-Stephen, p. 27.

nothing opens the eyes of men so readily as their interest, he was in no danger of falling, in this respect, into that abject superstition, which retained his people in subjection. From the commencement of his reign, in the government of his foreign dominions, as well as of England, he had shown a fixed purpose to repress clerical usurpations, and to maintain those prerogatives, which had been transmitted to him by his predecessors. During the schism of the papacy between Alexander and Victor, he had determined, for some time, to remain neuter: And when informed, that the archbishop of Roüen and the bishop of Mans had, from their own authority, acknowledged Alexander as legitimate pope, he was so enraged, that, though he spared the archbishop on account of his great age, he immediately issued orders for overthrowing the houses of the bishop of Mans, and archdeacon of Roüen;* and it was not till he had deliberately examined the matter, by those views, which usually enter into the councils of princes, that he allowed that pontiff to exercise authority over any of his dominions. In England, the mild character and advanced years of Theobald, archbishop of Canterbury, together with his merits in refusing to put the crown on the head of Eustace, son of Stephen, prevented Henry, during the life-time of that primate, from taking any measures against the multiplied encroachments of the clergy: But after his death, the king resolved to exert himself with more activity; and that he might be secure against any opposition, he advanced to that dignity Becket, his chancellor, on whose compliance, he thought, he could entirely depend.

June 3. Thomas a Becket, archbishop of Canterbury. Thomas a Becket, the first man of English descent, who, since the Norman conquest, had, during the course of a whole century, risen to any considerable station, was born of reputable parents in the city of London; and being endowed both with industry and capacity, he early insinuated himself into the favour of archbishop Theobald, and obtained from that prelate some preferments and offices. By their means, he was enabled to travel for improvement to Italy, where he studied the civil and canon law at Bologna; and on his return, he appeared to have made such proficiency in knowledge, that he was promoted by his patron to the archdeaconry of Canterbury, an office of considerable trust and profit. He was afterwards employed with success by Theobald in trans-

* See note [P] at the end of the volume.

CHAPTER VIII

acting business at Rome; and on Henry's accession, he was recommended to that monarch as worthy of farther preferment. Henry,
who knew that Becket had been instrumental in supporting that
resolution of the archbishop, which had tended so much to facilitate his own advancement to the throne, was already prepossessed
in his favour; and finding, on farther acquaintance, that his spirit
and abilities entitled him to any trust, he soon promoted him to the
dignity of chancellor, one of the first civil offices in the kingdom.
The chancellor, in that age, besides the custody of the great seal,
had possession of all vacant prelacies and abbies; he was the guardian of all such minors and pupils as were the king's tenants; all
baronies which escheated to the crown were under his administration; he was entitled to a place in council, even though he were
not particularly summoned; and as he exercised also the office of
secretary of state, and it belonged to him to countersign all com-
missions, writs, and letters-patent, he was a kind of prime minister,
and was concerned in the dispatch of every business of importance.[p] Besides exercising this high office, Becket, by the favour of the king or archbishop, was made provost of Beverley,
dean of Hastings, and constable of the Tower: He was put in
possession of the honours of Eye and Berkham, large baronies that
had escheated to the crown: And to complete his grandeur, he was
entrusted with the education of Prince Henry, the king's eldest
son, and heir of the monarchy.[q] The pomp of his retinue, the
sumptuousness of his furniture, the luxury of his table, the mu-
nificence of his presents, corresponded to these great preferments; or rather exceeded any thing that England had ever before
seen in any subject. His historian and secretary, Fitz-Stephens,[r]
mentions, among other particulars, that his apartments were every
day in winter covered with clean straw or hay, and in summer with
green rushes or boughs; lest the gentlemen, who paid court to him,
and who could not, by reason of their great number, find a place
at table, should soil their fine cloaths by sitting on a dirty floor.[s] A
great number of knights were retained in his service; the greatest

[p] Fitz-Steph. p. 13.   [q] Ibid. p. 15. Hist. Quad. p. 9, 14.   [r] p. 15.   [s] John
Baldwin held the manor of Oterarsfee in Aylesbury of the king in soccage,
by the service of finding litter for the king's bed, viz., in summer, grass or
herbs, and two grey geese, and in winter, straw and three eels, thrice in the
year, if the king should come thrice in the year to Aylesbury. Madox, Bar.
Anglica, p. 247.

barons were proud of being received at his table; his house was a place of education for the sons of the chief nobility; and the king himself frequently vouchsafed to partake of his entertainments. As his way of life was splendid and opulent, his amusements and occupations were gay, and partook of the cavalier spirit, which, as he had only taken deacon's orders, he did not think unbefitting his character. He employed himself at leisure hours in hunting, hawking, gaming, and horsemanship; he exposed his person in several military actions;[t] he carried over, at his own charge, seven hundred knights to attend the king in his wars at Toulouse; in the subsequent wars on the frontiers of Normandy, he maintained, during forty days, twelve hundred knights, and four thousand of their train;[u] and in an embassy to France, with which he was entrusted, he astonished that court by the number and magnificence of his retinue.

Henry, besides committing all his more important business to Becket's management, honoured him with his friendship and intimacy; and whenever he was disposed to relax himself by sports of any kind, he admitted his chancellor to the party.[w] An instance of their familiarity is mentioned by Fitz-Stephens, which, as it shows the manners of the age, it may not be improper to relate. One day, as the king and the chancellor were riding together in the streets of London, they observed a beggar, who was shivering with cold. Would it not be very praise-worthy, said the king, to give that poor man a warm coat in this severe season? It would, surely, replied the chancellor; and you do well, Sir, in thinking of such good actions. Then he shall have one presently, cried the king: And seizing the skirt of the chancellor's coat, which was scarlet, and lined with ermine, began to pull it violently. The chancellor defended himself for some time; and they had both of them like to have tumbled off their horses in the street, when Becket, after a vehement struggle, let go his coat; which the king bestowed on the beggar, who, being ignorant of the quality of the persons, was not a little surprised at the present.[x]

Becket, who, by his complaisance and good-humour, had rendered himself agreeable, and by his industry and abilities useful, to

[t] Fitz-Steph. p. 23. Hist. Quad. p. 9.   [u] Fitz-Steph. p. 19, 20, 22, 23.
[w] Ibid. p. 16. Hist. Quad. p. 8.   [x] Fitz-Steph. p. 16.

his master, appeared to him the fittest person for supplying the vacancy made by the death of Theobald. As he was well acquainted with the king's intentions[y] of retrenching, or rather confining within the ancient bounds, all ecclesiastical privileges, and always showed a ready disposition to comply with them,[z] Henry, who never expected any resistance from that quarter, immediately issued orders for electing him archbishop of Canterbury. But this resolution, which was taken contrary to the opinion of Matilda, and many of the ministers,[a] drew after it very unhappy consequences; and never prince of so great penetration, appeared, in the issue, to have so little understood the genius and character of his minister.

No sooner was Becket installed in this high dignity, which rendered him for life the second person in the kingdom, with some pretensions of aspiring to be the first, than he totally altered his demeanor and conduct, and endeavoured to acquire the character of sanctity, of which his former busy and ostentatious course of life might, in the eyes of the people, have naturally bereaved him. Without consulting the king, he immediately returned into his hands the commission of chancellor; pretending, that he must thenceforth detach himself from secular affairs, and be solely employed in the exercise of his spiritual function, but in reality, that he might break off all connexions with Henry, and apprise him, that Becket, as primate of England, was now become entirely a new personage. He maintained, in his retinue and attendants alone, his ancient pomp and lustre, which was useful to strike the vulgar: In his own person he affected the greatest austerity, and most rigid mortification, which, he was sensible, would have an equal or a greater tendency to the same end. He wore sack-cloth next his skin, which, by his affected care to conceal it, was necessarily the more remarked by all the world: He changed it so seldom, that it was filled with dirt and vermin: His usual diet was bread; his drink water, which he even rendered farther unpalatable by the mixture of unsavoury herbs: He tore his back with the frequent discipline which he inflicted on it: He daily on his knees washed, in imitation of Christ, the feet of thirteen beggars, whom he afterwards dis-

[y] Ibid. p. 17.   [z] Ibid. p. 23. Epist. St. Thom. p. 232.   [a] Epist. St. Thom. p. 167.

missed with presents:[b] He gained the affections of the monks by his frequent charities to the convents and hospitals: Every one, who made profession of sanctity, was admitted to his conversation, and returned full of panegyrics on the humility, as well as on the piety and mortification, of the holy primate: He seemed to be perpetually employed in reciting prayers and pious lectures, or in perusing religious discourses: His aspect wore the appearance of seriousness, and mental recollection, and secret devotion: And all men of penetration plainly saw, that he was meditating some great design, and that the ambition and ostentation of his character had turned itself towards a new and more dangerous object.

1163. Quarrel between the king and Becket.

Becket waited not till Henry should commence those projects against the ecclesiastical power, which, he knew, had been formed by that prince: He was himself the aggressor; and endeavoured to overawe the king by the intrepidity and boldness of his enterprizes. He summoned the earl of Clare to surrender the barony of Tunbridge, which, ever since the conquest, had remained in the family of that nobleman, but which, as it had formerly belonged to the see of Canterbury, Becket pretended his predecessors were prohibited by the canons to alienate. The earl of Clare, besides the lustre which he derived from the greatness of his own birth, and the extent of his possessions, was allied to all the principal families in the kingdom; his sister, who was a celebrated beauty, had farther extended his credit among the nobility, and was even supposed to have gained the king's affections; and Becket could not better discover, than by attacking so powerful an interest, his resolution of maintaining with vigour the rights, real or pretended, of his see.[c]

William de Eynsford, a military tenant of the crown, was patron of a living, which belonged to a manor that held of the archbishop of Canterbury; but Becket, without regard to William's right, presented, on a new and illegal pretext, one Laurence to that living, who was violently expelled by Eynsford. The primate, making himself, as was usual in spiritual courts, both judge and party, issued in a summary manner, the sentence of excommunication against Eynsford, who complained to the king, that he, who held

[b] Fitz-Steph. p. 25. Hist. Quad. p. 19.   [c] Fitz-Steph. p. 28. Gervase, p. 1384.

CHAPTER VIII

in capite of the crown, should, contrary to the practice established by the Conqueror, and maintained ever since by his successors, be subjected to that terrible sentence, without the previous consent of the sovereign.[d] Henry, who had now broken off all personal intercourse with Becket, sent him, by a messenger, his orders to absolve Eynsford; but received for answer, that it belonged not to the king to inform him whom he should absolve and whom excommunicate:[e] And it was not till after many remonstrances and menaces, that Becket, though with the worst grace imaginable, was induced to comply with the royal mandate.

Henry, though he found himself thus grievously mistaken in the character of the person whom he had promoted to the primacy, determined not to desist from his former intention of retrenching clerical usurpations. He was entirely master of his extensive dominions: The prudence and vigour of his administration, attended with perpetual success, had raised his character above that of any of his predecessors:[f] The papacy seemed to be weakened by a schism, which divided all Europe: And he rightly judged, that, if the present favourable opportunity were neglected, the crown must, from the prevalent superstition of the people, be in danger of falling into an entire subordination under the mitre.

The union of the civil and ecclesiastical power serves extremely, in every civilized government, to the maintenance of peace and order; and prevents those mutual incroachments, which, as there can be no ultimate judge between them, are often attended with the most dangerous consequences. Whether the supreme magistrate, who unites these powers, receives the appellation of prince or prelate, is not material: The superior weight, which temporal interests commonly bear in the apprehensions of men above spiritual, renders the civil part of his character most prevalent; and in time prevents those gross impostures and bigotted persecutions, which, in all false religions, are the chief foundation of clerical authority. But during the progress of ecclesiastical usurpations, the state, by the resistance of the civil magistrate, is naturally thrown into convulsions; and it behoves the prince, both for his own interest, and for that of the public, to provide, in time

---

[d] M. Paris, p. 7. Diceto, p. 536.   [e] Fitz-Steph. p. 28.   [f] Epist. St. Thom. p. 130.

sufficient barriers against so dangerous and insidious a rival. This precaution had hitherto been much neglected in England, as well as in other catholic countries; and affairs at last seemed to have come to a dangerous crisis: A sovereign of the greatest abilities was now on the throne: A prelate of the most inflexible and intrepid character was possessed of the primacy: The contending powers appeared to be armed with their full force, and it was natural to expect some extraordinary event to result from their conflict.

Among their other inventions to obtain money, the clergy had inculcated the necessity of pennance as an atonement for sin: and having again introduced the practice of paying them large sums as a commutation, or species of atonement, for the remission of those pennances, the sins of the people, by these means, had become a revenue to the priests; and the king computed, that, by this invention alone, they levied more money upon his subjects, than flowed, by all the funds and taxes, into the royal exchequer.[g] That he might ease the people of so heavy and arbitrary an imposition, Henry required, that a civil officer of his appointment should be present in all ecclesiastical courts, and should, for the future, give his consent to every composition which was made with sinners for their spiritual offences.

The ecclesiastics, in that age, had renounced all immediate subordination to the magistrate: They openly pretended to an exemption, in criminal accusations, from a trial before courts of justice; and were gradually introducing a like exemption in civil causes: Spiritual penalties alone could be inflicted on their offences: And as the clergy had extremely multiplied in England, and many of them were consequently of very low characters, crimes of the deepest dye, murders, robberies, adulteries, rapes, were daily committed with impunity by the ecclesiastics. It had been found, for instance, on enquiry, that no less than a hundred murders had, since the king's accession, been perpetrated by men of that profession, who had never been called to account for these offences;[h] and holy orders were become a full protection for all enormities. A clerk in Worcestershire, having debauched a gentleman's daughter, had, at this time, proceeded to murder the father; and the general indignation against this crime moved the king to

[g] Fitz-Steph. p. 32.   [h] Neubr. p. 394.

CHAPTER VIII

attempt the remedy of an abuse which was become so palpable, and to require that the clerk should be delivered up, and receive condign punishment from the magistrate.[i] Becket insisted on the privileges of the church; confined the criminal in the bishop's prison, lest he should be seized by the king's officers; maintained that no greater punishment could be inflicted on him than degradation: And when the king demanded, that, immediately after he was degraded, he should be tried by the civil power, the primate asserted, that it was iniquitous to try a man twice upon the same accusation, and for the same offence.[k]

Henry, laying hold of so plausible a pretence, resolved to push the clergy with regard to all their privileges, which they had raised to an enormous height, and to determine at once those controversies, which daily multiplied, between the civil and the ecclesiastical jurisdictions. He summoned an assembly of all the prelates of England; and he put to them this concise and decisive question. Whether or not they were willing to submit to the ancient laws and customs of the kingdom? The bishops unanimously replied, that they were willing, *saving their own order:*[l] A device, by which they thought to elude the present urgency of the king's demand, yet reserve to themselves, on a favourable opportunity, the power of resuming all their pretensions. The king was sensible of the artifice, and was provoked to the highest indignation. He left the assembly, with visible marks of his displeasure: He required the primate instantly to surrender the honours and castles of Eye and Berkham: The bishops were terrified, and expected still farther effects of his resentment. Becket alone was inflexible; and nothing but the interposition of the pope's legate and almoner, Philip, who dreaded a breach with so powerful a prince at so unseasonable a juncture, could have prevailed on him to retract the saving clause, and give a general and absolute promise of observing the ancient customs.[m]

But Henry was not content with a declaration in these general terms: He resolved, ere it was too late, to define expressly those

[i] Fitz-Steph. p. 33. Hist. Quad. p. 32. [k] Fitz-Steph. p. 29. Hist. Quad. p. 33, 45. Hoveden, p. 492. M. Paris, p. 72. Diceto, p. 536, 537. Brompton, p. 1058. Gervase, p. 1384. Epist. St. Thom. p. 208, 209. [l] Fitz-Steph. p. 31. Hist. Quad. p. 34. Hoveden, p. 492. [m] Hist. Quad. p. 37. Hoveden, p. 493. Gervase, p. 1385.

customs, with which he required compliance, and to put a stop to clerical usurpations, before they were fully consolidated, and could plead antiquity, as they already did a sacred authority, in their favour. The claims of the church were open and visible. After a gradual and insensible progress during many centuries, the mask had at last been taken off, and several ecclesiastical councils, by their canons, which were pretended to be irrevocable and infallible, had positively defined those privileges and immunities, which gave such general offence, and appeared so dangerous to the civil magistrate. Henry therefore deemed it necessary to define with the same precision the limits of the civil power; to oppose his legal customs to their divine ordinances; to determine the exact boundaries of the rival jurisdictions; and for this purpose, he summoned a general council of the nobility and prelates at Clarendon, to whom he submitted this great and important question.

The barons were all gained to the king's party, either by the reasons which he urged, or by his superior authority: The bishops were overawed by the general combination against them: And the following laws, commonly called the *Constitutions of Clarendon*, were voted without opposition by this assembly.[n] It was enacted, that all suits concerning the advowson and presentation of churches should be determined in the civil courts: That the churches, belonging to the king's fee, should not be granted in perpetuity without his consent: That clerks, accused of any crime, should be tried in the civil courts: That no person, particularly no clergyman of any rank, should depart the kingdom without the king's licence: That excommunicated persons should not be bound to give security for continuing in their present place of abode: That laics should not be accused in spiritual courts, except by legal and reputable promoters and witnesses: That no chief tenant of the crown should be excommunicated, nor his lands be put under an interdict, except with the king's consent: That all appeals in spiritual causes should be carried from the archdeacon to the bishop, from the bishop to the primate, from him to the king; and should be carried no farther without the king's consent: That if any law-suit arose between a layman and a clergyman concerning a tenant, and it be disputed whether the land be a lay or an ecclesiastical fee, it

*1164.
25th
Jan.*

Constitutions of Clarendon.

---

[n] Fitz-Steph. p. 33.

CHAPTER VIII

should first be determined by the verdict of twelve lawful men to what class it belonged, and if it be found to be a lay-fee, the cause should finally be determined in the civil courts: That no inhabitant in demesne should be excommunicated for non-appearance in a spiritual court, till the chief officer of the place, where he resides, be consulted, that he may compel him by the civil authority to give satisfaction to the church: That the archbishops, bishops, and other spiritual dignitaries should be regarded as barons of the realm; should possess the privileges and be subjected to the bur-thens belonging to that rank; and should be bound to attend the king in his great councils, and assist at all trials, till the sentence, either of death or loss of members, be given against the criminal: That the revenue of vacant sees should belong to the king; the chapter, or such of them as he pleases to summon, should sit in the king's chapel till they made the new election with his consent, and that the bishop-elect should do homage to the crown: That if any baron or tenant *in capite* should refuse to submit to the spiritual courts, the king should employ his authority in obliging him to make such submissions; if any of them throw off his allegiance to the king, the prelates should assist the king with their censures in reducing him: That goods, forfeited to the king, should not be protected in churches or church-yards: That the clergy should no longer pretend to the right of enforcing payment of debts con-tracted by oath or promise; but should leave these law-suits, equally with others, to the determination of the civil courts: And that the sons of villains should not be ordained clerks, without the consent of their lord.[o]

These articles, to the number of sixteen, were calculated to prevent the chief abuses, which had prevailed in ecclesiastical af-fairs, and to put an effectual stop to the usurpations of the church, which, gradually stealing on, had threatened the total destruction of the civil power. Henry, therefore, by reducing those ancient customs of the realm to writing, and by collecting them in a body, endeavoured to prevent all future dispute with regard to them; and by passing so many ecclesiastical ordinances in a national and civil assembly, he fully established the superiority of the legislature

[o] Hist. Quadr. p. 163. M. Paris, p. 70, 71. Spelm. Conc. vol. ii. p. 63. Gervase, p. 1386, 1387. Wilkins, p. 321.

above all papal decrees or spiritual canons, and gained a signal victory over the ecclesiastics. But as he knew, that the bishops, though overawed by the present combination of the crown and the barons, would take the first favourable opportunity of denying the authority, which had enacted these constitutions; he resolved, that they should all set their seal to them, and give a promise to observe them. None of the prelates dared to oppose his will; except Becket, who, though urged by the earls of Cornwal and Leicester, the barons of principal authority in the kingdom, obstinately withheld his assent. At last, Richard de Hastings, grand prior of the templars in England, threw himself on his knees before him; and with many tears, entreated him, if he paid any regard, either to his own safety or that of the church, not to provoke, by a fruitless opposition, the indignation of a great monarch, who was resolutely bent on his purpose, and who was determined to take full revenge on every one, that should dare to oppose him.[p] Becket, finding himself deserted by all the world, even by his own brethren, was at last obliged to comply; and he promised, *legally, with good faith, and without fraud or reserve,*[q] to observe the constitutions; and he took an oath to that purpose.[r] The king, thinking that he had now finally prevailed in this great enterprize, sent the constitutions to pope Alexander, who then resided in France; and he required that pontiff's ratification of them: But Alexander, who, though he had owed the most important obligations to the king, plainly saw, that these laws were calculated to establish the independancy of England on the papacy, and of the royal power on the clergy, condemned them in the strongest terms; abrogated, annulled, and rejected them. There were only six articles, the least important, which, for the sake of peace, he was willing to ratify.

Becket, when he observed, that he might hope for support in an opposition, expressed the deepest sorrow for his compliance; and endeavoured to engage all the other bishops in a confederacy to adhere to their common rights, and to the ecclesiastical privileges, in which he represented the interest and honour of God to be so deeply concerned. He redoubled his austerities in order to punish himself for his criminal assent to the constitutions of Clar-

---

[p] Hist. Quad. p. 38. Hoveden, p. 493.   [q] Fitz-Steph. p. 35. Epist. St. Thom. p. 25.   [r] Fitz-Steph. p. 45. Hist. Quad. p. 39. Gervase, p. 1386.

CHAPTER VIII

endon: He proportioned his discipline to the enormity of his supposed offence: And he refused to exercise any part of his archiepiscopal function, till he should receive absolution from the pope,
which was readily granted him. Henry, informed of his present
dispositions, resolved to take vengeance for this refractory behaviour; and he attempted to crush him, by means of that very power
which Becket made such merit in supporting. He applied to the
pope, that he should grant the commission of legate in his dominions to the archbishop of York; but Alexander, as politic as he,
though he granted the commission, annexed a clause, that it
should not impower the legate to execute any act in prejudice of
the archbishop of Canterbury:[s] And the king, finding how fruitless
such an authority would prove, sent back the commission by the
same messenger that brought it.[t]

The primate, however, who found himself still exposed to the
king's indignation, endeavoured twice to escape secretly from the
kingdom; but was as often detained by contrary winds: And Henry
hastened to make him feel the effects of an obstinacy, which he
deemed so criminal. He instigated John, mareschal of the exchequer, to sue Becket in the archiepiscopal court for some lands,
part of the manor of Pageham; and to appeal thence to the king's
court for justice.[u] On the day appointed for trying the cause, the
primate sent four knights, to represent certain irregularities in
John's appeal; and at the same time to excuse himself, on account
of sickness, for not appearing personally that day in the court. This
slight offence (if it even deserve the name) was represented as a
grievous contempt; the four knights were menaced, and with difficulty escaped being sent to prison, as offering falsehoods to the
court;* and Henry, being determined to prosecute Becket to the
utmost, summoned at Northampton a great council, which he
purposed to make the instrument of his vengeance against the
inflexible prelate.

The king had raised Becket from a low station to the highest
offices, had honoured him with his countenance and friendship,
had trusted to his assistance in forwarding his favourite project
against the clergy; and when he found him become of a sudden his

[s] Epist. St. Thom. p. 13, 14. [t] Hoveden, p. 493. Gervase, p. 1388.
[u] Hoveden, p. 494. M. Paris, p. 72. Diceto, p. 537. * See note [Q] at the
end of the volume.

most rigid opponent, while every one beside complied with his will, rage at the disappointment, and indignation against such signal ingratitude, transported him beyond all bounds of moderation; and there seems to have entered more of passion than of justice, or even of policy, in this violent prosecution.[w] The barons, notwithstanding, in the great council voted whatever sentence he was pleased to dictate to them; and the bishops themselves, who undoubtedly bore a secret favour to Becket, and regarded him as the champion of their privileges, concurred with the rest, in the design of oppressing their primate. In vain did Becket urge, that his court was proceeding with the utmost regularity and justice in trying the mareschal's cause, which however, he said, would appear, from the sheriff's testimony, to be entirely unjust and iniquitous: That he himself had discovered no contempt of the king's court; but on the contrary, by sending four knights to excuse his absence, had virtually acknowledged its authority: That he also, in consequence of the king's summons, personally appeared at present in the great council, ready to justify his cause against the mareschal, and to submit his conduct to their enquiry and jurisdiction: That even should it be found, that he had been guilty of non-appearance, the laws had affixed a very slight penalty to that offence: And that, as he was an inhabitant of Kent, where his archiepiscopal palace was seated, he was by law entitled to some greater indulgence than usual in the rate of his fine.[x] Notwithstanding these pleas, he was condemned as guilty of a contempt of the king's court, and as wanting in the fealty which he had sworn to his sovereign; all his goods and chattels were confiscated;[y] and that this triumph over the church might be carried to the utmost, Henry, bishop of Winchester, the prelate who had been so powerful in the former reign, was, in spite of his remonstrances, obliged, by order of the court, to pronounce the sentence against him.[z] The primate submitted to the decree; and all the prelates, except Folliot, bishop of London, who paid court to the king by this singularity, became sureties for him.[a] It is remarkable, that several Norman barons voted in this council; and we may conclude, with some probability, that a like practice had prevailed in many of the great councils

---

[w] Neubr. p. 394.   [x] Fitz-Steph. p. 37, 42.   [y] Hist. Quad. p. 47. Hoveden, p. 494. Gervase, p. 1389.   [z] Fitz-Steph. p. 37.   [a] Ibid.

CHAPTER VIII

summoned since the conquest. For the contemporary historian, who has given us a full account of these transactions, does not mention this circumstance as any wise singular;[b] and Becket, in all his subsequent remonstrances with regard to the severe treatment, which he had met with, never sounds any objection on an irregularity, which to us appears very palpable and flagrant. So little precision was there at that time in the government and constitution!

The king was not content with this sentence, however violent and oppressive. Next day, he demanded of Becket the sum of three hundred pounds, which the primate had levied upon the honours of Eye and Berkham, while in his possession. Becket, after premising that he was not obliged to answer to this suit, because it was not contained in his summons; after remarking, that he had expended more than that sum in the repairs of those castles, and of the royal palace at London; expressed however his resolution that money should not be any ground of quarrel between him and his sovereign: He agreed to pay the sum; and immediately gave sureties for it.[c] In the subsequent meeting, the king demanded five hundred marks, which, he affirmed, he had lent Becket during the war at Toulouse;[d] and another sum to the same amount, for which that prince had been surety for him to a Jew. Immediately after these two claims, he preferred a third of still greater importance: He required him to give in the accounts of his administration while chancellor, and to pay the balance due from the revenues of all the prelacies, abbies, and baronies, which had, during that time, been subjected to his management.[e] Becket observed, that, as this demand was totally unexpected, he had not come prepared to answer it; but he required a delay, and promised in that case to give satisfaction. The king insisted upon sureties; and Becket desired leave to consult his suffragans in a case of such importance.[f]

It is apparent, from the known character of Henry, and from the usual vigilance of his government, that, when he promoted Becket to the see of Canterbury, he was, on good grounds, well pleased with his administration in the former high office, with which he had entrusted him; and that, even if that prelate had

[b] Fitz-Steph. p. 36. [c] Ibid. p. 38. [d] Hist. Quad. p. 47. [e] Hoveden, p. 494. Diceto, p. 537. [f] Fitz-Steph. p. 38.

dissipated money beyond the income of his place, the king was satisfied that his expences were not blameable, and had in the main been calculated for his service.[g] Two years had since elapsed; no demand had during that time been made upon him; it was not till the quarrel arose concerning ecclesiastical privileges, that the claim was started, and the primate was, of a sudden, required to produce accounts of such intricacy and extent before a tribunal, which had shown a determined resolution to ruin and oppress him. To find sureties, that he should answer so boundless and uncertain a claim, which in the king's estimation amounted to 44,000 marks,[h] was impracticable; and Becket's suffragans were extremely at a loss what counsel to give him, in such a critical emergency. By the advice of the bishop of Winchester he offered two thousand marks as a general satisfaction for all demands: But this offer was rejected by the king.[i] Some prelates exhorted him to resign his see, on condition of receiving an acquittal: Others were of opinion, that he ought to submit himself entirely to the king's mercy:[k] But the primate, thus pushed to the utmost, had too much courage to sink under oppression: He determined to brave all his enemies, to trust to the sacredness of his character for protection, to involve his cause with that of God and religion, and to stand the utmost efforts of royal indignation.

After a few days, spent in deliberation, Becket went to church, and said mass, where he had previously ordered, that the introit to the communion service should begin with these words, *Princes sat and spake against me*; the passage appointed for the martyrdom of St. Stephen, whom the primate thereby tacitly pretended to resemble in his sufferings for the sake of righteousness. He went thence to court arrayed in his sacred vestments: As soon as he arrived within the palace-gate he took the cross into his own hands, bore it aloft as his protection, and marched in that posture into the royal apartments.[l] The king, who was in an inner room, was astonished at this parade, by which the primate seemed to menace him and his court with the sentence of excommunication; and he sent some of the prelates to remonstrate with him on account of such audacious behaviour. These prelates complained to Becket, that, by sub-

[g] Hoveden, p. 495.   [h] Epist. St. Thom. p. 315.   [i] Fitz-Steph. p. 38.
[k] Fitz-Steph. p. 39. Gervase, p. 1390.   [l] Fitz-Steph. p. 40. Hist. Quad. p. 53. Hoveden, p. 404. Neubr. p. 394. Epist. St. Thom. p. 43.

scribing, himself, to the constitutions of Clarendon, he had seduced them to imitate his example, and that now, when it was too late, he pretended to shake off all subordination to the civil power, and appeared desirous of involving them in the guilt, which must attend any violation of those laws, established by their consent and ratified by their subscriptions.[m] Becket replied, that he had indeed subscribed the constitutions of Clarendon, *legally, with good faith, and without fraud or reserve*; but in these words was virtually implied a salvo for the rights of their order, which, being connected with the cause of God and his church, could never be relinquished by their oaths and engagements: That if he and they had erred, in resigning the ecclesiastical privileges, the best atonement they could now make was to retract their consent, which in such a case could never be obligatory, and to follow the pope's authority, who had solemnly annulled the constitutions of Clarendon, and had absolved them from all oaths which they had taken to observe them: That a determined resolution was evidently embraced to oppress the church; the storm had first broken upon him; for a slight offence, and which too was falsely imputed to him, he had been tyrannically condemned to a grievous penalty; a new and unheard-of claim was since started, in which he could expect no justice; and he plainly saw, that he was the destined victim, who, by his ruin, must prepare the way for the abrogation of all spiritual immunities: That he strictly inhibited them who were his suffragans, from assisting at any such trial, or giving their sanction to any sentence against him; he put himself and his see under the protection of the supreme pontiff; and appealed to him against any penalty, which his iniquitous judges might think proper to inflict upon him: And that however terrible the indignation of so great a monarch as Henry, his sword could only kill the body; while that of the church, entrusted into the hands of the primate, could kill the soul, and throw the disobedient into infinite and eternal perdition.[n]

Appeals to the pope, even in ecclesiastical causes, had been abolished by the constitutions of Clarendon, and were become criminal by law; but an appeal in a civil cause, such as the king's

[m] Fitz-Steph. p. 35. [n] Fitz-Steph. p. 42, 44, 45, 46. Hist. Quad. p. 57. Hoveden, p. 495. M. Paris, p. 72. Epist. St. Thom. p. 45, 195.

demand upon Becket, was a practice altogether new and unprecedented; tended directly to the subversion of the government; and could receive no colour of excuse, except from the determined resolution, which was but too apparent, in Henry and the great council, to effectuate, without justice, but under colour of law, the total ruin of the inflexible primate. The king, having now obtained a pretext so much more plausible for his violence, would probably have pushed the affair to the utmost extremity against him; but Becket gave him no leisure to conduct the prosecution. He refused so much as to hear the sentence, which the barons, sitting apart from the bishops, and joined to some sheriffs and barons of the second rank,[o] had given upon the king's claim: He departed from the palace; asked Henry's immediate permission to leave Northampton; and upon meeting with a refusal, he withdrew secretly; wandered about in disguise for some time; and at last took shipping and arrived safely at Gravelines.

Banishment of Becket.

The violent and unjust prosecution of Becket, had a natural tendency to turn the public favour on his side, and to make men overlook his former ingratitude towards the king, and his departure from all oaths and engagements, as well as the enormity of those ecclesiastical privileges, of which he affected to be the champion. There were many other reasons, which procured him countenance and protection in foreign countries. Philip, earl of Flanders,[p] and Lewis, king of France,[q] jealous of the rising greatness of Henry, were well pleased to give him disturbance in his government; and forgetting that this was the common cause of princes, they affected to pity extremely the condition of the exiled primate; and the latter even honoured him with a visit at Soissons, in which city he had invited him to fix his residence.[r] The pope, whose interests were more immediately concerned in supporting him, gave a cold reception to a magnificent embassy, which Henry sent to accuse him; while Becket himself, who had come to Sens, in order to justify his cause before the sovereign pontiff, was re-

[o] Fitz-Steph. p. 46. This historian is supposed to mean the more considerable vassals of the chief barons: These had no title to sit in the great council, and the giving them a place there was a palpable irregularity: Which however is not insisted on in any of Becket's remonstrances. A farther proof how little fixed the constitution was at that time! [p] Epist. St. Thom. p. 35. [q] Ibid. p. 36, 37. [r] Hist. Quad. p. 76.

CHAPTER VIII

ceived with the greatest marks of distinction. The king, in revenge, sequestered the revenues of Canterbury; and by a conduct, which might be esteemed arbitrary, had there been at that time any regular check on royal authority, he banished all the primate's relations and domestics, to the number of four hundred, whom he obliged to swear, before their departure, that they would instantly join their patron. But this policy, by which Henry endeavoured to reduce Becket sooner to necessity, lost its effect: The pope, when they arrived beyond sea, absolved them from their oath, and distributed them among the convents in France and Flanders: A residence was assigned to Becket himself in the convent of Pontigny; where he lived for some years in great magnificence, partly from a pension granted him on the revenues of that abbey, partly from remittances made him by the French monarch.

The more to ingratiate himself with the pope, Becket resigned *1165.* into his hands the see of Canterbury, to which, he affirmed, he had been uncanonically elected, by the authority of the royal mandate; and Alexander in his turn, besides investing him anew with that dignity, pretended to abrogate by a bull the sentence, which the great council of England had passed against him. Henry, after attempting in vain to procure a conference with the pope, who departed soon after for Rome, whither the prosperous state of his affairs now invited him; made provisions against the consequences of that breach, which impended between his kingdom and the apostolic see. He issued orders to his justiciaries, inhibiting, under severe penalties, all appeals to the pope or archbishop; forbidding any one to receive any mandates from them, or apply in any case to their authority; declaring it treasonable to bring from either of them an interdict upon the kingdom, and punishable in secular clergymen, by the loss of their eyes and by castration, in regulars by amputation of their feet, and in laics with death; and menacing with sequestration and banishment the persons themselves, as well as their kindred, who should pay obedience to any such interdict: And he farther obliged all his subjects to swear to the observance of those orders.[5] These were edicts of the utmost importance, affected the lives and properties of all the subjects, and even changed, for the time, the national religion, by breaking off all

---

[5] Hist. Quad. p. 88, 167. Hoveden, p. 496. M. Paris, p. 73.

communication with Rome: Yet were they enacted by the sole authority of the king, and were derived entirely from his will and pleasure.

The spiritual powers, which, in the primitive church, were, in a great measure, dependant on the civil, had, by a gradual progress, reached an equality and independance; and though the limits of the two jurisdictions were difficult to ascertain or define, it was not impossible, but, by moderation on both sides, government might still have been conducted, in that imperfect and irregular manner which attends all human institutions. But as the ignorance of the age encouraged the ecclesiastics daily to extend their privileges, and even to advance maxims totally incompatible with civil government;[t] Henry had thought it high time to put an end to their pretensions, and formally, in a public council, to fix those powers which belonged to the magistrate, and which he was for the future determined to maintain. In this attempt, he was led to re-establish customs, which, though ancient, were beginning to be abolished by a contrary practice, and which were still more strongly opposed by the prevailing opinions and sentiments of the age. Principle, therefore, stood on the one side; power on the other; and if the English had been actuated by conscience, more than by present interest, the controversy must soon, by the general defection of Henry's subjects, have been decided against him. Becket, in order to forward this event, filled all places with exclamations against the violence which he had suffered. He compared himself to Christ, who had been condemned by a lay tribunal,[u] and who was crucified anew in the present oppressions under which his church laboured: He took it for granted, as a point incontestible, that his cause was the cause of God:[w] He assumed the character of champion for the patrimony of the divinity: He pretended to be the spiritual father of the king and all the people of England:[x] He even told Henry, that kings reign solely by the authority of the church:[y] And though he had thus torn off the veil more openly on the one side, than that prince had on the other, he seemed still,

[t] *Quis dubitet*, says Becket to the king, *sacerdotes Christi regum et principum omniumque fidelium patres et magistros censeri.* Epist. St. Thom. p. 97, 148.
[u] Epist. St. Thom. p. 63, 105, 194.   [w] Ibid. p. 29, 30, 31, 226.
[x] Fitz-Steph. p. 46. Epist. St. Thom. p. 52, 148.   [y] Brady's Append. N°. 56. Epist. St. Thom. p. 94, 95, 97, 99, 197. Hoveden, p. 497.

CHAPTER VIII

from the general favour borne him by the ecclesiastics, to have all the advantage in the argument. The king, that he might employ the weapons of temporal power remaining in his hands, suspended the payment of Peter's-pence; he made advances towards an alliance with the emperor, Frederic Barbarossa, who was at that time engaged in violent wars with pope Alexander; he discovered some intentions of acknowledging Pascal III. the present antipope, who was protected by that emperor; and by these expedients he endeavoured to terrify the enterprising, though prudent pontiff, from proceeding to extremities against him.

But the violence of Becket, still more than the nature of the controversy, kept affairs from remaining long in suspence between the parties. That prelate, instigated by revenge, and animated by the present glory attending his situation, pushed matters to a decision, and issued a censure, excommunicating the king's chief ministers by name, and comprehending in general all those who favoured or obeyed the constitutions of Clarendon: These constitutions he abrogated and annulled; he absolved all men from the oaths which they had taken to observe them; and he suspended the spiritual thunder over Henry himself, only that the prince might avoid the blow by a timely repentance.[z] *1166.*

The situation of Henry was so unhappy, that he could employ no expedient for saving his ministers from this terrible censure, but by appealing to the pope himself, and having recourse to a tribunal, whose authority he had himself attempted to abridge in this very article of appeals, and which, he knew, was so deeply engaged on the side of his adversary. But even this expedient was not likely to be long effectual. Becket had obtained from the pope a legantine commission over England; and in virtue of that authority, which admitted of no appeal, he summoned the bishops of London, Salisbury, and others, to attend him, and ordered, under pain of excommunication, the ecclesiastics, sequestered on his account, to be restored in two months to all their benefices. But John of Oxford, the king's agent with the pope, had the address to procure orders for suspending this sentence; and he gave the pontiff such hopes of a speedy reconcilement between the king

---

[z] Fitz-Steph. p. 56. Hist. Quad. p. 93. M. Paris, p. 74. Beaulieu Vie de St. Thom. p. 213. Epist. Thom. p. 149, 229. Hoveden, p. 499.

and Becket, that two legates, William of Pavia and Otho, were sent to Normandy, where the king then resided, and they endeavoured to find expedients for that purpose. But the pretensions of the parties were, as yet, too opposite to admit of an accommodation: The king required, that all the constitutions of Clarendon should be ratified: Becket, that previously to any agreement, he and his adherents should be restored to their possessions: And as the legates had no power to pronounce a definitive sentence on either side, the negotiation soon after came to nothing. The cardinal of Pavia also, being much attached to Henry, took care to protract the negotiation; to mitigate the pope, by the accounts which he sent of that prince's conduct; and to procure him every possible indulgence from the see of Rome. About this time, the king had also the address to obtain a dispensation for the marriage of his third son, Geoffrey, with the heiress of Britanny; a concession, which, considering Henry's demerits towards the church, gave great scandal both to Becket, and to his zealous patron, the king of France.

1167. The intricacies of the feudal law had, in that age, rendered the boundaries of power between the prince and his vassals, and between one prince and another, as uncertain as those between the crown and the mitre; and all wars took their origin from disputes, which, had there been any tribunal possessed of power to enforce their decrees, ought to have been decided only before a court of judicature. Henry, in prosecution of some controversies, in which he was involved with the count of Auvergne, a vassal of the dutchy of Guienne, had invaded the territories of that nobleman; who had recourse to the king of France, his superior lord, for protection, and thereby kindled a war between the two monarchs. But this war was, as usual, no less feeble in its operations, than it was frivolous in its cause and object; and after occasioning some mutual depredations,[a] and some insurrections among the barons of Poictou and Guienne, was terminated by a peace. The terms of this peace were rather disadvantageous to Henry, and prove, that that prince had, by reason of his contest with the church, lost the superiority, which he had hitherto maintained over the crown of France: An additional motive to him for accommodating those differences.

[a] Hoveden, p. 517. M. Paris, p. 75. Diceto, p. 547. Gervase, p. 1402, 1403. Robert de Monte.

CHAPTER VIII

The pope and the king began at last to perceive, that in the present situation of affairs, neither of them could expect a final and decisive victory over the other, and that they had more to fear than to hope from the duration of the controversy. Though the vigour of Henry's government had confirmed his authority in all his dominions, his throne might be shaken by a sentence of excommunication; and if England itself could, by its situation, be more easily guarded against the contagion of superstitious prejudices, his French provinces at least, whose communication was open with the neighbouring states, would be much exposed, on that account, to some great revolution or convulsion.[b] He could not, therefore, reasonably imagine, that the pope, while he retained such a check upon him, would formally recognize the constitutions of Clarendon, which both put an end to papal pretensions in England, and would give an example to other states of asserting a like independancy.[c] Pope Alexander, on the other hand, being still engaged in dangerous wars with the emperor Frederic, might justly apprehend, that Henry, rather than relinquish claims of such importance, would join the party of his enemy; and as the trials hitherto made of the spiritual weapons by Becket had not succeeded to his expectation, and every thing had remained quiet in all the king's dominions, nothing seemed impossible to the capacity and vigilance of so great a monarch. The disposition of minds on both sides, resulting from these circumstances, produced frequent attempts towards an accommodation; but as both parties knew, that the essential articles of the dispute could not then be terminated, they entertained a perpetual jealousy of each other, and were anxious not to lose the least advantage in the negociation. The nuncios, Gratian and Vivian, having received a commission to endeavour a reconciliation, met with the king in Normandy; and after all differences seemed to be adjusted, Henry offered to sign the treaty, with a salvo to his royal dignity; which gave such umbrage to Becket, that the negotiation, in the end, became fruitless, and the excommunications were renewed against the king's ministers. Another negotiation was conducted at Montmirail, in presence of the king of France and the French prelates; where Becket also offered to make his submissions, with a salvo to

1168.

[b] Epist. St. Thom. p. 230. [c] Ibid. p. 276.

the honour of God, and the liberties of the church; which, for a like reason, was extremely offensive to the king, and rendered the treaty abortive. A third conference, under the same mediation, was broken off, by Becket's insisting on a like reserve in his submissions; and even in a fourth treaty, when all the terms were adjusted, and when the primate expected to be introduced to the king, and to receive the kiss of peace, which it was usual for princes to grant in those times, and which was regarded as a sure pledge of forgiveness, Henry refused him that honour; under pretence, that, during his anger, he had made a rash vow to that purpose. This formality served, among such jealous spirits, to prevent the conclusion of the treaty; and though the difficulty was attempted to be overcome by a dispensation which the pope granted to Henry from his vow, that prince could not be prevailed on to depart from the resolution which he had taken.

1169.

In one of these conferences, at which the French king was present, Henry said to that monarch: "There have been many kings of England, some of greater, some of less authority than myself: There have also been many archbishops of Canterbury, holy and good men, and entitled to every kind of respect: Let Becket but act towards me with the same submission, which the greatest of his predecessors have paid to the least of mine, and there shall be no controversy between us." Lewis was so struck with this state of the case, and with an offer which Henry made to submit his cause to the French clergy, that he could not forbear condemning the primate, and withdrawing his friendship from him during some time: But the bigotry of that prince, and their common animosity against Henry, soon produced a renewal of their former good correspondence.

1170.
22d July.

Compromise with Becket.

All difficulties were at last adjusted between the parties; and the king allowed Becket to return, on conditions which may be esteemed both honourable and advantageous to that prelate. He was not required to give up any rights of the church, or resign any of those pretensions, which had been the original ground of the controversy. It was agreed, that all these questions should be buried in oblivion; but that Becket and his adherents should, without making farther submission, be restored to all their livings, and that even the possessors of such benefices as depended on the see of Canterbury, and had been filled during the primate's absence,

CHAPTER VIII

should be expelled, and Becket have liberty to supply the vacancies.[d] In return for concessions, which entrenched so deeply on
the honour and dignity of the crown, Henry reaped only the advantage of seeing his ministers absolved from the sentence of excommunication pronounced against them, and of preventing the
interdict, which, if these hard conditions had not been complied
with, was ready to be laid on all his dominions.[e] It was easy to see
how much he dreaded that event, when a prince of so high a spirit
could submit to terms so dishonourable, in order to prevent it. So
anxious was Henry to accommodate all differences, and to reconcile himself fully with Becket, that he took the most extraordinary
steps to flatter his vanity, and even on one occasion humiliated
himself so far as to hold the stirrup of that haughty prelate, while
he mounted.[f]

But the king attained not even that temporary tranquillity,
which he had hoped to reap from these expedients. During the
heat of his quarrel with Becket, while he was every day expecting
an interdict to be laid on his kingdom, and a sentence of excommunication to be fulminated against his person, he had thought it
prudent to have his son, prince Henry, associated with him in the
royalty, and to make him be crowned king, by the hands of Roger
archbishop of York. By this precaution, he both ensured the succession of that prince, which, considering the many past irregularities in that point, could not but be esteemed somewhat precarious; and he preserved at least his family on the throne, if the
sentence of excommunication should have the effect which he
dreaded, and should make his subjects renounce their allegiance to
him. Though this design was conducted with expedition and
secrecy, Becket, before it was carried into execution, had got intelligence of it; and being desirous of obstructing all Henry's measures, as well as anxious to prevent this affront to himself, who
pretended to the sole right, as archbishop of Canterbury, to officiate in the coronation, he had inhibited all the prelates of England
from assisting at this ceremony, had procured from the pope a
mandate to the same purpose,[g] and had incited the king of France

[d] Fitz-Steph. p. 68, 69. Hoveden, p. 520.   [e] Hist. Quad. p. 104. Brompton,
p. 1062. Gervase, p. 1408. Epist. St. Thom. p. 704, 705, 706, 707, 792, 793,
794. Benedict. Abbas, p. 70.   [f] Epist. 45. lib. 5.   [g] Hist. Quad. p. 103.
Epist. St. Thom. p. 682. Gervase, p. 1412.

to protest against the coronation of young Henry, unless the princess, daughter of that monarch, should at the same time receive
the royal unction. There prevailed in that age an opinion which
was akin to its other superstitions, that the royal unction was essential to the exercise of royal power:[h] It was therefore natural both
for the king of France, careful of his daughter's establishment, and
for Becket, jealous of his own dignity, to demand, in the treaty with
Henry, some satisfaction in this essential point. Henry, after apol-
ogizing to Lewis for the omission with regard to Margaret, and
excusing it on account of the secrecy and dispatch requisite for
conducting that measure, promised that the ceremony should be
renewed in the persons both of the prince and princess: And he
assured Becket, that, besides receiving the acknowledgments of
Roger and the other bishops for the seeming affront put on the see
of Canterbury, the primate should, as a farther satisfaction, recover his rights by officiating in this coronation. But the violent
spirit of Becket, elated by the power of the church, and by the
victory which he had already obtained over his sovereign, was not
content with this voluntary compensation, but resolved to make
the injury, which he pretended to have suffered, a handle for
taking revenge on all his enemies. On his arrival in England, he
met the archbishop of York and the bishops of London and Salisbury, who were on their journey to the king in Normandy: He
notified to the archbishop the sentence of suspension, and to the
two bishops that of excommunication, which, at his solicitation, the
pope had pronounced against them. Reginald de Warenne, and
Gervase de Cornhill, two of the king's ministers, who were employed on their duty in Kent, asked him, on hearing of this bold
attempt, whether he meant to bring fire and sword into the kingdom? But the primate, heedless of the reproof, proceeded, in the
most ostentatious manner, to take possession of his diocese. In
Rochester, and all the towns through which he passed, he was
received with the shouts and acclamations of the populace. As he
approached Southwark, the clergy, the laity, men of all ranks and
ages, came forth to meet him, and celebrated with hymns of joy his
triumphant entrance. And though he was obliged, by order of the
young prince, who resided at Woodstoke, to return to his diocese,

*Becket's
return
from ban-
ishment.*

[h] Epist. St. Thom. p. 708.

CHAPTER VIII

he found that he was not mistaken, when he reckoned upon the highest veneration of the public towards his person and his dignity. He proceeded, therefore, with the more courage to dart his spiritual thunders: He issued the sentence of excommunication against Robert de Broc, and Nigel de Sackville, with many others, who either had assisted at the coronation of the prince, or been active in the late persecution of the exiled clergy. This violent measure, by which he, in effect, denounced war against the king himself, is commonly ascribed to the vindictive disposition and imperious character of Becket; but as this prelate was also a man of acknowledged abilities, we are not, in his passions alone, to look for the cause of his conduct, when he proceeded to these extremities against his enemies. His sagacity had led him to discover all Henry's intentions; and he proposed, by this bold and unexpected assault, to prevent the execution of them.

The king, from his experience of the dispositions of his people, was become sensible, that his enterprize had been too bold, in establishing the constitutions of Clarendon, in defining all the branches of royal power, and in endeavouring to extort from the church of England, as well as from the pope, an express avowal of these disputed prerogatives. Conscious also of his own violence, in attempting to break or subdue the inflexible primate, he was not displeased to undo that measure, which had given his enemies such advantage against him; and he was contented, that the controversy should terminate in that ambiguous manner, which was the utmost that princes, in those ages, could hope to attain in their disputes with the see of Rome. Though he dropped for the present, the prosecution of Becket, he still reserved to himself the right of maintaining, that the constitutions of Clarendon, the original ground of the quarrel, were both the ancient customs and the present law of the realm: And though he knew, that the papal clergy asserted them to be impious in themselves, as well as abrogated by the sentence of the sovereign pontiff, he intended, in spite of their clamours, steadily to put those laws in execution;[i] and to trust to his own abilities, and to the course of events, for success in that perilous enterprize. He hoped, that Becket's experience of a six years' exile would, after his pride was fully gratified by his

[i] Epist. St. Thom. p. 837, 839.

restoration, be sufficient to teach him more reserve in his opposition: Or if any controversy arose, he expected thenceforth to
engage in a more favourable cause, and to maintain with advantage, while the primate was now in his power,[k] the ancient and
undoubted customs of the kingdom against the usurpations of the
clergy. But Becket, determined not to betray the ecclesiastical privileges by his connivance,[l] and apprehensive lest a prince of such
profound policy, if allowed to proceed in his own way, might
probably in the end prevail, resolved to take all the advantage
which his present victory gave him, and to disconcert the cautious
measures of the king, by the vehemence and rigour of his own
conduct.[m] Assured of support from Rome, he was little intimidated
by dangers, which his courage taught him to despise, and which,
even if attended with the most fatal consequences, would serve
only to gratify his ambition and thirst of glory.[n]

When the suspended and excommunicated prelates arrived at
Baieux, where the king then resided, and complained to him of the
violent proceedings of Becket, he instantly perceived the consequences; was sensible, that his whole plan of operations was
overthrown; foresaw, that the dangerous contest between the civil
and spiritual powers, a contest which he himself had first rouzed,
but which he had endeavoured, by all his late negociations and
concessions, to appease, must come to an immediate and decisive
issue; and he was thence thrown into the most violent commotion.
The archbishop of York remarked to him, that, so long as Becket
lived, he could never expect to enjoy peace or tranquillity: The
king himself, being vehemently agitated, burst forth into an excla-
mation against his servants, whose want of zeal, he said, had so
long left him exposed to the enterprizes of that ungrateful and
imperious prelate.[o] Four gentlemen of his household, Reginald
Fitz-Urse, William de Traci, Hugh de Moreville, and Richard
Brito, taking these passionate expressions to be a hint for Becket's
death, immediately communicated their thoughts to each other;
and swearing to avenge their prince's quarrel, secretly withdrew
from court.[p] Some menacing expressions, which they had
dropped, gave a suspicion of their design; and the king dispatched

[k] Fitz-Steph. p. 65. [l] Epist. St. Thom. p. 345. [m] Fitz-Steph. p. 74.
[n] Epist. St. Thom. p. 818, 848. [o] Gervase, p. 1414. Parker, p. 207. [p] M.
Paris, p. 86. Brompton, p. 1065. Benedict. Abbas, p. 10.

a messenger after them, charging them to attempt nothing against the person of the primate:[q] But these orders arrived too late to prevent their fatal purpose. The four assassins, though they took different roads to England, arrived nearly about the same time at Saltwoode near Canterbury; and being there joined by some assistants, they proceeded in great haste to the archiepiscopal palace. They found the primate, who trusted entirely to the sacredness of his character, very slenderly attended; and though they threw out many menaces and reproaches against him, he was so incapable of fear, that, without using any precautions against their violence, he immediately went to St. Benedict's church, to hear vespers. They followed him thither, attacked him before the altar, and having cloven his head with many blows, retired without meeting any opposition. This was the tragical end of Thomas a Becket, a prelate of the most lofty, intrepid, and inflexible spirit, who was able to cover, to the world and probably to himself, the enterprizes of pride and ambition, under the disguise of sanctity and of zeal for the interests of religion: An extraordinary personage, surely, had he been allowed to remain in his first station, and had directed the vehemence of his character to the support of law and justice; instead of being engaged, by the prejudices of the times, to sacrifice all private duties and public connexions to tyes, which he imagined, or represented, as superior to every civil and political consideration. But no man, who enters into the genius of that age, can reasonably doubt of this prelate's sincerity. The spirit of superstition was so prevalent, that it infallibly caught every careless reasoner, much more every one whose interest, and honour, and ambition, were engaged to support it. All the wretched literature of the times was inlisted on that side: Some faint glimmerings of common sense might sometimes pierce through the thick cloud of ignorance, or what was worse, the illusions of perverted science, which had blotted out the sun, and enveloped the face of nature: But those who preserved themselves untainted by the general contagion, proceeded on no principles which they could pretend to justify: They were more indebted to their total want of instruction, than to their knowledge, if they still retained some share of understanding: Folly was possessed of all the schools as well as all the

Decemb. 29. Murder of Thomas a Becket.

[q] Hist. Quad. p. 144. Trivet, p. 55.

churches; and her votaries assumed the garb of philosophers together with the ensigns of spiritual dignities. Throughout that large collection of letters, which bears the name of St. Thomas, we find, in all the retainers of that aspiring prelate, no less than in himself, a most entire and absolute conviction of the reason and piety of their own party, and a disdain of their antagonists: Nor is there less cant and grimace in their stile, when they address each other, than when they compose manifestos for the perusal of the public. The spirit of revenge, violence, and ambition, which accompanied their conduct, instead of forming a presumption of hypocrisy, are the surest pledges of their sincere attachment to a cause, which so much flattered these domineering passions.

Grief   Henry, on the first report of Becket's violent measures, had purposed to have him arrested, and had already taken some steps towards the execution of that design: But the intelligence of his murder threw the prince into great consternation; and he was immediately sensible of the dangerous consequences, which he had reason to apprehend from so unexpected an event. An archbishop of reputed sanctity, assassinated before the altar, in the exercise of his functions, and on account of his zeal in maintaining ecclesiastical privileges, must attain the highest honours of martyrdom; while his murderer would be ranked among the most bloody tyrants, that ever were exposed to the hatred and detestation of mankind. Interdicts and excommunications, weapons in themselves so terrible, would, he foresaw, be armed with double force, when employed in a cause so much calculated to work on the human passions, and so peculiarly adapted to the eloquence of popular preachers and declaimers. In vain would he plead his own innocence, and even his total ignorance of the fact: He was sufficiently guilty, if the church thought proper to esteem him such: And his concurrence in Becket's martyrdom, becoming a religious opinion, would be received with all the implicit credit, which belonged to the most established articles of faith. These considerations gave the king the most unaffected concern; and as it was extremely his interest to clear himself from all suspicion, he took no care to conceal the depth of his affliction.[r] He shut himself up from the light of day and from all commerce with his servants: He

[r] Ypod. Neust. p. 447. M. Paris, p. 87. Diceto, p. 556. Gervase, p. 1419.

even refused during three days all food and sustenance:[s] The courtiers, apprehending dangerous effects from his despair, were at last obliged to break in upon his solitude; and they employed every topic of consolation, induced him to accept of nourishment, and occupied his leisure in taking precautions against the consequences, which he so justly apprehended from the murder of the primate.

The point of chief importance to Henry was to convince the pope of his innocence; or rather, to persuade him, that he would reap greater advantages from the submissions of England than from proceeding to extremities against that kingdom. The archbishop of Roüen, the bishops of Worcester and Evreux, with five persons of inferior quality, were immediately dispatched to Rome,[t] and orders were given them to perform their journey with the utmost expedition. Though the name and authority of the court of Rome were so terrible in the remote countries of Europe, which were sunk in profound ignorance, and were entirely unacquainted with its character and conduct; the pope was so little revered at home that his inveterate enemies surrounded the gates of Rome itself, and even controuled his government in that city; and the ambassadors, who, from a distant extremity of Europe, carried to him the humble, or rather abject submissions of the greatest potentate of the age, found the utmost difficulty to make their way to him, and to throw themselves at his feet. It was at length agreed, that Richard Barre, one of their number, should leave the rest behind, and run all the hazards of the passage,[u] in order to prevent the fatal consequences which might ensue from any delay in giving satisfaction to his holiness. He found on his arrival, that Alexander was already wrought up to the greatest rage against the king, that Becket's partizans were daily stimulating him to revenge, that the king of France had exhorted him to fulminate the most dreadful sentence against England, and that the very mention of Henry's name before the sacred college was received with every expression of horror and execration. The Thursday before Easter was now approaching, when it is customary for the pope to denounce annual curses against all his enemies; and it was expected, that Henry

1171. and submission of the king.

---

[s] Hist. Quad. p. 143. [t] Hoveden, p. 526. M. Paris, p. 87. [u] Hoveden, p. 526. Epist. St. Thom. p. 863.

should, with all the preparations peculiar to the discharge of that sacred artillery, be solemnly comprehended in the number. But Barre found means to appease the pontiff, and to deter him from a measure which, if it failed of success, could not afterwards be easily recalled: The anathemas were only levelled in general against all the actors, accomplices, and abettors of Becket's murder. The abbot of Valasse, and the archdeacons of Salisbury and Lisieux, with others of Henry's ministers, who soon after arrived, besides asserting their prince's innocence, made oath before the whole consistory, that he would stand to the pope's judgment in the affair, and make every submission, that should be required of him. The terrible blow was thus artfully eluded; the cardinals Albert and Theodin were appointed legates to examine the cause, and were ordered to proceed to Normandy for that purpose; and though Henry's foreign dominions were already laid under an interdict by the archbishop of Sens, Becket's great partizan, and the pope's legate in France, the general expectation, that the monarch would easily exculpate himself from any concurrence in the guilt, kept every one in suspence, and prevented all the bad consequences, which might be dreaded from that sentence.

The clergy, mean while, though their rage was happily diverted from falling on the king, were not idle in magnifying the sanctity of Becket; in extolling the merits of his martyrdom; and in exalting him above all that devoted tribe, who, in several ages, had, by their blood, cemented the fabric of the temple. Other saints had only borne testimony by their sufferings to the general doctrines of Christianity; but Becket had sacrificed his life to the power and privileges of the clergy; and this peculiar merit challenged, and not in vain, a suitable acknowledgment to his memory. Endless were the panegyrics on his virtues; and the miracles, wrought by his reliques, were more numerous, more nonsensical, and more impudently attested, than those which ever filled the legend of any confessor or martyr. Two years after his death he was canonized by pope Alexander; a solemn jubilee was established for celebrating his merits; his body was removed to a magnificent shrine, enriched with presents from all parts of Christendom; pilgrimages were performed to obtain his intercession with heaven; and it was computed, that, in one year, above a hundred thousand pilgrims arrived in Canterbury, and paid their devotions at his tomb. It is

337

CHAPTER VIII

indeed a mortifying reflection to those who are actuated by the love of fame, so justly denominated the last infirmity of noble minds, that the wisest legislator and most exalted genius, that ever reformed or enlightened the world, can never expect such tributes of praise, as are lavished on the memory of pretended saints, whose whole conduct was probably, to the last degree, odious or contemptible, and whose industry was entirely directed to the pursuit of objects pernicious to mankind. It is only a conqueror, a personage no less intitled to our hatred, who can pretend to the attainment of equal renown and glory.

It may not be amiss to remark, before we conclude this subject of Thomas a Becket, that the king, during his controversy with that prelate, was on every occasion more anxious than usual to express his zeal for religion, and to avoid all appearance of a profane negligence on that head. He gave his consent to the imposing of a tax on all his dominions for the delivery of the holy land, now threatened by the famous Saladine: This tax amounted to two-pence a pound for one year, and a penny a pound for the four subsequent.[w] Almost all the princes of Europe laid a like imposition on their subjects, which received the name of Saladine's tax. During this period, there came over from Germany about thirty heretics of both sexes, under the direction of one Gerard; simple ignorant people, who could give no account of their faith, but declared themselves ready to suffer for the tenets of their master. They made only one convert in England, a woman as ignorant as themselves; yet they gave such umbrage to the clergy, that they were delivered over to the secular arm, and were punished by being burned on the forehead, and then whipped through the streets. They seemed to exult in their sufferings, and as they went along, sung the beatitude, *Blessed are ye, when men hate you and persecute you.*[x] After they were whipped, they were thrust out almost naked in the midst of winter, and perished through cold and hunger; no one daring, or being willing, to give them the least relief. We are ignorant of the particular tenets of these people: For it would be imprudent to rely on the representations left of them by the clergy, who affirm, that they denied the efficacy of the sacra-

[w] Chron. Gervase, p. 1399. M. Paris, p. 74.   [x] Neubr. p. 391. M. Paris, p. 74. Heming. p. 494.

ments, and the unity of the church. It is probable, that their departure from the standard of orthodoxy was still more subtile and minute. They seem to have been the first that ever suffered for heresy in England.

As soon as Henry found, that he was in no immediate dangers from the thunders of the Vatican, he undertook an expedition against Ireland; a design, which he had long projected, and by which he hoped to recover his credit, somewhat impaired by his late transactions with the hierarchy.

IX

HENRY II

State of Ireland – Conquest of that island –
The king's accommodation with the court of Rome –
Revolt of young Henry and his brothers – Wars
and insurrections – War with Scotland – Pennance
of Henry for Becket's murder – William, king of
Scotland, defeated and taken prisoner – The king's
accommodation with his sons – The king's equitable
administration – Crusades – Revolt of prince
Richard – Death and character of Henry –
Miscellaneous transactions of his reign

As Britain was first peopled from Gaul, so was Ireland probably from Britain; and the inhabitants of all these countries
seem to have been so many tribes of the Celtae, who derive their
origin from an antiquity, that lies far beyond the records of any
history or tradition. The Irish, from the beginning of time, had
been buried in the most profound barbarism and ignorance; and
as they were never conquered or even invaded by the Romans,
from whom all the western world derived its civility, they continued still in the most rude state of society, and were distinguished
by those vices alone, to which human nature, not tamed by education or restrained by laws, is for ever subject. The small principalities, into which they were divided, exercised perpetual rapine
and violence against each other; the uncertain succession of their
princes was a continual source of domestic convulsions; the usual

1172.
State of
Ireland.

title of each petty sovereign was the murder of his predecessor; courage and force, though exercised in the commission of crimes, were more honoured than any pacific virtues; and the most simple arts of life, even tillage and agriculture, were almost wholly unknown among them. They had felt the invasions of the Danes and the other northern tribes; but these inroads, which had spread barbarism in other parts of Europe, tended rather to improve the Irish; and the only towns, which were to be found in the island, had been planted along the coast by the freebooters of Norway and Denmark. The other inhabitants exercised pasturage in the open country; sought protection from any danger in their forests and morasses; and being divided by the fiercest animosities against each other, were still more intent on the means of mutual injury, than on the expedients for common or even for private interest.

Besides many small tribes, there were in the age of Henry II. five principal sovereignties in the island, Munster, Leinster, Meath, Ulster, and Connaught; and as it had been usual for the one or the other of these to take the lead in their wars, there was commonly some prince, who seemed, for the time, to act as monarch of Ireland. Roderic O Connor, king of Connaught, was then advanced to this dignity;[j] but his government, ill obeyed even within his own territory, could not unite the people in any measures, either for the establishment of order, or for defence against foreigners. The ambition of Henry had, very early in his reign, been moved, by the prospect of these advantages, to attempt the subjecting of Ireland; and a pretence was only wanting to invade a people, who, being always confined to their own island, had never given any reason of complaint to any of their neighbours. For this purpose, he had recourse to Rome, which assumed a right to dispose of kingdoms and empires; and not foreseeing the dangerous disputes, which he was one day to maintain with that see, he helped, for present, or rather for an imaginary, convenience, to give sanction to claims which were now become dangerous to all sovereigns. Adrian IV. who then filled the papal chair, was by birth an Englishman; and being, on that account, the more disposed to oblige Henry, he was easily persuaded to act as master of the world, and to make, without any hazard or expence, the acqui-

[j] Hoveden, p. 527.

CHAPTER IX

sition of a great island to his spiritual jurisdiction. The Irish had, by precedent missions from the Britons, been imperfectly converted to Christianity; and, what the pope regarded as the surest mark of their imperfect conversion, they followed the doctrines of their first teachers, and had never acknowledged any subjection to the see of Rome. Adrian, therefore, in the year 1156, issued a bull in favour of Henry; in which, after premising, that this prince had ever shown an anxious care to enlarge the church of God on earth, and to encrease the number of his saints and elect in heaven; he represents his design of subduing Ireland as derived from the same pious motives: He considers his care of previously applying for the apostolic sanction as a sure earnest of success and victory; and having established it as a point incontestible, that all Christian kingdoms belong to the patrimony of St. Peter, he acknowledges it to be his own duty to sow among them the seeds of the gospel, which might in the last day fructify to their eternal salvation: He exhorts the king to invade Ireland, in order to extirpate the vice and wickedness of the natives, and oblige them to pay yearly, from every house, a penny to the see of Rome: He gives him entire right and authority over the island, commands all the inhabitants to obey him as their sovereign, and invests with full power all such godly instruments as he should think proper to employ in an enterprize, thus calculated for the glory of God and the salvation of the souls of men.[z] Henry, though armed with this authority, did not immediately put his design in execution; but being detained by more interesting business on the continent, waited for a favourable opportunity of invading Ireland.

Dermot Macmorrogh, king of Leinster, had, by his licentious tyranny, rendered himself odious to his subjects, who seized with alacrity the first occasion that offered, of throwing off the yoke, which was become grievous and oppressive to them. This prince had formed a design on Dovergilda, wife of Ororic, prince of Breffny; and taking advantage of her husband's absence, who, being obliged to visit a distant part of his territory, had left his wife secure, as he thought, in an island, surrounded by a bog, he suddenly invaded the place, and carried off the princess.[a] This exploit,

[z] M. Paris, p. 67. Girald. Cambr. Spelm. Concil. vol. ii. p. 51. Rymer, vol. i. p. 15. [a] Girald. Cambr. p. 760.

though usual among the Irish, and rather deemed a proof of gallantry and spirit,[b] provoked the resentment of the husband; who, having collected forces, and being strengthened by the alliance of Roderic, king of Connaught, invaded the dominions of Dermot, and expelled him his kingdom. The exiled prince had recourse to Henry, who was at this time in Guienne, craved his assistance in restoring him to his sovereignty, and offered, on that event, to hold his kingdom in vassalage under the crown of England. Henry, whose views were already turned towards making acquisitions in Ireland, readily accepted the offer; but being at that time embarrassed by the rebellions of his French subjects, as well as by his disputes with the see of Rome, he declined, for the present, embarking in the enterprize, and gave Dermot no farther assistance than letters patent, by which he empowered all his subjects to aid the Irish prince in the recovery of his dominions.[c] Dermot supported by this authority, came to Bristol; and after endeavouring, though for some time in vain, to engage adventurers in the enterprize, he at last formed a treaty with Richard, sirnamed Strongbow, earl of Strigul. This nobleman, who was of the illustrious house of Clare, had impaired his fortune by expensive pleasures; and being ready for any desperate undertaking, he promised assistance to Dermot, on condition that he should espouse Eva, daughter of that prince, and be declared heir to all his dominions.[d] While Richard was assembling his succours, Dermot went into Wales; and meeting with Robert Fitz-Stephens, constable of Abertivi, and Maurice Fitz-Gerald, he also engaged them in his service, and obtained their promise of invading Ireland. Being now assured of succour, he returned privately to his own state; and lurking in the monastery of Fernes, which he had founded, (for this ruffian was also a founder of monasteries) he prepared every thing for the reception of his English allies.[e]

Conquest of that island. The troops of Fitz-Stephens were first ready. That gentleman landed in Ireland with thirty knights, sixty esquires, and three hundred archers; but this small body, being brave men, not unacquainted with discipline, and completely armed, a thing almost unknown in Ireland, struck a great terror into the barbarous in-

[b] Spencer, vol. vi.   [c] Girald. Cambr. p. 760.   [d] Ibid. p. 761.   [e] Ibid. p. 761.

CHAPTER IX

habitants, and seemed to menace them with some signal revolution. The conjunction of Maurice de Pendergail, who, about the
same time, brought over ten knights and sixty archers, enabled
Fitz-Stephens to attempt the siege of Wexford, a town inhabited by
the Danes; and after gaining an advantage, he made himself master of the place.[f] Soon after, Fitz-Gerald arrived with ten knights,
thirty esquires, and a hundred archers;[g] and being joined by the
former adventurers, composed a force which nothing in Ireland
was able to withstand. Roderic, the chief monarch of the island,
was foiled in different actions; the prince of Ossory was obliged to
submit, and give hostages for his peaceable behaviour; and Dermot, not content with being restored to his kingdom of Leinster,
projected the dethroning of Roderic, and aspired to the sole dominion over the Irish.

In prosecution of these views, he sent over a messenger to the
earl of Strigul, challenging the performance of his promise, and
displaying the mighty advantages which might now be reaped by
a reinforcement of warlike troops from England. Richard, not
satisfied with the general allowance given by Henry to all his subjects, went to that prince, then in Normandy; and having obtained
a cold or ambiguous permission, prepared himself for the execution of his designs. He first sent over Raymond, one of his
retinue, with ten knights and seventy archers, who, landing near
Waterford, defeated a body of three thousand Irish, that had ventured to attack him;[h] and as Richard himself, who brought over two
hundred horse, and a body of archers, joined, a few days after, the
victorious English, they made themselves masters of Waterford,
and proceeded to Dublin, which was taken by assault. Roderic, in
revenge, cut off the head of Dermot's natural son, who had been
left as a hostage in his hands; and Richard, marrying Eva, became
soon after, by the death of Dermot, master of the kingdom of
Leinster, and prepared to extend his authority over all Ireland.
Roderic, and the other Irish princes, were alarmed at the danger;
and combining together, besieged Dublin with an army of thirty
thousand men: But earl Richard, making a sudden sally at the
head of ninety knights, with their followers, put this numerous
army to rout, chaced them off the field, and pursued them with

[f] Ibid. p. 761, 762.   [g] Girald. Cambr. p. 766.   [h] Ibid. p. 767.

great slaughter. None in Ireland now dared to oppose themselves to the English.[i]

Henry, jealous of the progress, made by his own subjects, sent orders to recal all the English, and he made preparations to attack Ireland in person:[k] But Richard, and the other adventurers, found means to appease him, by making him the most humble submissions, and offering to hold all their acquisitions in vassalage to his crown.[l] That monarch landed in Ireland at the head of five hundred knights, besides other soldiers: He found the Irish so dispirited by their late misfortunes, that, in a progress which he made through the island, he had no other occupation than to receive the homages of his new subjects. He left most of the Irish chieftains or princes in possession of their ancient territories; bestowed some lands on the English adventurers; gave earl Richard the commission of seneschal of Ireland; and after a stay of a few months, returned in triumph to England. By these trivial exploits, scarcely worth relating, except for the importance of the consequences, was Ireland subdued, and annexed to the English crown.

The low state of commerce and industry, during those ages, made it impracticable for princes to support regular armies, which might retain a conquered country in subjection; and the extreme barbarism and poverty of Ireland could still less afford means of bearing the expence. The only expedient, by which a durable conquest could then be made or maintained, was by pouring in a multitude of new inhabitants, dividing among them the lands of the vanquished, establishing them in all offices of trust and authority, and thereby transforming the ancient inhabitants into a new people. By this policy, the northern invaders of old, and of late the duke of Normandy, had been able to fix their dominions, and to erect kingdoms, which remained stable on their foundations, and were transmitted to the posterity of the first conquerors. But the state of Ireland rendered that island so little inviting to the English, that only a few of desperate fortunes could be persuaded, from time to time, to transport themselves thither;[m] and instead of reclaiming the natives from their uncultivated manners, they were

[i] Girald. Cambr. p. 733.   [k] Ibid. p. 770.   [l] Ibid. p. 775.   [m] Brompton, p. 1069. Neubrig. p. 403.

CHAPTER IX

gradually assimilated to the antient inhabitants, and degenerated from the customs of their own nation. It was also found requisite to bestow great military and arbitrary powers on the leaders, who commanded a handful of men amidst such hostile multitudes; and law and equity, in a little time, became as much unknown in the English settlements as they had ever been among the Irish tribes. Palatinates were erected in favour of the new adventurers; independant authority conferred; the natives, never fully subdued, still retained their animosity against the conquerors; their hatred was retaliated by like injuries; and from these causes, the Irish, during the course of four centuries, remained still savage and untractable: It was not till the latter end of Elizabeth's reign, that the island was fully subdued; nor till that of her successor, that it gave hopes of becoming a useful conquest to the English nation.

Besides that the easy and peaceable submission of the Irish left Henry no farther occupation in that island, he was recalled from it by another incident, which was of the last importance to his interest and safety. The two legates, Albert and Theodin, to whom was committed the trial of his conduct in the murder of archbishop Becket, were arrived in Normandy; and being impatient of delay, sent him frequent letters, full of menaces, if he protracted any longer making his appearance before them.[n] He hastened therefore to Normandy, and had a conference with them at Savigny, where their demands were so exorbitant, that he broke off the negotiation, threatened to return to Ireland, and bade them do their worst against him. They perceived that the season was now past for taking advantage of that tragical incident; which, had it been hotly pursued by interdicts and excommunications, was capable of throwing the whole kingdom into combustion. But the time, which Henry had happily gained, had contributed to appease the minds of men: The event could not now have the same influence, as when it was recent; and as the clergy every day looked for an accommodation with the king, they had not opposed the pretensions of his partizans, who had been very industrious in representing to the people his entire innocence in the murder of the primate, and his ignorance of the designs formed by the assassins. The legates, therefore, found themselves obliged to lower their

[n] Girald. Cambr. p. 778.

terms; and Henry was so fortunate as to conclude an accommodation with them. He declared upon oath, before the reliques of the saints, that, so far from commanding or desiring the death of the archbishop, he was extremely grieved when he received intelligence of it: But as the passion, which he had expressed on account of that prelate's conduct, had probably been the occasion of his murder, he stipulated the following conditions, as an atone-

The king's accommodation with the court of Rome.

ment for the offence. He promised, that he should pardon all such as had been banished for adhering to Becket, and should restore them to their livings; that the see of Canterbury should be reinstated in all its antient possessions; that he should pay the templars a sum of money sufficient for the subsistance of two hundred knights during a year in the Holy Land; that he should himself take the cross at the Christmas following, and, if the pope required it, serve three years against the infidels, either in Spain or Palestine; that he should not insist on the observance of such customs, derogatory to ecclesiastical privileges, as had been introduced in his own time; and that he should not obstruct appeals to the pope in ecclesiastical causes, but should content himself with exacting sufficient security from such clergymen as left his dominions to prosecute an appeal, that they should attempt nothing against the rights of his crown.[o] Upon signing these concessions, Henry received absolution from the legates, and was confirmed in the grant of Ireland made by pope Adrian:[p] and nothing proves more strongly the great abilities of this monarch, than his extricating himself, on such easy terms, from so difficult a situation. He had always insisted, that the laws, established at Clarendon, contained not any new claims, but the ancient customs of the kingdom; and he was still at liberty, notwithstanding the articles of this agreement, to maintain his pretensions. Appeals to the pope were indeed permitted by that treaty; but as the king was also permitted to exact reasonable securities from the parties, and might stretch his demands on this head as far as he pleased, he had it virtually in his power to prevent the pope from reaping any advantage by this seeming concession. And on the whole, the constitutions of Clarendon remained still the law of the realm; though

[o] M. Paris, p. 88. Benedict. Abb. p. 34. Hoveden, p. 529. Diceto, p. 560. Chron. Gerv. p. 1422. [p] Brompton, p. 1071. Liber. Nig. Scac. p. 47.

CHAPTER IX

the pope and his legates seem so little to have conceived the king's power to lie under any legal limitations, that they were satisfied with his departing, by treaty, from one of the most momentous articles of these constitutions, without requiring any repeal by the states of the kingdom.

Henry, freed from this dangerous controversy with the ecclesiastics and with the see of Rome, seemed now to have reached the pinnacle of human grandeur and felicity, and to be equally happy in his domestic situation and in his political government. A numerous progeny of sons and daughters gave both lustre and authority to his crown, prevented the dangers of a disputed succession, and repressed all pretensions of the ambitious barons. The king's precaution also, in establishing the several branches of his family, seemed well calculated to prevent all jealousy among the brothers, and to perpetuate the greatness of his family. He had appointed Henry, his eldest son, to be his successor in the kingdom of England, the dutchy of Normandy, and the counties of Anjou, Maine, and Touraine; territories which lay contiguous, and which, by that means, might easily lend to each other mutual assistance, both against intestine commotions and foreign invasions. Richard, his second son, was invested in the dutchy of Guienne and county of Poictou; Geoffrey, his third son, inherited, in right of his wife, the dutchy of Britanny; and the new conquest of Ireland was destined for the appanage of John, his fourth son. He had also negociated, in favour of this last prince, a marriage with Adelais, the only daughter of Humbert, count of Savoy and Maurienne; and was to receive as her dowry considerable demesnes in Piedmont, Savoy, Bresse, and Dauphiny.[q] But this exaltation of his family excited the jealousy of all his neighbours, who made those very sons, whose fortunes he had so anxiously established, the means of embittering his future life and disturbing his government.

Young Henry, who was rising to man's estate, began to display his character, and aspire to independance: Brave, ambitious, liberal, munificent, affable; he discovered qualities, which give great lustre to youth; prognosticate a shining fortune; but, unless tem-

[q] Ypod. Neust. p. 448. Bened. Abb. p. 38. Hoveden, p. 532. Diceto, p. 562. Brompton, p. 1081. Rymer, vol. i. p. 33.

pered in mature age with discretion, are the forerunners of the greatest calamities.[r] It is said, that at the time when this prince received the royal unction, his father, in order to give greater dignity to the ceremony, officiated at table as one of the retinue; and observed to his son, that never king was more royally served. *It is nothing extraordinary,* said young Henry to one of his courtiers, *if the son of a count should serve the son of a king.* This saying, which might pass only for an innocent pleasantry, or even for an oblique compliment to his father, was however regarded as a symptom of his aspiring temper; and his conduct soon after justified the conjecture.

1173.

Henry, agreeably to the promise which he had given both to the pope and French king, permitted his son to be crowned anew by the hands of the archbishop of Roüen, and associated the princess Margaret, spouse to young Henry, in the ceremony.[s] He afterwards allowed him to pay a visit to his father-in-law at Paris, who took the opportunity of instilling into the young prince those ambitious sentiments, to which he was naturally but too much in-

Revolt of young Henry and his brothers.

clined.[t] Though it had been the constant practice of France, ever since the accession of the Capetian line, to crown the son during the life-time of the father, without conferring on him any present participation of royalty; Lewis persuaded his son-in-law, that, by this ceremony, which in those ages was deemed so important, he had acquired a title to sovereignty, and that the king could not, without injustice, exclude him from immediate possession of the whole, or at least a part of his dominions. In consequence of these extravagant ideas, young Henry, on his return, desired the king to resign to him either the crown of England or the dutchy of Normandy; discovered great discontent on the refusal; spake in the most undutiful terms of his father; and soon after, in concert with Lewis, made his escape to Paris, where he was protected and supported by that monarch.

While Henry was alarmed at this incident, and had the prospect

[r] Chron. Gerv. p. 1463. [s] Hoveden, p. 529. Diceto, p. 560. Brompton, p. 1080. Chron. Gerv. p. 1421. Trivet, p. 58. It appears from Madox's History of the Exchequer, that silk garments were then known in England, and that the coronation robes of the young king and queen cost eighty-seven pounds ten shillings and four pence, money of that age. [t] Girald. Cambr. p. 782.

CHAPTER IX

of dangerous intrigues, or even of a war, which, whether successful or not, must be extremely calamitous and disagreeable to him, he received intelligence of new misfortunes, which must have affected him in the most sensible manner. Queen Eleanor, who had disgusted her first husband by her gallantries, was no less offensive to her second, by her jealousy; and after this manner, carried to extremity, in the different periods of her life, every circumstance of female weakness. She communicated her discontents against Henry to her two younger sons, Geoffrey and Richard, persuaded them that they were also entitled to present possession of the territories assigned to them; engaged them to fly secretly to the court of France; and was meditating, herself, an escape to the same court, and had even put on man's apparel for that purpose; when she was seized by orders from her husband, and thrown into confinement. Thus, Europe saw with astonishment the best and most indulgent of parents at war with his whole family; three boys, scarcely arrived at the age of puberty, require a great monarch, in the full vigour of his age and height of his reputation, to dethrone himself in their favour; and several princes not ashamed to support them in these unnatural and absurd pretensions.

Henry, reduced to this perilous and disagreeable situation, had recourse to the court of Rome: Though sensible of the danger attending the interposition of ecclesiastical authority in temporal disputes, he applied to the pope, as his superior lord, to excommunicate his enemies, and by these censures to reduce to obedience his undutiful children, whom he found such reluctance to punish by the sword of the magistrate.ᵘ Alexander, well pleased to exert his power in so justifiable a cause, issued the bulls required of him: But it was soon found, that these spiritual weapons had not the same force as when employed in a spiritual controversy; and that the clergy were very negligent in supporting a sentence, which was nowise calculated to promote the immediate interests of their order. The king, after taking in vain this humiliating step, was obliged to have recourse to arms, and to enlist such auxiliaries, as

---

ᵘ Epist. Petri Bles. epist. 136. in Biblioth. Patr. tom. xxiv. p. 1048. His words are, *Vestrae jurisdictionis est regnum Angliae, et quantum ad feudatorii juris obligationem, vobis duntaxat obnoxius teneor.* The same strange paper is in Rymer, vol. i. p. 35. and Trivet, vol. i. p. 62.

are the usual resource of tyrants, and have seldom been employed by so wise and just a monarch.

The loose government which prevailed in all the states of Europe, the many private wars carried on among the neighbouring nobles, and the impossibility of enforcing any general execution of the laws, had encouraged a tribe of banditti to disturb every where the public peace, to infest the highways, to pillage the open country, and to brave all the efforts of the civil magistrate, and even the excommunications of the church, which were fulminated against them.[w] Troops of them were sometimes inlisted in the service of one prince or baron, sometimes in that of another: They often acted in an independant manner, under leaders of their own: The peaceable and industrious inhabitants, reduced to poverty by their ravages, were frequently obliged for subsistence to betake themselves to a like disorderly course of life: And a continual intestine war, pernicious to industry, as well as to the execution of justice, was thus carried on in the bowels of every kingdom.[x] Those desperate ruffians received the name sometimes of Brabançons, sometimes of Routiers or Cottereaux; but for what reason, is not agreed by historians: And they formed a kind of society or government among themselves, which set at defiance the rest of mankind. The greatest monarchs were not ashamed, on occasion, to have recourse to their assistance; and as their habits of war and depredation had given them experience, hardiness, and courage, they generally composed the most formidable part of those armies, which decided the political quarrels of princes. Several of them were enlisted among the forces levied by Henry's enemies;[y] but the great treasures amassed by that prince enabled him to engage more numerous troops of them in his service; and the situation of his affairs rendered even such banditti the only forces on whose fidelity he could repose any confidence. His licentious barons, disgusted with a vigilant government, were more desirous of being ruled by young princes, ignorant of public affairs, remiss in their conduct, and profuse in their grants;[z] and as the king had ensured to his sons the succession to every particular province of his dominions, the nobles dreaded no danger in adhering to those who, they

[w] Neubrig, p. 413.   [x] Chron. Gerv. p. 1461.   [y] Petr. Bles. epist. 47.
[z] Diceto, p. 570.

CHAPTER IX

knew, must some time become their sovereigns. Prompted by these motives, many of the Norman nobility had deserted to his son Henry; the Breton and Gascon barons seemed equally disposed to embrace the quarrel of Geoffrey and Richard. Disaffection had creeped in among the English; and the earls of Leicester and Chester in particular had openly declared against the king. Twenty thousand Brabançons, therefore, joined to some troops, which he brought over from Ireland, and a few barons of approved fidelity, formed the sole force, with which he intended to resist his enemies.

Lewis, in order to bind the confederates in a closer union, summoned at Paris an assembly of the chief vassals of the crown, received their approbation of his measures, and engaged them by oath to adhere to the cause of young Henry. This prince, in return, bound himself by a like tie never to desert his French allies; and having made a new great seal, he lavishly distributed among them many considerable parts of those territories, which he purposed to conquer from his father. The counts of Flanders, Boulogne, Blois, and Eu, partly moved by the general jealousy arising from Henry's power and ambition, partly allured by the prospect of reaping advantage from the inconsiderate temper and the necessities of the young prince, declared openly in favour of the latter. William, king of Scotland, had also entered into this great confederacy; and a plan was concerted for a general invasion on different parts of the king's extensive and factious dominions.

Hostilities were first commenced by the counts of Flanders and Boulogne on the frontiers of Normandy. Those princes laid siege to Aumale, which was delivered into their hands, by the treachery of the count of that name: This nobleman surrendered himself prisoner; and, on pretence of thereby paying his ransom, opened the gates of all his other fortresses. The two counts next besieged and made themselves masters of Drincourt: But the count of Boulogne was here mortally wounded in the assault; and this incident put some stop to the progress of the Flemish arms.

In another quarter, the king of France, being strongly assisted by his vassals, assembled a great army of seven thousand knights and their followers on horseback, and a proportionable number of infantry: Carrying young Henry along with him, he laid siege to Verneüil, which was vigorously defended by Hugh de Lacy and Hugh de Beauchamp, the governors. After he had lain a month

Wars and insurrections.

before the place, the garrison, being straitened for provisions, were obliged to capitulate; and they engaged, if not relieved within three days, to surrender the town, and to retire into the citadel. On the last of these days, Henry appeared with his army upon the heights above Verneüil. Lewis, dreading an attack, sent the archbishop of Sens and the count of Blois to the English camp, and desired that next day should be appointed for a conference, in order to establish a general peace, and terminate the difference between Henry and his sons. The king, who passionately desired this accommodation, and suspected no fraud, gave his consent; but Lewis, that morning, obliging the garrison to surrender, according to the capitulation, set fire to the place, and began to retire with his army. Henry, provoked at this artifice, attacked the rear with vigour, put them to rout, did some execution, and took several prisoners. The French army, as their time of service was now expired, immediately dispersed themselves into their several provinces; and left Henry free to prosecute his advantages against his other enemies.

The nobles of Britanny, instigated by the earl of Chester and Ralph de Fougeres, were all in arms; but their progress was checked by a body of Brabançons, which the king, after Lewis's retreat, had sent against them. The two armies came to an action near Dol; where the rebels were defeated, fifteen hundred killed on the spot, and the leaders, the earls of Chester and Fougeres, obliged to take shelter in the town of Dol. Henry hastened to form the siege of that place, and carried on the attack with such ardour, that he obliged the governor and garrison to surrender themselves prisoners. By these vigorous measures and happy successes, the insurrections were entirely quelled in Britanny; and the king, thus fortunate in all quarters, willingly agreed to a conference with Lewis, in hopes, that his enemies, finding all their mighty efforts entirely frustrated, would terminate hostilities on some moderate and reasonable conditions.

The two monarchs met between Trie and Gisors; and Henry had here the mortification to see his three sons in the retinue of his mortal enemy. As Lewis had no other pretence for war than supporting the claims of the young princes, the king made them such offers as children might be ashamed to insist on, and could be extorted from him by nothing but his parental affection or by the present necessity of his affairs.[a] He insisted only on retaining the sovereign authority in all his dominions; but offered young Henry half the revenues of England, with some places of surety in that kingdom; or, if he rather chose to reside in Normandy, half the revenues of that dutchy, with all those of Anjou. He made a like offer to Richard in Guienne; he promised to resign Britanny to Geoffrey; and if these concessions were not deemed sufficient, he agreed to add to them whatever the pope's legates, who were present, should require of him.[b] The earl of Leicester was also present at the negotiation; and either from the impetuosity of his temper, or from a view of abruptly breaking off a conference which must cover the allies with confusion, he gave vent to the most violent reproaches against Henry, and he even put his hand to his sword, as if he meant to attempt some violence against him. This furious action threw the whole company into confusion, and put an end to the treaty.[c]

The chief hopes of Henry's enemies seemed now to depend on the state of affairs in England, where his authority was exposed to the most imminent danger. One article of prince Henry's agreement with his foreign confederates, was, that he should resign Kent, with Dover and all its other fortresses, into the hands of the earl of Flanders:[d] Yet so little national or public spirit prevailed among the independant English nobility, so wholly bent were they on the aggrandizement each of himself and his own family, that, notwithstanding this pernicious concession, which must have produced the ruin of the kingdom, the greater part of them had conspired to make an insurrection and to support the prince's pretensions. The king's principal resource lay in the church and the bishops, with whom he was now in perfect agreement; whether that the decency of their character made them ashamed of supporting so unnatural a rebellion, or that they were entirely satisfied with Henry's atonement for the murder of Becket and for his former invasion of ecclesiastical immunities. That prince, however, had resigned none of the essential rights of his crown in the accommodation; he maintained still the same prudent jealousy of the court of Rome; admitted no legate into England, without his

[a] Hoveden, p. 539. [b] Ibid. p. 536. Brompton, p. 1088. [c] Hoveden, p. 536. [d] Hoveden, p. 533. Brompton, p. 1084. Neubr. p. 508.

swearing to attempt nothing against the royal prerogatives; and he had even obliged the monks of Canterbury, who pretended to a free election on the vacancy made by the death of Becket, to chuse Roger, prior of Dover, in the place of that turbulent prelate.*

War with Scotland.   The king of Scotland made an irruption into Northumberland, and committed great devastations; but being opposed by Richard de Lucy, whom Henry had left guardian of the realm, he retreated into his own country, and agreed to a cessation of arms. This truce enabled the guardian to march southwards with his army, in order to oppose an invasion, which the earl of Leicester, at the head of a great body of Flemings, had made upon Suffolk. The Flemings had been joined by Hugh Bigod, who made them masters of his castle of Framlingham; and marching into the heart of the kingdom, where they hoped to be supported by Leicester's vassals, they were met by Lucy, who, assisted by Humphry Bohun, the constable, and the earls of Arundel, Glocester, and Cornwal, had advanced to Farnham with a less numerous, but braver army, to oppose them. The Flemings, who were mostly weavers and artificers (for manufactures were now beginning to be established in Flanders) were broken in an instant, ten thousand of them were put to the sword, the earl of Leicester was taken prisoner, and the remains of the invaders were glad to compound for a safe retreat into their own country.

1174.   This great defeat did not dishearten the malcontents; who, being supported by the alliance of so many foreign princes, and encouraged by the king's own sons, determined to persevere in their enterprize. The earl of Ferrars, Roger de Moubray, Archetil de Mallory, Richard de Moreville, Hamo de Mascie, together with many friends of the earls of Leicester and Chester, rose in arms: The fidelity of the earls of Clare and Glocester were suspected; and the guardian, though vigorously supported by Geoffrey, Bishop of Lincoln, the king's natural son by the fair Rosamond, found it difficult to defend himself on all quarters, from so many open and concealed enemies. The more to augment the confusion, the king of Scotland, on the expiration of the truce, broke into the northern provinces with a great army[f] of 80,000 men; which, though undisciplined and disorderly, and better fitted for committing devastation, than for executing any military enterprize, was become

*Hoveden, p. 537.   [f] Heming. p. 501.

dangerous from the present factious and turbulent spirit of the kingdom. Henry, who had baffled all his enemies in France, and had put his frontiers in a posture of defence, now found England the seat of danger; and he determined by his presence to overawe the malcontents, or by his conduct and courage to subdue them. He landed at Southampton; and knowing the influence of super- stition over the minds of the people, he hastened to Canterbury, in order to make atonement to the ashes of Thomas a Becket, and tender his submissions to a dead enemy. As soon as he came within sight of the church of Canterbury, he dismounted, walked bare- foot towards it, prostrated himself before the shrine of the saint, remained in fasting and prayer during a whole day, and watched all night the holy reliques. Not content with this hypocritical de- votion towards a man, whose violence and ingratitude had so long disquieted his government, and had been the object of his most inveterate animosity, he submitted to a pennance, still more singu- lar and humiliating. He assembled a chapter of the monks, dis- robed himself before them, put a scourge of discipline into the hands of each, and presented his bare shoulders to the lashes which these ecclesiastics successively inflicted upon him. Next day, he received absolution; and departing for London, got soon after the agreeable intelligence of a great victory which his generals had obtained over the Scots, and which, being gained, as was reported, on the very day of his absolution, was regarded as the earnest of his final reconciliation with Heaven and with Thomas a Becket.

8th July. Pen- nance of Henry for Becket's murder.

William, king of Scots, though repulsed before the castle of Prudhow, and other fortified places, had committed the most hor- rible depredations upon the northern provinces: But on the ap- proach of Ralph de Glanville, the famous justiciary, seconded by Bernard de Baliol, Robert de Stuteville, Odonel de Umfreville, William de Vesci, and other northern barons, together with the gallant bishop of Lincoln, he thought proper to retreat nearer his own country, and he fixed his camp at Alnwic. He had here weak- ened his army extremely, by sending out numerous detachments in order to extend his ravages; and he lay absolutely safe, as he imagined, from any attack of the enemy. But Glanville, informed of his situation, made a hasty and fatiguing march to Newcastle; and allowing his soldiers only a small interval for refreshment, he immediately set out towards evening for Alnwic. He marched that

*13th
July.*

night above thirty miles; arrived in the morning, under cover of a mist, near the Scottish camp; and regardless of the great numbers of the enemy, he began the attack with his small, but determined, body of cavalry. William was living in such supine security, that he took the English at first for a body of his own ravagers, who were returning to the camp: But the sight of their banners convincing him of his mistake, he entered on the action with no greater body than a hundred horse, in confidence, that the numerous army, which surrounded him, would soon hasten to his relief. He was dismounted on the first shock, and taken prisoner; while his troops, hearing of this disaster, fled on all sides with the utmost precipitation. The dispersed ravagers made the best of their way to their own country; and discord arising among them, they proceeded even to mutual hostilities, and suffered more from each other's sword than from that of the enemy.

*William,
king of
Scotland,
defeated
and
taken
prisoner.*

This great and important victory proved at last decisive in favour of Henry, and entirely broke the spirit of the English rebels. The bishop of Durham, who was preparing to revolt, made his submissions; Hugh Bigod, though he had received a strong reinforcement of Flemings, was obliged to surrender all his castles, and throw himself on the king's mercy; no better resource was left to the earl of Ferrars and Roger de Moubray; the inferior rebels imitating the example, all England was restored to tranquillity in a few weeks; and as the king appeared to lie under the immediate protection of Heaven, it was deemed impious any longer to resist him. The clergy exalted anew the merits and powerful intercession of Becket; and Henry, instead of opposing this superstition, plumed himself on the new friendship of the saint, and propagated an opinion which was so favourable to his interests.[g]

Prince Henry, who was ready to embark at Gravelines with the earl of Flanders and a great army, hearing that his partizans in England were suppressed, abandoned all thoughts of the enterprize, and joined the camp of Lewis, who, during the absence of the king, had made an irruption into Normandy, and had laid siege to Roüen.[h] The place was defended with great vigour by the inhabitants;[i] and Lewis, despairing of success by open force, tried to gain the town by a stratagem, which, in that superstitious age, was deemed not very honourable. He proclaimed in his own camp

[g] Hoveden, p. 539.   [h] Brompton, p. 1096.   [i] Diceto, p. 578.

CHAPTER IX

a cessation of arms, on pretence of celebrating the festival of St. Laurence; and when the citizens, supposing themselves in safety, were so imprudent as to remit their guard, he purposed to take advantage of their security. Happily, some priests had, from mere curiosity, mounted a steeple, where the alarm-bell hung; and observing the French camp in motion, they immediately rang the bell, and gave warning to the inhabitants, who ran to their several stations. The French, who, on hearing the alarm, hurried to the assault, had already mounted the walls in several places; but being repulsed by the enraged citizens, were obliged to retreat with considerable loss.[k] Next day, Henry, who had hastened to the defence of his Norman dominions, passed over the bridge in triumph; and entered Roüen in sight of the French army. The city was now in absolute safety; and the king, in order to brave the French monarch, commanded the gates, which had been walled up, to be opened; and he prepared to push his advantages against the enemy. Lewis saved himself from this perilous situation by a new piece of deceit, not so justifiable. He proposed a conference for adjusting the terms of a general peace, which, he knew, would be greedily embraced by Henry; and while the king of England trusted to the execution of his promise, he made a retreat with his army into France.

There was, however, a necessity on both sides for an accommodation. Henry could no longer bear to see his three sons in the hands of his enemy; and Lewis dreaded, lest this great monarch, victorious in all quarters, crowned with glory, and absolute master of his dominions, might take revenge for the many dangers and disquietudes, which the arms, and still more the intrigues of France, had, in his disputes both with Becket and his sons, found means to raise him. After making a cessation of arms, a conference was agreed on near Tours; where Henry granted his sons much less advantageous terms than he had formerly offered; and he received their submissions. The most material of his concessions were some pensions which he stipulated to pay them, and some castles which he granted them for the place of their residence; together with an indemnity for all their adherents, who were restored to their estates and honours.[l]

The king's accommodation with his sons.

[k] Brompton, p. 1096. Neubrig. p. 411. Heming. p. 503. [l] Rymer, vol. i. p. 35. Bened. Abb. p. 88. Hoveden, p. 540. Diceto, p. 583. Brompton, p. 1098. Heming. p. 505. Chron. Dunst. p. 36.

Of all those who had embraced the cause of the young princes, William, king of Scotland, was the only considerable loser, by that invidious and unjust enterprize. Henry delivered from confinement, without exacting any ransom, about nine hundred knights whom he had taken prisoners; but it cost William the ancient independancy of his crown as the price of his liberty. He stipulated to do homage to Henry for Scotland and all his other possessions; he engaged that all the barons and nobility of his kingdom should also do homage; that the bishops should take an oath of fealty; that both should swear to adhere to the king of England against their native prince, if the latter should break his engagements; and that the fortresses of Edinburgh, Stirling, Berwic, Roxborough, and Jedborough should be delivered into Henry's hands, till the performance of articles.[m] This severe and humiliating treaty was executed in its full rigour. William, being released, brought up all his barons, prelates, and abbots; and they did homage to Henry in the cathedral of York, and acknowledged him and his successors for their superior lord.[n] The English monarch stretched still farther the rigour of the conditions which he exacted. He engaged the king and states of Scotland to make a perpetual cession of the fortresses of Berwic and Roxborough, and to allow the castle of Edinburgh to remain in his hands for a limited time. This was the first great ascendant which England obtained over Scotland; and indeed the first important transaction which had passed between the kingdoms. Few princes have been so fortunate as to gain considerable advantages over their weaker neighbours with less violence and injustice, than was practised by Henry against the king of Scots, whom he had taken prisoner in battle, and who had wantonly engaged in a war, in which all the neighbours of that prince, and even his own family, were, without provocation, combined against him.[o]

1175.
10th
Aug.

[m] M. Paris, p. 91. Chron. Dunst. p. 36. Hoveden, p. 545. M. West. p. 251. Diceto, p. 584. Brompton, p. 1103. Rymer, vol. i. p. 39. Liber Niger Scaccarii, p. 36.   [n] Bened. Abb. p. 113.   [o] Some Scotch historians pretend, that William paid, besides, 100,000 pounds of ransom, which is quite incredible. The ransom of Richard I, who, besides England, possessed so many rich territories in France, was only 150,000 marks, and yet was levied with great difficulty. Indeed, two thirds of it only could be paid before his deliverance.

CHAPTER IX

Henry, having thus, contrary to expectation, extricated himself with honour from a situation, in which his throne was exposed to great danger, was employed for several years in the administration of justice, in the execution of the laws, and in guarding against those inconveniences, which either the past convulsions of his state, or the political institutions of that age, unavoidably occasioned. The provisions, which he made, show such largeness of thought as qualified him for being a legislator; and they were commonly calculated as well for the future as the present happiness of his kingdom. *King's equitable administration.*

He enacted severe penalties against robbery, murder, false coining, arson; and ordained that these crimes should be punished by the amputation of the right hand and right foot.[p] The pecuniary commutation for crimes, which has a false appearance of lenity, had been gradually disused; and seems to have been entirely abolished by the rigour of these statutes. The superstitious trial by water ordeal, though condemned by the church,[q] still subsisted; but Henry ordained, that any man, accused of murder or any heinous felony by the oath of the legal knights of the county, should, even though acquitted by the ordeal, be obliged to abjure the realm.[r] *1176.*

All advances towards reason and good sense are slow and gradual. Henry, though sensible of the great absurdity attending the trial by duel or battle, did not venture to abolish it: He only admitted either of the parties to challenge a trial by an assize or jury of twelve freeholders.[s] This latter method of trial seems to have been very ancient in England, and was fixed by the laws of king Alfred: But the barbarous and violent genius of the age had of late given more credit to the trial by battle, which had become the general method of deciding all important controversies. It was never abolished by law in England; and there is an instance of it so late as the reign of Elizabeth: But the institution revived by this king, being found more reasonable and more suitable to a civilized people, gradually prevailed over it.

The partition of England into four divisions, and the appointment of itinerant justices to go the circuit in each division,

---

[p] Bened. Abb. p. 132. Hoveden, p. 549. [q] Seld. Spicileg. ad Eadm. p. 204. [r] Bened. Abb. p. 132. [s] Glanv. lib. ii. cap. 7.

and to decide the causes in the counties, was another important ordinance of this prince, which had a direct tendency to curb the oppressive barons, and to protect the inferior gentry and common people in their property.[t] Those justices were either prelates or considerable noblemen; who, besides carrying the authority of the king's commission, were able, by the dignity of their own character, to give weight and credit to the laws.

That there might be fewer obstacles to the execution of justice, the king was vigilant in demolishing all the new erected castles of the nobility, in England as well as in his foreign dominions; and he permitted no fortress to remain in the custody of those whom he found reason to suspect.[u]

But lest the kingdom should be weakened by this demolition of the fortresses, the king fixed an assize of arms, by which all his subjects were obliged to put themselves in a situation for defending themselves and the realm. Every man, possessed of a knight's fee, was ordained to have for each fee, a coat of mail, a helmet, a shield, and a lance; every free layman, possessed of goods to the value of sixteen marks, was to be armed in like manner; every one that possessed ten marks was obliged to have an iron gorget, a cap of iron, and a lance; all burgesses were to have a cap of iron, a lance and a wambais; that is, a coat quilted with wool, tow, or such like materials.[w] It appears, that archery, for which the English were afterwards so renowned, had not, at this time, become very common among them. The spear was the chief weapon employed in battle.

The clergy and the laity were during that age in a strange situation with regard to each other, and such as may seem totally incompatible with a civilized, and indeed with any species of government. If a clergyman were guilty of murder, he could be punished by degradation only: If he were murdered, the murderer was exposed to nothing but excommunication and ecclesiastical censures; and the crime was atoned for by pennances and submission.[x] Hence the assassins of Thomas a Becket himself, though guilty of the most atrocious wickedness, and the most repugnant to the sentiments of that age, lived securely in their own houses, without

---

[t] Hoveden, p. 590. [u] Benedict. Abbas, p. 202. Diceto, p. 585. [w] Bened. Abb. p. 305. Annal. Waverl. p. 161. [x] Petri Blessen. epist. 73. apud Bibl. Patr. tom. xxiv. p. 992.

CHAPTER IX

being called to account by Henry himself, who was so much concerned, both in honour and interest, to punish that crime, and who professed or affected on all occasions the most extreme abhorrence of it. It was not till they found their presence shunned by every one as excommunicated persons, that they were induced to take a journey to Rome, to throw themselves at the feet of the pontiff, and to submit to the pennances imposed upon them: After which, they continued to possess, without molestation, their honours and fortunes, and seem even to have recovered the countenance and good opinion of the public. But as the king, by the constitutions of Clarendon, which he endeavoured still to maintain,^y had subjected the clergy to a trial by the civil magistrate, it seemed but just to give them the protection of that power, to which they owed obedience: It was enacted, that the murderers of clergymen should be tried before the justiciary in the presence of the bishop or his official; and besides the usual punishment for murder, should be subjected to a forfeiture of their estates, and a confiscation of their goods and chattels.^z

The king passed an equitable law, that the goods of a vassal should not be seized for the debt of his lord, unless the vassal be surety for the debt; and that the rents of vassals should be paid to the creditors of the lord, not to the lord himself. It is remarkable, that this law was enacted by the king in a council which he held at Verneüil, and which consisted of some prelates and barons of England, as well as some of Normandy, Poictou, Anjou, Maine, Touraine, and Britanny; and the statute took place in all these last mentioned territories,^a though totally unconnected with each other:^b A certain proof how irregular the ancient feudal government was, and how near the sovereigns, in some instances, approached to despotism, though in others they seemed scarcely to possess any authority. If a prince, much dreaded and revered like Henry, obtained but the appearance of general consent to an ordi-

---

^y Chron. Gervase, p. 1433.   ^z Diceto, p. 592. Chron Gervase, p. 1433.
^a Bened. Abb. p. 248. It was usual for the kings of England, after the conquest of Ireland, to summon barons and members of that country to the English parliament. Molineux's case of Ireland, p. 64, 65, 66.
^b Spelman even doubts whether the law were not also extended to England. If it were not, it could only be because Henry did not choose it. For his authority was greater in that kingdom than in his transmarine dominions.

nance, which was equitable and just, it became immediately an established law, and all his subjects acquiesced in it. If the prince was hated or despised; if the nobles, who supported him, had small influence; if the humours of the times disposed the people to question the justice of his ordinance; the fullest and most authentic assembly had no authority. Thus all was confusion and disorder; no regular idea of a constitution; force and violence decided every thing.

The success, which had attended Henry in his wars, did not much encourage his neighbours to form any attempt against him; and his transactions with them, during several years, contain little memorable. Scotland remained in that state of feudal subjection, to which he had reduced it; and gave him no farther inquietude. He sent over his fourth son, John, into Ireland, with a view of making a more complete conquest of the island; but the petulance and incapacity of this prince, by which he enraged the Irish chieftains, obliged the king soon after to recall him.ᶜ The king of France had fallen into an abject superstition; and was induced by a devotion, more sincere than that of Henry, to make a pilgrimage to the tomb of Becket, in order to obtain his intercession for the cure of Philip, his eldest son. He probably thought himself well intitled to the favour of that saint, on account of their ancient intimacy; and hoped, that Becket, whom he had protected while on earth, would not now, when he was so highly exalted in heaven, forget his old friend and benefactor. The monks, sensible that their saint's honour was concerned in the case, failed not to publish, that Lewis's prayers were answered, and that the young prince was restored to health, by Becket's intercession. That king himself was soon after struck with an apoplexy, which deprived him of his understanding: Philip, though a youth of fifteen, took on him the administration, till his father's death, which happened soon after, opened his way to the throne; and he proved the ablest and greatest monarch that had governed that kingdom since the age of Charlemagne. The superior years, however, and experience of Henry, while they moderated his ambition, gave him such an ascendant over this prince, that no dangerous rivalship, for a long

1180.

ᶜ Bened. Abb. p. 437, &c.

CHAPTER IX

time, arose between them. The English monarch, instead of taking advantage of his own situation, rather employed his good offices in composing the quarrels which arose in the royal family of France; and he was successful in mediating a reconciliation between Philip and his mother and uncles. These services were but ill-requited by Philip, who, when he came to man's estate, fomented all the domestic discords in the royal family of England, and encouraged Henry's sons in their ungrateful and undutiful behaviour towards him.

Prince Henry, equally impatient of obtaining power, and incapable of using it, renewed to the king the demand of his resigning Normandy; and on meeting with a refusal, he fled with his consort to the court of France: But not finding Philip, at that time, disposed to enter into war for his sake, he accepted of his father's offers of reconciliation, and made him submissions. It was a cruel circumstance in the king's fortune, that he could hope for no tranquillity from the criminal enterprizes of his sons but by their mutual discord and animosities, which disturbed his family, and threw his state into convulsions. Richard, whom he had made master of Guienne, and who had displayed his valour and military genius, by suppressing the revolts of his mutinous barons, refused to obey Henry's orders, in doing homage to his elder brother for that dutchy; and he defended himself against young Henry and Geoffrey, who, uniting their arms, carried war into his territories.[d] The king with some difficulty composed this difference; but immediately found his eldest son engaged in conspiracies, and ready to take arms against himself. While the young prince was conducting these criminal intrigues, he was seized with a fever at Martel, a castle near Turenne, to which he had retired in discontent; and seeing the approaches of death, he was at last struck with remorse for his undutiful behaviour towards his father. He sent a message to the king, who was not far distant; expressed his contrition for his faults; and entreated the favour of a visit, that he might at least die with the satisfaction of having obtained his forgiveness. Henry, who had so often experienced the prince's ingratitude and violence, apprehended that his sickness was entirely feigned, and he

1183.

[d] Ypod. Neust. p. 451. Bened. Abb. p. 383. Diceto, p. 617.

*11th
June.
Death of
young
Henry.*

durst not entrust himself into his son's hands: But when he soon
after received intelligence of young Henry's death, and the proofs
of his sincere repentance, this good prince was affected with the
deepest sorrow; he thrice fainted away; he accused his own hard-
heartedness in refusing the dying request of his son; and he lamented, that he had deprived that prince of the last opportunity
of making atonement for his offences, and of pouring out his soul
in the bosom of his reconciled father.*e* This prince died in the
twenty-eighth year of his age.

The behaviour of his surviving children did not tend to give the
king any consolation for the loss. As prince Henry had left no
posterity, Richard was become heir to all his dominions; and the
king intended, that John, his third surviving son and favourite,
should inherit Guienne as his appanage: But Richard refused his
consent, fled into that dutchy, and even made preparations for
carrying on war, as well against his father as against his brother
Geoffrey, who was now put in possession of Britanny. Henry sent
for Eleanor, his queen, the heiress of Guienne, and required Richard to deliver up to her the dominion of these territories; which
that prince, either dreading an insurrection of the Gascons in her
favour, or retaining some sense of duty towards her, readily performed; and he peaceably returned to his father's court. No sooner
was this quarrel accommodated, than Geoffrey, the most vicious
perhaps of all Henry's unhappy family, broke out into violence;
demanded Anjou to be annexed to his dominions of Britanny; and

1185.

on meeting with a refusal, fled to the court of France, and levied
forces against his father.*f* Henry was freed from this danger by his
son's death, who was killed in a tournament at Paris.*g* The widow
of Geoffrey, soon after his decease, was delivered of a son, who
received the name of Arthur, and was invested in the dutchy of
Britanny, under the guardianship of his grandfather, who, as duke
of Normandy, was also superior lord of that territory. Philip, as
lord Paramount, disputed some time his title to this wardship; but
was obliged to yield to the inclinations of the Bretons, who preferred the government of Henry.

Crusades.

But the rivalship between these potent princes, and all their

---

e Bened. Abb. p. 393. Hoveden, p. 621. Trivet, vol. i. p. 84.   *f* Neubrig,
p. 422.   *g* Bened. Abb. p. 451. Chron. Gervase, p. 1480.

inferior interests, seemed now to have given place to the general passion for the relief of the Holy Land, and the expulsion of the Saracens. Those infidels, though obliged to yield to the immense inundation of Christians in the first crusade, had recovered courage after the torrent was past; and attacking on all quarters the settlements of the Europeans, had reduced these adventurers to great difficulties, and obliged them to apply again for succours from the west. A second crusade, under the emperor Conrade, and Lewis VII. king of France, in which there perished above 200,000 men, brought them but a temporary relief; and those princes, after losing such immense armies, and seeing the flower of their nobility fall by their side, returned with little honour into Europe. But these repeated misfortunes, which drained the western world of its people and treasure, were not yet sufficient to cure men of their passion for those spiritual adventures; and a new incident rekindled with fresh fury the zeal of the ecclesiastics and military adventures among the Latin Christians. Saladin, a prince of great generosity, bravery, and conduct, having fixed himself on the throne of Egypt, began to extend his conquests over the east; and finding the settlement of the Christians in Palestine an invincible obstacle to the progress of his arms, he bent the whole force of his policy and valour to subdue that small and barren, but important territory. Taking advantage of dissentions, which prevailed among the champions of the cross, and having secretly gained the count of Tripoli, who commanded their armies, he invaded the frontiers with a mighty power; and, aided by the treachery of that count, gained over them at Tiberiade a complete victory, which utterly *1187.* annihilated the force of the already languishing kingdom of Jerusalem. The holy city itself fell into his hands after a feeble resistance; the kingdom of Antioch was almost entirely subdued; and except some maritime towns, nothing considerable remained of those boasted conquests, which, near a century before, it had cost the efforts of all Europe to acquire.[h]

The western Christians were astonished on receiving this dismal intelligence. Pope Urban III. it is pretended, died of grief; and his successor, Gregory VIII. employed the whole time of his short pontificate in rouzing to arms all the Christians who acknowledged

[h] M. Paris, p. 100.

his authority. The general cry was, that they were unworthy of enjoying any inheritance in heaven, who did not vindicate from the dominion of the infidels the inheritance of God on earth, and deliver from slavery that country which had been consecrated by the footsteps of their Redeemer. William, archbishop of Tyre, having procured a conference between Henry and Philip near Gisors, enforced all these topics; gave a pathetic description of the miserable state of the eastern Christians; and employed every argument to excite the ruling passions of the age, superstition and jealousy of military honour.[i] The two monarchs immediately took the cross; many of their most considerable vassals imitated the example;[k] and as the emperor Frederic I. entered into the same confederacy, some well-grounded hopes of success were entertained; and men flattered themselves, that an enterprize, which had failed under the conduct of many independant leaders, or of imprudent princes, might at last, by the efforts of such potent and able monarchs, be brought to a happy issue.

The kings of France and England imposed a tax, amounting to the tenth of all moveable goods, on such as remained at home;[l] but as they exempted from this burden most of the regular clergy, the secular aspired to the same immunity; pretended that their duty obliged them to assist the crusade with their prayers alone; and it was with some difficulty they were constrained to desist from an opposition, which in them, who had been the chief promoters of those pious enterprizes, appeared with the worst grace imaginable.[m] This backwardness of the clergy is perhaps a symptom, that the enthusiastic ardour, which had at first seized the people for crusades, was now by time and ill success considerably abated; and that the frenzy was chiefly supported by the military genius and love of glory in the monarchs.

But before this great machine could be put in motion, there were still many obstacles to surmount. Philip, jealous of Henry's power, entered into a private confederacy with young Richard; and working on his ambitious and impatient temper, persuaded him, instead of supporting and aggrandizing that monarchy, which he was one day to inherit, to seek present power and independance, by disturbing and dismembering it. In order to give a pretence for hostilities between the two kings, Richard broke into

*1188.
21st January.*

*1189.
Revolt of prince Richard.*

[i] Bened. Abb. p. 531.　[k] Neubrig. p. 435. Heming. p. 512.　[l] Bened. Abb. p. 498.　[m] Petri Blessen. epist. 112.

the territories of Raymond, count of Toulouse, who immediately carried complaints of this violence before the king of France as his superior lord. Philip remonstrated with Henry; but received for answer, that Richard had confessed to the archbishop of Dublin, that his enterprize against Raymond had been undertaken by the approbation of Philip himself, and was conducted by his authority. The king of France, who might have been covered with shame and confusion by this detection, still prosecuted his design, and invaded the provinces of Berri and Auvergne, under colour of revenging the quarrel of the count of Toulouse.[n] Henry retaliated, by making inroads upon the frontiers of France, and burning Dreux. As this war, which destroyed all hopes of success in the projected crusade, gave great scandal, the two kings held a conference at the accustomed place between Gisors and Trie, in order to find means of accommodating their differences: They separated on worse terms than before; and Philip, to show his disgust, ordered a great elm, under which the conferences had been usually held, to be cut down;[o] as if he had renounced all desire of accommodation, and was determined to carry the war to extremities against the king of England. But his own vassals refused to serve under him in so invidious a cause;[p] and he was obliged to come anew to a conference with Henry, and to offer terms of peace. These terms were such as entirely opened the eyes of the king of England, and fully convinced him of the perfidy of his son, and his secret alliance with Philip, of which he had before only entertained some suspicion. The king of France required, that Richard should be crowned king of England in the life-time of his father, should be invested in all his transmarine dominions, and should immediately espouse Alice, Philip's sister, to whom he had formerly been affianced, and who had already been conducted into England.[q] Henry had experienced such fatal effects, both from the crowning of his eldest son, and from that prince's alliance with the royal family of France, that he rejected these terms; and Richard, in consequence of his secret agreement with Philip, immediately revolted from him,[r] did homage to the king of France for all the dominions which Henry held of that crown, and received the investitures, as if he had already been the lawful possessor. Several historians assert, that Henry himself had become enamoured of

[n] Bened. Abb. p. 508.   [o] Ibid. p. 517, 532.   [p] Ibid. p. 519.   [q] Bened. Abb. p. 521. Hoveden, p. 652.   [r] Brompton, p. 1149. Neubrig. p. 437.

young Alice, and mention this as an additional reason for his refusing these conditions: But he had so many other just and equitable motives for his conduct, that it is superfluous to assign a cause, which the great prudence and advanced age of that monarch render somewhat improbable.

Cardinal Albano, the pope's legate, displeased with these encreasing obstacles to the crusade, excommunicated Richard, as the chief spring of discord: But the sentence of excommunication, which, when it was properly prepared, and was zealously supported by the clergy, had often great influence in that age, proved entirely ineffectual in the present case. The chief barons of Poictou, Guienne, Normandy, and Anjou, being attached to the young prince, and finding that he had now received the investiture from their superior lord, declared for him, and made inroads into the territories of such as still adhered to the king. Henry, disquieted by the daily revolts of his mutinous subjects, and dreading still worse effects from their turbulent disposition, had again recourse to papal authority; and engaged the cardinal Anagni, who had succeeded Albano in the legateship, to threaten Philip with laying an interdict on all his dominions. But Philip, who was a prince of great vigour and capacity, despised the menace, and told Anagni, that it belonged not to the pope to interpose in the temporal disputes of princes, much less in those between him and his rebellious vassal. He even proceeded so far as to reproach him with partiality, and with receiving bribes from the king of England;[s] while Richard, still more outrageous, offered to draw his sword against the legate, and was hindered, by the interposition alone of the company, from committing violence upon him.[t]

The king of England was now obliged to defend his dominions by arms, and to engage in a war with France and with his eldest son, a prince of great valour, on such disadvantageous terms. Ferté-Barnard fell first into the hands of the enemy: Mans was next taken by assault; and Henry, who had thrown himself into that place, escaped with some difficulty:[u] Amboise, Chaumont, and Chateau de Loire, opened their gates on the appearance of Philip and Richard: Tours was menaced; and the king, who had retired to Saumur, and had daily instances of the cowardice or

[s] M. Paris, p. 104. Bened. Abb. p. 542. Hoveden, p. 652.   [t] M. Paris, p. 104.   [u] M. Paris, p. 105. Bened. Abb. p. 543. Hoveden, p. 652.

CHAPTER IX

infidelity of his governors, expected the most dismal issue to all his enterprizes. While he was in this state of despondency, the duke of Burgundy, the earl of Flanders, and the archbishop of Rheims interposed with their good offices; and the intelligence, which he received of the taking of Tours, and which made him fully sensible of the desperate situation of his affairs, so subdued his spirit, that he submitted to all the rigorous terms, which were imposed upon him. He agreed, that Richard should marry the princess Alice; that that prince should receive the homage and oath of fealty of all his subjects both in England and his transmarine dominions; that he himself should pay twenty thousand marks to the king of France as a compensation for the charges of the war; that his own barons should engage to make him observe this treaty by force, and in case of his violating it, should promise to join Philip and Richard against him; and that all his vassals, who had entered into confederacy with Richard, should receive an indemnity for the offence.[w]

But the mortification, which Henry, who had been accustomed to give the law in most treaties, received from these disadvantageous terms, was the least that he met with on this occasion. When he demanded a list of those barons, to whom he was bound to grant a pardon for their connections with Richard; he was astonished to find, at the head of them, the name of his second son, John;[x] who had always been his favourite, whose interests he had ever anxiously at heart, and who had even, on account of his ascendant over him, often excited the jealousy of Richard.[y] The unhappy father, already overloaded with cares and sorrows, finding this last disappointment in his domestic tenderness, broke out into expressions of the utmost despair, cursed the day in which he received his miserable being, and bestowed, on his ungrateful and undutiful children, a malediction which he never could be prevailed on to retract.[z] The more his heart was disposed to friendship and affection, the more he resented the barbarous return, which his four sons had successively made to his parental care; and this finishing blow, by depriving him of every comfort in life, quite broke his spirit, and threw him into a lingering fever, of which he expired, at the castle of Chinon near Saumur. His natural son, Geoffrey, who alone had behaved dutifully towards him, attended

6th July.
Death

[w] M. Paris, p. 106. Bened. Abb. p. 545. Hoveden, p. 653.   [x] Hoveden, p. 654.   [y] Bened. Abb. p. 541.   [z] Hoveden, p. 654.

his corpse to the nunnery of Fontervrault; where it lay in state in the abbey-church. Next day, Richard, who came to visit the dead body of his father, and who, notwithstanding his criminal conduct, was not wholly destitute of generosity, was struck with horror and remorse at the sight; and as the attendants observed, that, at that very instant, blood gushed from the mouth and nostrils of the corpse,[a] he exclaimed, agreeably to a vulgar superstition, that he was his father's murderer; and he expressed a deep sense, though too late, of that undutiful behaviour, which had brought his parent to an untimely grave.[b]

and character of Henry.   Thus died, in the fifty-eighth year of his age and thirty-fifth of his reign, the greatest prince of his time, for wisdom, virtue, and abilities, and the most powerful in extent of dominion of all those that had ever filled the throne of England. His character, in private as well as in public life, is almost without a blemish; and he seems to have possessed every accomplishment both of body and mind, which makes a man either estimable or amiable. He was of a middle stature, strong and well proportioned; his countenance was lively and engaging; his conversation affable and entertaining: His elocution easy, persuasive, and ever at command. He loved peace, but possessed both bravery and conduct in war; was provident without timidity; severe in the execution of justice without rigour; and temperate without austerity. He preserved health, and kept himself from corpulency, to which he was somewhat inclined, by an abstemious diet, and by frequent exercise, particularly hunting. When he could enjoy leisure, he recreated himself either in learned conversation or in reading; and he cultivated his natural talents by study, above any prince of his time. His affections, as well as his enmities, were warm and durable, and his long experience of the ingratitude and infidelity of men never destroyed the natural sensibility of his temper, which disposed him to friendship and society. His character has been transmitted to us by several writers, who were his contemporaries;[c] and it extremely resembles, in its most remarkable features, that of his maternal grandfather Henry I.: Excepting only, that ambition, which was a ruling passion in both, found not in the first Henry such unexceptionable

[a] Bened. Abb. p. 547. Brompton, p. 1151.   [b] M. Paris, p. 107.   [c] Petri Bles. epist. 46, 47, in Bibliotheca Patrum, vol. xxiv. p. 985, 986, &c. Girald. Camb. p. 783, &c.

CHAPTER IX

means of exerting itself, and pushed that prince into measures, which were both criminal in themselves, and were the cause of farther crimes, from which his grandson's conduct was happily exempted.

This prince, like most of his predecessors of the Norman line, except Stephen, passed more of his time on the continent than in this island: He was surrounded with the English gentry and nobility, when abroad: The French gentry and nobility attended him when he resided in England: Both nations acted in the government, as if they were the same people; and on many occasions, the legislatures seem not to have been distinguished. As the king and all the English barons were of French extraction, the manners of that people acquired the ascendant, and were regarded as the models of imitation. All foreign improvements, therefore, such as they were, in literature and politeness, in laws and arts, seem now to have been, in a good measure, transplanted into England; and that kingdom was become little inferior, in all the fashionable accomplishments, to any of its neighbours on the continent. The more homely, but more sensible manners and principles of the Saxons, were exchanged for the affectations of chivalry, and the subtilties of school philosophy: The feudal ideas of civil government, the Romish sentiments in religion, had taken entire possession of the people: By the former, the sense of submission towards princes was somewhat diminished in the barons; by the latter, the devoted attachment to papal authority was much augmented among the clergy. The Norman and other foreign families, established in England, had now struck deep root; and being entirely incorporated with the people, whom at first they oppressed and despised, they no longer thought that they needed the protection of the crown for the enjoyment of their possessions, or considered their tenure as precarious. They aspired to the same liberty and independance, which they saw enjoyed by their brethren on the continent, and desired to restrain those exorbitant prerogatives and arbitrary practices, which the necessities of war and the violence of conquest had at first obliged them to indulge in their monarch. That memory also of a more equal government under the Saxon princes, which remained with the English, diffused still farther the spirit of liberty, and made the barons both desirous of more independance to themselves, and willing to in-

Miscellaneous transactions of this reign.

dulge it to the people. And it was not long ere this secret revolution in the sentiments of men produced, first violent convulsions in the state, then an evident alteration in the maxims of government.

The history of all the preceding kings of England since the conquest, gives evident proofs of the disorders attending the feudal institutions; the licentiousness of the barons, their spirit of rebellion against the prince and laws, and of animosity against each other: The conduct of the barons in the transmarine dominions of those monarchs afforded perhaps still more flagrant instances of these convulsions; and the history of France, during several ages, consists almost entirely of narrations of this nature. The cities, during the continuance of this violent government, could neither be very numerous nor populous; and there occur instances, which seem to evince, that, though these are always the first seat of law and liberty, their police was in general loose and irregular, and exposed to the same disorders, with those by which the country was generally infested. It was a custom in London for great numbers, to the amount of a hundred or more, the sons and relations of considerable citizens, to form themselves into a licentious confederacy, to break into rich houses and plunder them, to rob and murder the passengers, and to commit with impunity all sorts of disorder. By these crimes, it had become so dangerous to walk the streets by night, that the citizens durst no more venture abroad after sun-set, than if they had been exposed to the incursions of a public enemy. The brother of the earl of Ferrars had been murdered by some of those nocturnal rioters; and the death of so eminent a person, which was much more regarded than that of many thousands of an inferior station, so provoked the king, that he swore vengeance against the criminals, and became thenceforth more rigorous in the execution of the laws.[d]

There is another instance given by historians, which proves to what a height such riots had proceeded, and how open these criminals were in committing their robberies. A band of them had attacked the house of a rich citizen, with an intention of plundering it; had broken through a stone-wall with hammers and wedges; and had already entered the house sword in hand; when the citizen, armed cap-a-pee and supported by his faithful ser-

[d] Bened. Abb. p. 196.

vants, appeared in the passage to oppose them: He cut off the right hand of the first robber that entered; and made such stout resistance, that his neighbours had leisure to assemble, and come to his relief. The man, who lost his hand, was taken; and was tempted by the promise of pardon to reveal his confederates; among whom was one John Senex, esteemed among the richest and best-born citizens in London. He was convicted by the ordeal; and though he offered five hundred marks for his life, the king refused the money, and ordered him to be hanged.[e] It appears from a statute of Edward I. that these disorders were not remedied even in that reign. It was then made penal to go out at night after the hour of the curfew, to carry a weapon, or to walk without a light or lanthorn.[f] It is said in the preamble to this law, that, both by night and by day, there were continual frays in the streets of London.

Henry's care in administering justice had gained him so great a reputation, that even foreign and distant princes made him arbiter, and submitted their differences to his judgment. Sanchez, king of Navarre, having some controversies with Alfonso, king of Castile, was contented, though Alfonso had married the daughter of Henry, to chuse this prince for a referee; and they agreed, each of them to consign three castles into neutral hands, as a pledge of their not departing from his award. Henry made the cause be examined before his great council, and gave a sentence, which was submitted to by both parties. These two Spanish kings sent each a stout champion to the court of England, in order to defend his cause by arms, in case the way of duel had been chosen by Henry.[g]

Henry so far abolished the barbarous and absurd practice of confiscating ships, which had been wrecked on the coast, that he ordained, if one man or animal were alive in the ship, that the vessel and goods should be restored to the owners.[h]

The reign of Henry was remarkable also for an innovation, which was afterwards carried farther by his successors, and was attended with the most important consequences. This prince was disgusted with the species of military force, which was established by the feudal institutions, and which, though it was extremely burdensome to the subject, yet rendered very little service to the

[e] Bened. Abb. p. 197, 198. [f] Observations on the ancient Statutes, p. 216.
[g] Rymer, vol. iv. p. 43. Bened. Abb. p. 172. Diceto, p. 597. Brompton, p. 1120. [h] Rymer, vol. i. p. 36.

sovereign. The barons, or military tenants, came late into the field; they were obliged to serve only forty days; they were unskilful and disorderly in all their operations; and they were apt to carry into the camp the same refractory and independant spirit, to which they were accustomed in their civil government. Henry, therefore, introduced the practice of making a commutation of their military service for money; and he levied scutages from his baronies and knights fees, instead of requiring the personal attendance of his vassals. There is mention made, in the history of the exchequer, of these scutages in his second, fifth, and eighteenth year;[i] and other writers give us an account of three more of them.[k] When the prince had thus obtained money, he made a contract with some of those adventurers, in which Europe at that time abounded: They found him soldiers of the same character with themselves who were bound to serve for a stipulated time: The armies were less numerous, but more useful, than when composed of all the military vassals of the crown: The feudal institutions began to relax: The kings became rapacious for money, on which all their power depended: The barons, seeing no end of exactions, sought to defend their property: And as the same causes had nearly the same effects, in the different countries of Europe, the several crowns either lost or acquired authority, according to their different success in the contest.

This prince was also the first that levied a tax on the moveables or personal estates of his subjects, nobles as well as commons. Their zeal for the holy wars made them submit to this innovation; and a precedent being once obtained, this taxation became, in following reigns, the usual method of supplying the necessities of the crown. The tax of Danegelt, so generally odious to the nation, was remitted in this reign.

It was a usual practice of the kings of England, to repeat the ceremony of their coronation thrice every year, on assembling the states at the three great festivals. Henry, after the first years of his reign, never renewed this ceremony, which was found to be very expensive and very useless. None of his successors revived it. It is considered as a great act of grace in this prince, that he mitigated

[i] Madox, p. 435, 436, 437, 438.　　[k] Tyrrel, vol. ii. p. 466, from the records.

375

CHAPTER IX

the rigour of the forest laws, and punished any transgressions of them, not capitally, but by fines, imprisonments, and other more moderate penalties.

Since we are here collecting some detached incidents, which show the genius of the age, and which could not so well enter into the body of our history, it may not be improper to mention the quarrel between Roger archbishop of York, and Richard archbishop of Canterbury. We may judge of the violence of military men and laymen, when ecclesiastics could proceed to such extremities. Cardinal Haguezun being sent, in 1176, as legate into Britain, summoned an assembly of the clergy at London; and as both the archbishops pretended to sit on his right hand, this question of precedency begat a controversy between them. The monks and retainers of archbishop Richard fell upon Roger, in the presence of the cardinal and of the synod, threw him to the ground, trampled him under foot, and so bruised him with blows, that he was taken up half dead, and his life was, with difficulty, saved from their violence. The archbishop of Canterbury was obliged to pay a large sum of money to the legate, in order to suppress all complaints with regard to this enormity.[l]

We are told by Gyraldus Cambrensis, that the monks and prior of St. Swithun threw themselves, one day, prostrate on the ground and in the mire before Henry, complaining, with many tears and much doleful lamentation, that the bishop of Winchester, who was also their abbot, had cut off three dishes from their table. How many has he left you, said the king? Ten only, replied the disconsolate monks. I myself, exclaimed the king, never have more than three; and I enjoin your bishop to reduce you to the same number.[m]

This king left only two legitimate sons, Richard, who succeeded him, and John, who inherited no territory, though his father had often intended to leave him a part of his extensive dominions. He was thence commonly denominated *Lackland*. Henry left three legitimate daughters; Maud, born in 1156, and married to Henry, duke of Saxony; Eleanor, born in 1162, and married to Alphonso,

---

[l] Bened. Abb. p. 138, 139. Brompton, p. 1109. Chron. Gerv. p. 1433. Neubrig. p. 413.　[m] Gir. Camb. cap. 5. in Anglia Sacra, vol. ii.

king of Castile; Joan, born in 1165, and married to William, king of Sicily.[n]

Henry is said by ancient historians to have been of a very amorous disposition: They mention two of his natural sons by Rosamond, daughter of lord Clifford, namely Richard Longespée, or Longsword, (so called from the sword he usually wore) who was afterwards married to Ela, the daughter and heir of the earl of Salisbury; and Geoffrey, first bishop of Lincoln, then archbishop of York. All the other circumstances of the story, commonly told of that lady, seem to be fabulous.

[n] Diceto, p. 616.

X

RICHARD I

The king's preparations for
the crusade – Sets out on the crusade –
Transactions in Sicily – King's arrival in Palestine –
State of Palestine – Disorders in Englar.d –
The king's heroic actions in Palestine –
His return from Palestine – Captivity in
Germany – War with France – The king's delivery –
Return to England – War with France – Death –
and character of the king –
Miscellaneous transactions of this reign

THE COMPUNCTION of Richard, for his undutiful behaviour   *1189.*
towards his father, was durable, and influenced him in the
choice of his ministers and servants after his accession. Those who
had seconded and favoured his rebellion, instead of meeting with
that trust and honour which they expected, were surprized to find,
that they lay under disgrace with the new king, and were on all
occasions hated and despised by him. The faithful ministers of
Henry, who had vigorously opposed all the enterprizes of his sons,
were received with open arms, and were continued in those offices
which they had honourably discharged to their former master.[o]
This prudent conduct might be the result of reflection; but in a
prince, like Richard, so much guided by passion, and so little by

[o] Hoveden, p. 655. Bened. Abb. p. 547. M. Paris, p. 107.

377

policy, it was commonly ascribed to a principle still more virtuous and more honourable.

Richard, that he might make atonement to one parent for his breach of duty to the other, immediately sent orders for releasing the queen-dowager from the confinement in which she had long been detained; and he entrusted her with the government of England, till his arrival in that kingdom. His bounty to his brother John was rather profuse and imprudent. Besides bestowing on him the county of Mortaigne in Normandy, granting him a pension of four thousand marks a year, and marrying him to Avisa, the daughter of the earl of Glocester, by whom he inherited all the possessions of that opulent family; he increased this appanage, which the late king had destined him, by other extensive grants and concessions. He conferred on him the whole estate of William Pevereli, which had escheated to the crown: He put him in possession of eight castles, with all the forests and honours annexed to them: He delivered over to him no less than six earldoms, Cornwal, Devon, Somerset, Nottingham, Dorset, Lancaster, and Derby. And endeavouring, by favours, to fix that vicious prince in his duty, he put it too much in his power, whenever he pleased, to depart from it.

The king's preparation for the crusade. The king, impelled more by the love of military glory than by superstition, acted, from the beginning of his reign, as if the sole purpose of his government had been the relief of the Holy Land, and the recovery of Jerusalem from the Saracens. This zeal against infidels, being communicated to his subjects, broke out in London on the day of his coronation, and made them find a crusade less dangerous, and attended with more immediate profit. The prejudices of the age had made the lending of money on interest pass by the invidious name of usury: Yet the necessity of the practice had still continued it, and the greater part of that kind of dealing fell every where into the hands of the Jews; who, being already infamous on account of their religion, had no honour to lose, and were apt to exercise a profession, odious in itself, by every kind of rigour, and even sometimes by rapine and extortion. The industry and frugality of this people had put them in possession of all the ready money, which the idleness and profusion, common to the English with other European nations, enabled them to lend at exorbitant and unequal interest. The monkish writers represent it as a great stain on the wise and equitable government of Henry,

CHAPTER X

that he had carefully protected this infidel race from all injuries and insults; but the zeal of Richard afforded the populace a pretence for venting their animosity against them. The king had issued an edict, prohibiting their appearance at his coronation; but some of them, bringing him large presents from their nation, presumed, in confidence of that merit, to approach the hall in which he dined: Being discovered, they were exposed to the insults of the bystanders; they took to flight; the people pursued them; the rumor was spread, that the king had issued orders to massacre all the Jews; a command so agreeable was executed in an instant on such as fell into the hands of the populace; those who had kept at home were exposed to equal danger; the people, moved by rapacity and zeal, broke into their houses, which they plundered, after having murdered the owners; where the Jews barricadoed their doors, and defended themselves with vigour, the rabble set fire to the houses, and made way through the flames to exercise their pillage and violence; the usual licentiousness of London, which the sovereign power with difficulty restrained, broke out with fury, and continued these outrages; the houses of the rich citizens, though Christians, were next attacked and plundered; and weariness and satiety at last put an end to the disorder: Yet when the king impowered Glanville, the justiciary, to enquire into the authors of these crimes, the guilt was found to involve so many of the most considerable citizens, that it was deemed more prudent to drop the prosecution; and very few suffered the punishment due to this enormity. But the disorder stopped not at London. The inhabitants of the other cities of England, hearing of this slaughter of the Jews, imitated the example: In York, five hundred of that nation, who had retired into the castle for safety, and found themselves unable to defend the place, murdered their own wives and children, threw the dead bodies over the walls upon the populace, and then setting fire to the houses, perished in the flames. The gentry of the neighbourhood, who were all indebted to the Jews, ran to the cathedral, where their bonds were kept, and made a solemn bonfire of the papers before the altar. The compiler of the annals of Waverley, in relating these events, blesses the Almighty for thus delivering over this impious race to destruction.[p]

[p] Gale's Collect. vol. iii. p. 165.

The ancient situation of England, when the people possessed little riches and the public no credit, made it impossible for sovereigns to bear the expence of a steady or durable war, even on their frontiers; much less could they find regular means for the support of distant expeditions like those into Palestine, which were more the result of popular frenzy than of sober reason or deliberate policy. Richard, therefore, knew, that he must carry with him all the treasure necessary for his enterprize, and that both the remoteness of his own country and its poverty made it unable to furnish him with those continued supplies, which the exigencies of so perilous a war must necessarily require. His father had left him a treasure of above a hundred thousand marks; and the king, negligent of every consideration, but his present object, endeavoured to augment this sum by all expedients, how pernicious soever to the public, or dangerous to royal authority. He put to sale the revenues and manors of the crown; the offices of greatest trust and power, even those of forester and sheriff, which anciently were so important,[q] became venal; the dignity of chief justiciary, in whose hands was lodged the whole execution of the laws, was sold to Hugh de Puzas, bishop of Durham, for a thousand marks; the same prelate bought the earldom of Northumberland for life;[r] many of the champions of the cross, who had repented of their vow, purchased the liberty of violating it; and Richard, who stood less in need of men than of money, dispensed, on these conditions, with their attendance. Elated with the hopes of fame, which in that age attended no wars but those against the infidels, he was blind to every other consideration; and when some of his wiser ministers objected to this dissipation of the revenue and power of the crown, he replied, that he would sell London itself could he find a purchaser.[s] Nothing indeed could be a stronger proof how negligent he was of all future interests in comparison of the crusade, than his selling, for so small a sum as 10,000 marks, the vassalage of Scotland, together with the fortresses of Roxborough and Berwic, the greatest acquisition that had been made by his father during the course of his victorious reign; and his accepting the homage of

---

[q] The sheriff had anciently both the administration of justice and the management of the king's revenue committed to him in the county. See *Hale of Sheriffs Accounts.*   [r] M. Paris, p. 109.   [s] W. Heming. p. 519. Knyghton, p. 2402.

CHAPTER X

William in the usual terms, merely for the territories which that prince held in England.[1] The English of all ranks and stations were oppressed by numerous exactions: Menaces were employed both against the innocent and the guilty, in order to extort money from them: And where a pretence was wanting against the rich, the king obliged them, by the fear of his displeasure, to lend him sums, which, he knew, it would never be in his power to repay.

But Richard, though he sacrificed every interest and consideration to the success of this pious enterprize, carried so little the appearance of sanctity in his conduct, that Fulk, curate of Neuilly, a zealous preacher of the crusade, who from that merit had acquired the privilege of speaking the boldest truths, advised him to rid himself of his notorious vices, particularly his pride, avarice, and voluptuousness, which he called the king's three favourite daughters. *You counsel well,* replied Richard; *and I hereby dispose of the first to the Templars, of the second to the Benedictines, and of the third to my prelates.*

Richard, jealous of attempts which might be made on England during his absence, laid prince John, as well as his natural brother Geoffrey, archbishop of York, under engagements, confirmed by their oaths, that neither of them should enter the kingdom till his return; though he thought proper, before his departure, to withdraw this prohibition. The administration was left in the hands of Hugh, bishop of Durham, and of Longchamp, bishop of Ely, whom he appointed justiciaries and guardians of the realm. The latter was a Frenchman of mean birth, and of a violent character; who by art and address had insinuated himself into favour, whom Richard had created chancellor, and whom he had engaged the pope also to invest with the legantine authority, that, by centering every kind of power in his person, he might the better ensure the public tranquillity. All the military and turbulent spirits flocked about the person of the king, and were impatient to distinguish themselves against the infidels in Asia; whither his inclinations, his engagements, led him, and whither he was impelled by messages from the king of France, ready to embark in this enterprize.

The emperor Frederic, a prince of great spirit and conduct, had already taken the road to Palestine at the head of 150,000

[1] Hoveden, p. 662. Rymer, vol. i. p. 64. M. West. p. 257.

men, collected from Germany and all the northern states. Having surmounted every obstacle thrown in his way by the artifices of the Greeks and the power of the infidels, he had penetrated to the borders of Syria; when, bathing in the cold river Cydnus, during the greatest heat of the summer-season, he was seized with a mortal distemper, which put an end to his life and his rash enterprize.[u] His army, under the command of his son Conrade, reached Palestine; but was so diminished by fatigue, famine, maladies, and the sword, that it scarcely amounted to eight thousand men; and was unable to make any progress against the great power, valour, and conduct of Saladin. These reiterated calamities, attending the crusades, had taught the kings of France and England the necessity of trying another road to the Holy Land; and they determined to conduct their armies thither by sea, to carry provisions along with them, and by means of their naval power to maintain an open communication with their own states, and with the western parts of Europe. The place of rendezvous was appointed in the plains of Vezelay, on the borders of Burgundy:[w] Philip and Richard, on their arrival there, found their combined army amount to 100,000 men;[x] a mighty force, animated with glory and religion, conducted by two warlike monarchs, provided with every thing which their several dominions could supply, and not to be overcome but by their own misconduct, or by the unsurmountable obstacles of nature.

*1190.
29th
June.*

*King sets
out on
the cru-
sade.*

The French prince and the English here reiterated their promises of cordial friendship, pledged their faith not to invade each other's dominions during the crusade, mutually exchanged the oaths of all their barons and prelates to the same effect, and subjected themselves to the penalty of interdicts and excommunications, if they should ever violate this public and solemn engagement. They then separated; Philip took the road to Genoa, Richard that to Marseilles, with a view of meeting their fleets, which were severally appointed to rendezvous in these harbours. They put to sea; and nearly about the same time, were obliged, by stress of weather, to take shelter in Messina, where they were detained during the whole winter. This incident laid the foundation of animosities, which proved fatal to their enterprize.

*14th
Sept.*

---

[u] Bened. Abb. p. 556.   [w] Hoveden, p. 660.   [x] Vinisauf. p. 305.

CHAPTER X

Richard and Philip were, by the situation and extent of their dominions, rivals in power; by their age and inclinations, competitors for glory; and these causes of emulation, which, had the princes been employed in the field against the common enemy, might have stimulated them to martial enterprizes, soon excited, during the present leisure and repose, quarrels between monarchs of such a fiery character. Equally haughty, ambitious, intrepid, and inflexible; they were irritated with the least appearance of injury, and were incapable, by mutual condescensions, to efface those causes of complaint, which unavoidably arose between them. Richard, candid, sincere, undesigning, impolitic, violent, laid himself open, on every occasion, to the designs of his antagonist; who, provident, interested, intriguing, failed not to take all advantages against him: And thus, both the circumstances of their disposition in which they were similar, and those in which they differed, rendered it impossible for them to persevere in that harmony, which was so necessary to the success of their undertaking.

The last king of Sicily and Naples was William II. who had married Joan, sister to Richard, and who, dying without issue, had bequeathed his dominions to his paternal aunt, Constantia, the only legitimate descendant surviving of Roger, the first sovereign of those states who had been honoured with the royal title. This princess had, in expectation of that rich inheritance, been married to Henry VI. the reigning emperor;[y] but Tancred, her natural brother, had fixed such an interest among the barons, that, taking advantage of Henry's absence, he had acquired possession of the throne, and maintained his claim, by force of arms, against all the efforts of the Germans.[z] The approach of the crusaders naturally gave him apprehensions for his unstable government; and he was uncertain, whether he had most reason to dread the presence of the French or of the English monarch. Philip was engaged in a strict alliance with the emperor his competitor: Richard was disgusted by his rigors towards the queen-dowager, whom the Sicilian prince had confined in Palermo; because she had opposed with all her interest his succession to the crown. Tancred, therefore, sensible of the present necessity, resolved to pay court to both these formidable princes; and he was not unsuccessful in his en-

Transactions in Sicily.

[y] Bened. Abb. p. 580.   [z] Hoveden, p. 663.

deavours. He persuaded Philip that it was highly improper for him to interrupt his enterprize against the infidels, by any attempt against a Christian state: He restored queen Joan to her liberty; and even found means to make an alliance with Richard, who stipulated by treaty to marry his nephew, Arthur, the young duke of Britanny, to one of the daughters of Tancred.[a] But before these terms of friendship were settled, Richard, jealous both of Tancred and of the inhabitants of Messina, had taken up his quarters in the suburbs, and had possessed himself of a small fort, which commanded the harbour; and he kept himself extremely on his guard against their enterprizes. The citizens took umbrage. Mutual insults and attacks passed between them and the English: Philip, who had quartered his troops in the town, endeavoured to accommodate the quarrel, and held a conference with Richard for that purpose. While the two kings, meeting in the open fields, were engaged in discourse on this subject, a body of those Sicilians seemed to be drawing towards them; and Richard pushed forwards, in order to enquire into the reason of this extraordinary movement.[b] The English, insolent from their power, and inflamed with former animosities, wanted but a pretence for attacking the Messinese: They soon chaced them off the field, drove them into the town, and entered with them at the gates. The king employed his authority to restrain them from pillaging and massacring the defenceless inhabitants; but he gave orders, in token of his victory, that the standard of England should be erected on the walls. Philip, who considered that place as his quarters, exclaimed against the insult, and ordered some of his troops to pull down the standard: But Richard informed him by a messenger, that, though he himself would willingly remove that ground of offence, he would not permit it to be done by others; and if the French king attempted such an insult upon him, he should not succeed but by the utmost effusion of blood. Philip, content with this species of haughty submission, recalled his orders:[c] The difference was seemingly accommodated; but still left the remains of rancour and jealousy in the breasts of the two monarchs.

Tancred, who, for his own security, desired to inflame their mutual hatred, employed an artifice, which might have been at-

[a] Hoveden, p. 676, 677. Bened. Abb. p. 615. [b] Bened. Abb. p. 608.
[c] Hoveden, p. 674.

CHAPTER X

tended with consequences still more fatal. He showed Richard a *1191.*
letter, signed by the French king, and delivered to him, as he
pretended, by the duke of Burgundy; in which that monarch desired Tancred to fall upon the quarters of the English, and promised to assist him in putting them to the sword, as common enemies. The unwary Richard gave credit to the information; but was
too candid not to betray his discontent to Philip, who absolutely
denied the letter, and charged the Sicilian prince with forgery
and falsehood. Richard either was, or pretended to be, entirely
satisfied.[d]

Lest these jealousies and complaints should multiply between
them, it was proposed, that they should, by a solemn treaty, obviate
all future differences, and adjust every point that could possibly
hereafter become a controversy between them. But this expedient
started a new dispute, which might have proved more dangerous
than any of the foregoing, and which deeply concerned the honour of Philip's family. When Richard, in every treaty with the late
king, insisted so strenuously on being allowed to marry Alice of
France, he had only sought a pretence of quarrelling; and never
meant to take to his bed a princess suspected of a criminal amour
with his own father. After he became master, he no longer spake
of that alliance: He even took measures for espousing Berengaria,
daughter of Sanchez, king of Navarre, with whom he had become
enamoured during his abode in Guienne:[e] Queen Eleanor was
daily expected with that princess at Messina:[f] and when Philip
renewed to him his applications for espousing his sister Alice,
Richard was obliged to give him an absolute refusal. It is pretended
by Hoveden and other historians,[g] that he was able to produce such
convincing proofs of Alice's infidelity, and even of her having born
a child to Henry, that her brother desisted from his applications,
and chose to wrap up the dishonour of his family in silence and
oblivion. It is certain, from the treaty itself, which remains,[h] that,
whatever were his motives, he permitted Richard to give his hand
to Berengaria; and having settled all other controversies with that
prince, he immediately set sail for the Holy Land. Richard awaited
some time the arrival of his mother and bride; and when they

[d] Ibid. p. 688. Bened. Abb. p. 642, 643. Brompton, p. 1195.   [e] Vinisauf.
p. 316.   [f] M. Paris, p. 112. Trivet, p. 102. W. Heming. p. 519.
[g] Hoveden, p. 688.   [h] Rymer, vol. i. p. 69. Chron. de Dunst. p. 44.

joined him, he separated his fleet into two squadrons, and set forward on his enterprize. Queen Eleanor returned to England; but Berengaria, and the queen-dowager of Sicily, his sister, attended him on the expedition.[i]

The English fleet, on leaving the port of Messina, met with a furious tempest; and the squadron, on which the two princesses were embarked, was driven on the coast of Cyprus, and some of the vessels were wrecked near Limisso in that island. Isaac, prince of Cyprus, who assumed the magnificent title of emperor, pillaged the ships that were stranded, threw the seamen and passengers into prison, and even refused to the princesses liberty, in their dangerous situation, of entering the harbour of Limisso. But Richard, who arrived soon after, took ample vengeance on him for the injury. He disembarked his troops; defeated the tyrant, who opposed his landing; entered Limisso by storm; gained next day a second victory; obliged Isaac to surrender at discretion; and established governors over the island. The Greek prince, being thrown into prison and loaded with irons, complained of the little regard with which he was treated: Upon which, Richard ordered silver fetters to be made for him; and this emperor, pleased with the distinction, expressed a sense of the generosity of his conqueror.[k]

The king here espoused Berengaria, who, immediately embarking, carried along with her to Palestine the daughter of the Cypriot prince; a dangerous rival, who was believed to have seduced the affections of her husband. Such were the libertine character and conduct of the heroes engaged in this pious enterprize!

The English army arrived in time to partake in the glory of the siege of Acre or Ptolemais, which had been attacked for above two years by the united force of all the Christians in Palestine, and had been defended by the utmost efforts of Saladin and the Saracens. The remains of the German army, conducted by the emperor Frederic, and the separate bodies of adventurers who continually poured in from the West, had enabled the king of Jerusalem to form this important enterprize:[l] But Saladin, having thrown a strong garrison into the place under the command of Caracos, his own master in the art of war, and molesting the besiegers with

12th April

12th May.

The king's arrival in Palestine.

---

[i] Bened. Abb. p. 644.   [k] Bened. Abb. p. 650. Ann. Waverl. p. 164. Vinisauf. p. 328. W. Heming. p. 523.   [l] Vinisauf. p. 269, 271, 279.

CHAPTER X

continual attacks and sallies, had protracted the success of the enterprize, and wasted the force of his enemies. The arrival of Philip and Richard inspired new life into the Christians; and these princes, acting by concert, and sharing the honour and danger of every action, gave hopes of a final victory over the infidels. They agreed on this plan of operations: When the French monarch attacked the town, the English guarded the trenches: Next day, when the English prince conducted the assault, the French succeeded him in providing for the safety of the assailants. The emulation between those rival kings and rival nations produced extraordinary acts of valour: Richard in particular, animated with a more precipitate courage than Philip, and more agreeable to the romantic spirit of that age, drew to himself the general attention, and acquired a great and splendid reputation. But this harmony was of short duration; and occasions of discord soon arose between these jealous and haughty princes.

The family of Boüillon, which had first been placed on the throne of Jerusalem, ending in a female, Fulk, count of Anjou, grandfather to Henry II. of England, married the heiress of that kingdom, and transmitted his title to the younger branches of his family. The Anjevin race ending also in a female, Guy de Lusignan, by espousing Sibylla, the heiress, had succeeded to the title; and though he lost his kingdom by the invasion of Saladin, he was still acknowledged by all the Christians for king of Jerusalem.[m] But as Sibylla died without issue, during the siege of Acre, Isabella, her younger sister, put in her claim to that titular kingdom, and required Lusignan to resign his pretensions to her husband, Conrade, marquis of Montserrat. Lusignan, maintaining that the royal title was unalienable and indefeazable, had recourse to the protection of Richard, attended on him before he left Cyprus, and engaged him to embrace his cause.[n] There needed no other reason for throwing Philip into the party of Conrade; and the opposite views of these great monarchs brought faction and dissention into the Christian army, and retarded all its operations. The Templars, the Genoese, and the Germans, declared for Philip and Conrade; the Flemings, the Pisans, the knights of the hospital of St. John, adhered to Richard and Lusignan. But notwithstanding these dis-

State of Palestine.

---

[m] Vinisauf. p. 281.   [n] Trivet, p. 104. Vinisauf. p. 342. W. Heming. p. 524.

12th July.

putes, as the length of the siege had reduced the Saracen garrison to the last extremity, they surrendered themselves prisoners; stipulated, in return for their lives, other advantages to the Christians, such as restoring of the Christian prisoners, and the delivery of the wood of the true cross;[o] and this great enterprize, which had long engaged the attention of all Europe and Asia, was at last, after the loss of 300,000 men, brought to a happy period.

But Philip, instead of pursuing the hopes of farther conquest, and of redeeming the holy city from slavery, being disgusted with the ascendant assumed and acquired by Richard, and having views of many advantages, which he might reap by his presence in Europe, declared his resolution of returning to France; and he pleaded his bad state of health as an excuse for his desertion of the common cause. He left, however, to Richard ten thousand of his troops, under the command of the duke of Burgundy; and he renewed his oath never to commence hostilities against that prince's dominions during his absence. But he had no sooner reached Italy than he applied, 'tis pretended, to pope Celestine III. for a dispensation from this vow; and when denied that request, he still proceeded, though after a covert manner, in a project, which the present situation of England rendered inviting, and which gratified, in an eminent degree, both his resentment and his ambition.

Disorders in England.

Immediately after Richard had left England, and begun his march to the holy land, the two prelates, whom he had appointed guardians of the realm, broke out into animosities against each other, and threw the kingdom into combustion. Longchamp, presumptuous in his nature, elated by the favour which he enjoyed with his master, and armed with the legantine commission, could not submit to an equality with the bishop of Durham: He even went so far as to arrest his colleague, and to extort from him a resignation of the earldom of Northumberland, and of his other dignities, as the price of his liberty.[p] The king, informed of these

---

[o] This true cross was lost in the battle of Tiberiade, to which it had been carried by the crusaders for their protection. Rigord, an author of that age, says, that after this dismal event, all the children who were born throughout all Christendom, had only twenty or twenty-two teeth, instead of thirty or thirty-two, which was their former complement, p. 14.   [p] Hoveden, p. 665. Knyghton, p. 2403.

CHAPTER X

dissentions, ordered, by letters from Marseilles, that the bishop
should be reinstated in his offices; but Longchamp had still the
boldness to refuse compliance, on pretence that he himself was
better acquainted with the king's secret intentions.[q] He proceeded
to govern the kingdom by his sole authority; to treat all the nobility
with arrogance; and to display his power and riches with an invidious ostentation. He never travelled without a strong guard of
fifteen hundred foreign soldiers, collected from that licentious
tribe, with which the age was generally infested: Nobles and
knights were proud of being admitted into his train: His retinue
wore the aspect of royal magnificence: And when, in his progress
through the kingdom, he lodged in any monastery, his attendants,
it is said, were sufficient to devour, in one night, the revenue of
several years.[r] The king, who was detained in Europe longer than
the haughty prelate expected, hearing of this ostentation, which
exceeded even what the habits of that age indulged in ecclesiastics;
being also informed of the insolent, tyrannical conduct of his minister; thought proper to restrain his power: He sent new orders,
appointing Walter archbishop of Roüen, William Mareshal earl of
Strigul, Geoffrey Fitz-Peter, William Briewere, and Hugh Bardolf,
counsellors to Longchamp, and commanding him to take no measure of importance without their concurrence and approbation.
But such general terror had this man impressed by his violent
conduct, that even the archbishop of Roüen and the earl of Strigul
durst not produce this mandate of the king's; and Longchamp still
maintained an uncontrouled authority over the nation. But when
he proceeded so far as to throw into prison Geoffrey archbishop of
York, who had opposed his measures, this breach of ecclesiastical
privileges excited such an universal ferment, that prince John,
disgusted with the small share he possessed in the government,
and personally disobliged by Longchamp, ventured to summon at
Reading a general council of the nobility and prelates, and cite him
to appear before them. Longchamp thought it dangerous to entrust his person in their hands, and he shut himself up in the
Tower of London; but being soon obliged to surrender that fortress, he fled beyond sea, concealed under a female habit, and was

[q] W. Heming. p. 528.   [r] Hoveden, p. 680. Bened. Abb. p. 626, 700.
Brompton, p. 1193.

deprived of his offices of chancellor and chief justiciary; the last of which was conferred on the archbishop of Roüen, a prelate of prudence and moderation. The commission of legate, however, which had been renewed to Longchamp by pope Celestine, still gave him, notwithstanding his absence, great authority in the kingdom, enabled him to disturb the government, and forwarded the views of Philip, who watched every opportunity of annoying Richard's dominions. That monarch first attempted to carry open war into Normandy; but as the French nobility refused to follow him in an invasion of a state which they had sworn to protect, and as the pope, who was the general guardian of all princes that had taken the cross, threatened him with ecclesiastical censures, he desisted from his enterprize, and employed against England the expedient of secret policy and intrigue. He debauched prince John from his allegiance; promised him his sister Alice in marriage; offered to give him possession of all Richard's transmarine dominions; and had not the authority of queen Eleanor, and the menaces of the English council, prevailed over the inclinations of that turbulent prince, he was ready to have crossed the seas, and to have put in execution his criminal enterprizes.

1192.

The king's heroic actions in Palestine.

The jealousy of Philip was every moment excited by the glory, which the great actions of Richard were gaining him in the east, and which, being compared to his own desertion of that popular cause, threw a double lustre on his rival. His envy, therefore, prompted him to obscure that fame, which he had not equalled; and he embraced every pretence of throwing the most violent and most improbable calumnies on the king of England. There was a petty prince in Asia, commonly called *The old man of the mountain*, who had acquired such an ascendant over his fanatical subjects, that they paid the most implicit deference to his commands; esteemed assassination meritorious, when sanctified by his mandate; courted danger, and even certain death, in the execution of his orders; and fancied, that when they sacrificed their lives for his sake, the highest joys of paradise were the infallible reward of their devoted obedience.[s] It was the custom of this prince, when he imagined himself injured, to dispatch secretly some of his subjects against the aggressor, to charge them with the execution of his

---

[s] W. Heming. p. 532. Brompton, p. 1243.

CHAPTER X

revenge, to instruct them in every art of disguising their purpose; and no precaution was sufficient to guard any man, however powerful, against the attempts of these subtle and determined ruffians. The greatest monarchs stood in awe of this prince of the assassins, (for that was the name of his people; whence the word has passed into most European languages) and it was the highest indiscretion in Conrade, marquis of Montserrat, to offend and affront him. The inhabitants of Tyre, who were governed by that nobleman, had put to death some of this dangerous people: The prince demanded satisfaction; for as he piqued himself on never beginning any offence,' he had his regular and established formalities in requiring atonement: Conrade treated his messengers with disdain: The prince issued the fatal orders: Two of his subjects, who had insinuated themselves in disguise among Conrade's guards, openly, in the streets of Sidon, wounded him mortally; and when they were seized and put to the most cruel tortures, they triumphed amidst their agonies, and rejoiced that they had been destined by heaven to suffer in so just and meritorious a cause.

Every one in Palestine knew from what hand the blow came. Richard was entirely free from suspicion. Though that monarch had formerly maintained the cause of Lusignan against Conrade, he had become sensible of the bad effects attending those dissentions, and had voluntarily conferred on the former the kingdom of Cyprus, on condition that he should resign to his rival all pretensions on the crown of Jerusalem." Conrade himself, with his dying breath, had recommended his widow to the protection of Richard;" the prince of the assassins avowed the action in a formal narrative which he sent to Europe;˟ yet, on this foundation, the king of France thought fit to build the most egregious calumnies, and to impute to Richard the murder of the marquis of Montserrat, whose elevation he had once openly opposed. He filled all Europe with exclamations against the crime; appointed a guard for his own person, in order to defend himself against a like attempt;ʸ and endeavoured, by these shallow artifices, to cover the infamy of attacking the dominions of a prince, whom he himself had deserted, and who was engaged with so much glory in a war,

ᵗ Rymer. vol. i. p. 71. ᵘ Vinisauf. p. 391. ʷ Brompton, p. 1243. ˟ Rymer, vol. i. p. 71. Trivet, p. 124. W. Heming. p. 544. Diceto, p. 680. ʸ W. Heming. p. 532. Brompton, p. 1245.

universally acknowledged to be the common cause of Christendom.

But Richard's heroic actions in Palestine were the best apology for his conduct. The Christian adventurers under his command determined, on opening the campaign, to attempt the siege of Ascalon, in order to prepare the way for that of Jerusalem; and they marched along the sea-coast with that intention. Saladin purposed to intercept their passage; and he placed himself on the road with an army, amounting to 300,000 combatants. On this occasion was fought one of the greatest battles of that age; and the most celebrated, for the military genius of the commanders, for the number and valour of the troops, and for the great variety of events which attended it. Both the right wing of the Christians, commanded by d'Avesnes, and the left, conducted by the duke of Burgundy, were, in the beginning of the day, broken and defeated; when Richard, who led on the main body, restored the battle; attacked the enemy with intrepidity and presence of mind; performed the part both of a consummate general and gallant soldier; and not only gave his two wings leisure to recover from their confusion, but obtained a complete victory over the Saracens, of whom forty thousand are said to have perished in the field.[z] Ascalon soon after fell into the hands of the Christians: Other sieges were carried on with equal success: Richard was even able to advance within sight of Jerusalem, the object of his enterprize; when he had the mortification to find, that he must abandon all hopes of immediate success, and must put a stop to his career of victory. The crusaders, animated with an enthusiastic ardor for the holy wars, broke at first through all regards to safety or interest in the prosecution of their purpose; and trusting to the immediate assistance of heaven, set nothing before their eyes but fame and victory in this world, and a crown of glory in the next. But long absence from home, fatigue, disease, want, and the variety of incidents which naturally attend war, had gradually abated that fury, which nothing was able directly to withstand; and every one, except the king of England, expressed a desire of speedily returning into Europe. The Germans and the Italians declared their resolution of desisting from the enterprize: The French were still more

---

[z] Hoveden, p. 698. Bened. Abb. p. 677. Diceto, p. 662. Brompton, p. 1214.

CHAPTER X

obstinate in this purpose: The duke of Burgundy, in order to pay court to Philip, took all opportunities of mortifying and opposing Richard:[a] And there appeared an absolute necessity of abandoning for the present all hopes of farther conquest, and of securing the acquisitions of the Christians by an accommodation with Saladin. Richard, therefore, concluded a truce with that monarch; and stipulated, that Acre, Joppa, and other seaport towns of Palestine, should remain in the hands of the Christians, and that every one of that religion should have liberty to perform his pilgrimage to Jerusalem unmolested. This truce was concluded for three years, three months, three weeks, three days, and three hours; a magical number, which had probably been devised by the Europeans, and which was suggested by a superstition well suited to the object of the war.

The liberty, in which Saladin indulged the Christians, to perform their pilgrimages to Jerusalem, was an easy sacrifice on his part; and the furious wars, which he waged in defence of the barren territory of Judea, were not with him, as with the European adventurers, the result of superstition, but of policy. The advantage indeed of science, moderation, humanity, was at that time entirely on the side of the Saracens; and this gallant emperor, in particular, displayed, during the course of the war, a spirit and generosity, which even his bigotted enemies were obliged to acknowledge and admire. Richard, equally martial and brave, carried with him more of the barbarian character; and was guilty of acts of ferocity, which threw a stain on his celebrated victories. When Saladin refused to ratify the capitulation of Acre, the king of England ordered all his prisoners, to the number of five thousand, to be butchered; and the Saracens found themselves obliged to retaliate upon the Christians by a like cruelty.[b] Saladin died at Damascus soon after concluding this truce with the princes of the crusade: It is memorable, that, before he expired, he ordered his winding-sheet to be carried as a standard through every street of the city; while a crier went before, and proclaimed with a loud voice, *This is all that remains to the mighty Saladin, the conqueror of the East.* By his last will, he ordered charities to be distributed to the poor, without distinction of Jew, Christian, or Mahometan.

[a] Vinisauf. p. 380. [b] Hoveden, p. 697. Bened. Abb. p. 673. M. Paris, p. 115. Vinisauf. p. 346. W. Heming. p. 531.

There remained, after the truce, no business of importance to detain Richard in Palestine; and the intelligence which he received, concerning the intrigues of his brother John, and those of the king of France, made him sensible, that his presence was necessary in Europe. As he dared not to pass through France, he sailed to the Adriatic; and being shipwrecked near Aquileia, he put on the disguise of a pilgrim, with a purpose of taking his journey secretly through Germany. Pursued by the governor of Istria, he was forced out of the direct road to England, and was obliged to pass by Vienna; where his expences and liberalities betrayed the monarch in the habit of the pilgrim; and he was arrested by orders of Leopold, duke of Austria. This prince had served under Richard at the siege of Acre; but being disgusted by some insult of that haughty monarch, he was so ungenerous as to seize the present opportunity of gratifying at once his avarice and revenge; and he threw the king into prison. The emperor Henry VI. who also considered Richard as an enemy, on account of the alliance contracted by him with Tancred, king of Sicily, dispatched messengers to the duke of Austria, required the royal captive to be delivered to him, and stipulated a large sum of money as a reward for this service. Thus the king of England, who had filled the whole world with his renown, found himself, during the most critical state of his affairs, confined in a dungeon, and loaded with irons, in the heart of Germany,[c] and entirely at the mercy of his enemies, the basest and most sordid of mankind.

     The English council was astonished on receiving this fatal intelligence; and foresaw all the dangerous consequences, which might naturally arise from that event. The queen-dowager wrote reiterated letters to pope Celestine; exclaiming against the injury which her son had sustained, representing the impiety of detaining in prison the most illustrious prince that had yet carried the banners of Christ into the Holy Land; claiming the protection of the apostolic see, which was due even to the meanest of those adventurers; and upbraiding the pope, that, in a cause where justice, religion, and the dignity of the church, were so much concerned; a cause which it might well befit his holiness himself to support by taking in person a journey to Germany, the spiritual

[c] Chron. T. Wykes, p. 35.

CHAPTER X

thunders should so long be suspended over those sacrilegious offenders.[d] The zeal of Celestine corresponded not to the impatience
of the queen-mother; and the regency of England were, for a long
time, left to struggle alone with all their domestic and foreign
enemies.

The king of France, quickly informed of Richard's confinement
by a message from the emperor,[e] prepared himself to take advantage of the incident: and he employed every means of force and
intrigue, of war and negotiation, against the dominions and the
person of his unfortunate rival. He revived the calumny of Richard's assassinating the marquis of Montserrat; and by that absurd
pretence, he induced his barons to violate their oaths, by which
they had engaged, that, during the crusade, they never would, on
any account, attack the dominions of the king of England. He
made the emperor the largest offers, if he would deliver into his
hands the royal prisoner, or at least detain him in perpetual captivity: He even formed an alliance by marriage with the king of
Denmark, desired that the ancient Danish claim to the crown of
England should be transferred to him, and solicited a supply of
shipping to maintain it. But the most successful of Philip's negotiations was with prince John, who, forgetting every tye to his
brother, his sovereign, and his benefactor, thought of nothing but
how to make his own advantage of the public calamities. That
traitor, on the first invitation from the court of France, suddenly
went abroad, had a conference with Philip, and made a treaty, of
which the object was the perpetual ruin of his unhappy brother.
He stipulated to deliver into Philip's hands a great part of Normandy;[f] he received, in return, the investiture of all Richard's
transmarine dominions; and it is reported by several historians,
that he even did homage to the French king for the crown of
England.

In consequence of this treaty, Philip invaded Normandy; and
by the treachery of John's emissaries, made himself master, without opposition, of many fortresses, Neuf-chatel, Neaufle, Gisors,
Pacey, Ivreé: He subdued the counties of Eu and Aumale; and
advancing to form the siege of Roüen, he threatened to put all the

*War with
France.*

---

[d] Rymer, vol. i. p. 72, 73, 74, 75, 76, &c.   [e] Rymer, vol. i. p. 70.   [f] Ibid.
p. 85.

inhabitants to the sword, if they dared to make resistance. Happily, Robert earl of Leicester appeared in that critical moment; a gallant nobleman, who had acquired great honour during the crusade, and who, being more fortunate than his master in finding his passage homewards, took on him the command in Roüen, and exerted himself, by his exhortations and example, to infuse courage into the dismayed Normans. Philip was repulsed in every attack; the time of service from his vassals expired; and he consented to a truce with the English regency, received in return the promise of 20,000 marks, and had four castles put into his hands, as security for the payment.[g]

Prince John, who, with a view of encreasing the general confusion, went over to England, was still less successful in his enterprizes. He was only able to make himself master of the castles of Windsor and Wallingford; but when he arrived in London, and claimed the kingdom as heir to his brother, of whose death he pretended to have received certain intelligence, he was rejected by all the barons, and measures were taken to oppose and subdue him.[h] The justiciaries, supported by the general affection of the people, provided so well for the defence of the kingdom, that John was obliged, after some fruitless efforts, to conclude a truce with them; and before its expiration, he thought it prudent to return into France, where he openly avowed his alliance with Philip.[i]

Mean while, the high spirit of Richard suffered in Germany every kind of insult and indignity. The French ambassadors, in their master's name, renounced him as a vassal to the crown of France, and declared all his fiefs to be forfeited to his liege-lord. The emperor, that he might render him more impatient for the recovery of his liberty, and make him submit to the payment of a larger ransom, treated him with the greatest severity, and reduced him to a condition worse than that of the meanest malefactor. He was even produced before the diet of the empire at Worms, and accused by Henry of many crimes and misdemeanors; of making an alliance with Tancred, the usurper of Sicily; of turning the arms of the Crusade against a Christian prince, and subduing Cyprus; of affronting the duke of Austria before Acre; of obstructing the

[g] Hoveden, p. 730, 731. Rymer, vol. i. p. 81. [h] Hoveden, p. 724.
[i] W. Heming. p. 536.

CHAPTER X

progress of the Christian arms by his quarrels with the king of France; of assassinating Conrade, marquis of Montserrat; and of concluding a truce with Saladin, and leaving Jerusalem in the hands of the Saracen emperor.[k] Richard, whose spirit was not broken by his misfortunes, and whose genius was rather rouzed by these frivolous or scandalous imputations; after premising, that his dignity exempted him from answering before any jurisdiction, except that of heaven; yet condescended, for the sake of his reputation, to justify his conduct before that great assembly. He observed, that he had no hand in Tancred's elevation, and only concluded a treaty with a prince, whom he found in possession of the throne: That the king, or rather tyrant of Cyprus, had provoked his indignation by the most ungenerous and unjust proceedings; and though he chastised this aggressor, he had not retarded a moment the progress of his chief enterprize: That if he had at any time been wanting in civility to the duke of Austria, he had already been sufficiently punished for that sally of passion; and it better became men, embarked together in so holy a cause, to forgive each other's infirmities, than to pursue a slight offence with such unrelenting vengeance: That it had sufficiently appeared by the event, whether the king of France or he were most zealous for the conquest of the Holy Land, and were most likely to sacrifice private passions and animosities to that great object: That if the whole tenor of his life had not shown him incapable of a base assassination, and justified him from that imputation in the eyes of his very enemies, it was in vain for him, at present, to make his apology, or plead the many irrefragable arguments, which he could produce in his own favour: And that, however he might regret the necessity, he was so far from being ashamed of his truce with Saladin, that he rather gloried in that event; and thought it extremely honourable, that, though abandoned by all the world, supported only by his own courage and by the small remains of his national troops, he could yet obtain such conditions from the most powerful and most warlike emperor that the East had ever yet produced. Richard, after thus deigning to apologize for his conduct, burst out into indignation at the cruel treatment which he had met with; that he, the champion of the cross, still wearing that honourable badge, should, after expending the blood and treasure of his subjects in the common cause of Christendom, be intercepted by Christian princes in his return to his own country, be thrown into a dungeon, be loaded with irons, be obliged to plead his cause, as if he were a subject and a malefactor; and what he still more regretted, be thereby prevented from making preparations for a new crusade, which he had projected, after the expiration of the truce, and from redeeming the sepulchre of Christ, which had so long been profaned by the dominion of infidels. The spirit and eloquence of Richard made such impression on the German princes, that they exclaimed loudly against the conduct of the emperor; the pope threatened him with excommunication; and Henry, who had hearkened to the proposals of the king of France and prince John, found that it would be impracticable for him to execute his and their base purposes, or to detain the king of England any longer in captivity. He therefore concluded with him a treaty for his ransom, and agreed to restore him to his freedom for the sum of 150,000 marks, about 300,000 pounds of our present money: of which 100,000 marks were to be paid before he received his liberty, and sixty-seven hostages delivered for the remainder.[1] The emperor, as if to gloss over the infamy of this transaction, made at the same time a present to Richard of the kingdom of Arles, comprehending Provence, Dauphiny, Narbonne, and other states, over which the empire had some antiquated claims; a present which the king very wisely neglected.

The king's delivery.

The captivity of the superior lord was one of the cases provided for by the feudal tenures; and all the vassals were in that event obliged to give an aid for his ransom. Twenty shillings were therefore levied on each knight's fee in England; but as this money came in slowly, and was not sufficient for the intended purpose, the voluntary zeal of the people readily supplied the deficiency. The churches and monasteries melted down their plate, to the amount of 30,000 marks; the bishops, abbots, and nobles, paid a fourth of their yearly rent; the parochial clergy contributed a tenth of their tythes: And the requisite sum being thus collected, queen Eleanor, and Walter archbishop of Roüen, set out with it for Germany; paid the money to the emperor and the duke of Austria at Mentz;

1194. 4th Feb.

[1] Rymer, vol. i. p. 84.

CHAPTER X

delivered them hostages for the remainder; and freed Richard from captivity. His escape was very critical. Henry had been detected in the assassination of the bishop of Liege, and in an attempt of a like nature on the duke of Louvaine; and finding himself extremely obnoxious to the German princes on account of these odious practices, he had determined to seek support from an alliance with the king of France; to detain Richard, the enemy of that prince, in perpetual captivity; to keep in his hands the money which he had already received for his ransom; and to extort fresh sums from Philip and prince John, who were very liberal in their offers to him. He therefore gave orders that Richard should be pursued and arrested; but the king, making all imaginable haste, had already embarked at the mouth of the Schelde, and was out of sight off land, when the messengers of the emperor reached Antwerp.

The joy of the English was extreme on the appearance of their monarch, who had suffered so many calamities, who had acquired so much glory, and who had spread the reputation of their name into the farthest East, whither their fame had never before been able to extend. He gave them, soon after his arrival, an opportunity of publickly displaying their exultation, by ordering himself to be crowned anew at Winchester; as if he intended, by that ceremony, to reinstate himself in his throne, and to wipe off the ignominy of his captivity. Their satisfaction was not damped, even when he declared his purpose of resuming all those exorbitant grants, which he had been necessitated to make before his departure for the Holy Land. The barons also, in a great council, confiscated, on account of his treason, all prince John's possessions in England; and they assisted the king in reducing the fortresses which still remained in the hands of his brother's adherents.[m] Richard, having settled every thing in England, passed over with an army into Normandy; being impatient to make war on Philip, and to revenge himself for the many injuries which he had received from that monarch.[n] As soon as Philip heard of the king's deliverance from captivity, he wrote to his confederate, John, in these terms: *Take care of yourself: The devil is broken loose.*[o]

King's return to England. 20th March.

[m] Hoveden, p. 737. Ann. Waverl. p. 165. W. Heming. p. 540.
[n] Hoveden, p. 740.   [o] Hoveden, p. 739.

When we consider such powerful and martial monarchs, inflamed with personal animosity against each other, enraged by
mutual injuries, excited by rivalship, impelled by opposite interests, and instigated by the pride and violence of their own temper;
our curiosity is naturally raised, and we expect an obstinate and
furious war, distinguished by the greatest events, and concluded
by some remarkable catastrophe. Yet are the incidents, which attended those hostilities, so frivolous, that scarce any historian can
entertain such a passion for military descriptions as to venture on
a detail of them: A certain proof of the extreme weakness of
princes in those ages, and of the little authority they possessed over
their refractory vassals! The whole amount of the exploits on both
sides is, the taking of a castle, the surprise of a straggling party, a
rencounter of horse, which resembles more a rout than a battle.
Richard obliged Philip to raise the siege of Verneüil; he took
Loches, a small town in Anjou; he made himself master of Beaumont, and some other places of little consequence; and after these
trivial exploits, the two kings began already to hold conferences for
an accommodation. Philip insisted, that, if a general peace were
concluded, the barons on each side should for the future be prohibited from carrying on private wars against each other: But
Richard replied, that this was a right claimed by his vassals, and he
could not debar them from it. After this fruitless negociation, there
ensued an action between the French and English cavalry at Fret-
teval, in which the former were routed, and the king of France's
cartulary and records, which commonly at that time attended his
person, were taken. But this victory leading to no important advantages, a truce for a year was at last, from mutual weakness,
concluded between the two monarchs.

During this war, prince John deserted from Philip, threw himself at his brother's feet, craved pardon for his offences, and by the
intercession of queen Eleanor, was received into favour. *I forgive
him,* said the king, *and hope I shall as easily forget his injuries, as he will
my pardon.* John was incapable even of returning to his duty, without committing a baseness. Before he left Philip's party, he invited
to dinner all the officers of the garrison, which that prince had
placed in the citadel of Evreux; he massacred them during the
entertainment; fell, with the assistance of the townsmen, on the

garrison, whom he put to the sword; and then delivered up the place to his brother.

The king of France was the great object of Richard's resentment and animosity: The conduct of John, as well as that of the emperor and duke of Austria, had been so base, and was exposed to such general odium and reproach, that the king deemed himself sufficiently revenged for their injuries; and he seems never to have entertained any project of vengeance against any of them. The duke of Austria about this time, having crushed his leg by the fall of his horse at a tournament, was thrown into a fever; and being struck, on the approaches of death, with remorse for his injustice to Richard, he ordered, by will, all the English hostages in his hands to be set at liberty, and the remainder of the debt due to him to be remitted: His son, who seemed inclined to disobey these orders, was constrained by his ecclesiastics to execute them.[p] The emperor also made advances for Richard's friendship, and offered to give him a discharge of all the debt, not yet paid to him, provided he would enter into an offensive alliance against the king of France; a proposal which was very acceptable to Richard, and was greedily embraced by him. The treaty with the emperor took no effect; but it served to rekindle the war between France and England before the expiration of the truce. This war was not distinguished by any more remarkable incidents than the foregoing. After mutually ravaging the open country, and taking a few insignificant castles, the two kings concluded a peace at Louviers, and made an exchange of some territories with each other.[q] Their inability to wage war occasioned the peace: Their mutual antipathy engaged them again in war before two months expired. Richard imagined, that he had now found an opportunity of gaining great advantages over his rival, by forming an alliance with the counts of Flanders, Toulouse, Boulogne, Champagne, and other considerable vassals of the crown of France.[r] But he soon experienced the insincerity of those princes; and was not able to make any impression on that kingdom, while governed by a monarch of so much vigour and activity as Philip. The most remarkable inci-

1195.

1196.

---

[p] Rymer, vol. i. p. 88, 102. [q] Rymer, vol. i. p. 91. [r] W. Heming. p. 549. Brompton, p. 1273. Rymer, vol. i. p. 94.

dent of this war was the taking prisoner in battle the bishop of Beauvais, a martial prelate, who was of the family of Dreux, and a near relation of the French king's. Richard, who hated that bishop, threw him into prison, and loaded him with irons; and when the pope demanded his liberty, and claimed him as his son, the king sent to his holiness the coat of mail which the prelate had worn in battle, and which was all besmeared with blood: And he replied to him, in the terms employed by Jacob's sons to that patriarch, *This have we found: Know now whether it be thy son's coat or no.'* This new war between England and France, though carried on with such animosity, that both kings frequently put out the eyes of their prisoners, was soon finished, by a truce of five years; and immediately after signing this treaty, the kings were ready, on some new offence, to break out again into hostilities; when the mediation of the cardinal of St. Mary, the pope's legate, accommodated the difference.' This prelate even engaged the princes to commence a treaty for a more durable peace; but the death of Richard put an end to the negociation.

1199. Vidomar, viscount of Limoges, a vassal of the king's, had found a treasure, to which he sent part to that prince as a present. Richard, as superior lord, claimed the whole; and at the head of some Brabançons, besieged the viscount in the castle of Chalus, near Limoges, in order to make him comply with his demand." The garrison offered to surrender; but the king replied, that, since he had taken the pains to come thither and besiege the place in person, he would take it by force, and would hang every one of them. The same day, Richard, accompanied by Marcadée, leader of his Brabançons, approached the castle in order to survey it; when one Bertrand de Gourdon, an archer, took aim at him, and pierced his *28th* shoulder with an arrow. The king, however, gave orders for the *March.* assault, took the place, and hanged all the garrison, except Gourdon, who had wounded him, and whom he reserved for a more deliberate and more cruel execution.^w

The wound was not in itself dangerous; but the unskilfulness of the surgeon made it mortal: He so rankled Richard's shoulder in pulling out the arrow, that a gangrene ensued; and that prince was

' Genesis, chap. xxxvii. ver. 32. M. Paris, p. 128. Brompton, p. 1273. ' Rymer, vol. i. p. 109, 110. " Hoveden, p. 791. Knyghton, p. 2413. ^w Ibid.

CHAPTER X

now sensible that his life was drawing towards a period. He sent for Gourdon, and asked him, *Wretch, what have I ever done to you, to oblige you to seek my life? –What have you done to me?* replied coolly the prisoner: *You killed with your own hands my father, and my two brothers; and you intended to have hanged myself: I am now in your power, and you may take revenge, by inflicting on me the most severe torments: But I shall endure them all with pleasure, provided I can think that I have been so happy as to rid the world of such a nuisance.*[x] Richard, struck with the reasonableness of this reply, and humbled by the near approach of death, ordered Gourdon to be set at liberty, and a sum of money to be given him; but Marcadée, unknown to him, seized the unhappy man, flead him alive, and then hanged him. Richard died in the tenth year of his reign, and the forty-second of his age; and he left no issue behind him.

8th April. Death

The most shining part of this prince's character are his military talents. No man, even in that romantic age, carried personal courage and intrepidity to a greater height; and this quality gained him the appellation of the lion-hearted, *coeur de lion.* He passionately loved glory, chiefly military glory; and as his conduct in the field was not inferior to his valour, he seems to have possessed every talent necessary for acquiring it. His resentments also were high; his pride unconquerable; and his subjects, as well as his neighbours, had therefore reason to apprehend, from the continuance of his reign, a perpetual scene of blood and violence. Of an impetuous and vehement spirit, he was distinguished by all the good, as well as the bad qualities, incident to that character: He was open, frank, generous, sincere, and brave; he was revengeful, domineering, ambitious, haughty, and cruel; and was thus better calculated to dazzle men by the splendor of his enterprizes, than either to promote their happiness or his own grandeur, by a sound and well regulated policy. As military talents make great impression on the people, he seems to have been much beloved by his English subjects; and he is remarked to have been the first prince of the Norman line that bore any sincere regard to them. He passed however only four months of his reign in that kingdom: The crusade employed him near three years; he was detained about fourteen months in captivity; the rest of his reign was spent either in

and character of the king.

---

[x] Hoveden, p. 791. Brompton, p. 1277. Knyghton, p. 2413.

war, or preparations for war, against France; and he was so pleased with the fame which he had acquired in the East, that he determined, notwithstanding his past misfortunes, to have farther exhausted his kingdom, and to have exposed himself to new hazards, by conducting another expedition against the infidels.

Miscellaneous transactions of this reign. Though the English pleased themselves with the glory which the king's martial genius procured them, his reign was very oppressive, and somewhat arbitrary, by the high taxes which he levied on them, and often without consent of the states or great council. In the ninth year of his reign, he levied five shillings on each hyde of land; and because the clergy refused to contribute their share, he put them out of the protection of law, and ordered the civil courts to give them no sentence for any debts which they might claim.[y] Twice in his reign he ordered all his charters to be sealed anew, and the parties to pay fees for the renewal.[z] It is said that Hubert, his justiciary, sent him over to France, in the space of two years, no less a sum than 1,100,000 marks, besides bearing all the charges of the government in England. But this account is quite incredible, unless we suppose that Richard made a thorough dilapidation of the demesnes of the crown, which is not likely he could do with any advantage after his former resumption of all grants. A king, who possessed such a revenue, could never have endured fourteen months captivity, for not paying 150,000 marks to the emperor, and be obliged at last to leave hostages for a third of the sum. The prices of commodities in this reign are also a certain proof, that no such enormous sum could be levied on the people. A hyde of land, or about a hundred and twenty acres, was commonly let at twenty shillings a year, money of that time. As there were 243,600 hydes in England, it is easy to compute the amount of all the landed rents of the kingdom. The general and stated price of an ox was four shillings; of a labouring horse the same; of a sow, one shilling; of a sheep with fine wool, ten-pence; with coarse wool, six-pence.[a] These commodities seem not to have advanced in their price since the conquest,[*] and to have still been ten times cheaper than at present.

[y] Hoveden, p. 743. Tyrrel, vol. ii. p. 563.   [z] Prynne's Chronol. Vindic. tom. i. p. 1133.   [a] Hoveden, p. 745.   [*] See note [R] at the end of the volume.

CHAPTER X

Richard renewed the severe laws against transgressors in his forests, whom he punished by castration and putting out their eyes, as in the reign of his great-grandfather. He established by law one weight and measure throughout his kingdom.[b] A useful institution, which the mercenary disposition and necessities of his successor engaged him to dispense with for money.

The disorders in London, derived from its bad police, had risen to a great height during this reign; and in the year 1196, there seemed to be formed so regular a conspiracy among the numerous malefactors, as threatened the city with destruction. There was one William Fitz-Osbert, commonly called *Longbeard*, a lawyer, who had rendered himself extremely popular among the lower rank of citizens; and by defending them on all occasions, had acquired the appellation of the advocate or saviour of the poor. He exerted his authority, by injuring and insulting the more substantial citizens, with whom he lived in a state of hostility, and who were every moment exposed to the most outrageous violences from him and his licentious emissaries. Murders were daily committed in the streets; houses were broken open and pillaged in day-light; and it is pretended, that no less than fifty-two thousand persons had entered into an association, by which they bound themselves to obey all the orders of this dangerous ruffian. Archbishop Hubert, who was then chief justiciary, summoned him before the council to answer for his conduct; but he came so well attended, that no one durst accuse him, or give evidence against him; and the primate, finding the impotence of law, contented himself with exacting from the citizens hostages for their good behaviour. He kept, however, a watchful eye on Fitz-Osbert; and seizing a favourable opportunity, attempted to commit him to custody; but the criminal, murdering one of the public officers, escaped with his concubine to the church of St. Mary le Bow, where he defended himself by force of arms. He was at last forced from his retreat, condemned, and executed, amidst the regrets of the populace, who were so devoted to his memory, that they stole his gibbet, paid the same veneration to it as to the cross, and were equally zealous in propagating and attesting reports of the miracles wrought by it.[c] But

[b] M. Paris, p. 109, 134. Trivet, p. 127. Ann. Waverl. p. 165. Hoveden, p. 774.   [c] Hoveden, p. 765. Diceto, p. 691. Neubrig. p. 492, 493.

though the sectaries of this superstition were punished by the justiciary,[d] it received so little encouragement from the established clergy, whose property was endangered by such seditious practices, that it suddenly sunk and vanished.

It was during the crusades, that the custom of using coats of arms was first introduced into Europe. The knights cased up in armour, had no way to make themselves be known and distinguished in battle, but by the devices on their shields; and these were gradually adopted by their posterity and families, who were proud of the pious and military enterprizes of their ancestors.

King Richard was a passionate lover of poetry: There even remain some poetical works of his composition: and he bears a rank among the Provençal poets or *Trobadores,* who were the first of the modern Europeans, that distinguished themselves by attempts of that nature.

[d] Gervase, p. 1551.

XI

JOHN

Accession of the king – His marriage – War with France – Murder of Arthur, duke of Britanny – The king expelled from all the French provinces – The king's quarrel with the court of Rome – Cardinal Langton appointed archbishop of Canterbury – Interdict of the kingdom – Excommunication of the king – The king's submission to the pope – Discontents of the barons – Insurrection of the barons – Magna Charta – Renewal of the civil wars – Prince Lewis called over – Death – and character of the king

☙ ☙ ☙

THE NOBLE AND FREE genius of the ancients, which made the government of a single person be always regarded as a species of tyranny and usurpation, and kept them from forming any conception of a legal and regular monarchy, had rendered them entirely ignorant both of the rights of *primogeniture* and a *representation* in succession; inventions so necessary for preserving order in the lines of princes, for obviating the evils of civil discord and of usurpation, and for begetting moderation in that species of government, by giving security to the ruling sovereign. These innovations arose from the feudal law; which, first introducing the right of primogeniture, made such a distinction between the families of the elder and younger brothers, that the son of the former

1199.
Accession of the king.

was thought entitled to succeed to his grandfather, preferably to his uncles, though nearer allied to the deceased monarch. But though this progress of ideas was natural, it was gradual. In the age of which we treat, the practice of representation was indeed introduced, but not thoroughly established; and the minds of men fluctuated between opposite principles. Richard, when he entered on the holy war, declared his nephew, Arthur duke of Britanny, his successor; and by a formal deed, he set aside, in his favour, the title of his brother John, who was younger than Geoffrey, the father of that prince.ᵉ But John so little acquiesced in that destination, that, when he gained the ascendant in the English ministry, by expelling Longchamp, the chancellor and great justiciary, he engaged all the English barons to swear, that they would maintain his right of succession; and Richard, on his return, took no steps towards restoring or securing the order which he had at first established. He was even careful, by his last will, to declare his brother John heir to all his dominions;ᶠ whether, that he now thought Arthur, who was only twelve years of age, incapable of asserting his claim against John's faction, or was influenced by Eleanor, the queen-mother, who hated Constantia, mother of the young duke, and who dreaded the credit which that princess would naturally acquire if her son should mount the throne. The authority of a testament was great in that age, even where the succession of a kingdom was concerned; and John had reason to hope, that this title, joined to his plausible right in other respects, would ensure him the succession. But the idea of representation seems to have made, at this time, greater progress in France than in England: The barons of the transmarine provinces, Anjou, Maine, and Touraine, immediately declared in favour of Arthur's title, and applied for assistance to the French monarch as their superior lord. Philip, who desired only an occasion to embarrass John, and dismember his dominions, embraced the cause of the young duke of Britanny, took him under his protection, and sent him to Paris to be educated, along with his own son Lewis.ᵍ In this emergence, John hastened to establish his authority in the chief members of the monarchy; and after sending Eleanor into Poictou and Guienne, where her right was incontestible, and was readily acknowledged,

ᵉ Hoveden, p. 677. M. Paris, p. 112. Chron. de Dunst. p. 43. Rymer, vol. i. p. 66, 68. Bened. Abb. p. 619. ᶠ Hoveden, p. 791. Trivet, p. 138. ᵍ Hoveden, p. 792. M. Paris, p. 137. M. West. p. 263. Knyghton, p. 2414.

CHAPTER XI

he hurried to Roüen, and having secured the dutchy of Normandy, he passed over, without loss of time, to England. Hubert, archbishop of Canterbury, William Mareschal, earl of Strigul, who also passes by the name of earl of Pembroke, and Geoffrey Fitz-Peter, the justiciary, the three most favoured ministers of the late king, were already engaged on his side;[h] and the submission or acquiescence of all the other barons put him, without opposition, in possession of the throne.

The king soon returned to France, in order to conduct the war against Philip, and to recover the revolted provinces from his nephew, Arthur. The alliances, which Richard had formed with the earl of Flanders,[i] and other potent French princes, though they had not been very effectual, still subsisted, and enabled John to defend himself against all the efforts of his enemy. In an action between the French and Flemings, the elect bishop of Cambray was taken prisoner by the former; and when the cardinal of Capua claimed his liberty, Philip, instead of complying, reproached him with the weak efforts which he had employed in favour of the bishop of Beauvais, who was in a like condition. The legate, to show his impartiality, laid at the same time the kingdom of France and the dutchy of Normandy under an interdict, and the two kings found themselves obliged to make an exchange of these military prelates.

Nothing enabled the king to bring this war to a happy issue so much as the selfish, intriguing character of Philip, who acted in the provinces that had declared for Arthur, without any regard to the interests of that prince. Constantia, seized with a violent jealousy, that he intended to usurp the entire dominion of them,[k] found means to carry off her son secretly from Paris: She put him into the hands of his uncle; restored the provinces which had adhered to the young prince; and made him do homage for the dutchy of Britanny, which was regarded as a rere-fief of Normandy. From this incident, Philip saw, that he could not hope to make any progress against John; and being threatened with an interdict on account of his irregular divorce from Ingelburga, the Danish princess, whom he had espoused, he became desirous of concluding a peace with England. After some fruitless confer-

1200.

---

[h] Hoveden, p. 793. M. Paris, p. 137.   [i] Rymer, vol. i. p. 114. Hoveden, p. 794. M. Paris, p. 138.   [k] Hoveden, p. 795.

ences, the terms were at last adjusted; and the two monarchs seemed in this treaty to have an intention, besides ending the present quarrel, of preventing all future causes of discord, and of obviating every controversy which could hereafter arise between them. They adjusted the limits of all their territories; mutually secured the interests of their vassals; and to render the union more durable, John gave his niece, Blanche of Castile, in marriage to prince Lewis, Philip's eldest son, and with her the baronies of Issoudun and Graçai, and other fiefs in Berri. Nine barons of the king of England, and as many of the king of France, were guarantees of this treaty; and all of them swore, that, if their sovereign violated any article of it, they would declare themselves against him, and embrace the cause of the injured monarch.[1]

The King's marriage. John, now secure, as he imagined, on the side of France, indulged his passion for Isabella, the daughter and heir of Aymar Tailleffer, count of Angouleme, a lady with whom he had become much enamoured. His queen, the heiress of the family of Glocester, was still alive: Isabella was married to the count de la Marche, and was already consigned to the care of that nobleman; though, by reason of her tender years, the marriage had not been consummated. The passion of John made him overlook all these obstacles: He persuaded the count of Angouleme to carry off his daughter from her husband; and having, on some pretence or other, procured a divorce from his own wife, he espoused Isabella; regardless both of the menaces of the pope, who exclaimed against these irregular proceedings, and of the resentment of the injured count, who soon found means of punishing his powerful and insolent rival.

1201. John had not the art of attaching his barons either by affection or by fear. The count de la Marche, and his brother the count d'Eu, taking advantage of the general discontent against him, excited commotions in Poictou and Normandy; and obliged the king to have recourse to arms, in order to suppress the insurrection of his vassals. He summoned together the barons of England, and required them to pass the sea under his standard, and to quell the rebels: He found that he possessed as little authority in that king-

---

[1] Norman. Duchesnii, p. 1055. Rymer, vol. i. p. 117, 118, 119. Hoveden, p. 814. Chron. Dunst. vol. i. p. 47.

CHAPTER XI

dom as in his transmarine provinces. The English barons unanimously replied, that they would not attend him on this expedition, unless he would promise to restore and preserve their privileges:[m] The first symptom of a regular association and plan of liberty among those noblemen! But affairs were not yet fully ripe for the revolution projected. John, by menacing the barons, broke the concert; and both engaged many of them to follow him into Normandy, and obliged the rest, who staid behind, to pay him a scutage of two marks on each knight's fee, as the price of their exemption from the service.

The force, which John carried abroad with him, and that which joined him in Normandy, rendered him much superior to his malcontent barons; and so much the more, as Philip did not publickly give them any countenance, and seemed as yet determined to persevere steadily in the alliance, which he had contracted with England. But the king, elated with his superiority, advanced claims, which gave an universal alarm to his vassals, and diffused still wider the general discontent. As the jurisprudence of those times required, that the causes in the lord's court should chiefly be decided by duel, he carried along with him certain bravos, whom he retained as champions, and whom he destined to fight with his barons, in order to determine any controversy which he might raise against them.[n] The count de la Marche, and other noblemen, regarded this proceeding as an affront, as well as an injury; and declared, that they would never draw their sword against men of such inferior quality. The king menaced them with vengeance; but he had not vigour to employ against them the force in his hands, or to prosecute the injustice, by crushing entirely the nobles who opposed it.

This government, equally feeble and violent, gave the injured barons courage as well as inclination to carry farther their opposition: They appealed to the king of France; complained of the denial of justice in John's court; demanded redress from him as their superior lord; and entreated him to employ his authority, and prevent their final ruin and oppression. Philip perceived his advantage, opened his mind to great projects, interposed in behalf of the French barons, and began to talk in a high and menacing

War with France.

[m] Annal. Burton, p. 2621.   [n] Ibid.

style to the king of England. John, who could not disavow Philip's authority, replied, that it belonged to himself first to grant them a trial by their peers in his own court; it was not till he failed in this duty, that he was answerable to his peers in the supreme court of the French king;[o] and he promised, by a fair and equitable judicature, to give satisfaction to his barons. When the nobles, in consequence of this engagement, demanded a safe-conduct, that they might attend his court, he at first refused it: Upon the renewal of Philip's menaces, he promised to grant their demand; he violated this promise; fresh menaces extorted from him a promise to surrender to Philip the fortresses of Tillieres and Boutavant, as a security for performance; he again violated this engagement; his enemies, sensible both of his weakness and want of faith, combined still closer in the resolution of pushing him to extremities; and a new and powerful ally soon appeared to encourage them in their invasion of this odious and despicable government.

The young duke of Britanny, who was now rising to man's estate, sensible of the dangerous character of his uncle, determined to seek both his security and elevation by an union with Philip and the malcontent barons. He joined the French army, which had begun hostilities against the king of England: He was received with great marks of distinction by Philip; was knighted by him; espoused his daughter Mary; and was invested not only in the dutchy of Britanny, but in the counties of Anjou and Maine, which he had formerly resigned to his uncle.[p] Every attempt succeeded with the allies. Tillieres and Boutavant were taken by Philip, after making a feeble defence: Mortimar and Lyons fell into his hands almost without resistance. That prince next invested Gournai; and opening the sluices of a lake, which lay in the neighbourhood, poured such a torrent of water into the place, that the garrison deserted it, and the French monarch, without striking a blow, made himself master of that important fortress. The progress of the French arms was rapid, and promised more considerable success than usually in that age attended military enterprizes. In answer to every advance which the king made towards peace, Philip still insisted, that he should resign all his transmarine dominions to his nephew, and rest contented with the kingdom of Eng-

[o] Philipp. lib. 6.   [p] Trivet, p. 142.

CHAPTER XI

land; when an event happened, which seemed to turn the scales in favour of John, and to give him a decisive superiority over his enemies.

Young Arthur, fond of military renown, had broken into Poictou at the head of a small army; and passing near Mirebeau, he heard, that his grandmother, Queen Eleanor, who had always opposed his interests, was lodged in that place, and was protected by a weak garrison, and ruinous fortifications.[q] He immediately determined to lay siege to the fortress, and make himself master of her person: But John, rouzed from his indolence by so pressing an occasion, collected an army of English and Brabançons, and advanced from Normandy with hasty marches to the relief of the queen-mother. He fell on Arthur's camp before that prince was aware of the danger; dispersed his army; took him prisoner, together with the count de la Marche, Geoffrey de Lusignan, and the most considerable of the revolted barons; and returned in triumph to Normandy.[r] Philip, who was lying before Arques in that dutchy, raised the siege and retired, upon his approach.[s] The greater part of the prisoners were sent over to England; but Arthur was shut up in the castle of Falaise.

1st August.

The king had here a conference with his nephew; represented to him the folly of his pretensions; and required him to renounce the French alliance, which had encouraged him to live in a state of enmity with all his family: But the brave, though imprudent, youth, rendered more haughty from misfortunes, maintained the justice of his cause; asserted his claim, not only to the French provinces, but to the crown of England; and in his turn, required the king to restore the son of his elder brother to the possession of his inheritance.[t] John, sensible, from these symptoms of spirit, that the young prince, though now a prisoner, might hereafter prove a dangerous enemy, determined to prevent all future peril by dispatching his nephew; and Arthur was never more heard of. The circumstances which attended this deed of darkness, were, no doubt, carefully concealed by the actors, and are variously related by historians: But the most probable account is as follows. The king, it is said, first proposed to William de la Braye, one of his

Murder of Arthur duke of Britanny.

[q] Ann. Waverl. p. 167. M. West. p. 264.   [r] Ann. Marg. p. 213. M. West. p. 264.   [s] M. West. p. 264.   [t] Ibid.

servants, to dispatch Arthur; but William replied, that he was a gentleman, not a hangman; and he positively refused compliance. Another instrument of murder was found, and was dispatched with proper orders to Falaise; but Hubert de Bourg, chamberlain to the king, and constable of the castle, feigning that he himself would execute the king's mandate, sent back the assassin, spread the report that the young prince was dead, and publickly performed all the ceremonies of his interment: But finding, that the Bretons vowed revenge for the murder, and that all the revolted barons persevered more obstinately in their rebellion, he thought it prudent to reveal the secret, and to inform the world that the duke of Britanny was still alive, and in his custody. This discovery proved fatal to the young prince: John first removed him to the castle of Roüen; and coming in a boat, during the night-time, to that place, commanded Arthur to be brought forth to him. The young prince, aware of his danger, and now more subdued by the continuance of his misfortunes, and by the approach of death, threw himself on his knees before his uncle, and begged for mercy: But the barbarous tyrant, making no reply, stabbed him with his own hands; and fastening a stone to the dead body, threw it into the Seine.

All men were struck with horror at this inhuman deed; and from that moment the king, detested by his subjects, retained a very precarious authority over both the people and the barons in his dominions. The Bretons, enraged at this disappointment in their fond hopes, waged implacable war against him; and fixing the succession of their government, put themselves in a posture to revenge the murder of their sovereign. John had got into his power his niece, Eleanor, sister to Arthur, commonly called *the damsel of Britanny*; and carrying her over to England, detained her ever after in captivity:" But the Bretons, in despair of recovering this princess, chose Alice for their sovereign; a younger daughter of Constantia, by her second marriage with Gui de Thouars; and they entrusted the government of the dutchy to that nobleman. The states of Britanny meanwhile carried their complaints before Philip as their liege lord, and demanded justice for the violence committed by John on the person of Arthur, so near a relation,

---

" Trivet, p. 145. T. Wykes, p. 36. Ypod. Neust. p. 459.

CHAPTER XI

who, notwithstanding the homage which he did to Normandy, was always regarded as one of the chief vassals of the crown. Philip received their application with pleasure; summoned John to stand a trial before him; and on his non-appearance, passed sentence, with the concurrence of the peers, upon that prince; declared him guilty of felony and parricide; and adjudged him to forfeit to his superior lord all his seignories and fiefs in France.[w]

The king of France, whose ambitious and active spirit had been hitherto confined, either by the sound policy of Henry, or the martial genius of Richard, seeing now the opportunity favourable against this base and odious prince, embraced the project of expelling the English, or rather the English king, from France, and of annexing to the crown so many considerable fiefs, which, during several ages, had been dismembered from it. Many of the other great vassals, whose jealousy might have interposed, and have obstructed the execution of this project, were not at present in a situation to oppose it; and the rest either looked on with indifference, or gave their assistance to this dangerous aggrandizement of their superior lord. The earls of Flanders and Blois were engaged in the holy war: The count of Champagne was an infant, and under the guardianship of Philip: The dutchy of Britanny, enraged at the murder of their prince, vigorously promoted all his measures: And the general defection of John's vassals made every enterprize easy and successful against him. Philip, after taking several castles and fortresses beyond the Loire, which he either garrisoned or dismantled, received the submissions of the count of Alençon, who deserted John, and delivered up all the places under his command to the French: Upon which, Philip broke up his camp, in order to give the troops some repose after the fatigues of the campaign. John, suddenly collecting some forces, laid siege to Alençon; and Philip, whose dispersed army could not be brought together in time to succour it, saw himself exposed to the disgrace of suffering the oppression of his friend and confederate. But his active and fertile genius found an expedient against this evil. There was held at that very time a tournament at Moret in the Gatinois; whither all the chief nobility of France and the neighbouring countries had resorted, in order to signalize their prowess

The king expelled from the French provinces.

[w] W. Heming. p. 455. M. West. p. 264. Knyghton, p. 2420.

and address. Philip presented himself before them; craved their assistance in his distress; and pointed out the plains of Alençon as the most honourable field, in which they could display their generosity and martial spirit. Those valorous knights vowed, that they would take vengeance on the base parricide, the stain of arms and of chivalry; and putting themselves, with all their retinue, under the command of Philip, instantly marched to raise the siege of Alençon. John, hearing of their approach, fled from before the place; and in the hurry abandoned all his tents, machines, and baggage, to the enemy.

This feeble effort was the last exploit of that slothful and cowardly prince for the defence of his dominions. He thenceforth remained in total inactivity at Roüen; passing all his time, with his young wife, in pastimes and amusements, as if his state had been in the most profound tranquillity, or his affairs in the most prosperous condition. If he ever mentioned war, it was only to give himself vaunting airs, which, in the eyes of all men, rendered him still more despicable and ridiculous. *Let the French go on,* said he, *I will retake in a day what it has cost them years to acquire.*[x] His stupidity and indolence appeared so extraordinary, that the people endeavoured to account for the infatuation by sorcery, and believed, that he was thrown into this lethargy by some magic or witchcraft. The English barons, finding that their time was wasted to no purpose, and that they must suffer the disgrace of seeing, without resistance, the progress of the French arms, withdrew from their colours, and secretly returned to their own country.[y] No one thought of defending a man, who seemed to have deserted himself; and his subjects regarded his fate with the same indifference, to which, in this pressing exigency, they saw him totally abandoned.

John, while he neglected all domestic resources, had the meanness to betake himself to a foreign power, whose protection he claimed: He applied to the pope, Innocent III. and entreated him to interpose his authority between him and the French monarch. Innocent, pleased with any occasion of exerting his superiority, sent Philip orders to stop the progress of his arms, and to make peace with the king of England. But the French barons received the message with indignation; disclaimed the temporal authority

[x] M. Paris, p. 146. M. West. p. 266. [y] M. Paris, p. 146. M. West. p. 264.

CHAPTER XI

assumed by the pontiff; and vowed, that they would, to the utter-
most, assist their prince against all his enemies: Philip, seconding
their ardour, proceeded, instead of obeying the pope's envoys, to
lay siege to Chateau Gaillard, the most considerable fortress which
remained to guard the frontiers of Normandy.

Chateau Gaillard was situated partly on an island in the river
Seine, partly on a rock opposite to it; and was secured by every
advantage, which either art or nature could bestow upon it. The
late king, having cast his eye on this favourable situation, had
spared no labour or expence in fortifying it; and it was defended
by Roger de Laci, constable of Chester, a determined officer, at the
head of a numerous garrison. Philip, who despaired of taking the
place by force, purposed to reduce it by famine; and that he might
cut off its communication with the neighbouring country, he threw
a bridge across the Seine, while he himself with his army blockaded
it by land. The earl of Pembroke, the man of greatest vigour and
capacity in the English court, formed a plan for breaking through
the French entrenchments, and throwing relief into the place. He
carried with him an army of 4000 infantry and 3000 cavalry, and
suddenly attacked, with great success, Philip's camp in the night-
time; having left orders, that a fleet of seventy flatbottomed vessels
should sail up the Seine, and fall at the same instant on the bridge.
But the wind and the current of the river, by retarding the vessels,
disconcerted this plan of operations; and it was morning before
the fleet appeared; when Pembroke, though successful in the beginning of the action, was already repulsed with considerable loss,
and the king of France had leisure to defend himself against these
new assailants, who also met with a repulse. After this misfortune,
John made no farther efforts for the relief of Chateau Gaillard;
and Philip had all the leisure requisite for conducting and finishing the siege. Roger de Laci defended himself for a twelvemonth
with great obstinacy; and having bravely repelled every attack, and
patiently born all the hardships of famine, he was at last overpowered by a sudden assault in the night-time, and made prisoner
of war, with his garrison.[z] Philip, who knew how to respect valour
even in an enemy, treated him with civility, and gave him the whole
city of Paris for the place of his confinement.

When this bulwark of Normandy was once subdued, all the

[z] Trivet, p. 144. Gul. Britto, lib. 7. Ann. Waverl. p. 168.

province lay open to the inroads of Philip; and the king of England despaired of being any longer able to defend it. He secretly prepared vessels for a scandalous flight; and that the Normans might no longer doubt of his resolution to abandon them, he ordered the fortifications of Pont de l'Arche, Moulineaux, and Monfort l'Amauri to be demolished. Not daring to repose confidence in any of his barons, whom he believed to be universally engaged in a conspiracy against him, he entrusted the government of the province to Archas Martin and Lupicaire, two mercenary Brabançons, whom he had retained in his service. Philip, now secure of his prey, pushed his conquests with vigour and success against the dismayed Normans. Falaise was first besieged; and Lupicaire, who commanded in this impregnable fortress, after surrendering the place, inlisted himself with his troops in the service of Philip, and carried on hostilities against his ancient master. Caen, Coutance, Seez, Evreux, Baïeux soon fell into the hands of the French monarch, and all the lower Normandy was reduced under his dominion. To forward his enterprizes on the other division of the province, Gui de Thouars, at the head of the Bretons, broke into the territory, and took Mount St. Michael, Avranches, and all the other fortresses in that neighbourhood. The Normans, who abhorred the French yoke, and who would have defended themselves to the last extremity, if their prince had appeared to conduct them, found no resource but in submission; and every city opened its gates, as soon as Philip appeared before it. Roüen alone, Arques, and Verneuil determined to maintain their liberties; and formed a confederacy for mutual defence. Philip began with the siege of Roüen: The inhabitants were so inflamed with hatred to France, that, on the appearance of his army, they fell on all the natives of that country, whom they found within their walls, and put them to death. But after the French king had begun his operations with success, and had taken some of their outworks, the citizens, seeing no resource, offered to capitulate; and demanded only thirty days to advertise their prince of their danger, and to require succours against the enemy. Upon the expiration of the term, as no supply had arrived, they opened their gates to Philip;[a] and the whole province soon after imitated the example, and submitted to the victor. Thus was

1205.

1st June.

---

[a] Trivet, p. 147. Ypod. Neust. p. 459.

CHAPTER XI

this important territory re-united to the crown of France, about three centuries after the cession of it by Charles the Simple to Rollo, the first duke: And the Normans, sensible that this conquest was probably final, demanded the privilege of being governed by French laws; which Philip, making a few alterations on the ancient Norman customs, readily granted them. But the French monarch had too much ambition and genius to stop in his present career of success. He carried his victorious army into the western provinces; soon reduced Anjou, Maine, Touraine, and part of Poictou;[b] and in this manner, the French crown, during the reign of one able and active prince, received such an accession of power and grandeur, as, in the ordinary course of things, it would have required several ages to attain.

John, on his arrival in England, that he might cover the disgrace of his own conduct, exclaimed loudly against his barons, who, he pretended, had deserted his standard in Normandy; and he arbitrarily extorted from them a seventh of all their moveables, as a punishment for the offence.[c] Soon after he forced them to grant him a scutage of two marks and a half on each knight's fee for an expedition into Normandy; but he did not attempt to execute the service, for which he pretended to exact it. Next year, he summoned all the barons of his realm to attend him on this foreign expedition, and collected ships from all the sea-ports; but meeting with opposition from some of his ministers, and abandoning his design, he dismissed both fleet and army, and then renewed his exclamations against the barons for deserting him. He next put to sea with a small army, and his subjects believed, that he was resolved to expose himself to the utmost hazard for the defence and recovery of his dominions: But they were surprized, after a few days, to see him return again into harbour, without attempting any thing. In the subsequent season, he had the courage to carry his hostile measures a step farther. Gui de Thouars, who governed Britanny, jealous of the rapid progress made by his ally, the French king, promised to join the king of England with all his forces; and John ventured abroad with a considerable army, and landed at Rochelle. He marched to Angers; which he took and reduced to ashes. But the approach of Philip with an army threw him into a

1206.

[b] Trivet, p. 149. [c] M. Paris, p. 146. M. West, p. 265.

panic; and he immediately made proposals for peace, and fixed a place of interview with his enemy: But instead of keeping this engagement, he stole off with his army, embarked at Rochelle, and returned, loaded with new shame and disgrace, into England. The mediation of the pope procured him at last a truce for two years with the French monarch;[d] almost all the transmarine provinces were ravished from him; and his English barons, though harassed with arbitrary taxes and fruitless expeditions, saw themselves and their country baffled and affronted in every enterprize.

In an age, when personal valour was regarded as the chief accomplishment, such conduct as that of John, always disgraceful, must be exposed to peculiar contempt; and he must thenceforth have expected to rule his turbulent vassals with a very doubtful authority. But the government, exercised by the Norman princes, had wound up the royal power to so high a pitch, and so much beyond the usual tenor of the feudal constitutions, that it still behoved him to be debased by new affronts and disgraces, ere his barons could entertain the view of conspiring against him, in order to retrench his prerogatives. The church, which, at that time, declined not a contest with the most powerful and most vigorous monarchs, took first advantage of John's imbecillity; and with the most aggravating circumstances of insolence and scorn, fixed her yoke upon him.

1207.

The king's quarrel with the court of France.

The papal chair was then filled by Innocent III. who, having attained that dignity at the age of thirty-seven years, and being endowed with a lofty and enterprizing genius, gave full scope to his ambition, and attempted, perhaps more openly than any of his predecessors, to convert that superiority, which was yielded him by all the European princes, into a real dominion over them. The hierarchy, protected by the Roman pontiff, had already carried to an enormous height its usurpations upon the civil power; but in order to extend them farther, and render them useful to the court of Rome, it was necessary to reduce the ecclesiastics themselves under an absolute monarchy, and to make them entirely dependant on their spiritual leader. For this purpose, Innocent first attempted to impose taxes at pleasure upon the clergy; and in the first year of this century, taking advantage of the popular frenzy

[d] Rymer, vol. i. p. 141.

CHAPTER XI

for crusades, he sent collectors over all Europe, who levied by his authority the fortieth of all ecclesiastical revenues, for the relief of the Holy Land, and received the voluntary contributions of the laity to a like amount.*e* The same year Hubert, archbishop of Canterbury, attempted another innovation, favourable to ecclesiastical and papal power: In the king's absence, he summoned, by his legantine authority, a synod of all the English clergy, contrary to the inhibition of Geoffrey Fitz-Peter, the chief justiciary; and no proper censure was ever passed on this encroachment, the first of the kind, upon the royal power. But a favourable incident soon after happened, which enabled so aspiring a pontiff as Innocent, to extend still farther his usurpations on so contemptible a prince as John.

Hubert, the primate, died in 1205; and as the monks or canons of Christ-church, Canterbury, possessed a right of voting in the election of their archbishop, some of the juniors of the order, who lay in wait for that event, met clandestinely the very night of Hubert's death; and without any congé d'elire from the king, chose Reginald, their sub-prior, for the successor; installed him in the archi-episcopal throne before midnight; and having enjoined him the strictest secrecy, sent him immediately to Rome, in order to solicit the confirmation of his election.*f* The vanity of Reginald prevailed over his prudence; and he no sooner arrived in Flanders, than he revealed to every one the purpose of his journey, which was immediately known in England.*g* The king was enraged at the novelty and temerity of the attempt, in filling so important an office without his knowledge or consent: The suffragan bishops of Canterbury, who were accustomed to concur in the choice of their primate, were no less displeased at the exclusion given them in this election: The senior monks of Christ-church were injured by the irregular proceedings of their juniors: The juniors themselves, ashamed of their conduct, and disgusted with the levity of Reginald, who had broken his engagements with them, were willing to set aside his election:*h* And all men concurred in the design of remedying the false measures, which had been taken. But as John knew, that this affair would be canvassed before a superior tribu-

e Rymer, vol. i. p. 119.   *f* M. Paris, p. 148. M. West. p. 266.   *g* Ibid.
h M. West. p. 266.

nal, where the interposition of royal authority, in bestowing ecclesiastical benefices, was very invidious; where even the cause of suffragan bishops was not so favourable as that of monks; he determined to make the new election entirely unexceptionable: He submitted the affair wholly to the canons of Christ-church; and departing from the right, claimed by his predecessors, ventured no farther than to inform them privately, that they would do him an acceptable service, if they chose John de Gray, bishop of Norwich, for their primate.[i] The election of that prelate was accordingly made without a contradictory vote; and the king, to obviate all contests, endeavoured to persuade the suffragan bishops not to insist on their claim of concurring in the election: But those prelates, persevering in their pretensions, sent an agent to maintain their cause before Innocent; while the king, and the convent of Christ-church, dispatched twelve monks of that order to support, before the same tribunal, the election of the bishop of Norwich.

Thus there lay three different claims before the pope, whom all parties allowed to be the supreme arbiter in the contest. The claim of the suffragans, being so opposite to the usual maxims of the papal court, was soon set aside: The election of Reginald was so obviously fraudulent and irregular, that there was no possibility of defending it: But Innocent maintained, that, though this election was null and invalid, it ought previously to have been declared such by the sovereign pontiff, before the monks could proceed to a new election; and that the choice of the bishop of Norwich was of course as uncanonical as that of his competitor.[k] Advantage was, therefore, taken of this subtlety for introducing a precedent, by which the see of Canterbury, the most important dignity in the church after the papal throne, should ever after be at the disposal of the court of Rome.

While the pope maintained so many fierce contests, in order to wrest from princes the right of granting investitures, and to exclude laymen from all authority in conferring ecclesiastical benefices, he was supported by the united influence of the clergy, who, aspiring to independance, fought, with all the ardour of ambition, and all the zeal of superstition, under his sacred banners. But no sooner was this point, after a great effusion of blood, and the

[i] M. Paris, p. 149. M. West. p. 266. [k] M. Paris, p. 155. Chron. de Mailr. p. 182.

convulsions of many states, established in some tolerable degree, than the victorious leader, as is usual, turned his arms against his own community, and aspired to centre all power in his person. By the invention of reserves, provisions, commendams, and other devices, the pope gradually assumed the right of filling vacant benefices; and the plenitude of his apostolic power, which was not subject to any limitations, supplied all defects of title in the person on whom he bestowed preferment. The canons which regulated elections were purposely rendered intricate and involved: Frequent disputes arose among candidates: Appeals were every day carried to Rome: The apostolic see, besides reaping pecuniary advantages from these contests, often exercised the power of setting aside both the litigants, and on pretence of appeasing faction, nominated a third person, who might be more acceptable to the contending parties.

The present controversy about the election to the see of Canterbury afforded Innocent an opportunity of claiming this right; and he failed not to perceive and avail himself of the advantage. He sent for the twelve monks deputed by the convent to maintain the cause of the bishop of Norwich; and commanded them, under the penalty of excommunication, to chuse for their primate, cardinal Langton, an Englishman by birth, but educated in France, and connected, by his interests and attachments, with the see of Rome.[l] In vain did the monks represent, that they had received from their convent no authority for this purpose; that an election, without a previous writ from the king, would be deemed highly irregular; and that they were merely agents for another person, whose right they had no power or pretence to abandon. None of them had the courage to persevere in this opposition, except one; Elias de Brantefield: All the rest, overcome by the menaces and authority of the pope, complied with his orders, and made the election required of them.

Cardinal Langton appointed archbishop of Canterbury.

Innocent, sensible that this flagrant usurpation would be highly resented by the court of England, wrote John a mollifying letter; sent him four golden rings set with precious stones; and endeavoured to enhance the value of the present, by informing

[l] M. Paris, p. 155. Ann. Waverl. p. 169. W. Heming. p. 553. Knyghton, p. 2415.

him of the many mysteries implied in it. He begged him to consider seriously the *form* of the rings, their *number*, their *matter*, and their *colour*. Their form, he said, being round, shadowed out Eternity, which had neither beginning nor end; and he ought thence to learn his duty of aspiring from earthly objects to heavenly, from things temporal to things eternal. The number four, being a square, denoted steadiness of mind, not to be subverted either by adversity or prosperity, fixed for ever on the firm basis of the four cardinal virtues. Gold, which is the matter, being the most precious of metals, signified Wisdom, which is the most valuable of all accomplishments, and justly preferred by Solomon to riches, power, and all exterior attainments. The blue colour of the saphire represented Faith; the verdure of the emerald, Hope; the redness of the ruby, Charity; and the splendor of the topaz, Good Works.[m] By these conceits, Innocent endeavoured to repay John for one of the most important prerogatives of his crown, which he had ravished from him; conceits probably admired by Innocent himself. For it is easily possible for a man, especially in a barbarous age, to unite strong talents for business with an absurd taste for literature and in the arts.

John was inflamed with the utmost rage, when he heard of this attempt of the court of Rome;[n] and he immediately vented his passion on the monks of Christ-church, whom he found inclined to support the election made by their fellows at Rome. He sent Fulk de Cantelupe, and Henry de Cornhulle, two knights of his retinue, men of violent tempers and rude manners, to expel them the convent, and take possession of their revenues. These knights entered the monastery with drawn swords, commanded the prior and the monks to depart the kingdom, and menaced them, that, in case of disobedience, they would instantly burn them with the convent.[o] Innocent, prognosticating, from the violence and imprudence of these measures, that John would finally sink in the contest, persevered the more vigorously in his pretensions, and exhorted the king not to oppose God and the church any longer, nor to persecute that cause, for which the holy martyr, St. Thomas, had sacrificed his life, and which had exalted him equal to the highest saints in heaven:[p] A clear hint to John to profit by the

---

[m] Rymer, vol. i. p. 139. M. Paris, p. 155.   [n] Rymer, vol. i. p. 143.   [o] M. Paris, p. 156. Trivet, p. 151. Ann. Waverl. p. 169.   [p] M. Paris, p. 157.

example of his father, and to remember the prejudices and established principles of his subjects, who bore a profound veneration to that martyr, and regarded his merits as the subject of their chief glory and exultation.

Innocent, finding that John was not sufficiently tamed to submission, sent three prelates, the bishops of London, Ely, and Worchester, to intimate, that, if he persevered in his disobedience, the sovereign pontiff would be obliged to lay the kingdom under an interdict.[q] All the other prelates threw themselves on their knees before him, and entreated him, with tears in their eyes, to prevent the scandal of this sentence, by making a speedy submission to his spiritual Father, by receiving from his hands the new elected primate, and by restoring the monks of Christ-church to all their rights and possessions. He burst out into the most indecent invectives against the prelates; swore by God's teeth, his usual oath, that, if the pope presumed to lay his kingdom under an interdict, he would send to him all the bishops and clergy of England, and would confiscate all their estates; and threatened, that, if thenceforth he caught any Romans in his dominions, he would put out their eyes, and cut off their noses, in order to set a mark upon them, which might distinguish them from all other nations.[r] Amidst all this idle violence, John stood on such bad terms with his nobility, that he never dared to assemble the states of the kingdom, who, in so just a cause, would probably have adhered to any other monarch, and have defended with vigour the liberties of the nation against these palpable usurpations of the court of Rome. Innocent, therefore, perceiving the king's weakness, fulminated at last the sentence of interdict, which he had for some time held suspended over him.[s]

Interdict of the kingdom.

The sentence of interdict was at that time the great instrument of vengeance and policy employed by the court of Rome; was denounced against sovereigns for the lightest offences; and made the guilt of one person involve the ruin of millions, even in their spiritual and eternal welfare. The execution of it was calculated to strike the senses in the highest degree, and to operate with irresistible force on the superstitious minds of the people. The nation was of a sudden deprived of all exterior exercise of its religion: The

[q] M. Paris, p. 157. [r] Ibid. [s] Ibid. Trivet, p. 152. Ann. Waverl. p. 170. M. West. p. 268.

altars were despoiled of their ornaments: The crosses, the reliques, the images, the statues of the saints were laid on the ground; and as if the air itself were profaned, and might pollute them by its contact, the priests carefully covered them up, even from their own approach and veneration. The use of bells entirely ceased in all the churches: The bells themselves were removed from the steeples, and laid on the ground with the other sacred utensils. Mass was celebrated with shut doors; and none but the priests were admitted to that holy institution. The laity partook of no religious rite, except baptism to new-born infants, and the communion to the dying: The dead were not interred in consecrated ground: They were thrown into ditches, or buried in common fields; and their obsequies were not attended with prayers or any hallowed ceremony. Marriage was celebrated in the church-yards;[t] and that every action in life might bear the marks of this dreadful situation, the people were prohibited the use of meat, as in Lent, or times of the highest pennance; were debarred from all pleasures and entertainments; and were forbidden even to salute each other, or so much as to shave their beards, and give any decent attention to their person and apparel. Every circumstance carried symptoms of the deepest distress, and of the most immediate apprehension of divine vengeance and indignation.

The king, that he might oppose *his* temporal to *their* spiritual terrors, immediately, from his own authority, confiscated the estates of all the clergy who obeyed the interdict;[u] banished the prelates, confined the monks in their convent, and gave them only such a small allowance from their own estates, as would suffice to provide them with food and rayment. He treated with the utmost rigour all Langton's adherents, and every one that showed any disposition to obey the commands of Rome: And in order to distress the clergy in the tenderest point, and at the same time expose them to reproach and ridicule, he threw into prison all their concubines, and required high fines as the price of their liberty.[w]

After the canons, which established the celibacy of the clergy, were, by the zealous endeavours of archbishop Anselm, more rigorously executed in England, the ecclesiastics gave, almost univer-

---

[t] Chron. Dunst. vol. i. p. 51.   [u] Ann. Waverl. p. 170.   [w] M. Paris, p. 158. Ann. Waverl. p. 170.

CHAPTER XI

sally and avowedly, into the use of concubinage; and the court of Rome, which had no interest in prohibiting this practice, made very slight opposition to it. The custom was become so prevalent, that, in some cantons of Swisserland, before the reformation, the laws not only permitted, but, to avoid scandal, enjoined the use of concubines to the younger clergy;[x] and it was usual every where for priests to apply to the ordinary, and obtain from him a formal liberty for this indulgence. The bishop commonly took care to prevent the practice from degenerating into licentiousness: He confined the priest to the use of one woman, required him to be constant to her bed, obliged him to provide for her subsistance and that of her children; and, though the offspring was, in the eye of the law, deemed illegitimate, this commerce was really a kind of inferior marriage, such as is still practised in Germany among the nobles; and may be regarded by the candid, as an appeal from the tyranny of civil and ecclesiastical institutions, to the more virtuous and more unerring laws of nature.

The quarrel between the king and the see of Rome continued for some years; and though many of the clergy, from the fear of punishment, obeyed the orders of John, and celebrated divine service, they complied with the utmost reluctance, and were regarded, both by themselves and the people, as men who betrayed their principles, and sacrificed their conscience to temporal regards and interests. During this violent situation, the king, in order to give a lustre to his government, attempted military expeditions, against Scotland, against Ireland, against the Welsh;[y] and he commonly prevailed, more from the weakness of his enemies than from his own vigour or abilities. Meanwhile, the danger, to which his government stood continually exposed from the discontents of the ecclesiastics, encreased his natural propension to tyranny; and he seems to have even wantonly disgusted all orders of men, especially his nobles, from whom alone he could reasonably expect support and assistance. He dishonoured their families by his licentious amours; he published edicts, prohibited them from hunting feathered game, and thereby restrained them from their favourite occupation and amusement;[z] he ordered all the hedges and fences

---

[x] Padre Paolo, Hist. Conc. Trid. lib. 1.   [y] W. Heming. p. 556. Ypod. Neust. p. 460. Knyghton, p. 2420.   [z] M. West. p. 268.

1208.

near his forests to be levelled, that his deer might have more ready access into the fields for pasture; and he continually loaded the nation with arbitrary impositions. Conscious of the general hatred which he had incurred, he required his nobility to give him hostages for security of their allegiance; and they were obliged to put into his hands their sons, nephews, or near relations. When his messengers came with like orders to the castle of William de Braouse, a baron of great note, the lady of that nobleman replied, that she would never entrust her son into the hands of one who had murdered his own nephew, while in his custody. Her husband reproved her for the severity of this speech; but, sensible of his danger, he immediately fled with his wife and son into Ireland, where he endeavoured to conceal himself. The king discovered the unhappy family in their retreat; seized the wife and son, whom he starved to death in prison; and the baron himself narrowly escaped, by flying into France.

1209.

The court of Rome had artfully contrived a gradation of sentences; by which he kept offenders in awe, still afforded them an opportunity of preventing the next anathema by submission; and in case of their obstinacy, was able to refresh the horror of the people against them, by new denunciations of the wrath and vengeance of heaven. As the sentence of interdict had not produced the desired effect on John, and as his people, though extremely discontented, had hitherto been restrained from rising in open rebellion against him, he was soon to look for the sentence of excommunication: And he had reason to apprehend, that, notwithstanding all his precautions, the most dangerous consequences might ensue from it. He was witness of the other scenes, which, at that very time, were acting in Europe, and which displayed the unbounded and uncontrouled power of the papacy. Innocent, far from being dismayed at his contests with the king of England, had excommunicated the emperor Otho, John's nephew;[a] and soon brought that powerful and haughty prince to submit to his authority. He published a crusade against the Albigenses, a species of enthusiasts in the south of France, whom he denominated heretics; because, like other enthusiasts, they neglected the rites of the church, and opposed the power and influ-

[a] M. Paris, p. 160. Trivet, 154. M. West. p. 269.

CHAPTER XI

ence of the clergy: The people from all parts of Europe, moved by their superstition and their passion for wars and adventures, flocked to his standard: Simon de Montfort, the general of the crusade, acquired to himself a sovereignty in these provinces: The count of Toulouse, who protected, or perhaps only tolerated the Albigenses, was stripped of his dominions: And these sectaries themselves, though the most innocent and inoffensive of mankind, were exterminated with all the circumstances of extreme violence and barbarity. Here were therefore both an army and a general, dangerous from their zeal and valour, who might be directed to act against John; and Innocent, after keeping the thunder long suspended, gave at last authority to the bishops of London, Ely, and Worcester, to fulminate the sentence of excommunication against him.[b] These prelates obeyed; though their brethren were deterred from publishing, as the pope required of them, the sentence in the several churches of their dioceses.

Excommunication of the king.

No sooner was the excommunication known, than the effects of it appeared. Geoffrey, archdeacon of Norwich, who was entrusted with a considerable office in the court of exchequer, being informed of it while sitting on the bench, observed to his colleagues the danger of serving under an excommunicated king; and he immediately left his chair, and departed the court. John gave orders to seize him, to throw him into prison, to cover his head with a great leaden cope; and by this and other severe usage, he soon put an end to his life:[c] Nor was there any thing wanting to Geoffrey, except the dignity and rank of Becket, to exalt him to an equal station in heaven with that great and celebrated martyr. Hugh de Wells, the chancellor, being elected by the king's appointment, bishop of Lincoln, upon a vacancy in that see, desired leave to go abroad, in order to receive consecration from the archbishop of Roüen; but he no sooner reached France, than he hastened to Pontigny, where Langton then resided, and paid submissions to him as his primate. The bishops, finding themselves exposed either to the jealousy of the king or hatred of the people gradually stole out of the kingdom; and at last there remained only three prelates to perform the functions of the episcopal office.[d] Many of

[b] M. Paris, p. 159. M. West. p. 270.   [c] M. Paris, p. 159.   [d] Ann. Waverl. p. 170. Ann. Marg. p. 14.

the nobility, terrified by John's tyranny, and obnoxious to him on different accounts, imitated the example of the bishops; and most of the others, who remained, were with reason suspected of having secretly entered into a confederacy against him.ᵉ John was alarmed at his dangerous situation; a situation, which prudence, vigour, and popularity, might formerly have prevented, but which no virtues or abilities were now sufficient to retrieve. He desired a conference with Langton at Dover; offered to acknowledge him as primate, to submit to the pope, to restore the exiled clergy, even to pay them a limited sum as a compensation for the rents of their confiscated estates. But Langton, perceiving his advantage, was not satisfied with these concessions: He demanded, that full restitution and reparation should be made to all the clergy; a condition so exorbitant, that the king, who probably had not the power of fulfilling it, and who foresaw that this estimation of damages might amount to an immense sum, finally broke off the conference.ᶠ

1212. The next gradation of papal sentences was to absolve John's subjects from their oaths of fidelity and allegiance, and to declare every one excommunicated who had any commerce with him, in public or in private; at his table, in his council, or even in private conversation:ᵍ And this sentence was accordingly, with all imaginable solemnity, pronounced against him. But as John still persevered in his contumacy, there remained nothing but the sentence of deposition; which, though intimately connected with the former, had been distinguished from it by the artifice of the court of Rome; and Innocent determined to dart this last thunder-bolt against the refractory monarch. But as a sentence of this kind required an armed force to execute it, the pontiff, casting his eyes around, fixed at last on Philip, king of France, as the person, into whose powerful hand he could most properly entrust that weapon, the ultimate resource of his ghostly authority. And he offered the monarch, besides the remission of all his sins and endless spiritual benefits, the property and possession of the kingdom of England, as the reward of his labour.ʰ

It was the common concern of all princes to oppose these exorbitant pretensions of the Roman pontiff, by which they them-

ᵉ M. Paris, p. 162. M. West. p. 270, 271. ᶠ Ann. Waverl. p. 171. ᵍ M. Paris, p. 161. M. West. p. 270. ʰ M. Paris, p. 161. M. West. p. 271.

CHAPTER XI

selves were rendered vassals, and vassals totally dependant, of the papal crown: Yet even Philip, the most able monarch of the age, was seduced, by present interest, and by the prospect of so tempting a prize, to accept this liberal offer of the pontiff, and thereby to ratify that authority, which, if he ever opposed its boundless usurpations, might, next day, tumble him from the throne. He levied a great army; summoned all the vassals of the crown to attend him at Roüen; collected a fleet of 1700 vessels, great and small, in the sea-ports of Normandy and Picardy; and partly from the zealous spirit of the age, partly from the personal regard universally paid him, prepared a force, which seemed equal to the greatness of his enterprize. The king, on the other hand, issued out writs, requiring the attendance of all his military tenants at Dover, and even of all able-bodied men, to defend the kingdom in this dangerous extremity. A great number appeared; and he selected an army of 60,000 men; a power invincible, had they been united in affection to their prince, and animated with a becoming zeal for the defence of their native country.[i] But the people were swayed by superstition, and regarded their king with horror, as anathematized by papal censures: The barons, besides lying under the same prejudices, were all disgusted by his tyranny, and were, many of them, suspected of holding a secret correspondence with the enemy: And the incapacity and cowardice of the king himself, ill-fitted to contend with those mighty difficulties, made men prognosticate the most fatal effects from the French invasion.

Pandolf, whom the pope had chosen for his legate, and appointed to head this important expedition, had, before he left Rome, applied for a secret conference with his master, and had asked him, whether, if the king of England, in this desperate situation, were willing to submit to the apostolic see, the church should, without the consent of Philip, grant him any terms of accommodation?[k] Innocent, expecting from his agreement with a prince so abject both in character and fortune, more advantages than from his alliance with a great and victorious monarch, who, after such mighty acquisitions, might become too haughty to be bound by spiritual chains, explained to Pandolf the conditions on which he was willing to be reconciled to the king of England. The

[i] M. Paris, p. 163. M. West. p. 271.   [k] M. Paris, p. 162.

legate, therefore, as soon as he arrived in the north of France, sent over two knights templars to desire an interview with John at Dover, which was readily granted: He there represented to him, in such strong, and probably in such true colours, his lost condition, the disaffection of his subjects, the secret combination of his vassals against him, the mighty armament of France, that John, yielded at discretion,[l] and subscribed to all the conditions which Pandolf was pleased to impose upon him. He promised, among other articles, that he would submit himself entirely to the judgment of the pope; that he would acknowledge Langton for primate; that he would restore all the exiled clergy and laity, who had been banished on account of the contest; that he would make them full restitution of their goods, and compensation for all damages, and instantly consign eight thousand pounds, in part of payment; and that every one outlawed or imprisoned for his adherence to the pope, should immediately be received into grace and favour.[m] Four barons swore, along with the king, to the observance of this ignominious treaty.[n]

13th May. The king's submission to the pope.

But the ignominy of the king was not yet carried to its full height. Pandolf required him, as the first trial of obedience, to resign his kingdom to the church; and he persuaded him, that he could no wise so effectually disappoint the French invasion, as by thus putting himself under the immediate protection of the apostolic see. John, lying under the agonies of present terror, made no scruple of submitting to this condition. He passed a charter, in which he said, that, not constrained by fear, but of his own freewill, and by the common advice and consent of his barons, he had, for remission of his own sins and those of his family, resigned England and Ireland to God, to St. Peter and St. Paul, and to pope Innocent and his successors in the apostolic chair: He agreed to hold these dominions as feudatory of the church of Rome, by the annual payment of a thousand marks; seven hundred for England, three hundred for Ireland: And he stipulated, that, if he or his successors should ever presume to revoke or infringe this charter, they should instantly, except upon admonition they repented of their offence, forfeit all right to their dominion.[o]

---

[l] M. West. p. 271.   [m] Rymer, vol. 1. p. 166. M. Paris, p. 163. Annal. Burt. p. 268.   [n] Rymer, vol. i. p. 170. M. Paris, p. 163.   [o] Rymer, vol. i. p. 176. M. Paris, p. 165.

CHAPTER XI

In consequence of this agreement, John did homage to Pandolf *15th*
as the pope's legate, with all the submissive rites which the feudal *May.*
law required of vassals before their liege-lord and superior. He
came disarmed into the legate's presence, who was seated on a
throne; he flung himself on his knees before him; he lifted up his
joined hands, and put them within those of Pandolf; he swore
fealty to the pope; and he paid part of the tribute, which he owed
for his kingdom as the patrimony of St. Peter. The legate, elated
by this supreme triumph of sacerdotal power, could not forbear
discovering extravagant symptoms of joy and exultation: He trampled on the money, which was laid at his feet, as an earnest of the
subjection of the kingdom: An insolence, of which, however offensive to all the English, no one present, except the archbishop of
Dublin, dared to take any notice. But though Pandolf had brought
the king to submit to these base conditions, he still refused to free
him from the excommunication and interdict, till an estimation
should be taken of the losses of the ecclesiastics, and full compensation and restitution should be made them.

John, reduced to this abject situation under a foreign power,
still showed the same disposition to tyrannize over his subjects,
which had been the chief cause of all his misfortunes. One Peter of
Pomfret, a hermit, had foretold, that the king, this very year,
should lose his crown; and for that rash prophecy, he had been
thrown into prison in Corfe-castle. John now determined to bring
him to punishment as an impostor; and though the man pleaded,
that his prophecy was fulfilled, and that the king had lost the royal
and independent crown which he formerly wore, the defence was
supposed to aggravate his guilt: He was dragged at horses tails, to
the town of Warham, and there hanged on a gibbet with his son.*p*

When Pandolf, after receiving the homage of John, returned to
France, he congratulated Philip on the success of his pious enterprize; and informed him, that John, moved by the terror of the
French arms, had now come to a just sense of his guilt; had returned to obedience under the apostolic see; had even consented
to do homage to the pope for his dominions; and having thus
made his kingdom a part of St. Peter's patrimony, had rendered it
impossible for any Christian prince, without the most manifest and

p M. Paris, p. 165. Chron. Dunst. vol. i. p. 56.

most flagrant impiety, to attack him.[q] Philip was enraged on receiving this intelligence: He exclaimed, that having, at the pope's
instigation, undertaken an expedition, which had cost him above
60,000 pounds sterling, he was frustrated of his purpose, at the
time when its success was become infallible: He complained, that
all the expence had fallen upon him; all the advantages had accrued to Innocent: He threatened to be no longer the dupe of
these hypocritical pretences: And assembling his vassals, he laid
before them the ill-treatment which he had received, exposed the
interested and fraudulent conduct of the pope, and required their
assistance to execute his enterprize against England, in which, he
told them, that, notwithstanding the inhibitions and menaces of
the legate, he was determined to persevere. The French barons
were in that age little less ignorant and superstitious than the
English: Yet, so much does the influence of those religious principles depend on the present dispositions of men! they all vowed
to follow their prince on his intended expedition, and were resolute not to be disappointed of that glory and those riches, which
they had long expected from this enterprize. The earl of Flanders
alone, who had previously formed a secret treaty with John, declaring against the injustice and impiety of the undertaking, retired with his forces;[r] and Philip, that he might not leave so dangerous an enemy behind him, first turned his arms against the
dominions of that prince. Meanwhile, the English fleet was assembled under the earl of Salisbury, the king's natural brother; and
though inferior in number, received orders to attack the French in
their harbours. Salisbury performed this service with so much
success, that he took three hundred ships; destroyed a hundred
more:[s] And Philip, finding it impossible to prevent the rest from
falling into the hands of the enemy, set fire to them himself, and
thereby rendered it impossible for him to proceed any farther in
his enterprize.

John, exulting in his present security, insensible to his past
disgrace, was so elated with this success, that he thought of no less
than invading France in his turn, and recovering all those provinces which the prosperous arms of Philip had formerly ravished

[q] Trivet, p. 160.   [r] M. Paris, p. 166.   [s] M. Paris, p. 166. Chron. Dunst.
vol. i. p. 59. Trivet, p. 157.

CHAPTER XI

from him. He proposed this expedition to the barons, who were already assembled for the defence of the kingdom. But the English nobles both hated and despised their prince: They prognosticated no success to any enterprize conducted by such a leader: And pretending, that their time of service was elapsed, and all their provisions exhausted, they refused to second his undertaking.[t] The king, however, resolute in his purpose, embarked with a few followers, and sailed to Jersey, in the foolish expectation, that the barons would at last be ashamed to stay behind.[u] But finding himself disappointed, he returned to England; and raising some troops, threatened to take vengeance on all his nobles for their desertion and disobedience. The archbishop of Canterbury, who was in a confederacy with the barons, here interposed; strictly inhibited the king from thinking of such an attempt; and threatened him with a renewal of the sentence of excommunication, if he pretended to levy war upon any of his subjects, before the kingdom were freed from the sentence of interdict.[w]

The church had recalled the several anathemas pronounced against John, by the same gradual progress with which she had at first issued them. By receiving his homage, and admitting him to the rank of a vassal, his deposition had been virtually annulled, and his subjects were again bound by their oaths of allegiance. The exiled prelates had then returned in great triumph, with Langton at their head; and the king hearing of their approach, went forth to meet them, and throwing himself on the ground before them, he entreated them with tears to have compassion on him and the kingdom of England.[x] The primate, seeing these marks of sincere penitence, led him to the chapter-house of Winchester, and there 2oth administered an oath to him, by which he again swore fealty and July. obedience to pope Innocent and his successors; promised to love, maintain, and defend holy church and the clergy; engaged that he would re-establish the good laws of his predecessors, particularly those of St. Edward, and would abolish the wicked ones; and expressed his resolution of maintaining justice and right in all his dominions.[y] The primate next gave him absolution in the requisite forms, and admitted him to dine with him, to the great joy of all the

[t] M. Paris, p. 166. [u] M. Paris, p. 166. [w] M. Paris, p. 167. [x] M. Paris, p. 166. Ann. Waverl. p. 178. [y] M. Paris, p. 166.

people. The sentence of interdict, however, was still upheld against the kingdom. A new legate, Nicholas, bishop of Frescati, came into England, in the room of Pandolf; and he declared it to be the pope's intentions never to loosen that sentence till full restitution were made to the clergy of every thing taken from them, and ample reparation for all damages which they had sustained. He only permitted mass to be said with a low voice in the churches, till those losses and damages could be estimated to the satisfaction of the parties. Certain barons were appointed to take an account of the claims; and John was astonished at the greatness of the sums, to which the clergy made their losses to amount. No less than twenty thousand marks were demanded by the monks of Canterbury alone; twenty-three thousand for the see of Lincoln; and the king, finding these pretensions to be exorbitant and endless, offered the clergy the sum of a hundred thousand marks for a final acquittal. The clergy rejected the offer with disdain; but the pope, willing to favour his new vassal, whom he found zealous in his declarations of fealty, and regular in paying the stipulated tribute to Rome, directed his legate to accept of forty thousand. The issue of the whole was, that the bishops and considerable abbots got reparation beyond what they had any title to demand: The inferior clergy were obliged to sit down contented with their losses: And the king, after the interdict was taken off, renewed, in the most solemn manner, and by a new charter, sealed with gold, his professions of homage and obedience to the see of Rome.

1214.   When this vexatious affair was at last brought to a conclusion, the king, as if he had nothing farther to attend to but triumphs and victories, went over to Poictou, which still acknowledged his authority;[z] and he carried war into Philip's dominions. He besieged a castle near Angiers; but the approach of prince Lewis, Philip's son, obliged him to raise the siege with such precipitation, that he left his tents, machines, and baggage behind him; and he returned to England with disgrace. About the same time, he heard of the great and decisive victory gained by the king of France at Bovines over the emperor Otho, who had entered France at the head of 150,000 Germans; a victory which established for ever the glory of

---

[z] Queen Eleanor died in 1203 or 1204.

CHAPTER XI

Philip, and gave full security to all his dominions. John could, therefore, think henceforth of nothing farther, than of ruling peaceably his own kingdom; and his close connexions with the pope, which he was determined at any price to maintain, ensured him, as he imagined, the certain attainment of that object. But the last and most grievous scene of this prince's misfortunes still awaited him; and he was destined to pass through a series of more humiliating circumstances than had ever yet fallen to the lot of any other monarch.

The introduction of the feudal law into England by William the Conqueror had much infringed the liberties, however imperfect, enjoyed by the Anglo-Saxons in their ancient government, and had reduced the whole people to a state of vassalage under the *Discontents of the barons.* king or barons, and even the greater part of them to a state of real slavery. The necessity also of entrusting great power in the hands of a prince, who was to maintain military dominion over a vanquished nation, had engaged the Norman barons to submit to a more severe and absolute prerogative than that to which men of their rank, in other feudal governments, were commonly subjected. The power of the crown, once raised to a high pitch, was not easily reduced; and the nation, during the course of a hundred and fifty years, was governed by an authority, unknown, in the same degree, to all the kingdoms founded by the northern conquerors. Henry I. that he might allure the people to give an exclusion to his elder brother Robert, had granted them a charter, favourable in many particulars to their liberties; Stephen had renewed the grant; Henry II. had confirmed it: But the concessions of all these princes had still remained without effect; and the same unlimited, at least irregular authority, continued to be exercised both by them and their successors. The only happiness was, that arms were never yet ravished from the hands of the barons and people: The nation, by a great confederacy, might still vindicate its liberties: And nothing was more likely, than the character, conduct, and fortunes of the reigning prince, to produce such a general combination against him. Equally odious and contemptible, both in public and private life, he affronted the barons by his insolence, dishonoured their families by his gallantries, enraged them by his tyranny, and gave discontent to all ranks of men by his endless exactions and impositions.[a] The effect of these lawless practices had already appeared in the general demand made by the barons of a restoration of their privileges; and after he had reconciled himself to the pope, by abandoning the independance of the kingdom, he appeared to all his subjects in so mean a light, that they universally thought they might with safety and honour insist upon their pretensions.

But nothing forwarded this confederacy so much as the concurrence of Langton, archbishop of Canterbury, a man, whose memory, though he was obtruded on the nation by a palpable incroachment of the see of Rome, ought always to be respected by the English. This prelate, whether he was moved by the generosity of his nature and his affection to public good; or had entertained an animosity against John, on account of the long opposition made by that prince to his election; or thought that an acquisition of liberty to the people would serve to encrease and secure the privileges of the church; had formed the plan of reforming the government, and had prepared the way for that great innovation, by inserting those singular clauses above-mentioned in the oath, which he administered to the king, before he would absolve him from the sentence of excommunication. Soon after, in a private meeting of some principal barons at London, he showed them a copy of Henry I.'s charter, which, he said, he had happily found in a monastery; and he exhorted them to insist on the renewal and observance of it: The barons swore, that they would sooner lose their lives than depart from so reasonable a demand.[b] The confederacy began now to spread wider, and to comprehend almost all the barons in England; and a new and more numerous meeting was summoned by Langton at St. Edmondsbury, under colour of devotion. He again produced to the assembly the old charter of Henry; renewed his exhortations of unanimity and vigour in the prosecution of their purpose; and represented in the strongest colours the tyranny to which they had so long been subjected, and from which it now behoved them to free themselves and their posterity.[c] The barons, inflamed by his eloquence, incited by the sense of their own wrongs, and encouraged by the appearance of

November.

[a] Chron. Mailr. p. 188. T. Wykes, p. 36. Ann. Waverl. p. 181. W. Heming. p. 557.   [b] M. Paris, p. 167.   [c] Ibid. p. 175.

their power and numbers, solemnly took an oath before the high altar, to adhere to each other, to insist on their demands, and to make endless war on the king, till he should submit to grant them.[d] They agreed, that, after the festival of Christmas, they would prefer in a body their common petition; and in the mean time, they separated, after mutually engaging, that they would put themselves in a posture of defence, would inlist men and purchase arms, and would supply their castle with the necessary provisions.

The barons appeared in London on the day appointed and demanded of the king, that, in consequence of his own oath before the primate, as well as in deference to their just rights, he should grant them a renewal of Henry's charter, and a confirmation of the laws of St. Edward. The king, alarmed with their zeal and unanimity, as well as with their power, required a delay; promised, that, at the festival of Easter, he would give them a positive answer to their petition; and offered them the archbishop of Canterbury, the bishop of Ely, and the earl of Pembroke, the Mareschal, as sureties for his fulfilling this engagement.[e] The barons accepted of the terms, and peaceably returned to their castles. *1215.* *6th Jan.*

During this interval, John, in order to break or subdue the league of his barons, endeavoured to avail himself of the ecclesiastical power, of whose influence he had, from his own recent misfortunes, had such fatal experience. He granted to the clergy a charter, relinquishing for ever that important prerogative, for which his father and all his ancestors had zealously contended; yielding to them the free election on all vacancies; reserving only the power to issue a congé d'elire, and to subjoin a confirmation of the election; and declaring, that, if either of these were with-held, the choice should nevertheless be deemed just and valid.[f] He made a vow to lead an army into Palestine against the infidels, and he took on him the cross; in hopes, that he should receive from the church that protection, which she tendered to every one that had entered into this sacred and meritorious engagement.[g] And he sent to Rome his agent, William de Mauclerc, in order to appeal to the pope against the violence of his barons, and procure him a favourable sentence from that powerful tribunal.[h] The barons also were *15th* *Jan.*

[d] Ibid. p. 176. [e] M. Paris, p. 176. M. West. p. 273. [f] Rymer, vol. i. p. 197. [g] Rymer, vol. i. p. 200. Trivet, p. 162. T. Wykes, p. 37. M. West. p. 273. [h] Rymer, vol. i. p. 184.

not negligent on their part in endeavouring to engage the pope in their interests: They dispatched Eustace de Vescie to Rome; laid their case before Innocent as their feudal lord; and petitioned him to interpose his authority with the king, and oblige him to restore and confirm all their just and undoubted privileges.[i]

Innocent beheld with regret the disturbances which had arisen in England, and was much inclined to favour John in his pretensions. He had no hopes of retaining and extending his newly acquired superiority over that kingdom, but by supporting so base and degenerate a prince, who was willing to sacrifice every consideration to his present safety: And he foresaw, that, if the administration should fall into the hands of those gallant and high-spirited barons, they would vindicate the honour, liberty, and independance of the nation, with the same ardour which they now exerted in defence of their own. He wrote letters therefore to the prelates, to the nobility, and to the king himself. He exhorted the first to employ their good offices in conciliating peace between the contending parties, and putting an end to civil discord: To the second, he expressed his disapprobation of their conduct in employing force to extort concessions from their reluctant sovereign: The last, he advised to treat his nobles with grace and indulgence, and to grant them such of their demands as should appear just and reasonable.[k]

The barons easily saw, from the tenor of these letters, that they must reckon on having the pope, as well as the king, for their adversary; but they had already advanced too far to recede from their pretensions, and their passions were so deeply engaged, that it exceeded even the power of superstition itself any longer to controul them. They also foresaw, that the thunders of Rome, when not seconded by the efforts of the English ecclesiastics, would be of small avail against them; and they perceived, that the most considerable of the prelates, as well as all the inferior clergy, professed the highest approbation of their cause. Besides, that these men were seized with the national passion for laws and liberty; blessings, of which they themselves expected to partake; there concurred very powerful causes to loosen their devoted attachment to the apostolic see. It appeared, from the late usurpa-

[i] Ibid.　[k] Ibid. p. 196, 197.

tions of the Roman pontiff, that he pretended to reap alone all the advantages accruing from that victory, which, under his banners, though at their own peril, they had every where obtained over the civil magistrate. The pope assumed a despotic power over all the churches: Their particular customs, privileges, and immunities, were treated with disdain: Even the canons of general councils were set aside by his dispensing power: The whole administration of the church was centered in the court of Rome: All preferments ran of course in the same channel: and the provincial clergy saw, at least felt, that there was a necessity for limiting these pretensions. The legate, Nicholas, in filling those numerous vacancies which had fallen in England during an interdict of six years, had proceeded in the most arbitrary manner; and had paid no regard, in conferring dignities, to personal merit, to rank, to the inclination of the electors, or to the customs of the country. The English church was universally disgusted; and Langton himself, though he owed his elevation to an incroachment of the Romish see, was no sooner established in his high office, than he became jealous of the privileges annexed to it, and formed attachments with the country subjected to his jurisdiction. These causes, though they opened slowly the eyes of men, failed not to produce their effect: They set bounds to the usurpations of the papacy: The tide first stopped, and then turned against the sovereign pontiff: And it is otherwise inconceivable, how that age, so prone to superstition, and so sunk in ignorance, or rather so devoted to a spurious erudition, could have escaped falling into an absolute and total slavery under the court of Rome.

About the time that the pope's letters arrived in England, the malcontent barons, on the approach of the festival of Easter, when they were to expect the king's answer to their petition, met by agreement at Stamford; and they assembled a force, consisting of above 2000 knights, besides their retainers and inferior persons without number. Elated with their power, they advanced in a body to Brackley, within fifteen miles of Oxford, the place where the court then resided; and they there received a message from the king, by the archbishop of Canterbury and the earl of Pembroke, desiring to know what those liberties were which they so zealously challenged from their sovereign. They delivered to these messengers a schedule, containing the chief articles of their demands;

Insurrection of the barons.

27th April.

which was no sooner shown to the king, than he burst into a furious passion, and asked, why the barons did not also demand of him his kingdom? swearing, that he would never grant them such liberties as must reduce himself to slavery.[l]

No sooner were the confederated nobles informed of John's reply, than they chose Robert Fitz-Walter their general, whom they called *the mareschal of the army of God and of holy church;* and they proceeded without farther ceremony to levy war upon the king. They besieged the castle of Northampton during fifteen days, though without success.[m] The gates of Bedford castle were willingly opened to them by William Beauchamp, its owner: They advanced to Ware in their way to London, where they held a correspondence with the principal citizens: They were received without opposition into that capital: And finding now the great superiority of their force, they issued proclamations, requiring the other barons to join them, and menacing them, in case of refusal or delay, with committing devastation on their houses and estates.[n] In order to show what might be expected from their prosperous arms, they made incursions from London, and laid waste the king's parks and palaces; and all the barons, who had hitherto carried the semblance of supporting the royal party, were glad of this pretence for openly joining a cause, which they always had secretly favoured. The king was left at Odiham in Surrey with a poor retinue of only seven knights; and after trying several expedients to elude the blow, after offering to refer all differences to the pope alone, or to eight barons, four to be chosen by himself, and four by the confederates,[o] he found himself at last obliged to submit at discretion.

24th May.

Magna Charta, 15th June.

A conference between the king and the barons was appointed at Runnemede, between Windsor and Staines; a place which has ever since been extremely celebrated, on account of this great event. The two parties encamped a-part, like open enemies; and after a debate of a few days, the king, with a facility somewhat suspicious, signed and sealed the charter which was required of him. This famous deed, commonly called the GREAT CHARTER, either granted or secured very important liberties and privileges to

19th June.

[l] M. Paris, p. 176. [m] M. Paris, p. 177. Chron. Dunst. vol. i. p. 71. [n] M. Paris, p. 177. [o] Rymer, vol. i. p. 200.

443

every order of men in the kingdom; to the clergy, to the barons, and to the people.

The freedom of elections was secured to the clergy: The former charter of the king was confirmed, by which the necessity of a royal congé d'elire and confirmation was superseded: All check upon appeals to Rome was removed, by the allowance granted every man to depart the kingdom at pleasure: And the fines to be imposed on the clergy, for any offence, were ordained to be proportional to their lay estates, not to their ecclesiastical benefices.

The privileges granted to the barons were either abatements in the rigour of the feudal law, or determinations in points which had been left by that law, or had become by practice, arbitrary and ambiguous. The reliefs of heirs succeeding to a military fee were ascertained; an earl's and baron's at a hundred marks, a knight's at a hundred shillings. It was ordained by the charter, that, if the heir be a minor, he shall, immediately upon his majority, enter upon his estate, without paying any reliefs: The king shall not sell his wardship: He shall levy only reasonable profits upon the estate, without committing waste or hurting the property: He shall uphold the castles, houses, mills, parks, and ponds: And if he commit the guardianship of the estate to the sheriff or any other, he shall previously oblige them to find surety to the same purpose. During the minority of a baron, while his lands are in wardship, and are not in his own possession, no debt which he owes to the Jews shall bear any interest. Heirs shall be married without disparagement; and before the marriage be contracted, the nearest relations of the person shall be informed of it. A widow, without paying any relief, shall enter upon her dower, the third part of her husband's rents: She shall not be compelled to marry, so long as she chuses to continue single; she shall only give security never to marry without her lord's consent. The king shall not claim the wardship of any minor, who holds lands by military tenure of a baron, on pretence that he also holds lands of the crown, by soccage or any other tenure. Scutages shall be estimated at the same rate as in the time of Henry I.; and no scutage or aid, except in the three general feudal cases, the king's captivity, the knighting of his eldest son, and the marrying of his eldest daughter, shall be imposed but by the great council of the kingdom; the prelates, earls, and great barons, shall be called to this great council, each by a particular writ; the lesser barons by a general summons of the sheriff. The king shall not seize any baron's land for a debt to the crown, if the baron possesses as many goods and chattels as are sufficient to discharge the debt. No man shall be obliged to perform more service for his fee than he is bound to by his tenure. No governor or constable of a castle shall oblige any knight to give money for castle-guard, if the knight be willing to perform the service in person, or by another able-bodied man; and if the knight be in the field himself, by the king's command, he shall be exempted from all other service of this nature. No vassal shall be allowed to sell so much of his land as to incapacitate himself from performing his service to his lord.

These were the principal articles, calculated for the interest of the barons; and had the charter contained nothing farther, national happiness and liberty had been very little promoted by it, as it would only have tended to encrease the power and independance of an order of men, who were already too powerful, and whose yoke might have become more heavy on the people than even that of an absolute monarch. But the barons, who alone drew and imposed on the prince this memorable charter, were necessitated to insert in it other clauses of a more extensive and more beneficent nature: They could not expect the concurrence of the people, without comprehending, together with their own, the interests of inferior ranks of men; and all provisions, which the barons, for their own sake, were obliged to make, in order to ensure the free and equitable administration of justice, tended directly to the benefit of the whole community. The following were the principal clauses of this nature.

It was ordained, that all the privileges and immunities abovementioned, granted to the barons against the king, should be extended by the barons to their inferior vassals. The king bound himself not to grant any writ, empowering a baron to levy aids from his vassals, except in the three feudal cases. One weight and one measure shall be established throughout the kingdom. Merchants shall be allowed to transact all business, without being exposed to any arbitrary tolls and impositions: They and all free men shall be allowed to go out of the kingdom and return to it at pleasure: London, and all cities and burghs, shall preserve their ancient liberties, immunities, and free customs: Aids shall not be

CHAPTER XI

required of them but by the consent of the great council: No towns or individuals shall be obliged to make or support bridges but by ancient custom: The goods of every freeman shall be disposed of according to his will: If he die intestate, his heirs shall succeed to them. No officer of the crown shall take any horses, carts, or wood, without the consent of the owner. The king's courts of justice shall be stationary, and shall no longer follow his person: They shall be open to every one; and justice shall no longer be sold, refused, or delayed by them. Circuits shall be regularly held every year. The inferior tribunals of justice, the county court, sheriff's turn, and court-leet shall meet at their appointed time and place: The sheriffs shall be incapacitated to hold pleas of the crown; and shall not put any person upon his trial, from rumour or suspicion alone, but upon the evidence of lawful witnesses. No freeman shall be taken or imprisoned, or dispossessed of his free tenement and liberties, or outlawed, or banished, or any wise hurt or injured, unless by the legal judgment of his peers, or by the law of the land; and all who suffered otherwise in this or the two former reigns, shall be restored to their rights and possessions. Every freeman shall be fined in proportion to his fault; and no fine shall be levied on him to his utter ruin: Even a villain or rustic shall not by any fine be bereaved of his carts, ploughs, and implements of husbandry. This was the only article calculated for the interests of this body of men, probably at that time the most numerous in the kingdom.

It must be confessed, that the former articles of the Great Charter contain such mitigations and explanations of the feudal law as are reasonable and equitable; and that the latter involve all the chief outlines of a legal government, and provide for the equal distribution of justice, and free enjoyment of property; the great objects for which political society was at first founded by men, which the people have a perpetual and unalienable right to recal, and which no time, nor precedent, nor statute, nor positive institution, ought to deter them from keeping ever uppermost in their thoughts and attention. Though the provisions made by this charter might, conformably to the genius of the age, be esteemed too concise, and too bare of circumstances, to maintain the execution of its articles, in opposition to the chicanery of lawyers, supported by the violence of power; time gradually ascertained the sense of all the ambiguous expressions; and those generous barons, who first extorted this concession, still held their swords in their hands, and could turn them against those who dared, on any pretence, to depart from the original spirit and meaning of the grant. We may, now, from the tenor of this charter, conjecture what those laws were of king Edward, which the English nation, during so many generations, still desired, with such an obstinate perseverance, to have recalled and established. They were chiefly these latter articles of *Magna Charta;* and the barons, who, at the beginning of these commotions, demanded the revival of the Saxon laws, undoubtedly thought, that they had sufficiently satisfied the people, by procuring them this concession, which comprehended the principal objects, to which they had so long aspired. But what we are most to admire, is the prudence and moderation of those haughty nobles themselves, who were enraged by injuries, inflamed by opposition, and elated by a total victory over their sovereign. They were content, even in this plenitude of power, to depart from some articles of Henry I.'s charter, which they made the foundation of their demands, particularly from the abolition of wardships, a matter of the greatest importance; and they seem to have been sufficiently careful not to diminish too far the power and revenue of the crown. If they appear, therefore, to have carried other demands to too great a height, it can be ascribed only to the faithless and tyrannical character of the king himself, of which they had long had experience, and which, they foresaw, would, if they provided no farther security, lead him soon to infringe their new liberties, and revoke his own concessions. This alone gave birth to those other articles, seemingly exorbitant, which were added as a rampart for the safeguard of the Great Charter.

The barons obliged the king to agree, that London should remain in their hands, and the Tower be consigned to the custody of the primate, till the 15th of August ensuing, or till the execution of the several articles of the Great Charter.[p] The better to ensure the same end, he allowed them to chuse five and twenty members from their own body, as conservators of the public liberties; and no bounds were set to the authority of these men either in extent or duration. If any complaint were made of a violation of the charter, whether attempted by the king, justiciaries, sheriffs, or foresters,

[p] Rymer, vol. i. p. 201. Chron. Dunst. vol. i. p. 73.

CHAPTER XI

any four of these barons might admonish the king to redress the grievance: If satisfaction were not obtained, they could assemble the whole council of twenty-five; who, in conjunction with the great council, were empowered to compel him to observe the charter, and, in case of resistance, might levy war against him, attack his castles, and employ every kind of violence, except against his royal person, and that of his queen and children. All men, throughout the kingdom, were bound, under the penalty of confiscation, to swear obedience to the twenty-five barons; and the freeholders of each county were to chuse twelve knights, who were to make report of such evil customs as required redress, conformably to the tenor of the Great Charter.[q] The names of those conservators were the earls of Clare, Albemarle, Glocester, Winchester, Hereford, Roger Bigod, earl of Norfolk, Robert de Vere, earl of Oxford, William Mareschal the younger, Robert Fitz-Walter, Gilbert de Clare, Eustace de Vescey, Gilbert Delaval, William de Moubray, Geoffrey de Say, Roger de Mombezon, William de Huntingfield, Robert de Ros, the constable of Chester, William de Aubenie, Richard de Perci, William Malet, John Fitz-Robert, William de Lanvalay, Hugh de Bigod, and Roger de Montfichet.[r] These men were, by this convention, really invested with the sovereignty of the kingdom: They were rendered co-ordinate with the king, or rather superior to him, in the exercise of the executive power: And as there was no circumstance of government, which, either directly or indirectly, might not bear a relation to the security or observance of the Great Charter; there could scarcely occur any incident, in which they might not lawfully interpose their authority.

John seemed to submit passively to all these regulations, however injurious to majesty: He sent writs to all the sheriffs, ordering them to constrain every one to swear obedience to the twenty-five barons.[s] He dismissed all his foreign forces: He pretended, that his government was thenceforth to run in a new tenor, and be more indulgent to the liberty and independance of his people. But he only dissembled, till he should find a favourable opportunity for annulling all his concessions. The injuries and indignities, which

[q] This seems a very strong proof that the house of commons was not then in being; otherwise the knights and burgesses from the several counties could have given into the lords a list of grievances, without so unusual an election.   [r] M. Paris, p. 181.   [s] M. Paris, p. 182.

he had formerly suffered from the pope and the king of France, as they came from equals or superiors, seemed to make but small impression on him: But the sense of this perpetual and total subjection under his own rebellious vassals, sunk deep in his mind, and he was determined, at all hazards, to throw off so ignominious a slavery.[t] He grew sullen, silent, and reserved: He shunned the society of his courtiers and nobles: He retired into the Isle of Wight, as if desirous of hiding his shame and confusion; but in this retreat he meditated the most fatal vengeance against all his enemies.[u] He secretly sent abroad his emissaries to inlist foreign soldiers, and to invite the rapacious Brabançons into his service, by the prospect of sharing the spoils of England, and reaping the forfeitures of so many opulent barons, who had incurred the guilt of rebellion, by rising in arms against him.[w] And he dispatched a messenger to Rome, in order to lay before the pope the Great Charter, which he had been compelled to sign, and to complain, before that tribunal, of the violence, which had been imposed upon him.[x]

Innocent, considering himself as feudal lord of the kingdom, was incensed at the temerity of the barons, who, though they pretended to appeal to his authority, had dared, without waiting for his consent, to impose such terms on a prince, who, by resigning to the Roman pontiff his crown and independance, had placed himself immediately under the papal protection. He issued, therefore, a bull, in which, from the plenitude of his apostolic power, and from the authority, which God had committed to him, to build and destroy kingdoms, to plant and overthrow, he annulled and abrogated the whole charter, as unjust in itself, as obtained by compulsion, and as derogatory to the dignity of the apostolic see. He prohibited the barons from exacting the observance of it: He even prohibited the king himself from paying any regard to it: He absolved him and his subjects from all oaths, which they had been constrained to take to that purpose: And he pronounced a general sentence of excommunication against every one, who should persevere in maintaining such treasonable and iniquitous pretensions.[y]

[t] Ibid. p. 183.   [u] Ibid.   [w] M. Paris, p. 183. Chron. Dunst. vol. i. p. 72. Chron. Mailr. p. 188.   [x] M. Paris, p. 183. Chron. Dunst. vol. i. p. 73. [y] Rymer, vol. i. p. 203, 204, 205, 208. M. Paris, p. 184, 185, 187.

CHAPTER XI

The king, as his foreign forces arrived along with this bull, now *Renewal* ventured to take off the mask; and, under sanction of the pope's *of the* decree, recalled all the liberties which he had granted to his sub- *civil* jects, and which he had solemnly sworn to observe. But the spiri- *wars.* tual weapon was found upon trial to carry less force with it, than he had reason from his own experience to apprehend. The primate refused to obey the pope in publishing the sentence of excommunication against the barons; and though he was cited to Rome, that he might attend a general council, there assembled, and was suspended, on account of his disobedience to the pope, and his secret correspondence with the king's enemies.[z] Though a new and particular sentence of excommunication was pronounced by name against the principal barons;[a] John still found, that his nobility and people, and even his clergy, adhered to the defence of their liberties, and to their combination against him: The sword of his foreign mercenaries was all he had to trust to for restoring his authority.

The barons, after obtaining the Great Charter, seem to have been lulled into a fatal security, and to have taken no rational measures, in case of the introduction of a foreign force, for reassembling their armies. The king was from the first master of the field; and immediately laid siege to the castle of Rochester, which was obstinately defended by William de Albiney, at the head of a hundred and forty knights with their retainers, but was at last reduced by famine. John, irritated with the resistance, intended to *30th* have hanged the governor and all the garrison; but on the repre- *Nov.* sentation of William de Mauleon, who suggested to him the danger of reprizals, he was content to sacrifice, in this barbarous manner, the inferior prisoners only.[b] The captivity of William de Albiney, the best officer among the confederated barons, was an irreparable loss to their cause; and no regular opposition was thenceforth made to the progress of the royal arms. The ravenous and barbarous mercenaries, incited by a cruel and enraged prince, were let loose against the estates, tenants, manors, houses, parks of the barons, and spread devastation over the face of the kingdom. Nothing was to be seen but the flames of villages and castles reduced to ashes, the consternation and misery of the inhabitants,

[z] M. Paris, p. 189. [a] Rymer, vol. i. p. 211. M. Paris, p. 192. [b] M. Paris, p. 187.

tortures exercised by the soldiery to make them reveal their concealed treasures, and reprizals no less barbarous, committed by the barons and their partizans on the royal demesnes, and on the estates of such as still adhered to the crown. The king, marching through the whole extent of England, from Dover to Berwic, laid the provinces waste on each side of him; and considered every state, which was not his immediate property, as entirely hostile and the object of military execution. The nobility of the north in particular, who had shewn greatest violence in the recovery of their liberties, and who, acting in a separate body, had expressed their discontent even at the concessions made by the Great Charter; as they could expect no mercy, fled before him with their wives and families, and purchased the friendship of Alexander, the young king of Scots, by doing homage to him.

Prince Lewis called over.

The barons, reduced to this desperate extremity, and menaced with the total loss of their liberties, their properties, and their lives, employed a remedy no less desperate; and making applications to the court of France, they offered to acknowledge Lewis, the eldest son of Philip, for their sovereign; on condition, that he would afford them protection from the violence of their enraged prince. Though the sense of the common rights of mankind, the only rights that are entirely indefeasible, might have justified them in the deposition of their king; they declined insisting before Philip, on a pretension, which is commonly so disagreeable to sovereigns, and which sounds harshly in their royal ears. They affirmed, that John was incapable of succeeding to the crown, by reason of the attainder, passed upon him during his brother's reign; though that attainder had been reversed, and Richard had even, by his last will, declared him his successor. They pretended, that he was already legally deposed by sentence of the peers of France, on account of the murder of his nephew; though that sentence could not possibly regard any thing but his transmarine dominions, which alone he

1216.

held in vassalage to that crown. On more plausible grounds, they affirmed, that he had already deposed himself by doing homage to the pope, changing the nature of his sovereignty, and resigning an independant crown for a see under a foreign power. And as Blanche of Castile, the wife of Lewis, was descended by her mother from Henry II. they maintained, though many other princes stood before her in the order of succession, that they had not shaken off the royal family, in chusing her husband for their sovereign.

CHAPTER XI

Philip was strongly tempted to lay hold on the rich prize which was offered to him. The legate menaced him with interdicts and excommunications, if he invaded the patrimony of St. Peter, or attacked a prince, who was under the immediate protection of the holy see.[c] But as Philip was assured of the obedience of his own vassals, his principles were changed with the times, and he now undervalued as much all papal censures, as he formerly pretended to pay respect to them. His chief scruple was with regard to the fidelity, which he might expect from the English barons in their new engagements, and the danger of entrusting his son and heir into the hands of men, who might, on any caprice or necessity, make peace with their native sovereign, by sacrificing a pledge of so much value. He therefore exacted from the barons twenty-five hostages of the most noble birth in the kingdom;[d] and having obtained this security, he sent over first a small army to the relief of the confederates; then more numerous forces, which arrived with Lewis himself at their head.

The first effect of the young prince's appearance in England was the desertion of John's foreign troops, who, being mostly levied in Flanders, and other provinces of France, refused to serve against the heir of their monarchy.[e] The Gascons and Poictevins alone, who were still John's subjects, adhered to his cause; but they were too weak to maintain that superiority in the field, which they had hitherto supported against the confederated barons. Many considerable noblemen deserted John's party, the earls of Salisbury, Arundel, Warrene, Oxford, Albemarle, and William Mareschal the younger: His castles fell daily into the hands of the enemy: Dover was the only place, which, from the valour and fidelity of Hubert de Burgh, the governor, made resistance to the progress of Lewis:[f] And the barons had the melancholy prospect of finally succeeding in their purpose, and of escaping the tyranny of their own king, by imposing on themselves and the nation a foreign yoke. But this union was of short duration between the French and English nobles; and the imprudence of Lewis, who, on every occasion, showed too visible a preference to the former, encreased that jealousy, which it was so natural for the latter to entertain in their present situation.[g] The viscount of Melun, too, it

[c] M. Paris, p. 194. M. West. p. 275.   [d] M. Paris, p. 193. Chron. Dunst. vol. i. p. 74.   [e] M. Paris, p. 195.   [f] Ibid. p. 198. Chron. Dunst. vol. i. p. 75, 76.   [g] W. Heming. p. 559.

is said, one of his courtiers, fell sick at London, and finding the approaches of death, he sent for some of his friends among the English barons, and warning them of their danger, revealed Lewis's secret intentions of exterminating them and their families as traitors to their prince, and of bestowing their estates and dignities on his native subjects, in whose fidelity he could more reasonably place confidence.[h] This story, whether true or false, was universally reported and believed; and concurring with other circumstances, which rendered it credible, did great prejudice to the cause of Lewis. The earl of Salisbury and other noblemen deserted again to John's party;[i] and as men easily change sides in a civil war, especially where their power is founded on an hereditary and independant authority, and is not derived from the opinion and favour of the people, the French prince had reason to dread a sudden reverse of fortune. The king was assembling a considerable army, with a view of fighting one great battle for his crown; but passing from Lynne to Lincolnshire, his road lay along the sea-shore, which was overflowed at high water; and not chusing the proper time for his journey, he left in the inundation all his carriages, treasure, baggage, and regalia. The affliction for this disaster, and vexation from the distracted state of his affairs, encreased the sickness under which he then laboured; and though he reached the castle of Newark, he was obliged to halt there, and his distemper soon after put an end to his life, in the forty-ninth year of his age, and eighteenth of his reign; and freed the nation from the dangers, to which it was equally exposed, by his success or by his misfortunes.

17th Octob. Death

The character of this prince is nothing but a complication of vices, equally mean and odious; ruinous to himself, and destructive to his people. Cowardice, inactivity, folly, levity, licentiousness, ingratitude, treachery, tyranny, and cruelty, all these qualities appear too evidently in the several incidents of his life, to give us room to suspect that the disagreeable picture has been anywise overcharged, by the prejudices of the ancient historians. It is hard to say, whether his conduct to his father, his brother, his nephew, or his subjects, was most culpable; or whether his crimes in these respects were not even exceeded by the baseness, which

and character of the king.

[h] M. Paris, p. 199. M. West. p. 277.   [i] Chron. Dunst. vol. i. p. 78.

CHAPTER XI

appeared in his transactions with the king of France, the pope, and the barons. His European dominions, when they devolved to him by the death of his brother, were more extensive than have ever, since his time, been ruled by any English monarch: But he first lost by his misconduct the flourishing provinces in France, the ancient patrimony of his family: He subjected his kingdom to a shameful vassalage under the see of Rome: He saw the prerogatives of his crown diminished by law, and still more reduced by faction. And he died at last, when in danger of being totally expelled by a foreign power, and of either ending his life miserably in prison, or seeking shelter as a fugitive from the pursuit of his enemies.

The prejudices against this prince were so violent, that he was believed to have sent an embassy to the Miramoulin or emperor of Morocco, and to have offered to change his religion and become Mahometan, in order to purchase the protection of that monarch. But though this story is told us, on plausible authority, by Matthew Paris,[k] it is in itself utterly improbable; except, that there is nothing so incredible but may be believed to proceed from the folly and wickedness of John.

The monks throw great reproaches on this prince for his impiety and even infidelity; and as an instance of it, they tell us, that, having one day caught a very fat stag, he exclaimed, *How plump and well fed is this animal! and yet I dare swear, he never heard mass.*[l] This sally of wit, upon the usual corpulency of the priests, more than all his enormous crimes and iniquities, made him pass with them for an atheist.

John left two legitimate sons behind him, Henry, born on the first of October, 1207, and now nine years of age; and Richard, born on the sixth of January, 1209; and three daughters, Jane afterwards married to Alexander king of Scots; Eleanor married first to William Mareschal the younger, earl of Pembroke, and then to Simon Mountfort, earl of Leicester; and Isabella married to the emperor Frederic II. All these children were born to him by Isabella of Angoulesme, his second wife. His illegitimate children were numerous; but none of them were any wise distinguished.

It was this king, who, in the ninth year of his reign, first gave by charter to the city of London, the right of electing annually a

[k] P. 169. [l] M. Paris, 170.

mayor out of its own body, an office which was till now held for life. He gave the city also power to elect and remove its sheriffs at pleasure, and its common-council-men annually. London bridge was finished in this reign: The former bridge was of wood. Maud the empress was the first that built a stone bridge in England.

APPENDIX II
THE FEUDAL
AND ANGLO-NORMAN
GOVERNMENT
AND MANNERS

Origin of the feudal law –
Its progress – Feudal government of England –
The feudal parliament – The commons –
Judicial power – Revenue of the crown –
Commerce – The church –
Civil Laws – Manners

THE FEUDAL LAW is the chief foundation, both of the political government and of the jurisprudence, established by the Normans in England. Our subject therefore requires, that we should form a just idea of this law, in order to explain the state, as well of that kingdom, as of all other kingdoms of Europe, which, during those ages, were governed by similar institutions. And though I am sensible, that I must here repeat many observations and reflections, which have been communicated by others;[m] yet, as every book, agreeably to the observation of a great historian,[n] should be as complete as possible within itself, and should never refer, for any thing material, to other books, it will be necessary, in this place, to deliver a short plan of that prodigious fabric, which,

[m] L'Esprit de Loix. Dr. Robertson's History of Scotland.   [n] Padre Paolo Hist. Conc. Trid.

for several centuries, preserved such a mixture of liberty and oppression, order and anarchy, stability and revolution, as was never experienced in any other age or any other part of the world.

Origin of the feudal law. After the northern nations had subdued the provinces of the Roman empire, they were obliged to establish a system of government, which might secure their conquests, as well against the revolt of their numerous subjects, who remained in the provinces, as from the inroads of other tribes, who might be tempted to ravish from them their new acquisitions. The great change of circumstances made them here depart from those institutions, which prevailed among them, while they remained in the forests of Germany; yet was it still natural for them to retain, in their present settlement, as much of their ancient customs as was compatible with their new situation.

The German governments, being more a confederacy of independant warriors, than a civil subjection, derived their principal force from many inferior and voluntary associations, which individuals formed under a particular head or chieftain, and which it became the highest point of honour to maintain with inviolable fidelity. The glory of the chief consisted in the number, the bravery, and the zealous attachment of his retainers: The duty of the retainers required, that they should accompany their chief in all wars and dangers, that they should fight and perish by his side, and that they should esteem his renown or his favour a sufficient recompence for all their services.[*o*] The prince himself was nothing but a great chieftain, who was chosen from among the rest, on account of his superior valour or nobility; and who derived his power from the voluntary association or attachment of the other chieftains.

When a tribe governed by these ideas, and actuated by these principles, subdued a large territory, they found, that, though it was necessary to keep themselves in a military posture, they could neither remain united in a body, nor take up their quarters in several garrisons, and that their manners and institutions debarred them from using these expedients; the obvious ones, which, in a like situation, would have been employed by a more civilized nation. Their ignorance in the art of finances, and perhaps the devastations inseparable from such violent conquests,

[*o*] Tacit. de Mor. Germ.

rendered it impracticable for them to levy taxes sufficient for the pay of numerous armies; and their repugnance to subordination, with their attachment to rural pleasures, made the life of the camp or garrison, if perpetuated during peaceful times, extremely odious and disgustful to them. They seized, therefore, such a portion of the conquered lands as appeared necessary; they assigned a share for supporting the dignity of their prince and government; they distributed other parts, under the title of fiefs, to the chiefs; these made a new partition among their retainers; the express condition of all these grants was, that they might be resumed at pleasure, and that the possessor, so long as he enjoyed them, should still remain in readiness to take the field for the defence of the nation. And though the conquerors immediately separated, in order to enjoy their new acquisitions, their martial disposition made them readily fulfil the terms of their engagement: They assembled on the first alarm; their habitual attachment to the chieftain made them willingly submit to his command; and thus a regular military force, though concealed, was always ready, to defend, on any emergence, the interest and honour of the community.

We are not to imagine, that all the conquered lands were seized by the northern conquerors; or that the whole of the land thus seized was subjected to those military services. This supposition is confuted by the history of all the nations on the continent. Even the idea, given us of the German manners by the Roman historian, may convince us, that that bold people would never have been content with so precarious a subsistence, or have fought to procure establishments, which were only to continue during the good pleasure of their sovereign. Though the northern chieftains accepted of lands, which, being considered as a kind of military pay, might be resumed at the will of the king or general; they also took possession of estates, which, being hereditary and independant, enabled them to maintain their native liberty, and support, without court-favour, the honour of their rank and family.

But there is a great difference, in the consequences, between the distribution of a pecuniary subsistence, and the assignment of lands burthened with the condition of military service. The delivery of the former, at the weekly, monthly, or annual terms of payment, still recalls the idea of a voluntary gratuity from the *Progress of the feudal law.*

prince, and reminds the soldier of the precarious tenure by which he holds his commission. But the attachment, naturally formed with a fixed portion of land, gradually begets the idea of something like property, and makes the possessor forget his dependant situation, and the condition which was at first annexed to the grant. It seemed equitable, that one who had cultivated and sowed a field, should reap the harvest: Hence fiefs, which were at first entirely precarious, were soon made annual. A man, who had employed his money in building, planting, or other improvements, expected to reap the fruits of his labour or expence: Hence they were next granted during a term of years. It would be thought hard to expel a man from his possessions, who had always done his duty, and performed the conditions on which he originally received them: Hence the chieftains, in a subsequent period, thought themselves entitled to demand the enjoyment of their feudal lands during life. It was found, that a man would more willingly expose himself in battle, if assured, that his family should inherit his possessions, and should not be left by his death in want and poverty: Hence fiefs were made hereditary in families, and descended, during one age, to the son, then to the grandson, next to the brothers, and afterwards to more distant relations.[p] The idea of property stole in gradually upon that of military pay; and each century made some sensible addition to the stability of fiefs and tenures.

In all these successive acquisitions, the chief was supported by his vassals; who, having originally a strong connexion with him, augmented by the constant intercourse of good offices, and by the friendship arising from vicinity and dependance, were inclined to follow their leader against all his enemies, and voluntarily, in his private quarrels, paid him the same obedience, to which by their tenure they were bound in foreign wars. While he daily advanced new pretensions to secure the possession of his superior fief, they expected to find the same advantage, in acquiring stability to their subordinate ones; and they zealously opposed the intrusion of a new lord, who would be inclined, as he was fully intitled, to bestow the possession of their lands on his own favourites and retainers. Thus the authority of the sovereign gradually decayed; and each

[p] Lib. Feud. lib. 1. tit. 1.

APPENDIX II

noble, fortified in his own territory by the attachment of his vassals, became too powerful to be expelled by an order from the
throne; and he secured by law what he had at first acquired by
usurpation.

During this precarious state of the supreme power, a difference
would immediately be experienced between those portions of territory which were subjected to the feudal tenures, and those which
were possessed by an allodial or free title. Though the latter possessions had at first been esteemed much preferable, they were
soon found, by the progressive changes introduced into public and
private law, to be of an inferior condition to the former. The
possessors of a feudal territory, united by a regular subordination
under one chief, and by the mutual attachments of the vassals, had
the same advantages over the proprietors of the other, that a
disciplined army enjoys over a dispersed multitude; and were enabled to commit with impunity all injuries on their defenceless
neighbours. Every one, therefore, hastened to seek that protection
which he found so necessary; and each allodial proprietor, resigning his possessions into the hands of the king, or of some
nobleman respected for power or valour, received them back with
the condition of feudal services;[q] which, though a burden somewhat grievous, brought him ample compensation, by connecting
him with the neighbouring proprietors, and placing him under the
guardianship of a potent chieftain. The decay of the political government thus necessarily occasioned the extension of the feudal:
The kingdoms of Europe were universally divided into baronies,
and these into inferior fiefs: And the attachment of vassals to their
chief, which was at first an essential part of the German manners,
was still supported by the same causes from which it at first arose;
the necessity of mutual protection, and the continued intercourse,
between the head and the members, of benefits and services.

But there was another circumstance, which corroborated these
feudal dependancies, and tended to connect the vassals with their
superior lord by an indissoluble bond of union. The northern
conquerors, as well as the more early Greeks and Romans, embraced a policy, which is unavoidable to all nations that have made
slender advances in refinement: They every where united the civil

[q] Marculf. Form. 47. apud Lindenbr. p. 1238.

jurisdiction with the military power. Law, in its commencement, was not an intricate science, and was more governed by maxims of equity, which seem obvious to common sense, than by numerous and subtile principles, applied to a variety of cases by profound reasonings from analogy. An officer, though he had passed his life in the field, was able to determine all legal controversies which could occur within the district committed to his charge; and his decisions were the most likely to meet with a prompt and ready obedience, from men who respected his person, and were accustomed to act under his command. The profit, arising from punishments, which were then chiefly pecuniary, was another reason for his desiring to retain the judicial power; and when his fief became hereditary, this authority, which was essential to it, was also transmitted to his posterity. The counts and other magistrates, whose power was merely official, were tempted, in imitation of the feudal lords, whom they resembled in so many particulars, to render their dignity perpetual and hereditary; and in the decline of the regal power, they found no difficulty in making good their pretensions. After this manner the vast fabric of feudal subordination became quite solid and comprehensive; it formed every where an essential part of the political constitution; and the Norman and other barons, who followed the fortunes of William, were so accustomed to it, that they could scarcely form an idea of any other species of civil government.[r]

The Saxons, who conquered England, as they exterminated the ancient inhabitants, and thought themselves secured by the sea against new invaders, found it less requisite to maintain themselves in a military posture: The quantity of land, which they annexed to offices, seems to have been of small value; and for that reason continued the longer in its original situation, and was always possessed during pleasure by those who were intrusted with the command. These conditions were too precarious to satisfy the Norman barons, who enjoyed more independant possessions and jurisdictions in their own country; and William was obliged, in the new distribution of land, to copy the tenures, which were now become

---

[r] The ideas of the feudal government were so rooted, that even lawyers, in those ages, could not form a notion of any other constitution. *Regnum* (says Bracton, lib. 2. cap. 34.) *quod ex comitabus & baronibus dicitur esse constitutum.*

APPENDIX II

universal on the continent. England of a sudden became a feudal kingdom;[s] and received all the advantages, and was exposed to all the inconveniencies, incident to that species of civil polity.

According to the principles of the feudal law, the king was the supreme lord of the landed property: All possessors, who enjoyed the fruits or revenue of any part of it, held those privileges, either mediately or immediately, of him; and their property was conceived to be, in some degree, conditional.[t] The land was still apprehended to be a species of *benefice,* which was the original conception of a feudal property; and the vassal owed, in return for it, stated services to his baron, as the baron himself did for his land to the crown. The vassal was obliged to defend his baron in war; and the baron, at the head of his vassals, was bound to fight in defence of the king and kingdom. But besides these military services, which were casual, there were others imposed of a civil nature, which were more constant and durable.

The northern nations had no idea, that any man, trained up to honour, and enured to arms, was ever to be governed, without his own consent, by the absolute will of another; or that the administration of justice was ever to be exercised by the private opinion of any one magistrate, without the concurrence of some other persons, whose interest might induce them to check his arbitrary and iniquitous decisions. The king, therefore, when he found it necessary to demand any service of his barons or chief tenants, beyond what was due by their tenures, was obliged to assemble them, in order to obtain their *consent:* And when it was necessary to determine any controversy, which might arise among the barons themselves, the question must be discussed in their presence, and be decided according to their opinion or *advice.* In these two circumstances of consent and advice, consisted chiefly the civil services of the ancient barons; and these implied all the considerable incidents of government. In one view, the barons regarded this attendance as their principal *privilege;* in another, as a grievous *burden.* That no momentous affairs could be transacted without their consent and advice, was in *general* esteemed the great security of their possessions and dignities: But as they reaped no immediate profit

The feudal government of England.

---

[s] Coke Comm. on Lit. p. 1, 2, ad sect. 1.   [t] Somner of Gavelk. p. 109. Smith de Rep. lib. 3. cap. 10.

from their attendance at court, and were exposed to great inconvenience and charge by an absence from their own estates, every one was glad to exempt himself from each *particular* exertion of this power; and was pleased both that the call for that duty should seldom return upon him, and that others should undergo the burden in his stead. The king, on the other hand, was usually anxious, for several reasons, that the assembly of the barons should be full at every stated or casual meeting: This attendance was the chief badge of their subordination to his crown, and drew them from that independance which they were apt to affect in their own castles and manors; and where the meeting was thin or ill attended, its determinations had less authority, and commanded not so ready an obedience from the whole community.

The case was the same with the barons in their courts as with the king in the supreme council of the nation. It was requisite to assemble the vassals, in order to determine by their vote any question which regarded the barony; and they sat along with the chief in all trials, whether civil or criminal, which occurred within the limits of their jurisdiction. They were bound to pay suit and service at the court of their baron; and as their tenure was military, and consequently honourable, they were admitted into his society, and partook of his friendship. Thus, a kingdom was considered only as a great barony, and a barony as a small kingdom. The barons were peers to each other in the national council, and, in some degree, companions to the king: The vassals were peers to each other in the court of barony, and companions to their baron.[u]

But though this resemblance so far took place, the vassals, by the natural course of things, universally, in the feudal constitutions, fell into a greater subordination under the baron, than the baron himself under his sovereign; and these governments had a necessary and infallible tendency to augment the power of the nobles. The great chief, residing in his country-seat, which he was commonly allowed to fortify, lost, in a great measure, his connexion or acquaintance with the prince; and added every day new force to his authority over the vassals of the barony. They received

---

[u] Du Cange Gloss. in verb. *Par.* Cujac. Commun. in Lib. Feud. lib. 1. tit. p. 18. Spelm. Gloss. in verb.

from him education in all military exercises: His hospitality invited them to live and enjoy society in his hall: Their leisure, which was great, made them perpetual retainers on his person, and partakers of his country sports and amusements: They had no means of gratifying their ambition but by making a figure in his train: His favour and countenance was their greatest honour: His displeasure exposed them to contempt and ignominy: And they felt every moment the necessity of his protection, both in the controversies which occurred with other vassals, and what was more material, in the daily inroads and injuries which were committed by the neighbouring barons. During the time of general war, the sovereign, who marched at the head of his armies, and was the great protector of the state, always acquired some accession to his authority, which he lost during the intervals of peace and tranquility: But the loose police, incident to the feudal constitutions, maintained a perpetual, though secret hostility, between the several members of the state; and the vassals found no means of securing themselves against the injuries, to which they were continually exposed, but by closely adhering to their chief, and falling into a submissive dependance upon him.

If the feudal government was so little favourable to the true liberty even of the military vassal, it was still more destructive of the independance and security of the other members of the state, or what in a proper sense we call the people. A great part of them were *serfs*, and lived in a state of absolute slavery or villainage: The other inhabitants of the country paid their rent in services, which were in a great measure arbitrary; and they could expect no redress of injuries, in a court of barony, from men, who thought they had a right to oppress and tyrannize over them: The towns were situated either within the demesnes of the king, or the lands of the great barons, and were almost entirely subjected to the absolute will of their master. The languishing state of commerce kept the inhabitants poor and contemptible; and the political institutions were calculated to render that poverty perpetual. The barons and gentry, living in rustic plenty and hospitality, gave no encouragement to the arts, and had no demand for any of the more elaborate manufactures: Every profession was held in contempt but that of arms: And if any merchant or manufacturer rose by industry and frugality to a degree of opulence, he found himself but the more exposed to injuries, from the envy and avidity of the military nobles.

These concurring causes gave the feudal governments so strong a bias towards aristocracy, that the royal authority was extremely eclipsed in all the European states, and, instead of dreading the growth of monarchical power, we might rather expect, that the community would every where crumble into so many independant baronies, and lose the political union, by which they were cemented. In elective monarchies, the event was commonly answerable to this expectation; and the barons, gaining ground on every vacancy of the throne, raised themselves almost to a state of sovereignty, and sacrificed to their power both the rights of the crown and the liberties of the people. But hereditary monarchies had a principle of authority, which was not so easily subverted; and there were several causes, which still maintained a degree of influence in the hands of the sovereign.

The greatest baron could never lose view entirely of those principles of the feudal constitution, which bound him, as a vassal, to submission and fealty towards his prince; because he was every moment obliged to have recourse to those principles, in exacting fealty and submission from his own vassals. The lesser barons, finding that the annihilation of royal authority left them exposed without protection to the insults and injuries of more potent neighbours, naturally adhered to the crown, and promoted the execution of general and equal laws. The people had still a stronger interest to desire the grandeur of the sovereign; and the king, being the legal magistrate, who suffered by every internal convulsion or oppression, and who regarded the great nobles as his immediate rivals, assumed the salutary office of general guardian or protector of the commons. Besides the prerogatives, with which the law invested him; his large demesnes and numerous retainers rendered him, in one sense, the greatest baron in his kingdom; and where he was possessed of personal vigour and abilities (for his situation required these advantages) he was commonly able to preserve his authority, and maintain his station as head of the community, and the chief fountain of law and justice.

The first kings of the Norman race were favoured by another circumstance, which preserved them from the encroachments of

APPENDIX II

their barons. They were generals of a conquering army, which was obliged to continue in a military posture, and to maintain great subordination under their leader, in order to secure themselves from the revolt of the numerous natives, whom they had bereaved of all their properties and privileges. But though this circumstance supported the authority of William and his immediate successors, and rendered them extremely absolute, it was lost as soon as the Norman barons began to incorporate with the nation, to acquire a security in their possessions, and to fix their influence over their vassals, tenants, and slaves. And the immense fortunes, which the Conqueror had bestowed on his chief captains, served to support their independance, and make them formidable to the sovereign.

He gave, for instance, to Hugh de Abrincis, his sister's son, the whole county of Chester, which he erected into a palatinate, and rendered by his grant almost independant of the crown.[w] Robert, earl of Mortaigne had 973 manors and lordships: Allan, earl of Britanny and Richmond, 442: Odo, bishop of Baieux, 439:[x] Geoffrey, bishop of Coutance, 280:[y] Walter Giffard, earl of Buckingham, 107: William, earl Warrenne, 298, besides 28 towns or hamlets in Yorkshire: Todenei, 81: Roger Bigod, 123: Robert, earl of Eu, 119: Roger Mortimer, 132, besides several hamlets: Robert de Stafford, 130: Walter de Eurus, earl of Salisbury, 46: Geoffrey de Mandeville, 118: Richard de Clare, 171: Hugh de Beauchamp, 47: Baldwin de Ridvers, 164: Henry de Ferrers, 222: William de Percy, 119:[z] Norman d'Arcy, 33.[a] Sir Henry Spelman computes, that, in the large county of Norfolk, there were not, in the Conqueror's time, above sixty-six proprietors of land.[b] Men, possessed of such princely revenues and jurisdictions, could not long be retained in the rank of subjects. The great earl Warrenne, in a subsequent reign, when he was questioned concerning his right to the lands which he possessed, drew his sword, which he produced as his title; adding, that William the Bastard did not conquer the

---

[w] Cambd. in Chesh. Spel. Gloss. in verb. *Comes Palatinut.* [x] Brady's Hist. p. 198, 200. [y] Order. Vital. [z] Dugdale's Baronage, from Domesday-book, vol. i. p. 60, 74, iii, 112, 132, 136, 138, 156, 174, 200, 207, 223, 254, 257, 269. [a] Ibid. p. 369. It is remarkable that this family of d'Arcy, seems to be the only male descendants of any of the Conqueror's barons now remaining among the peers. Lord Holdernesse is the heir of that family. [b] Spel. Gloss. in verb. *Domesday.*

kingdom himself; but that the barons, and his ancestor among the rest, were joint adventurers in the enterprize.[c]

The feudal parliament. The supreme legislative power of England was lodged in the king and great council, or what was afterwards called the parliament. It is not doubted but the archbishops, bishops, and most considerable abbots were constituent members of this council. They sat by a double title: By prescription, as having always possessed that privilege, through the whole Saxon period, from the first establishment of Christianity; and by their right of baronage, as holding of the king *in capite* by military service. These two titles of the prelates were never accurately distinguished. When the usurpations of the church had risen to such a height, as to make the bishops affect a separate dominion, and regard their seat in parliament as a degradation of their episcopal dignity; the king insisted, that they were barons, and, on that account, obliged, by the general principles of the feudal law, to attend on him in his great councils.[d] Yet there still remained some practices, which supposed their title to be derived merely from ancient possession: When a bishop was elected, he sat in parliament before the king had made him restitution of his temporalities; and during the vacancy of a see, the guardian of the spiritualities was summoned to attend along with the bishops.

The barons were another constituent part of the great council of the nation. These held immediately of the crown by a military tenure: They were the most honourable members of the state, and had a *right* to be consulted in all public deliberations: They were the immediate vassals of the crown, and owed as a *service* their attendance in the court of their supreme lord. A resolution, taken without their consent, was likely to be but ill executed: And no determination of any cause or controversy among them had any validity, where the vote and advice of the body did not concur. The dignity of earl or count was official and territorial, as well as hereditary; and as all the earls were also barons, they were considered as military vassals of the crown, were admitted in that capacity into the general council, and formed the most honourable and powerful branch of it.

[c] Dug. Bar. vol. i. p. 79. Ibid. Origines Juridicales, p. 13.   [d] Spel. Gloss. in verb. *Baro.*

APPENDIX II

But there was another class of the immediate military tenants of the crown, no less or probably more numerous than the barons, the tenants *in capite* by knights service; and these, however inferior in power or property, held by a tenure, which was equally honourable with that of the others. A barony was commonly composed of several knights fees: And though the number seems not to have been exactly defined, seldom consisted of less than fifty hydes of land:[f] But where a man held of the king only one or two knights fees, he was still an immediate vassal of the crown, and as such had a title to have a seat in the general councils. But as this attendance was usually esteemed a burthen, and one too great for a man of slender fortune to bear constantly; it is probable, that, though he had a title, if he pleased, to be admitted, he was not obliged, by any penalty, like the barons, to pay a regular attendance. All the immediate military tenants of the crown amounted not fully to 700, when Domesday-book was framed; and as the members were well pleased, on any pretext, to excuse themselves from attendance, the assembly was never likely to become too numerous for the dispatch of public business.

So far the nature of a general council or ancient parliament is determined without any doubt or controversy. The only question seems to be with regard to the commons, or the representatives of counties and boroughs; whether they were also, in more early times, constituent parts of parliament? This question was once disputed in England with great acrimony: But such is the force of time and evidence, that they can sometimes prevail even over faction; and the question seems, by general consent, and even by their own, to be at last determined against the ruling party. It is agreed, that the commons were no part of the great council, till some ages after the conquest; and that the military tenants alone of the crown composed that supreme and legislative assembly.

The commons.

The vassals of a baron were by their tenure immediately dependant on him, owed attendance at his court, and paid all their duty to the king, through that dependance which their lord was

---

[f] Four hydes made one knight's fee: The relief of a barony was twelve times greater than that of a knight's fee; whence we may conjecture its usual value. Spelm. Gloss. in verb. *Feodum.* There were 243,600 hydes in England, and 60,215 knights fees; whence it is evident that there were a little more than four hydes in each knight's fee.

obliged by *his* tenure to acknowledge to his sovereign and superior. Their land, comprehended in the barony, was represented in parliament by the baron himself, who was supposed, according to the fictions of the feudal law, to possess the direct property of it; and it would have been deemed incongruous to give it any other representation. They stood in the same capacity to him, that he and the other barons did to the king: The former were peers of the barony; the latter were peers of the realm: The vassals possessed a subordinate rank within their district; the baron enjoyed a superior dignity in the great assembly: They were in some degree his companions at home; he the king's companion at court: And nothing can be more evidently repugnant to all feudal ideas, and to that gradual subordination, which was essential to those ancient institutions, than to imagine that the king would apply either for the advice or consent of men, who were of a rank so much inferior, and whose duty was immediately paid to the *mesne* lord, that was interposed between them and the throne.[f]

If it be unreasonable to think, that the vassals of a barony, though their tenure was military and noble and honourable, were ever summoned to give their opinion in national councils, much less can it be supposed, that the tradesmen or inhabitants of boroughs, whose condition was so much inferior, would be admitted to that privilege. It appears from Domesday, that the greatest boroughs were, at the time of the conquest, scarcely more than country villages; and that the inhabitants lived in entire dependance on the king or great lords, and were of a station little better than servile.[g] They were not then so much as incorporated; they formed no community; were not regarded as a body politic; and being really nothing but a number of low dependant tradesmen, living, without any particular civil tie, in neighbourhood together, they were incapable of being represented in the states of the kingdom. Even in France, a country which made more early advances in arts and civility than England, the first corporation is sixty years posterior to the conquest under the duke of Normandy; and the erecting of these communities was an invention of Lewis

[f] Spelm. Gloss. in verb. *Baro.* [g] *Liber homo* anciently signified a gentleman: For scarce any one beside was entirely free. Spelm. Gloss. in verbo.

APPENDIX II

the Gross, in order to free the people from slavery under the lords, and to give them protection, by means of certain privileges and a separate jurisdiction.[h] An ancient French writer calls them a new and wicked device, to procure liberty to slaves, and encourage them in shaking off the dominion of their masters.[i] The famous charter, as it is called, of the Conqueror to the city of London, though granted at a time when he assumed the appearance of gentleness and lenity, is nothing but a letter of protection, and a declaration that the citizens should not be treated as slaves.[k] By the English feudal law, the superior lord was prohibited from marrying his female ward to a burgess or a villain;[l] so near were these two ranks esteemed to each other, and so much inferior to the nobility and gentry. Besides possessing the advantages of birth, riches, civil powers and privileges, the nobles and gentlemen alone were armed; a circumstance, which gave them a mighty superiority, in an age when nothing but the military profession was honourable, and when the loose execution of laws gave so much encouragement to open violence, and rendered it so decisive in all disputes and controversies.[m]

The great similarity among the feudal governments of Europe is well known to every man, that has any acquaintance with ancient history; and the antiquaries of all foreign countries, where the question was never embarrassed by party disputes, have allowed, that the commons came very late to be admitted to a share in the legislative power. In Normandy particularly, whose constitution was most likely to be William's model in raising his new fabric of English government, the states were entirely composed of the clergy and nobility; and the first incorporated boroughs or communities of that dutchy were Roüen and Falaise, which enjoyed their privileges by a grant of Philip Augustus in the year 1207.[n] All the ancient English historians, when they mention the great council of the nation, call it an assembly of the baronage, nobility, or great men; and none of their expressions, though several hundred passages might be produced, can, without the utmost violence, be

[h] Du Cange's Gloss. in verb. *commune, communitas.*   [i] Guibertus, de vita sua, lib. 3. cap. 7.   [k] Stat. of Merton, 1235. cap. 6.   [l] Holingshed, vol. iii. p. 15.   [m] Madox's Baron. Angl. p. 19.   [n] Norman. Du Chesnii, p. 1066. Du Cange Gloss. in verb. *commune.*

tortured to a meaning, which will admit the commons to be constituent members of that body.⁰ If in the long period of 200 years,
which elapsed between the Conquest and the latter end of Henry
III. and which abounded in factions, revolutions, and convulsions
of all kinds, the house of commons never performed one single
legislative act, so considerable as to be once mentioned by any of
the numerous historians of that age, they must have been totally
insignificant: And in that case, what reason can be assigned for
their ever being assembled? Can it be supposed, that men of so
little weight or importance possessed a negative voice against the
king and the barons? Every page of the subsequent histories dis-
covers their existence; though these histories are not written with
greater accuracy than the preceding ones, and indeed scarcely
equal them in that particular. The *Magna Charta* of king John
provides, that no scutage or aid should be imposed, either on the
land or towns, but by consent of the great council; and for more
security, it enumerates the persons entitled to a seat in that assembly, the prelates and immediate tenants of the crown, without any
mention of the commons: An authority so full, certain, and explic-
ite, that nothing but the zeal of party could ever have procured
credit to any contrary hypothesis.

It was probably the example of the French barons, which first
emboldened the English to require greater independance from
their sovereign: It is also probable, that the boroughs and corporations of England were established in imitation of those of
France. It may, therefore, be proposed as no unlikely conjecture,

---

⁰ Sometimes the historians mention the people, *populus*, as a part of the
parliament: But they always mean the laity, in opposition to the clergy.
Sometimes, the word, *communitas*, is found; but it always means *communitas
baronagii*. These points are clearly proved by Dr. Brady. There is also
mention sometimes made of a crowd or multitude that thronged into the
great council on particular interesting occasions; but as deputies from
boroughs are never once spoke of, the proof, that they had not then any
existence, becomes the most certain and undeniable. These never could
make a crowd, as they must have had a regular place assigned them, if they
had made a regular part of the legislative body. There were only 130
boroughs who received writs of summons from Edward I. It is expressly
said in Gesta Reg. Steph. p. 932, that it was usual for the populace, *vulgus*,
to crowd into the great councils; where they were plainly mere spectators,
and could only gratify their curiosity.

APPENDIX II

that both the chief privileges of the peers in England and the liberty of the commons were originally the growth of that foreign country.

In ancient times, men were little solicitous to obtain a place in the legislative assemblies; and rather regarded their attendance as a burden, which was not compensated by any return of profit or honour, proportionate to the trouble and expence. The only reason for instituting those public councils, was; on the part of the subject, that they desired some security from the attempts of arbitrary power; and on the part of the sovereign, that he despaired of governing men of such independant spirits without their own consent and concurrence. But the commons, or the inhabitants of boroughs, had not as yet reached such a degree of consideration, as to desire *security* against their prince, or to imagine, that, even if they were assembled in a representative body, they had power or rank sufficient to enforce it. The only protection, which they aspired to, was against the immediate violence and injustice of their fellow-citizens; and this advantage each of them looked for, from the courts of justice, or from the authority of some great lord, to whom, by law or his own choice, he was attached. On the other hand, the sovereign was sufficiently assured of obedience in the whole community, if he procured the concurrence of the nobles; nor had he reason to apprehend, that any order of the state could resist his and their united authority. The military sub-vassals could entertain no idea of opposing both their prince and their superiors: The burgesses and tradesmen could much less aspire to such a thought: And thus, even if history were silent on the head, we have reason to conclude, from the known situation of society during those ages, that the commons were never admitted as members of the legislative body.

The *executive* power of the Anglo-Norman government was lodged in the king. Besides the stated meetings of the national council at the three great festivals of Christmas, Easter, and Whitsuntide,[p] he was accustomed, on any sudden exigence, to summon them together. He could at his pleasure command the attendance of his barons and their vassals, in which consisted the military force of the kingdom; and could employ them, during forty days, either

[p] Dugd. Orig. Jurid. p. 15. Spelm. Gloss. in verbo *parliamentum*.

in resisting a foreign enemy, or reducing his rebellious subjects. And what was of great importance, the whole *judicial* power was ultimately in his hands, and was exercised by officers and ministers of his appointment.

Judicial power. The general plan of the Anglo-Norman government was, that the court of barony was appointed to decide such controversies as arose between the several vassals or subjects of the same barony; the hundred-court and county-court, which were still continued as during the Saxon times,[q] to judge between the subjects of different baronies,[r] and the *curia Regis* or king's court, to give sentence among the barons themselves.[s] But this plan, though simple, was attended with some circumstances, which, being derived from a very extensive authority, assumed by the Conqueror, contributed to increase the royal prerogative; and as long as the state was not disturbed by arms, reduced every order of the community to some degree of dependance and subordination.

The king himself often sat in his court, which always attended his person:[t] He there heard causes and pronounced judgment;[u] and though he was assisted by the advice of the other members, it is not to be imagined that a decision could easily be obtained contrary to his inclination or opinion. In his absence the chief justiciary presided, who was the first magistrate in the state, and a kind of viceroy, on whom depended all the civil affairs of the kingdom.[w] The other chief officers of the crown, the constable,

[q] Ang. Sacra, vol. i. p. 334, &c. Dugd. Orig. Jurid. p. 27, 29. Madox Hist. of Exch. p. 75, 76. Spelm. Gloss. in verbo *hundred*.   [r] None of the feudal governments in Europe had such institutions as the county-courts, which the great authority of the Conqueror still retained from the Saxon customs. All the freeholders of the county, even the greatest barons, were obliged to attend the sheriffs in these courts, and to assist them in the administration of justice. By this means, they received frequent and sensible admonitions of their dependance on the king or supreme magistrate: They formed a kind of community with their fellow barons and freeholders: They were often drawn from their individual and independant state, peculiar to the feudal system; and were made members of a political body: And perhaps, this institution of county-courts in England has had greater effects on the government than has yet been distinctly pointed out by historians or traced by antiquaries. The barons were never able to free themselves from this attendance on the sheriffs and itinerant justices till the reign of Henry III.   [s] Brady Pref. p. 143.   [t] Madox Hist. of Exch. p. 103.   [u] Bracton, lib. 3. cap. 9. § I. cap. 10. § I.   [w] Spelm. Gloss. in verbo *justiciarii*.

mareschal, seneschal, chamberlain, treasurer, and chancellor,[x] were members, together with such feudal barons as thought proper to attend, and the barons of the exchequer, who at first were also feudal barons, appointed by the king.[y] This court, which was sometimes called the King's court, sometimes the court of Exchequer, judged in all causes, civil and criminal, and comprehended the whole business, which is now shared out among four courts, the Chancery, the King's Bench, the Common Pleas, and the Exchequer.[z]

Such an accumulation of powers was itself a great source of authority, and rendered the jurisdiction of the court formidable to all the subjects; but the turn, which judicial trials took soon after the Conquest, served still more to increase its authority, and to augment the royal prerogatives. William, among the other violent changes, which he attempted and effected, had introduced the Norman law into England,[a] had ordered all the pleadings to be in that tongue, and had interwoven, with the English jurisprudence, all the maxims and principles, which the Normans, more advanced in cultivation, and naturally litigious, were accustomed to observe in the distribution of justice. Law now became a science, which at first fell entirely into the hands of the Normans; and which, even after it was communicated to the English, required so much study and application, that the laity, in those ignorant ages, were incapable of attaining it, and it was a mystery almost solely confined to the clergy, and chiefly to the monks.[b] The great officers of the crown and the feudal barons, who were military men, found themselves unfit to penetrate into those obscurities; and though they were entitled to a seat in the supreme judicature, the business of the court was wholly managed by the chief justiciary and the law barons, who were men appointed by the king, and entirely at his disposal.[c] This natural course of things was forwarded by the multiplicity of business, which flowed into that court, and which daily augmented by the appeals from all the subordinate judicatures of the kingdom.

[x] Madox Hist. Exch. p. 27, 29, 33, 38, 41, 54. The Normans introduced the practice of sealing charters; and the chancellor's office was to keep the Great Seal. *Ingulph. Dudg.* p. 33, 34.　[y] Madox Hist. of the Exch. p. 134, 135. Gerv. Dorob. p. 1387.　[z] Madox Hist. of the Exch. p. 56, 70.　[a] Dial. de Scac. p. 30. apud Madox Hist. of the Exchequer.　[b] Malmes. lib. 4. p. 123.　[c] Dugd. Orig. Jurid. p. 25.

In the Saxon times, no appeal was received in the king's court, except upon the denial or delay of justice by the inferior courts; and the same practice was still observed in most of the feudal kingdoms of Europe. But the great power of the Conqueror established at first in England an authority, which the monarchs in France were not able to attain till the reign of St. Lewis, who lived near two centuries after: He empowered his court to receive appeals both from the courts of barony and the county-courts, and by that means brought the administration of justice ultimately into the hands of the sovereign.[d] And lest the expence or trouble of a journey to court should discourage suitors, and make them acquiesce in the decision of the inferior judicatures, itinerant judges were afterwards established, who made their circuits throughout the kingdom, and tried all causes that were brought before them.[e] By this expedient, the courts of barony were kept in awe; and if they still preserved some influence, it was only from the apprehensions, which the vassals might entertain, of disobliging their superior, by appealing from his jurisdiction. But the county-courts were much discredited; and as the freeholders were found ignorant of the intricate principles and forms of the new law, the lawyers gradually brought all business before the king's judges, and abandoned the ancient simple and popular judicature. After this manner, the formalities of justice, which, though they appear tedious and cumbersome, are found requisite to the support of liberty in all monarchical governments, proved at first, by a combination of causes, very advantageous to royal authority in England.

Revenue of the crown. The power of the Norman kings was also much supported by a great revenue; and by a revenue, that was fixed, perpetual, and independant of the subject. The people, without betaking themselves to arms, had no check upon the king, and no regular security for the due administration of justice. In those days of violence,

[d] Madox Hist. of the Exch. p. 65. Glanv. lib. 12. cap. 1. 7. LL. Hen. I. § 31. apud Wilkins, p. 248. Fitz Stephens, p. 36. Coke's Comment. on the Statute of Mulbridge, cap. 20.   [e] Madox Hist. of the Exch. p. 83, 84, 100. Gerv. Dorob. p. 1410. What made the Anglo-Norman barons more readily submit to appeals from their court to the King's court of Exchequer, was, their being accustomed to like appeals in Normandy to the ducal court of Exchequer. See Gilbert's History of the Exchequer, p. 1, 2.; though the author thinks it doubtful, whether the Norman court was not rather copied from the English, p. 6.

many instances of oppression passed unheeded; and soon after were openly pleaded as precedents, which it was unlawful to dispute or controul. Princes and ministers were too ignorant to be themselves sensible of the advantages attending an equitable administration; and there was no established council or assembly which could protect the people, and, by withdrawing supplies, regularly and peaceably admonish the king of his duty, and ensure the execution of the laws.

The first branch of the king's stated revenue was the royal demesnes or crown-lands, which were very extensive, and comprehended, beside a great number of manors, most of the chief cities of the kingdom. It was established by law, that the king could alienate no part of his demesne, and that he himself, or his successor, could, at any time, resume such donations:[f] But this law was never regularly observed; which happily rendered in time the crown somewhat more dependant. The rent of the crown-lands, considered merely as so much riches, was a source of power: The influence of the king over his tenants and the inhabitants of his towns, encreased this power: But the other numerous branches of his revenue, besides supplying his treasury, gave, by their very nature, a great latitude to arbitrary authority, and were a support of the prerogative; as will appear from an enumeration of them.

The king was never content with the stated rents, but levied heavy talliages at pleasure on the inhabitants both of town and country, who lived within his demesne. All bargains of sale, in order to prevent theft, being prohibited, except in boroughs and public markets,[g] he pretended to exact tolls on all goods which were there sold.[h] He seized two hogsheads, one before and one behind the mast, from every vessel that imported wine. All goods payed to his customs a proportional part of their value:[i] Passage over bridges and on rivers was loaded with tolls at pleasure:[k] And though the boroughs by degrees brought the liberty of farming these impositions, yet the revenue profited by these bargains, new sums were often exacted for the renewal and confirmation of their

---

[f] Fleta, lib. 1. cap. 8. § 17. lib. 3. cap. 6. § 3. Bracton, lib. 2. cap. 5. [g] LL. Will. I. cap. 61. [h] Madox, p. 530. [i] Ibid. p. 529. This author says a fifteenth. But it is not easy to reconcile this account to other authorities. [k] Madox, p. 529.

charters,[l] and the people were thus held in perpetual dependance.

Such was the situation of the inhabitants within the royal demesnes. But the possessors of land, or the military tenants, though they were better protected, both by law, and by the great privilege of carrying arms, were, from the nature of their tenures, much exposed to the inroads of power, and possessed not what we should esteem in our age a very durable security. The Conqueror ordained, that the barons should be obliged to pay nothing beyond their stated services,[m] except a reasonable aid to ransom his person if he were taken in war, to make his eldest son a knight, and to marry his eldest daughter. What should, on these occasions, be deemed a reasonable aid, was not determined; and the demands of the crown were so far discretionary.

The king could require in war the personal attendance of his vassals, that is, of almost all the landed proprietors; and if they declined the service, they were obliged to pay him a composition in money, which was called a scutage. The sum was, during some reigns, precarious and uncertain; it was sometimes levied without allowing the vassal the liberty of personal service;[n] and it was a usual artifice of the king's to pretend an expedition, that he might be entitled to levy the scutage from his military tenants. Danegelt was another species of land-tax levied by the early Norman kings, arbitrarily, and contrary to the laws of the Conqueror.[o] Moneyage was also a general land-tax of the same nature, levied by the two first Norman kings, and abolished by the charter of Henry I.[p] It was a shilling paid every three years by each hearth, to induce the king not to use his prerogative in debasing the coin. Indeed, it appears from that charter, that, though the Conqueror had granted his military tenants an immunity from all taxes and talliages, he and his son William had never thought themselves bound to observe that rule, but had levied impositions at pleasure on all the landed estates of the kingdom. The utmost that Henry grants, is, that the land cultivated by the military tenant himself shall not be so burdened; but he reserves the power of taxing the farmers: And as it is known, that Henry's charter was never observed in any one article, we may be assured, that this prince and

---

[l] Madox's Hist. of the Exch. p. 275, 276, 277, &c.　[m] LL. Will. Conq. § 55.
[n] Gervase de Tilbury, p. 25.　[o] Madox's Hist. of the Exch. p. 475.
[p] Matth. Paris, p. 38.

APPENDIX II

his successors retracted even this small indulgence, and levied arbitrary impositions on all the lands of all their subjects. These taxes were sometimes very heavy; since Malmesbury tells us, that, in the reign of William Rufus, the farmers, on account of them, abandoned tillage, and a famine ensued.[q]

The escheats were a great branch both of power and of revenue, especially during the first reigns after the conquest. In default of posterity from the first baron, his land reverted to the crown, and continually augmented the king's possessions. The prince had indeed by law a power of alienating these escheats; but by this means he had an opportunity of establishing the fortunes of his friends and servants, and thereby enlarging his authority. Sometimes he retained them in his own hands; and they were gradually confounded with the royal demesnes, and became difficult to be distinguished from them. This confusion is probably the reason why the king acquired the right of alienating his demesnes.

But besides escheats from default of heirs, those which ensued from crimes or breach of duty towards the superior lord, were frequent in ancient times. If the vassal, being thrice summoned to attend his superior's court, and do fealty, neglected or refused obedience, he forfeited all title to his land.[r] If he denied his tenure, or refused his service, he was exposed to the same penalty.[s] If he sold his estate without licence from his lord,[t] or if he sold it upon any other tenure or title than that by which he himself held it,[u] he lost all right to it. The adhering to his lord's enemies,[w] deserting him in war,[x] betraying his secrets,[y] debauching his wife or his near relations,[z] or even using indecent freedoms with them,[a] might be punished by forfeiture. The higher crimes, rapes, robbery, murder, arson, &c. were called felony; and being interpreted want of fidelity to his lord, made him lose his fief.[b] Even where the felon was vassal to a baron, though his immediate lord enjoyed the forfeiture, the king might retain possession of his estate during a twelvemonth, and had the right of spoiling and destroying it, unless the baron paid him a reasonable composition.[c] We have not

[q] So also Chron. Abb. St. Petri de Burgo, p. 55. Knyghton, p. 2366. [r] Hottom. de Feud. Disp. cap. 38. col. 886. [s] Lib. Feud. lib. 3. tit. 1.; lib. 4. tit. 21. 39. [t] Lib. Feud. lib. 1. tit. 21. [u] Id. lib. 4. tit. 44. [w] Lib. Feud. lib. 3. tit. 1. [x] Id. lib. 4. tit. 14. 21. [y] Id. lib. 4. tit. 14. [z] Id. lib. 1. tit. 14. 21. [a] Id. lib. 1. tit. 1. [b] Spelm. Gloss. in verb. *Felonia.* [c] Spelm. Gloss. in verb. *Felonia.* Glanville, lib. 7. cap. 17.

here enumerated all the species of felonies, or of crimes by which forfeiture was incurred: We have said enough to prove, that the possession of feudal property was anciently somewhat precarious, and that the primary idea was never lost, of its being a kind of *fee* or *benefice*.

When a baron died, the king immediately took possession of the estate; and the heir, before he recovered his right, was obliged to make application to the crown, and desire that he might be admitted to do homage for his land, and pay a composition to the king. This composition was not at first fixed by law, at least by practice: The king was often exorbitant in his demands, and kept possession of the land till they were complied with.

If the heir were a minor, the king retained the whole profit of the estate till his majority; and might grant what sum he thought proper for the education and maintenance of the young baron. This practice was also founded on the notion, that a fief was a benefice, and that, while the heir could not perform his military services, the revenue devolved to the superior, who employed another in his stead. It is obvious, that a great proportion of the landed property must, by means of this device, be continually in the hands of the prince, and that all the noble families were thereby held in perpetual dependance. When the king granted the wardship of a rich heir to any one, he had the opportunity of enriching a favourite or minister: If he sold it, he thereby levied a considerable sum of money. Simon de Mountfort paid Henry III. 10,000 marks, an immense sum in those days, for the wardship of Gilbert de Umfreville.[d] Geoffrey de Mandeville payed to the same prince the sum of 20,000 marks, that he might marry Isabel countess of Gloucester, and possess all her lands and knights fees. This sum would be equivalent to 300,000, perhaps 400,000 pounds in our time.[e]

If the heir were a female, the king was entitled to offer her any husband of her rank he thought proper; and if she refused him, she forfeited her land. Even a male heir could not marry without the royal consent, and it was usual for men to pay large sums for the liberty of making their own choice in marriage.[f] No man could dispose of his land, either by sale or will, without the consent of his

[d] Madox's Hist. of the Exch. p. 223. [e] Id. p. 322. [f] Id. p. 320.

479

superior. The possessor was never considered as full proprietor: He was still a kind of beneficiary; and could not oblige his superior to accept of any vassal, that was not agreeable to him.

Fines, amerciaments, and oblatas, as they were called, were another considerable branch of the royal power and revenue. The ancient records of the exchequer, which are still preserved, give surprizing accounts of the numerous fines and amerciaments levied in those days,[g] and of the strange inventions fallen upon to exact money from the subject. It appears, that the ancient kings of England put themselves entirely on the foot of the barbarous eastern princes, whom no man must approach without a present, who sell all their good offices, and who intrude themselves into every business, that they may have a pretence for extorting money. Even justice was avowedly bought and sold; the king's court itself, though the supreme judicature of the kingdom, was open to none that brought not presents to the king; the bribes given for the expedition, delay,[h] suspension, and, doubtless, for the perversion of justice, were entered in the public registers of the royal revenue, and remain as monuments of the perpetual iniquity and tyranny of the times. The barons of the exchequer, for instance, the first nobility of the kingdom, were not ashamed to insert, as an article in their records, that the county of Norfolk paid a sum, that they might be fairly dealt with;[i] the borough of Yarmouth, that the king's charters, which they have for their liberties, might not be violated;[k] Richard, son of Gilbert, for the king's helping him to recover his debt from the Jews;[l] Serlo, son of Terlavaston, that he might be permitted to make his defence, in case he were accused of a certain homicide;[m] Walter de Burton for free law, if accused of wounding another;[n] Robert de Essart, for having an inquest to find whether Roger, the butcher, and Wace and Humphrey, accused him of robbery and theft out of envy and ill-will, or not;[o] William Buhurst, for having an inquest to find whether he were accused of the death of one Godwin out of ill-will or for just cause.[p] I have selected these few instances from a great number of a like kind, which Madox had selected from a still greater number, preserved in the ancient rolls of the exchequer.[q]

[g] Id. p. 272. [h] Madox's Hist. of Exch. p. 274, 309. [i] Id. p. 295. [k] Id. ibid. [l] Id. p. 296. He paid 200 marks, a great sum in those days. [m] Id. p. 296. [n] Id. ibid. [o] Id. p. 298. [p] Id. p. 302. [q] Chap. xii.

HISTORY OF ENGLAND

Sometimes the party litigant offered the king a certain portion, a half, a third, a fourth, payable out of the debts, which he, as the executor of justice, should assist him in recovering.[r] Theophania de Westland agreed to pay the half of 212 marks, that she might recover that sum against James de Fughleston;[s] Solomon the Jew engaged to pay one mark out of every seven that he should recover against Hugh de la Hose;[t] Nicholas Morrel promised to pay sixty pounds, that the earl of Flanders might be distrained to pay him 343 pounds, which the earl had taken from him; and these sixty pounds were to be paid out of the first money that Nicholas should recover from the earl.[u]

As the king assumed the entire power over trade, he was to be paid for a permission to exercise commerce or industry of any kind.[w] Hugh Oisel paid 400 marks for liberty to trade in England:[x] Nigel de Havene gave fifty marks for the partnership in merchandize which he had with Gervase de Hanton:[y] The men of Worcester paid 100 shillings, that they might have the liberty of selling and buying dyed cloth, as formerly:[z] Several other towns paid for a like liberty.[a] The commerce indeed of the kingdom was so much under the controul of the king, that he erected gilds, corporations and monopolies, wherever he pleased; and levied sums for these exclusive privileges.[b]

There were no profits so small as to be below the king's attention. Henry, son of Arthur, gave ten dogs, to have a recognition against the countess of Copland for one knight's fee.[c] Roger, son of Nicholas, gave twenty lampreys and twenty shads for an inquest to find, whether Gilbert, son of Alured, gave to Roger 200 muttons to obtain his confirmation for certain lands, or whether Roger took them from him by violence:[d] Geoffrey Fitz-Pierre, the chief justiciary, gave two good Norway hawks, that Walter le Madine might have leave to export a hundred weight of cheese out of the king's dominions.[e]

It is really amusing to remark the strange business in which the king sometimes interfered, and never without a present: The wife of Hugh de Nevile gave the king 200 hens, that she might lie with

[r] Madox's Hist. of Exch. p. 311.   [s] Id. ibid.   [t] Id. p. 79, 312.   [u] Id. p. 312.   [w] Id. p. 323.   [x] Id. ibid.   [y] Id. ibid.   [z] Id. p. 324.   [a] Id. ibid. [b] Id. p. 232, 233, &c.   [c] Id. p. 298.   [d] Madox's Hist. of Exch. p. 305. [e] Id. p. 325.

APPENDIX II

her husband one night;[f] and she brought with her two sureties, who answered each for a hundred hens. It is probable that her husband was a prisoner, which debarred her from having access to him. The abbot of Rucford paid ten marks, for leave to erect houses and place men upon his land near Welhang, in order to secure his wood there from being stolen:[g] Hugh archdeacon of Wells, gave one tun of wine for leave to carry 600 summs of corn whither he would:[h] Peter de Perariis gave twenty marks for leave to salt fishes, as Peter Chevalier used to do.[i]

It was usual to pay high fines, in order to gain the king's goodwill, or mitigate his anger. In the reign of Henry II. Gilbert, the son of Fergus, fines in 919 pounds 9 shillings to obtain that prince's favour; William de Chataignes a thousand marks that he would remit his displeasure. In the reign of Henry III. the city of London fines in no less a sum than 20,000 pounds on the same account.[k]

The king's protection and good offices of every kind were bought and sold. Robert Grislet paid twenty marks of silver, that the king would help him against the earl of Mortaigne in a certain plea:[l] Robert de Cundet gave thirty marks of silver, that the king would bring him to an accord with the bishop of Lincoln:[m] Ralph de Breckham gave a hawk, that the king would protect him;[n] and this is a very frequent reason for payments: John, son of Ordgar, gave a Norway hawk, to have the king's request to the king of Norway to let him have his brother Godard's chattels.[o] Richard de Neville gave twenty palfreys to obtain the king's request to Isolda Bisset, that she should take him for a husband:[p] Roger Fitz-Walter gave three good palfreys to have the king's letter to Roger Bertram's mother, that she should marry him:[q] Eling, the dean, paid 100 marks, that his whore and his children might be let out upon bail:[r] The bishop of Winchester gave one tun of good wine for his not putting the king in mind to give a girdle to the countess of Albemarle:[s] Robert de Veaux gave five of the best palfreys, that the king would hold his tongue about Henry Pinel's wife.[t] There are in the records of exchequer many other singular instances of a like

[f] Id. p. 326. [g] Id. ibid. [h] Id. p. 320. [i] Id. p. 326. [k] Id. p. 327, 329.
[l] Id. p. 329. [m] Madox's Hist. of Exch. p. 330. [n] Id. p. 332. [o] Id. ibid.
[p] Id. p. 333. [q] Id. ibid. [r] Id. p. 342. *Pro habenda amica sua & filiis, &c.*
[s] Id. p. 352. [t] Id. ibid. *Ut rex taceret de uxore Henrici Pinel.*

nature." It will however be just to remark, that the same ridiculous practices and dangerous abuses prevailed in Normandy, and probably in all the other states of Europe." England was not in this respect more barbarous than its neighbours.

These iniquitous practices of the Norman kings were so well known, that, on the death of Hugh Bigod, in the reign of Henry II. the best and most just of these princes, the eldest son and the widow of this nobleman came to court, and strove, by offering large presents to the king, each of them to acquire possession of that rich inheritance. The king was so equitable as to order the cause to be tried by the great council! But, in the mean time, he seized all the money and treasure of the deceased.ˣ Peter of Blois, a judicious, and even an elegant writer for that age, gives a pathetic description of the venality of justice and the oppressions of the poor, under the reign of Henry: And he scruples not to complain to the king himself of these abuses.ʸ We may judge what the case

ᵘ *We shall gratify the reader's curiosity by subjoining a few more instances from* Madox, p. 332. Hugh Oisel was to give the king two robes of a good green colour, to have the king's letters patent to the merchants of Flanders with a request to render him 1000 marks, which he lost in Flanders. The abbot of Hyde paid thirty marks, to have the king's letters of request to the archbishop of Canterbury, to remove certain monks that were against the abbot. Roger de Trihanton paid twenty marks and a palfrey, to have the king's request to Richard de Umfreville to give him his sister to wife, and to the sister that she would accept of him for a husband: William de Cheveringworth paid five marks, to have the king's letter to the abbot of Perfore, to let him enjoy peaceably his tythes as formerly; Matthew de Hereford, clerk, paid ten marks for a letter of request to the bishop of Landaff, to let him enjoy peaceably his church of Schenfrith; Andrew Neulun gave three Flemish caps, for the king's request to the prior of Chikesand, for performance of an agreement made between them; Henry de Fontibus gave a Lombardy horse of value, to have the king's request to Henry Fitz-Hervey, that he would give him his daughter to wife: Roger, son of Nicholas, promised all the lampreys he could get, to have the king's request to earl William Mareshal, that he would grant him the manor of Langeford at Ferm. The burgesses of Glocester promised 300 lampreys, that they might not be distrained to find the prisoners of Poictou with necessaries, unless they pleased. Id. p. 352. Jordan, son of Reginald, paid twenty marks to have the king's request to William Paniel, that he would grant him the land of Mill Nierenuit, and the custody of his heirs; and if Jordan obtained the same, he was to pay the twenty marks, otherwise not. Id. p. 333. ʷ Madox's Hist. of Exch. p. 359. ˣ Bened. Abb. p. 180, 181. ʸ Petri Bles. Epist. 95. apud Bibl. Patrum, tom. 24. p. 2014.

483

would be under the government of worse princes. The articles of enquiry concerning the conduct of sheriffs, which Henry promulgated in 1170, show the great power as well as the licentiousness of these officers.[z]

Amerciaments or fines for crimes and trespasses were another considerable branch of the royal revenue.[a] Most crimes were atoned for by money; the fines imposed were not limited by any rule or statute; and frequently occasioned the total ruin of the person, even for the slightest trespasses. The forest-laws, particularly, were a great source of oppression. The king possessed sixty-eight forests, thirteen chaces, and seven hundred and eighty-one parks, in different parts of England;[b] and considering the extreme passion of the English and Normans for hunting, these were so many snares laid for the people, by which they were allured into trespasses, and brought within the reach of arbitrary and rigorous laws, which the king had thought proper to enact by his own authority.

But the most barefaced acts of tyranny and oppression were practised against the Jews, who were entirely out of the protection of law, were extremely odious from the bigotry of the people, and were abandoned to the immeasurable rapacity of the king and his ministers. Besides many other indignities, to which they were continually exposed, it appears, that they were once all thrown into prison, and the sum of 66,000 marks exacted for their liberty:[c] At another time, Isaac the Jew paid alone 5100 marks;[d] Brun, 3000 marks;[e] Jurnet, 2000; Bennet, 500: At another, Licorica, widow of David, the Jew of Oxford, was required to pay 6000 marks; and she was delivered over to six of the richest and discreetest Jews in England, who were to answer for the sum.[f] Henry III. borrowed 5000 marks from the earl of Cornwal; and for his repayment consigned over to him all the Jews in England.[g] The revenue arising from exactions upon this nation was so considerable, that there was a particular court of exchequer set apart for managing it.[h]

We may judge concerning the low state of commerce among the English, when the Jews, notwithstanding these oppressions, *Commerce.*

[z] Hoveden, Chron. Gerv. p. 1410.   [a] Madox, chap. xiv.   [b] Spelm. Gloss. in verbo *Foresta.*   [c] Madox's Hist. of the Exch. p. 151. This happened in the reign of king John.   [d] Id. p. 151.   [e] Id. p. 153.   [f] Id. p. 168.   [g] Id. p. 156.   [h] Id. chap. vii.

could still find their account in trading among them, and lending them money. And as the improvements of agriculture were also much checked, by the immense possessions of the nobility, by the disorders of the times, and by the precarious state of feudal property; it appears, that industry of no kind could then have place in the kingdom.[i]

It is asserted by Sir Harry Spellman,[k] as an undoubted truth, that, during the reigns of the first Norman princes, every edict of the king, issued with the consent of his privy-council, had the full force of law. But the barons surely were not so passive as to entrust a power, entirely arbitrary and despotic, into the hands of the sovereign. It only appears, that the constitution had not fixed any precise boundaries to the royal power; that the right of issuing proclamations on any emergence and of exacting obedience to them, a right which was always supposed inherent in the crown, is very difficult to be distinguished from a legislative authority; that the extreme imperfection of the ancient laws, and the sudden exigencies, which often occurred in such turbulent governments, obliged the prince to exert frequently the latent powers of his prerogative; that he naturally proceeded, from the acquiescence of the people, to assume, in many particulars of moment, an authority, from which he had excluded himself by express statutes, charters, or concessions, and which was, in the main, repugnant to the general genius of the constitution; and that the lives, the personal liberty, and the properties of all his subjects were less secured by law against the exertion of his arbitrary authority, than by the independant power and private connexion of each individual. It appears from the great charter itself, that not only John, a tyrannical prince, and Richard, a violent one, but their father, Henry, under whose reign the prevalence of gross abuses is the least to be suspected, were accustomed, from their sole authority,

[i] We learn from the extracts given us of Domesday by Brady in his Treatise of Boroughs, that almost all the boroughs of England had suffered in the shock of the Conquest, and had extremely decayed between the death of the Confessor, and the time when Domesday was framed. [k] Gloss. in verb. *judicium Dei*. The author of the *Miroir des justices*, complains, that ordinances are only made by the king and his clerks, and by aliens and others, who dare not contradict the king, but study to please him. Whence, he concludes, laws are oftener dictated by will than founded on right.

APPENDIX II

without process of law, to imprison, banish, and attaint the free-men of their kingdom.

A great baron, in ancient times, considered himself as a kind of sovereign within his territory; and was attended by courtiers and dependants more zealously attached to him than the ministers of state and the great officers were commonly to *their* sovereign. He often maintained in his court the parade of royalty, by establishing a justiciary, constable, mareschal, chamberlain, seneschal, and chancellor, and assigning to each of these officers a separate prov-ince and command. He was usually very assiduous in exercising his jurisdiction; and took such delight in that image of sovereignty, that it was found necessary to restrain his activity, and prohibit him by law from holding courts too frequently.[l] It is not to be doubted, but the example, set him by the prince, of a mercenary and sordid extortion, would be faithfully copied; and that all his good and bad offices, his justice and injustice, were equally put to sale. He had the power, with the king's consent, to exact talliages even from the free-citizens who lived within his barony; and as his necessities made him rapacious, his authority was usually found to be more oppressive and tyrannical than that of the sovereign.[m] He was ever engaged in hereditary or personal animosities or confederacies with his neighbours, and often gave protection to all desperate adventurers and criminals, who could be useful in serving his violent purposes. He was able alone, in times of tranquillity, to obstruct the execution of justice within his territories; and by com-bining with a few malcontent barons of high rank and power, he could throw the state into convulsions. And on the whole, though the royal authority was confined within bounds, and often within very narrow ones, yet the check was irregular, and frequently the source of great disorders; nor was it derived from the liberty of the people, but from the military power of many petty tyrants, who were equally dangerous to the prince and oppressive to the subject.

The power of the church was another rampart against royal authority; but this defence was also the cause of many mischiefs and inconveniencies. The dignified clergy, perhaps, were not so prone to immediate violence as the barons; but as they pretended *The church.*

[l] Dugd. Jurid. Orig. p. 26.   [m] Madox Hist. of Exch. p. 520.

HISTORY OF ENGLAND

to a total independance on the state, and could always cover themselves with the appearances of religion, they proved, in one respect, an obstruction to the settlement of the kingdom, and to the
regular execution of the laws. The policy of the conqueror was in
this particular liable to some exception. He augmented the superstitious veneration for Rome, to which that age was so much inclined; and he broke those bands of connexion, which, in the
Saxon times, had preserved an union between the lay and the
clerical orders. He prohibited the bishops from sitting in the
county-courts; he allowed ecclesiastical causes to be tried in spiritual courts only;[n] and he so much exalted the power of the clergy,
that of 60,215 knights fees, into which he divided England, he
placed no less than 28,015 under the church.[o]

Civil
laws.
 The right of primogeniture was introduced with the feudal law:
An institution, which is hurtful by producing and maintaining an
unequal division of private property; but is advantageous, in another respect, by accustoming the people to a preference in favour
of the eldest son, and thereby preventing a partition or disputed
succession in the monarchy. The Normans introduced the use of
sirnames, which tend to preserve the knowledge of families and
pedigrees. They abolished none of the old absurd methods of trial,
by the cross or ordeal; and they added a new absurdity, the trial by
single combat,[p] which became a regular part of jurisprudence, and
was conducted with all the order, method, devotion, and solemnity
imaginable.[q] The ideas of chivalry also seem to have been imported
by the Normans: No traces of those fantastic notions are to be
Manners. found among the plain and rustic Saxons. The feudal institutions,
by raising the military tenants to a kind of sovereign dignity, by
rendering personal strength and valour requisite, and by making
every knight and baron his own protector and avenger, begat that
martial pride and sense of honour, which, being cultivated and
embellished by the poets and romance writers of the age, ended in
chivalry. The virtuous knight fought not only in his own quarrel;

[n] Char. Will. apud Wilkins, p. 230. Spel. Conc. vol. ii. p. 14.   [o] Spel. Gloss.
in verb. *manus mortua.* We are not to imagine, as some have done, that the
church possessed lands in this proportion, but only that they and their
vassals enjoyed such a proportionable part of the landed property.   [p] LL.
Will. cap. 68.   [q] Spel. Gloss. in verb. *campus.* The last instance of these
duels was in the 15th of Eliz. So long did that absurdity remain.

but in that of the innocent, of the helpless, and above all, of the fair, whom he supposed to be for ever under the guardianship of his valiant arm. The uncourteous knight, who, from his castle, exercised robbery on travellers, and committed violence on virgins, was the object of his perpetual indignation; and he put him to death, without scruple or trial or appeal, wherever he met with him. The great independance of men made personal honour and fidelity the chief tie among them; and rendered it the capital virtue of every true knight, or genuine professor of chivalry. The solemnities of single combat, as established by law, banished the notion of every thing unfair or unequal in rencounters; and maintained an appearance of courtesy between the combatants, till the moment of their engagement. The credulity of the age grafted on this stock the notion of giants, enchanters, dragons, spells,ʳ and a thousand wonders, which still multiplied during the times of the Crusades; when men, returning from so great a distance, used the liberty of imposing every fiction on their believing audience. These ideas of chivalry infected the writings, conversation, and behaviour of men, during some ages; and even after they were, in a great measure, banished by the revival of learning, they left modern *gallantry* and the *point of honour,* which still maintain their influence, and are the genuine offspring of those ancient affectations.

The concession of the Great Charter, or rather its full establishment (for there was a considerable interval of time between the one and the other), gave rise, by degrees, to a new species of government, and introduced some order and justice into the administration. The ensuing scenes of our history are therefore somewhat different from the preceding. Yet the Great Charter contained no establishment of new courts, magistrates, or senates, nor abolition of the old. It introduced no new distribution of the powers of the commonwealth, and no innovation in the political or public law of the kingdom. It only guarded, and that merely by verbal clauses, against such tyrannical practices as are incompatible with civilized government, and, if they become very frequent, are incompatible with all government. The barbarous licence of

---

ʳ In all legal single combats, it was part of the champion's oath, that he carried not about him any herb, spell, or inchantment, by which he might procure victory. Dugd. Orig. Jurid. p. 82.

the kings, and perhaps of the nobles, was thenceforth somewhat more restrained: Men acquired some more security for their properties and their liberties: And government approached a little nearer to that end, for which it was originally instituted, the distribution of justice, and the equal protection of the citizens. Acts of violence and iniquity in the crown, which before were only deemed injurious to individuals, and were hazardous chiefly in proportion to the number, power, and dignity of the persons affected by them, were now regarded, in some degree, as public injuries, and as infringements of a charter, calculated for general security. And thus, the establishment of the Great Charter, without seeming anywise to innovate in the distribution of political power, became a kind of epoch in the constitution.

NOTES TO THE
FIRST VOLUME

NOTE [A], p. 12

This question has been disputed with as great zeal and even acrimony between the Scotch and Irish antiquaries, as if the honour of their respective countries were the most deeply concerned in the decision. We shall not enter into any detail on so uninteresting a subject; but shall propose our opinion in a few words. It appears more than probable, from the similitude of language and manners, that Britain either was originally peopled, or was subdued, by the migration of inhabitants from Gaul, and Ireland from Britain: The position of the several countries, is an additional reason that favours this conclusion. It appears also probable, that the migrations of that colony of Gauls or Celts, who peopled or subdued Ireland, was originally made from the north west parts of Britain; and this conjecture (if it do not merit a higher name) is founded both on the Irish language, which is a very different dialect from the Welsh and from the language anciently spoken in South Britain, and on the vicinity of Lancashire, Cumberland, Galloway and Argyleshire to that island. These events, as they passed long before the age of history and records, must be known by reasoning alone, which in this case seems to be pretty satisfactory: Caesar and Tacitus, not to mention a multitude of other Greek and Roman authors, were guided by like inferences. But besides these primitive facts, which lie in a very remote antiquity, it is a matter of positive and undoubted testimony, that the Roman province of Britain, during the time of the lower empire, was much infested by bands of robbers or pyrates, whom the provincial Britons called Scots or Scuits; a name which was probably used as a term of reproach, and which these banditti themselves did not acknowledge or assume. We may infer from two passages in Claudian, and from one in Orosius and another in Isidore, that the chief fear of these Scots was in Ireland. That some part of the Irish freebooters migrated back to the north-west parts of Britain, whence their ancestors had probably been derived in a more remote age is positively asserted by Bede, and implied in Gildas. I grant, that neither Bede nor Gildas are Caesars or Tacituses; but such as they are, they remain the sole testimony on the subject, and therefore must be relied on for want of better: Happily, the frivolousness of the question corresponds to the weakness of the authorities. Not to mention, that, if any part of the traditional history of a barbarous people can be relied on, it is the genealogy of nations, and even sometimes that of families. It is in vain to argue against these facts from the supposed warlike disposition of the Highlanders and unwarlike of the ancient Irish. Those arguments are still much weaker than the authorities. Nations change very quickly in these particulars. The Britons were unable to resist the Picts and Scots, and invited over the Saxons for their defence, who repelled those invaders: Yet the same Britons valiantly resisted for 150 years not only this victorious band of Saxons, but infinite numbers more, who poured in upon them from all quarters. Robert Bruce in 1322 made a peace, in which England, after many defeats, was constrained to acknowledge the independance of his country: Yet in no more distant period than ten years after, Scotland was totally subdued by a small handful of English, led by a few private noblemen. All history is full of such events. The Irish Scots, in the course of two or three centuries, might find time and opportunities sufficient to settle in North Britain, though we can neither assign the period nor causes of that revolution. Their barbarous manner of life rendered them much fitter than the Romans for subduing these mountaineers. And in a word, it is clear, from the language of the two countries, that the Highlanders and the Irish are the same people, and that the one are a colony from the other. We have positive evidence, which, though from neutral persons, is not perhaps the best that may be wished for, that the former, in the third or fourth century, sprang from the latter: We have no evidence at all that the latter sprang from the former. I shall add, that the name of Erse or Irish, given by the low-country Scots to the language of the Scotch Highlanders, is a certain proof of the traditional opinion, delivered from father to son, that the latter people came originally from Ireland.

NOTE [B], p. 96

There is a seeming contradiction in ancient historians with regard to some circumstances in the story of Edwy and Elgiva. It is agreed, that this prince had a violent passion for his second or third cousin, Elgiva, whom he married, though within the degrees prohibited by the canons. It is also agreed, that he was dragged from a lady on the day of his coronation, and that the lady was afterwards treated with the singular barbarity above mentioned. The only difference is, that Osborne and some others call her his strumpet, not his wife, as she is said to be by Malmesbury. But this difference is easily reconciled: For if Edwy married her contrary to the canons, the monks would be sure to deny her to be his wife, and would insist that she could be nothing but his strumpet: So that, on the whole, we may esteem this representation of the matter as certain; at least, as by far the most probable. If Edwy had only kept a mistress, it is well known, that there are methods of accommodation with the church, which would have prevented the clergy from proceeding to such extremities against him: But his marriage, contrary to the canons, was an insult on their authority, and called for their highest resentment.

NOTES TO THE FIRST VOLUME

NOTE [C], p. 97

Many of the English historians make Edgar's ships amount to an extravagant number, to 3000, or 3600: See Hoveden, p. 426. Flor. Wigorn. p. 607. Abbas Rieval p. 360. Brompton, p. 869, says that Edgar had 4000 vessels. How can these accounts be reconciled to probability, and to the state of the navy in the time of Alfred? W. Thorne makes the whole number amount only to 300, which is more probable. The fleet of Ethelred, Edgar's son, must have been short of 1000 ships; yet the Saxon Chronicle, p. 137, says it was the greatest navy that ever had been seen in England.

NOTE [D], p. 116

Almost all the ancient historians speak of this massacre of the Danes as if it had been universal, and as if every individual of that nation throughout England had been put to death. But the Danes were almost the sole inhabitants in the kingdoms of Northumberland and East Anglia, and were very numerous in Mercia. This representation therefore of the matter is absolutely impossible. Great resistance must have been made, and violent wars ensued; which was not the case. This account given by Wallingford, though he stands single, must be admitted as the only true one. We are told, that the name *Lurdane, lord Dane,* for an idle lazy fellow, who lives at other people's expence, came from the conduct of the Danes, who were put to death. But the English princes had been intirely masters for several generations; and only supported a military corps of that nation. It seems probable, therefore, that it was these Danes only that were put to death.

NOTE [E], p. 136

The ingenious author of the article GODWIN, in the Biographia Britannica, has endeavoured to clear the memory of that nobleman, upon the supposition, that all the English annals had been falsified by the Norman historians after the conquest. But that this supposition has not much foundation, appears hence, that almost all these historians have given a very good character of his son Harold, whom it was much more the interest of the Norman cause to blacken.

NOTE [F], p. 145

The whole story of the transactions between Edward, Harold, and the duke of Normandy, is told so differently by the ancient writers, that there are few important passages of the English history liable to so great uncertainty. I have followed the account, which appeared to me the most consistent and probable. It does not seem likely, that Edward ever executed a will in the duke's favour, much less that he got it ratified by the states of the kingdom, as is affirmed by some. The will would have been known to all, and would have been produced by the Conqueror, to whom it gave so plausible, and really so just a title; but the doubtful and ambiguous manner in which he seems always to have mentioned it, proves, that he could only plead the known intentions of that monarch in his favour, which he was desirous to call a will. There is indeed a charter of the Conqueror preserved by Dr. Hickes, vol. i. where he calls himself *rex hereditarius*, meaning heir by will; but a prince, possessed of so much power, and attended with so much success, may employ what pretence he pleases: It is sufficient to refute his pretences to observe, that there is a great difference and variation among historians, with regard to a point, which, had it been real, must have been agreed upon by all of them.

Again, some historians, particularly Malmsbury and Matthew of Westminster, affirm that Harold had no intention of going over to Normandy, but that taking the air in a pleasure-boat on the coast, he was driven over by stress of weather to the territories of Guy count of Ponthieu: But besides that this story is not probable in itself, and is contradicted by most of the ancient historians, it is contradicted by a very curious and authentic monument lately discovered. It is a tapestry, preserved in the ducal palace of Roüen, and supposed to have been wrought by orders of Matilda, wife to the emperor: At least it is of very great antiquity. Harold is there represented as taking his departure from king Edward in execution of some commission, and mounting his vessel with a great train. The design of redeeming his brother and nephew, who were hostages is the most likely cause that can be assigned; and is accordingly mentioned by Eadmer, Hoveden, Brompton, and Simeon of Durham. For a farther account of this piece of tapestry, see Histoire de l'Academie de Litterature, tom. ix. page 535.

NOTE [G], p. 163

It appears from the ancient translations of the Saxon annals and laws, and from king Alfred's translation of Bede, as well as from all the ancient historians, that *comes* in Latin, *alderman* in Saxon, and *earl* in Dano-Saxon were quite synonimous. There is only a clause in a law of king Athelstan's, (see Spelm. Conc. p. 406.) which has stumbled some antiquaries, and has made them imagine that an earl was superior to an alderman. The weregild or the price of an earl's blood is there fixed at 15,000 thrimsas, equal to that of an archbishop; whereas that of a bishop and alderman is only 8000 thrimsas. To solve this difficulty we must have recourse to Selden's conjecture, (see his Titles of Honour, chap. v. p. 603, 604) that the term of earl was in the age of Athelstan just beginning to be in use in England, and stood at that time for the atheling or prince of the blood, heir to the crown. This he confirms by a law of Canute, § 55. where an atheling and an archbishop are put upon the same footing. In another law of the same Athelstan the weregild of the prince or atheling is said to be 15,000 thrimsas. See Wilkins, p. 71. He is therefore the same who is called earl in the former law.

NOTE [H], p. 203

There is a paper or record of the family of Sharneborne, which pretends, that that family, which was Saxon, was restored upon proving their innocence, as well as other Saxon families, which were in the same situation. Though this paper was able to impose on such great antiquaries as Spellman (see Gloss. in verbo *Drenges*) and Dugdale, (see Baron. vol. i. p. 118.) it is proved by Dr. Brady (see Answ. to Petyt, p. 11, 12.) to have been a forgery; and is allowed as such by Tyrrel, though a pertinacious defender of his party notions (see his hist. vol. ii. introd. p. 51, 73.) Ingulf, p. 70 tells us, that very early Hereward, though absent during the time of the conquest, was turned out of all his estate, and could not obtain redress. William even plundered the monasteries. Flor. Wigorn. p. 636. Chron. Abb. St. Petri de Burgo, p. 48. M. Paris, p. 5. Sim. Dun. p. 200. Diceto, p. 482. Brompton, p. 967. Knyghton, p. 2344. Alur. Beverl. p. 130. We are told by Ingulf, that Ivo de Taillebois plundered the monastery of Croyland of a great part of its land; and no redress could be obtained.

NOTE [I], p. 203

The obliging of all the inhabitants to put out their fires and lights at certain hours, upon the sounding of a bell, called the *courfeu*, is represented by Polydore Virgil, lib. 9. as a mark of the servitude of the English. But this was a law of police, which William had previously established in Normandy. See du Moulin, hist. de Normandie, p. 160. The same law had place in Scotland. LL. Burgor, cap. 86.

NOTE [J], p. 209

What these laws were of Edward the Confessor, which the English, every reign during a century and a half, desire so passionately to have restored, is much disputed by antiquaries, and our ignorance of them seems one of the greatest defects in the ancient English history. The collection of laws in Wilkins, which pass under the name of Edward, are plainly a posterior and an ignorant compilation. Those to be found in Ingulf are genuine; but so imperfect, and contain so few clauses favourable to the subject, that we see no great reason for their contending for them so vehemently. It is probable, that the English meant the *common law*, as it prevailed during the reign of Edward; which we may conjecture to have been more indulgent to liberty than the Norman institutions. The most material articles of it were afterwards comprehended in Magna Charta.

NOTE [K], p. 227

Ingulf, p. 70. H. Hunt. p. 370, 372. M. West. p. 225. Gul. Neub. p. 357. Alured. Beverl. p. 124. De gest. Angl. p. 333. M. Paris. p. 4. Sim. Dun. p. 206. Brompton, p. 962, 980, 1161. Gervase Tilb. lib. i. cap. 16. Textus Roffensis apud Seld. Spicileg. ad Eadm. p. 197. Gul. Pict. p. 206. Ordericus Vitalis, p. 521, 666, 853. Epist. St. Thom. p. 801. Gul. Malmes. p. 52, 57. Knyghton, p. 2354. Edmer, p. 110. Thom. Rudborne in Ang. Sacra, vol. i. p. 248. Monach. Roff. in Ang. Sacra, vol. ii. p. 276. Girald. Camb. in eadem, vol. ii. p. 413. Hist. Elyensis, p. 516. The words of this last historian, who is very ancient, are remarkable, and worth transcribing. *Rex itaque factus Willielmus, quid in principes Anglorum, qui tantae cladi superesse poterant, fecerit, dicere, cum nihil prosit, omitto. Quid enim prodesset, si nec unum in toto regno de illis dicerem pristina potestate uti permissum, sed omnes aut in gravem paupertatis aerumnam detrusos, aut exhaeredatos, patria pulsos, aut effossis oculis, vel caeteris amputatis membris, opprobrium hominum factos, aut certe miserrime afflictos, vita privatos. Simili modo utilitate carere existimo dicere quid in minorem populum, non solum ab eo, sed a suis actum sit, cum id dictu sciamus difficile, et ob immanem crudelitatem fortassis incredibile.*

NOTE [L], p. 272

Henry, by the feudal customs, was intitled to levy a tax for the marrying of his eldest daughter, and he exacted three shillings a hyde on all England. H. Hunt. p. 379. Some historians (Brady, p. 270. and Tyrrel, vol. ii. p. 182.) heedlessly make this sum amount to above 800,000 pounds of our present money: But it could not exceed 135,000. Five hydes, sometimes less, made a knight's fee, of which there were about 60,000 in England, consequently near 300,000 hydes; and at the rate of three shillings a hyde, the sum would amount to 45,000 pounds, or 135,000 of our present money. See Rudburne, p. 257. In the Saxon times, there were only computed 243,600 hydes in England.

NOTE [M], p. 276

The legates *a latere,* as they were called, were a kind of delegates, who possessed the full power of the pope in all the provinces committed to their charge, and were very busy in extending, as well as exercising it. They nominated to all vacant benefices, assembled synods, and were anxious to maintain ecclesiastical privileges, which never could be fully protected without incroachments on the civil power. If there were the least concurrence or opposition, it was always supposed that the civil power was to give way: Every deed, which had the least pretence of holding of any thing spiritual, as marriages, testaments, promissory oaths, were brought into the spiritual court, and could not be canvassed before a civil magistrate. These were the established laws of the church; and where a legate was sent immediately from Rome, he was sure to maintain the papal claims with the utmost rigour: But it was an advantage to the king to have the archbishop of Canterbury appointed legate, because the connexions of that prelate with the kingdom tended to moderate his measures.

NOTE [N], p. 301

William of Newbridge, p. 383. (who is copied by later historians) asserts, that Geoffrey had some title to the counties of Maine and Anjou. He pretends, that count Geoffrey, his father, had left him these dominions by a secret will, and had ordered that his body should not be buried, till Henry should swear to the observance of it, which he, ignorant of the contents, was induced to do. But besides, that this story is not very likely in itself, and savours of monkish fiction, it is found in no other ancient writer, and is contradicted by some of them, particularly the monk of Marmoutier, who had better opportunities than Newbridge of knowing the truth. See Vita Gauf. Duc. Norman. p. 103.

NOTE [O], p. 304

The sum scarcely appears credible; as it would amount to much above half the rent of the whole land. Gervase is indeed a cotemporary author; but churchmen are often guilty of strange mistakes of that nature, and are commonly but little acquainted with the public revenues. This sum would make 540,000 pounds of our present money. The Norman Chronicle, p. 995. says, that Henry raised only 60 Angevin shillings on each knight's fee in his foreign dominions: This is only a fourth of the sum which Gervase says he levied on England: An inequality no wise probable. A nation may by degrees be brought to bear a tax of 15 shillings in the pound, but a sudden and precarious tax can never be imposed to that amount, without a very visible necessity, especially in an age so little accustomed to taxes. In the succeeding reign, the rent of a knight's fee was computed at four pounds a year. There were 60,000 knights fees in England.

NOTE [P], p. 306

Fitz-Stephen, p. 18. This conduct appears violent and arbitrary; but was suitable to the strain of administration in those days. His father, Geoffrey, though represented as a mild prince, set him an example of much greater violence. When Geoffrey was master of Normandy, the chapter of Seez presumed, without his consent, to proceed to the election of a bishop; upon which he ordered all of them with the bishop elect to be castrated, and made all their testicles be brought him in a platter. Fitz-Steph. p. 44. In the war of Toulouse, Henry laid a heavy and an arbitrary tax on all the churches within his dominions. See Epist. St. Thom. p. 232.

NOTE [Q], p. 317

I follow here the narrative of Fitz-Stephens, who was secretary to Becket; though, no doubt, he may be suspected of partiality towards his patron. Lord Lyttelton chuses to follow the authority of a manuscript letter, or rather manifesto, of Folliot, bishop of London, which is addressed to Becket himself, at the time when the bishop appealed to the pope from the excommunication pronounced against him by his primate. My reasons, why I give the preference to Fitz-Stephens are, (1.) If the friendship of Fitz-Stephens might render him partial to Becket even after the death of that prelate, the declared enmity of the bishop must, during his lifetime, have rendered him more partial on the other side. (2.) The bishop was moved by interest, as well as enmity, to calumniate Becket. He had himself to defend against the sentence of excommunication, dreadful to all, especially to a prelate: And no more effectual means than to throw all the blame on his adversary. (3.) He has actually been guilty of palpable calumnies in that letter. Among these, I reckon the following: He affirms, that, when Becket subscribed the Constitutions of Clarendon, he said plainly to all the bishops of England, *It is my master's pleasure, that I should forswear myself, and at present I submit to it, and do resolve to incur a perjury, and repent afterwards as I may.* However barbarous the times, and however negligent zealous churchmen were then of morality, these are not words which a primate of great sense and of much seeming sanctity would employ in an assembly of his suffragans: He might act upon these principles, but never surely would publickly avow them. Folliot also says, that all the bishops were resolved obstinately to oppose the Constitutions of Clarendon, but the primate himself betrayed them from timidity, and led the way to their subscribing. This is contrary to the testimony of all the historians, and directly contrary to Becket's character, who surely was not destitute either of courage or of zeal for ecclesiastical immunities. (4.) The violence and injustice of Henry, ascribed to him by Fitz-Stephens, is of a piece with the rest of the prosecution. Nothing could be more iniquitous, than, after two years silence, to make a sudden and unprepared demand upon Becket to the amount of 44,000 marks (equal to a sum of near a million in our time) and not allow him the least interval to bring in his accounts. If the king was so palpably oppressive in one article, he may be presumed to be equally so in the rest. (5.) Though Folliot's letter, or rather manifesto, be addressed to Becket himself, it does not acquire more authority on that account. We know not what answer was made by Becket: The collection of letters cannot be supposed quite complete. But that the collection was not made by one (whoever he were) very partial to that primate, appears from the tenor of them, where there are many passages very little favourable to him: Insomuch that the editor of them at Brussels, a Jesuit, thought proper to publish them with great omissions, particularly of this letter of Folliot's. Perhaps, Becket made no answer at all, as not deigning to write to an excommunicated person, whose very commerce would contaminate him; and the bishop, trusting to this arrogance of his primate, might calumniate him the more freely. (6.) Though the sentence, pronounced on Becket by the great council, implies that he had refused to make any answer to the king's court, this does not fortify the narrative of Folliot. For if his excuse was rejected as false and frivolous, it would be treated as no answer. Becket submitted so far to the sentence of confiscation of goods and chattels, that he gave surety, which is a proof, that he meant not at that time to question the authority of the king's courts. (7.) It may be worth observing, that both the author of Historia quadraparrita, and Gervase, contemporary writers, agree with Fitz-Stephens; and the latter is not usually very partial to Becket. All the ancient historians give the same account.

NOTE [R], p. 404

Madox, in his Baronia Anglica, cap. 14. tells us, That in the 30th of Henry II. thirty-three cows and two bulls cost but eight pounds seven shillings, money of that age; 500 sheep, twenty-two pounds ten shillings, or about ten pence three farthings per sheep; sixty-six oxen, eighteen pounds three shillings; fifteen breeding mares, two pounds twelve shillings and six-pence; and twenty-two hogs, one pound two shillings. Commodities seem then to have been about ten times cheaper than at present; all except the sheep, probably on account of the value of the fleece. The same author in his Formulare Anglicanum, p. 17. says, That in the 10th year of Richard I. mention is made of ten per cent. paid for money: But the Jews frequently exacted much higher interest.